WebLogic™
The Definitive Guide

D1411437

Jon Mountjoy and Avinash Chugh

O'REILLY®

Beijing · Cambridge · Farnham · Köln · Paris · Sebastopol · Taipei · Tokyo

WebLogic™: The Definitive Guide
by Jon Mountjoy and Avinash Chugh

Published by O'Reilly Media, Inc., 1005 Gravenstein Highway North, Sebastopol, CA 95472.

O'Reilly & Associates books may be purchased for educational, business, or sales promotional use. Online editions are also available for most titles (*safari.oreilly.com*). For more information, contact our corporate/institutional sales department: (800) 998-9938 or *corporate@oreilly.com*.

Editor:	Brett McLaughlin
Production Editor:	Mary Brady
Cover Designer:	Emma Colby
Interior Designer:	David Futato

Printing History:

February 2004:   First Edition.

ISBN: 0-596-00432-X
[M]

Table of Contents

Preface

WebLogic™ Server is one of the leading J2EE-compliant application servers, produced by BEA Systems. It implements the full range of J2EE technologies, and provides many more additional features such as advanced management, clustering, and web services. It forms the core of the WebLogic Platform, and provides a stable framework for building scalable, highly available, and secure applications. You can gauge the extent of its acceptance by exploring the list of customers who have embraced WebLogic Server from all segments of the industry. A number of partners also are collaborating with BEA to build a diverse range of products that integrate with WebLogic Server and the WebLogic Platform. This information on customers and partners involved with WebLogic is available on BEA's web site, *http://www.bea.com/*. Clearly, WebLogic Server has established a strong presence in the market.

BEA is serious about WebLogic Server. It is one of the influential members on the various committees that decide on the future direction of the J2EE revolution. It has invested much financial and intellectual capital toward making WebLogic Server the leading Java™ application server in the industry. Its dev2dev web site and newsgroups bring together developers, architects, and experts from different domains, all collaborating to make WebLogic Server as popular as it is. Over the years, two factors have determined the growth of WebLogic Server. First, WebLogic has consistently maintained compliance with the J2EE standards. Second, BEA has always been committed to ensuring that WebLogic meets and exceeds the needs of its customers, and provides a feature set that delivers a viable platform for building enterprise solutions. The combination of both of these factors has contributed to the widespread popularity of WebLogic Server.

WebLogic continues to maintain its edge by offering robust implementation of current and upcoming J2EE technologies. It also offers a lot more, extending the base platform with features that let you build real enterprise solutions with cutting-edge technologies. A quick preview of some of its features will convince you that WebLogic is a force to contend with.

- Support for a wide range of platforms, including Windows 2000, XP, and 2003, Solaris, Red Hat and SuSE Linux, HP Tru64, HP-UX, IBM AIX, and other Unix flavors.

- A rich set of client options: HTTP clients, Java clients over RMI/IIOP and the native T3 protocol, and web service clients that support JAX-RPC or SOAP.

- A robust implementation of standard J2EE APIs, and support for the standard J2EE components such as servlets, JSP pages and custom tags, EJB and RMI objects, JMS producers and consumers, J2EE connectors, and more.

- An innovative strategy for deploying J2EE applications across multiple servers.

- The ability to interoperate with industry-strength HTTP servers, LDAP servers, relational DBMS products, messaging software, enterprise information systems, load balancers, firewalls, and more.

- An easy, flexible way to configure the different J2EE containers, and the ability to benefit from practical extensions and optimizations.

- Designed to operate in a distributed environment with extensive support for failover and load balancing through clustering.

- An intuitive framework for organizing the different WebLogic resources in a domain, with an emphasis on performance and scalability.

- A stable, production-ready JMS server that supports distributed JMS destinations, configurable delivery options, extended acknowledgment modes, and much more.

- A comprehensive suite of security features that help protect the various applications and resources deployed in your WebLogic environment.

- Rich support for XML features, including a streaming and XPath API.

- A distributed management infrastructure that can be configured dynamically through JMX, and integrated into a larger SNMP framework.

- A distributed logging framework and support for i18n and l10n.

- A rich implementation of web services for building standards-compliant web services over existing J2EE components, with features such as SOAP security and reliable SOAP messaging.

- An integral component of the WebLogic Platform, over which other technologies such as WebLogic Integration and WebLogic Portal are built.

Finally, WebLogic Server also comes bundled with an IDE, WebLogic Workshop. This IDE provides a fast route to implementing J2EE and web service components, featuring automatic code generation and graphical component composition.

With these kinds of ingredients, we believe WebLogic Server has realized the perfect recipe to deal with other competing J2EE application servers. As you read on, we're certain you, too, will be convinced.

Who Should Read This Book?

J2EE is a mature platform for building enterprise-scale applications. This book caters to developers who are presently working on the WebLogic platform, and those J2EE programmers who are considering doing so in the future. If you are a programmer responsible for developing J2EE applications on WebLogic, an administrator who needs to manage the entire logical and physical setup for your application, or an architect responsible for evaluating which technologies, tools, and products should be used, this book is for you!

Let's clarify how we believe this book can help the different groups within our target audience:

Developers

For the most part, we assume that developers reading this book are familiar with the J2EE platform. Developers should turn to other books, online resources, and published specifications for learning the intricate details of each J2EE technology. With the help of this book, you can then take that knowledge to the next level by putting that theory into practice when using WebLogic Server. Our aim is to guide you through the world of WebLogic and show how you can apply your J2EE expertise to build and manage applications on WebLogic. We reveal how WebLogic implements the various J2EE features, demonstrate how WebLogic enhances these services in interesting and useful ways, and explain how your applications can benefit from these features.

Administrators

Any group of users that is responsible for managing a WebLogic-based setup will find that this book has all the material needed to build a fundamental understanding of creating, managing, and maintaining WebLogic domains and services. This includes users who need to interact with the system in some nonprogrammatic way—for instance, the application assemblers, the deployers, and the tool providers. We explain how to manage the runtime WebLogic environment, discuss the performance implications and trade-offs, and examine the different design and security constraints.

System architects

A system architect needs to have a good understanding of the overall capabilities of the application server if he is to design effective solutions. For instance, he must be aware of the different system architectures supported by WebLogic, the overall organization of a WebLogic domain and supporting network infrastructure, how WebLogic resources cooperate in a clustered environment, what additional features and services are offered, and how to extract optimal performance from the application setup. He needs to be able to extrapolate the possibilities, but also understand the limitations and trade-offs of adopting a WebLogic-based solution. Our book attempts to provide a 360-degree view of WebLogic. We not only highlight its features and strengths, but also point out any shortcomings and issues of which you need to be aware.

We expect our target audience to have an understanding of the J2EE platform.

Developers, at the very least, should have some previous experience with programming servlets, creating JSP pages, using the JDBC API, and building EJBs. We encourage those who don't to read other books from the O'Reilly catalogue that cover the entire gamut of J2EE technologies. The various J2EE specifications published by Sun Microsystems also serve as a useful reference. This book aims to build on that J2EE know-how, and guides you through the different J2EE technologies and enterprise services supported by WebLogic.

For system administrators, this book serves as a complete guide for managing a WebLogic environment. We expect that you will have had past experience with administering an enterprise application, perhaps on a different platform using other technologies.

For Java architects, this book reveals how other WebLogic enterprise services can enrich your solutions with exciting possibilities. It also advances your understanding of how to achieve the best performance out of your application architecture. We expect you will have had some previous experience in building and designing multi-tier system architectures, and some level of awareness of the capabilities of the J2EE technology stack.

Organization

The first chapter provides a quick tour of WebLogic Server. It offers an overview of the J2EE and other enterprise features supported by WebLogic. We explore the fundamental WebLogic resources such as domains, servers, and clusters. We also look at essential administration tasks such as starting and stopping the server. The remaining chapters in the book can be grouped into three categories: those that deal with J2EE, those that deal with WebLogic management, and finally, those that focus on WebLogic's own enterprise APIs.

WebLogic and J2EE

The first part of the book examines WebLogic's rich support for the various J2EE services. WebLogic is a fully compliant J2EE application server, and it provides a mature environment for building robust, server-side, component-based applications.

Chapters 2 and 3 give in-depth coverage of how to build web applications on WebLogic. We examine how to configure servlets and JSP pages on WebLogic Server. We look at how to incorporate custom JSP tags and filters into your web applications, and we explain how to package and deploy your web applications on WebLogic. We also learn about WebLogic-specific custom tags and filters, and how to create tag libraries from prebuilt EJBs. We look at how to configure the behavior of the servlet engine (web container) using the XML deployment descriptors for a web application. We discuss how WebLogic manages server-side HTTP sessions in a clustered environment, how to restrict access to specific web resources, and how to use commercial web servers to proxy requests to WebLogic Server. Moreover, we explore the many ways WebLogic lets you configure its HTTP server.

Chapter 4 explains how resources are published over WebLogic's JNDI service. We examine how WebLogic's JNDI operates in a clustered environment. Later, we look at how to build RMI applications, and explore the various optimizations intrinsic to WebLogic's RMI. Finally, we learn how RMI objects can be accessible to both T3 and IIOP clients. Chapter 5 looks at WebLogic's support for JDBC connection pools and how data sources enable you to access these pools. Chapter 6 examines the use of distributed transactions in WebLogic. Chapter 7 looks at how to use JCA-compliant resource adapters to enable WebLogic applications to connect to proprietary enterprise stores. Chapter 8 provides an in-depth look at creating JMS applications and using WebLogic-specific features such as quotas, flow control, timed delivery options, XML-formatted messages, and bridging with other JMS providers. Chapter 9 succinctly covers how to configure JavaMail on WebLogic, thereby allowing deployed applications to send and receive electronic mail.

The next two chapters investigate WebLogic's support for Enterprise JavaBeans™ (EJBs). In Chapter 10, we learn about the various EJB types and how to package and deploy EJB components. We also describe the behavior of WebLogic's EJB container and the various ways you can influence the runtime behavior of your EJBs. We demonstrate how you can adjust the size of the free pool of EJBs and the in-memory EJB cache. We also look at the various optimizations for EJBs, such as network and transactional collocation, optimistic concurrency strategy, and read-only entity beans that can rely on a multicast invalidation framework. Most importantly, we explore how WebLogic incorporates load-balancing and failover support for EJBs deployed in a clustered environment.

Chapter 11 explains how to create container-managed persistence (CMP) entity beans, while concurrently introducing the features of WebLogic's CMP engine. Later, we look at how to implement container-managed relationships (CMR) between entity beans. We also examine the EJB-Query Language (EJB QL) syntax, and learn about the WebLogic-specific extensions to EJB QL.

Managing the WebLogic Environment

The middle portion of the book examines the post-development aspects of WebLogic applications. We look at how to package and deploy your applications, configure and optimize the runtime WebLogic environment, and deal with security issues. Chapter 12 explains how to package J2EE applications using available WebLogic tools. We also learn about WebLogic's classloader hierarchy and its impact on your deployment. Finally, we discuss the new two-phase deployment strategy in WebLogic Server, and the usefulness of application staging. Chapter 13 looks at how to manage the different resources and services that live in a WebLogic domain spread across multiple machines. It also covers monitoring the health of servers in the domain, configuring network resources, and planning for additional capacity.

Chapter 14 provides an understanding of WebLogic's support for clustering, with a strong emphasis on its load-balancing and failover capabilities. It examines how various J2EE resources behave in a clustered environment. It also analyzes the performance and design implications of adopting different clustered solutions for your application's architecture. Chapter 15 explains the implications of tuning various performance-related configuration settings, and how to improve the performance of the JVM, the applications deployed to WebLogic, and the server itself. Chapter 16 provides all the details necessary to configure WebLogic's SSL support, and create your own programs that use WebLogic's SSL support. Chapter 17 explores the many services implemented under the hood of WebLogic's default security realm. It explains the behavior of WebLogic's security providers, its authentication framework, and declarative security for various J2EE components.

WebLogic Enterprise APIs

In the last section of the book, we examine important enterprise WebLogic services that would attract many more developers and administrators. Chapter 18 looks at WebLogic's support for XML, including XML Registries, application-scoped XML parsers, event-driven parsing using the Streaming API, and other miscellaneous extensions. Chapter 19 describes how to create WebLogic web services over existing J2EE components. It explains how you can build JAX-RPC clients that interact with deployed web services, generate the necessary support for custom types, and set up a chain of handlers that can intercept SOAP request messages and SOAP response messages. It also describes how you can secure WebLogic web services and write clients that can invoke these protected web services. Finally, it explains how to publish and then inquire about web services advertised over the local UDDI registry.

Chapter 20 provides an overview of WebLogic's JMX services and how you can use managed beans (MBeans) to programmatically administer and/or monitor WebLogic resources. Chapter 21 covers WebLogic's support for internationalization and logging. Chapter 22 looks at how administrators can integrate WebLogic into an SNMP-compliant management infrastructure. It provides an overview of the SNMP agent model and how you can implement an SNMP view of the WebLogic Server.

Online Documentation

BEA's documentation on WebLogic Server is available at *http://edocs.bea.com/*, and can also be downloaded in HTML or PDF formats. BEA's dev2dev Online (*http://dev2dev.bea.com*) is another good source of tools, utilities, articles, and white papers.

BEA also maintains a newsgroup site on the WebLogic Platform, *nntp://newsgroups. bea.com/*, which provides the ideal forum for discussions and support, and the opportunity for closer interaction between WebLogic developers, architects, administrators, and experts.

All of these resources, as well as related books, have contributed to the material covered in this book. The most significant source for our book has been BEA's online documentation.

BEA also produces helpful white papers. Tom Barnes's white paper, "JMS Performance Guide," deserves a special mention because it helped clarify a number of issues related to WebLogic's JMS implementation.

Conventions Used in This Book

We use the following formatting conventions in this book:

Italic

> Used for filenames, pathnames, hostnames, domain names, URLs, email addresses, script names, folder names, and new terms where they are defined.

`Constant width`

> Used for code examples, program fragments, and console output. It is also used for Java keywords, names of Java classes, variables, and methods, SQL table and column names, XML elements and tags, and for shell commands and scripting variables.

`Constant width italic`

> Used to indicate text that is replaceable. For example, in `BeanNamePK`, the `BeanName` may be replaced with a particular bean name.

`Constand width bold`

> Used for emphasis in some code examples.

The term "WebLogic" is often used to refer to WebLogic Server, which is BEA's J2EE-compliant application server. This must not be confused with the "WebLogic Platform," which refers to a host of BEA technologies built around the core WebLogic Server product.

 This icon signifies a tip, suggestion, or general note.

 This icon indicates a warning or caution.

Using Code Examples

This book is here to help you get your job done. In general, you may use the code in this book in your programs and documentation. You do not need to contact us for permission unless you're reproducing a significant portion of the code. For example, writing a program that uses several chunks of code from this book does not require permission. Selling or distributing a CD-ROM of examples from O'Reilly books does require permission. Answering a question by citing this book and quoting example code does not require permission. Incorporating a significant amount of example code from this book into your product's documentation does require permission.

We appreciate, but do not require, attribution. An attribution usually includes the title, author, publisher, and ISBN. For example: "*WebLogic: The Definitive Guide*, by Jon Mountjoy and Avinash Chugh. Copyright 2004 O'Reilly & Associates, Inc., 0-596-00432-X."

If you feel your use of code examples falls outside fair use or the permission given above, feel free to contact us at *permissions@oreilly.com*.

Comments and Questions

Please address comments and questions concerning this book to the publisher:

> O'Reilly & Associates, Inc.
> 1005 Gravenstein Highway North
> Sebastopol, CA 95472
> (800) 998-9938 (in the United States or Canada)
> (707) 829-0515 (international or local)
> (707) 829-0104 (fax)

There's a web page for this book that lists errata, examples, and any additional information. You can access this page at:

> *http://www.oreilly.com/catalog/weblogictdg*

To comment or ask technical questions about this book, send email to:

> *bookquestions@oreilly.com*

For more information about books, conferences, Resource Centers, and the O'Reilly Network, see the O'Reilly web site at:

> *http://www.oreilly.com*

Acknowledgments

It is our pleasure to acknowledge the assistance of many friends and colleagues who encouraged us to complete this book and provided constructive criticism of the manuscript. Our thanks to our editor, Brett McLaughlin, and to Deepak Vohra for reviewing drafts of our chapters. Melissa Chaika, formerly of BEA, was kind enough to keep us updated on current and future changes to WebLogic Server. We'd also like to thank the production staff at O'Reilly. Mary Brady and her team did a super job of transforming an ugly manuscript into a good-looking book.

Many people have dispensed with their free time and energy to respond to our queries on WebLogic's newsgroups over the years. These include Joe Weinstein, Tom Barnes, Bruce Stephens, Slava Imeshev, Cameron Purdy, Rob Woolen, and Andy Piper. We'd also like to thank those who took the time to review drafts of this manuscript because this book owes a lot to their thoughts and ideas. We are particularly grateful to many folk at BEA who took time out of their busy schedules to help us: Joe Weinstein, Tom Barnes, Sanjeev Chopra, Cedric Beust, Peter Bower, and Tony Vlatas. Cameron was also gracious enough to review a chapter at short notice.

On a more personal note, Jon would like to thank his wife for the constant support and nourishment through trying conditions, and the Cowan family of Eastside Farm for their company, kindness, and excellent Lagavulin.

Avinash would like to thank his family and friends for their support and understanding, not just throughout the time he has been involved with this book, but also in helping him to get through his father's death. He would have liked his dad to just hold the final manuscript, even if the contents inside wouldn't have made much sense to him.

CHAPTER 1

Introduction

WebLogic Server is one of the leading J2EE application servers on the market today. It is a robust, mature, scalable implementation of the J2EE specification. It also lies at the heart of the WebLogic Platform, a unified, extensible platform for developing and deploying enterprise solutions such as enterprise information portals and systems integration solutions. This chapter provides an overview of WebLogic Server, and offers a perspective of its place within the WebLogic Platform. You'll also get a flavor of the various J2EE and enterprise features of WebLogic that you'll encounter in this book.

As you shall see, WebLogic offers much more than a full-fledged implementation of the J2EE standards. This chapter introduces some of the extensions to the J2EE technology stack, such as WebLogic's management framework and its robust support for web services. In addition, this chapter prepares the groundwork for the rest of the book, and helps you get started with using WebLogic Server.

Overview of WebLogic Server

WebLogic is a Java Application Server, a server-side Java program that provides a number of enterprise services for the benefit of the various applications and components running on the server. These services include the HTTP service, session handling, distributed naming and lookup, database access, persistence, transaction management, caching, concurrency, messaging, security, and much more. Server-side applications can use these services to implement their application logic, while external clients can either use the published services or directly interact with the applications. Once installed, WebLogic provides various command-line scripts for starting up the server. In fact, many of the WebLogic tools are Java programs that run within a console or as a GUI-based Java application. For this reason, stable releases of WebLogic Server are available on a wide range of platforms, including Windows 2000 Server/Professional, Windows XP, Solaris OS, Red Hat Linux, Tru64, HP-UX, IBM AIX, and other Unix variants.

WebLogic is designed to operate in a distributed environment. This means that you can easily set up an environment where multiple WebLogic instances are running on separate machines within the network, each configured with its own set of applications and services. Alternatively, you may need to design a "cluster" of WebLogic instances distributed across multiple machines over the network, each configured with the same set of applications and services. If you're blessed with powerful, multi-CPU machines, you even may opt to host multiple servers on a single machine. Moreover, WebLogic provides tools that enable you to set up these different scenarios and effectively manage the applications and other resources spread across all the servers. The ease and flexibility with which you can adapt your WebLogic configuration to suit your performance and scalability needs make WebLogic Server a very attractive platform for building real-world enterprise applications.

WebLogic provides a rich set of client options—it can interact with web clients that use HTTP, Java clients that use RMI-IIOP, JAX-RPC clients for web services over SOAP, and mobile devices that use WAP. It also provides comprehensive support for enterprise Java technologies. In fact, WebLogic is a fully certified J2EE application server. It means that you don't need to live under any illusions about the capabilities of WebLogic Server. At the very least, WebLogic will continue to support the full J2EE technology stack and adhere to all of the constraints that it imposes on interoperability. But WebLogic offers more and implements enterprise services that go beyond the J2EE standard, anticipating future trends in the enterprise Java application server market.

Effectively managing the applications and services deployed across the various servers on separate machines can prove to be a formidable challenge. WebLogic rises to the occasion by providing a rich, robust management infrastructure for administering the applications, resources, and other services running on separate WebLogic instances. As we shall see, WebLogic relies on the notion of a "domain" to sketch out a region of servers, WebLogic services, network and application resources, and security policies. All resources that lie within the scope of the domain are under the central control of the Administration Server. All domain administration tasks are routed via the Administration Server, which is responsible for the entire domain configuration. The domain can rely on Node Managers—one on each machine that is responsible for the health of all servers running on it. In addition, the domain may include a number of clusters, where each cluster is composed of multiple servers, possibly running on different physical machines.

Security is another important consideration when planning the system architecture for an enterprise application. WebLogic is capable of handling security issues at various levels of your setup—at the JVM level through JVM-specific policies, at the connection level through filtering and the Secure Sockets Layer (SSL), at the application level through application-specific policy constraints, and at the server level through security providers that let you transparently change various aspects of WebLogic's default security implementation. Restricted access to particular services (read ports), firewalls and demilitarized zones (DMZs), and database access privileges further reinforces the security within your application setup and makes it less vulnerable to malicious attacks and unauthorized access.

The WebLogic Platform

Before we take a closer look at WebLogic's features, let's examine how WebLogic fits in the larger scheme of things. As we mentioned earlier, WebLogic Server forms the core of the WebLogic Platform. Other WebLogic technologies, including the Portal, Integration, and Workshop, are built on top of WebLogic Server. Figure 1-1 depicts the conceptual layout of the technologies that make up the WebLogic Platform.

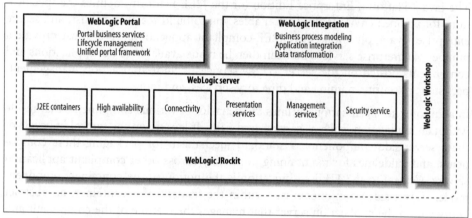

Figure 1-1. The WebLogic Platform

Clearly, WebLogic provides a range of enterprise technologies that cater to different business problems and solution paradigms:

WebLogic JRockit
    JRockit is BEA's high-performance JVM optimized for server-side performance and scalability.

WebLogic Workshop
    Workshop is a visual development environment that allows you to build enterprise-class applications on WebLogic Server.

WebLogic Portal
    WebLogic Portal is an enterprise portal platform that allows you to develop and manage custom portals that support various business processes such as commerce, content management, and interaction management.

WebLogic Integration
    WebLogic Integration provides a unified platform for developing, deploying, and integrating enterprise applications and business processes in a collaborative framework. It provides business process modeling tools, data transformation tools, a message broker, and integration adapters for a wide range of applications and formats.

This book focuses on WebLogic Server, which serves as the foundation for higher-level WebLogic technologies. A good understanding of WebLogic Server will help you appreciate how other WebLogic technologies operate. The next two sections survey the extent of WebLogic's support for the J2EE standard, as well as how WebLogic augments these features in interesting and useful ways. We also examine the enterprise features WebLogic offers on top of the existing set of J2EE features—the features that distinguish WebLogic from the rest of the crowd.

WebLogic as a J2EE Product

The Java 2 Platform, Enterprise Edition (or the J2EE Platform) defines the specifications for an open environment that enables you to build scalable, robust, and secure enterprise Java applications. Any J2EE-compliant application server must provide a number of enterprise services that can then be made available to the applications and components hosted on the server. These services include transaction management, persistence, security, naming and directory services, and more.

In addition, the specification outlines the behavior of various components that reside within an application, such as servlets and EJBs. It lays down the typical life cycle of these server-side components, a standard mechanism for packaging these components, and guidelines for maintaining portability across other compliant application servers. Central to the J2EE specification is the notion of the container-component model. Server-side components run within the context of a container, an abstract entity within the application server that manages the lifetime of the component and provides access to a host of available services. Like a cocoon, a container nurtures and protects the various components deployed to the server. Servlets and JSP pages typically run within a web container, while the EJBs run within an EJB container.

Versions 8.1 and 7.0 of WebLogic Server embrace the J2EE 1.3 specification. Because the J2EE 1.3 specification is backward-compatible with J2EE 1.2, you can run J2EE 1.2–compliant applications on WebLogic Server 8.1 and 7.0 as well. Remember, the J2EE standard defines only the *minimum* set of enterprise services that any compliant application server must implement. WebLogic also offers a whole lot more. We'll look at these additional exciting enterprise features of WebLogic Server in the following section. Let's first inspect the standard J2EE features that are part of WebLogic Server.

Servlets, JSPs, and the web container

WebLogic Server is equipped with a full-featured servlet engine that complies with the Servlet 2.3 and JSP 1.2 specifications. This means that you can build web applications that contain HTTP servlets and JSP pages for generating dynamic responses to web requests. You also may configure multiple filters that process a web request before it has been handled or after the web response has been generated. You can incorporate custom JSP tags into your JSP pages, where each tag encapsulates a well-defined, reusable piece of functionality. Clearly, these components have access to other J2EE services as well, such as JNDI lookups, JDBC API calls, distributed transactions, remote EJBs, and more. Of course, you can deploy multiple web applications to WebLogic Server, and utilize third-party tag libraries in your existing web applications.

WebLogic offers several enhancements to the web container. During development mode, WebLogic supports automatic reloading of servlets and JSPs. It provides different ways of caching the response to web requests, and how and when the cached responses ought to be refreshed. You may choose to configure WebLogic's cache filter for specific web requests, or rely on WebLogic's custom JSP cache tags to cache specific portions of the JSP page. WebLogic also provides advanced session-handling features with support for failover, whereby a user's session data can be replicated to another WebLogic instance or persisted to a file or a database. This mechanism guarantees high availability for web applications deployed to a cluster. WebLogic also provides an "EJB-to-JSP" tool that lets you automatically generate a set of JSP tags from EJBs that you've already developed.

So, WebLogic has an established framework for handling dynamic HTTP requests. But WebLogic is also a robust, mature HTTP server, which means that you can use WebLogic to serve requests for the static content in your web applications, such as HTML pages, images, text files, and more. You even can configure virtual hosts, HTTP tunneling, and SSL for WebLogic's HTTP server. You also can set up the HTTP server to act as a proxy server so that it proxies dynamic requests for servlets and JSPs to another WebLogic instance. The same behavior can be achieved using commercial web servers. WebLogic provides custom proxy plug-ins for popular web servers such as Apache, Microsoft's Internet Information Service (IIS), and Netscape's Enterprise Server (NES). These plug-ins ensure that only specific requests for dynamic content are forwarded to a WebLogic instance. In this way, you can continue to use your high-performance web servers, while your backend WebLogic instance(s) are responsible for handling all the dynamic web requests.

JDBC and distributed transactions

Most Java applications use the JDBC API to interact with backend relational databases. Because WebLogic supports the JDBC 2.0 specification, you can configure a ready pool of database connections on WebLogic using any JDBC 2.0–compliant driver. The connection pool provides access to the backend DBMS—you would be hard-pressed to find a DBMS for which a JDBC driver isn't shipped. Server-side applications and external clients then can transparently access the connection pool using configured data sources. WebLogic also supports distributed transaction-aware (XA-aware) data sources, in which case connections obtained from the data source can participate in distributed transactions. If the data source is attached to a pool of non XA-aware connections, WebLogic can still emulate the two-phase commit protocol, and ensure that the data source can participate in distributed transactions, albeit with some limitations.

Besides making JDBC connection pools accessible to both server-side applications and external clients, WebLogic allows you to set up a multipool where a number of connection pools can collaborate to achieve load balancing or high availability for JDBC connection requests, even in a single-server environment. You can then transparently access the multipool through each connection pool's configured data sources. Furthermore, WebLogic can optimize JDBC access by supplying a statement cache with every connection pool. WebLogic can then cache a number of prepared statements (or callable statements) used by clients of the connection pool. Statement caching can offer a significant performance boost if the most-often used statements fill the cache. You also can configure application-scoped JDBC resources. As these are packaged with the application, they make it easy to duplicate the configuration on different application server instances.

In addition, WebLogic's multi-tier drivers provide clients with direct access to server-side connection pools, automatic enrollment in distributed transactions, and clustered access to connection pools through their data sources. Multi-tier drivers enable connection requests to a data source that is targeted to a cluster of WebLogic instances to fail over to another connection pool if one of the servers fails.

The Java Transaction API (JTA) provides the higher-level client access to distributed transactions. Clients need to explicitly initiate distributed transactions when multiple EJBs are needed to fulfill a client request or when the default container-managed transactions are inadequate to implement the business logic. WebLogic extends the capabilities of the JTA by enabling clients to access the current transaction associated with the thread or to obtain a reference to the transaction manager. Moreover, WebLogic allows you to monitor, log, and recover transactions through its transaction recovery service.

JNDI and RMI

Java Naming and Directory Interface (JNDI) provides the standard way for interacting with naming and directory services. J2EE applications use the JNDI API to access various resources that have been configured for the server, including data sources, user transactions, Remote Method Invocation (RMI) objects, EJB home objects, mail sessions, JMS connection factories, JMS topics/queues, and much more. WebLogic's JNDI framework extends over an entire cluster, across all its available members. The cluster-wide JNDI tree manages the JNDI bindings for all clusterable objects. These bindings are automatically replicated across all WebLogic instances in the cluster. Each server maintains a local copy of the global JNDI tree holding replicas of all JNDI bindings in the global JNDI tree. In addition, the local JNDI tree holds bindings for any server-specific resources that must be made available only to the particular WebLogic instance.

The RMI specification initiated the wave of distributed Java computing. It established an intuitive framework for enabling Java method invocations across JVMs. WebLogic's

RMI is a highly optimized implementation, incorporating high-performance serialization logic and avoiding the overhead of marshalling and unmarshalling when both the client and the server-side RMI objects run within the same VM. WebLogic's RMI usually relies on its native transport protocol, called the *T3 protocol*. However, WebLogic also supports RMI clients that need to talk over *Internet Inter-ORB Protocol* (IIOP), a protocol that allows interoperability with CORBA objects.

Moreover, WebLogic's RMI Registry is a thin veneer over its JNDI service. In fact, RMI objects can be published directly over WebLogic's JNDI tree. WebLogic's JNDI service and clusterable RMI stubs collaborate to provide failover and load-balancing facilities to clients. WebLogic lets you compile and bind RMI objects into this clustered environment. Any client that looks up the RMI object from the JNDI tree obtains a *cluster-aware stub*—a stub that is aware of all its replicas on all available servers in the cluster. Thus, WebLogic's implementation of JNDI and RMI provides a transparent and elegant way for supporting failover and load balancing of RMI objects in a clustered environment.

EJBs

EJBs are reusable server-side Java components that usually encapsulate the business logic of an enterprise application. EJBs typically interact with backend databases and almost always participate in distributed transactions. WebLogic fully supports all the different EJB component types defined in the EJB 2.0 specification: session beans, message-driven beans, and entity beans.

J2EE applications can use these EJB types to implement their business logic. Even though WebLogic Server supports EJBs that are compliant with the 1.1 standard, most developers find it inadequate for their needs, and eventually need to deal with business requirements where it is just as convenient to upgrade to the EJB 2.0 standard.

Typically, your EJB components form the "object tier" of an enterprise application that services requests from other servlets and JSP pages, or even external clients. You can even choose to deploy only your EJB components separately to a cluster of WebLogic instances. This division of labor between WebLogic instances—one set of servers that handles the web/presentation aspects of the enterprise application, and another set of servers that manages the EJB components—lets you benefit from WebLogic's load-balancing and failover features. The flexibility of options that are available to you when designing a WebLogic-based architecture also adds to its appeal.

WebLogic's EJB container provides many additional enhancements. WebLogic supports a free pool of EJB instances for stateless session beans, message-driven beans, and entity beans. It also provides an in-memory cache of EJB instances for stateful session beans and entity beans. The WebLogic-specific deployment descriptors allow you to adjust the size of the free pool and the EJB cache. A properly configured free pool and EJB cache can significantly improve the performance of your EJBs. Most importantly, EJBs can operate easily in a clustered environment. Client requests to the EJB home object or method calls on an EJB object can be load-balanced across all available servers in a cluster. Failover on method calls also can be achieved under certain conditions. In addition, WebLogic supports failover for stateful session EJBs that have been deployed to a cluster. Just like HTTP sessions, WebLogic achieves this behavior by replicating the state of the session EJB onto another server in the cluster.

WebLogic dedicates a whole array of optimizations to entity beans. For instance, WebLogic's EJB container supports value-change checks to ensure that only those persistent fields that have been modified are written to the database. This can improve the performance of your EJBs if their persistent fields map to long-valued columns (large chars, varchars, blobs, clobs, etc.). It also supports read-only entity beans where the in-memory state of the EJB can be refreshed at regular intervals. In this way, WebLogic's EJB container can avoid persisting the EJB's state to the underlying database. In addition, WebLogic incorporates a multicast invalidation framework, whereby an EJB update can invalidate all cached EJB instances on other servers. This mechanism avoids unnecessary loading of EJB data. You even can configure WebLogic's EJB container so that all updates made during a transaction are deferred until transaction commit.

WebLogic's CMP engine is equipped with a rich set of features. Its RDBMS persistence framework allows you to map an entity bean's container-managed fields to columns spread across multiple tables. You can specify precisely when the in-memory state of the entity EJB is written to the database. In addition, WebLogic supports an "optimistic concurrency" strategy for entity EJBs, which ensures that no locks are held by WebLogic or the database. Instead, the EJB container performs a smart update by checking that the data hasn't been modified since the start of the transaction. In this way, optimistic concurrency allows you to dramatically improve the concurrency of your entity EJBs. Other features, such as batching and fetch groups, provide you with extreme control over when and how the database is accessed.

WebLogic also implements a superset of the standard EJB QL. It allows you to define EJB queries that provide ordering and aggregation, and that remove duplicates from matching EJB instances. These extensions are identical to their SQL counterparts: ORDER BY, GROUP BY, and SELECT DISTINCT.

JMS

Java Messaging Service (JMS) equips you with a powerful programming model based on asynchronous, decoupled communication. It allows you to build J2EE applications on top of existing message-oriented middleware. WebLogic's JMS implementation is compliant with the 1.02b release of the JMS standard, and is chock-full of practical enhancements. For instance, WebLogic enables producers and consumers to exchange XML-formatted messages. The message filters can be specified using

XPath expressions that can then filter out any message whose body doesn't match the given XPath query.

For better scalability, WebLogic provides fine control of message delivery and handling. For instance, you can delay the delivery of messages or configure specific time periods during which the messages are delivered. WebLogic's support for message paging gives you additional control over resource usage by moving messages out of main memory under predefined conditions. It also provides flow control mechanisms that let you throttle the production of messages during peak message load conditions. All these features ensure WebLogic's JMS server cannot degrade the performance of other WebLogic services.

Depending on your message delivery needs, WebLogic lets you choose from a range of acknowledgment modes, from guaranteed to unacknowledged message delivery. If no acknowledgment is required, WebLogic relies on multicast broadcasts to deliver your messages. WebLogic's JMS service is integrated with its clustering services. It lets you transparently masquerade multiple JMS destinations that reside on separate servers behind a virtual destination name. This feature yields seamless failover and load balancing when delivering messages to the "distributed" JMS destination. The messaging bridge tops off all these features by allowing you to integrate WebLogic JMS with other JMS providers.

JCA

Java Connector Architecture (JCA) provides a standard framework for connecting J2EE application servers to enterprise information systems. Server-side applications and external clients can use the configured resource adapter to interact with the enterprise information system (EIS). Just like JDBC drivers, WebLogic lets you set up a pool of connections to the underlying EIS. These connections may participate in distributed transactions, along with other transaction-aware resources. WebLogic also can reliably detect connection leaks by relying on the garbage collector and an idle timer setting. This ensures that the pool doesn't run out of available connections, in case clients of the resource adapter aren't properly releasing their connections. You'll also find that WebLogic's security infrastructure extends to resource adapters.

Additional Enterprise Features of WebLogic

We've just looked at some of the standard features that are compulsory for any J2EE-compliant application server, and how WebLogic's implementation enhances these features. Beyond this, WebLogic provides a slew of additional functionality that enhances your experience of developing and managing applications in a WebLogic environment. You'll find that these enterprise features of WebLogic Server enable you to build more secure, manageable, and scalable solutions.

WebLogic's security framework

WebLogic provides a comprehensive suite of security features with which you can protect your domain resources. For instance, WebLogic augments the security of your network by letting you set up connection filters that can deny access to connections according to custom criteria. In addition, WebLogic supports the use of SSL, which can be configured to use mutual authentication. Plus, you can programmatically rely on SSL to communicate with other systems. At the server level, WebLogic lets you set up fine-grained control over access to resources such as JDBC connection pools, EJBs, web services, and specific branches of the JNDI hierarchy.

WebLogic's security infrastructure is based on a modular, extensible set of security service provider interfaces (SSPIs). A domain can use either the default implementation of the security providers, or custom security providers that extend the default providers according to your needs. For instance, WebLogic's authentication framework allows you to store all authentication information to a Lightweight Directory Access Protocol (LDAP) or to a JDBC-based repository. In fact, WebLogic comes with its own embedded LDAP server. The traditional J2EE role-based security also relies on a role-mapping provider. WebLogic lets you transparently plug in a custom role-mapping provider and thereby benefit from an alternative implementation.

WebLogic in a clustered environment

You can easily set up a cluster of WebLogic instances, all working together to provide support for load balancing and failover. Your applications and related resources can be deployed homogenously across all the servers in the cluster. External clients can interact with any member of the cluster, and fall back on another server in case of a failure. WebLogic's support for clustering provides an intuitive way for enhancing the scalability of your architecture. New servers can transparently join the cluster and grab their share of the overall load on the cluster. Your applications continue to be highly available because other servers can take over in case a peer server fails.

Clusters are especially relevant when designing a multi-tier architecture for an enterprise application. Client requests for a web application can be distributed across a bank of WebLogic instances. EJB method calls from a servlet or JSP page can again be distributed across a cluster of WebLogic instances that host all the EJB components. This division of labor is vital if you have differing performance constraints for your web applications and your EJBs, and therefore need to ensure your application tiers can scale independently.

Clearly, there's little point in considering these architectures if WebLogic services cannot adapt to a clustered environment. Fortunately, most J2EE services can benefit from WebLogic clusters. This includes load-balancing and failover support for HTTP requests, method calls to EJB home objects and EJB objects, JDBC connection requests, JMS distributed destinations, and much more. Stateful services also can operate in a clustered environment. For instance, WebLogic supports in-memory replication of HTTP sessions and stateful session EJBs. As discussed earlier, the interplay between the cluster-wide JNDI tree and clusterable RMI stubs is crucial to the support for load balancing and failover. For singleton services such as JMS, WebLogic allows you to migrate the service to another peer server in the cluster, thereby ensuring high availability.

XML support

XML has become all-important in the J2EE world, and WebLogic provides extensive support for these technologies. First, WebLogic is bundled with Apache's Xerces XML parsers and Xalan XSLT implementations. WebLogic also includes an optimized nonvalidating SAX parser, ideal for small to medium-size documents such as those that occur in the world of web services. All of these parsers can be used through the standard JAXP interface, which provides better control over the XML parser that is used under a given situation. WebLogic also lets you configure particular XML parsers on a per-server and per-application basis.

On top of all this, WebLogic includes an XML Streaming API, which allows you to parse XML documents using a pull-based approach. Under the right conditions, pull-based parsing can be more optimal than event-driven SAX parsing or the DOM-based approach. WebLogic 8.1 also provides an XML XPath API, which can integrate with the Streaming API.

Web services

A *web service* is a distributed, interoperable, web-based interface that transparently wraps some well-defined piece of functionality. Clients can locate the desired web service from a registry and then invoke the web service. The actual implementation behind the web service can manifest itself in various ways. For instance, WebLogic makes it very easy for you to create web services that wrap ordinary Java objects, stateless session EJBs, and JMS destinations.

Support for web services is going to be an essential requirement in the next release of the J2EE specification. WebLogic has preemptively implemented a rich set of facilities that enable you to easily create and deploy industry-strength web services. Its GUI-based tool, WebLogic Workshop, is dedicated to building and deploying web services on WebLogic Server. WebLogic relies on the standard SOAP 1.1 protocol with attachments message format for delivering data during web service invocations. Descriptions of web services deployed to WebLogic Server adhere to the WSDL 1.1 standard. Moreover, WebLogic lets you automatically generate these descriptions, along with HTML pages that allow you to test your web services. You can publish the web services on WebLogic through the UDDI service that runs within WebLogic. Clients can locate desired web services by questioning the UDDI 2.0 registry.

WebLogic 8.1 also supports a reliable SOAP message transport, which allows clients to use guaranteed SOAP message delivery. In addition to this, you can invoke web service operations asynchronously. With this style of invocation, you can either periodically poll for a result, or create a listener that will receive a notification when the operation's result comes in. WebLogic 8.1 can secure SOAP message exchanges through token-based identification, digital signatures, and data encryption. Finally, WebLogic supports the JAX-RPC standard for invoking web services running on either WebLogic Server or any other compatible platform. The combination of these features makes WebLogic's web services implementation quite formidable.

Management features

The Java Management Extensions (JMX) specification defines the architecture, services, and Java APIs for the distributed management of resources. WebLogic's built-in MBean server provides access to a host of JMX MBeans that enable you to programmatically fiddle around with the static and runtime configuration settings of various resources of a WebLogic domain. You can use these MBeans to build your own management and configuration tools, or simply use them to monitor the performance of the different WebLogic services.

The Simple Network Management Protocol (SNMP) is used to monitor many different types of managed resources, from hardware to software products. JMX services also serve as inputs for WebLogic's SNMP agent. WebLogic's SNMP agent allows you to seamlessly integrate a WebLogic domain within a larger network management framework of your enterprise. In this way, your WebLogic domain can be treated just like any other network resource. Both JMX and SNMP give you exceptional control over the overall management of a WebLogic domain.

Both of WebLogic's JMX and SNMP systems can interact with the distributed logging infrastructure. This allows you to centrally manage all logging activity and create advanced components that listen and react to error situations.

WebLogic Server Tools

As much as WebLogic's enterprise features may entrance you, you still need the right set of tools to assemble and deploy your applications, manage your WebLogic environment, and monitor the runtime state of all deployed services, applications, and resources. Fortunately, WebLogic takes care of all these needs, and more.

System administration console

The Administration Console is a comprehensive, browser-based GUI application for configuring, managing, and monitoring all of the resources in a WebLogic domain. Some of its capabilities include managing the domain configuration, starting and stopping servers, monitoring the performance of the server and application components, viewing server logs, initiating deployment tasks, and editing deployment descriptors.

Deployment and development tools

With Java applications, deployment has never been easy. In a clustered environment, it can be even trickier. The Administration Console lets you deploy, redeploy, and undeploy J2EE applications and modules to specific server instances and to all members of a cluster. WebLogic's Deployer utility, `weblogic.Deployer`, is a command-line tool for managing the deployment of J2EE applications.

EJBGen is another useful tool that can generate the EJB deployment descriptors, and the home and remote interfaces from the source of the EJB's bean class annotated with predefined JavaDoc tags. WebLogic's Marathon utility (DDInit) can examine the contents of a staging folder and generate the standard J2EE and WebLogic-specific deployment descriptors for both web applications and EJB modules. WebLogic also supplies a Client Deployer tool that can extract the client-side JAR from an EAR file to create a deployable JAR file.

WebLogic also provides a number of utility Ant tasks that ease the build and deployment process. For instance, the `appc` task lets you generate the container classes for your EJBs, as well as generate an EJB JAR that can be deployed to WebLogic Server. It can also be used to precompile your JSP pages. The `wsdl2service` task takes a WSDL file as input and generates the *web-services.xml* deployment descriptor, and a raw Java source file that can be used as a starting point for implementing the web service. You'll learn about other Ant tasks provided by WebLogic as you read the rest of the book!

WebLogic Builder

Assembling a J2EE application, creating and editing its deployment descriptors, and later deploying it to WebLogic Server is not a trivial task. WebLogic Builder fulfills these requirements. It is a graphical tool used for assembling a J2EE application, creating and editing its deployment descriptors, and deploying it to a WebLogic instance.

WebLogic Workshop

WebLogic Workshop is a tool that deserves special mention and a book of its own. WebLogic Server comes with an IDE, WebLogic Workshop, which can be used to compose web services and other components using a very high level of abstraction.

The IDE lets you create and compose enterprise applications in a graphical way— simply drag the components that you want to use onto the same screen and wire them together. All and all, it provides a very quick route to application creation. Here are some of the features of WebLogic Workshop:

- It provides a visual and textual coding environment.
- The code generated by Workshop is annotated with JavaDoc tags indicating behavior. For example, Workshop can be used to create EJBs. These EJBs are annotated using the tags supported by EJBGen, which is described in Chapter 10.

- Workshop provides a framework that abstracts the complexities of the J2EE. Instead of writing J2EE infrastructure code, most of the Java you need to write is simply business logic and a little wiring.

- Workshop offers a component model in the form of Java controls. Controls can be created for almost all J2EE concepts, such as web services, EJBs, JMS destinations, web applications, and databases. You can write your own controls and embed controls within others.

- Because of the Java Control model adopted by Workshop, you can reuse controls from previous projects, download controls from BEA, and even buy controls to supplement the controls distributed with Workshop.

- Workshop integrates tightly with WebLogic Server during development. Deployment, testing, and debugging are made very easy.

- Workshop also can be used to easily construct web applications based on Apache's Struts framework. Visual designers are provided, as well as data-binding tag libraries. Navigation in the web application is controlled by a combination of page flows and controller logic.

It is beyond the scope of this book to discuss how to use WebLogic Workshop in depth. It is a powerful, comprehensive tool that provides a different route to creating applications than that described in the rest of this book. However, Chapter 19 provides a detailed, low-level look at the web services framework supported by WebLogic. Creating web services using this framework requires coding, descriptor files, and Ant build files. On the other hand, you can create web services in Workshop with a few drags of the mouse. Both techniques have their place.

Software and Versions

This book examines features and services of WebLogic Server. We've used WebLogic Server 8.1 SP 1, and WebLogic 7.0 SP 2. We recommend that you apply the latest service packs after installing WebLogic Server to ensure all known issues have been resolved. Most of the changes between WebLogic 7.0 and WebLogic 8.1 occur in the form of new features or in slight changes to the Administration Console. We have tried hard not to litter the book with sections relevant to only one particular version, or with distracting warnings about which features are in which version. Rather, we have tried to be discrete. So, for example, when we say at the beginning of a section that "WebLogic 8.1 introduces a new feature that ...," you can be sure that the feature is in WebLogic 8.1 only, and not in 7.0.

Customers can choose the particular edition of WebLogic Server that best suits their needs. If you intend to develop pure web applications that consist of static web resources and incorporate dynamic content through servlets and JSPs, you can perhaps opt for the WebLogic Express edition. If you need to build full enterprise systems using EJBs, JMS, and distributed transactions, you will need WebLogic Server instead. Each comes in two different flavors: versions that support clustering and versions that don't.

Your WebLogic distribution is shipped with a stable release of the J2SE SDK. WebLogic 8.1 ships with a 1.4 JDK, and WebLogic 7.0 with a 1.3 JDK. All shell scripts and batch command files within WebLogic reference the JRE contained within this JDK.

WebLogic Server is fully compliant with the J2EE 1.3 standard. This means that you can incorporate any other third-party custom components, such as JSP tags that conform to the JSP 1.2 specification or entity beans that conform to the EJB 2.0 standard. Moreover, WebLogic applications can interact with any LDAP server for which the vendor supplies a JNDI 1.1–compliant service provider. In addition, you can deploy any third-party resource adapter that conforms to the JCA 1.1 standard.

Typically, WebLogic interacts with a backend DBMS through a configured pool of JDBC connections. We've used Microsoft's SQL Server 2000 Service Pack 3 and PostgreSQL to run many of the code samples illustrated here. In fact, you may use any industry-strength RDBMS for which a JDBC 2.0–compliant driver is available, including Oracle 8.0 or higher, IBM's DB2 or Informix, and many others.

Finally, even though WebLogic comes equipped with JAXP-compliant XML parsers, you may choose to utilize other implementations.

Getting Started with WebLogic Server

As we've already seen, all WebLogic instances and their resources exist within the context of an organizational unit called a WebLogic domain. Within the domain, you can set up multiple servers, customize their network configurations, and deploy multiple J2EE applications and any required resources. You may even set up WebLogic clusters using a subset of the servers in the domain. All servers in the cluster can then work together to provide support for failover and load balancing.

One server in the domain is vital to its existence: the Administration Server that manages the configuration for the entire domain. This includes the configuration of all servers within the domain, and all applications and services deployed to these servers. Other servers in the domain, called Managed Servers, host the actual J2EE applications and resources such as JDBC connection pools, data sources, JMS connection factories, topics and queues, RMI objects, and so on. The Administration Server merely manages the entire configuration of these servers. In a single-server domain, you have little choice but to deploy your applications to the Administration Server itself. However, in a production environment, we recommend you deploy your applications to a separate server.

WebLogic is fairly flexible about how you configure the servers in the domain. So long as all Managed Servers in the domain can reach the Administration Server over the same network, WebLogic doesn't care whether the servers in the domain run on the same machine or on their own hardware.

Let's now quickly look at how to create a single-server WebLogic domain so that you can start the Administration Server. Once you're able to access the domain's configuration using the Administration Console, you know that you have a working WebLogic domain. This should be a good starting point for you to start building J2EE applications for WebLogic, and trying out any examples that you encounter as you read this book. Chapter 13 shows you how to expand on this configuration to build more complex domains.

Creating a Domain

In order to set up a running WebLogic instance that you can work with, you need to first create a WebLogic domain. When you've successfully done so, you can deploy your J2EE applications to the Administration Server itself. Later on, as you become more comfortable with WebLogic Server, you can add more servers to the domain and move your applications to the Managed Servers.

For WebLogic 8.1, start up the Domain Configuration Wizard by selecting the program from your operating system's Start menu. Select the Basic WebLogic Server Domain option from the list, and choose the express setup route. You then need to supply the username and password for the system administrator. Remember these details, as you won't be able to start or access the Administration Console successfully without them. After selecting from the installed SDKs to use, provide a name for the domain and a location on the filesystem where you want to store the domain. Finally, choose Create. The domain set up in this manner will automatically bind to all available IP addresses and listen on port 7001.

For WebLogic 7.0, start up the Domain Configuration Wizard by running the *dmwiz* script located under the *WL-HOME/common/bin* folder, or by selecting the program from your operating system's Start menu. Select the WLS Domain option from the list, supply a name for the new domain, and then choose the Single Server (Standalone Server) option. Then you need to supply the full path of the directory under which all domain-related files are stored. After this, you need to configure the standalone server. For this, you need to specify the server's name, IP address or hostname, and the listen port on which the server is available. If you do not specify an address for the standalone Administration Server, the server automatically binds to all available IP addresses. Finally, you need to supply the username and password for the system administrator. Ensure that the single server doesn't run as an OS service.

In order to run the standalone server, you need to navigate to the domain's root directory, locate the *startweblogic* shell script for your OS, and run it. The server won't start unless you also supply the username and password of the administrator configured earlier during the creation of the domain. Ensure that you've installed the proper WebLogic licenses or else the server aborts its boot sequence. You'll know that the server has successfully completed its startup sequence when you see the following in the console log window:

```
<20-Apr-03 23:26:57 BST> <Notice> <WebLogicServer> <000365> <Server state changed to
RUNNING>
<20-Apr-03 23:26:57 BST> <Notice> <WebLogicServer> <000360> <Server started in
RUNNING mode>
```

Well done, you've successfully configured a new WebLogic domain and started the standalone Administration Server.

 The Domain Configuration Wizard lets you install domains already populated with applications. The "examples" domain is very useful, as it contains code and examples for most aspects of WebLogic.

Under the domain's root directory, you'll find the *config.xml* file that captures the entire configuration of the domain. Any changes made to the domain's configuration are persisted to the *config.xml* file. The domain log file *domain-name.log* also lives under the domain's root folder. Log files for the Administration Server are placed under the *domain-name/server-name* folder.

uver — Weblogic

Pwd — Reddy212

Using the Administration Console

Once you've successfully started the domain's Administration Server, you can use the Administration Console to configure, manage, and monitor the domain and all its resources. Now if you've bound the Administration Server to the IP address 10.0.10. 10, for instance, and set its listen port to 7001, you can invoke the Administration Console through your web browser by navigating to *http://10.0.10.10:7001/console/*. Here again, you need to supply the administrator's login credentials (username/password) in order to view the domain's configuration.

Once the user's credentials have been successfully authenticated, you can access all areas of the Administration Console. On the left pane, you'll notice a graphical tree menu that lets you navigate to the different resources located in a WebLogic domain. Ensure that you have installed a Java plug-in for the browser, or else the menu applet will not render successfully.

Figure 1-2 illustrates the navigation menu for the Administration Console. We recommend that you familiarize yourself with these menu options. The rest of the book frequently will refer to the left pane of the Administration Console because it provides the primary means for manipulating the domain's configuration. For instance, you'll often come across the instruction "Select the desired server instance from the left pane of the Administration Console." Assuming that you've configured the server *myserver* within a WebLogic domain *mydomain*, this means that you need to navigate to the mydomain/Servers/myserver node of the tree menu in the left pane. Then, clicking the *myserver* node from the left pane automatically displays the server's configuration settings in the right frame of your browser window.

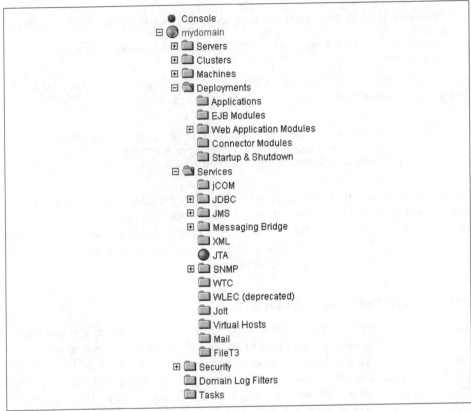

Figure 1-2. Navigation menu of the Administration Console

Similarly, by clicking any WebLogic resource from the left pane, you can view and modify the associated configuration settings in the right pane of the Administration Console. Moreover, WebLogic maintains runtime statistics for each deployed resource, which you can view through the Monitoring tab in the right pane.

The graphical tree menu also lets you perform specific operations on a resource by right-clicking the particular tree node. For instance, you can view the server's JNDI tree by right-clicking the *myserver* node in the left pane, and then choosing the "View JNDI tree" option from the pop-up menu.

Now that you've set up your domain and understand the essentials of using the Administration Console to view the domain's configuration and monitor the various domain resources, you are ready to proceed on a journey into the world of WebLogic Server.

CHAPTER 2

Web Applications

Many of today's enterprise applications implement a web frontend. They choose to expose their business functions via a web user interface, most often accessed from the client's browser. These applications may access other enterprise services such as XML transformers, JNDI, database resources, and connection factories to fulfill their service contracts. WebLogic Server provides the ideal environment for creating rich web applications—it offers an extensive range of tools for assembling and configuring web components. Like any servlet engine, WebLogic supports all the functionality needed to host multiple web applications, which we shall cover in detail in later chapters.

In this chapter, we look at the internal structure of web applications and their associated XML deployment descriptors. We shall see how WebLogic eases the task of building and assembling web applications, and examine some of the deployment issues of WebLogic Server. We also look at how you can configure the various web components.

We take a peek at WebLogic's JSP compiler, and then examine JSP configuration issues when deploying a web application. Custom JSP tags are a useful mechanism for adding dynamic content to a JSP page. WebLogic provides a number of tag libraries. One such tag library offers useful caching functionality. Similar caching functionality is made available in the form of a servlet filter. WebLogic also provides a tool that can automatically create a JSP tag library from EJB components.

You also will learn about WebLogic's servlet support, such as session tracking and session persistence. WebLogic provides a number of ways to persist session state. File-, memory-, and cookie-based persistence mechanisms are supported. When using servlets in a cluster, in-memory session replication also can be used. This chapter examines these mechanisms, and looks at how to set up a simple web cluster with session replication.

Finally, we look at various ways in which you can secure a web application using declarative and programmatic techniques. Setting up the HTTP over SSL (HTTPS) listen port and the associated SSL configuration is covered in Chapter 16. Chapter 3 concludes the discussion of the web environment—it describes how you can use and configure WebLogic's HTTP server and proxy plug-ins.

Packaging and Deployment

As a J2EE-compliant web container, WebLogic Server can host a number of web applications. Each *web application* is a logical collection of servlets, JSPs, client-side applets, and static *web resources* such as HTML pages, images, multimedia documents, etc. In addition, a web application may use filters, JSP tag libraries, utility Java classes, and JavaBean components. Each web application is executed in its own runtime environment provided by the web container—a handle to this environment is provided by ServletContext. We refer to JSPs and servlets as *web components*. These web components also have access to external resources and WebLogic enterprise services such as deployed EJB components, JDBC data sources, JMS destinations, XML parser factories, and much more through access to ServletContext.

Structure of a Web Application

A web application is structured as a hierarchy of directories—the root directory serves as the *document root* for all resources in the web application. These directories contain all the JSPs, servlets, and other, static resources such as images that are referenced by the application. A special directory named *WEB-INF* holds all resources that aren't part of the public document tree of the application. So, a web client will not have direct access to any file stored under the *WEB-INF* directory, which is quite useful for protecting from clients specific resources in the web application. However, the contents of the *WEB-INF* directory are exposed to the server side. Both the methods getResource( ) and getResourceAsStream( ) of the ServletContext object and the forward( ) and include( ) methods of the RequestDispatcher object can access the contents of the *WEB-INF* folder.

The *WEB-INF* folder also includes the following files:

- A *web.xml* deployment descriptor, which is the standard J2EE XML document that describes the contents of the web application
- A *weblogic.xml* deployment descriptor, which contains the WebLogic-specific deployment information about the web application
- A *classes* subdirectory, which is the base directory for all compiled servlets, filters, precompiled JSPs, implementation classes for custom JSP tags, and utility classes
- A *lib* folder, which is the location for all JAR files that may be useful to the web application, including custom JSP tag libraries

Example 2-1 lists the contents of a typical web application.

Example 2-1. Directory layout for a simple web application

```
/index.html
/home.jsp
/error.jsp
/demos/products.swf
/images/banner.jpg
/WEB-INF/web.xml
/WEB-INF/weblogic.xml
/WEB-INF/classes/com/oreilly/bar/MyServlet.class
/WEB-INF/classes/com/oreilly/bar/MyFilter.class
/WEB-INF/classes/com/oreilly/bar/MyTagImpl.class
/WEB-INF/lib/mylibs.jar
```

Assembling a WAR

A web archive (WAR) can be created very simply by placing the contents of the WAR in a staging directory—for instance, *wardir*—and then using the jar tool that comes with your JDK to create the archive:

```
jar cvf mywar.war -C wardir
```

Alternatively, you can use a standard Ant task:

```
<war warfile="mywar.war" webxml="web.xml" manifest="manifest.txt">
  <zipfileset dir="." prefix="WEB-INF" includes="weblogic.xml"/>
  <zipfileset dir="." prefix="images" includes="*.gif,*.jpg"/>
  <classes dir="classes" includes="**/MyServlet.class"/>
  <fileset dir="." includes="*.jsp,*.html"/>
</war>
```

This has an advantage over the jar command because the different components of the WAR are not required to be in any particular fixed directory structure before creation. The war task can be part of an Ant script, which is used to build and deploy the web application.

Chapter 19 shows how you can use WebLogic's tools to package web service components within a WAR file.

XML Deployment Descriptors

A web application needs a standard J2EE *web.xml* descriptor and an optional WebLogic-specific *weblogic.xml* descriptor before it is ready for deployment. You can use these XML documents to define the web components and set up the operating environment for the web application. The *web.xml* descriptor is defined in the Servlet specification. It can be used to specify application-specific initialization parameters, servlets, filters and event listeners, MIME types, sessions tag libraries, security, and references to external resources.

Some web applications may require a *weblogic.xml* descriptor, which defines deployment properties specific to the runtime environment in WebLogic Server. In

WebLogic Server 8.1, the *weblogic.xml* descriptor must be a valid XML document conforming to the DTD, published at *http://www.bea.com/servers/wls810/dtd/weblogic810-web-jar.dtd*. You can use this deployment descriptor to specify:

- HTTP session parameters (for the session tracking cookie, session persistence, and URL rewriting).
- JSP parameters (compilation settings for WebLogic's JSP compiler).
- Container attributes (configure whether you require reauthentication for forwarded requests and whether redirects use absolute or relative URLs).
- Character-set mappings and parameters.
- JNDI names for references to external resources defined in the *web.xml* descriptor file (including EJBs, data sources, security realms, etc.).
- Custom classes for URL pattern matching.
- Security role assignments to one or more principals in the realm.
- Virtual directories for mapping other document roots for a specific set of requests. For example, images for a web application may be stored in a separate location and need not be under the document root for the web application. If one or more virtual directories have been mapped, WebLogic Server will inspect the virtual directories for the resource before looking at the document root for the web application.

All of these issues are covered in this chapter and in Chapter 3.

Chapter 12 provides a number of techniques that may be used to edit deployment descriptors of web applications.

WebLogic's JSP Compiler

WebLogic's internal JSP compiler translates JSP pages into servlet classes. By default, WebLogic automatically compiles JSPs without any user intervention. This compilation occurs when a JSP has been requested and the servlet class file has not yet been generated or the servlet class is older than the actual JSP page. This means that the compilation occurs automatically whenever a new JSP is invoked, or when the client has invoked a JSP that has been modified since the last time it was compiled. Therefore, you don't ever *need* to invoke the JSP compiler directly (although you may want to, as detailed in this section). Later, we shall see how you can register a JSP page as a servlet, and set it to load and initialize when the server starts up. In that case, the JSP compilation occurs during startup, even before a request is received from a client browser.

You also can configure WebLogic Server to precompile all JSP pages when a web application is deployed (or redeployed) or when the server starts up. To enable JSP precompilation, you need to set a JSP configuration parameter within the jsp-descriptor element in the *weblogic.xml* descriptor file:

```
<jsp-descriptor>
  <jsp-param>
    <param-name>precompile</param-name>
    <param-value>true</param-value>
  </jsp-param>
</jsp-descriptor>
```

Alternatively, you may directly compile all JSPs, thereby avoiding the need for compilation while the server is running. This functionality is made available through the *weblogic.appc* compiler. The JSP compiler parses and translates the JSP files, generating Java source files, which it then compiles. The following command will validate the descriptors in the given WAR, compile the JSP files, and update the WAR with the resulting class files:

```
java weblogic.appc -keepgenerated -verbose myWebApp.war
```

You can also simply point it to a directory containing a web application:

```
java weblogic.appc -keepgenerated webappDirectory
```

Table 2-1 lists various options available to the JSP compiler.

Table 2-1. JSP compiler options

Option	Description	Default
-classpath	This option customizes the classpath used by the JSP compiler. On a Windows NT/2000 platform, the classpath must be a semi-colon-separated list of the names of directories, ZIP, and/or JAR files. On Unix platforms, the classpath must be a colon-separated list of names.	none
-compiler	This option specifies the compiler to be used for compiling *.java* files. It defaults to the first `javac` binary in your PATH environment variable.	javac
-output file	Usually the compiler updates the web archive, adding to its current contents. If you want to send the output to a different WAR, specify the filename here.	none
-forceGeneration	By default, the compiler compiles only those files that it thinks should be compiled, judging by timestamps. If you supply this option, it will recompile everything.	false
-g	This option instructs the compiler to include debugging information in the class file.	none
-keepgenerated	This instructs the compiler to not delete the intermediate *.java* source file once the JSP file has successfully compiled. In the absence of JSP debugging tools, this flag is extremely useful for tracking down bugs in your JSP code.	none
-O	This tells the compiler to compile generated *.java* files with the optimization flag on (overrides –g flag).	none
-verbose	This option determines whether the JSP compiler runs in a verbose mode.	false
-verboseJavac	This option passes the `verbose` flag to the Java compiler when compiling intermediate *.java* files.	false

You also can define JSP compiler settings for the web application in the WebLogic-specific *weblogic.xml* deployment descriptor, as detailed in the following section.

Deploying a Web Application

A web application can be packaged in two ways before it is ready for deployment:

Exploded directory format
> Here the contents of the web application are placed in a folder. This is recommended during the development stages, when you must directly modify the resources within the web application, without the need for repackaging.

Archived format
> Alternatively, you can create a WAR, where the contents of the web application are bundled into a JAR file with a *.war* extension. This approach is recommended for a production environment.

Thus, you have the flexibility of deploying your web application in exploded format, if it is undergoing constant changes during development stages. Otherwise, you may package the contents within a standard WAR file, and then simply deploy the web application in a production environment. In fact, WebLogic provides two modes of operation that impact how you deploy your web applications:

Development mode
> Enable this mode during the development stages, when your web application is under construction and the team members are concurrently making changes to its contents. Its key benefit is the ease with which you can directly modify the resources within the web application, and then instantly see the results of the changes without having to redeploy the entire web application.

Production mode
> Use the production mode when you need to make infrequent changes to your web applications. Typically, you will package the web application in archived format when deploying it to a server running in this mode. So, if you update any Java class files or modify any of the deployment descriptors, you must redeploy the entire WAR. Unfortunately, redeploying a web application means WebLogic loses all active HTTP sessions associated with that web application. If the web application is targeted to other Managed Servers, your network must also endure a surge in traffic while all changes are propagated to all the servers.

On top of this, you can decide whether a web application will be deployed as a standalone application or as a J2EE module within an enterprise application, alongside other web applications, EJB components, resource adapters, and library JARs. Refer to Chapter 12 for more information on how to package enterprise applications and later introduce them to a WebLogic environment. Chapter 12 also introduces WebLogic's split directory development structure, which can be used as an alternative to deploying web applications during development.

The *applications* folder under the domain's root directory provides a convenient store for standalone applications that are deployed to WebLogic. In the development mode, you can deploy a web application to WebLogic simply by placing the WAR file (or a directory, if it exists in an exploded format) under the domain's *applications* directory. WebLogic also supports an *auto-deploy* feature in the development mode, which greatly eases the task of updating your web applications:

- If your web application is packaged as a WAR file, you can redeploy the web application simply by modifying the WAR file (or replacing it with a new copy).

- If your web application exists in the exploded form, any changes you make to resources within the web application are automatically reflected without having to redeploy it. Any changes to static files (such as HTML pages, images, etc.) and JSP pages are automatically picked up by WebLogic.

- You can refresh compiled Java classes used by the web application. This means that you can *hot-deploy* changes to servlets, filters, JSP tag implementations, and classes located under the *WEB-INF/classes* folder without the need for redeployment.

Another neat little trick WebLogic provides is its ability to redeploy the web application whenever you touch a *REDEPLOY* file in the *WEB-INF* directory. All of these features are supported by default in the development mode. The value of the command-line parameter weblogic.ProductionModeEnabled determines whether WebLogic operates in the development mode. The following command shows how to start a server in the production mode:

```
java -classpath %CLASSPATH%  -Dweblogic.Name=myserver  -Dbea.home=%BEA_HOME%  \
  -Dweblogic.management.username=%WL_USER%  -Dweblogic.management.password=%WL_PW% \
  -Djava.security.policy=... -Dweblogic.security.SSL.trustedCAKeyStore=... \
  -Dweblogic.ProductionModeEnabled=true ...
weblogic.Server
```

Chapter 12 looks at how to use the Administration Console or WebLogic's Deployer tool to manage deployed applications in a WebLogic environment.

Class Loaders

WebLogic Server provides a separate class loader for each web application deployed as part of an EAR. This class loader ensures that all servlets and classes in a web application are loaded within the same scope. This eliminates the possibility of classes loaded from the web application conflicting with WebLogic Server implementation classes. For instance, even though WebLogic needs XML parsers to process deployment descriptors, a web application can still load parsers supporting different SAX or DOM versions, without conflicting with the server's copy. So, separating the scope of classes in a web application from the server's bootstrap classes resolves this issue quite elegantly.

WebLogic provides an option for changing the default class-loading mechanism for a web application. This option, called Prefer Web-Inf Classes, can be set by modifying the *weblogic.xml* descriptor file:

```
<container-descriptor>
    <prefer-web-inf-classes>true</prefer-web-inf-classes>
</container-descriptor>
```

In WebLogic 7.0, this option is available in the Configuration/Other tab of a web application. The default mechanism in most class-loading hierarchies is that if a child class loader is asked for a class, and it doesn't have it in memory, it asks its parent to load the class. Only if the parents fail does the child load the class. So, if we have a servlet in a web application that requires a class that has not been loaded by the web application class loader, the web application should pass the request on to its parent class loader. By setting the prefer-web-inf-classes element to true, WebLogic changes the class-loading logic to allow the web application class loader to immediately try and load the class, without first asking the parent. This rather delicate setting could be used in esoteric cases where you want the web application class files to take priority over parent class loaders, perhaps the EAR class loader, because of possible class implementation differences.

A second issue related to class loading is that the J2EE standard specifies that any class loader for a web application is required to load classes from the *classes* folder before loading any classes from the JARs in the *lib* folder. For instance, if a class exists both in the *classes* folder and in JARs in the *lib* folder, WebLogic Server will always load the class from the *classes* folder.

Usually, the contents of the */WEB-INF/classes* folder won't conflict with the JARs located under the */WEB-INF/lib* folder. The *classes* folder will typically contain the servlet and utility classes, whereas the *lib* folder will contain other supporting library JARs needed by the web application, including tag library JARs.

The Class-Path entry in the manifest file *META-INF/MANIFEST.MF* for a WAR also can be used to reference any supporting JARs. This manifest entry for extending the CLASSPATH to include other WAR dependencies must follow the standard JAR manifest format. You can find more information on the standard extension mechanism for JAR files at *http://java.sun.com/j2se/1.4/docs/guide/extensions/spec.html*. Chapter 12 provides an extensive overview of WebLogic's classloader hierarchy.

Configuring Web Applications

The configuration for a web application deployed on WebLogic is spread across the application's deployment descriptors and the server configuration file. For instance:

- The session timeout for the web application can be configured using the session-timeout element within the standard *web.xml* deployment descriptor.

- The JSP compilation parameters for a web application are defined in the WebLogic-specific *weblogic.xml* deployment descriptor.
- The *staging mode setting*, which determines how a web application is deployed, can be found in the server's *config.xml* file.

The easiest approach to editing the deployment descriptors is to use either the Administration Console or WebLogic Builder. The following sections examine WebLogic-specific configuration settings related to web applications.

Context Root

A web application is rooted at a specific path within the web server, called the *context root*. For example, if the context root for a web application is set to here, you could access it by using a URL of the form *http://server:port/here/index.html*. If you do not explicitly set a context root for the web application, its default value depends on how the web application has been packaged:

- If the web application is deployed in the exploded format, its default context root is the name of the folder that holds the contents of the web application.
- If the contents of the web application have been packaged as a web archive, its default context root is the name of the web archive itself. An example of this is if you deploy the web application *myWar.war* to WebLogic, you can invoke a resource—say, *index.html*—using the URL *http://server:port/myWar/index.html*.

There are two ways to configure the context root for a web application:

- If it is deployed as a standalone application, you can set the context-root element within the *weblogic.xml* descriptor for the web application:

```
<weblogic-web-app>
  <context-root>ourwebapp</context-root>
</weblogic-web-app>
```

- If it exists as a J2EE module within an enterprise application, you can configure the context-root element in the standard *application.xml* deployment descriptor for the enterprise application:

```
<module>
  <web>
    <web-uri>mywebapp</web-uri>
    <context-root>ourwebapp</context-root>
  </web>
</module>
```

As shown in Chapter 3, setting the default web application for the web server or virtual host means that the context path can be omitted altogether from URLs that access the web application.

Directory Listings

If a client makes a partial request that resolves to a directory that doesn't contain any of the pages specified in the list of welcome files, WebLogic Server returns a 404 response. However, if you have checked the Index Directories flag for the web application, WebLogic then will return a directory listing to the client instead. By default, if no welcome files are defined, WebLogic looks for the following files in order and serves the first one it finds: *index.html*, *index.htm*, and *index.jsp*.

The Index Directory Enabled flag can be reached by selecting the web application in the Administration Console and moving to the Configuration/Descriptor tab. If you have enabled this option, you also can specify the sort order of the directory listing. This can be done only in the *weblogic.xml* descriptor file. Here is how to enable directory listings and specify a sort order:

```
<container-descriptor>
    <index-directory-enabled>true</index-directory-enabled>
    <index-directory-sort-by>SIZE</index-directory-sort-by>
</container-descriptor>
```

In WebLogic 7.0, this option is available in the Configuration/Files tab of a web application. The valid sort orders are SIZE, NAME, or LAST_MODIFIED.

Serving Static Files

By default, WebLogic uses an internal servlet, weblogic.servlet.FileServlet, to serve requests for static resources in a web application. You can modify this default behavior by mapping a custom servlet to the URL pattern /. Your custom servlet will then respond to requests for all files except those with the extension *.htm* or *.html*, which still will be handled by FileServlet. If your custom servlet must also handle requests for HTML files, you need to explicitly associate the HTML files with your servlet.

The following portion from the *web.xml* descriptor file shows how to override the default FileServlet for all web resources:

```
<!-- web.xml entries -->
<servlet-mapping>
    <servlet-name>MyServlet</servlet-name>
    <url-pattern>/</url-pattern>
</servlet-mapping>
<!-- Map HTML files to the servlet -->
<servlet-mapping>
    <servlet-name>MyServlet</servlet-name>
    <url-pattern>*.htm*</url-pattern>
</servlet-mapping>
```

Enabling CGI Scripts

WebLogic can be configured so that web applications can support Common Gateway Interface (CGI) scripts. Your WebLogic distribution is shipped with a CGI servlet, weblogic.servlet.CGIServlet, which provides a gateway to such scripts. Example 2-2 shows how you can configure the CGI servlet to invoke shell scripts.

Example 2-2. Enabling CGI for a web application

```
<servlet>
  <servlet-name>CGIServlet</servlet-name>
  <servlet-class>weblogic.servlet.CGIServlet</servlet-class>
  <init-param>
    <param-name>cgiDir</param-name>
    <param-value>scripts</param-value>
  </init-param>
  <init-param>
    <param-name>*.sh</param-name>
    <param-value>d:\cygwin\bin\bash</param-value>
  </init-param>
</servlet>
...
<servlet-mapping>
  <servlet-name>CGIServlet</servlet-name>
  <url-pattern>/cgi/*</url-pattern>
</servlet-mapping>
```

CGIServlet requires the following initialization parameters:

cgiDir

>   This parameter specifies a list of the names of directories containing your CGI scripts. For Unix platforms, you must remember to use a colon (:) to separate multiple folder names. By default, WebLogic looks for scripts in the *cgi-bin* directory under the document root for the web application.

Extension mappings

>   These parameters let you map a file extension to an interpreter or an executable that can run the scripts. You can define any number of these mappings, mapping different file extensions to either the same (or different) interpreter.

If you have configured the CGI servlet for a web application as shown in Example 2-2, you can invoke the script *helloworld.sh* by simply navigating to the URL *http://server:port/webapp/cgi/helloworld.sh*. You must place the *helloworld.sh* file into the *scripts* directory of your web application.

>   Ensure that the CGI script returns an exit code of 0 when it ends successfully. Otherwise, WebLogic concludes the script has failed, and will report a server error (500) to the browser.

Reloading Files

WebLogic automatically picks up any changes to static content within a web application in the *development* mode. In fact, WebLogic is able to detect changes to servlets, filters, JSP tag implementation classes, and any classes found under the *WEB-INF/classes* folder. This is possible because WebLogic regularly inspects the filesystem for changes in web resources. You can adjust the frequency with which WebLogic looks at the filesystem for changes in the contents of the web application.

Select the web application from under the Deployments/Web Application Modules node in the left pane of the Administration Console. Then, from the Configuration/Settings tab in the right pane, adjust the value of the Servlet Reload Check Secs setting. WebLogic 7.0 users can find this in the Configuration/Files tab.

Changes to JSP files also are picked up provided you've set a nonnegative value for the pageCheckSeconds element in the *weblogic.xml* descriptor for the web application.

Resources References

The J2EE specification defines how to configure the naming environment, which allows web applications to easily access resources and external information without actually knowing how that information is named or organized. Depending on the resource, you will use one or more of the following elements in the standard *web.xml* descriptor: the env-entry, ejb-ref, ejb-local-ref, resource-ref, security-role-ref, and resource-env-ref elements. At runtime, you can use these elements to access objects registered in the JNDI namespace for the web container. The *weblogic.xml* descriptor file must be configured to map these references to real resources that have been deployed to the server. For instance, suppose you've configured WebLogic with a data source, which you've placed in the JNDI with its name set to myDataSource. Now you can define the following entries in the deployment descriptors for the web application:

```
<!-- web.xml entry: -->
<resource-ref>
  <res-ref-name>jdbc/myds</res-ref-name>
  <res-type>javax.sql.DataSource</res-type>
  <res-auth>Container</res-auth>
</resource-ref>

<!-- weblogic.xml entry: -->
<resource-description>
  <res-ref-name>jdbc/myds</res-ref-name>
  <jndi-name>myDataSource</jndi-name>
</resource-description>
```

Then, you can access this data source using the resource reference jdbc/myds as follows:

```
javax.sql.DataSource ds =
  (javax.sql.DataSource) ctx.lookup("java:comp/env/jdbc/myds");
```

Note that your Java code doesn't have to explicitly reference the global JNDI name myDataSource—instead, you can use the alias jdbc/myds.

Similarly, suppose you've defined the following entries in the deployment descriptors for a web application:

```
<!-- web.xml entry: -->
<ejb-ref>
  <ejb-ref-name>ejb/foohome</ejb-ref-name>
```

```
    <ejb-ref-type>Session</ejb-ref-type>
    <home>com.foo.bar.FooHome</home>
    <remote>com.foo.bar.Foo</remote>
</ejb-ref>

<!-- weblogic.xml entry: -->
<ejb-reference-description>
  <ejb-ref-name>ejb/foohome</ejb-ref-name>
  <jndi-name>FooHome</jndi-name>
</ejb-reference-description>
```

Here the standard *web.xml* descriptor file declares an EJB reference to a session bean, and the *weblogic.xml* descriptor file maps the EJB reference to its actual JNDI name. You then can access the session bean registered in the global JNDI tree under the name FooHome using the EJB reference *ejb/foohome* as follows:

```
Object home = ctx.lookup("java:comp/env/ejb/foohome");
FooHome fh = (FooHome) PortableRemoteObject.narrow(home, FooHome.class);
```

Again, we have not used the session EJB's actual JNDI name within our code. Instead we used its alias *ejb/foohome*.

The WebLogic Builder tool provides an easy way to declare these references.

Response Caching

WebLogic supplies a cache servlet filter that permits page-level caching of responses. Setting up such a filter is very easy. Example 2-3 establishes a cache filter that works on all files ending with a *.html* extension, and configures the cache to be application-wide.

Example 2-3. A cache filter for all HTML files in a web application

```
<filter>
  <filter-name>HTML</filter-name>
  <filter-class>weblogic.cache.filter.CacheFilter</filter-class>
  <init-params>
    <param-name>scope</param-name>
    <param-value>application</param-value>
  </init-params>
</filter>

<filter-mapping>
  <filter-name>HTML</filter-name>
  <url-pattern>*.html</url-pattern>
</filter-mapping>
```

The cache filter automatically caches the Content-Type and Last-Modified response header fields. A cached page is served only if the If-Modified-Since request header is more recent than the Last-Modified response header—otherwise, the filter sends back an SC_NOT_MODIFIED(302) status with no content. The filter can be configured in various ways depending on the values of the initialization parameters. You can define the following parameters:

name

> Specifies the name for the cache; defaults to the request URI.

timeout

> Determines the amount of time to wait between cache updates. The default unit of time is seconds, but this can be changed by specifying a value followed by ms (milliseconds), s (seconds), m (minutes), h (hours), or d (days). Note that the value of an item is refreshed only when it is requested and timed out, not if it is only timed out.

scope

> Determines whether the scope of the cache is for the request, session, application, or cluster. The default scope is application.

size

> Determines the number of different unique key values that are cached. It defaults to infinity (limited by memory because of the soft reference implementation).

key

> Ordinarily the key will be the URL requested. You can use this attribute to specify a comma-separated list of additional keys. The value of this attribute will be the name of the variable whose value you wish to use as a key into the cache. You additionally can specify a scope by prepending the scope to the key. For example, a value of application.mykey implies the target resource will carry an additional key—i.e., the value of the attribute mykey in the context for the web application. If no scope is prepended, WebLogic will search through the scopes in the order shown earlier.

Cache filters are extremely useful; they provide a reusable and configurable way for caching various parts of your web application without requiring any code changes. When configured properly, cache filters can provide a significant performance boost to your web application. The next chapter shows how WebLogic's JSP cache tags support a slightly richer version of this caching behavior. It also provides more examples on the use of keys.

Servlets and JSPs

WebLogic supports HTTP servlets as defined in the Servlet 2.3 specification, as well as JSP pages and tag extensions as defined in the JSP 1.2 specification. Typically, you will use servlets alongside JSPs to build a web application. WebLogic provides a number of useful additions to standard servlet and JSP configuration. For example, you can assign custom execute queues to critical servlets, and install servlets to serve static files and act as a CGI gateway.

Configuring a Custom Execute Queue

By default, all J2EE applications (except JMS resources) share the same pool of server threads for their operation. This includes the servlets and JSPs that rely on the default execute queue configured for a particular WebLogic instance. However, WebLogic also lets you assign a custom execute queue that is dedicated to an individual servlet (or JSP). In this way, you can ensure that a dedicated pool of threads is always available for a particular servlet and that it doesn't need to compete with other services for a free server thread. Execute queues are explained is more detail in Chapter 15.

To assign an execute queue to a servlet, you need to modify the *weblogic.xml* descriptor file to include a dispatch-policy element for the servlet. The value of this element should match the name of a preconfigured execute queue. Here is an example:

```
<servlet-descriptor>
  <servlet-name>FooServlet</servlet-name>
    <init-as-principal-name>system</init-as-principal-name>
    <destroy-as-principal-name>system</destroy-as-principal-name>
    <dispatch-policy>MyCustomExecuteQ</dispatch-policy>
</servlet-descriptor>
```

In this way, you can configure each servlet with its own execute queue, or perhaps even force multiple servlets to share the same execute queue.

Threading Issues

When using multithreaded servlets, you must make adequate provisions for concurrent access within the service methods. Your servlet code needs to guard against sharing violations on access to shared resources and member variables. That said, wherever possible, avoid synchronization because it blocks other servlet threads until the current thread has completed. Limit sharing across threads by defining variables within the scope of the service methods. If you are accessing external resources such as databases, JMS destinations, etc., you need to synchronize on the class level, or whenever possible, encapsulate your work in a transaction.

Single-threaded servlets

An instance of a servlet that implements the SingleThreadModel interface is guaranteed never to be invoked concurrently by multiple threads. WebLogic creates multiple instances of a single-threaded servlet so that it can serve multiple client requests simultaneously. This pool of servlet instances is created initially when the servlet is first requested. You can use the single-threaded-servlet-pool-size element in the *weblogic.xml* file to specify the initial number of servlet instances that are created. Typically, you will set the value of this attribute to the average number of concurrent requests that the servlet is likely to receive. In WebLogic 8.1, you can configure this setting from the Administration Console. Select the web application in the left frame, and then, from the Configuration/Descriptor tab, supply a value for the Single Threaded Servlet Pool Size setting. By default, WebLogic initializes the pool with five servlet instances.

Because WebLogic creates a pool of servlet instances (one for each thread), you effectively multiply the memory requirements of the servlet, at least for all the nonstatic attributes of the servlet. If you have declared shared class variables (for instance, a static attribute), even though it will be accessed in a single-threaded manner, there could be many such single-threaded instances potentially accessing the same resource. You must be careful to ensure that you avoid all synchronization issues.

Custom URL Pattern Matching

The servlet-mapping declaration in the *web.xml* deployment descriptor allows you to specify the URL pattern that must be matched to invoke a particular servlet. WebLogic provides an extension to the URL matching mechanism and allows you to plug in a richer pattern matcher—for instance, a matching scheme that goes beyond the use of just the / and * metacharacters. To configure this scheme, you must use the url-match-map element in the *weblogic.xml* descriptor file to specify the fully qualified name of a class that provides the actual logic for custom URL matching:

```
<url-match-map>
   com.oreilly.wlguide.servlets.OReillyURLMatchMap
</url-match-map>
```

This class must implement the following interface, found in the weblogic.servlet. utils package:

```
public interface URLMapping {
  public void put(String pattern, Object value);
  public Object get(String uri);
  public void remove(String pattern)
  public void setDefault(Object defaultObject);
  public Object getDefault();
  public void setCaseInsensitive(boolean ci);
  public boolean isCaseInsensitive();
  public int size();
  public Object[] values();
  public String[] keys();
}
```

By default, WebLogic Server uses the J2EE-standard URL pattern-matching scheme. This is set up because the value of the url-match-map element defaults to weblogic. servlet.utils.URLMatchMap.

Configuring JSPs

Just as you can when deploying servlets, you can use the servlet element in the standard *web.xml* deployment descriptor to register a JSP page:

```
<servlet>
  <servlet-name>home</servlet-name>
  <jsp-file>home.jsp</jsp-file>
</servlet>

<servlet-mapping>
  <servlet-name>home</servlet-name>
  <url-pattern>/home</url-pattern>
</servlet-mapping>
```

Here, a request to the URL */home* will cause */home.jsp* to be invoked. In Chapter 18, you'll see how a similar mapping enables XSLT conversion from within a JSP. By registering a JSP as a servlet in this way, you can do the following:

- Specify the load order of JSP pages
- Define any initialization parameters for those pages
- Restrict access by applying security roles to JSP pages

The jsp-descriptor element in the *weblogic.xml* descriptor file allows you to specify additional settings for JSP compilation. Each JSP configuration parameter is defined as a name/value pair within a jsp-param subelement. Here is an example of how to configure the translator to retain generated Java files:

```
<jsp-descriptor>
  <jsp-param>
    <param-name>keepgenerated</param-name>
    <param-value>true</param-value>
  </jsp-param>
</jsp-descriptor>
```

Table 2-2 provides a complete list of JSP configuration parameters that may be defined in the jsp-descriptor element. Remember, you need to define a separate jsp-param element for each configuration parameter.

Table 2-2. JSP configuration parameters

Parameter name	Description	Default
compileCommand	This specifies the full pathname of the standard Java compiler used to compile *.java* files generated from a JSP. By default, the compiler uses javac (from your PATH environment variable) or the compiler set in the server configuration for WebLogic Server.	javac

compileFlags	This parameter specifies one or more flags to be used by the standard Java compiler. Multiple flags should be enclosed in quotes:
	
	`<jsp-param>`
	`  <param-name>compileFlags</param-name>`
	`  <param-value>"-g -v"</param-value>`
	`</jsp-param>`
		none

debug	If this parameter is set to true, the JSP compiler adds JSP line numbers to the generated source files (as an aid to debugging).	false

Table 2-2. JSP configuration parameters (continued)

Parameter name	Description	Default
encoding	This parameter defines the default character set used by JSPs. If no value is set, the character encoding for your platform becomes the default encoding for all JSPs. You can override this setting by declaring a contentType page directive in your JSP: `<%@ page contentType="text/html; charset=ISO-8859-1" %>`	default platform encoding
keepgenerated	This tells the JSP compiler to not delete the intermediate *.java* source file once it has compiled successfully.	false
noTryBlocks	If this parameter's value is set to true, try/catch blocks are not generated for JSPs that use nonempty tags. Because tag library descriptor (TLD) files do not allow you to specify valid tag nestings, the compiler cannot enforce how custom tags ought to be nested. This means you could accidentally nest a custom tag within another, and erroneously rely on a "dependency" that may not occur at runtime (e.g., a shared object with page scope may be unavailable to an inner tag). To avoid any nasty consequences, the JSP compiler emits try/catch blocks around each tag. You could avoid try/catch blocks altogether by setting this parameter to true, but it may mean you have to deal with more obscure runtime errors if you use the tags incorrectly.	false
packagePrefix	This sets the package prefix for generated HTTP servlets.	jsp_servlet
superclass	This parameter specifies the super class for the generated servlet. The supplied value must be a subclass of javax.servlet.http.HttpServlet or javax.servlet.GenericServlet.	weblogic.servlet.jsp.JspBase
pageCheckSeconds	This specifies the interval (in seconds) at which WebLogic Server checks to see whether the JSP files have been modified and need recompiling (WebLogic also checks dependencies and reloads them as required). If this parameter's value is set to 0, pages are checked on every request; if it is set to −1, page checking and recompilation are disabled.	1
precompile	If this parameter's value is set to true, WebLogic Server automatically precompiles all JSP resources when the web application is deployed (or redeployed).	false
verbose	If this parameter's value is set to true, debugging information is printed out to the browser, console, and WebLogic Server log files.	true
workingDir	This specifies the directory where WebLogic places compiled JSP classes (and intermediate Java source files, if keepgenerated is true).	A directory generated internally by WebLogic Server
printNulls	Setting this parameter to true tells the compiler to treat null values in JSP expressions as empty strings.	false

You can set the "JSP page check seconds," "Keep Generated," "verbose," "debug line numbers," and "compiler command" settings using the Administration Console. These settings can be found on the Configuration/Descriptor tab of a web application.

By default, WebLogic automatically checks for modifications to JSP pages in a web application, and automatically recompiles a JSP if it is invoked after it has been modified. By setting the pageCheckSeconds configuration parameter to −1, you avoid the overhead WebLogic incurs when it needs to monitor changes to JSP source files that belong to the web application. In this scenario, the JSPs will be updated only when the entire web application is redeployed. This is particularly useful in production deployments in which you typically want compilation to occur only under the explicit control of a deployer. We have found that this setting does affect performance.

Note that WebLogic places all compiled JSPs into an internally generated directory. As a new directory is created every time the server is started, you will lose all of the compiled JSPs. If you want to avoid this and retain the compiled JSPs across server startups, specify a `workingDir` to use.

JSP Tag Libraries

JSP tag libraries provide a simple, elegant way of embedding dynamic server-side request handling into a JSP page. WebLogic Server provides a tag library with custom tags that you may use in your JSP pages; this library defines the cache, repeat, and process tags. Other tags also are supplied, though these are not discussed, as much of their functionality can now be found in more standard tag library implementations, such as the Java Standard Template Library (JSTL). WebLogic also provides a tool to automatically generate a tag library for an EJB.

WebLogic's Tag Library

WebLogic's tag library JAR (*weblogic-tags.jar*) is located in *WL_HOME/server/ext*. It packages the tag library descriptor, the tag handler classes, and several other support classes. In order to use these tags in your JSP pages, you need to make the library available to your web application. Copy the JAR to the */WEB-INF/lib* folder under the document root of the web application, and define a `taglib` element in the standard *web.xml* deployment descriptor:

```
<taglib>
  <taglib-uri>/weblogic-tags</taglib-uri>
  <taglib-location>/WEB-INF/lib/weblogic-tags.jar</taglib-location>
</taglib>
```

Now you can import the tag library into your JSP pages as follows:

```
<%@ taglib uri="/weblogic-tags" prefix="wl" %>
```

Let's take a closer look at the features and capabilities of these three tags.

The cache tag

The cache tag enables you to cache the output generated within the body of the tag. Because the output is usually some function of parameter or attribute values, the tag also allows you to cache the values of input parameters or attributes that uniquely generate a particular response. The caches are implemented using soft references to prevent the cache mechanism from hogging memory. Let's examine important attributes of the cache tag.

A cache tag may specify a unique name for the cache, if it is to be used across multiple JSP pages. A random name is generated if you do not specify one. By default, the cache tag uses an application-wide scope. You may specify a custom scope for the cache tag using one of the following values for the scope attribute: page, request, session, or application. For example, if you need to cache the contents of the tag's body for each HTTP session, you should use the cache tag as follows:

```
<wl:cache name="foo" scope="session">...</wl:cache>
```

The tag's body content will be evaluated once when the JSP is requested after an HTTP session has been created, and then cached forever until the session is invalidated (or the cache is manually flushed).

You may also specify a timeout value, after which the cache contents become invalid. The tag content is not refreshed automatically after the timeout. Instead, it is reevaluated only when the JSP is invoked for the first time after the timeout occurs. You may use any of the following time units, as appropriate: ms (milliseconds), s (seconds), m (minutes), h (hours), or d (days). The default timeout value is -1, which implies that the cache data will never be refreshed. The following example illustrates how you can use the cache tag to refresh news content every 15 minutes:

```
<wl:cache name="news" timeout="15m">
 <%-- HTML News Feed --%>
</wl:cache>
```

Often the contents of the tag's body will be evaluated based on the value of a certain request parameter or perhaps an object associated with the request or session attribute. For instance, you could generate news items on the basis of a URL submitted via a request parameter to the JSP. In that case, you need to be able to associate the content generated with the name of that parameter or the object attribute used to evaluate the content. The key attribute allows you to specify the name of a parameter/attribute, whose value will be used as a key to locate the cached response generated within the tag's body. In fact, you may specify a comma-separated list of key values. The following example shows how to cache the tag contents, using the value of the url request parameter as the key:

```
<wl:cache key="parameter.url" timeout="15m" size="10">
 <%-- JSP body that uses the url parameter, perhaps to fetch a news item --%>
</wl:cache>
```

The contents of the tag's body are evaluated the first time a JSP is invoked, and the response is cached using the specified value for the url parameter. If the JSP is subsequently invoked with the same value for the url parameter, the cached response will be returned as long as it's not more than 15 minutes old. Otherwise, the contents of the tag will be reevaluated and the cache updated. The size attribute instructs the JSP container to cache the content for no more than 10 unique url values. The least recently used items are expelled from the cache if new items need to be inserted and the cache has reached maximum capacity. The default value for the size attribute is -1, which means the cache supports an unlimited number of entries.

The following example caches the contents of the tag's body based on the value of a session attribute:

```
<wl:cache key="session.userid">
 <%-- JSP body that generates HTML form with details of current user --%>
</wl:cache>
```

In this case, the output is cached until the particular session is invalidated. Notice how the key uses a prefix to specify a scope for the parameter or attribute. You can choose from the following prefixes: parameter, page, request, session, and application. If the key does not have a scope prepended to it, the container will search through the scopes in the same order listed earlier.

The cache tag also supports *input caching*, whereby the tag caches values that are calculated within the tag's body. The vars attribute allows you to specify a list of the names of variables whose values should be cached along with the body of the tag. Just like the key attribute, you may prefix the variable name with a scope. When the cache is retrieved, the values that were cached are restored, allowing you to access them from their respective scopes outside the cache tag body. For instance, say that we calculate some value, calculatedvalue, and store it as a request attribute. The calculated value will then be made available after the cache tag:

```
Attribute value before is: <%= request.getAttribute("calculatedvalue") %>
<wl:cache timeout="10s" vars="request.calculatedvalue">
  <!-- This will only be evaluated once every 10 seconds -->
  <% request.setAttribute("calculatedvalue", new Date().toString()); %>
</wl:cache>
Attribute value after is: <%= request.getAttribute("calculatedvalue") %>
```

Here is the output when we access this page a number of times over a 10-second window:

```
Attribute value before is: null
Attribute value after is: Mon Feb 10 09:27:58 GMT 2003
Attribute value before is: null
Attribute value after is: Mon Feb 10 09:27:58 GMT 2003
Attribute value before is: null
Attribute value after is: Mon Feb 10 09:27:58 GMT 2003
Attribute value before is: null
Attribute value after is: Mon Feb 10 09:28:08 GMT 2003
```

Notice how the attribute value is retained by the cache and reinserted into the request scope after execution of the cache tag, making it available to the rest of the JSP page.

You also can set the async attribute to true, which means WebLogic will attempt to update the cache asynchronously if the cached entries are set to time out. In this case, a JSP request that generates a cache hit may still use the old cached response while the new values are concurrently evaluated and cached for future use.

Finally, the cache tag enables you to flush all cached values. If you set the flush attribute's value to true, the JSP container will flush all entries associated with the cache. Whenever you set the flush attribute, the cache tag must have an empty body. The following example shows how to flush a cache with session scope:

```
<wl:cache name="foo" flush="true" scope="session"/>
```

If the cache does not have a name, you must identify the cache using its vars, keys, and scope attributes.

You can refresh all caches in a particular scope by setting the _cache_refresh attribute's value to true. For instance, if you want to refresh all caches associated with a user's session, you should invoke the following from a session-aware JSP page:

```
<% session.setAttribute("_cache_refresh", "true"); %>
```

If you want all caches to be refreshed, you should set the attribute in the application scope. And, if you want to flush all caches associated with the current request, you should set the request attribute (or parameter) to true.

Table 2-3 provides a summary of the cache options.

Table 2-3. Cache tag attributes

Parameter name	Description
name	You can use this parameter to provide a unique name for the cache, allowing it to be shared across multiple JSP pages.
timeout	The timeout determines the time after which the cache will be refreshed if accessed again.
scope	The scope determines the scope in which the data is cached. It can be one of page, parameter, request, session, or application.
key	The key specifies additional values that should be used when evaluating whether to cache the values contained within the tag.
async	If this parameter is true, the cache will be updated asynchronously if possible.
size	This parameter determines the maximum size of the cache. If set to −1, it is unlimited. Otherwise, an LRU scheme is used to maintain the cache.
vars	This parameter specifies a set of scoped variables that should be cached along with the contents of the cache tag, and made available to the rest of JSP after execution of the tag.
flush	If this parameter is set to true, the cache is flushed.

The process tag

The process tag allows you to customize the flow control within a JSP page using query parameters supplied to it. You can configure the tag to include the body based on the following:

- The existence (or absence) of a query parameter (the value of the name attribute defaults to submit, if it isn't specified):

```
<wl:process name="foo">
<!-- include body if the query parameter foo has been
  passed to enclosing JSP -->
</wl:process>
```

```
<wl:process notname="foo">
<!-- include body if the query parameter foo has not been
    passed to enclosing JSP -->
</wl:process>
```

- A condition that a specific parameter has a particular value (or doesn't have a specific value):

```
<wl:process name="foo" value="bar">
<!-- include body if the query parameter foo has value "bar" -->
</wl:process>
```

```
<wl:process name="foo" notvalue="bar">
<!-- include body if the query parameter foo has value other than "bar" -->
</wl:process>
```

Clearly, process tags provide a simple, declarative way of including/excluding JSP portions.

The repeat tag

The repeat tag allows you to repeatedly evaluate the body of a tag, while iterating over the elements in a collection. The tag supports all kinds of collections—arrays, vectors, enumerations, JDBC result sets, hash-table keys, etc. The set attribute allows you to specify the collection that will be used to iterate over. The body of the tag will be evaluated for each iteration, using the current element of the configured set. Let's look at few examples of how you can use the repeat tag:

- Display the details of the first 10 users:

```
<wl:repeat id="user" set="<%= (ArrayList) request.getAttribute("users") %>"
    type="com.foo.bar.AUser" count="10">
<%--print details of each user--%>
    Username: <%= user.getUsername() %> <br>
    Full Name: <%= user.getFullname() %> <br>
    DOB: <%= user.getDob() %> <br>
</wl:repeat>
```

- List all product items in an HTML dropdown:

```
<select name="products">
<wl:repeat id="product"
    set="<%= (String []) application.getAttribute("products") %>">
<%--print all products--%>
    <option><%= product %></option>
</wl:repeat>
</select>
```

The id attribute defines the name of the object that holds a reference to the element of the set during each iteration. You can specify the type of each element in the collection using the type attribute. By default, the repeat tag expects the type of each element to be String. You also can specify a count attribute, which forces the tag to iterate only over the first count entries.

Building Tag Libraries for EJBs

WebLogic Server provides a tool that generates a tag library from an EJB JAR file—one for each EJB in the JAR file. The custom tags in the library provide an easy, elegant way for invoking methods on the enterprise bean. Take, for example, the following remote interface for a session bean:

```
public interface User extends javax.ejb.EJBObject {
    public AUser[] list(int realmid) throws java.rmi.RemoteException;
    public boolean add(int realmid, AUser user) throws java.rmi.RemoteException;
    public boolean update(int realmid, AUser user) throws java.rmi.RemoteException;
    public boolean delete(int realmid, String userid) throws java.rmi.RemoteException;
}
```

Using the EJB-to-JSP integration tool, you can generate a tag library that is custom-made for the session bean. The tag library will contain a tag for each method, so you can invoke the EJB from within a JSP page as follows:

```
<% taglib uri="/WEB-INF/user-tags.tld" prefix="user" %>

<b>List Users: </b><br>

<%-- value of _return attribute is the scripting variable
 that will hold the return value for the EJB method --%>
<user:list realmid="101" _return="users"/>

<wl:repeat id="user" set="<%= users %>" type="com.foo.bar.AUser" count="10">
<!-- print details of first 10 users -->
  Username: <%= user.getUsername() %> <br>
  Full Name: <%= user.getFullname() %> <br>
  DOB: <%= user.getDob() %> <br>
</wl:repeat>
```

The attributes for the tags correspond to the parameters for the EJB method call. The tag handlers for the custom tags provide the implementation for the actual EJB invocations. Because the custom tag hides away all the messy details of invoking an EJB method, the resulting JSP is clean and elegant. The EJB-JSP integration tool supports tag libraries for session beans (stateful and stateless) and for entity beans.

The ejb2jsp tool

You can run the EJB-to-JSP integration tool in graphical mode as follows:

```
java weblogic.servlet.ejb2jsp.gui.Main
```

Initially, no project files are loaded, so you need to create a new ejb2jsp project by choosing an EJB JAR file. Once you have created an ejb2jsp project, you can modify the project settings, save the project, and reload ejb2jsp projects created earlier. The structure of the tag library is fairly straightforward:

- The ejb2jsp tool inspects the EJB JAR file to determine the type of the EJB, home and bean interfaces, and the JNDI name needed to look up the EJB home object.

- A custom tag is generated for each remote method of the EJB. Tag implementation consists of the tag handler and tag-extra info classes.

- The EJB specification allows an EJB home interface to declare methods that are neither create( ) nor find( ) methods. The ejb2jsp tool generates custom tags for these methods as well. By default, the tool adds home- prefixes to the names for custom tags associated with EJB home methods.

You can use the Project Build Options panel to configure how the ejb2jsp tool will generate the associated tag library. In fact, you must specify the following items:

- The Java compiler to be used during the build process (defaults to javac)

- Additional compilation flags for the compiler

- How you want the tag library to be built (as a tag library JAR under the /WEB-INF/lib folder, or in the *directory format*, which is where the tag classes go under the /WEB-INF/classes and the TLD file goes in the /WEB-INF folder)

- The package name for the tag handler classes

- The full path of the document root for the web application

- The locations for the TLD file and *classes* folder (if you're building the project in directory format)

- A location for the tag library JAR (if your tag library will be packaged in a JAR)

- A temporary folder needed during the build process

When you create a new ejb2jsp project using the selected EJB JAR file, the ejb2jsp tool cannot generate the tags based only on information acquired from introspecting the bean interface classes. It needs the source for the EJB classes as well, before it can assign meaningful names for the tag attributes. You can adjust the source path for the EJB JAR under the Project Build Options panel. By default, the ejb2jsp tool assumes that the source files are in the same folder that contains the EJB JAR file. Once you have set the source path, you can select File/Resolve Attributes to resolve the tag attribute names to method parameter names. You can build the tag library only after you have meaningful names for all tag attributes.

Resolving conflicts

The ejb2jsp tool tries to resolve attribute names based on the EJB source and compiled classes. Despite this, a project may generate errors or conflicts while building the tag library. This may happen for several reasons:

- The ejb2jsp project is missing important build settings, such as a Java compiler or an invalid location for the web application. Make sure you have specified all the build options needed to generate the tag library.

- The `ejb2jsp` project contains duplicate tag names because the particular bean interface declares one or more *overloaded methods* (i.e., methods with the same name but different signatures). You can resolve this in one of two ways:
  — Rename the duplicate tag.
  — Disable the duplicate tag so that it doesn't participate in the build process.
- A custom tag has duplicate attribute names. This can happen when a method accepts multiple arguments with the same name. You must ensure that every tag has unique attribute names within its definition.

 It's perfectly acceptable for two tags to have an attribute with the same name; however, each attribute *within* a tag must have a unique name.

- A custom tag has meaningless attribute names such as `arg0` and `arg1`. This can happen when the `ejb2jsp` tool is unable to generate meaningful names after parsing the EJB source files. In such a case, you need to manually supply valid attribute names for the affected custom tags.

Once you have generated the tag library, you can save the current project for later use. You even can configure certain attributes of the custom tag to accept default values. The `ejb2jsp` tool allows you to set the default value for an attribute in two ways:

- By specifying a simple expression that evaluates to the value of the attribute.
- By supplying a method body that returns a value for the attribute. The method will be embedded within the tag handler for the JSP, so it will have access to the `pageContext` for the enclosing JSP page.

Attributes with default values need not be specified when their associated custom tag is used in a JSP page.

Custom tags for stateful beans and entity beans

In a typical scenario involving stateful beans or entity beans, a client looks up the bean in the JNDI tree and acquires a reference to the EJB's home interface; it then invokes multiple methods on the bean instance. The custom tags generated for the enterprise bean preserve the same semantics. Custom tags corresponding to methods of the bean's remote interface must be nested within the tag associated with the `find( )` or `create( )` method of the bean's home interface. So, all EJB methods are invoked using the bean instance created (or found) by the enclosing `create` (or `find`) tag. WebLogic's JSP container generates a runtime exception if the EJB method tag is not enclosed within the tag of one of the EJB's home methods.

Consider the following EJB code:

```
/** bean home interface */
public interface UserHome extends EJBHome {
```

```
public User create(String userid, String fullname,
                    String username, String password, boolean alive);
public User findByPrimaryKey(String userid);
public Collection findDeadUsers();
}

/** bean remote interface */
public interface User extends EJBObject {
  public String getUserID();
  public String getFullName();
  public void changePassword(String oldpw, String newpw);
}
```

After generating the tag library, you can invoke the entity bean from a JSP page as follows:

```
<% taglib uri="/WEB-INF/user-ejb.tld" prefix="user" %>

<user:home-create
  userid="<%= request.getParameter("userid") %>"
  fullname="<%= request.getParameter("fullname") %>"
  username="<%= request.getParameter("username") %>"
  password="<%= request.getParameter("password") %>"
  alive="<%= true %>"
  _return="user">

  <user:changePassword oldpw="<%= request.getParameter("oldpw") %>"
    newpw="<%= request.getParameter("newpw") %>" />
  <%= user.getFullName() %>: Your password has been successfully changed.

</user:home-create>
```

The _return attribute in the home-create tag determines the name of the page variable that holds a reference to the newly created (or found) bean instance. Entity bean finder methods will typically return a collection of EJB instances that match the select criteria. If a home tag for an entity bean returns a collection of EJB instances, the body of the tag will be evaluated for each item in the collection. In this case, the _return attribute for the find tag corresponds to the bean instance used in the current iteration. The following example generates an HTML list of all deceased users:

```
<b>All Deceased Users:</b>
<ul>
<user:home-findDeadUsers _return="user">
  <li> User <%= user.getFullName() %> is dead! </li>
</user:home-findDeadUsers>
</ul>
```

The ejb2jsp tool is useful for generating reusable tag libraries for your enterprise beans. It allows for rapid prototyping of JSP pages and provides a quick way for testing EJB functionality. Custom tags for the EJB methods hide all the details of invoking the bean.

Session Tracking

HTTP is, by design, a stateless protocol. Many web applications require that a series of requests from a client be associated with one another. For example, an online store will need to maintain the state of a user's shopping cart across HTTP requests. The HttpSession object allows servlets and JSPs to manage client-specific state on the server. You can associate object-valued attributes to the HttpSession by name. Any object bound to the session is available to any other servlet within the same servlet context. You can even declare JavaBean components within JSPs that have session-wide scope.

In order to implement server-side HTTP sessions, WebLogic needs to associate session data across browser requests with the same client. This is done by associating a unique tag (called the *session ID*) with every client, and ensuring that this tag is transferred with every request. The mechanism by which WebLogic binds the client to its session data is called *session tracking*. WebLogic supports two mechanisms for tracking session-state information: cookies and URL rewriting.

Session Tracking with Cookies

Every J2EE-compliant servlet engine is required to support session tracking using cookies. When an HttpSession is created, a unique ID is associated with it. WebLogic then attempts to store the session ID by sending a cookie back to the client. Once a cookie is set, the browser will return the cookie on each subsequent request. The server then is able to parse the cookie and return the associated session object when you invoke the getSession( ) method on the servlet. The servlet specification demands that this session-tracking cookie be named JSESSIONID.

Using cookies with SSL

Requests sent using HTTP and HTTPS use different ports, and some browsers treat the same address with different ports as two different locations. Hence a cookie created using one port may not be associated with the cookie using the other port. As a result, you may find new sessions being created when browser requests alternate between the HTTP and HTTPS protocols. To get around this problem, you need to configure the CookieDomain parameter within the session-descriptor element in the *weblogic.xml* descriptor file:

```
<!-- weblogic.xml entry -->
<session-descriptor>
  <session-param>
    <param-name>CookieDomain</param-name>
    <param-value>domainname.com</param-value>
  </session-param>
</session-descriptor>
```

The browser will then be instructed to include the proper cookies for all requests to the web application under any of the hosts in the domain *domainname.com*

Session Tracking with URL Rewriting

URL rewriting is an alternate mechanism for session tracking. If the client browser does not accept cookies, you must encode the session ID into all URLs sent back to the client through the response stream. The encodeURL() method on the HttpServletResponse object allows you to encode the session ID into a URL as a path parameter. The servlet specification demands that the session ID parameter have the name jsessionid. For example, the URI /catalog/index.html could be encoded as *http://www.myserver.com/catalog/index.html;jsessionid=1234*. This means that when a client browser requests a web resource using the encoded URL, WebLogic extracts the session ID from the URL and fetches the associated session object.

To ensure your code handles URL rewriting properly, you must encode all URLs sent back to the client:

```
out.println("<a href=\"" + response.encodeURL("/catalog/index.jsp")
  + "\">Catalog Index</a>");
```

However, WebLogic detects whether the client supports cookies before encoding URLs. So, the encodeURL() method leaves the URL unchanged if the client does accept cookies. Likewise, when you redirect to another servlet or JSP, you must encode the target URL as well:

```
if (loggedin) {
  response.sendRedirect(response.encodeRedirectURL("/welcomeUser.jsp"));
}
```

Regardless of the settings, WebLogic automatically uses URL rewriting when creating a new session because the server needs more than one visit to ensure that the client supports cookies. Servlets can determine whether the session ID came from a cookie or a URL by invoking the isRequestedSessionIdFromCookie() method on the HttpServletRequest object.

You can disable URL rewriting explicitly by setting the UrlRewritingEnabled session parameter to false. This session parameter is defined within the session-descriptor element in the *weblogic.xml* descriptor file:

```
<!-- weblogic.xml entry -->
<session-descriptor>
  <session-param>
    <param-name>UrlRewritingEnabled</param-name>
    <param-value>false</param-value>
  </session-param>
</session-descriptor>
```

By default, URL rewriting is enabled for all web applications in WebLogic Server.

URL rewriting for WAP

The WAP protocol does not support cookies, so URL rewriting must always be used if the web application needs to cater to WAP-enabled browsers. Additionally, many

WAP devices have a limit on the length of the URL. To cater for this, you can set the IDLength parameter in the session-descriptor element:

```
<!-- weblogic.xml entry -->
<session-descriptor>
  <session-param>
    <param-name>IDLength</param-name>
    <param-value>104</param-value>
  </session-param>
</session-descriptor
```

This value for the IDLength parameter defaults to 52, and can range from 8 to Integer.MAX_VALUE.

Session Security and Single Sign-on

Once a client has authenticated itself with a web server, the user is associated with both session data and authentication data. The authentication data is stored both as part of the user's session and as part of the server context. This authentication information can persist independent of the session data. Therefore, in order to effectively log the user out of the web server, you need to remove his authentication and session data. If the user is logged in to a single web application, you could invoke invalidate() on the user's HttpSession object, effectively logging the user out of the web server. If a web client can log into multiple web applications, you will need to invalidate all of the user's active sessions and remove the user's authentication data from the web server.

WebLogic permits a *single sign-on* for multiple web applications. This means that once a client has authenticated itself to the web server, the user has access to all web applications running on the server. When a user leaves a web server or "logs off" from one of the web applications, you want to be able to invalidate all his active sessions and remove his authentication data. We need a *single sign-off* so that after a client logs off, the user cannot access any of the web applications unless he authenticates himself again. The servlet specification provides no mechanism for this. However, WebLogic Server does.

The weblogic.servlet.security.ServletAuthentication class allows you to effectively log a client out of all web applications:

```
logout(HttpServletRequest req)
```

The logout() method removes authentication data associated with a client from the web server and all active sessions the user has logged into. The session associated with the user remains alive.

```
invalidateAll(HttpServletRequest req)
```

The invalidateAll() method invalidates all the sessions associated with the user and removes the authentication data. Because the cookie binding the user to the session is no longer needed, the cookie is invalidated too.

```
killCookie(HttpServletRequest req)
```

The `killCookie( )` method invalidates the current cookie, ensuring that it expires as soon as the response is sent back to the client. The session will remain active until it times out. Note that for this to successfully invalidate the cookie, the browser must receive the response holding the invalidated cookie.

Avoiding single sign-on

As you can see from the previous discussion, the single sign-on mechanism is the default mechanism in WebLogic—all web applications will share the security data. If you do not want a web application to participate in the single sign-on facility, you can specify a different cookie name for the session-tracking cookie. By changing the value of the `CookieName` parameter within the `session-descriptor` element in the *weblogic.xml* descriptor file, you can ensure that the client is always required to sign on and authenticate itself when it visits a servlet, JSP, or any static resource that belongs to the web application.

Session Persistence

Session persistence involves persisting the data stored in the HTTP session object. This typically is done to support failover across a cluster of servers. For instance, if the session state is duplicated between two running servers, and if one goes down, the other server can take over and no data is lost. WebLogic supports five different mechanisms for persisting session state information:

Memory (single-server, nonreplicated)
  The session data is stored on a single server in memory.

File
  The session data is stored on a shared filesystem.

JDBC
  The session data is stored in a database table.

Cookie-based
  The session data is stored at the client end in a cookie.

In-memory replication
  The session data is stored in memory on multiple servers.

By default, WebLogic stores session state information in memory in a nonreplicated manner. The other four persistence mechanisms are desirable when the web application is deployed in a WebLogic cluster. Session persistence allows WebLogic Server to support automatic *session failover*. Session failover ensures that a server failure remains transparent to the user—another server will seamlessly pick up the backup of the session data. Because the session data is now persistent and accessible to multiple server instances, session information isn't lost when the server goes down. Clearly, session persistence will be more expensive than just storing the session data in memory on a single server. The session caching mechanism can help alleviate this cost.

We will examine each persistence mechanism in detail later in this chapter, with a separate section dedicated to in-memory replication. Usually, any kind of Java object can be bound to the session. However, if you want to use session persistence, certain restrictions are imposed. If you have configured the session persistence to use either file, JDBC, or in-memory replication, an object must implement the java.io. Serializable interface before it can be bound in the session. If you have configured session persistence to use cookies instead, only strings may be bound in the HTTP session.

Configuring Session Persistence

The following properties can be set in the session-descriptor element in the *weblogic.xml* configuration file.

CacheSize

> This property determines the number of sessions that are cached in memory. The default value is 256. If your site holds a large number of sessions, but these sessions are not always active, you will want to cache the most-often used sessions. A *Least-Recently Used (LRU) algorithm* is used to swap sessions out to whichever persistence store is in use if the cache size is reached, and to swap them back in again when needed. Of course, the persistence mechanism has to be configured for this to work. Otherwise, the value is ignored and the number of sessions held in memory is limited only by the amount of memory available. The minimum value is 16 and the maximum is Integer.MAX_VALUE.

InvalidationIntervalSecs

> This parameter determines the period between the executions of the house-cleaning tasks. If a session is deleted or times out after session-timeout minutes, the house-cleaning task removes all data associated with the session, freeing up server resources. You typically will set this value to less than the value of the session-timeout element. The minimum value is 1, the maximum is 604800 (a week), and the default is 60.

PersistentStoreType

> This property sets the type of the persistence mechanism to be used. Its value can be one of the following values: memory, file, jdbc, cookie, or replicated. The default value for this setting is memory.

You can set the session timeout and session invalidation interval from the Administration Console. These settings can be configured from the Configuration/Descriptor tab for a selected web application.

Memory Persistence

By default, WebLogic stores all the session-state information for a server in memory. This implies that the number of concurrent sessions is limited by the amount of heap space available to the particular server instance. If you do not specify a sufficiently large heap size when you start WebLogic Server, you may run out of memory under severe load. It also means that if the server is stopped or fails for some reason, you lose all the session information.

Thus, by default, session data isn't persistent and cannot survive the lifetime of the server. For development environments, the default setting is sufficient. In a production environment where your deployment consists of multiple servers, you will require session failover when one of the servers fails. The other four possible values for the PersistentStoreType property provide automatic session failover. No further configuration is necessary for memory persistence.

File-Based Persistence

Setting the persistence type to file enables WebLogic to persist session-state information on the filesystem. In addition, you may specify the directory on the filesystem where the session information will be stored, using the PersistentStoreDir session parameter in the *weblogic.xml* descriptor file:

```
<!-- weblogic.xml entry -->
<session-descriptor>
  <session-param>
    <param-name>PersistentStoreType</param-name>
    <param-value>file</param-value>
  </session-param>
  <session-param>
    <param-name>PersistentStoreDir</param-name>
    <param-value>tmp_sessions</param-value>
  </session-param>
</session-descriptor>
```

If you do not specify a directory, WebLogic Server will automatically create a temporary directory. Note that if you are using file-based session persistence in a cluster, you must ensure the attribute is set to a shared directory that is accessible to all the servers in the cluster. Typically, this directory will reside on high-performance disks with built-in support for failover.

JDBC Persistence

Setting the persistence type to jdbc enables WebLogic to store session data in a database table. If you choose to use the database for persisting session data, you must also specify the name of the connection pool that will provide JDBC connections to the database. The PersistentStorePool session parameter defined in the session-descriptor element in the *weblogic.xml* descriptor file lets you specify the name of the connection pool:

```
<!-- weblogic.xml entry -->
<session-descriptor>
```

```
  <session-param>
    <param-name>PersistentStoreType</param-name>
    <param-value>jdbc</param-value>
  </session-param>
  <session-param>
    <param-name>PersistentStorePool</param-name>
    <param-value>myJDBCPool</param-value>
  </session-param>
  <session-param>
    <param-name>JDBConnectionTimeoutSecs</param-name>
    <param-value>60</param-value>
  </session-param>
</session-descriptor>
```

The JDBConnectionTimeoutSecs property determines how long the persistence mechanism will wait to retrieve session data from the database. It defaults to 120 seconds. You must ensure the JDBC pool is accessible to all permitted users. Otherwise, the server will fail to save the session data.

An SQL table called wl_servlet_sessions must also be created. The database user associated with the connection pool must have read/write access to this table. Table 2-4 defines the structure of this database table, listing the name and type of each column.

Table 2-4. Table definition for wl_servlet_sessions

Column name	Type
wl_id	A variable-width alphanumeric column holding up to 100 characters
wl_context_path	Same as wl_id
wl_is_new	A single character column
wl_create_time	A numeric column of length 20
wl_is_valid	A single character column
wl_session_values	A large binary column
wl_access_time	A numeric column of length 20
wl_max_inactive_interval	An integer column

The primary key for this table is a compound key comprising two columns: wl_id and wl_context_path. Example 2-4 provides the SQL needed to create such a table on an Oracle database.

Example 2-4. SQL for creating the table to store session persistence information
for JDBC-based session persistence

```
create table wl_servlet_sessions
  ( wl_id VARCHAR2(100) NOT NULL,
    wl_context_path VARCHAR2(100) NOT NULL,
    wl_is_new CHAR(1),
    wl_create_time NUMBER(20),
    wl_is_valid CHAR(1),
```

```
    wl_session_values LONG RAW,
    wl_access_time NUMBER(20),
    wl_max_inactive_interval INTEGER,
  PRIMARY KEY (wl_id, wl_context_path) );
```

The SQL script needed to create the table on other DBMS products will closely resemble the previous SQL statement. Note that although JDBC persistence provides the most robust way of persisting session data, its performance is also by far the poorest.

Cookie Persistence

Setting the persistence type to cookie enables WebLogic to store session data on the client browser itself. Unlike other persistence mechanisms, which store the session data on the WebLogic Server, this approach saves the session data on the client side, and the data then gets transported between the client and the server. In order to effectively use cookie-based persistence, you should persist only small amounts of session data because the cookie data needs to be transferred to and fro many times. Nevertheless, cookie-based persistence does have a significant advantage: because there is no server-side state, you don't need to configure any failover support for the cluster, and the servers can be stopped and started without losing session data.

You also can use the PersistentStoreCookieName property to specify the name of the cookie used for session persistence:

```
<!-- weblogic.xml entry -->
<session-descriptor>
  <session-param>
    <param-name>PersistentStoreType</param-name>
    <param-value>cookie</param-value>
  </session-param>
  <session-param>
    <param-name>PersistentStoreCookieName</param-name>
    <param-value>MYWLCOOKIE</param-value>
  </session-param>
</session-descriptor>
```

The default name for the session persistence cookie is WLCOOKIE. There are limitations to using this form of persistence:

- The user's browser must be configured to accept cookies.
- Only string-valued attributes may be stored in the session. WebLogic will throw an IllegalArgumentException if you attempt to assign any other type of object to a session attribute.

- Cookies are written in an HTTP response header, which must be written before any content. For this reason, you should not flush the HTTP response, or else cookie data cannot be written. Note that buffers are automatically flushed when they reach the default buffer size (12 KB), in which case the cookie data will not be updated. (You can change the default buffer size by calling the setBufferSize( ) method on the ServletResponse object.)
- You may use only basic, browser-based authentication.
- By default, the session data stored in a cookie is not encrypted in any way. If your session is holding sensitive information that must never be tampered with, you should consider the potential security risks of exposing this data to the client's browser.

Clusters and Replicated Persistence

Setting the persistence type to replicated enables WebLogic to replicate the session state in memory itself. Like the default memory persistence scheme, session data is stored in memory. Unlike the default memory persistence, this scheme works closely with the notion of primary and secondary servers in the cluster, as discussed later in Chapter 14. WebLogic creates the primary session state on the server that a client first connects to, and then transparently replicates the session-state information onto a secondary server instance. The process of copying session state from one server instance to another in the cluster is called *in-memory replication*. The replica is kept up-to-date so that the secondary server can take over when the original server instance that holds the session data fails.

In-memory session-state replication will work only for those object-valued attributes in the session that are Serializable objects. Changes to the session object will be replicated only if you use the setAttribute( ) and removeAttribute( ) methods on the HttpSession object. These methods ensure that any changes to the attributes of the session are mirrored onto the secondary server for the client. Remember that only nontransient attributes of an object in the session will be replicated to the secondary server. All transient attributes of the object will be ignored.

If you modify the state of an object stored in the session using another object reference, those changes will not be automatically replicated across. For instance, suppose you access a session attribute and modify its value as follows:

```
HttpSession session = request.getSession(false);
com.oreilly.user.AUser foo = (AUser) session.getAttribute("user");
foo.setName("Ali Cowan");
```

The changes to the AUser object will be replicated only if you subsequently invoke the setAttribute( ) method:

```
session.setAttribute("user", foo);
```

This means that changes to the session data are replicated *only* after explicit calls to either the setAttribute( ) or removeAttribute( ) methods on the HttpSession object.

Disadvantages of Session-State Replication

Even though session-state replication guarantees failover, there are a few downsides of which you should be aware. There is a slight cost of additional network traffic when the session data is actually replicated to the secondary server. Clearly, the demands on network resources will grow as the number of active sessions grows and as more server instances are added to the cluster. There is also the additional cost associated with serializing the session data every time an attribute is added.

The benefits of HTTP session failover are offset by overheads of additional network traffic due to session-state replication. In Chapters 14 and 15, we will look at how you can plan for network capacity and manage some of these issues.

Session Replication

Although Chapter 14 covers the use and configuration of clusters, we need to understand a little here in order to fully grasp replicated persistence. In essence, in-memory replicated persistence requires two things:

Redundancy
> A secondary server that holds and maintains a copy of the session data

Failover
> The ability to let the secondary server transparently take over when the primary server fails

Earlier, we saw that WebLogic handles session replication through its implementation of the setAttribute( ) and removeAttribute( ) methods on the HttpSession object. Now we investigate how the failover is handled transparently.

Transparent failover of session data can occur only when you access the WebLogic cluster through a web server fitted with a WebLogic proxy plug-in, a WebLogic instance equipped with the HttpClusterServlet, or load-balancing hardware supported by WebLogic.

Session Failover

For the software approach to work, you need to use either the HttpClusterServlet or a combination of HTTP servers with identically configured plug-ins. WebLogic currently supports proxy plug-ins for Apache, IIS, and NES. Even though we will talk about session failover using proxy plug-ins, the same discussion holds if you use WebLogic Server with an HttpClusterServlet.

Figure 2-1 illustrates how session replication works in a WebLogic cluster. The plug-in maintains a list of all active servers in the cluster. When a new session is created, the server that handles this request becomes the primary server (Server A in the diagram), and WebLogic will ensure that any future requests are routed to this same server. Thus, sessions are said to be "sticky."

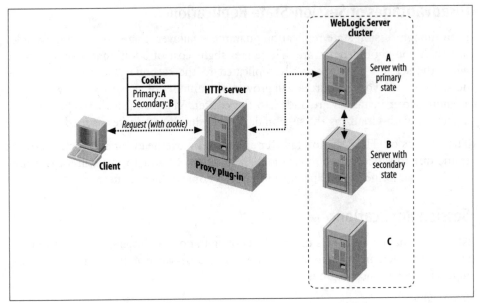

Figure 2-1. Session replication in a cluster

After a primary server has been selected, a secondary server is selected (perhaps using a preferred replication group, which is discussed later in Chapter 14). In our example, Server B is chosen to hold a copy of the session state held in Server A. From now on, all changes to the client's session state in Server A will be replicated to Server B. When the result page is sent back to the client, information is attached that identifies the primary and secondary locations. This information is attached in the form of a cookie or, if cookies are disabled, embedded using URL rewriting.

The interesting bit happens when there is a failure. As the plug-ins hold an active server list for the cluster, a plug-in will know whether the primary server for an incoming request is live. If the server is not live, the plug-in will examine the cookie for the location of the secondary server and automatically route the request to that server. The secondary server now becomes the primary server, and a new server is located and chosen as the secondary server. The session state then is replicated to the new secondary server, and a new cookie (which holds updated locations for the primary and secondary servers) is returned to the client.

In the special case of a cluster having only two server instances, if one server goes down, there will be no available secondary server. Then, if another server does come up at some later stage, it will automatically become the secondary for all the session data.

Configuring a Simple Web Cluster

Whenever you deploy a web application to a WebLogic cluster, you need something sitting *before* the cluster (i.e., between the client and the cluster) that can direct incoming requests to the appropriate server that hosts the primary session state. There are many ways in which you can accomplish this:

Hardware load balancer
> A hardware load balancer can be placed in front of the cluster. In this case, all client requests to the cluster must pass through the load balancer. The load balancer can distribute requests across the available members of the cluster, and direct requests involved in a session to the appropriate server holding the primary state.

Web server with proxy plug-in
> A web server can be augmented with a *proxy plug-in*, a piece of software supplied with WebLogic that will redirect certain requests (for example, those to servlets and JSPs) through to the cluster. Clients accessing the web server then can be served up static content by the web server directly and transparently proxied through to the cluster behind the web server for the dynamic content.

WebLogic with the HttpClusterServlet
> The HttpClusterServlet is an alternative to a proxy plug-in. A WebLogic instance can be configured to host the servlet, which can forward requests across to the cluster in the same way as the proxy plug-in.

The main ways in which you can architect your cluster and web tiers are discussed in much more detail in Chapter 14. Here we will give a brief introduction to setting up the HttpClusterServlet, leaving the configuration of the proxy plug-ins, an almost identical task, to Chapter 3.

Configuring HttpClusterServlet

As its name suggests, the HttpClusterServlet is a servlet. It is supplied with WebLogic. To put the servlet into action, create a simple web application with the servlet configured as part of the web application. You need to then deploy the web application to the machine that is going to serve as the main gateway to your cluster, as suggested by Figure 2-2.

As detailed in Figure 2-2, the idea is that requests that go to the server instance called Front Server are to be redirected to one of the servers in the cluster. If Server A and Server B form a cluster, then the HttpClusterServlet will load-balance new requests between the servers, and session replication and failover will occur as detailed in the previous section. The cluster servlet maintains a list of all the servers participating in the cluster and avoids redirecting to failed servers. The client has direct access to the Front Server only, and remains unaware of the actual cluster member that eventually processes its requests.

The configuration entails several tasks, and we will use the architecture in Figure 2-2 in our configuration details.

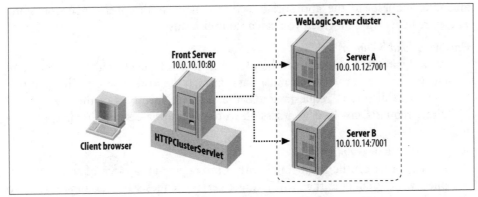

Figure 2-2. Example clustering setup

- The HttpClusterServlet servlet has to be registered in the web application, and the web application must be deployed on Front Server. You typically would make the web application the default web application.

- You have to configure the servlet engine to send certain URL patterns through to the HttpClusterServlet servlet. The servlet will then pass these on to the cluster and return the results.

- You have to configure the HttpClusterServlet so that it knows the addresses of the servers participating in the cluster.

- You must deploy your web application to the cluster. Make sure the web application has its PersistentStoreType attribute set to replicated.

Registering the servlet is like registering any other servlet. The class name for the servlet is weblogic.servlet.proxy.HttpClusterServlet, and it is included within WebLogic's runtime libraries. The following snippet from the *web.xml* descriptor file does the job:

```
<servlet>
    <servlet-name>HttpClusterServlet</servlet-name>
    <servlet-class>
        weblogic.servlet.proxy.HttpClusterServlet
    </servlet-class>
    <!-- optional init-params go here -->
</servlet>
```

As shown earlier in this chapter, you can create a servlet mapping to determine the set of URLs to pass to the servlet. For instance, we would like a request such as *http://10.0.10.10/index.jsp* to result in the cluster servlet being invoked, which will in turn proxy through to the appropriate server in the cluster. The easiest way to establish a mapping for all files is to use the special shortcut URL pattern, /, together with explicit mappings for HTML and JSP files:

```
<!-- Map almost everything to the servlet -->
<servlet-mapping>
```

```
    <servlet-name>HttpClusterServlet</servlet-name>
    <url-pattern>/</url-pattern>
  </servlet-mapping>
  <!-- Map JSP files to the servlet -->
  <servlet-mapping>
    <servlet-name>HttpClusterServlet</servlet-name>
    <url-pattern>*.jsp</url-pattern>
  </servlet-mapping>
  <!-- Map HTML files to the servlet -->
  <servlet-mapping>
    <servlet-name>HttpClusterServlet</servlet-name>
    <url-pattern>*.html</url-pattern>
  </servlet-mapping>
```

The servlet also has to be configured with the addresses of the servers in the cluster and other information. This must be done with the servlet initialization parameters. The most important parameter, `WebLogicCluster`, configures the addresses and ports of the members of the cluster. For the preceding example, you need the following:

```
<init-param>
  <param-name>WebLogicCluster</param-name>
  <param-value>
    10.0.10.12:7001:7002|10.0.10.14:7001:7002
  </param-value>
</init-param>
```

The servlet can take a whole host of additional parameters, all of which are detailed in the proxy plug-in documentation in Chapter 3.

Once the cluster servlet has been configured and deployed, requests to the server Front Server will be mapped to the appropriate server in the cluster. So, assuming we have a web application deployed to the cluster, accessing *http://10.0.10.10/index.jsp* will result in the following activity:

1. WebLogic's servlet engine on Front Server will find a matching URL pattern and will send the request to the cluster servlet.

2. The cluster servlet will consult its internal list of available cluster members and forward the request to either Server A or Server B. In fact, it also will check to see if the request is associated with a user in a session, in which case it will try and forward to the server hosting the primary session state.

3. The server in the cluster tier will execute the request, feeding the result back to the cluster servlet, which will in turn feed the result back to the user.

Debugging the Configuration

The `HttpClusterServlet` supports the `DebugConfigInfo` initialization parameter, which is useful for debugging the servlet's configuration. If you've specified this initialization parameter for the `HTTPClusterServlet`, the servlet returns the details of its configuration whenever you invoke a servlet along with the query parameter `__Web-LogicBridgeConfig`, instead of passing the request through to the cluster. In order to debug the servlet's configuration, you need to use the *web.xml* descriptor file to specify the initialization parameter for the HttpClusterServlet:

```
<init-param>
    <param-name>DebugConfigInfo</param-name>
    <param-value>ON</param-value>
</init-param>
```

Now you can view the configuration of the HttpClusterServlet by navigating to a URL similar to *http://10.0.10.10/index.jsp?__WebLogicBridgeConfig*. In the case of our example cluster setup, we obtain the following details on the servlet's configuration:

```
Query String: __WebLogicBridgeConfig

Primary Server: 10.0.10.12:7001:7002

General Server List:
10.0.10.12:7001:7002
10.0.10.14:7001:7002

ConnectRetrySecs: 2
ConnectTimeoutSecs: 10
CookieName: JSESSIONID
Debug: false
DebugConfigInfo: true
DefaultFileName: null
DisableCookie2Server: false
DynamicServerList: true
FileCaching: true
HungServerRecoverSecs: 300
Idempotent: true
KeepAliveEnabled: true
KeepAliveSecs: 30
MaxPostSize: -1
MaxSkipTime: 10
PathPrepend: null
PathTrim: null
TrimExt: null
SecureProxy: false
WLLogFile: c:/temp/wlproxy.log
WLProxySSL: false
```

Note how the output lists the servers participating in the cluster, and also indicates the primary server to which the request has been bound (if any).

Security Configuration

WebLogic provides several ways to secure a web application:

- You can declaratively configure web authentication for clients that access your web application. You can restrict access to resources in a web application by applying security constraints to a collection of web resources.

- A servlet/JSP can programmatically check whether the client has sufficient privileges before executing a particular piece of code.
- You can programmatically log in a user, bypassing the standard J2EE mechanisms.

Authentication

The login-config element in the standard *web.xml* deployment descriptor allows you to set up authentication for a web application. You can specify the authentication method using the auth-method element. WebLogic supports the following authentication methods:

HTTP basic authentication (BASIC)
 Here the web server authenticates the client against the security realm using the supplied username and password combination.

Form-based authentication (FORM)
 Here the client authenticates using a custom HTML form, which resembles:

```
<form method="post" action="j_security_check">
  <input type="text" name="j_username">
  <input type="password" name="j_password">
</form>
```

If you choose form-based authentication, you must specify the locations for the login page that initially will be displayed, and the error page that will be used when the user fails to authenticate himself. Use the form-login-page subelement to specify the login page, and the form-error-page subelement to specify the error page.

Here's a sample configuration for a web application that uses form-based authentication:

```
<!-- web.xml entry: -->
<login-config>
  <auth-method>FORM</auth-method>
  <realm-name>foo</realm-name>
  <form-login-config>
    <form-login-page>/login.html</form-login-page>
    <form-error-page>/error.html</form-error-page>
  </form-login-config>
</login-config>
```

Client certificates (CLIENT-CERT)
 Here the web server authenticates the client using a client certificate or some form of perimeter authentication.

Use the realm-name subelement to specify the name of a security realm used during client authentication.

Always associate the appropriate security realm with a web application. Otherwise, a client may fail to authenticate.

WebLogic also supports a single sign-on mechanism between different web applications, as described earlier in this chapter.

Declarative Security

The J2EE specification defines a standard way to restrict access to resources in a web application. A *security constraint* is a declarative way of protecting web resources. It is defined in terms of one or more security roles that apply to collections of web resources. A *security role* maps to one or more principals in the security realm. A *principal* maps to either users or groups of users. The collection of web resources is specified via a URL pattern. In addition, you can configure whether SSL is required when clients access any resource in the collection.

The following portion from the *web.xml* descriptor illustrates how to enforce a security constraint to web resources:

```
<!-- web.xml entry: -->
<security-constraint>
  <web-resource-collection>
    <web-resource-name>Admin Resources</web-resource-name>
    <description>security constraints for admin stuff</description>
    <url-pattern>/admin/*</url-pattern>
    <http-method>POST</http-method>
    <http-method>GET</http-method>
  </web-resource-collection>
  <auth-constraint>
    <role-name>admin</role-name>
  </auth-constraint>
  <user-data-constraint>
    <transport-guarantee>NONE</transport-guarantee>
  </user-data-constraint>
</security-constraint>
```

The security-constraint element in the standard *web.xml* descriptor file ensures that only users in the admin role are granted access to web resources under the *admin* directory.

The security setup isn't complete. You still need to specify a security role and WebLogic principals that are associated with the role. For this, use the security-role element in the *web.xml* descriptor file to configure the security role, and use the security-role-assignment element in the *weblogic.xml* descriptor file to associate one or more WebLogic principals with the role. The role assignment maps actual WebLogic users and groups to the security role. Given the earlier constraint on a resource, you then can set up the following security role assignment:

```
<!-- web.xml entry: -->
<security-role>
  <role-name>admin</role-name>
</security-role>

<!-- weblogic.xml entry: -->
<security-role-assignment>
  <role-name>admin</role-name>
  <principal-name>jmountjoy</principal-name>
  <principal-name>achugh</principal-name>
</security-role-assignment>
```

In this case, the WebLogic users achugh and jmountjoy are placed into the admin role, so they will have access to any resources for which this role is authorized. Alternatively, you can indicate that the role actually maps to a security role that already has been configured within WebLogic's security realm using the Administration Console. In this case, you need to use the global-role element to refer to the security role:

```
<!-- weblogic.xml entry for Administration Console assignment: -->
<security-role-assignment>
  <role-name>admin</role-name>
  <global-role/>
</security-role-assignment>
```

You must now use the Administration Console to configure a security role and assign users and/or groups to this role, and also ensure that it is available to the web application. Chapter 17 explains the global-role element in more detail, and also describes how you can configure WebLogic users, groups, and roles.

Web applications can interact with the declarative security using three methods that can be invoked on the HttpServletRequest object:

getRemoteUser( )
> This method returns the username the client used to authenticate itself (null, if the user was not authenticated).

isUserInRole( )
> This method returns true if the remote user is in a specified role (false if the user has not been authenticated).

getUserPrincipal( )
> This method returns the principal associated with the current user (returns a java.security.Principal object).

In order for WebLogic to determine whether a remote user does belong to a particular role, you need to set up the security role and then assign one or more principals to the role as we have just done.

You also can configure an alias for the security role, which can then be used from within your servlet code. The security-role-ref element within the *web.xml* descriptor file shows how to define this alias for this security role:

```
<!-- web.xml entry: -->
<servlet>
...
  <security-role-ref>
    <role-name>administrator</role-name>
    <role-link>admin</role-link>
  </security-role-ref>
...
</servlet>
```

Note that the role-link element maps to the actual name of the security role as defined in the *web.xml* descriptor. Once you have configured this alias for the role, you can programmatically check whether the user is in a given role:

```
if (req.isUserInRole("administrator")) {
  // if user is also an administrator
}
else {
  // for non-administrators
}
```

Although we've covered the basics of web security here, WebLogic provides a far richer security API to control every aspect of security in an enterprise deployment. We cover this extensively in Chapters 16 and 17.

Programmatic Security

In some instances, you may want to implement your own authentication scheme, bypassing the standard basic-, form-, or certificate-based authentication altogether. In this case, you can use the programmatic authentication API supplied by WebLogic, which is available via the weblogic.servlet.security. ServletAuthentication class. You may want to read this in conjunction with the material in Chapter 17 if you are unfamiliar with the terminology being used here.

The ServletAuthentication.runAs( ) method accepts two arguments: an authenticated Subject, and the HTTP request object. When you execute this method, it effectively logs the subject into the web application by associating it with the current session. For all intents and purposes, it is as if the client authenticated itself using traditional web authentication. To create the subject, you need to use another helper method, weblogic.security.services.Authentication.login( ). This method accepts the username and password of the WebLogic user, authenticates the credentials, and returns a Subject populated with all principals associated with the subject. The username and password must be passed in the form of a callback handler.

The following JSP page illustrates these points nicely:

```
<%@ page import ="javax.security.auth.callback.*,javax.security.auth.*" %>
<%
out.println("Principal before authentication is " + request.getUserPrincipal() +
    "<br>");
CallbackHandler handler =
```

```
    new weblogic.security.SimpleCallbackHandler("jon", "12341234");
Subject mySubject =
    weblogic.security.services.Authentication.login(handler);
weblogic.servlet.security.ServletAuthentication.runAs(mySubject, request);
out.println("Principal after authentication is " + request.getUserPrincipal() +
    "<br>");
%>
```

When you invoke this JSP page from a browser, you get the following output:

```
Principal before authentication is null
Principal after authentication is jon
```

If you invoke this page again, you get the following output:

```
Principal before authentication is jon
Principal after authentication is jon
```

This is to be expected because once the client has been authenticated, the credentials are associated for the duration of the client's session. In Chapter 3, we look at how to enforce the single sign-on mechanism, in which case the client's authenticated subject persists across all web applications available on a web server or virtual host.

Securing Servlet Initialization and Destruction

Some users need to run a servlet's init( ) and destroy( ) methods under a different principal, generally because of access to some protected resource. You can configure this in WebLogic by modifying the *weblogic.xml* descriptor and including something such as the following for each servlet:

```
<servlet-descriptor>
  <servlet-name>MyServletName</servlet-name>
  <run-as-principal-name>system</run-as-principal-name>
  <init-as-principal-name>systeminit</init-as-principal-name>
  <destroy-as-principal-name>systeminit</destroy-as-principal-name>
</servlet-descriptor>
```

Authenticated Dispatching

WebLogic provides servlet request dispatching in the standard way. For instance, the following code sample shows how to forward a servlet request to another JSP page, *page.jsp*, within the same web application:

```
// Perform some processing, perhaps writing some output
ServletContext sc = getServletConfig( ).getServletContext( );
RequestDispatcher rd = sc.getRequestDispatcher("page.jsp");
rd.forward(request,response);
```

Similarly, a JSP page also can forward a request to another servlet in the web application:

```
<jsp:forward page="/MyServlet" />
```

By default, a web application isn't required to authenticate on requests forwarded to another web resource. However, you can force WebLogic to reauthenticate the client whenever a request is forwarded. If you specify the check-auth-on-forward element in the *weblogic.xml* descriptor file for the web application, any client request forwarded to a protected resource will require the client to reauthenticate itself:

```
<!-- weblogic.xml entry: -->
<container-descriptor>
  <check-auth-on-forward/>
</container-descriptor>
```

Ordinarily, once a client has authenticated itself to WebLogic, the web application will continue to use the same security context when any request is forwarded to another web resource. The check-auth-on-forward element lets you deviate from this standard behavior by enforcing an extra authentication check when client requests are forwarded to a protected resource.

Monitoring Web Applications

You can monitor web applications, and the servlets and JSPs contained in them, by using the Administration Console. Choose the Deployments/Web Application Modules to list each web application, together with its context root and deployment order. If you customize the view, you will be able to view further information, such as the security authentication realm associated with the web application and the servlet's reload period.

From the Servlets tab (the Monitoring tab in WebLogic 7.0), you can view statistics on each servlet, such as the number of times it has been invoked and its average execution time. You also can customize the view and obtain further information, such as the full classname of the servlet and the number of times the servlet was reloaded. By default, the servlet with the name /* is the FileServlet, which serves any request for static files. JSPs also are listed here because they, too, are servlets.

You can gather further statistics about sessions, but to do so you have to first enable session monitoring. You can do this by selecting the Sessions tab and enabling the option. You also can enable this option for a web application from its Configuration/ Descriptor tab. Once you've enabled session monitoring, you can then view the list of active sessions from the Monitoring/Sessions tab. This includes data such as the session identifier, the server to which the session is bound, and at the time the session was last accessed.

CHAPTER 3

Managing the Web Server

As a J2EE-compliant servlet engine, WebLogic Server is able to serve dynamic content through servlets, filters, JSPs, and custom tag libraries. It supports multiple web applications, each providing a distinct piece of functionality, and each having access to an array of configured enterprise services. It supports robust server-side session-state management, which is vital for constructing rich enterprise applications that use a client browser as their interface. It provides standard web authentication mechanisms to log in users and provides a secure operating environment. As a full-featured HTTP server, WebLogic also can be used as the primary web server for static content such as HTML pages, applets, images, multimedia files, etc.

WebLogic Server can do a lot more than just serve the static file contents of a web application. It supports many features found in other web servers, such as multiple *virtual hosts*, whereby a single WebLogic Server instance or cluster can host multiple web sites. Even though each logical web server has its own hostname, Domain Name Service (DNS) may map each of them to the same IP address (or cluster IP address). WebLogic extracts the hostname from the HTTP request headers, and redirects the request to the appropriate "web site." The same web application can then be targeted to multiple virtual hosts, as if it were deployed on separate web servers. In this chapter, we look at how to configure the web server and HTTP protocol, and how to create multiple virtual hosts. We also will look at how you can configure the logging of HTTP requests.

WebLogic Server also can integrate with other web servers, such as the Apache HTTP Server, Microsoft's IIS, and the NES. You can proxy HTTP requests for static content through WebLogic to another web server. Alternatively, you can install a native plug-in (provided by your WebLogic distribution) on the web server so that the web server forwards requests for servlets and JSPs to a WebLogic server or cluster. We examine both of these scenarios in this chapter.

We'll also see how a plug-in can function like the HttpClusterServlet, described in Chapter 2. In this case, it acts not only as a proxy, but also as a load balancer that takes into account server failure.

Configuring WebLogic's HTTP Server

WebLogic's HTTP server forms an implicit part of its support for a number of different protocols. For example, it supports HTTP, HTTPS, T3, T3S, IIOP, and IIOPS. This chapter concentrates on its support for HTTP only, while Chapter 13 examines the other protocols. The HTTP protocol can be configured from the Administration Console by selecting the Server node from the navigation tree in the left frame, and then choosing the Protocols/HTTP tab from the right frame. As the next section will explain, identical HTTP settings can be configured for a number of virtual hosts as well. Table 3-1 lists the general settings for the HTTP server (or virtual host).

Table 3-1. Settings for configuring the HTTP server

Parameter	Description	Default
Default Server Name	Sets the hostname returned in the HTTP response header when the web server redirects a request.	none
Enable Keepalives	Use this to set HTTP keepalives. You generally want this set to `true`.	`true`
Duration	The number of seconds to wait before closing an inactive HTTP connection.	30
HTTPS Duration	The number of seconds to wait before closing an inactive HTTPS connection.	60

The Default Server Name is useful when you are using a firewall or a load balancer, and redirected requests from the browser should go to a particular hostname. For example, suppose that you set the hostname to xena, and the server is configured with the listen address 10.0.10.10. Now suppose that when a client submits a request for the URL *http://10.0.10.10:7001/*, the web server redirects the request to the main welcome page—say, *index.jsp*. The Default Server Name setting ensures that the supplied hostname is included in the redirected URL *http://xena:7001/index.jsp*.

Three additional attributes, available in the advanced section, also are relevant if you have some frontend, such as a load balancer or firewall. If the frontend causes inaccurate information to be delivered in the incoming HTTP headers, such as erroneous hostname or port number information, you may want WebLogic to ignore the information received in the header, and instead configure WebLogic with this data. The frontend host and ports parameters allow you to do just this.

Denial-of-Service Attacks

POST *denial-of-service attacks* attempt to put a web server out of service by overloading it with HTTP POSTs. The first three configuration settings described in Table 3-2 help prevent these attacks from overwhelming a server. WebLogic supports two additional settings that are useful in guarding against more general denial-of-service attacks.

Table 3-2. Settings for preventing denial-of-service attacks

Parameter	Description	Default
Post Timeout Secs	This setting limits the amount of time that the server waits between receiving chunks of data in an HTTP POST. It defaults to 30 seconds.	30
Max Post Size	This setting limits the maximum amount of data that WebLogic will receive for an HTTP POST. If this size is exceeded, a `MaxPostSizeExceeded` exception is thrown and the message "POST size exceeded the parameter MaxPostSize" is written to the server log. In this case, an HTTP error code also is sent back to the client: code `413` (`Request Entity too large`).	-1
HTTP Max Message Size	Set this attribute to specify the maximum HTTP message size allowable in a message header. This helps prevent attacks that try and force the server to allocate more memory than is available, increasing response time.	-1
HTTP Message Timeout	Set this attribute to specify the maximum number of seconds that WebLogic waits for a complete HTTP message to be received. This helps prevent attacks where callers tie up connections by indicating that they will be sending a message of a certain size, which they never finish sending.	-1

You should configure these settings appropriately according to the performance needs of your network and application.

WAP Options

There are two options that can be used to configure WAP support. Both of these are available under the advanced options of the Protocols/HTTP tab and are listed in Table 3-3.

Table 3-3. WAP settings for the web container

Parameter	Description	Default
WAP Enabled	If this is selected, the session ID will not include JVM information. This can be used to limit the size of URLs when using URL rewriting on WAP devices.	`Disabled`
Send Server Header	If set to `false`, the server name is not sent with the HTTP response. This is useful for saving header space for WAP applications.	`true`

Setting the Default Web Application

Each server or virtual host can be configured with a default web application that responds to HTTP requests that can't be resolved to any of the targeted web applications. This means that a client can access any resource within the default web application, even without a context path in its URL. For instance, if a web application called webapp is the default web application for WebLogic Server, a file *hello.jsp* under the document root can be accessed through the URL *http://server:port/hello.jsp*. Whenever a client invokes a URL that uses a context path that cannot be resolved to any of the deployed web applications, WebLogic automatically forwards the request to the default web application (if it exists). If the resource cannot be found within the default web application, or if no default web application has been configured for the server (or virtual host), the client will receive an `HTTP 404, Resource Not Found` error.

Setting up a web application as the default requires nothing more than setting its context root to `/`. To set the context path, you must set the `context-root` element within the *weblogic.xml* descriptor for the web application. Here is an example:

```
<weblogic-web-app>
  <context-root>/</context-root>
</weblogic-web-app>
```

Be sure to target the web application to the particular server or virtual host.

 Past versions of WebLogic let you set the default web application for a server/virtual host from the Administration Console. In the 8.1 release, the default web application is determined at deploy time based on the `context-root` property for the web application.

Virtual Hosting

Virtual hosting is the ability to run multiple web sites—say, *www.domain1.com* and *www.domain2.com*—on a single web server. *Name-based virtual hosting* implies that you map multiple domain names (or *logical hosts*) to the same IP address. The fact that both web sites run on the same server is not apparent to the clients. WebLogic Server allows you to create a virtual host for any number of different domain names. For instance, using DNS you could create two different domain names—*v1.oreilly.com* and *v2.oreilly.com*—pointing to the same physical WebLogic instance. On this single instance you can create two virtual hosts—say, v1 and v2.

If you have two virtual hosts, you can configure the web server to behave in the following ways:

- You can modify the HTTP behavior of each virtual host independently. For instance, each virtual host can have its own HTTP access logs.

- You can associate a different default web application with each virtual host in the same way that you associate a default web application with a WebLogic Server.

- You can target different WebLogic servers or clusters to different virtual hosts. For instance, if you have mapped different web applications to the virtual hosts, and targeted the web applications to different WebLogic servers, you can effectively target the virtual hosts to the appropriate servers.

Identical web applications are then isolated from each other when they are targeted to different virtual hosts.

 The Servlet specification demands that each logical virtual host must have its own servlet context, and that servlet contexts cannot be shared across virtual hosts.

Creating Virtual Hosts

Before you set up virtual hosts on WebLogic Server, you need to ensure that you have mapped the desired domain names to the same IP address. In our earlier example, the DNS server would have mapped *v1.oreilly.com* and *v2.oreilly.com* to the machine's IP address. Now to create a virtual host, you need to perform the following steps from the Administration Console:

1. Select the Services node, then the Virtual Hosts node.
2. Choose "Configure a new Virtual Host" in the right frame.
3. Enter a name for the virtual host. This is needed only to identify the Virtual Host entry in the domain.
4. Enter the names of the virtual hosts as you've configured them in the DNS server. In our example, the name of the virtual host would be *v1.oreilly.com*. In fact, you can enter the names of multiple virtual hosts here (one per line). This ensures that you have identical settings for each virtual host.
5. You may additionally configure the HTTP logging settings, and HTTP configuration parameters that are specific to the virtual host(s).

Once you have created a virtual host, you will notice an additional entry for it under the Target tab of any web application. If you want to target an application to a virtual host, select the virtual host as a target, and then move to the Target & Deploy tab to deploy the application to the targeted virtual host.

 In order to set up the virtual host, you should remember to configure the server instances or cluster that will respond to the virtual host and target the web applications to the particular virtual host(s). If you omit either of these steps, the virtual host will not respond properly.

A Virtual Hosting Scenario

Let us consider a small scenario and examine how WebLogic resolves URLs to particular web resources. Imagine that your WebLogic deployment consists of two virtual hosts, corresponding to the two domains *v1.oreilly.com* and *v2.oreilly.com*. Let's target an application app1 to host v1 only, and app2 to v1 and v2. Furthermore, imagine that app1 has a context root of app1, and app2 has a context root of /.

Now, consider what happens when a client requests the following URLs:

http://v1.oreilly.com/index.jsp
> This URL requests *index.jsp* from the default web application targeted to host v1. This implies the URL resolves to *index.jsp* from the web application app2.

http://v2.oreilly.com/index.jsp
> Again, this URL requests *index.jsp* from the default web application targeted to host v2. This implies the URL resolves to *index.jsp* from the web application app2.

http://v2.oreilly.com/app1/index.jsp
> This URL attempts to request *index.jsp* from the web application app1. In this case, the client will receive an HTTP 404 Resource Not Found error response because the web application app1 has not been not targeted to host v2.

http://v1.oreilly.com/app1/someservlet
> This URL points to the servlet mapped to */someservlet* within the web application app1. A client will be able to access this resource because app1 was targeted to host v1.

HTTP Access Logs

HTTP access logs maintain a record of all HTTP requests received by WebLogic Server. You can separately configure HTTP logging for each web server or virtual host defined in your WebLogic domain. The information in the access logs may be written in one of two formats: either the *Common Log Format* or the *Extended Log Format*. The Common Log Format is the default format based on standard conventions. The Extended Log Format enables you to customize the information that is recorded in the access logs.

To configure the HTTP logging facilities for a web server, start the Administration Console, then go to the Servers node in the left frame and choose the Logging/HTTP tab. To configure logging for a virtual host, select the host from the Services/Virtual Hosts node and then choose the Configuration/Logging tab. Note that the logging facilities also include a "log rotation" mechanism, which means that WebLogic Server continues to use a log file until its size reaches a certain limit or for a certain time period. After that, WebLogic renames the log file and creates a new one in its place. Table 3-4 provides a description of the configuration settings for the HTTP logging facility.

Table 3-4. Configuration settings for HTTP logging

Parameter	Description	Default
Enabled HTTP Logging	This setting enables logging of HTTP requests for the particular server or virtual host.	true
Log File Name	This setting determines the filename to which the log messages are written. If you provide a relative filename, it is assumed to be relative to the root directory of the machine on which the server or virtual host is running.	*ServerName/access.log*

Table 3-4. Configuration settings for HTTP logging (continued)

Parameter	Description	Default
Format	This setting specifies the format for the HTTP access logs. Its value can be either common or extended.	common
Log File Buffer and Flush Seconds	This setting instructs the server to check every Flush seconds whether the internal HTTP log buffer has reached Buffer KB in size. If so, the contents of the log buffer are then written to the log file. As file writes are usually slow, this allows you to optimize how much data is written to the physical log file at one time, and how often.	8Kb and 60s
Log Rotation Type	This setting specifies how the access logs are to be rotated: when the size of the log file reaches a certain limit (size), or after a certain amount of time has elapsed (date).	size
Max Log File Size KB	If log rotation is based on size, this setting determines the size limit for the current log file before it is rotated.	5000
Rotation Period and Rotation Time	If log rotation is based on date, the log files are rotated at an hourly interval determined by the Period attribute. Such a rotation will begin at the time specified by the Rotation Time attribute.	1440
Limit Number of Retained Files and Number to Retain	If you have configured log file rotation, you can use these settings to limit the number of log files that will be retained.	No limit

Let's now examine the two formats for the HTTP access logs.

Common Log Format

The *Common Log Format* is the default log format used by WebLogic. This format is supported by many different web servers and is documented by the W3C organization. A typical entry in the HTTP access logs matches the following pattern:

```
remotehost RFC931 authuser [day/month/year:hour:minute:second
    UTC_offset] "request" status bytes
```

Here's a brief description of the fields used in the log entry:

remotehost
> This field indicates the DNS name or IP address of the remote host.

RFC931
> This field indicates the identifier associated with the remote user. WebLogic just inserts a – here.

authuser
> This field indicates the name of the authenticated user making the request.

date
> This field indicates the date and time of the HTTP request. It appears in the format [day/month/year:hour:minute:second UTC_Offset], where the offset is the difference (in hours) between the local time and GMT enclosed in square brackets.

request
> This field indicates the first line of the request submitted by the client, enclosed in double quotes.

status
> This field indicates the HTTP status code returned by the server, or - otherwise.

bytes
> This field indicates the number of bytes listed as the content length in the HTTP header, or - otherwise.

Extended Log Format

The *Extended Log Format* is based on a draft W3C specification titled "Extended Log File Format." This format is more extensible, can be more easily parsed, and is highly configurable. The Extended Log Format allows you to define the type and the order of the information that is recorded for each HTTP request. WebLogic also allows you to define custom user-defined fields, and implement a Java class that generates the output for the fields.

The Extended Log Format allows you to customize which fields get recorded, and in what order. The actual log file defines a series of field directives in the head of the file. These directives determine the fields that ought to be recorded. Each directive begins on a new line and starts with a #. If the log file doesn't exist already, WebLogic creates a new log file with a default set of directives. WebLogic then will use the directives at the start of the log file to determine the format in which the HTTP access data should be logged.

For instance, we could create a log file with the following directives at the beginning:

```
#Version: 1.0
#Fields: date time bytes, sc-status x-com.oreilly.wl.httplog.MyField
```

These directives instruct WebLogic to record the date and time of the HTTP request, the HTTP status code returned by the server, and a user-defined field identifier whose output is generated by a Java class. For a complete description of other "standard" fields available under the Extended Log Format, refer to the draft specification available at *http://www.w3.org/TR/WD-logfile.html*.

All custom field identifiers are designated by an x- followed by the fully qualified name of a Java class that generates the output for the field. This Java class must implement the weblogic.servlet.logging.CustomELFLogger interface. This interface requires you to implement the logField( ) method, which gets invoked whenever HTTP access data ought to be logged. The method accepts two parameters:

- An HttpAccountingInfo object that provides access to the HTTP request and response data
- A FormatStringBuffer object that is used to generate the output

Here is an example of a Java class that implements a custom field identifier:

```
package com.oreilly.wl.httplog;
// imports omitted
public class MyField implements CustomELFLogger {
  public void logField(HttpAccountingInfo info,FormatStringBuffer out) {
    out.appendValueOrDash(info.getQueryString(););
  }
}
```

This method of logging is extremely powerful. The HttpAcccountingInfo gives total access to HTTP header information, information about the servlet (such as user principals), and session and parameter data. Nevertheless, custom user-defined fields should be used with some discretion. Because the logField( ) method gets invoked whenever a client accesses the HTTP server, you should ensure that the method performs its task in as short a time as possible!

Understanding Proxies

Even though WebLogic Server can operate as a full-featured HTTP 1.1 server, its real power lies in its ability to serve dynamic content through servlets and JSPs. A number of companies have adopted commercial web servers to host their corporate web sites. WebLogic provides integration with these web servers in the form of a web server *proxy plug-in*. This plug-in allows the web server to communicate with the WebLogic Server (or cluster). You then can have the web server serving up the usual static content, while it passes requests for JSPs and servlets to WebLogic. A proxy plug-in offloads the task of serving static content to a commercial web server.

Here are the various architectural scenarios you should consider:

- You could use WebLogic's built-in web server as your primary HTTP server, eliminating the need for other web servers.
- You can have WebLogic Server act as the primary HTTP server and servlet engine; additionally it proxies through certain requests for static requests to a commercial web server.
- You can have a commercial web server acting as your primary HTTP server; additionally it transparently proxies requests for servlets and JSPs through to WebLogic.

The choice of which configuration you adopt is largely dependent on the type of content being served up, the performance of the various HTTP servers, and other deployment parameters. For instance, if you are serving up mostly dynamic content (using JSPs and servlets), a pure WebLogic solution should be sufficient. If you are integrating with an existing framework, proxying to WebLogic Server may work better.

We have already seen how to establish WebLogic as your primary web server, including the configuration of virtual hosts. The following section shows how you can extend this by configuring WebLogic to proxy to a secondary web server. For more information on how to set up a web tier, refer to Chapter 14.

Proxying to a Secondary Web Server

WebLogic Server can be configured so that its built-in web server services requests for servlets and JSPs, while other requests for static web resources are redirected to a secondary server. This approach ensures WebLogic primarily handles all dynamic requests, while requests for static files are handled by some other web server. In order to implement this scenario, you need to configure an HttpProxyServlet for the web application and then map one or more URL patterns to the Proxy servlet. This way, whenever WebLogic Server receives a request that matches one of the URL patterns, the HttpProxyServlet gets invoked and simply redirects the request to the value of the redirectURL parameter.

To set up the proxy, register the class weblogic.t3.srvr.HttpProxyServlet, and set up a redirectURL initialization parameter. Here is a snippet from a *web.xml* deployment descriptor that illustrates how you should declare the Proxy servlet:

```
<servlet>
  <servlet-name>ProxyServlet</servlet-name>
  <servlet-class>weblogic.t3.srvr.HttpProxyServlet</servlet-class>
  <init-param>
    <param-name>redirectURL</param-name>
    <param-value>http://someserver:port/</param-value>
  </init-param>
</servlet>
```

Now you need to simply map a series of URL patterns to the servlet. You can have any number of these; again, these go in the *web.xml* descriptor file. Here is an example that shows how you can map all files ending in *.jpg* to the Proxy servlet:

```
<servlet-mapping>
  <servlet-name>ProxyServlet</servlet-name>
  <url-pattern>*.jpg</url-pattern>
</servlet-mapping>
```

Now, any request for a resource ending in *.jpg* will invoke the Proxy servlet, which then redirects the request to the configured URL.

Web Server Plug-ins

Let us now examine the scenario where an industry-strength web server is configured as the primary HTTP server, proxying certain client requests (usually requests for servlets and JSPs) through to WebLogic Server. WebLogic implements this configuration by providing web server plug-ins that augment the primary server with proxying logic. As mentioned in Chapter 2, a proxy plug-in enhances the web server by allowing it to delegate requests for dynamic content to WebLogic Server. Currently, WebLogic supports plug-ins for three web servers: the Apache HTTP Server, IIS, and NES.

The web server continues to serve static content, such as HTML pages, images, text files, and other web resources, and uses the plug-in to redirect requests for servlets and JSPs to WebLogic Server, which may be running on a different process, or may even be located on a different host. This internal delegation of requests for dynamic content to WebLogic Server occurs transparently. The client browser remains unaware of the existence of WebLogic Server. Configuring the proxy plug-in is a two-stage process:

1. First, the proxy plug-in has to be installed on the web server. Refer to the WebLogic documentation for more information on how to install the plug-in on your web server. After that, you need to specify the conditions under which the web server will delegate client requests to the plug-in.

2. Second, the proxy plug-in itself has to be configured. You must supply a list of name-value pairs that define the behavior of the web server plug-in.

Let us now look at some of the issues you need to consider when configuring proxy plug-ins on web servers.

Installing a Proxy

The rest of this section looks at how to use a proxy plug-in in general. In particular, we discuss how to configure the plug-in for the popular Apache 2.0 HTTP Server. The same configuration issues apply to proxy plug-ins for other well-known web servers. The only major change lies in how you set up the plug-ins on these servers. For instance, Apache's web server requires you to simply edit its configuration file, while Microsoft's IIS provides a GUI Console to establish the plug-in configuration. Though the exact syntax and configuration mechanism may differ, the overall intent and functionality remain unaltered. Refer to WebLogic's documentation for more information on how to install and configure the proxy plug-in on other supported web servers.

To install the proxy plug-in for Apache 2.0, you simply need to copy the proxy plug-in implementation into the *modules* subdirectory of your Apache installation. The Apache plug-in library is in fact included within your WebLogic installation, and is located at *WL_HOME/server/bin/mod_wl_20.so*. After this, you need to include the following line in the configuration file, *httpd.conf*:

```
LoadModule weblogic_module modules/mod_wl_20.so
```

That's it—your Apache web server is now equipped with WebLogic's proxy plug-in. The same configuration file also holds any changes to the plug-in's configuration.

Types of Proxying

You can configure the web server to proxy requests in two ways:

Proxying by path
    It can use a portion of the request URL.

Proxying by file extension
    It can use the MIME type of the web resource requested.

Proxying by path involves instructing the web server to pass to WebLogic Server any requests that begin with a particular path. For instance, you could set up the Apache plug-in to proxy by path by adding the following to Apache's configuration file:

```
<IfModule mod_weblogic.c>
    WebLogicHost wl.oreilly.com
    WebLogicPort 7001
</IfModule>
<Location /dynamic>
    SetHandler weblogic-handler
</Location>
```

In this case, a request URL such as *http://www.servername.com/dynamic/myservlet* will get passed on to WebLogic Server, which then invokes myservlet on the target web application dynamic on the host running at *w1.oreilly.com:7001*. Once the servlet has completed servicing the request, WebLogic Server feeds the response back to the proxy on the web server, which in turn feeds it back to the client.

Proxying by MIME type or extension involves having the web server proxy through to WebLogic Server all requests that map to a particular extension. The following example shows how to set up the Apache plug-in to proxy all requests for *.jsp* and *.xyz* through to WebLogic:

```
<IfModule mod_weblogic.c>
    WebLogicHost wl.oreilly.com
    WebLogicPort 7001
    MatchExpression *.jsp
    MatchExpression *.xyz
</IfModule>
```

As you would expect, requests for JSPs would go through to the server at *w1.oreilly. com:7001*, and WebLogic will fetch and then process the required JSP file. *.xyz* is an arbitrary file extension that you could use to proxy requests for servlets through to WebLogic Server. For instance, you could invoke myservlet using a URL such as *http://www.servername.com/myservlet/foo.xyz*.

If a request URL matches both criteria, the request is proxied by path. Later, we will examine additional parameters that you can define to customize the behavior of the web server plug-in.

Connection Pools and Keep-Alive Connections

The web server plug-ins support a reusable pool of HTTP connections to the WebLogic Server. The plug-in uses HTTP 1.1 keep-alive connections to the WebLogic Server behind it. It reuses the same connection from the pool for subsequent requests from the same client. You can set the duration that a connection is kept alive by setting the KeepAliveSecs parameter. By default, an inactive connection is reclaimed by the plug-in after 30 seconds and returned to the pool. You can disable this feature by setting the KeepAliveEnabled parameter to false.

Proxying to a Cluster

A proxy plug-in really comes into its own when it is placed before a bank of WebLogic instances. Figure 3-1 describes this scenario where incoming requests to a web server are then distributed between two WebLogic instances, Server A and Server B.

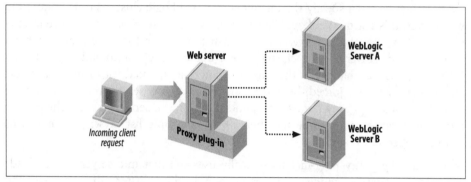

Figure 3-1. Proxying to a cluster

In this case, the plug-in not only proxies requests through, but also load-balances these requests and avoids servers that may become unavailable. Such a front-tier architecture is discussed in more detail in Chapter 14. The following configuration shows how to set up the Apache proxy plug-in when it sits in front of a WebLogic cluster:

```
<IfModule mod_weblogic.c>
    WebLogicCluster 10.0.10.10:7003,10.0.10.10:7005
    MatchExpression *.jsp
</IfModule>
```

In this case, we have instructed the plug-in to proxy/load-balance JSP requests between two servers in a cluster, running on the same machine, 10.0.10.10, on ports 7003 and 7005.

Connection Failures

The web server plug-in uses the ConnectTimeoutSecs parameter to determine how long it has to wait for connections to WebLogic Server. Once connected, it uses the HungServerRecoverSecs parameter to determine how long to wait for a response from WebLogic Server. If the plug-in doesn't receive a response within the specified duration, it marks the server as dead. If the plug-in fails to connect or doesn't receive a server response, it will try connecting to another server in the cluster.

The ConnectRetrySecs parameter determines how long the plug-in sleeps before trying to connect to another member in the cluster. If no member of a WebLogic cluster responds to the connection request, the plug-in returns an HTTP 503 (Service

Unavailable) error response. The number of times WebLogic tries to connect before returning a 503 response is determined by the value of (ConnectTimeoutSecs)/ (ConnectRetrySecs).

Dynamic Server List

Even though you can specify the members of a WebLogic cluster sitting behind the web server, this list of WebLogic Servers is only a starting point. Once a request is redirected to one of the servers, a new dynamic server list is returned with an updated list of servers in the cluster. These updates occur automatically with the HTTP response as changes to the cluster occur. The updated list includes any new servers that may have joined the cluster, and removes any servers that are no longer part of the cluster or may not have responded to the web server plug-in. The plug-in then load-balances among the members of this dynamic list of servers, unless, of course, the request is sticky.

By default, the proxy plug-in automatically uses the dynamic server list for load-balancing requests among the members of the cluster. If you set the DynamicServerList parameter to OFF, the plug-in ignores any changes to the WebLogic cluster at runtime and sticks to the original static definition of the servers in the cluster.

We've already discussed how WebLogic provides HTTP session failover—by keeping track of the primary server and the secondary server that replicates the session state. If the proxy fails to connect to the primary server, it attempts to connect to the secondary server. If both primary and secondary servers fail to respond, the session information is lost and the proxy plug-in chooses a new server from the dynamic server list.

SSL and Web Server Plug-ins

You may use SSL to protect the connections used between the web server plug-in and WebLogic Server. Using HTTPS connections between the plug-in and WebLogic guarantees security and confidentiality. The SSL protocol allows the web server proxy to authenticate itself to WebLogic Server so that only trusted principals are accessing WebLogic Server. In order to use secure proxies, you need to do the following:

1. Configure SSL on WebLogic Server (and the SSL listen port).
2. Specify two additional parameters for the proxy plug-in:
    a. Enable secure proxies by setting the SecureProxy parameter to ON.
    b. Using the TrustedCAFile parameter, specify the file that contains the digital certificates for trusted CAs for the plug-in.

Configuration Parameters

Once you have configured *which* URLs the proxy plug-in should respond to, you are in a position to specify *where* and *how* the plug-in should redirect incoming requests. As mentioned earlier, you need to specify a list of name-value pairs in order to configure the proxy plug-in. For instance, in order to configure WebLogic's plug-in for Apache's Web Server, you can include the following in the server's configuration file:

```
<IfModule mod_weblogic.c>
    WebLogicHost wl.oreilly.com
    WebLogicPort 7001
    MatchExpression *.jsp
    MatchExpression *.xyz
</IfModule>
```

Let us consider the important configuration parameters:

WebLogicHost

> This must be set when the web server needs to proxy to a single host, not a cluster. In this case, you must supply the hostname or virtual hostname of the server that will handle the request.

WebLogicPort

> This specifies the port number of WebLogic Server (server or virtual host) that will handle proxied requests.

WebLogicCluster

> This specifies the cluster address that will handle requests redirected by the proxy plug-in. This parameter will be a comma-delimited list of *host:port* entries.

PathTrim

> This specifies a string that is to be trimmed from the beginning of the original URI, before the request is passed on to WebLogic. Imagine you have configured a default web application for your WebLogic deployment. This means you can access the web application without a context-path. Then, if you set the value of the PathTrim parameter to */dynamic*, the plug-in will redirect the modified request to WebLogic after having removed */dynamic*. For instance, a request to the URL *http://www.servername.com/dynamic/myservlet* could then be forwarded to *http://weblogic.servername.com:7001/myservlet*.

PathPrepend

> This specifies a string that should be prefixed to the URI after it has been trimmed. For instance, this approach can be used to ensure that certain requests are routed to a particular web application, by specifying the context path for the web application as the path prefix.

Debug

> This determines the level of logging. It can take one of the values discussed in the following list.

OFF
> Debugging is disabled (this is the default value).

ON
> Log info and error messages.

HFC
> Logs headers from client, in addition to usual debugging info.

HTC
> Logs headers sent to client, in addition to usual debugging info.

HFW
> Logs headers from WebLogic Server, in addition to usual debugging info.

HTW
> Logs headers sent to WebLogic Server, in addition to usual debugging info.

ALL
> Logs all headers, in addition to usual debugging info.

WLLogFile
> This specifies the path and name of the log file to be used, when debugging is switched on.

DebugConfigInfo
> This can be set to either OFF or ON. If ON, any request that is proxied to WebLogic and that also includes the query parameter __WebLogicBridgeConfig retrieves the configuration data and runtime statistics from the configured proxy plug-in. Typically, you will enable this parameter for debugging purposes only.

CookieName
> This is set to the cookie name that you have configured for your web application. This defaults to JSESSIONID, which is also the default for a web application.

Clearly, a proxy plug-in is very useful for transparently integrating a WebLogic Server (or a cluster) with a commercial web server.

Example Configurations

Let's take a closer look at sample plug-in configurations that also let you debug. Here is an example configuration that enables logging of debug information when the configured proxy is used:

```
<IfModule mod_weblogic.c>
    WebLogicHost 10.0.10.10
    WebLogicPort 7001
    MatchExpression *.jsp
    Debug ON
    WLLogFile weblogic.log
</IfModule>
```

As the proxy plug-in is used, you will see a lot of debug information being placed into the log. This includes your SSL configuration, the dynamic server lists, cookies, and more. The next configuration shows how to support dynamic queries for the plug-in's setup and runtime statistics:

```
<IfModule mod_weblogic.c>
    WebLogicHost 10.0.10.10
    WebLogicPort 7001
    MatchExpression *.jsp
    DebugConfigInfo ON
</IfModule>
```

You can then retrieve the plug-in's configuration and runtime statistics by pointing your browser to a URL, similar to *http://webserver/a.jsp?__WebLogicBridgeConfig*.

If you need to set up the plug-in to proxy to a WebLogic cluster using file extensions, consider the following configuration:

```
<IfModule mod_weblogic.c>
    WebLogicCluster 10.0.10.10:7003,10.0.10.10:7005
    MatchExpression *.jsp
</IfModule>
```

You can achieve quite complex things if you use the full expression language syntax. You also may combine proxying by path with a cluster using the following setup:

```
<Location /dynamic>
    SetHandler weblogic-handler
    PathTrim /dynamic
</Location>
<IfModule mod_weblogic.c>
    WebLogicCluster 10.0.10.10:7003,10.0.10.10:7005
</IfModule>
```

In this case, all requests that include /dynamic in their paths are then sent through to the default web application configured for the servers within the cluster. The following example instructs the plug-in to proxy requests for *.jsp* and *.asp* files to separate clusters:

```
<IfModule mod_weblogic.c>
    MatchExpression *.jsp WebLogicCluster=10.0.10.10:7003,10.0.10.10:7005
    MatchExpression *.asp WebLogicCluster=10.0.10.11:7003,10.0.10.11:7005
</IfModule>
```

The web server in turn allows you to configure many more advanced scenarios. For instance, you can benefit from exciting web server features such as virtual hosting, path matching using regular expressions, and more.

CHAPTER 4
Using JNDI and RMI

The *Java Naming and Directory Interface* (JNDI) provides a standard way of accessing naming and directory services. The API describes how objects can be bound in a distributed directory service, and how clients of the directory can locate and retrieve these objects. It plays a critical role in any J2EE environment, providing the central naming and directory service API used by containers, J2EE resources, deployed applications, and external clients.

JNDI has an open architecture that permits the integration of a number of different implementations of directory services. These service provider implementations map vendor-neutral JNDI calls to the operations supported by the underlying directory service. For instance, your Java SDK distribution comes equipped with service providers for LDAP, CORBA Naming Services, and Java's Remote Method Invocation (RMI) Registry. Other service providers are also available for Sun's Network Information Service (NIS), Novell's Network Directory Service (NDS), DNS, and Windows Registry. Everything from Java objects to email addresses can be stored in the various types of directories, making them useful for a variety of things. In fact, WebLogic uses an embedded LDAP repository to store security information about WebLogic users, groups, security policies, and much more. The JNDI provides a standard interface to all of these types of directory services, and in WebLogic you will find a robust, distributed JNDI implementation that provides the naming and directory support for all J2EE applications.

WebLogic's JNDI implementation is used primarily as the standard J2EE mechanism that allows clients to publish, locate, and retrieve objects in a distributed fashion. For instance, when a JDBC data source or EJB is deployed, it is made available in a global JNDI tree, bound to its configured JNDI name. A Java client then can use the JNDI name to look up and gain access to the resource. Other J2EE resources such as JMS connection factories, JTA transactions, and RMI objects also may be bound in the JNDI tree.

In this chapter, we will look at how WebLogic's JNDI implementation can be accessed and used, as well as how you can bind your own objects into the JNDI tree.

You also will learn how WebLogic's JNDI implementation can take advantage of clusters, providing transparent global replication of bound services or objects across the members of the cluster. This cluster-wide JNDI tree may appear as a single, global hierarchy, but it actually is replicated across each member of the cluster. The JNDI implementation supports both *replicated* objects (or services), where the objects are replicated across all members of the cluster, and *pinned* objects, where the object (or service) is bound to a single server but still is accessible to the cluster.

The *RMI framework* is the standard technology underlying distributed object programming in Java. It enables a Java client to transparently access remote RMI objects by creating stubs that proxy requests through to the remote object and marshal the return values. WebLogic provides a high-performance implementation of RMI that complements the JNDI and clustering frameworks; in this chapter, you will learn how to create your own RMI objects that can take advantage of these features. For instance, you can easily create cluster-aware stubs that proxy requests through to a server hosting the runtime object. These cluster-aware stubs maintain a list of all servers in the cluster that host the object, allowing the stub to transparently provide load-balancing and failover facilities to the client. Moreover, the RMI registry that allows clients to locate the RMI objects with which they want to interact can be accessed using WebLogic's JNDI implementation. In fact, this technology is used in the implementation of many other J2EE resources within WebLogic, such as EJB home objects that provide failover and load-balancing facilities.

The final topic covered in this chapter is the use of CORBA and its IIOP transport protocol as an alternative to RMI. WebLogic can generate Interface Definition Language (IDL) descriptions of RMI objects, which then can be used to create clients on any language platform. These clients can interact with WebLogic using the standard CORBA/IIOP framework, providing a basis for rich interoperability.

Using WebLogic's JNDI

Each WebLogic server maintains a local JNDI tree. Typically, you will bind various J2EE resources to the JNDI tree, such as JDBC data sources, EJB home objects, JMS connection factories, and more. You can use the Administration Console to view the contents and structure of the JNDI tree on a server. Select a server from the left frame of the Administration Console, right-click the server node, and choose the "View JNDI tree" option from the pop-up menu. This launches a new window that displays the contents of the JNDI tree for the selected server. You can now navigate the JNDI tree and view the various objects bound to it.

In the following sections, you will learn how to programmatically establish a connection to WebLogic's JNDI server, from both an external client and an internal J2EE component, and how to use the connection to locate and bind objects. As the JNDI tree also permits authorization policies, we also will look at a few security issues surrounding the use of a JNDI tree.

Creating a Context

In order to access WebLogic's JNDI tree, you need to establish a standard JNDI InitialContext representing the context root of the server's directory service. You can do this by passing a Hashtable of property/value pairs to the javax.naming. InitialContext() constructor. The Hashtable represents environment properties that are used to establish the context; in an external client, you typically will need to supply at least a URL property that points to a server you wish to access, and a context factory class that represents the service provider to use in the construction of the context.

Example 4-1 shows how a Java client can obtain an initial JNDI context to a WebLogic Server.

Example 4-1. Obtaining the initial JNDI context

```
import javax.naming.*;

private static InitialContext ctx = null;
...
public static InitialContext getInitialContext() throws NamingException {
  if (ctx == null) {
    Hashtable env = new Hashtable();
    env.put(Context.INITIAL_CONTEXT_FACTORY,
            "weblogic.jndi.WLInitialContextFactory");
    env.put(Context.PROVIDER_URL,
            "t3://myserver:8001");
    ctx = new InitialContext(env);
  }
  return ctx;
}
```

The PROVIDER_URL property specifies the URL of the server whose JNDI tree we want to access. The INITIAL_CONTEXT_FACTORY property contains the fully qualified class name of WebLogic's context factory, specifying the service provider to use. If you need to access WebLogic's JNDI tree, you should always establish the context using the class name weblogic.jndi.WLInitialContextFactory.

 It is customary to cache the InitialContext object once it's created, and to use the cached object for subsequent requests for the initial JNDI context.

Table 4-1 provides the list of environment properties that may be used to customize the initial JNDI context. In the next section, we will examine other properties relevant to the use of JNDI in a clustered environment.

Table 4-1. Environment properties for the initial JNDI context

Context property	Description	Default
INITIAL_CONTEXT_FACTORY	Use this property to specify the name of the initial context factory. WLInitialContextFactory must be used to access WebLogic's JNDI service.	none
PROVIDER_URL	Use this property to set the URL of the WebLogic Server or cluster that you want to contact.	*t3://localhost:7001*
SECURITY_PRINCIPAL	If the client needs to authenticate itself to the server, use this property to specify the identity of a WebLogic user.	guest
SECURITY_CREDENTIALS	Use this property to specify the password for the WebLogic user.	guest

WebLogic providers a helper class, `weblogic.jndi.Environment`, which eases the creation of the initial context. The class provides type-safe methods for setting and accessing common JNDI properties, and assumes sensible defaults for many of the JNDI properties needed to access the JNDI tree on WebLogic Server. The following code sample shows how to obtain the initial JNDI context using the `Environment` object:

```
Environment env = new Environment();
env.setProviderUrl("t3://servername:7001");
env.setSecurityPrincipal("jon");
env.setSecurityCredentials("jonpassword");
Context ctx = env.getInitialContext();
...
```

A client should use the `close()` method to release any resources allocated to the JNDI Context. We recommend that you always invoke the `close()` method when you no longer require the JNDI context:

```
Context ctx = null;
try {
  // Create the context using the code in Example 4.1
  ctx = getInitialContext();
  //now use the JNDI Context to look up objects
}
catch (NamingException ene) {
  //handle JNDI Exceptions
}
finally {
  try {
    if (ctx != null) ctx.close();
  }
  catch (Exception ignored) {}
}
```

Server-side objects, such as servlets and EJBs, do not need to provide any environment properties when creating an initial JNDI context. When a server-side object invokes the `InitialContext()` constructor, the JNDI context will always connect to the local server that hosts the server-side object. This means that if you need only to access objects bound to the local JNDI tree, a server-side object can simply create the initial JNDI context, without explicitly specifying any environment properties. For example, if a servlet needs to look up the home object for an EJB that is deployed on the same server, a call to the default `InitialContext` constructor will suffice:

```
Context ctx = new InitialContext();
Object home = ic.lookup("java:comp/env/ejb/MyEJBHome");
MyEJBHome ejbHome = (MyEJBHome)
PortableRemoteObject.narrow(home, org.foo.bar.MyEJBHome.class);
// now use the EJB home object to obtain an EJB instance
```

Of course, you could pass the security credentials of a valid WebLogic user if you need to establish and use the context under a particular security scope.

Security in a Context

As you'll see later in Chapter 17, WebLogic allows an administrator to set up authorization policies that can restrict access to any arbitrary branch of the JNDI tree. You can view and change these policies by using the Administration Console's JNDI viewer. Right-click a node to view the policy for that node. As the policies are inherited, by applying a policy to the root node you will effectively be applying it to all nodes of the tree. By applying such a policy, you are creating an authorization requirement on the actual *lookup* in the JNDI tree. You also can create authorization policies that apply to the objects bound in the JNDI tree itself. So, for instance, you can create a policy that restricts the lookup of a connection pool, and another that restricts the use of the connection pool.

The default policy on the root of the JNDI tree grants access to the anonymous user (in fact, to the group Everyone). Thus, if you do not specify the credentials of a WebLogic user when establishing an initial context, the anonymous user is automatically used to verify access control to the JNDI tree. So, by default, you do have the necessary authorization to access the JNDI tree. If the thread already has been associated with a WebLogic user, that security principal is used for all authorization checks when you subsequently access the JNDI tree. Hence, if a security policy has been defined on a specific branch of the JNDI tree, you need to ensure that a valid principal is associated with the thread, and that it has sufficient privileges to access the branch. There are two ways in which you can establish an identity under which the JNDI tree ought to be accessed:

- Supply values for the `SECURITY_PRINCIPAL` and `SECURITY_CREDENTIALS` environment properties when creating an initial context. When you create a JNDI context in this way, the security scope is valid for the lifetime of the context. It is terminated when you invoke the `close()` method on the `Context` object. The security context actually is associated with the thread running the code. This has important implications. Establishing a new context will replace any previous security context associated with the thread. Thus, you should not try to establish a nested context using differing security principals. In that case, *all* code will run using the most recently created context.

- Use the `weblogic.security.Security.runAs( )` method to apply a security context to your code. In this case, you should use the standard JAAS login procedure to create and populate a security subject. The `runAs( )` method accepts two arguments: the code that needs to be executed, and the subject under which it ought to be executed. The thread's security context is then propagated to any subsequent JNDI contexts created from within your code. Any such JNDI lookup will be authorized using the credentials of the current subject associated with the thread.

JAAS-based authentication is covered in Chapter 17, which also discusses how to use SSL certificates and mutual authentication to provide additional security when creating a JNDI context.

Using a Context

Once you have obtained the initial JNDI context, you can look up any named object bound in the context. Example 4-2 shows how you can look up a transactional data source and `UserTransaction` from the JNDI tree, and use them to create JDBC connections that participate in a JTA transaction.

Example 4-2. Using the initial JNDI context to look up a named object

```
javax.naming.Context ctx = null;
javax.transaction.UserTransaction tx = null;
javax.sql.DataSource ds = null;
java.sql.Connection con = null;

//set up the JNDI environment

try {
  ctx = new InitialContext(env);
  //use the JNDI tree to look up a configured TxDataSource
  ds = (DataSource) ctx.lookup("myTxDs");

  //use the JNDI tree to initiate a new JTA transaction
  tx = (UserTransaction) ctx.lookup("java:comp/UserTransaction");

  //initiate the transaction
  tx.begin();

  con = ds.getConnection();
  //perform your JDBC updates here...

  //commit the transaction
  tx.commit();
}
catch (Exception e) {
  // exceptions code goes here
}
finally {
  try {
```

```
    if (ctx != null) ctx.close( );
    //release other JDBC resources here...
  }
  catch (Exception ignored) {}
}
```

You also may use the Context object to bind custom objects to WebLogic's JNDI context. The following code shows how you can bind an instance of a custom Java class, com.oreilly.custom.Foo, to the JNDI tree under the name myObj:

```
try {
    // env represents an instance of weblogic.jndi.Environment
    ctx = env.getInitialContext( );
    ctx.bind("myObj", new com.oreilly.custom.Foo( ));
}
catch (NamingException e) {
    //handle exception in case an object is already bound under the same name
}
```

A call to the bind( ) method for custom objects will not succeed if another object has already been bound to the JNDI tree under the same name. Instead, you should use the rebind( ) method to overwrite any previous binding and bind the new custom object under the same name:

```
try {
    ctx = env.getInitialContext( );
    ctx.rebind("myObj", new com.oreilly.custom.Foo( ));
}
catch (NamingException e) {
}
```

Remember that a custom object can be bound to the JNDI tree only if its class implements the java.io.Serializable interface. Typically, you should implement a WebLogic startup class that binds any needed custom objects at server startup. This approach is described later in this chapter in the section "Using a WebLogic Startup Class to Register an RMI Object."

Using JNDI in a Clustered Environment

WebLogic's JNDI implementation can be used in a clustered environment. Indeed, it is JNDI that provides the bedrock of many of WebLogic's clustered services. For instance, an EJB may be deployed to a number of servers in an object-tier cluster. Servlets in the web tier can look up the EJB in the object tier's JNDI and obtain access to one of the servers hosting the EJB; context objects even can use load-balancing logic to choose a server instance. When an EJB is deployed to several servers in the clustered object tier, the JNDI tree is updated with a cluster-aware EJB stub that records the location of each server instance hosting the EJB. Moreover, this knowledge is automatically distributed throughout the JNDI trees in the cluster. This magic is implemented partly by WebLogic's clustered JNDI implementation, which we will now look at.

Creating a Context in a Cluster

In a clustered environment, an object may be bound to the JNDI tree of an individual server, or it may be replicated and bound to all servers in the cluster. If the JNDI binding manifests in one server only, a client must explicitly connect to that server when establishing the initial context, as discussed earlier. In most cases, the JNDI binding actually will be replicated to all servers in the JNDI tree, in which case you need only specify a name representing the WebLogic cluster, not an individual server member. When creating an initial context to a cluster, WebLogic automatically chooses between the members of the cluster and creates a single context to that one member.

The next example shows how a client can look up an object that is available to a cluster-wide JNDI tree:

```
Context ctx = null;
Hashtable env = new Hashtable();
env.put(Context.INITIAL_CONTEXT_FACTORY,
        weblogic.jndi.WLInitialContextFactory");
env.put(Context.PROVIDER_URL, "t3://mycluster:8001");

//connect to the cluster-wide JNDI tree
ctx = new InitialContext(env);
//now use the JNDI Context to look up objects
```

In this case, the value for the PROVIDER_URL property uses the DNS name mycluster, which resolves to the addresses of each server in the cluster.

Typically, the address is represented as a DNS name. Alternatively, you could specify a comma-delimited list of server addresses to access the cluster-wide JNDI tree:

```
env.put(Context.PROVIDER_URL,"t3://ManagedServer1:7001,
    ManagedServer2:7002,ManagedServer3:7003");
```

If all the members of the cluster use the same T3 listen port, you also could set the same property as follows:

```
env.put(Context.PROVIDER_URL,"t3://ManagedServer1,
    ManagedServer2,ManagedServer3:7001");
```

There are two crucial aspects to consider when establishing a JNDI context in a clustered environment:

At creation time, the context factory performs a round robin between available servers
> If you supply multiple addresses or a DNS name that is mapped to multiple addresses, successive requests for a Context object perform a round robin between the supplied addresses, before it attaches to a particular cluster member. If one of the servers in the list becomes unavailable, the initial requests to create a new Context object continue to perform round robins between the remaining available servers in the list.

A lookup( ) *on the* Context *object can transparently fail over to another live server*
Even though the Context object is bound to a particular server in the list based on a round-robin scheme, it is cluster-aware—i.e., it is aware of the locations of all members participating in the cluster. If the server to which the Context object is bound fails, calls to the Context object will automatically fail over to another available server.

Let's take the following code as an example, where we have two servers in a cluster, as well as a data source targeted to the cluster:

```
Hashtable env = new Hashtable();
env.put(Context.INITIAL_CONTEXT_FACTORY,
        "weblogic.jndi.WLInitialContextFactory");
env.put(Context.PROVIDER_URL, "t3://10.0.10.14:7001,10.0.10.10:7001");
Context c = null;
for (int i = 0; i < 5000; i++) {
  ctx = new InitialContext(env);
  DataSource ds = (DataSource) c.lookup("myds");
  // Do some work
}
```

Because we create a Context object inside the loop, the context will continue to perform a round robin between the two servers in the cluster. Thus, every time we look up the data source, the data source alternately will be returned from the first and second server. If we bring down one of the two servers, this round-robin behavior will end. The context factory will detect the failed server, and the data source will then continue to be returned from the running server only.

Ordinarily, you would not create the context in a loop as we have done here, but rather, create it once, and then use this cached Context object multiple times. The example, however, is indicative of what happens when multiple calls are made to create an initial context. The behavior is slightly different if we change the code a little:

```
Hashtable env = new Hashtable();
env.put(Context.INITIAL_CONTEXT_FACTORY,
        "weblogic.jndi.WLInitialContextFactory");
env.put(Context.PROVIDER_URL, "t3://10.0.10.14:7001,10.0.10.10:7001");
Context c = new InitialContext(env);
for (int i = 0; i < 5000; i++) {
  DataSource ds = (DataSource) c.lookup("DS");
  // Do some work
}
```

In this case, the context immediately will be bound to one of the servers supplied in the provider URL, again using a round-robin scheme. Now, each time we execute the JNDI lookup within the loop, the *same* data source will be returned. Because we've created the context only once, the resulting context will not switch over to another server unless there is a failure.

In both cases, if the server to which the context is bound fails, the context will switch to the next server using a round-robin algorithm, and continue to return the data source replica bound to that server.

J2EE Resources and RMI Stubs

WebLogic's JNDI primarily serves as a naming service for J2EE resources. Each such service is represented by an RMI stub bound in the JNDI tree. For example, when you create and deploy an EJB, an RMI stub representing the EJB is bound in the JNDI tree, and thereby made available to other servers. The stub marshals incoming requests from a client to the actual J2EE resource, typically using RMI, allowing clients to access J2EE resources on remote machines.

To be more precise, WebLogic binds *cluster-aware* RMI stubs for J2EE resources in the JNDI tree. A cluster-aware RMI stub is aware of the locations of all servers to which the J2EE resource is deployed. If the EJB is deployed to a cluster, the RMI stub that is bound to each JNDI tree records the locations of the servers hosting the actual resource—in this case, the servers to which the EJB was deployed. RMI stubs are small in size and can be easily replicated across all the members of a WebLogic cluster. While the actual RMI object may reside on a single server, the RMI stubs can be replicated cheaply across the cluster.

In a clustered environment, each member of the cluster maintains its own copy of the cluster-wide JNDI tree. Thus, when a new server joins a WebLogic cluster and resources are deployed to it, two things happen:

- The cluster-aware RMI stubs on other servers are updated to include the location of the newly deployed object on the server. So, for instance, if an EJB is deployed to a cluster including the new server, when the new server deploys the EJB, the cluster-aware RMI stubs of the EJB on the other servers are updated to include the new server as a hosting location for that EJB.

- The new server builds its own copy of the JNDI tree after collecting information about all cluster-aware J2EE resources and all objects that are pinned to the server itself.

If an existing server fails, the RMI stubs bound to other servers are updated to reflect the server's failure.

This behavior reinforces the way we think about initial contexts. When you create an initial context to a cluster, a single server instance is chosen and you interact with the JNDI tree on that server instance. However, because cluster-aware RMI stubs representing J2EE resources are replicated to the JNDI trees on each server, it shouldn't matter which server instance you connected to when you created the context.

Binding Custom Objects

Usually J2EE resources are represented by RMI objects, which are bound at deployment in the cluster-wide JNDI tree. You also can programmatically bind a custom, non-RMI object to a cluster-wide JNDI tree. By default, a custom object bound to the JNDI tree is replicated automatically across all members of the WebLogic cluster. In this way, the JNDI binding is available across all servers in the cluster. However, if the original server used to bind the custom object fails, the object is removed from the remaining servers in the cluster. So, even though the object is replicated, if the host server fails, the object is removed from the cluster-wide JNDI tree. For this reason, WebLogic's JNDI tree is *not* an ideal candidate for a distributed object cache implementation!

In addition, if you alter the state of an object that is already bound to the cluster-wide JNDI tree, those changes will not be replicated to other servers in the cluster. The changes to the object's state will be broadcast to other members of the WebLogic cluster *only* if you subsequently unbind and rebind the custom object. This further emphasizes that the JNDI should not be used as a distributed object cache. We recommend using third-party solutions if such functionality is needed.

You can, however, alter the default behavior and disable the replication of JNDI bindings. The `weblogic.jndi.WLContext` interface supports properties that can be used when establishing the initial JNDI context in a clustered environment. The value of the `REPLICATE_BINDINGS` property determines whether any modifications to the server's JNDI tree are replicated across other members of the WebLogic cluster. The following code sample shows how an object can be bound to the server's JNDI tree, without replicating the binding to other servers in the cluster:

```
Hashtable env = new Hashtable();
env.put(Context.INITIAL_CONTEXT_FACTORY,
        weblogic.jndi.WLInitialContextFactory");
env.put(Context.PROVIDER_URL, "t3://ManagedServer1:7001");
env.put(WLContext.REPLICATE_BINDINGS, "false");
try {
  //connect to the server's JNDI tree
  Context ctx = new InitialContext(env);
  //bind a custom object
  ctx.bind("foo_bar", myObject);
}
catch (NamingException ene) {
  //handle JNDI exceptions
}
```

Here the `Context.PROVIDER_URL` property is assigned the address of a single server within a WebLogic cluster, and the `REPLICATE_BINDINGS` property is set to `false`. This means that any changes to the server's JNDI tree as a result of the bind operation will not be propagated to other servers in the cluster. It also means that a client must look up the custom object from the server to which the object was bound. The custom object will *not* be visible in JNDI trees on other servers.

This behavior can be put to good use. As we have learned, custom objects that are replicated in the cluster-wide JNDI tree are owned by some hosting server; when that server goes down, they are removed from the cluster-wide JNDI tree. If you really need to make a custom object available to all members of the cluster and ensure that the binding is resistant to server failures, you should deploy it to all servers in the cluster individually, as shown in the previous example, without replicating the JNDI bindings.

To summarize, custom objects can be bound to a cluster-wide JNDI tree in two ways:

- In the default mode, bind a custom, non-RMI object to the server's JNDI tree and it is automatically replicated to other servers in the cluster. Any changes to the state of a custom object are not propagated unless you later unbind and rebind the object. If the original server that hosts the custom object fails, the object is removed from all other servers in the cluster.

- Bind the custom object individually to each server in the cluster, while disabling the replication of JNDI bindings. In this way, the custom object is available across all members of the cluster, and is accessible from other servers even if one of the servers in the cluster fails. However, any changes to the custom object on a particular server will not be replicated to other cluster members, even if you unbind and rebind the object. Your only recourse is to implement custom logic to ensure objects bound to the server's JNDI tree are automatically updated when any one of its replicas on the other servers are updated.

Pinned Services

In certain situations, you may require a single instance of a service, which is made available to all members of a WebLogic cluster. For RMI objects, which behave differently from custom objects, you can simply deploy the object to an individual server. The default JNDI replication will make RMI stubs available to the JNDI trees on all the other servers. In this way, the RMI object is accessible from any member of the cluster, while residing on only a single member.

The situation is not as simple for non-RMI objects. To pin a custom object, you need to bind it to a server instance, ensuring that the REPLICATE_BINDINGS property is set to false. As a consequence, you need to contact the actual server that hosts the custom object when creating an initial JNDI context for a JNDI lookup on the custom object. To get around this rather clunky solution, you can alternatively implement an RMI object that serves as a remote proxy for the custom object. The custom object and RMI object could be deployed on the same server, and the RMI stub then can be replicated across the cluster-wide JNDI tree. Using this trick, the custom object is accessible to all members of the WebLogic cluster via the proxy RMI stub. A very good example of this in action is in WebLogic's JMS implementation. A JMS server is a pinned object, but accessible on all JNDI contexts throughout the cluster.

Remember that a custom object will continue to be available only while the original server remains alive. A pinned object cannot provide automatic failover support if the original server fails. Instead, you need to guarantee high availability for the original server and the hardware that supports the pinned service(s). This solution should allow you to restart WebLogic in the event of a failure with little or no disruption to availability of the pinned object or service.

Using WebLogic's RMI

RMI is the standard model for distributed object programming in Java. Using RMI, a Java client can access a remote object seamlessly on another JVM, and invoke methods on the object as if it were located within the client's JVM. In addition, RMI incorporates various reference semantics for remote objects, such as lazy activation, live (or nonpersistent) references, and persistent references.

WebLogic RMI is an integral part of the server framework. It enables a Java client to transparently access RMI objects that live on WebLogic Server. This includes access to any EJB components and other J2EE resources that have been deployed to WebLogic. It allows you to build fast, reliable, standards-compliant RMI applications. It also incorporates support for load balancing and failover when RMI objects are deployed to a WebLogic cluster. WebLogic RMI is fully compatible with the RMI specification, but provides extensions not available under the standard RMI implementation. Here's a brief overview of some of the extra benefits of using WebLogic's version of RMI.

Performance and scalability

WebLogic incorporates a highly optimized implementation of RMI. It handles all the implementation issues that relate to the support for RMI: managing threads and sockets, garbage collection, and serialization. Standard RMI relies on separate socket connections between the client and the server, and between the client and the RMI Registry. WebLogic RMI multiplexes all this network traffic onto a single socket connection between the client and the server. The same socket connection is reused for other kinds of J2EE interaction as well, such as JDBC requests and JMS connections. By minimizing the network connections between the client and WebLogic, the RMI implementation is able to scale well under load, and support a large number of RMI clients simultaneously. It also relies on high-performance serialization logic. All these features mean a significant performance gain in client-server communication.

In addition, WebLogic automatically optimizes client-server interactions when the client runs within the same VM as the RMI object. It ensures that you don't incur any performance penalty because of marshalling or unmarshalling of arguments during a call to a remote method. Instead, WebLogic uses Java's pass-by-reference semantics when the client and the server object are collocated, and when the class-loader hierarchy permits it.

Interclient communication

WebLogic's RMI provides asynchronous, bidirectional socket connections between the client and the server. An RMI client can invoke methods exposed by server-side RMI objects, and by other client-side RMI objects that have registered their remote interfaces over WebLogic's RMI Registry. Thus, a client application can publish RMI objects through the server registry, and other clients or servers can use these client-resident objects just as they would use any server-resident objects. In this way, you can create applications that involve peer-to-peer, bidirectional communication between RMI clients.

RMI Registry

The RMI Registry runs automatically whenever WebLogic is started. WebLogic ignores attempts to create multiple instances of the RMI Registry, and simply returns a reference to the existing registry.

WebLogic's RMI Registry is fully integrated with the JNDI framework. You may use either the JNDI or the RMI Registry to bind or look up server-side RMI objects. In fact, the RMI Registry is merely a thin façade over WebLogic's JNDI tree. We recommend that you directly use the JNDI API for registering and naming RMI objects, bypassing calls to the RMI Registry altogether. JNDI offers the prospect of publishing RMI objects over other enterprise naming and directory services, such as LDAP.

Tunneling

RMI clients can use URLs based on a variety of schemes: the standard *rmi://* scheme, or the *http://* and *iiop://* schemes that tunnel RMI requests over HTTP and IIOP, respectively. This enables RMI calls from the client to penetrate through most firewalls.

Dynamic generation of stubs and skeletons

WebLogic supports dynamic generation of client-side stubs and server-side skeletons, eliminating the need to generate client-side stubs and server-side skeletons for the RMI object. WebLogic will automatically generate the necessary stubs and skeletons when the object is deployed to the RMI Registry or JNDI. The only time you need to explicitly create stubs is when the server-side RMI object needs to be accessed by either clusterable or IIOP clients.

Programming Issues

Let's now look at some of the important ways in which WebLogic RMI allows you to depart from the standard RMI programming model. We'll use the example of a simple server-side object that returns the sum of two incoming arguments. Here's an example of a remote interface that exposes a single method, add( ):

```
package com.oreilly.rmi;
public interface Add extends java.rmi.Remote {
  /* Returns the sum */
  int add(int a, int b) throws java.rmi.RemoteException;
}
```

Here, java.rmi.Remote represents the marker interface that all RMI objects are required to implement.

 If you would like to use the WebLogic RMI counterpart to java.rmi.Remote, you could use the weblogic.rmi.Remote interface instead. If you do, we recommend that you do not mix the standard RMI classes and interfaces with their WebLogic RMI counterparts (use either all WebLogic RMI classes or all Sun-standard RMI classes).

Now, we need to provide an implementation for this interface. Example 4-3 shows a simple implementation for the Add interface.

Example 4-3. Implementation class for the com.oreilly.rmi.Add interface

```
package com.oreilly.rmi;

public class AddImpl implements Add, java.io.Serializable {
 // With WebLogic RMI, the implementation class doesn't need to extend
 // java.rmi.server.UnicastRemoteObject
  public AddImpl( ) throws java.rmi.RemoteException {
    super( );
  }
  /* Implements the remote method signature */
  public int add(int a, int b) throws java.rmi.RemoteException {
    return  a+b;
  }
}
```

The AddImpl class provides the implementation for the add( ) method exposed by the remote interface. WebLogic doesn't require that the implementation class for the RMI object extend UnicastRemoteObject. Instead, it is the WebLogic RMI base class stub that mimics the java.rmi.server.UnicastRemoteObject class. In this way, the implementation class can inherit any application-specific Java class and still continue to function like a server-side RMI object. It also doesn't require you to explicitly declare that each remote method throws a java.rmi.RemoteException. Your remote interface also may declare method signatures that rely on application-specific exceptions, including any subclasses of java.lang.RuntimeException. This means you won't need to change any exception-handling code for your existing RMI implementation classes. Both of these extensions add convenience, but you must remember that the resulting code will be less portable if you use them.

 WebLogic's RMI will not dynamically load classes delivered from an external client. Thus, you must ensure all RMI interfaces and implementation classes (and any classes needed by them) are available under the server's classpath.

Publishing the RMI object is equally easy, as shown in Example 4-4.

Example 4-4. Publishing an RMI object

```
package com.oreilly.rmi;

import javax.naming.*;
import java.util.Hashtable;

public class AddBind {

  // The factory to use when creating our initial context
  public final static String JNDI_FACTORY="weblogic.jndi.WLInitialContextFactory";

  /**
   * Create an instance of the Implementation class
   * and bind it in the registry.
   */
  public static void main(String args[]) {
    // Creating and installing the SecurityManager is not required
    if (System.getSecurityManager( ) == null)
      System.setSecurityManager(new weblogic.rmi.RMISecurityManager( ));

    try {
      Context ctx = getInitialContext("t3://localhost:7001");
      ctx.bind("AddServer", new AddImpl( ));
      System.out.println("AddImpl created and bound to the JNDI");
    }
    catch (Exception e) {
        System.out.println("AddImpl.main: an exception occurred!");
        e.printStackTrace(System.out);
    }
  }

  /* Creates the Initial JNDI Context */
  private static InitialContext getInitialContext(String url) throws NamingException {
    Hashtable env = new Hashtable( );
    env.put(Context.INITIAL_CONTEXT_FACTORY, JNDI_FACTORY);
    env.put(Context.PROVIDER_URL, url);
    return new InitialContext(env);
  }
}
```

The main( ) method is responsible for creating an instance of the implementation class and then publishing it to the RMI Registry. In this case, we've bound the server object to the name AddServer. Notice how WebLogic's RMI supports naming and lookup via JNDI. Alternatively, we could have used the java.rmi.Naming class to bind and look up objects published over the server registry.

WebLogic doesn't require you to assign a SecurityManager in order to incorporate security into the RMI object. Instead, WebLogic relies on a richer security framework covered in Chapter 17. WebLogic RMI supports the setSecurityManager( ) method for portability reasons only.

Once you have compiled the server classes and published the RMI object over the registry, you then can create an RMI client that looks up the object in the registry and invokes the remote methods exposed by its remote interface. Example 4-5 shows how to invoke the Add RMI object we published earlier.

Example 4-5. Invoking the published RMI object

```
package com.oreilly.rmi;

import javax.naming.*;
import java.util.Hashtable;

public class AddClient {

  public static void main(String[] argv) throws Exception {
    try {
      InitialContext ic = getInitialContext("t3://localhost:7001");
      Add obj = (Add) ic.lookup("AddServer");
      System.out.println("Successfully connected to AddServer " + obj.add(3,4) );
    }
    catch (Throwable t) {
      t.printStackTrace( );
    }
  }

  /* Creates the Initial JNDI Context. */
  private static InitialContext getInitialContext(String url)
    throws NamingException {
    Hashtable env = new Hashtable( );
    env.put(Context.INITIAL_CONTEXT_FACTORY,
            "weblogic.jndi.WLInitialContextFactory";
    env.put(Context.PROVIDER_URL, url);
    return new InitialContext(env);
  }
}
```

If this client runs within the same server JVM that hosts the RMI object, you effectively bypass the need for marshalling and unmarshalling of method arguments and the return value. Instead of pass-by-value, WebLogic RMI automatically ensures that the "remote" method call defaults to standard Java pass-by-reference semantics. This will be subject to classloader concerns. Chapter 12 provides a detailed look at the interaction of the classloader and application packaging and how it can affect this RMI optimization.

Using a WebLogic Startup Class to Register an RMI Object

Earlier we wrote a client application that was responsible for registering an instance of the remote object with the RMI Registry. If you want to always make a remote object available to the server instance, you should consider writing a WebLogic startup class that performs the same task. Startup classes are a proprietary feature in WebLogic

Server. WebLogic invokes all startup classes targeted to it as part of its runtime initialization. Creating a startup class is a simple procedure:

1. Write and compile the startup class.
2. Make the startup class available to the server's classpath.
3. Register the startup class via the Administration Console.
4. Restart the server.

Example 4-6 lists the code for a startup class that binds an RMI object to the server's JNDI tree.

Example 4-6. Startup class for registering custom RMI objects

```java
public class InitRMIObjects implements T3StartupDef {
  private T3ServicesDef services;
  //Defines the JNDI context factory
  public final static String JNDI_FACTORY=
      "weblogic.jndi.WLInitialContextFactory";

  /**
   * A T3StartupDef callback method
   */
  public void setServices(T3ServicesDef services) {
    this.services = services;
  }

  /**
   * A T3StartupDef callback method
   * Registers the RMI Object to the JNDI tree
   */
  public String startup(String name, Hashtable args) throws Exception {
    String foo = (String) args.get("foo");
    try {
      Context ctx = new InitialContext();
      ctx.bind("AddServer", new AddImpl());
      System.out.println("AddImpl created and bound in the registry to the name
AddServer");
    }
    catch (Exception e) {
      System.out.println("AddImpl.error: " +
        e.printStackTrace());
    }
    return "";
  }
}
```

WebLogic requires that each startup class implement the two callback methods of the `weblogic.common.T3StartupDef` interface. The `T3ServicesDef` object lets you access proprietary WebLogic resources. For the most part, the `setServices()` method can remain empty.

The startup( ) method implements the actual task that needs to be performed during server bootstrap. WebLogic invokes the startup( ) method with two parameters:

- A name parameter that represents the registered name for the startup class
- An args parameter that represents a hash map of arguments and key/value pairs that are specified when you register the startup class using the Administration Console

Once you've compiled the startup class and made it available to the server's classpath, you need to register it with a particular server instance. Choose the Deployments/ Startup and Shutdown node from the left pane of the Administration Console, and then select the Configure a New Startup Class link from the right pane. You must then specify a name and the fully qualified class name of the startup class. You also can specify arguments to the startup class using a comma-separated list of key/value pairs:

```
propA=value,propB=value,...
```

If you select the "Failure is Fatal" option, WebLogic aborts its initial bootstrap if the startup class fails for whatever reason. Finally, you can choose when the startup class should be executed, with respect to the startup process of WebLogic and the applications deployed to it. The default is to execute the startup class after applications are deployed. If you choose the "Run before application deployments" option, the startup class will run before any services have been initialized or applications deployed. See Chapter 12 for a detailed explanation of these states.

Once you've saved these configuration settings, you must target the startup class to a WebLogic Server instance. After this, you can restart the server and you'll find an RMI object bound to the server's JNDI tree under the name AddServer as soon as server initialization has completed.

Similarly, WebLogic lets you create shutdown classes that encapsulate various tasks that must be executed automatically when the server shuts down. You can target a number of startup and shutdown classes to a server, or across all members of a WebLogic cluster.

WebLogic's RMI Compiler

Many RMI compilers generate proxies for server-side RMI objects. Method calls from the client are routed via the proxy to the server-side object. The proxy class is responsible for marshalling and unmarshalling method parameters and return values of the method call. WebLogic's RMI compiler relies on dynamically generated client-side stubs and server-side skeletons instead, so you don't need any additional classes bundled with the RMI object. The only reason you need to explicitly invoke the RMI compiler is when the remote object needs to serve IIOP clients, or when the RMI object needs to be deployed to a cluster.

Here's how you can invoke WebLogic's RMI compiler:

```
java weblogic.rmic [options] rmi-class-name ...
```

The RMI compiler will accept any option supported by the Java compiler. For example, `-d /serverclasses` instructs the RMI compiler to place generated files in the */serverclasses* folder. Table 4-2 lists the various options available to the RMI compiler for general and cluster usage.

Table 4-2. General and cluster options available to WebLogic's RMI compiler

Option	Description
General options	
-help	This option prints a description of all options available to `weblogic.rmic`.
-d <directory>	This option specifies the output folder for the generated files.
-version	This option prints out version information.
-compiler <javac>	This option allows you to specify the location of the Java compiler to use.
-classpath <path>	This option specifies the classpath to be used during compilation.
-nontransactional	This option indicates that the RMI object must not participate in a transaction. If a transaction exists, it must be suspended before the remote method is invoked, and later resumed when the method call completes.
-descriptor	This option instructs the RMI compiler to create a descriptor for each remote class.
-oneway	This option indicates that all calls to the remote object will be one-way calls (i.e., all methods of the remote interface return `void`).
-keepgenerated	This option keeps the generated source files after the RMI compiler has completed.
Cluster options	
-clusterable	This option instructs the compiler to mark the remote object as being *clusterable*. This means the RMI object can be hosted by multiple servers in a WebLogic cluster. Each replica of the RMI object will be bound under the same JNDI name. Any client that looks up the JNDI name will obtain a cluster-aware RMI stub that maintains a list of all replicas of the remote object. This allows the stub to perform failover and load balancing among available replicas of the RMI object.
-loadAlgorithm <algo>	This option specifies a custom load-balancing strategy. You can choose from one of the following values: `round-robin`, `random`, or `weight-based`. This option may be used if the RMI object is marked as clusterable.
-callRouter <call-router-class>	This option specifies a custom call-routing class. A `CallRouter` class is invoked before each method call to the RMI object. It determines which one of the servers hosting the RMI object should be chosen, based on the method parameters supplied. If it returns `null`, the current load-balancing strategy is used. Again, this option may be used only if the RMI object has been marked as clusterable.

Table 4-2. General and cluster options available to WebLogic's RMI compiler (continued)

Option	Description
Cluster options	
-methodsAreIdempotent	This option indicates that all methods of the RMI object are idempotent. This way, a cluster-aware stub can retry the method call if the previous attempt failed. By default, a cluster-aware stub will retry the method call only if the failure occurred *before* the previous attempt. You may use this option provided the RMI object also has been marked as clusterable.
-stickToFirstServer	This option indicates that the stub ought to be constrained by "sticky" load balancing—i.e., the cluster member chosen to service the first request is then used for all subsequent requests from the same client. Again, this option may be used only alongside the clusterable option.

When you run the RMI compiler with the -clusterable option, it generates an XML descriptor file that captures all cluster options that apply to the RMI object. For instance, the RMI compiler generates an *AddImplRTD.xml* descriptor file if you invoke it using one or more cluster options:

```
java weblogic.rmic -clusterable -loadAlgorithm round-robin
    -methodsAreIdempotent com.oreilly.rmi.AddImpl
```

The XML descriptor file must then be made available to the server's CLASSPATH, and WebLogic will ensure the RMI stubs for the remote object adhere to the cluster options captured in the descriptor file.

RMI Objects in a Cluster

The behavior of RMI objects in a cluster depends on whether the object is made clusterable, and on the value of the REPLICATE_BINDINGS property when the object is bound in the cluster. Let's look at these scenarios in more detail.

Consider a WebLogic cluster that consists of three servers (A, B, C). Suppose you register a clusterable RMI object to Servers A and B. Now, if the RMI implementation class was bound to the server's JNDI tree with REPLICATE_BINDINGS enabled, the RMI stub will be available on all three servers A, B, and C. When a client executes a JNDI lookup, the RMI stub can be obtained from all three servers. However, method calls to the remote object will be load-balanced between Servers A and B only, according to the load-balancing strategy chosen during RMI compilation.

Suppose you deploy the clusterable RMI object to Servers A and B, but this time with REPLICATE_BINDINGS set to false. This means that if the client performs a JNDI lookup on Server A, it obtains a *pinned* RMI stub that refers to the remote object on Server A only. Similarly, if the client executes a JNDI lookup on Server B, the RMI stub it gets refers to the remote object on Server B. Of course, because the bindings were not replicated, the object will not be made available to Server C, and any JNDI lookup on Server C will fail with a NameNotFoundException error. In this situation, suppose the client obtains the RMI stub from Server A, and Server A fails before the client is able to invoke one of the remote methods. Because the RMI stub is cluster-able, it will do another JNDI lookup for the RMI stub from the remaining servers in the cluster that are still alive. The method call will succeed if Server B is chosen on the next attempt, and will fail with a `NameNotFoundException` error if the request is routed to Server C.

Now suppose you bind a nonclusterable RMI object to the server's JNDI tree with `REPLICATE_BINDINGS` set to `false`. This means that when a client performs a JNDI lookup on Server A, it obtains an RMI stub that points to the object on Server A. The same holds true for any other servers to which the RMI object has been deployed. No failover is possible in this scenario; if a remote method call fails, it will not be redirected to any of the other servers in the cluster.

 You cannot bind a nonclusterable RMI object to the server's JNDI tree with `REPLICATE_BINDINGS` set to `true`. In a cluster, only one server may host a nonclusterable RMI object.

Cluster Example

It is a simple matter to put this theory into practice! Let's create a clusterable version of the `Add` RMI object created earlier, bind it to a number of servers in a cluster, and access it from a client.

The first thing you want to do is create a clusterable version of the RMI object. This is done easily with the `rmic` compiler, where we have specified that we want a cluster-able object with round-robin load balancing:

```
java weblogic.rmic -clusterable -loadAlgorithm round-robin
    -methodsAreIdempotent com.oreilly.rmi.AddImpl
```

This just creates an XML file, *AddImplRTD.xml*, which you should place in the server's `CLASSPATH` along with the `Add` class and implementation. You can publish the object to JNDI by binding an instance of the object to a server. However, because the object is clusterable and we want to test these features, we bind it to two servers in a cluster:

```
Context ctx = getInitialContext("t3://ServerA:7001");
ctx.bind("AddServer", new AddImpl( ));
ctx.close( );
ctx = getInitialContext("t3://ServerB:7001");
ctx.bind("AddServer", new AddImpl( ));
ctx.close( );
```

According to the rules given in the previous sections, a single clusterable RMI stub will be bound in each JNDI tree in the cluster. Moreover, the RMI stub will record the location of each server hosting the actual object—in this case, `ServerA` and `ServerB`. Using the clustered RMI object is no different from using any other RMI object. The following code creates a context, performs a lookup, and invokes the add( ) method on the object a number of times:

```
Context ctx = getInitialContext("t3://ServerA,ServerB:7001");
obj = (Add) ic.lookup("AddServer");
for (int i=0; i<10; i++)
  System.out.println("Calling add: " + obj.add(2,i);
```

Note the following about the behavior of this code, illustrating the powerful features of WebLogic's RMI:

- Each invocation of add( ) in the loop will alternate between ServerA and ServerB because we invoked the rmic compiler with the round-robin load-balancing argument. This load balancing is transparent, and obviously simple to use. Choosing a different load-balancing scheme is just a matter of passing different arguments to the rmic compiler.

- The RMI stub that we are using is clusterable, and hence can tolerate failover. For instance, we can take ServerB down during the loop without any ill effect— all calls will just be routed to ServerA.

Using a Custom CallRouter Class with an RMI Object

WebLogic supports parameter-based load balancing using custom call-routing classes. The RMI compiler lets you associate a custom call-routing class with a clusterable RMI object. The class is invoked before each method call to the RMI object, allowing you to programmatically determine which server hosting the RMI object should be chosen, based on the method parameters in the call.

A custom call router for an RMI object must implement the weblogic.rmi.cluster. CallRouter interface. The interface method getServerList( ) will be called before each invocation of an RMI method and must return a list of server names. The call then will be routed to the first server in the list, or to others in the list if the first server has failed. If getServerList( ) returns null, the default load-balancing strategy for the stub is used. The getServerList( ) method is passed the method that is being called, as well as the parameters to that method; you can use any of this data in the decision-making process.

Let's modify our running example by creating a custom call router, which directs the addition of all large numbers (where we define "large" as the first parameter being greater than 5) to ServerA, and all smaller numbers to ServerB. Example 4-7 lists the code for our call-router class.

Example 4-7. A custom call router

```
public class NumberRouter implements weblogic.rmi.cluster.CallRouter {
  private static final String[] bigServers =
    { "ServerA" };
  private static final String[] smallServers =
    { "ServerB" };
```

Example 4-7. A custom call router (continued)

```
public String[] getServerList(Method m, Object[] params) {
    if ( ((Integer)params[0]).intValue() > 5)
        return bigServers;
    else
        return smallServers;
    }
}
```

Once you've compiled the call router, you can then register it with the RMI object using WebLogic's RMI compiler:

```
java weblogic.rmic -clusterable -loadAlgorithm round-robin \
        -callRouter com.oreilly.rmi.NumberRouter com.oreilly.rmi.AddImpl
```

Deployment proceeds in the same way as before, except you must additionally include the NumberRouter class file in your server's CLASSPATH.

Using WebLogic's RMI over IIOP

RMI over IIOP (or RMI-IIOP) enables Java-based RMI objects to interoperate with CORBA-based application components. By using the OMG standard IIOP as the underlying transport protocol, Java clients can invoke CORBA objects, and likewise, CORBA clients can remotely invoke RMI objects. CORBA components may be written in a variety of languages, including C++, Smalltalk, Java, COBOL, and many more. RMI-IIOP combines the ease of use of RMI with cross-language interoperability provided by the CORBA/IIOP architecture.

WebLogic's RMI-IIOP implementation provides several options for implementing Java-based RMI and CORBA/IDL clients:

Standalone RMI clients
> You can implement an RMI client that uses the JDK's IIOP implementation. This is ORB-based, and will not use any WebLogic libraries. As a result, the client can be kept quite trim, although this approach cannot make use of J2EE features such as transactions.

WebLogic fat clients
> By simply changing the context factory used in the standalone RMI client, and including *weblogic.jar*, you can create a client that still communicates using IIOP, but doesn't use a client-side ORB. Instead, it uses an optimized WebLogic-specific RMI-IIOP implementation. As a result, the client is faster and more scalable, and can benefit from WebLogic features. Of course, the client will be quite large now.

J2EE clients
> J2EE clients are application clients that are typically bundled with J2EE applications. These clients make use of the JDK 1.4 client-side ORB, and need to have WebLogic's thin client support library. As a result, these clients support WebLogic clustering and other J2EE features such as transactions and security.

CORBA/IDL clients

> CORBA/IDL clients are typically clients written in some other language, using interfaces generated by an IDL compiler. These clients would not include WebLogic libraries, and would use IIOP with standard ORBs.

Standalone RMI Clients

By default, an RMI client uses WebLogic's T3 protocol when talking with RMI objects hosted by WebLogic Server. The J2EE 1.3 framework also requires that an RMI client is able to talk to RMI objects using the industry-standard IIOP as the underlying protocol. In principle, such a client is similar to Example 4-5, except that it uses the IIOP protocol and therefore must have access to an ORB. For instance, it could use the CORBA 2.3–compliant ORB shipped with Sun's Java SDK 1.3 distribution. Furthermore, the client doesn't require any of the WebLogic classes. It's simply an RMI client that communicates over the IIOP protocol. For this reason, it does not support enterprise features such as transactions or security.

Earlier we developed a simple RMI client-server program that used WebLogic's T3 protocol as the underlying transport mechanism. In order for the client to communicate with the RMI object over IIOP, you need to execute the following steps:

1. After you've compiled the remote interface *Add.java* and the implementation class `AddImpl.java`, run the RMI compiler over the implementation class `AddImpl.class` using the -iiop option:

   ```
   java weblogic.rmic -iiop com.oreilly.rmi.AddImpl
   ```

2. Make sure that the class files generated from the remote interface, the implementation classes, and the stub classes are available to the server's classpath. This type of client does not use dynamic proxies.

3. Modify the RMI client `AddClient.java` in the following way:

   a. Use `com.sun.jndi.cosnaming.CNCtxFactory` as the value for the JNDI context factory when creating the initial JNDI context. In this way, the client relies on Sun's JNDI client, which defaults to Sun's RMI-IIOP ORB implementation.

   b. Make sure you've specified an *iiop://* scheme as the value for the client's `Context.PROVIDER_URL` property. This allows the client to tunnel RMI requests over IIOP. For example, we will connect to the local server using the URL *iiop://localhost:7001*.

   c. After the client performs a JNDI lookup, make sure it invokes the `narrow( )` method on the `javax.rmi.PortableRemoteObject` class. This method checks to see whether the object of the remote interface may be cast to the desired type:

   ```
   Add obj = (Add) javax.rmi.PortableRemoteObject.narrow(
               ic.lookup("AddServer"), Add.class);
   ```

The following code fragment encapsulates all the code changes needed to AddClient. java, before it can talk over IIOP:

```
public static void main(String[] argv) throws Exception {
  try {
    Hashtable env = new Hashtable( );
    env.put(Context.INITIAL_CONTEXT_FACTORY,
        "com.sun.jndi.cosnaming.CNCtxFactory");
    env.put(Context.PROVIDER_URL, "iiop://localhost:7001");
    InitialContext ctx = new InitialContext(env);

    Add obj = (Add) javax.rmi.PortableRemoteObject.narrow(
            ic.lookup("AddServer"), Add.class);
    System.out.println("Successfully connected to AddServer " + obj.add(3,4) );
  }
  catch (Throwable t) {
    t.printStackTrace( );
  }
}
```

Once you've registered the RMI object to the server's JNDI tree, you should get the following output when you run the client com.oreilly.rmi.AddClient:

```
Successfully connected to AddServer 7
```

Make sure that when you run the client, you use Sun's JDK 1.3.1_01 distribution or higher.

We have already seen a use of the -iiop option for WebLogic's rmic compiler. The compiler supports additional IIOP-related options, as documented in Table 4-3.

Table 4-3. IIOP options available to WebLogic's RMI compiler

Option	Description
-idl	This option instructs the RMI compiler to generate IDL files for the remote interfaces.
-idlOverwrite	This option directs the RMI compiler to overwrite any existing IDL files.
-idlDirectory <directory>	This option specifies the location of the folder where the IDL files should be generated.
-idlStrict	This option generates IDL files that conform to the OMG standard.
-idlFactories	This option directs the RMI compiler to generate factory methods for all value types.
-idlNoValueTypes	This option directs the RMI compiler to ignore all value types and any methods or attributes that refer to them.
-idlOrbix	This option instructs the RMI compiler to generate IDL files compliant with Orbix 2000 C++.
-idlVisibroker	This option directs the RMI compiler to generate IDL files compliant with Visibroker 4.5 C++.

Table 4-3. IIOP options available to WebLogic's RMI compiler (continued)

Option	Description
-iiop	This option generates IIOP stubs for the server objects.
-iiopDirectory <directory>	This option specifies the location of the folder where the IIOP stubs ought to be generated.

Make sure that you include *%JAVA_HOME%\lib\tools.jar* in your CLASSPATH before you attempt to generate the IIOP stubs for the RMI objects. WebLogic's RMI compiler relies on Sun's RMI compiler to generate the IIOP stubs.

WebLogic Fat Clients

The previous approach used the standard JDK classes, including the ORB supplied with the JDK. You also could vary this by using WebLogic's RMI-IIOP implementation on the client instead. In addition, the client must use WebLogic's initial context factory when contacting the server's JNDI:

```
Hashtable env = new Hashtable( );
env.put(Context.INITIAL_CONTEXT_FACTORY, "weblogic.jndi.WLInitialContextFactory");
env.put(Context.PROVIDER_URL,  "iiop://myserver:8001");
Context ctx = new InitialContext(env);
```

In return, though, you will find that the resulting client will no longer use an ORB, scales better, and can make use of all the standard WebLogic features available to clients.

J2EE Thin Clients

The J2EE supports application clients, which typically are shipped with a J2EE application and which can make use of J2EE features such as contexts and user transactions. This distinguishes these J2EE clients from ordinary Java clients. You can augment these clients with a WebLogic library, in which case the clients can utilize WebLogic features such as clustering and SSL. These clients (which in WebLogic 8.1 must run on a JDK 1.4 JVM) will use standard IIOP and the JVM's CORBA 2.4 ORB. J2EE thin clients created using this approach look similar to the fat clients. The only difference lies in the underlying mechanism:

```
Hashtable env = new Hashtable( );
env.put(Context.INITIAL_CONTEXT_FACTORY, "weblogic.jndi.WLInitialContextFactory");
env.put(Context.PROVIDER_URL,  "iiop://myserver:8001");
Context ctx = new InitialContext(env);
```

Note that regardless of the protocol specified in the provider URL, WebLogic will always use IIOP (or IIOPS as appropriate). If the client does not use JMS, simply bundle it with the *wlclient.jar* library, located in the *WL_HOME/server/lib* directory. If it does use JMS, include the *wljmsclient.jar* located in the same folder. Because early versions of the JDK 1.4 had errors in the CORBA implementation, we recommend you use the latest JVM edition for running your clients.

CORBA/IDL Clients

Let's now examine how you can write a CORBA/IDL client that can communicate with an RMI object through its IDL interface. WebLogic's RMI compiler (rmic) allows you to generate the IDL interface from a given RMI implementation class. You then can use a vendor-specific IDL compiler to generate the IIOP stubs and skeletons using the IDL interface. A CORBA/IDL client can use these generated classes to contact WebLogic Server, and access the remote interface exposed by the RMI object. WebLogic's ORB implements the objects-by-value specification. If you decide to use this feature, ensure that your client ORB also follows the specification.

In the following example, we will develop a Java-based CORBA client that uses the ORB implementation that comes with a standard JDK distribution. Let's assume that you've generated the class files for the remote interface and implementation class for some RMI object. In our earlier example, we generated the class files for *com/oreilly/rmi/Add.java* and *com/oreilly/rmi/AddImpl.java*. You can derive the IDL interface file from the implementation class using WebLogic's RMI compiler as follows:

```
java weblogic.rmic -idl com.oreilly.rmi.AddImpl
```

The RMI compiler generates the file *com/oreilly/rmi/Add.idl*, which captures the IDL interface for the RMI object. This IDL interface then can be passed through an IDL compiler to generate the IIOP stubs needed by our Java-based CORBA/IDL client. In this case, we will use the IDL compiler (idlj) that is included with Sun's Java SDK distribution:

```
%JAVA_HOME%\bin\idlj com\oreilly\rmi\Add.idl
```

If you examine the IDL interface generated for the RMI object, you will see that it contains an include directive:

```
#include orb.idl
```

This IDL file is supplied by the ORB vendor. Because we are using Sun's Java SDK, we use the IDL located at *%JAVA_HOME%\lib\orb.idl*. The IDL file *orb.idl* in turn contains another include directive:

```
#include ir.idl
```

This file also is located in the same folder. You must copy these two IDL files to the folder from which you intend to run the IDL compiler.

Now, all that remains is your Java-based CORBA client that will invoke the RMI object. Example 4-8 lists the code for a Java-based CORBA client *AddIIOPClient.java* that will invoke the RMI object.

Example 4-8. Java-based CORBA client for the RMI object

```
package com.oreilly.rmi;

import org.omg.CosNaming.*;  // AddClient will use the naming service.
import org.omg.CORBA.*;      // All CORBA applications need these classes.
```

Example 4-8. Java-based CORBA client for the RMI object (continued)

```java
public class AddIIOPClient {

  public static void main(String args[]) {
    try {
      // Create and initialize the ORB
      ORB orb = ORB.init(args, null);

      // Get the root naming context
      org.omg.CORBA.Object objRef = orb.resolve_initial_references("NameService");
      NamingContext ncRef = NamingContextHelper.narrow(objRef);

      // Look up the naming service for the RMI object
      NameComponent nc = new NameComponent("AddServer", "");
      NameComponent path[] = {nc};
      Add obj = AddHelper.narrow(ncRef.resolve(path));

      // Invoke the remote method on the RMI object
      System.out.println("Successfully invoked AddServer " + obj.add(3,4));

    } catch(Exception e) {
      System.out.println("ERROR : " + e);
      e.printStackTrace(System.out);
    }
  }
}
```

The code fragment in Example 4-8 is very similar to the RMI-IIOP version of AddClient.java. Like its RMI-IIOP counterpart, the CORBA client first attempts to acquire the root naming context, uses it to obtain a reference to the RMI object from the naming service, and finally invokes the methods exposed by its remote IDL interface. When you compile *com/oreilly/rmi/AddClient.java*, you find that the auxiliary source files generated previously by the IDL compiler are also compiled. Now, in order to run the client, you need to specify arguments for the hostname and port that identify where the naming service can be found:

```
java com.oreilly.rmi.AddClient -OrbInitialHost localhost -ORBInitialPort 7001
```

Here, the hostname and port refer to the listen address and listen port on which your WebLogic Server instance is running. If the client executes successfully, you should get the following output:

```
Successfully invoked AddServer 7
```

Configuring RMI-IIOP

In order to view or adjust the IIOP configuration settings for WebLogic Server, select a server from the left pane of the Administration Console and then choose the Protocols/ IIOP tab.* Select the Enable IIOP checkbox to enable the server to listen for IIOP requests. You also can specify the username and password to set up a default identity for all clients who have established IIOP connections with the particular server. By default, the anonymous user will be used. Use the IIOP Max Message Size field to set the maximum size (in bytes) of an IIOP request. Use the IIOP Message Timeout field to set the timeout duration (in seconds) for an IIOP request. These two fields help prevent denial-of-service (DOS) attacks to WebLogic Server.

No additional configuration is needed to set up RMI-over-IIOP. If your RMI objects have been bound to the JNDI tree properly, they will be available automatically to all (authorized) clients that can talk over RMI or RMI-over-IIOP. Typically, RMI objects are bound to the JNDI tree when the server starts up, and EJB home objects are bound when the actual EJB component is deployed to the server instance. WebLogic also supports RMI-IIOP with SSL for RMI and CORBA/IDL clients. Chapter 16 provides information on how you can configure SSL support for WebLogic Server.

* In WebLogic 7.0, choose the Connections/Protocols tab.

CHAPTER 5

JDBC

JDBC is the standard API for accessing relational databases in the Java platform. It provides a vendor-neutral abstraction for accessing databases. The JDBC interfaces are implemented for every major database, and these implementations are distributed as third-party drivers. The JDBC specification has evolved over time to support many features, including batched execution of SQL commands, statement caching, connection pooling, transactions, and disconnected rowsets. The current release, JDBC 3.0, is included in your JDK 1.4 distribution. The JDBC API provides a standard way for Java applications to interact with a relational database. It includes the following two packages:

java.sql
> This package contains the Java classes and interfaces that let you connect to a database, run SQL commands, insert and update rows, retrieve results, and access database metadata.

javax.sql
> This package contains the Java classes and interfaces that allow you to utilize the data source abstractions, pooled connections, distributed transactions, and rowsets.

WebLogic offers a number of services that use the JDBC, including container-managed entity beans, persistent messages, durable topic subscriptions, and JDBC-based HTTP session-state replication.

This chapter focuses on WebLogic's support for JDBC. We look at the various JDBC drivers that are compatible with WebLogic. We examine how WebLogic lets you configure and monitor a connection pool, or a pool of reusable connections to the database. WebLogic also lets you set up a pool of multiple connection pools, or a *multipool*. A multipool allows you to achieve high availability and load balancing across connection requests, even in a single-server environment. In addition, we examine how to set up a data source that you can use to dip into a JDBC pool.

We look at WebLogic's support for statement caching, which can offer a significant performance boost. We cover WebLogic's support for the wrapper drivers, which provide clients with an alternative access route to the configured JDBC pools. We also explain how data sources and connection pools should be set up in a clustered environment and how multi-tier JDBC connections support high availability and load balancing.

The JDBC 2.0 API introduces the rowset API as a standard extension. WebLogic provides a disconnected (cached) rowset implementation, which acts as a serializable container for transporting row data. It also supports various synchronization policies that determine how the data in a rowset should be synchronized with the underlying database. In addition, we look at how to export (or import) the rowset data and metadata to an XML document and schema.

Overview of JDBC Resources

In order to enable a JDBC application to obtain a connection to a database, you need to install a two-tier JDBC driver on WebLogic Server. Only then can you use the JDBC driver to configure a connection pool on the server. This pool of reusable database connections then is available to all server-side applications and to any remote clients of WebLogic. Typically, a JDBC application will access the connection pool through a data source associated with the pool. A multipool provides additional load-balancing and failover capabilities over a number of connection pools. Let's take a closer look at these JDBC resources.

JDBC Drivers for WebLogic Server

A JDBC driver provides the actual connectivity to a vendor's DBMS product, as well as provides the implementation of the standard JDBC interfaces and classes. WebLogic supports two kinds of JDBC drivers:

Two-tier drivers
> These JDBC drivers provide vendor-specific database access to WebLogic Server and the applications running on it. You can use a two-tier JDBC driver to configure a pool of reusable connections to the underlying database. Two-tier drivers include the JDBC drivers for Oracle, Sybase, and Microsoft shipped with WebLogic and third-party drivers such as the Oracle Thin Driver, Microsoft SQL Server 2000 JDBC driver, Sybase jConnect Driver, or the IBM JDBC drivers for Informix and DB2. A two-tier driver typically will provide native support for distributed transactions (WebLogic's jDriver for Oracle XA, Microsoft SQL Server 2000 JDBC driver, etc.).

Wrapper drivers
> WebLogic is equipped internally with wrapper drivers (also called multi-tier drivers) that provide vendor-neutral access to a pool of database connections already configured for the server. They wrap the connection pools created by the two-tier drivers, providing different ways of accessing the pools. WebLogic supports three wrapper JDBC drivers, which we describe in the list shown next.

The Pool Driver
> Server-side components (servlets, EJBs, etc.) can use this driver to acquire database connections directly from a connection pool.

The JTS Driver
> Server-side applications can use this driver to obtain database connections from a connection pool that also can participate in distributed transactions.

The RMI Driver
> Client (and server) JDBC applications can use this Type 3 JDBC driver to remotely access server-side connection pools via their data sources. The RMI Driver replaces the functionality of both the Pool Driver and JTS Driver.

A data source internally uses WebLogic's RMI Driver. When a remote client looks up the name of a data source in the JNDI tree in order to access the pool, it transparently uses the wrapper driver to dip into the connection pool. Because by default a data source is configured to honor distributed transactions, the RMI Driver ensures that the connections returned from the pool also can participate in distributed transactions.

Later, we examine how WebLogic's RMI Driver provides transparent access to connection pools that may be targeted to multiple server instances.

Connection Pools

JDBC connections are valuable resources because creating a connection to the database often can be a costly operation. For this reason, WebLogic lets you prepare a pool of reusable database connections, where each member of the pool has the same connection properties. Each connection in the pool connects to the same database server instance and uses the same database. All connections in the pool are associated with the same database user—i.e., the same username and password is used to create the connections. WebLogic is responsible for maintaining this pool of physical connections, which is in fact a collection of PooledConnection objects. When a program requests a connection from the pool, it obtains a Connection object that represents a logical connection to the database. Behind the scenes, WebLogic dips into the pool and associates a physical connection with the logical connection. So, the client's Connection object is a handle to the actual PooledConnection object.

If there are no available connections in the pool when a connection is requested, WebLogic increases the size of the pool by creating new physical connections. When the pool reaches its maximum capacity and no connections are available, WebLogic can force the client to wait for an available connection. If a connection still doesn't become available, WebLogic simply returns a connection failure. Once the client has completed its database access and invoked the close() method on the logical Connection object, the actual PooledConnection object is returned back to the pool.

A connection pool greatly enhances the performance and scalability of enterprise applications because the same physical connection can be shared by multiple applications, including servlets, EJBs, JMS message consumers, and even ordinary Java clients. Here are some of the important benefits of a connection pool:

- Applications can avoid the costly overhead of repeatedly creating connections at runtime. Even the DBMS performs better when it needs only to deal with a dedicated pool of prepared connections, instead of responding to random connection requests from the client.

- The database connection properties used to define a connection pool are shared by all members of the pool. A client can simply dip into the connection pool without having to hardwire the actual connection attributes within its code.

- A connection pool enables you to better manage the number of concurrent database users because all the connections share the same user credentials. This is crucial if you have a DBMS license that imposes certain constraints, such as a limit on the number of licensed database users or a limit on the number of concurrent users.

Connection pools also are needed by other WebLogic services such as CMP entity beans and durable JMS messages, where WebLogic needs access to a set of JDBC connections to the underlying database. Later in this chapter we shall see how you can access a server-side JDBC pool using either a data source or one of WebLogic's wrapper JDBC drivers.

Multipools

WebLogic also lets you set up a multipool—a pool of multiple connection pools that then can be targeted to either a single server or a cluster. A multipool defines a configurable algorithm for choosing a connection from one of the connection pools in the multipool. You can configure the multipool to operate in two modes:

High availability
  If a connection pool fails, the database connection is picked from the next pool in the list. The next pool in the ordered list is examined *only* if there is a problem with the current pool. This could happen if the current pool is disabled or if the actual database becomes unavailable. Otherwise, the multipool continues to behave like any ordinary connection pool.

Load balancing
  Connection requests are distributed evenly across the pools in a round-robin fashion.

Thus, you can set up the multipool so that either all connection pools evenly share the load of the connection requests, or a connection pool handles all the requests until it becomes inactive and then another "backup" pool is selected.

A multipool encapsulates access to multiple connection pools, where each connection pool is configured individually. All connections within a pool are configured to the same database, database user, and connection attributes. The attributes of the different pools in the multipool should vary in some significant way so that when one connection pool fails, the others are not also invalidated. You could even associate a different database user with each connection pool, if the DBMS has a limit on the number of simultaneous open connections per database user.

Typically, the JDBC pools within a multipool will point to distinct instances of the same database. If your DBMS configuration uses a high-availability solution (such as one based on data replication), you may use a multipool configured for high availability. If your DBMS configuration uses a number of servers running in parallel, and the database lives on shared, external (preferably fault-tolerant) storage, you may consider using a load-balancing multipool. However, if your DBMS runs on a single server or the DBMS automatically provides a single point of access to the cluster, as well as automatically handles failover, an ordinary connection pool will suffice.

It makes sense to configure multipools only if your application is independent of any specific connection pool. If each connection pool within the multipool points to a different database, multipools are useful provided your application does not depend on access to a particular database, or the databases are somehow kept in sync.

 A multipool does not provide failover from a connection pool on one server to a connection pool on another. They are simply a façade that lets you choose between multiple connection pools on the same server.

Data Sources

The DataSource interface is the preferred way for obtaining database connections. The data source allows you to map a logical name to a connection pool. An application then can access the connection pool directly by looking up the data source from the JNDI tree. The application need not be aware of the database setup or the actual connection properties. These settings are configured separately for the underlying connection pool. A server-side application can access a connection pool in several ways:

- You can use a data source that references the connection pool, or you can use a Pool Driver.
- If you need support for distributed transactions as well, you can use an XA-aware data source that references the connection pool, or you can use the JTS Driver.

Remember, the Pool and JTS Drivers are available only to server-side applications. We recommend that you look up the data source in the JNDI tree, and use it to access the connection pool. Later we shall see how you can use the Administration Console to set up the data source and its associated connection pool.

Configuring JDBC Connectivity

The Administration Console allows you to configure various JDBC resources: connection pools, multipools, and data sources. First you need to create one or more connection pools. You may want to create a multipool in order to benefit from additional load-balancing or failover capabilities. Next, set up the data sources, which provide access to the JDBC pools. These resources then can be targeted to multiple servers and/or clusters and accessed by multiple enterprise applications. After this, you can use either the Administration Console or the command-line `weblogic.Admin` tool to manage and monitor JDBC connectivity.

An alternative approach would be to configure an application-specific data source and connection pool, in which case the JDBC resources are isolated to a particular enterprise application. In this instance, the J2EE application fully captures the configuration of all JDBC resources that it needs, without having to rely on the proper configuration of the servers to which the application is deployed.

Using Third-Party JDBC Drivers

Once you have installed a third-party JDBC driver, you need to make the driver classes visible to WebLogic Server when it starts up. This means that you need to modify WebLogic startup scripts so that the system classpath includes the libraries for the JDBC driver. For instance, if you wish to use Microsoft's SQL Server 2000 JDBC Driver, you need to modify the *startWeblogic* script to include the library JARs:

```
set JDBC_LIB=f:\shared\jdbc\lib
set CLASSPATH=%JDBC_LIB%\msbase.jar;%JDBC_LIB%\msutil.jar;
    %JDBC_LIB%\mssqlserver.jar;%CLASSPATH%
```

In this case, the JDBC driver library JARs are in the *f:\shared\jdbc\lib* directory. Some JDBC drivers also require you to install native code libraries. Ensure that these libraries are included in the system PATH before you start WebLogic.

However, if you intend to use the Oracle Thin Driver 9.2.0 (*ojdbc14.jar*) or Sybase jConnect Driver v4.5 (*jConnect.jar*) or v5.5 (*jconn2.jar*)—which are shipped with your WebLogic distribution—you don't need to adjust the system classpath. These drivers are installed in the *WL_HOME\server\lib* directory, *and* the manifest file for *weblogic.jar* is configured to automatically load them. WebLogic also includes a version of the Oracle driver that provides additional debugging support. This driver can be found in the *WL_HOME\server\ext\jdbc\oracle\920* directory. If you want to use this particular driver, or any other updates to these libraries, you can either overwrite the library loaded from the *WL_HOME\server\lib* directory, or prepend its location to the classpath, just as you would for any other installed driver.

You can configure new connection pools to use the installed JDBC driver once the library classes for the JDBC driver are made available to the server.

Configuring a Connection Pool

A connection pool provides the database connectivity for applications deployed on WebLogic Server. You can use the Administration Console to do the following:

- Create a new connection pool
- Adjust the connection properties of an existing pool, including the connection reservation policy
- Assign the pool to servers and/or clusters
- Test, monitor, and control the state of all active JDBC pools

Let's take a closer look at how to manage connection pools on WebLogic Server.

Creating a pool

In WebLogic 8.1, the Administration Console provides assistants to help set up JDBC connection pools and data sources. These assistants simplify the configuration of the connection pools for the more popular JDBC drivers, by automatically populating crucial settings such as the driver classname, the connection URL, and driver properties.

In order to set up a connection pool, you need to navigate to the Services/JDBC/Connection Pools node from the left pane of the Administration Console. Here, you can select the "Configure a new JDBC Connection Pool" option to create a new pool. You must choose the database type (Oracle, DB2, Informix, MySQL, etc.), after which you are presented with a list of JDBC drivers available for that particular database. Choose the one that matches your installed JDBC driver. Note that most installed JDBC drivers come in two flavors: the ordinary JDBC driver, which supports local transactions, and an alternative version of the JDBC driver, whose connections can participate fully in distributed transactions. The latter drivers usually have an "XA" prefix.

Finally, you are prompted for the database name, the hostname, and the port number for the database server, as well as the login credentials (i.e., username and password) of a valid database user. WebLogic will use this supplied data to automatically construct a connection pool with the appropriate driver classname, driver URL, and driver properties. Once you've created the pool, you can create and test a connection. If you don't want to use these assistants, simply select Other as the database type. In that case, you must manually configure values for all the driver properties, including the fully qualified class name of the driver and the driver-specific JDBC URL.

You also can right-click an existing connection pool in the Administration Console and choose the Clone Connection Pool option. This creates a new pool with the same configuration, which you then can reconfigure as per your needs.

A connection pool may be targeted to multiple servers in the domain, effectively creating multiple copies of the pool. This makes the pool available to all server-side applications deployed to that server. A server-side application may access a local connection pool using either a data source configured for the JDBC pool, or the Pool and JTS wrapper drivers. An external client also can access a server-side connection pool using either a data source or the wrapper RMI Driver.

General pool configuration

The Configuration/General tab for a chosen connection pool displays the general settings for the connection pool. Most of them are listed in Table 5-1. You will already have encountered most of them while setting up the connection pool.

Table 5-1. General connection pool configuration options

Parameter	Description
URL	This attribute identifies the JDBC URL needed to create the connections in the pool. This setting is driver-specific, so you should consult the documentation for the driver to find the correct value for this setting.
Driver Classname	This attribute specifies the fully qualified class name of the two-tier JDBC driver used to create physical connections between WebLogic and the DBMS.
Properties	This attribute lists other connection properties needed by the JDBC driver — e.g., database name, name of database user, password, etc. You must specify a name=value for each property on a separate line.
Open String Password	If your DBMS uses an XA open string, this field will hold the encrypted form of the password. This setting overrides any plaintext password that you may have defined in the driver properties.
Password	Use this field to set the password for the database user. This setting overrides any plain text password that may have been specified in the property list passed to the JDBC driver. The value is stored in the domain's *config.xml* configuration file in encrypted form, and is hidden away from the Administration Console view.

The properties that are defined for a connection pool are driver-specific. Typically, you use the Properties field to configure connection attributes such as the database name, database user, server name, and port number. For instance, if you must configure a JDBC pool using Microsoft's SQL Server 2000 JDBC Driver, the following entry in the domain's *config.xml* file illustrates the bare configuration settings for the connection pool:

```
<JDBCConnectionPool
    Name="mssqlPool"
    DriverName="com.microsoft.jdbc.sqlserver.SQLServerDriver"
    URL="jdbc:microsoft:sqlserver://dbserver:1433"
    Properties="DatabaseName=master;User=sa;SelectMethod=Cursor"
    Password="{3DES}WvzaSHwL1Dj1oMVWjtybVw=="
    Targets="myServer"  />
```

If you intend to set up a pool using IBM's JDBC Driver for Informix, the following entry in the domain's *config.xml* file describes the settings for the connection pool:

```
<JDBCConnectionPool
    Name="ifxPool"
    DriverName="com.informix.jdbc.IfxDriver"
```

```
URL="jdbc:informix-sqli:ifxserver:1543"
Password="{3DES}WvzaSHwL1Dj1oMVWjtybVw=="
Properties="informixserver=ifxserver;user=informix"
Targets="myServer" />
```

Similarly, if you intend to set up a pool of XA connections, you must use the XA version of the JDBC driver. For instance, Microsoft's SQL Server 2000 Driver for JDBC supports distributed transactions, provided the connection pool is configured as follows:

```
<JDBCConnectionPool
    Name="mssqlPool"
    DriverName="com.microsoft.jdbc.sqlserver.SQLServerXADataSource"
    URL="jdbc:microsoft:sqlserver"
    Properties="DatabaseName=master;User=sa;SelectMethod=Cursor;ServerName=dbserver;
            PortNumber=1433"
    Password="{3DES}WvzaSHwL1Dj1oMVWjtybVw=="
    Targets="myServer" />
```

In this case, the DriverName property for the JDBC pool has been set to a class that implements the javax.sql.XADataSource interface.

Controlling the pool size

Table 5-2 lists configuration operations that control the size of the pool. These options are available in the Configuration/Connections tab of a selected connection pool.

Table 5-2. Configuration settings for controlling the pool size

Parameter	Description	Default
Initial Capacity	This setting determines the number of physical connections that are created when the connection pool is initialized. The size of the pool will never fall below the initial capacity.	1
Maximum Capacity	This setting determines the maximum number of physical connections that the pool can grow to.	15 or 25
Capacity Increment	This attribute determines the amount by which the connection pool is expanded when there are no available connections to service a connection request. WebLogic will continue to create new physical connections so long as all the connections in the pool are busy and the current pool size has not yet reached maximum capacity.	1
Allow Shrinking	This setting indicates whether the connection pool can be shrunk back to its initial capacity when database connections are idle.	true
Shrink Frequency	This attribute defines the time (in seconds) to wait before shrinking a pool back to its initial capacity.	900
Connection Creation Retry Frequency	This setting defines how often WebLogic should retry to create connections. This setting is used, for example, if a failure is detected while creating additional connections for a pool.	0
Login Delay	This setting defines the delay (in seconds) before creating a physical database connection. You may want to use this to control how fast WebLogic creates physical connections.	0

By default, the maximum capacity for a newly created pool is 15 if the server runs in development mode, and 25 if it runs in production mode. In fact, these are also the default number of threads configured for the server's default execute queue. In general, the size of the connection pool need not be any greater than the maximum concurrency configured for your application server.

By default, the initial capacity for a connection pool is set to 1. This means that only a single physical connection is created when the pool is initialized. If your server runs in a production environment, you will pay a price for the new connections that are created while servicing client requests. Clearly, this is not an ideal situation. Instead, you should set the pool's initial capacity equal to its maximum capacity, in which case the pool will be fully populated with physical connections before any client requests are made.

A connection pool grows whenever its existing capacity is unable to satisfy new connection requests—i.e., all the connections in the pool are busy when a new connection request arrives. A connection pool will never grow to more than its maximum capacity. It also can shrink when the extra capacity is no longer being used. Shrinking involves removing idle connections from the pool. By default, WebLogic tries to shrink the pool after every 900 seconds, either to its initial capacity or to the number of connections that are currently in use, whichever is the greater.

Be careful when you set the initial and maximum capacity for a connection pool, especially when it will be assigned to multiple servers in the domain. When you target a JDBC pool to multiple servers, the pool is initialized separately on each server. For instance, if you assign a connection pool to three Managed Servers, you effectively create three separate pools, one for each server. When all the servers are up and running, you will end up with three times as many physical database connections configured for the pool.

Connection reservation

The ability to control how connections within the pool are reserved is useful, particularly if you want finer control over transaction timeouts and the behavior of the pool under load. Table 5-3 lists the important configuration parameters that influence the pool's connection reservation behavior.

Table 5-3. Connection reservation configuration parameters

Parameter	Description	Default
Connection Reserve Timeout	This property determines the number of seconds after which a call to create a connection call will timeout, once the pool has reached its maximum capacity and all connections have been reserved. This attribute defaults to 10 seconds. If the pool still cannot return a connection within this wait period, the connection request will fail with a PoolLimitSQLException exception. If you set this timeout to –1, all clients of the pool wait indefinitely for a connection. Alternatively, you can set the timeout to 0 to disable the wait altogether.	10

Table 5-3. Connection reservation configuration parameters (continued)

Parameter	Description	Default
Maximum Waiting for Connection	This attribute determines the maximum number of clients that can concurrently block while waiting to reserve a connection. In other words, this is the maximum number of waiting connection requests. If you set this to 0, connections requests will not wait. It defaults to MAX-INT, which effectively means *all* connection requests will wait for a connection.	MAX-INT
Inactive Connection Timeout	This property determines how often WebLogic attempts to reap inactive reserved connections. It defaults to 0, which means this feature is disabled by default. Generally, inactive reserved connections occur due to errors in your code—for example, failing to release a connection after use. A positive value for this property helps manage the impact of idle reserved connections.	0

Let's observe how WebLogic reserves a JDBC connection from a pool, in response to a client connection request. If there is an available connection in the pool, it is simply returned to the client. If there are no connections available and the pool has not yet reached its maximum capacity, WebLogic increases the size of the pool by manufacturing the number of new connections specified in the Capacity Increment setting before returning one of these new connections to the client.

If the pool has reached its maximum capacity, WebLogic instructs the client to wait for the number of seconds specified in the Connection Reserve Timeout setting for one to be made available. No more than the number of requests to the pool specified in the Maximum Waiting for Connection setting may wait for a connection in this manner. If a connection becomes available during this wait period, it's returned to the client. Otherwise, the client's connection request fails with a `PoolLimit-SQLException`.

You should set a sensible limit on the number of connection requests to the pool that may wait in this fashion. Your application performance could degrade if too many connection requests wait for a connection to become available. By default, any request to reserve a connection from the pool times out after 10 seconds. This reservation timeout has implications on the transactional behavior of applications that use the connection pool. If the connection from the pool is involved in a transaction and the reservation timeout expires, an exception is raised and the transaction is rolled back.

None of these pool settings affects the way in which a multipool operates. For example, if a client attempts to reserve a connection from a multipool, and the pool has reached its maximum capacity, it will simply wait for a connection to become available, just like a client of a connection pool would do. Just because a connection pool is at maximum capacity and has no available connections to service the connection request, does not mean that WebLogic will attempt to reserve a connection from the next pool in the multipool.

Connection testing

In order to maintain a healthy connection pool, you need to maintain the health of its connections. You can configure a connection pool to automatically test its connections, and re-create new ones if a test fails. Table 5-4 lists the configuration parameters.

Table 5-4. Connection pool testing parameters

Parameter	Description	Default
Test Table Name	This setting specifies a table name used when testing a physical connection. By default, WebLogic uses the following query to test a database connection: `select count(*) from TestTableName` TestTableName must exist and be accessible to the database user. If this parameter begins with SQL, the rest of the string will be treated as the actual SQL statement used to test the database connection.	none
Test Frequency	This parameter determines how often WebLogic tests unused connections. Set this to 0 to disable testing.	0
Test Reserved Connections	If true, WebLogic tests a connection after creating it, but before returning it to the client.	false
Test Released Connections	If true, WebLogic tests a connection after a user closes it, but before releasing it back to the connection pool.	false
Test Created Connections	If true, WebLogic tests a connection after creating it, but before adding it to the connection pool.	false
Maximum Connections Made Unavailable	This parameter determines the maximum number of connections that will be unavailable to clients, due to testing. For example, setting this parameter to 2 allows WebLogic to test two connections from the pool at a time. However, during this test, these two connections will not be available to clients of the pool.	0

Connection testing occurs only if you have configured the Test Table Name parameter, and either selected a Test Frequency or specified exactly when the pool's connection ought to be tested. When a test fails, WebLogic closes the physical connection, removes it from the pool, and creates a new physical connection. Be careful when you enable connection testing, as it will cause a delay. For example, if you enable the Test Reserved Connection flag for a connection pool, WebLogic executes the configured test whenever the pool receives a connection request from a client. A ConnectionDeadSQLException exception is generated if a client tries to reserve a connection and the connection test fails.

Advanced distributed transaction control

If you configure a connection pool using an XA-aware JDBC driver, WebLogic provides additional parameters under the Advanced options in the Configuration/ Connections tab. All these settings default to false, though WebLogic does choose appropriate values for specific settings if you use the JDBC assistants to create your connection pools. The XA-specific parameters for a connection pool are listed in Table 5-5.

Table 5-5. Advanced XA connection pool options

Parameter	Description
Keep XA Connection Till Transaction Complete	This option ensures that distributed transactions are started and stopped in the same physical connection. This forces WebLogic to reserve the same connection for the duration of the distributed transaction. Sybase and DB2 use this feature.
Need Transaction Context On Close	Set this option to `true` if the XA driver must require a distributed transaction context when closing JDBC resources (such as result sets, etc.).
New XA Connection For Commit	Set this option to `true` if you require a dedicated XA connection to be used for commit or rollback processing.
XA End Only Once	If this option is enabled, the `XAResource.end( )` method will be called only once for each pending `XAResource.start( )`. Here, `XAResource.end(TMSUSPEND)` and `XAResource.end(TMSUCCESS)` will not be called successively.
Keep Connection Open On Release	If this option is `true`, the logical JDBC connection is kept open when the physical XA connection is returned to the connection pool.
Supports Local Transaction	Set this option to `true` if the XA connections created using the JDBC driver also can be used in a nontransactional context.

Initializing pool connections

You also can use the Init SQL setting for the connection pool to specify SQL that must be executed whenever a new connection is created. In this way, you can prime the JDBC connections in some DBMS-specific way. Any string that you supply should begin with SQL. Here is an example:

```
SQL SET LOCK MODE TO WAIT
```

Monitoring JDBC pools

The Monitoring tab lets you monitor each connection pool on a per-server basis. WebLogic captures a number of statistics on the pool, including the number of active connections, the number of clients waiting for a connection, the average length of the wait time, the current capacity, and the state of the pool (whether it is active, suspended, or unhealthy).

Managing the connection pool

The Control tab for a connection pool gives you explicit, immediate control over the connection pool. Here you can perform any of the following operations:

Shrink

Select this option to immediately shrink the connection pool.

Reset

Use this option to close and re-create all the physical connections in the selected pool. You may need to reset the pool, for instance, if your database server has crashed. Of course, you should reset the pool only after the database server has been restarted.

Clear Statement Cache

Use this option to clear the statement cache for each connection in the pool.

Suspend, Force Suspend, and Resume

Use this option to suspend a connection pool, which effectively suspends all operations on the pool's connections, until you later resume them. If you forcibly suspend a pool, the server additionally disconnects all users from the pool. Any applications that continue to use a connection from a suspended pool will get an exception.

Destroy and Force Destroy

Use this option if you choose to destroy a pool. All connections are released and the pool will no longer be available. This operation fails if any of the pool connections are in use, unless you *forcibly* destroy the pool, in which case all current users of the pool also are disconnected.

Note that if an application attempts to reserve a connection from a suspended connection pool, it will receive a `PoolDisabledSQLException` exception.

Using the physical connection

WebLogic provides you with a way to retrieve the physical connection associated with a logical connection. The `weblogic.jdbc.extensions.WLConnection` interface provides this access:

```
// ds is a reference to a DataSource object...
java.sql.Connection con = ds.getConnection( );
java.sql.Connection pCon = ((WLConnection)con)).getVendorConnection( )
```

In general, you should not use the underlying physical connection because the approach suffers from a number of limitations:

- You lose all the benefits WebLogic's connection management features, including support for error handling, prepared statement caching, connection testing, and distributed transactions.

- Only server-side applications may use the actual physical connection obtained from the pool.

- WebLogic is unable to reuse the physical connections. By default, when you close a physical connection, it is not returned to the pool. Instead, WebLogic discards it and replaces it with a new connection in the pool. Thus, your applications suffer a performance loss because the pool's connections cannot be reused. In addition, any statement cache that may have been active for the previous connection is no longer valid for the new connection in the pool.

For the core hacker, WebLogic does allow you to alter this default behavior and ensure that the physical connection is returned to the pool when you close it. If you set the MBean attribute `RemoveInfectedConnectionsEnabled` for the connection pool to `false`, WebLogic places the physical connection back into the pool when you close it. In this case, you must ensure that the actual JDBC connection is fit for use by other clients of the connection pool. Later, we will see how this same interface provides direct access to the prepared statement cache.

Configuring a Data Source

Now that you have created a connection pool, you can associate a data source with it and make it available in the JNDI tree. The data source then becomes the conduit for accessing the connection pool. You can create data source objects by navigating to the Services/JDBC/Data Sources node in the left frame of the Administration Console. Choose "Configure a new Data Source" to create a new data source.

Table 5-6 lists the configuration settings for a data source.

Table 5-6. Configuration settings for a data source

Parameter	Description	Default
Name	This setting specifies a name for the data source.	Required
JNDI Name	This setting specifies the JNDI name to which the data source will be bound in the server's JNDI tree.	Required
Pool Name	This setting specifies the logical name of a connection pool (or multi-pool) that is associated with the data source.	Required
Honors Global Transactions	If this flag is selected, the data source may participate in distributed transactions.	`true`
Row Prefetch Enabled	This setting improves application performance by enabling multiple rows to be prefetched when an external client is using the data source. Row prefetching is disabled when the client and WebLogic Server are running in the same JVM.	`false`
Row Prefetch Size	This attribute determines the number of rows to be prefetched when an external client accesses the data source.	`48`
Stream Chunk Size	This attribute specifies the chunk size (in bytes) used when retrieving streaming data types (such as character or byte streams). It can take on any value between 0 and 65,536.	`256`

Thus, in order to properly configure a data source, you must specify the JNDI name to which the data source will be available in the server's JNDI tree, as well as the name of the JDBC pool that will be used to supply the connections. The data source refers to a connection pool or multipool that you've already configured.

The row-prefetch options determine how an external client of the data source behaves when it invokes the ResultSet.next( ) method. This is explained later in this chapter in the section "The RMI Driver."

Setting up an XA-aware data source

As described in Chapter 6, there are two types of transactions. A *local transaction* is one whose scope is bound by the lifetime of a single connection to a resource (e.g., a

JDBC connection or a transacted JMS session). A *distributed transaction* is one that involves updates to multiple resources (e.g., a JDBC connection, a JMS server), coordinated using a two-phase commit protocol.

Consequently, WebLogic supports two kinds of data source objects: those that are configured to only support local transactions, and those that can participate in distributed transactions. The Honors Global Transactions flag determines whether the configured data source can participate in distributed transactions. By default, this flag is enabled, which means that by default, any data source you create is configured to participate in distributed transactions. We'll use the term *XA-aware data source* to refer to a data source that also can participate in distributed transactions.

If you set the Honors Global Transactions flag to false, any connection obtained from the data source can never participate in distributed transactions. You may explicitly disable support for distributed transactions in this way, if you are certain your application can perform multiple JDBC updates satisfactorily within the lifetime of a single JDBC connection. You will need to configure an XA-aware data source if your application has any of the following requirements:

- Your code uses the JTA to support multiple database updates within a single transaction. That is, your code uses client-initiated transactions or EJBs that support bean-managed transactions.

- Your application uses EJBs that support container-managed transactions (e.g., CMP entity beans).

- Your code uses multiple resources such as databases, JMS, etc., within the scope of a single transaction.

If multiple EJBs are involved in database updates, you will certainly need transactions that can span multiple connections. There are two ways to configure XA-aware data sources:

- Associate the data source with a connection pool that has been created using an XA-aware JDBC driver. This yields a first-class XADataSource that can participate fully in any distributed transaction, just like any other XA resource.

- If the connection pool has been configured using a JDBC driver that does not support XA, you can still create an XADataSource in this scenario, so long as you also enable the Emulate Two-Phase Commit for non-XA Driver flag for the data source. You can find this option in the advanced section of the Configuration tab for a data source. Obviously, you do not need to enable this flag if your connection pool is XA-aware.

There are a number of caveats associated with two-phase commit emulation, which we discuss in Chapter 6.

Using a configured data source

Now that you have configured the data source and its connection pool, you can use it to obtain a connection from the pool from within any server-side application. The following example shows how a servlet can look up the configured data source and use it to request a JDBC connection from the pool:

```java
public void doGet(HttpServletRequest req, HttpServletResponse res)
        throws ServletException, IOException {

    DataSource ds = null;
    Connection con = null;

    try {
      //typically, you would obtain a reference to the data source
      //in the servlet's init method
      InitialContext ctx = new InitialContext();
      ds = (DataSource) ctx.lookup("myds");
      con = ds.getConnection();

      //use the database connection to service the request
    }
    catch (NamingException ene) {
      //handle naming exceptions
    }
    catch (SQLException esql) {
      //handle SQL exceptions
    }
    finally {
      /* release connection and other JDBC resources here,
         ensure JDBC objects are properly closed, even if an exception occurs */
      try {
        if (con != null) con.close();
      }
      catch(IOException eio) {}
    }
}
```

For an external client, the only change is the way in which you set up the initial JNDI context:

```java
try {
  Hashtable env = new Hashtable();
  env.put(Context.INITIAL_CONTEXT_FACTORY,
        "weblogic.jndi.WLInitialContextFactory");
  env.put(Context.PROVIDER_URL,
        "t3://server:port");  //URL of a running WebLogic Server instance

  InitialContext ctx = new InitialContext(env);
  DataSource ds = (DataSource) ctx.lookup("mytxds");

  javax.transaction.UserTransaction tx =
        (javax.transaction.UserTransaction) ctx.lookup("java:comp/
UserTransaction");
  tx.begin();
  Connection con = ds.getConnection();

  //you now have a handle that wraps the actual physical connection
```

```
    //make sure to release connection and related resources when you are done

    tx.commit();
}
catch (NamingException ene) {
    //handle naming exceptions
}
catch (SQLException esql) {
    //handle SQL exceptions
    try {
      tx.rollback();
    }
    catch (SystemException ese) {
}
```

Notice how the JDBC connection is being used within the context of a JTA transaction. In this case, we are assuming that an XA-aware data source has been configured and bound to the server's JNDI tree under the name mytxds.

Targeting the data source

In order to deploy a data source to the server, you must target both the data source and its associated JDBC pool to the server. The connection pool is then accessible to all server-side applications, as well as to any clients of the server. In fact, you can target both the data source and the connection pool to one or more Managed Servers. To do this, you must choose the data source (or the connection pool) from the left pane of the Administration Console, and then select the Targets and Deploy tab to assign the JDBC resource to the selected Managed Servers (or cluster).

Remember, a client can access a data source only if *both* the data source and the JDBC pool are assigned to the server as a combination. You must not target a data source to a Managed Server without also targeting its JDBC pool to the same server. In a WebLogic cluster, you can configure the data source in two ways:

- Assign the data source and connection pool uniformly to the cluster by targeting them both to every Managed Server belonging to the cluster.
- Target the data source and the connection pool to the cluster. In this case, the data source is now "cluster-aware." When a client requests a connection from the cluster-aware data source, the request can be redirected to any one of the Managed Servers in the cluster.

Because a connection pool isn't cluster-aware, targeting a JDBC pool to a cluster merely assigns it to all the members of the cluster. It is a convenience feature only. You will create as many instances of the connection pool as there are members in the cluster. Thus, you can target the data source and connection pool to different servers or clusters, but they must be applied to each server as a combination. Later, we will examine the implications of using data sources and JDBC pools in a clustered environment.

Never configure multiple XA-aware data sources that point to the same connection pool. This may result in a runtime exception (XA_PROTO error).

Application-Scoped Data Sources and Connection Pools

Connection pools and data sources generally are treated as managed objects. You must explicitly configure the server with the necessary data sources and connection pools needed by all applications deployed on that server. In this case, the deployed applications rely on proper configuration of the servers to which they are deployed, for any JDBC resources they may require. Alternatively, you can create data sources and connection pools that are specific to an enterprise application. The *weblogic-application.xml* descriptor file for an enterprise application lets you configure application-scoped pools and data sources that are, in effect, created when the application is deployed. The advantage of this approach is that the enterprise application carries the configuration of all JDBC resources that it needs. A similar mechanism also is available for XML parser factories, which we explore in Chapter 18.

WebLogic eases the configuration of application-scoped JDBC resources by allowing you to also refer to a data source factory created in your WebLogic domain. A *data source factory* stores the default values for any application-scoped connection pools. These defaults can be overridden in the *weblogic-application.xml* deployment descriptor when you define the application-scoped pool.

Remember, WebLogic creates an instance of the application-scoped pool whenever it creates an instance of the enterprise application. Thus, WebLogic creates an instance of the pool on all servers to which the owning application is deployed.

Creating a data source factory

To create a data source factory, choose the Services/JDBC/Data Source Factories node from the left pane of the Administration Console and select the "Create a new Data Source Factory" option. You will be asked to supply a name for the factory, together with the configuration details for the connection pool—namely, the JDBC URL, the driver classname, driver properties, and the username and password that should be used to create the connections. Note, however, that a data source factory doesn't actually create a connection pool—it merely provides the default values for any application-scoped pool that chooses to reference this factory.

Editing the deployment descriptor

Application-scoped data sources and connection pools can be defined using only the *weblogic-application.xml* descriptor file for an enterprise application. The easiest way to edit the descriptor file is to use WebLogic Builder. The entire configuration occurs under the jdbc-connection-pool element. The following portion from the *weblogic-application.xml* descriptor file shows how to configure an application-scoped data source and pool:

```
<jdbc-connection-pool>
  <data-source-name>myDS</data-source-name>
  <connection-factory>
    <!-- Set connection properties not covered by the data source factory,
         or override the defaults in the data source factory -->
    <factory-name>myds_factory</factory-name>
    <connection-properties>
      <user-name>sa</user-name>
      <url>jdbc:microsoft:sqlserver://10.0.10.10:1443</url>
      <driver-class-name>com.microsoft.jdbc.sqlserver.SQLServerDriver</driver-class-
name>
      <connection-params>
        <parameter>
          <param-name>databaseName</param-name>
          <param-value>DYNOLIFE</param-value>
        </parameter>
        <parameter>
          <param-name>password</param-name>
          <param-value>pssst</param-value>
        </parameter>
      </connection-params>
    </connection-properties>
  </connection-factory>
  <pool-params>
    <!-- Set the pool capacity limits, shrinking behavior, num-waiters, etc. -->
  </pool-params>
  <driver-params>
    <!-- Define profiling, prepared statement caching, etc. -->
  </driver-params>
</jdbc-connection-pool>
```

As you can see, the descriptor file simply holds an XML description of a connection pool and its runtime behavior. In this case, the optional factory-name element refers to a data source factory already configured in your WebLogic domain. Once you reference a data source factory from within an application-scoped pool, you need to set only those connection properties not covered already by the data source factory, since the pool automatically inherits the defaults defined in the data source factory. Alternatively, an application-scoped pool can override any of the default values inherited from the factory. If an application-scoped pool does not reference a data source factory, you must explicitly set all of the required connection properties in the descriptor file. Otherwise, you will get a configuration error when you later deploy the enterprise application.

Using an application-scoped data source

The data-source-name subelement defines the name of an application-scoped data source that will be associated with the pool. Once an application-scoped data source has been targeted to a server, it can then use this name to look up the data source from the local Environment Naming Context (ENC), available under *java:comp/env*.

In the previous example, any component within the enterprise application can access the application-scoped data source as follows:

```
DataSource ds = (DataSource) ctx.lookup("java:comp/env/myDS");
java.sql.Connection con = ds.getConnection( );
//...
```

 An application-scoped data source is always XA-aware.

The Administration Console allows you to access the configuration of application-scoped JDBC resources within a deployed application EAR. If you select the application EAR from the under the Deployments/Applications node, the Administration Console lists all the modules that are contained in the EAR, including any EJBs or WARs. In this case, you also can view the configuration of the application-scoped data source and pool. If you click the application-scoped data source, you get direct access to the configuration of the connection pool associated with the application-scoped data source. This includes the same properties and operations that are available for any traditional, server-specific connection pool. For example, you can monitor the connection pool and target the data source to one or more servers (or clusters). Be sure to target the data source to the same servers that will run code that accesses the data source.

Encrypting the passwords

When you define an application-scoped connection pool in the *weblogic-application.xml* descriptor file, you will notice that the login credentials of the database user appear in clear text:

```
<parameter>
  <param-name>password</param-name>
  <param-value>pssst</param-value>
</parameter>
```

This is a potential security risk because the credentials of the database user associated with the connection pool are now in full view of anyone who has access to the descriptor file. WebLogic provides a utility that you can use to encrypt the database password. The utility simply searches for all database passwords and replaces them with their encrypted versions. To run the utility, enter the following command:

```
java weblogic.j2ee.PasswordEncrypt descriptorFile domainDir
```

Here, the descriptorFile argument refers to the location of the *weblogic-application.xml* descriptor file, and the domainDir argument refers to the location of the root directory of your domain. After running the utility, the descriptor file portions that contain the database passwords will change into something like this:

```
<parameter>
  <param-name>password</param-name>
```

```
<param-value>{3DES}WvzaSHwL1Dj1oMVWjtybVw==</param-value>
</parameter>
```

If you want to change the database password, you need to simply change it in the *weblogic-application.xml* descriptor and rerun the utility. You must rerun the utility if you choose to move the application to a different installation of WebLogic Server, or if you deploy the application under a domain directory different from the one that was referenced when you ran the utility. Even if you delete the domain directory and create another one with the same name, you still will have to rerun the utility.

Managing the Statement Cache

WebLogic can be configured to maintain a statement cache for each connection in a connection pool. Whenever you create a prepared statement (or callable statement) using a connection obtained from the pool, WebLogic caches the compiled statement so that it can be reused later. Statement caching occurs transparently, without affecting any clients of the pool. In this way, WebLogic can avoid recompiling the prepared statement the next time it is used. This improves the performance of most JDBC applications.

Thus, when an application creates a prepared or callable statement on a connection obtained from the pool, WebLogic attempts to use cached copy of the statement, if it exists. Otherwise, WebLogic stores the new, compiled statement in the cache so that other clients of the pool can reuse it. WebLogic uses the precise SQL command and the result set type and concurrency options (if any) as the key to later retrieve the statement from the cache. If the statement cache is full, WebLogic evicts the least-recently used statement from the cache before introducing the new statement. WebLogic also supports an *immutable* statement cache per connection, which remains unchanged as soon as the statement cache is full, and until the physical connection is closed or the statement cache is cleared.

Enabling statement caching

By default, statement caching is enabled for any connection pool. In order to configure the statement cache for the pool, select the connection pool from the left frame of the Administration Console, and then navigate to the Configuration/Connections tab in the right frame. Here, you can adjust the following configuration settings for the statement cache:

Statement Cache Size
> This parameter determines the number of prepared or callable statements that are cached for each connection in the pool. By default, WebLogic caches 10 statements per pool connection. You can disable statement caching simply by setting the cache size to 0.

*Statement Cache Type**

Use this parameter to configure the eviction policy for the connection pool. By default, WebLogic supports an LRU cache, which means that it replaces the least-recently used statement in the cache with the new statement when the cache is full. Generally, this option offers optimum JDBC performance. Alternatively, you can set the cache type to Fixed, in which case the prepared or callable statements are cached only until the cache becomes full. Once the cache is full, its contents no longer will change, until the physical connection is closed or the statement cache is cleared.

Remember, the statement cache is available to all clients of the pool. WebLogic caches the prepared or callable statements regardless of who created the statement. You should experiment with the cache size to find the optimal setting for your application.

Clearing the statement cache

The WLConnection interface also lets you remove prepared or callable statements from the cache. When a prepared or callable statement is inserted into the cache, it is indexed by the precise SQL that was used and the result set type and concurrency options (if any). Given this information, you then can use either of these methods to remove a statement from the cache:

```
boolean WLConnection.clearCallableStatement(String sql, int rsType, int
    rsConcurrency);
boolean WLConnection.clearPreparedStatement(String sql, int rsType, int
    rsConcurrency);
```

Here is an example:

```
boolean succeeded =
    ((WLConnection) con).clearPreparedStatement("SELECT * FROM foo WHERE goo > ?",
        ResultSet.TYPE_SCROLL_INSENSITIVE, ResultSet.CONCUR_READ_ONLY);
```

For a statement that doesn't return a result set, you need to supply only the SQL that was used to create the statement:

```
boolean WLConnection.clearCallableStatement(String sql);
boolean WLConnection.clearPreparedStatement(String sql);
```

Each clear*XXX*Statement() method returns false if the statement could not be found within the cache. You also can clear the entire statement cache associated with the connection:

```
if (((WLConnection) con).clearStatementCache()) {
    // successfully cleared the statement cache for the connection
}
```

---

* WebLogic 7.0 doesn't support the LRU statement cache. So, you must persist with the default Fixed type statement cache.

Limitations of statement caching

By default, WebLogic maintains a cache of 10 statements for each connection in the pool. Even though a statement cache can dramatically improve the performance of your applications, there are certain restrictions you should be aware of when caching prepared or callable statements:

- When using the `setNull()` method on a `PreparedStatement` object, make sure that you use the correct datatype for the parameter. For example, if the first parameter expects a value of type `VARCHAR`, you should use `ps.setNull(1, java.sql.Types.VARCHAR)` to set a `null` value.

- Beware of caching prepared statements that refer to database objects whose structure subsequently may be modified. If you perform a data definition language (DDL) operation on a database object that is referenced in a cached prepared statement, the prepared statement will fail the next time it is executed. For instance, if you already have cached a statement that refers to an SQL table, and then subsequently drop and re-create the table, the cached statement no longer will remain valid. A prepared statement is bound to database objects that were in existence when the statement was added to the cache, and not when it is executed.

- Similarly, a prepared statement is bound to the datatypes of columns that were in use when the statement was cached. If you subsequently add or delete columns, or modify any of the columns involved, the cached statement most likely will fail the next time it is used.

- Caching a prepared statement may require the DBMS to reserve a dedicated open cursor for the statement. Open cursors are finite resources, and most databases impose a certain limit on the number of open cursors. If you cache too many prepared statements, you may run out of open cursors. In that case, you must either increase the number of allowed cursors or reduce the size of the statement cache.

If you do encounter unexpected JDBC problems when using prepared or callable statements, try disabling the cache. Then trace the actual problem and determine whether the cache is the cause of the problem. Statement caching can be disabled simply by setting the cache's size to 0.

Validating Database Connections

WebLogic Server is equipped with utilities that allow you to test JDBC connections using installed two-tier and wrapper JDBC drivers. The dbping utility lets you test JDBC connections when you're using two-tier JDBC drivers shipped with WebLogic. In order to invoke the dbping utility, you need to adjust the environment so that the *weblogic.jar* and JDBC driver classes are included in the system classpath. The syntax for the dbping utility is:

```
java utils.dbping DBMS user password DB
```

Here, the value for the DBMS argument can be one of the following constants: ORACLE, ORACLE_THIN, JCONNECT, JCONN2, INFORMIX4, or MSSQLSERVER4. Thus, to test whether you can use WebLogic's jDriver to connect to your Oracle installation, you can run the following command:

```
java utils.dbping ORACLE joebloggs secretpassword mydb
```

To test whether you can use WebLogic's jDriver to connect to an MS SQL Server database, run the following command:

```
java utils.dbping MSSQLSERVER4 sa secretpassword mydb@localhost:1433
```

The t3dbping utility lets you test JDBC connections when you're using a third-party JDBC driver. The t3dbping utility uses the RMI Driver to access the underlying JDBC driver:

```
java utils.t3dbping weblogicURL username password DB driverClass driverURL
```

The command requires a T3 URL to connect to a WebLogic instance (e.g., *t3://server:port*), the username and password of a valid database user, the name of the database, and the fully qualified class name and URL for the JDBC driver. Here's how you can ping an SQL Server database using Microsoft's SQL Server 2000 JDBC Driver:

```
java  utils.t3dbping  t3://localhost:7001
    sa somepassword   myDB@localhost:1433
    com.microsoft.jdbc.sqlserver.SQLServerDriver
    jdbc:microsoft:sqlserver
```

To ping an Oracle database using WebLogic's jDriver for Oracle, you would run the following command:

```
java  utils.t3dbping  t3://localhost:7001
    joebloggs somepassword myDB
    weblogic.jdbc.oci.Driver
    jdbc:weblogic:oracle
```

In this way, you can check whether the third-party JDBC drivers have been installed properly on the server.

WebLogic's Wrapper Drivers

In this section, we examine how you can use WebLogic's wrapper drivers to access preconfigured connection pools. Even though a data source is the recommended way for accessing a connection pool, you may need to use wrapper drivers for existing or legacy applications that are based on the JDBC 1.x API. WebLogic supports three kinds of wrapper drivers:

WebLogic RMI Driver
    Client-side applications can use the RMI Driver to access server-side connection pools.

WebLogic Pool Driver

Server-side applications can use the Pool Driver to access the connection pools directly.

WebLogic JTS Driver

The JTS Driver is identical to the Pool Driver, except that the database connections also can participate in distributed transactions.

Each driver provides vendor-neutral access to connection pools already configured in WebLogic. The J2EE standard recommends that you use a data source to access the pool.

The RMI Driver

WebLogic's RMI Driver is a Type 3 JDBC driver that enables client-side applications to access connection pools configured on WebLogic Server. The RMI Driver returns JDBC connections through the data source configured for the pool. The connection pool is configured as usual using a two-tier JDBC driver. As its name suggests, the RMI Driver provides RMI access to a server-side JDBC pool.

Let's look at how a client application obtains a JDBC connection from a connection pool:

```
java.sql.Driver wlDriver = (java.sql.Driver)
    Class.forName("weblogic.jdbc.rmi.Driver").newInstance( );

String url = "jdbc:weblogic:rmi";
java.util.Properties props = new java.util.Properties( );
props.put("weblogic.server.url", "t3://localhost:7001");
props.put("weblogic.jdbc.datasource", "myds");

//if a security policy applies to the data source,
//you need to set the following two properties as well
props.put("weblogic.user", "system");
props.put("weblogic.credential", "wlpassword");

java.sql.Connection conn = wlDriver.connect(url, props);
```

First, you need to create an instance of the WebLogic RMI Driver. Then you must specify a set of properties before you can invoke the connect( ) method on the driver. These properties include the T3 URL for the server, the name of the data source, and optional user credentials. The connect( ) method also takes a JDBC URL as a parameter; the value jdbc:weblogic:rmi is specific to the RMI Driver.

Once you invoke the connect( ) method, the RMI Driver on behalf of the client application contacts the server, performs the JNDI lookup using the name of the data source, and then invokes the getConnection( ) method on the data source obtained. Make sure that you include the *WL_HOME\server\lib\weblogic.jar* in your system classpath so that the RMI Driver classes are accessible to the external client.

Just like the data source, a client application that uses the RMI Driver benefits from row prefetching. Caching multiple rows on the client's end saves costly round trips to WebLogic whenever the client application scrolls through a ResultSet. However, row prefetching is enabled only if the type of the ResultSet is TYPE_FORWARD_ONLY or CONCUR_READ_ONLY. It is disabled when the client application runs in the same VM as the server. It also may be disabled if the ResultSet includes columns of types LONGVARCHAR, LONGVARBINARY, NULL, BLOB, CLOB, ARRAY, REF, STRUCT, or JAVA_OBJECT. In addition, certain methods of the ResultSet may not be supported if row prefetching is enabled. These methods relate to the streaming datatypes, datatypes not supported when row prefetching is enabled, and indiscriminate scrolling across the ResultSet. A data source has to be configured explicitly to use prefetching. Remember, row prefetching is not used if the client and server are running in the same JVM.

The Pool Driver

WebLogic's Pool Driver is a JDBC driver that provides access to connection pools for server-side applications (such as servlets, EJBs, etc.) running on WebLogic Server. The Pool Driver obtains connections from a JDBC pool that uses a two-tier JDBC driver installed on WebLogic Server. Just like the RMI Driver, you create an instance of the Pool Driver and then create a connection by supplying the URL for the Pool Driver and the name of a connection pool. You can either append the name of the JDBC pool to the driver URL or specify the name of the connection pool in a java.util.Properties object.

Here's how a servlet could request access to a connection pool using the Pool Driver:

```
java.sql.Driver wlDriver = (java.sql.Driver)
    Class.forName("weblogic.jdbc.pool.Driver").newInstance();

String url = "jdbc:weblogic:pool";
Properties props = new Properties();
props.put("connectionPoolID", "myPool");
Connection con = wlDriver.connect(url, props);

//this would have worked as well...
//Connection con = wlDriver.connect("jdbc:weblogic:pool:myPool", null);
```

Notice how we use the connect() method on the Driver object to obtain a database connection, instead of using the connect() method on DriverManager. This approach yields better performance because the connect() method on the Driver object is not synchronized. When you are done, you should invoke the close() method on the Connection object so that it can be released back to the pool.

 We recommend that you use a data source instead of a Pool Driver. Data sources are a standard J2EE feature and provide a more portable way of accessing connections.

The JTS Driver

Like the Pool Driver, WebLogic's JTS Driver is a server-side JDBC driver that returns connections from a JDBC pool that can participate in distributed transactions. The JTS Driver obtains connections from a JDBC pool that uses a two-tier JDBC driver configured for WebLogic Server. Here's an example of how you can access a connection pool using the JTS Driver:

```
//set up a transaction context before you use the JTS Driver
UserTransaction tx = (UserTransaction) ctx.lookup("java:comp/UserTransaction");
tx.begin();

//load the JTS driver
java.sql.Driver wlDriver = (java.sql.Driver)
   Class.forName("weblogic.jdbc.jts.Driver").newInstance();

// obtain a tx-aware connection from the pool
String url = "jdbc:weblogic:jts";
Properties props = new Properties();
props.put("connectionPoolID", "myPool");
Connection con = wlDriver.connect(url, props);

//this would have worked as well...
//Connection con = wlDriver.connect("jdbc:weblogic:jts:myPool", null);

// use the connection to perform any updates...
// close the connection when you're done...
con.close();

// commit all changes
tx.commit();
```

Once you've loaded the JTS Driver, you create a connection by supplying the URL for the JTS Driver and the name of the JDBC pool. You can either append the name of the JDBC pool to the driver URL, or specify the name in a java.util.Properties object.

Notice how we set up a transaction context *before* we use the JTS Driver to obtain a connection from the pool. Because the JTS Driver avoids two-phase commit, the distributed transaction may perform only those updates that use the JTS Driver to access the same connection pool. If you attempt to access another connection pool within the same transaction, you will get an exception when you later commit or roll back the transaction. Note that the connection isn't returned to the pool when you invoke the close() method. This happens only when the transaction commits or rolls back. In case of a transaction commit, WebLogic returns the connections to the pool after it commits the local transactions on all connections obtained during the lifetime of the distributed transaction in the current thread.

 We recommend that you use a data source backed by an XA-aware JDBC driver instead of a JTS Driver. Data sources are a standard J2EE feature and provide a more portable way of accessing connections.

Rowsets

A rowset is a container for tabular data, encapsulating a number of rows that have been retrieved from a data source. Rowsets were introduced as a standard extension in JDBC 2.0. The javax.sql.RowSet interface extends the java.sql.ResultSet interface with support for additional capabilities, such as using a data source to populate the rowset and assigning listeners that can be notified when the rowset is manipulated.

WebLogic comes with its own implementation of a *disconnected* rowset, sometimes called a *cached* rowset. This rowset can be populated in two ways: either from an existing ResultSet or using an SQL query that is executed against a data source. The rowset then can be sent to some remote client, updated at the client's end, and later returned to the server and synchronized with the underlying database. Because the population of the rowset and the synchronization of the rowset data with the database typically will occur in separate transactions, WebLogic provides a number of nifty optimistic concurrency features that you can employ to control the synchronization. You also can export the rowset and its metadata to an XML document and schema, respectively. Likewise, XML data can be imported into the rowset. WebLogic's rowset implementation can be found in the weblogic.jdbc.rowset package.

To illustrate the features of WebLogic's cached rowsets, we shall refer to a database table, stockitems, which is defined as follows:

```
CREATE TABLE stockitems (
    id        integer primary key,
    name      varchar(50),
    available integer
)
```

Moreover, we assume that you've configured a data source with the JNDI name myds.

Creating and Populating Rowsets

A disconnected rowset is manufactured from a RowSetFactory instance. The following example shows how to create a WLCachedRowSet instance:

```
import weblogic.jdbc.rowset.RowSetFactory;
import weblogic.jdbc.rowset.WLCachedRowSet;
//...
RowSetFactory factory = RowSetFactory.newInstance();
WLCachedRowSet rs = factory.newCachedRowSet();
```

Once you have created an empty cached rowset, you need to populate it with data. Often, this can be done using the rows of an existing ResultSet object, obtained from an earlier JDBC call:

```
javax.sql.DataSource ds = ctx.lookup("myds");
java.sql.Connection con = ds.getConnection();
java.sql.Statement st = con.createStatement("select id,name,available from
stockitems");
```

```
ResultSet resultSet = st.executeQuery( );
rs.populate(resultSet);
con.close( );
```

Another way to populate the rowset is to configure a data source and then issue an SQL query that returns one or more rows:

```
javax.sql.DataSource ds = ctx.lookup("myds");
rs.setDataSource(ds);
rs.setCommand("select id,name,available from stockitems");
rs.execute( );
```

In this case, when you invoke the execute( ) method on the rowset, WebLogic uses the configured data source to obtain a connection from the pool, and then uses the SQL query to load the rowset with the returned rows. Later in this chapter in the section "XML and Rowsets" we shall see how to also import the data from an XML document into a rowset.

Once a rowset is populated, it no longer holds on to any open cursors or connections with the database. The rowset is disconnected from the database, and provides an in-memory copy of the data held in the database at the time of population. No locks are held, either by the database or by the rowset.

Manipulating Rowsets

Because the RowSet interface extends the standard ResultSet interface, you can iterate over the rows using the next( ) method, and use the appropriate get*XXX*( ) methods to read the columns of each row. The following example illustrates this straightforward approach:

```
rs.beforeFirst( );
while (rs.next( )) {
    pw.println("Got " + rs.getInt("id") + ": " + rs.getString("name") +
            ":" + rs.getInt("available"));
}
```

Inserting rows into an existing rowset is equally easy. The following example shows how to insert rows into our cached rowset:

```
rs.moveToInsertRow( );              // move to the special "insert" row
rs.updateInt("id", count++);
rs.updateString("name", "carrots");
rs.updateInt("available", 3+count);
rs.insertRow( );                    // mark the row for insertion
rs.updateInt("id", count++);
rs.updateString("name", "pears");
rs.updateInt("available", 3+count);
rs.insertRow( );                    // mark the row for insertion
rs.acceptChanges( );
rs.moveToCurrentRow( );             // return to the current position in the rowset
```

Because the rowset represents an in-memory copy of data held in the database, any updates you make to the rowset occur in memory. For this reason, you must invoke the acceptChanges( ) method on the rowset to flush any rowset changes back to the database. In the preceding example, the synchronization is handled by the rowset implementation, which issues the appropriate SQL INSERT commands to the underlying database.

Because the cached rowset implements the java.io.Serializable interface, you can send the cached rowset either as an RMI parameter or a return value. If you do send it to a remote client, typically the client will not need to invoke the acceptChanges( ) method. Instead, it will modify the rowset and send it back to the server, which will perform a more advanced synchronization.

To update or delete existing rows within a rowset, you often need to manipulate the metadata associated with the rowset. In general, when you populate the rowset using an SQL query, the rowset implementation relies on the ResultSetMetaData interface to learn about the tables and column names of the data in the rowset. Unfortunately, not all JDBC drivers will supply the metadata for the set of rows returned after issuing the SQL query. For instance, a JDBC driver may return an empty string when asked for the table name that is associated with a particular column. Without the table name, the rowset can be used only in a read-only fashion. In such cases, you often will need to step in and fill in some of the gaps in the rowset metadata. For example, suppose you wish to update the second row loaded into the rowset:

```
// Updates the second row of the rowset
rs.beforeFirst();
rs.next(); rs.next();
rs.updateString("name", "peanuts");
rs.updateRow();    // always call updateRow after update
rs.acceptChanges();
```

Even though this code looks pretty bland, you will get the following exception when you execute this code against our setup:

```
java.sql.SQLException: Unable to determine the table name for column: 'id'. Please
ensure that you've called WLRowSetMetaData.setTableName to set a table name for this
column.
```

A similar situation arises if you try and delete rows from the rowset:

```
rs.beforeFirst();
rs.next();          // Find the row to delete
rs.deleteRow();     // Mark it for deletion
rs.next();          // Find the next one to delete
rs.deleteRow();     // Mark it for deletion
rs.acceptChanges(); // Perform the deletions
```

The reason for this is clear—sadly, our JDBC driver has taken the liberty of supplying incomplete metadata for the rowset. To rectify this situation, and to ensure that your code works across JDBC drivers, you need to manipulate the rowset metadata so that any in-memory row updates or deletes can be synchronized properly with the database. The following code shows how to retrieve the metadata for the rowset, set the table name for all columns in the rowset, and identify the primary key column:

```
WLRowSetMetaData metaData = (WLRowSetMetaData) rs.getMetaData( );
metaData.setTableName("stockitems");
metaData.setPrimaryKeyColumn("id", true);
```

Given these changes to the rowset metadata, the earlier row updates and deletes will now succeed. Note that when you set a column to be the primary key, that column is made read-only. Thus, if you need to manipulate the primary key column, you must call the setReadOnly( ) method to make it read-write:

```
metadata.setReadOnly("id",false);
```

Fortunately, you also can minimize the amount of metadata hacking by invoking the executeAndGuessTableName( ) method on the WLCachedRowSet instance. Not only does this method populate the cached rowset, but it also parses the SQL query and extracts the table name (the first word following the SQL FROM keyword within the query). The executeAndGuessTableNameAndPrimaryKeys( ) method, in addition, looks up the table in java.sql.DatabaseMetaData and tries to determine the table's primary key columns. The following code sample shows how to avoid metadata hacking and eliminate the earlier SQLException:

```
rs.setDataSource(ds);
rs.setCommand("select id,name,available from stockitems");
rs.executeAndGuessTableNameAndPrimaryKeys( );
// find the row you want to delete, then
rs.updateString("name", "peanuts");
rs.updateRow( );
rs.acceptChanges( );
```

Finally, if the SQL query used to populate a rowset uses a column alias, you need to update the rowset metadata and specify the name of the actual column that should be associated with the alias so that the rowset implementation knows which table column to update. Here is how you specify the true column name for the alias:

```
metadata.setWriteColumnName("aliasName", "tableColumnName");
```

Transactions and Rowsets

WebLogic's rowsets can participate in transactions, just like any other JDBC resource. If the rowset needs to participate in a distributed transaction, you must ensure that the rowset is assigned an XA-aware data source. In this case, any optimistic conflicts that arise during synchronization will cause the distributed transaction to roll back. If the rowset is not being used within a distributed transaction, the rowset will use a simple local transaction. During the synchronization, the rowset implementation will first execute a setAutoCommit(false) on the connection obtained from the pool, execute any SQL statements to reflect the in-memory changes to the rowset, and finally invoke the commit( ) on the same connection. If an optimistic conflict occurs in this scenario, the local transaction rolls back, and of course, the database remains unchanged.

Synchronizing Rowsets

WebLogic's RowSet objects implement the java.io.Serializable interface. This means you can pass rowsets as an argument to an EJB method, or define an EJB method that returns a rowset populated with data from a data source. For example, you could define an EJB method that returns all items that need to be restocked. The EJB method easily could use a RowSet object as the container for the data. Now imagine a supplier that remotely updates the rowset. When the rowset is sent back to the EJB so that it can update its stock availability, it must synchronize the data in the rowset with the actual data in the database. Of course, you have no guarantee that the database hasn't changed since the rowset was last populated.

WebLogic provides a number of optimistic concurrency schemes that it can use to synchronize the rowset. Some of these schemes are reminiscent of the optimistic concurrency setting for EJBs, discussed in Chapter 11. Optimistic concurrency requires WebLogic to conditionally update the database, based on SQL that matches the rowset data and database data. By default, the rowset implementation performs a consistency check against all modified columns. In the rest of this section, we look at the various optimistic concurrency schemes for rowsets using a number of SQL updates as examples. The same discussion holds for any calls to the deleteRow( ) method on the rowset as well.

You need to access the rowset metadata and set the optimistic concurrency policy before you synchronize the rowset changes with the database. As usual, you must invoke the acceptChanges( ) method on the WLCachedRowset instance to execute the synchronization. The constants that define the different optimistic concurrency schemes are available in the WLRowSetMetaData interface. Here is an example:

```
try {
  WLRowSetMetaData metaData = (WLRowSetMetaData) rs.getMetaData( );
  metaData.setOptimisticPolicy(WLRowSetMetaData.VERIFY_READ_COLUMNS);
  rs.acceptChanges( );
} catch (OptimisticConflictException e_oc) {
  // Handle this in whichever way is suited to your application
}
```

If the rowset implementation detects that the underlying data in the database has changed since the time the rowset was populated, the synchronization attempt fails with an OptimisticConflictException, as indicated earlier. The choice as to which optimistic concurrency should be used will depend on the needs of your application. Your decision will be a simple trade-off between data consistency and the probability of an optimistic conflict.

Assume that you've read a single row from the stockitems table, updated the value of the available field, and now need to persist these changes back to the database. The following code sample illustrates this scenario:

```
//Assume that for id=1, name="melons", available=4
rs.setCommand("select id,name,available from stockitems where id=1");
```

```
rs.executeAndGuessTableNameAndPrimaryKeys( );
rs.next( );
rs.updateInt("available", 10);
rs.updateRow( );
rs.acceptChanges( );
```

Now we are in a position to examine the different optimistic concurrency schemes.

VERIFY_READ_COLUMNS

This option is the default optimistic concurrency policy. Any updates or deletes that occur during synchronization must ensure that none of the columns in the rowset has changed. This scheme provides you with the strongest consistency check during synchronization. Refer to the VERIFY_AUTO_VERSION_COLUMNS policy for a cheaper implementation. For the example, this means that the rowset implementation will synchronize the update by issuing the following SQL:

```
UPDATE stockitems SET available=10
    WHERE id=1 AND name='melons' AND available=4
```

VERIFY_AUTO_VERSION_COLUMNS

This optimistic concurrency policy assumes that the underlying database table has an additional version column, of integer type. It uses the specified version column to check for consistency, and automatically increments the version column as part of the database update. The next example shows how to enable this scheme. It assumes that a version column called version is present in the stockitems table:

```
WLRowSetMetaData metaData = (WLRowSetMetaData) rs.getMetaData( );
metaData.setOptimisticPolicy(WLRowSetMetaData.VERIFY_AUTO_VERSION_COLUMNS);
metaData.setAutoVersionColumn("version", true);
metaData.acceptChanges( );
```

Thus, if the version column was set to 1 when the rowset was populated, the rowset update will be synchronized using the following SQL:

```
UPDATE stockitems SET available=10, version=2 WHERE id=1
    AND version=1
```

In this way, auto-versioning provides you with a very strong consistency check, at little cost. However, any other clients that update the stockitems table must also update the version column appropriately.

VERIFY_VERSION_COLUMNS

This policy behaves just like the VERIFY_AUTO_VERSION_COLUMNS policy, except that the rowset implementation does not increment the version column. Choose this optimistic concurrency policy, for instance, if you have assigned a database trigger that automatically increments the version column when the row is updated. In our example, the rowset implementation will use the following SQL to synchronize the update:

```
UPDATE stockitems SET available=10 WHERE id=1
    AND version=1
```

VERIFY_MODIFIED_COLUMNS

This optimistic concurrency policy ensures that only the updated columns are checked for consistency. Of course, the primary key columns also are matched. This scheme ignores any nonprimary key columns that were not updated. For our example, this means that the rowset will be synchronized using the following SQL:

```
UPDATE stockitems SET available=10 WHERE id=1
    AND available=4
```

VERIFY_SELECTED_COLUMNS

This optimistic concurrency policy matches the primary key columns and enforces the consistency checks on a selected number of columns only. This scheme ignores any nonprimary key columns and columns not selected for consistency checks. You must call the setVerifySelectedColumn( ) method to explicitly select those columns that you want verified during synchronization. The next example shows how to force the verification of the available column:

```
WLRowSetMetaData metaData = (WLRowSetMetaData) rs.getMetaData( );
metaData.setOptimisticPolicy(WLRowSetMetaData.VERIFY_SELECTED_COLUMNS);
metaData.setVerifySelectedColumn("available", true);
rs.acceptChanges( );
```

This results in the following SQL being used to synchronize the rowset update:

```
UPDATE stockitems SET available=10 WHERE id=1
    AND available=4
```

VERIFY_NONE

This optimistic concurrency policy matches only the primary key columns. No consistency checks are made, and the rowset implementation blindly overwrites changes to the table without verifying whether the underlying data has changed. For our example, this means the following SQL is used to synchronize the rowset update:

```
UPDATE stockitems SET available=10 WHERE id=1
```

Caveats

Regardless of the optimistic concurrency policy you choose, the following caveats always hold true during synchronization:

- Only rows that are marked for update or delete are verified against the database. Read-only rows are not verified against the database.
- BLOB or CLOB columns are never verified against the database.
- If a rowset spans multiple database tables, only the updated tables are verified.

The easiest way to debug synchronization problems is to view the SQL that is being generated. Call the WLRowSetMetaData.setVerboseSQL( ) method to enable this debugging capability. When this debugging is enabled for the rowset, the rowset implementation sends the generated SQL to System.out during synchronization.

Group deletes and JDBC batching

WebLogic provides two ways to optimize how a rowset synchronizes its in-memory updates with the database:

Group deletes

Normally when you delete multiple rows from a rowset, the rowset implementation emits an SQL DELETE statement for each deleted row during synchronization. By enabling group deletes, you can determine the number of delete operations that should be issued in a single SQL DELETE statement. In the case of the earlier examples, depending on your optimistic policy, the rowset implementation will generate the following SQL command:

```
// Deletes two items in a single delete
DELETE FROM stockitems WHERE
   (id=1 AND version = 1) OR  (id=2 AND version = 1)
```

The following code enables this feature, and sets the group delete size for the rowset:

```
metaData.setGroupDeletes(true);
metaData.setGroupDeleteSize(42);
```

JDBC batching

WebLogic's rowset implementation also supports JDBC 2.0 statement batching. Instead of sending each individual statement to the JDBC driver, the rowset implementation sends a collection of statements in a batch. To enable statement batching, you should invoke the setBatchInserts( ), setBatchDeletes( ), or setBatchUpdates( ) method on a WLCachedRowSet instance. By default, statement batching is disabled. These methods must be invoked before you synchronize any rowset changes using the acceptChanges( ) method.

For Oracle JDBC drivers, the rowset implementation handles statement batching slightly differently. Here, batch updates automatically generate an additional SELECT query, which is used to determine whether an optimistic conflict occurred. Furthermore, batch deletes in Oracle are executed as a group delete.

Rowsets Spanning Multiple Tables

The data in a rowset could be populated from a join of a number of tables. For example, suppose your database also includes the following table:

```
CREATE TABLE itemprice (
   id         integer primary key,
   price      double
)
```

In that case, you could populate the rowset with the following SQL query:

```
rs.setCommand("select i.id,i.name,p.price from stockitems as i join itemprice as p on
i.id = p.id");
rs.execute( );
```

When a rowset spans multiple tables, any in-memory updates and deletes as well as the optimistic concurrency policy all work slightly differently:

- During synchronization, only the tables pertaining to those columns that have changed are checked, no matter which optimistic concurrency policy you configure for the rowset. In our example, if we change the item price in a row, the name of the item will never be checked for consistency.

- Rowset synchronization doesn't take foreign keys or any other constraints into account. This may lead to potential problems when updating multiple tables.

- If the rowset is populated by a join, a deleteRow( ) on the rowset will delete all of the records involved. In our example, if we invoke the deleteRow( ) on the rowset, records will be deleted from the stockitems and the itemprice tables during synchronization.

Often, you will need a much simpler delete policy. For example, if you have a one-to-many relationship between two tables, you may want to delete only the records in the table on the "many" side of the relationship. To achieve this delete behavior, you simply need to call the WLRowSetMetaData.setWriteTableName( ) method. The following example shows how a deleteRow( ) causes only the related record in the itemprice table to be deleted during synchronization:

```
WLRowSetMetaData metaData = (WLRowSetMetaData)rs.getMetaData( );
metaData.setTableName("price", "itemprice");  // Help the metadata
metaData.setWriteTableName("itemprice");      // Only touch the itemprice table
rs.beforeFirst( );  rs.next( );               // Delete the first row
rs.deleteRow( );
rs.acceptChanges( );
```

The setWriteTableName( ) method effectively marks any column that doesn't belong to the write table as read-only.

XML and Rowsets

The data in a rowset can be exported to an XML document. In addition, the rowset metadata can be exported to an XML schema that describes the structure of the XML document. This provides an alternative way to serialize a rowset. An XML document and schema also can be used to construct a rowset, thereby providing an alternative way to populate a rowset. Use the writeXML( ) method on a WLCachedRowSet instance to export the rowset to an XML document, and use the writeXMLSchema( ) method on the WLRowSetMetaData instance to export the metadata to an XML schema. These methods use WebLogic's XML Streaming API, described later in Chapter 18. The following example shows how to create a schema and XML output file from a rowset:

```
XMLOutputStreamFactory xof = XMLOutputStreamFactory.newInstance( );
XMLOutputStream xos = null;
FileOutputStream os = new FileOutputStream("/tmp/stockitems.xsd");
xos = xof.newDebugOutputStream(os);
```

```
metaData.writeXMLSchema(xos);
os.close( );
xos.close( );
os = new FileOutputStream("/tmp/stockitems.xml");
xos = xof.newDebugOutputStream(oss);
rs.writeXML(xos);
os.close( );
xos.close( );
```

Here is an example of the generated XML that represents the state of the rowset:

```
<TableRowSet  xmlns="http://www.openuri.org"
  xmlns:xsi="http://www.w3.org/2001/XMLSchema-instance"
  xmlns:wld="http://www.bea.com/2002/10/weblogicdata"
  xsi:schemaLocation="http://www.openuri.org/TableRowSet.xsd">
  <TableRow   wld:RowId="0">
  <id>1</id>
  <name>carrots</name>
  <available>52</available>
  </TableRow>
</TableRowSet>
```

Populating a rowset from an XML document and schema is equally easy. Use the loadXMLSchema( ) method to load the rowset metadata, and use the loadXML( ) method to load the data into the rowset itself:

```
XMLInputStreamFactory xif = XMLInputStreamFactory.newInstance( );
WLCachedRowSet rs = factory.newCachedRowSet( );

//load the metadata information from the XML schema
WLRowSetMetaData metaData = (WLRowSetMetaData) rs.getMetaData( );
FileInputStream fis = new FileInputStream("/tmp/stockitems.xsd");
XMLInputStream xis = xif.newInputStream(fis);
metaData.loadXMLSchema(xis);
fis.close( );
xis.close( );

//load the rowset data from the XML file
fis = new FileInputStream("/tmp/stockitems.xml");
xis = xif.newInputStream(fis);
rs.loadXML(xis);
fis.close( );
xis.close( );
```

Table 5-7 explains how the JDBC types are mapped to XML schema types.

Table 5-7. How JDBC types are mapped to XML schema types

JDBC type	XML schema type
BIGINT	xsd:long
BINARY	xsd:base64Binary
BIT	xsd:boolean
BLOB	xsd:base64Binary

Table 5-7. How JDBC types are mapped to XML schema types (continued)

JDBC type	XML schema type
BOOLEAN	xsd:boolean
CHAR	xsd:string
DATE	xsd:dateTime
DECIMAL	xsd:decimal
DOUBLE	xsd:decimal
FLOAT	xsd:float
INTEGER	xsd:int
LONGVARBINARY	xsd:base64Binary
LONGVARCHAR	xsd:string
NUMERIC	xsd:integer
REAL	xsd:double
SMALLINT	xsd:short
TIME	xsd:dateTime
TIMESTAMP	xsd:dateTime
TINYINT	xsd:byte
VARBINARY	xsd:base64Binary
VARCHAR	xsd:string

Table 5-8 describes how XML schema types are mapped to equivalent JDBC types.

Table 5-8. Mapping between XML schema types and JDBC types

XML schema type	JDBC type
base64Binary	BINARY
boolean	BOOLEAN
byte	SMALLINT
dateTime	DATE
decimal	DECIMAL
double	DOUBLE
float	FLOAT
hexBinary	BINARY
int	INTEGER
integer	NUMERIC
long	BIGINT
short	SMALLINT
string	VARCHAR

Clustering and JDBC Connections

WebLogic Server supports *clustered JDBC*, which means that some of the JDBC objects are aware of the cluster and will behave differently in a cluster. For instance, a connection pool is not cluster-aware. Assigning a connection pool to a cluster is equivalent to assigning it individually to each server in the cluster, and thus, there is no change in its behavior. A data source, on the other hand, *is* cluster-aware. If you assign a data source to a cluster, it behaves differently from a data source that is targeted to each member of the cluster individually. In this case, it can distribute connection requests across all copies of the pool assigned to the different members of the cluster. A data source internally uses WebLogic's RMI Driver to obtain a connection from the pool. The RMI Driver then directs the connection request to a pool on one of the clustered servers. The client is then "pinned" to that server for the duration of the database transaction, and until the connection is released.

Now, if we consider a data source that is targeted to a cluster, and each Managed Server in the cluster has a JDBC pool associated with the data source, WebLogic ensures the JDBC requests to the data source are handled uniformly by all members of the cluster. When an external client requests a connection from a data source assigned to the cluster, it obtains a *replica-aware* stub for the data source. The replica-aware stub maintains a list of all active servers in the cluster that host the particular data source. The clustered stub encapsulates the load-balancing logic and can distribute the connection requests evenly across the Managed Servers in the cluster. Because a data source is cluster-aware, if one of the Managed Servers fails, the client can make another connection request, which then will be handled by any one of the remaining members of the cluster.

A cluster-aware data source, however, behaves differently for local connection requests. If a server-side application (such as a servlet, EJB, etc.) running on one of the Managed Servers in a cluster requests a connection from a cluster-aware data source targeted to that same cluster, the connection is returned from the local JDBC pool on the same server, and not from any other member of the cluster. So, a server-side request for a JDBC connection from a clustered data source always will resolve to the *local* connection pool (or multipool) assigned to it, and never to a *remote* connection pool on another cluster server. The connection is then "pinned" to the local server for the duration of the database transaction, and until the connection is released.

Failover and Load Balancing

By default, WebLogic doesn't support connection failover. If a server instance dies, all active JDBC connections are killed, all active transactions are aborted and rolled back, and all JDBC objects associated with the dead connections become invalid. However, clustered JDBC does enable a client to reconnect when an existing connection fails. The cluster-aware nature of data sources allows an external client to request another connection when the Managed Server that held the original JDBC connection dies. A server-side application, on the other hand, fails to reconnect to the database when its local connection pool dies because a cluster-aware data source always resolves to the local pool. If you need failover for server-side applications, use a multipool configured for high availability. Only then can WebLogic fail over to another connection pool if the existing pool fails.

If you have replicated, synchronized database instances, you can achieve database failover using a multipool operating in high-availability mode. The multipool would be configured with several connection pools, each pointing to different instances of the same database. In high-availability mode, WebLogic continues to return connections from the first pool in the list, until it fails for some reason. Only then does WebLogic try to obtain a connection from the next pool in the list. If the multipool directs a connection request to a connection pool that has reached maximum capacity and an available connection can't be obtained within the configured wait period, a PoolLimitSQLException is generated. It does *not* mean that the connection request is forwarded automatically to the next pool in the multipool. The only way to resolve this issue is to either increase the capacity of the connection pool, or increase the wait period.

 A multipool operating in high-availability mode can support connection failover only if the TestConnectionsOnReserve attribute has been enabled for the connection pools. It uses the test to determine whether it has a bad connection; if so, it fails over to the next pool in the multipool.

A cluster-aware data source provides limited support for balancing the load of connection requests from external clients. This is because the replica-aware stub simply distributes the connection requests evenly across the members of the cluster. It does not react to the current load of the connection pools. For instance, a connection request to a clustered data source still could be redirected to a Managed Server where the connection pool has reached maximum capacity and all connections are busy.

On the other hand, you could use a multipool to balance the load of JDBC connections over its ordered list of connection pools. In this case, you assign the multipool to the cluster and the connection pools to all Managed Servers, and use a data source to tap into the multipool. In a load-balancing multipool, the connection pools are accessed in a round-robin scheme. For each successive client request, the list is rotated so that the next pool can be tapped.

CHAPTER 6

Transactions

A Java program typically will use the JDBC API to access the underlying database in some transactional context. Transactions are used to ensure that multiple operations are executed as an atomic unit, and to maintain a consistent view of data during concurrent access. All JDBC-compliant products are required to offer support for local transactions, including features such as auto-commit, transaction isolation levels, and savepoints (if the product is JDBC 3.0–compliant). Some J2EE services, such as entity beans and transactional JMS message delivery, require distributed transactions that span multiple connections and/or resources.

The Java Transaction API (JTA) provides high-level client access to distributed transactions. This framework defines a transaction manager that controls transaction boundaries and upholds the two-phase commit (2PC) semantics across multiple resource managers. WebLogic Server acts as the Transaction Processing (TP) monitor, providing the runtime support for managing the boundaries of your transactions. It protects the integrity of your transactions and ensures that all resources participating in a transaction are updated correctly, even after a system failure.

This chapter focuses on WebLogic's support for transactions. We look at distributed transactions, transaction attributes, and the role of the 2PC protocol. We examine how the EJB container manages EJBs when they are involved in distributed transactions, and how EJBs can create their own transaction boundaries. We also look at WebLogic's transaction service, its features, and how you can use the JTA interface to initiate your own transactions. In addition, we look at how to configure JTA transactions and monitor them through WebLogic's transaction logs. Finally, we explore how WebLogic allows you to recover failed transactions after a server crash, and offload the transaction recovery onto a backup server, if needed.

Overview

A transaction encapsulates a sequence of operations that are treated as a single *atomic* unit. The results of the operations within a transaction are committed only if all the operations are completed successfully. Otherwise, the transaction is rolled back and all changes resulting from the operations are abandoned. Regardless of whether the changes are committed or rolled back, the resources participating in the transaction must always be left in a *consistent* state. Intermediate changes made during the lifetime of a transaction are *isolated* from the outside world—they remain invisible until the transaction has completed. A transaction, if completed successfully, must ensure the changes are persistent or *durable*.

WebLogic Server provides the infrastructure for transaction management and guarantees the integrity of your transactions. As a TP monitor, WebLogic can manage transactions and coordinate access across various enterprise stores, including a relational database, JMS servers, or any transaction-aware resource. WebLogic guarantees that updates to multiple resources occur correctly and accurately when a transaction completes successfully, and the entire transaction rolls back if any of the operations fail.

JDBC Transactions

The JDBC API supports local transactions, where the scope of the JDBC transaction does not extend beyond the lifetime of the associated JDBC connection. If a connection has auto-commit enabled, the JDBC driver is forced to commit any changes made after the completion of every SQL statement. In effect, every SQL statement executed against the Connection object is encapsulated in a transaction. If auto-commit is disabled for a connection, the JDBC client is required to manually commit the transaction by invoking the commit( ) method on the Connection object. Alternatively, the JDBC client can indicate failure and drop all changes made by calling the rollback( ) method on the Connection object. The commit( ) and rollback( ) methods also are required to release any database locks held by the associated Connection object.

An orthogonal issue to JDBC transactions is the level of concurrent access from within a current transaction—i.e., the isolation level between multiple transactions. There are three ways in which two concurrent transactions can interact:

Dirty reads
    These occur when Transaction A can see uncommitted changes to data made by Transaction B.

Nonrepeatable reads
    These occur in the following scenario: Transaction A reads a row, Transaction B modifies the same row, and then Transaction A rereads the updated row and gets differing results.

Phantom reads
    Phantom reads can occur in the following situation: Transaction A reads rows that satisfy a WHERE clause, Transaction B inserts additional rows that satisfy the same search criteria, and then Transaction A reevaluates the WHERE clause to get new "phantom" rows.

A JDBC driver can support the following isolation levels, depending on the kind of interactions you would like to allow:

TRANSACTION_READ_UNCOMMITTED
A transaction is allowed to read uncommitted changes to data.

TRANSACTION_READ_COMMITTED
Any changes within a transaction remain invisible to the outside world, until the transaction is committed.

TRANSACTION_REPEATABLE_READ
Dirty and nonrepeatable reads are disallowed, but phantom reads may occur.

TRANSACTION_SERIALIZABLE
This is the most restrictive isolation level, and emulates serial execution of both transactions. Dirty, nonrepeatable, and phantom reads are disallowed.

The JDBC driver determines the default isolation level for a connection. Typically, it is the default isolation level for the underlying database. Use the setTransactionIsolation() method to adjust the isolation level for a Connection object. A JDBC driver that doesn't support a particular isolation level can replace it with a higher, more restrictive isolation level. The higher the isolation level, the lower the degree of concurrent access. So, the isolation level for a connection has a direct impact on the performance of your applications. If a JDBC driver does not support transactions, the getTransactionIsolation() method on the Connection object returns the value TRANSACTION_NONE.

Distributed Transactions

A distributed transaction involves updates that span multiple connections to resource managers (databases, EJBs, JMS, etc.). A transaction manager coordinates these updates across multiple resource managers using the two-phase commit protocol. Here are the major players involved in a distributed transaction:

- A transactional application is one that initiates the transaction context. This could be a client Java application, the EJB container, or even a JMS message producer.
- A transaction manager maintains the transactional boundaries on behalf of the application and coordinates all resource managers participating in a transaction.
- A resource manager manages the underlying data. In the context of JDBC, the DBMS server is the resource manager.

The two-phase commit protocol involves the following two phases:

A prepare phase
All updates involved are recorded in a transaction log, and each resource manager (on behalf of the resource) indicates whether it can make the requested change.

A commit phase

    If all resource managers vote to commit, all the resources participating in the transaction are updated permanently. If any resource manager votes to roll back, all the resources participating in the transaction roll back to their previous consistent state.

WebLogic Server provides full transaction support for applications that use EJBs or the JTA interface.

A J2EE application that needs support for distributed transactions must use the JTA. Later in this chapter, in the section "Using JTA Transactions," we look at an example of how an application can employ JTA transactions.

If an application performs JDBC updates as part of a distributed transaction, it must use transaction-aware data sources. Thus, you need to interface with the configured connection pool using an XA-aware data source that has been bound to the JNDI tree. You must use transactional data sources especially if your application uses enterprise beans that support container-managed transactions. If the JDBC driver is not XA-compliant and your transactions involve updates to other resources as well, you must enable two-phase commit emulation for the XA-aware data source. Only then can a connection obtained from the data source participate in XA transactions.

EJB Transactions

WebLogic supports two flavors of EJB transactions:

Container-managed transactions

    Here, the EJB container manages the transaction boundaries. The standard *ejb-jar.xml* deployment descriptor contains transaction attributes that determine how the EJB container handles transactions across method invocations.

Bean-managed transactions

    Here, the EJB implementation is responsible for demarcating transaction boundaries. The bean provider typically uses the transaction methods on the Connection object or the UserTransaction object to ensure all updates occur atomically.

The transaction-type element in the standard *ejb-jar.xml* descriptor file indicates whether the EJB will manage its own transaction boundaries, or defer all transaction management responsibilities to the EJB container. Both models have their benefits and limitations, and both impose certain restrictions on your EJB code.

Container-Managed Transactions

Container-managed transactions simplify your EJB code because you no longer need to explicitly mark transaction boundaries. You can configure your EJBs so that

WebLogic's EJB container automatically creates a new transaction context before delegating the call to the actual EJB method, and commits the transaction just before the method exits. The EJB container rolls back the transaction if a system exception is raised or if the method indicates a rollback should occur. Alternatively, you can indicate that an EJB method must never be executed within a transaction context. Of course, an EJB method need not support transactions at all. All of these options can be configured transparently, without any changes to your EJB code.

Each method call is associated with, at most, one transaction. The J2EE framework does not allow for nested or multiple transactions.

With container-managed transactions, the transactional behavior for your EJBs is determined at deployment time. The standard *ejb-jar.xml* deployment file lets you specify the transaction attributes for your EJB methods. A *transaction attribute* determines the scope of a transaction when an EJB method is invoked. It specifies whether an EJB method executes within an existing transaction context. An EJB method can have one of the following transaction attributes:

Never

> The method must never execute within an existing transaction context. If the client invokes such a method within a transaction context, the EJB container must throw a RemoteException (EJBException for local client).

NotSupported

> The EJB container ensures that the method doesn't execute in a transaction context. If one exists, the container suspends the transaction for the duration of the EJB method, and resumes the transaction once the method exits.

Supports

> The method executes with or without an existing transaction context. A new transaction isn't created before the method starts, but if one exists, it will be used, and it may influence the outcome of the transaction.

Required

> The method requires a transaction context before it is invoked. If one doesn't exist, a new transaction is created before the method starts.

Mandatory

> The method must never execute without a transaction context. If an existing transaction context doesn't exist, the EJB container must throw a TransactionRequiredException.

RequiresNew

> A new transaction is created regardless of whether a client transaction context exists. The existing transaction is suspended, the new transaction is created for the duration of the method call, and the existing transaction is resumed once the method terminates.

The following XML fragment shows how you can adjust the transaction settings for the remote EJB methods of the Registration EJB, using the `container-transaction` element in the *ejb-jar.xml* deployment descriptor:

```xml
<!-- ejb-jar.xml entry -->
<assembly-descriptor>
  <container-transaction>
    <method>
      <ejb-name>RegistrationEJB</ejb-name>
      <method-intf>Remote</method-intf>
      <method-name>registerForCourse</method-name>
    </method>
    ...
    <trans-attribute>Required</trans-attribute>
  </container-transaction>
  <container-transaction>
    <method>
      <ejb-name>RegistrationEJB</ejb-name>
      <method-intf>Remote</method-intf>
      <method-name>getCourses</method-name>
    </method>
    ...
    <trans-attribute>Supports</trans-attribute>
  </container-transaction>
  ...
</assembly-descriptor>
```

The value of the `trans-attribute` element in the *ejb-jar.xml* descriptor sets the transaction attribute for EJB methods. In this case, the `registerForCourse( )` EJB method must be invoked only from within an existing transaction. If the EJB client doesn't initiate a JTA transaction before invoking the `Registration` EJB, the EJB container will create one automatically before delegating the call to the method. The `getCourses( )` EJB method is configured to support transactions. So, if an EJB client created a transaction before invoking the method, the method will participate in the eventual outcome of the transaction.

In WebLogic Server, if an EJB supports container-managed transactions, the default transaction attribute for the EJB methods is `Supports`. This means any EJB method that runs within the context of an existing transaction can affect its outcome. Thus, if an EJB method throws a system exception, the EJB container must roll back the existing transaction. However, if an EJB method has a transaction setting of `NotSupported` or `RequiresNew`, the EJB container needs to suspend the current transaction before it can delegate the call to the method. In this case, the EJB method will have no effect on the outcome of the original transaction.

An EJB method can cause the EJB container to roll back a transaction in two ways:

- It can throw a system exception (a `RuntimeException` or an `EJBException`).
- It can invoke the `setRollbackOnly( )` method on the `EJBContext`.

In either case, any transaction-aware updates made by the EJB method will be rolled back. An EJB method that supports container-managed transactions must not interfere explicitly with an existing transaction context. So, within an EJB method:

- You must not invoke the `commit()`, `setAutoCommit()`, and `rollback()` methods on the `Connection` object.
- You must not call the `getUserTransaction()` method on the `EJBContext` or use the `UserTransaction` object.

These operations are allowed only if the EJB needs to explicitly demarcate transaction boundaries—i.e., if the EJB methods support bean-managed transactions.

Bean-Managed Transactions

Container-managed transactions have a limitation. A call to an EJB method can be associated with, at most, one transaction at a time. If this constraint makes it difficult for you to write your EJB code, you should consider using bean-managed transactions. *Bean-managed transactions* allow you to explicitly set the transaction boundaries for your EJB methods. For instance, now you could write an EJB method that updates the database as follows:

```
begin transaction
...
update table-A
...
if (condition-x) {
  commit transaction
}
else if (condition-y) {
  update table-B
  commit transaction
}
else {
  rollback transaction
  begin transaction
  update table-C
  commit transaction
}
...
```

If the EJB supports bean-managed transactions, you must ensure that the transaction-type element in the standard *ejb-jar.xml* descriptor file has the value Bean. In this case, the EJB method must use the `UserTransaction` interface to explicitly demarcate transaction boundaries. The following example shows how an EJB method can perform multiple updates using the `UserTransaction` interface:

```
public void doUpdates(int id) {
  try {
    //create a UserTransaction instance using the EJBContext for the bean
    UserTransaction tx = ctx.getUserTransaction();

    tx.begin();
```

```
    //ds is a reference to an XA-aware data source
    Connection con = ds.getConnection();
    Statement st = con.createStatement();
    st.executeUpdate("update tableA set ... where id=" + id);

    Connection con2 = ds.getConnection();
    st = con2.createStatement();
    st.executeUpdate("update tableB set ... where id=" + id);
    tx.commit();
}
catch (Exception ex) {
  try {
    tx.rollback();
    throw new EJBException("Tx Failed:" + ex.getMessage());
  }
  catch (SystemException ese) {
    throw new EJBException("Tx Rollback Failed:" + ese.getMessage());
  }
}
finally {
  //release open connections
}
}
```

Here, the distributed transaction is bound by the calls to the begin( ) and commit( ) methods on the UserTransaction object. Note that we're using an XA-aware data source to return JDBC connections so that they can participate in the JTA transaction. You also can look in the JNDI tree under *java:comp/UserTransaction* in order to obtain a reference to the UserTransaction object:

```
InitialContext ctx = new InitialContext();
UserTransaction tx =
  (UserTransaction) ic.lookup("java:comp/UserTransaction");
```

This is functionally equivalent to calling the getUserTransaction( ) method on the EJBContext.

With bean-managed transactions, your EJB code must explicitly specify when the JDBC updates are committed and when the changes are rolled back. The EJB container remains a silent spectator in this respect because the EJB method itself is entirely responsible for marking the boundaries of the transaction(s). If a transaction context does exist before the invocation of an EJB method that supports bean-managed transactions, the existing transaction is suspended for the duration of the EJB method and resumed once the method exits.

Bean-managed transactions impose certain restrictions on the EJB code as well:

- Only session and message-driven beans may implement bean-managed transactions. Entity beans may use only container-managed transactions.

- An' EJB that uses bean-managed transactions must never invoke the getRollbackOnly( ) and setRollbackOnly( ) methods on the EJBContext interface. Instead, the EJB should use the getStatus( ) and rollback( ) methods on the UserTransaction interface.

- An EJB must not attempt to manipulate JDBC transactions from within the EJB method. Thus, you must not invoke the `commit( )` or `rollback( )` methods on the JDBC Connection object.

Because the EJB container is not involved in the transaction, the EJB method must explicitly commit (or roll back) the transaction before it exits. This holds true for stateless session beans and message-driven beans. A stateful session bean isn't required to do so. An EJB method may initiate a transaction and then complete without committing or rolling back the transaction. In this case, the EJB container is required to maintain the association between the transaction and subsequent method calls until the EJB instance commits (or rolls back) the transaction.

The Transaction Service

WebLogic Server provides a transaction service that allows J2EE applications to manage their own transaction boundaries. WebLogic's transaction service supports multithreaded clients—i.e., a client can make concurrent requests for transactions in multiple threads. WebLogic Server implements *flat transactions*, which means that multiple transactions cannot be associated with the same thread at the same time. WebLogic supports distributed transactions that may span multiple WebLogic servers, clusters, and even domains.

The EJB container uses WebLogic's transaction service to coordinate transactions across EJB components. EJBs that support bean-managed transactions and J2EE applications both use the JTA to explicitly manage their own transactions. J2EE clients can obtain the UserTransaction and TransactionManager objects from the JNDI tree and use these interfaces to demarcate their transaction boundaries. This allows lightweight clients to begin and commit transactions, and delegate the actual responsibility of coordinating the transaction to the remote transaction manager running on WebLogic Server.

Using JTA Transactions

The JTA defines the contract between the transaction manager and all resources involved in a distributed transaction—i.e., the application, the application server, and the resource manager. It allows you to coordinate updates to multiple resources in a safe, elegant way, regardless of the transaction manager. The transaction manager is the standard façade to the transaction service. It manages the transaction boundaries on behalf of the J2EE applications. Ideally, a J2EE application should use the javax.transaction.UserTransaction interface to create a new transaction context. You can use the JTA transactions from within a J2EE client application or a server-side component, such as a servlet, a JMS message consumer, or any EJB that supports bean-managed transactions.

Here's an example that illustrates how you can use JTA transactions from within a servlet:

```java
public void doPost(HttpServletRequest req, HttpServletResponse res)
            throws ServletException, IOException {
    Connection con = null;
    Statement st = null;
    UserTransaction tx = null;

    try {
      InitialContext ic = new InitialContext( );

      //get reference to XA-aware data source(s) from JNDI tree
      DataSource db1 = ic.lookup("java:comp/env/jdbc/xads1");
      DataSource db2 = ic.lookup("java:comp/env/jdbc/xads2");

      tx = (UserTransaction) ic.lookup("java:comp/UserTransaction");
      tx.begin( ); //start a new transaction

      //update some table in db1
      con = db1.getConnection( );
      st = con.createStatement( );
      st.executeUpdate("update foo ...");
      st.close( );

      //update some table in db2
      con2 = db2.getConnection( );
      st = con2.createStatement( );
      st.executeUpdate("delete from foobar ...");
      st.close( );

      tx.commit( ); //commit all changes

      //indicate success to client browser
    } catch (Exception e) {
      if (tx != null) tx.rollback( ); //rollback current transaction
      throw new ServletException(e);
    } finally {
      //release all db resources
      try {
        if (con != null) con.close( );
        if (con2 != null) con2.close( );
      }
      catch (Exception ignored) {}
    }
}
```

Unlike with EJBs, where you can use the EJBContext object to acquire a UserTransaction object, a servlet needs to look it up in the JNDI tree. WebLogic Server makes the UserTransaction object available to all application components in the JNDI tree under *java:comp/UserTransaction*. You then can invoke the begin( ) method to initiate a transaction, and later the commit( ) method to indicate that all updates may be committed. If an error occurs during the lifetime of the transaction, you can invoke the rollback( ) method to indicate that the transaction must be aborted.

If an external client uses JTA transactions, the only change is in the way you obtain the UserTransaction object:

```
Context ctx = null;

Hashtable env = new Hashtable( );
env.put(Context.INITIAL_CONTEXT_FACTORY,
          "weblogic.jndi.WLInitialContextFactory");
env.put(Context.PROVIDER_URL, "t3://localhost:7001");
env.put(Context.SECURITY_PRINCIPAL, "joebloggs");
env.put(Context.SECURITY_CREDENTIALS, "somepassword");

ctx = new InitialContext(env);
UserTransaction tx = (UserTransaction)
  ctx.lookup("javax.transaction.UserTransaction");
```

This code sample shows how an external client needs to provide additional information, such as the T3 URL of a running server, and details of the WebLogic principal who is authorized to access the specified branch of the JNDI tree. For an external client, WebLogic Server makes the UserTransaction object available in the JNDI tree under *javax.transaction.UserTransaction*.

Using XA Versus Non-XA Drivers in JTA Transactions

Recall how a JDBC connection pool can be configured using either an XA-aware JDBC driver or a non-XA driver. If an XA-aware driver is used, the XA-aware data source associated with this connection pool can participate fully in distributed transactions. If the connection pool has been configured using a non-XA JDBC driver, the associated data source can still participate in JTA transactions, provided you instruct WebLogic to emulate two-phase commit for the data source. Thus, an XA-aware data source configured using a pool of non-XA connections can honor distributed transactions only if you've enabled two-phase commit emulation on the data source. You do have to pay a price for this emulation, though.

First, WebLogic manages connections from a non-XA driver and an XA-aware driver in different ways. When a non-XA connection is involved in a distributed transaction, WebLogic holds onto the physical JDBC connection for the duration of the transaction until it is committed or rolled back. Thus, for a non-XA pool, the number of concurrent transactions is limited by the size of the connection pool. XA connections, on the other hand, are more flexible. In this case, WebLogic doesn't need to hold onto the physical JDBC connection until the transaction completes. Clearly, an XA pool is more scalable because the number of active transactions isn't limited by the size of the pool.

Second, a distributed transaction can handle only one XA-aware data source configured for two-phase commit emulation. This means that WebLogic cannot manage multiple XA-aware data sources enabled with the two-phase commit emulation within the same JTA transaction. If you attempt to enlist non-XA connections obtained from two (or more) XA-aware data sources configured for two-phase commit emulation within a JTA transaction, WebLogic will throw an SQLException.

You must adhere to some programming guidelines when using a XA-aware data source:

- By default, auto-commit is disabled for all connections obtained from the XA-aware data source. So, you must not attempt to enable auto-commit on any connections obtained from the XA-aware data source. For example, a call to the Connection.setAutoCommit(true) method within an existing transaction context will throw an SQLException.

- In addition, if a JTA transaction is currently active, you must not commit any local transactions on the actual Connection itself. This means that you must not invoke the commit( ) or rollback( ) methods on the Connection object while in the middle of a distributed transaction. If you're using a JDBC 3.0–compliant driver, you must not invoke the setSavePoint( ) method on the Connection object either.

Finally, if the XA-aware data source is configured to use a non-XA pool of connections, the connection obtained from the data source will be enlisted in a distributed transaction only if you obtain the connection *after* the transaction has been initiated. Thus, for any XA-aware data source using two-phase commit emulation, you should request a connection from the data source only after beginning a new transaction context:

```
InitialContext ctx = new InitialContext( );

//get reference to XA-aware data source from JNDI tree
DataSource ds = ic.lookup("java:comp/env/jdbc/txds");

tx = (UserTransaction) ic.lookup("java:comp/UserTransaction");
tx.begin( ); //start a new transaction

//now create a connection so that it can be enlisted in the transaction
Connection con = ds.getConnection( );
...
```

However, if the XA-aware data source has been configured using an XA-aware JDBC driver, it makes no difference whether you acquire the Connection object before or after the JTA transaction has been initiated. Also, ensure that you close an XA connection after the transaction has been committed. In fact, we recommend that you create and release XA connections from outside the scope of a transaction context. This way, an XA connection is enlisted for the duration of the JTA transaction, until it has been committed.

Data integrity problems with two-phase commit emulation

You should use two-phase commit emulation with caution because it is not a perfect strategy and can result in some data integrity problems. Two-phase commit emulation is designed to ensure that the non-XA connection always succeeds in the prepare phase of the distribution transaction. The local transaction on the non-XA connection commits only when all other XA-aware resources involved in the distributed transaction are ready to commit. Only when this commit on the non-XA connection succeeds does the overall distributed transaction commit its work. If any of the other XA-aware resources involved in the transaction need to roll back, the overall distributed transaction as well as the local transaction on the non-XA connection also roll back.

If the commit or rollback on the local transaction fails, a heuristic error results, which may lead to data integrity errors. A similar error can occur if, say, a network error occurs after a commit message has been sent to all XA resources in the distributed transaction. The transaction manager will automatically abort the commit on all participating resources, but the non-XA resource will have committed its work, thereby resulting in a heuristic completion. For these reasons, ensure that your applications can tolerate potential heuristic completions when using an XA-aware data source configured for two-phase commit emulation.

WebLogic Extensions to the JTA

The JTA defines the following interfaces:

- The UserTransaction interface that allows a J2EE application to explicitly control transaction boundaries
- The TransactionManager interface that allows WebLogic to manage EJBs that support container-managed transactions
- The Status interface that encapsulates information about the current status of a transaction
- The Synchronization interface that allows interested parties to be notified before and after the transaction
- Various interfaces that allow the transaction manager to work with XA-compliant resources (XAResource interface) and obtain the Xid interface

WebLogic Server extends the capabilities of the JTA interfaces in the following ways:

- It makes the TransactionManager interface available to external clients and EJBs through the JNDI tree. A J2EE client or an EJB that supports bean-managed transactions can then suspend the transaction associated with the current thread and later resume it (just like the EJB container).
- WebLogic's extension to the TransactionManager interface allows you to register (or deregister) XA-compliant resources, force suspension of the transaction for the current thread, and force resumption of a suspended transaction.

- It extends the `Transaction` interface by enabling you to get the transaction identifier, access transaction properties, specify a reason for the rollback, and determine whether the transaction has timed out.

- It provides a convenience helper class (`weblogic.transaction.TxHelper`) that lets you access the transaction context or the transaction manager associated with the current thread.

Refer to the API documentation for a more detailed explanation of these extensions.

Managing WebLogic JTA

The Administration Console lets you configure and monitor the transaction service for a WebLogic domain. The configuration settings for JTA are persisted in the domain's *config.xml* configuration file. You can specify values for the transaction timeouts, set the behavior of the transaction manager, and define how transaction logs are maintained. The JTA configuration attributes apply at the domain level, while the monitoring and logging tasks apply at the individual server level. You can access the configuration attributes for the JTA by selecting the domain from the left panel and then choosing the Configuration/JTA tab. All of these JTA settings can be altered dynamically while the servers are running. Here's a description of the JTA settings you can modify for the domain:

Timeout Seconds
> This determines the transaction timeout for active transactions. This is relevant to active transactions that have not yet entered the prepare phase (defaults to 30 seconds).

Abandon Timeout Seconds
> The server will abandon a transaction after this amount of time has passed (defaults to 24hrs). A transaction can be abandoned after it has entered the prepare phase of a two-phase commit.

Before Completion Iteration Limit
> This setting determines the limit on the number of `Synchronization` objects that can be registered for a transaction (defaults to 10).

Max Transactions
> This setting determines the maximum number of simultaneous transactions allowed on a WebLogic Server instance (defaults to 10000).

Max Unique Name Statistics
> This determines the maximum number of transactions for which statistics will be maintained (defaults to 1000).

Checkpoint Interval Seconds
> This setting determines the duration after which WebLogic's transaction manager creates a new transaction log and checks old log files to see whether they can be deleted (defaults to 5 minutes).

Forget Heuristics

If this setting has a value of true, the transaction manager instructs all registered XA-compliant resources to "forget" about the heuristically completed transaction branch. This means that when a resource manager reports a heuristic exception, the transaction manager records the heuristic outcome and invokes the forget() method on the participating XAResource. By default, this setting is enabled. Refer to the sidebar "Heuristic Completions" in this chapter for more information on distributed transactions that result in a heuristic outcome.

Abandoning Transactions

In a two-phase commit protocol, the transaction manager coordinates all resource managers involved in a transaction. After all resource managers have voted to commit or roll back, the transaction manager conveys the final decision to all resource managers in the second phase. Then, the transaction manager will continue to wait until completion of the transaction—until all resource managers have successfully completed their work. The AbandonTimeoutSeconds attribute defines the maximum amount of time that the transaction manager will wait for the resource managers to complete their work. After the timeout expires, the transaction manager will abandon the transaction and make no further attempt to resolve resources that have failed to acknowledge their outcome. If the transaction had completed its prepare phase, the transaction manager will roll it back and report a heuristic error in the server log.

The transaction timeout is a fundamental setting because it determines the timeout behavior of all distributed transactions. You also can override the transaction timeout on a case-by-case basis, as the following code illustrates:

```
UserTransaction tx =
    (UserTransaction) ctx.lookup("java:comp/UserTransaction");
tx.setTransactionTimeout(120);
tx.begin();
// now do your work within the new transaction context ...
```

Monitoring Transactions

You can use the Administration Console to monitor transaction activity for each server instance. In fact, you even can use the Console to manually roll back or commit active transactions. You can view transaction statistics for each server by selecting the server in the left frame and then selecting the Monitoring/JTA tab. These statistics include the total number of transactions, transactions with a specific outcome (committed, rolled back, heuristic completions), rollbacks by specific reasons, abandoned transactions, and average commit time. You also can display further information on active transactions. If you choose the "Monitor all Transactions by Name" option, you can list all named transactions. And if you choose the "Monitor

Heuristic Completions

The transaction manager coordinates updates to all resources involved in a distributed transaction. Depending on how the resource managers vote during the prepare phase, a decision will be made as to whether all resources may commit their updates. A *heuristic completion* occurs when a resource makes a unilateral decision (without waiting for a decision from the transaction manager) to commit or roll back all updates. A heuristic decision can occur due to several reasons—for instance, if a network failure occurs that results in a premature rollback, or if the transaction times out. Whenever a heuristic decision is made, there is a risk that the decision may conflict with the eventual decision of the transaction manager, and therefore result in loss of data integrity.

A heuristic outcome can occur in one of four ways:

HeuristicCommit

> A resource participating in a transaction decides independently to commit its work, without waiting for a decision. If the transaction manager later decides to roll back, the decision of the participating resource was incorrect and could lead to data inconsistency.

HeuristicRollback

> A resource participating in a transaction decides independently to roll back its work, without waiting for a decision. If the transaction manager later decides to commit, the decision of the participating resource was incorrect and could result in inconsistencies.

HeuristicMixed

> The transaction manager is aware that the transaction has resulted in a mixed outcome because some participating resources decided independently to commit their changes, while others decided to roll back their changes, without waiting for a decision.

HeuristicHazard

> The transaction manager is aware that the transaction may have resulted in a mixed outcome, but because of system or resource failures, it is unable to verify whether a mixed outcome definitely occurred.

When a resource takes a heuristic decision that contravenes the eventual outcome of the transaction, it is still responsible for reporting its action to the transaction manager. In fact, we need to consider two scenarios:

- If the heuristic decision is consistent with the eventual outcome of the transaction, the transaction manager invokes the forget( ) method on the XAResource— i.e., it forgets about the heuristic decision made by the resource. No further action is required because the heuristic decision was in line with the outcome of the transaction.

—Continued

- If the heuristic decision is in conflict with the eventual outcome of the transaction, the resource consults its records of the decision and then returns one of the heuristic outcome exceptions.

Usually, a message indicating the nature of the heuristic outcome is added to the server logs, and retained until the resource is instructed by the transaction manager to "forget" about the transaction.

all Transactions by Resource" option, you can list all transactional resources that can be accessed by the server. So, for example, if you have configured a connection pool using an XA-aware driver, the connection pool is listed here together with statistics on all transactions associated with the pool. These statistics include the total number of transactions and the number of transactions that have committed and rolled back.

The "Monitor all Inflight Transactions" option is probably the most powerful. This option lists all the currently active transactions on the server. Note that this list is a snapshot, and it's conceivable that by the time you click an active transaction, the transaction may no longer be active. WebLogic simply informs you of this if it happens. If the transaction is still active by the time you click it, you can view information about the selected transaction, including: the transaction identifier; the name of the server coordinating the transaction; the transaction status; the number of seconds that the transaction has been active; servers participating in the transaction; XA resources participating in the transaction; and any properties assigned to the transaction by the application that created it.

You also have the option of manually resolving the transaction, by using menu controls in the Administration Console that let you manually commit or roll back the transaction. The controls that are available to you will depend on the current state of the transaction. Table 6-1 lists the various states of a transaction, as well as which controls are offered for that state.

Table 6-1. Transaction state and manual control

Status	Definition	Controls
Active	This state defines an active transaction. No commit has been issued yet.	Rollback
Preparing	This state defines the time that has elapsed from the point when the resources have been called on to prepare, up to the point when all participants have responded that they are ready to commit.	Rollback
Prepared	This state defines the time that has elapsed from the point when all participants have responded to prepare, up to the point when the commit or rollback has been initiated.	Commit/Rollback
Committing	This state defines the time that has elapsed from the Prepared state to the point when all participants have been informed of the outcome.	Commit

Table 6-1. Transaction state and manual control (continued)

Status	Definition	Controls
Committed	This state defines a committed transaction. Check to see whether the transaction completed heuristically.	Commit
Rolling Back	This state defines the time that has elapsed from the point when roll-back processing is initiated, up to the point when all resources have been instructed to roll back.	Rollback
Rolled Back	This state defines a rolled-back transaction. Check to see whether the transaction completed heuristically.	Rollback
Marked Roll Back	This state defines a transaction that has been marked for rollback, perhaps as a result of a call to the `setRollbackOnly( )` method.	Rollback
Unknown	This status is shown if the current status cannot be determined.	Commit/Rollback

For example, if your transaction is in the Preparing state, you will be allowed to manually roll back the transaction (but not force a commit). Each control is presented in two forms: a global and a local form. For example, if you are allowed to commit a transaction, you will find options to Force Local Commit and to Force Global Commit:

- The Force Local Commit and Force Local RollBack options act only on those participating resources that are hosted on the current server instance. If you select either option, WebLogic issues a commit (or rollback) on all participating resources hosted on the selected server only, after which the transaction is removed from the local transaction manager.

- On the contrary, the Force Global Commit and Force Global RollBack options act on all resources involved in the distributed transaction. If you select either option, the server on which the transaction originated (i.e., the coordinating server) asynchronously issues a local commit (or rollback) on all servers participating in the transaction. However, if the coordinating server cannot be reached, a `javax.transaction.SystemException` will be thrown.

Transaction Logs

Each WebLogic Server instance has a transaction log that captures information about committed transactions that may not have completed. The transaction log enables WebLogic Server to recover transactions that could not be completed before the server failed. This recovery procedure is executed the next time you restart the server after a system crash or network failure. As part of the recovery procedure, the server inspects the transaction log for incomplete transactions and tries to complete them.

Log files for the transaction log cannot be viewed because they are in binary format. You can locate the transaction files (*.tlog* files) in the server's folder in the domain's directory. If you wish to modify the default location of the transaction log files, you can use the Administration Console to set a value for the Transaction Log File Prefix setting for the server. You can access this setting for the server under the Logging/ JTA tab.

The transaction logs maintain a log of transactions that are ready to commit but have not yet completed. The log files are vital to WebLogic's transaction recovery when the server restarts after a failure. Therefore, in order to maintain data integrity, it is recommended that you do not delete the transaction log files manually. WebLogic automatically deletes them when the records in the log file are no longer required.

Transaction log files are critical for the WebLogic transaction service, so you should ensure that log files are stored on highly available filesystems (such as on a RAID disk, dual-ported SCSI disk, or a SAN [Storage Area Network] solution). When migrating a server to another machine, you must transfer the transaction log files as well. Too many log files are an indication of many long-running transactions that haven't yet completed, due to either a resource failure or perhaps a large timeout value for the transaction. WebLogic throws a SystemException on a commit if the filesystem holding the transaction logs runs out of space.

Transaction Recovery

WebLogic Server is able to recover failed transactions that occur because of a system crash or even crashes that happen during recovery. The *Transaction Recovery Service* automatically tries to recover transactions after restarting a failed server. The recovery service, which owns the transaction logs for the server, looks for incomplete transactions in the log files and attempts to complete them. Because WebLogic Server is designed to gracefully handle transaction recovery after a system crash, you should restart the failed server and allow the Transaction Recovery Service to complete pending transactions.

WebLogic executes a series of steps as part of the transaction recovery procedure:

1. If a transaction has reached the second phase of a two-phase commit and a commit decision has been made, the recovery service commits all updates for the transaction.

2. For transactions that already have been prepared with a resource manager, the recovery service invokes the recover( ) method for each XAResource and then resolves each Xid returned by the recover( ) method by invoking either the commit( ), rollback( ), or forget( ) method on the XAResource.

3. If a transaction has recorded a heuristic completion, the recovery service records the heuristic exception in the server log, and tells the transaction manager to forget about the heuristically completed transaction (that is, if the Forget Heuristics attribute has been enabled for the server).

The Transaction Recovery Service provides predictable, consistent handling of failed transactions. If a transaction is ready to commit (or to roll back) but has not been committed (or rolled back) before the crash, and the recover( ) method on the

XAResource resolves to the same transaction ID, the recovery service consistently tries to commit (or roll back) the transaction. This way, the transaction recovery after a crash can never result in heuristic completions. Also, the transaction manager persists in trying to resolve each pending transaction to either a commit or a rollback. Only a timeout attribute forces the Transaction Recovery Service to abandon the recovery for that transaction.

Handling Failed Servers

If you are unable to restart a failed server within a reasonable amount of time, you need to be able to offload the task of recovering incomplete transactions to a backup server. In the case of a nonclustered server, you can manually move the transaction log files from the failed server to the new server. Alternatively, you can make them available to the new server if you are using a shared storage solution. You need to adjust the Transaction Log File Prefix setting to the path for the log files and start the new server. The new server instance will then attempt to recover the failed transactions using the log files.

If a clustered server crashes, you can use the Administration Console to manually migrate the Transaction Recovery Service to another member of the same cluster. You can migrate the recovery service from the Control/JTA Migrate tab for the failed server. This way, the recovery service on the backup server takes ownership of the transaction log files for the failed server and attempts to resolve all pending transactions. Make sure that the failed server is not running when you attempt this. Once the Transaction Recovery Service has completed all failed transactions, the backup server relinquishes control over the service and the log files. The failed server can reclaim the recovery service and the log files the next time it is restarted. If the failed server is restarted while the backup server is recovering transactions, the backup server abandons recovery, does some internal cleanup, and relinquishes control of the recovery service and log files so that the failed server can handle them properly. You can use the Control/JTA Migration Configuration tab to specify which members of the cluster can access the transaction logs of the selected server, and hence which servers can perform a JTA migration if this server fails.

Migrating the Transaction Recovery Service to a backup server imposes certain constraints as well:

- You can migrate the Transaction Recovery Service only from a failed server or a server instance that is not running. You must stop a server instance if you decide to manually migrate the recovery service.
- The backup server processes incomplete transactions only and does not handle heuristic log files.
- Backup servers must have access to the same transaction log files, so they must reside on a shared storage device.

Remember, WebLogic is designed to handle transaction recovery when it's restarted after a system crash. You should consider moving the transaction logs or migrating the recovery service to a backup server only if you are unable to restart the server within a reasonable time period.

Interdomain Transactions

You also can configure WebLogic so that distributed transactions can span multiple domains. Multiple servers across WebLogic domains can participate in interdomain transactions. However, only domains that trust each other can participate in interdomain transactions.

 Resources using the two-phase commit emulation may not participate in an interdomain transaction.

Chapter 17 shows how to enable this trust between two WebLogic domains.

CHAPTER 7

J2EE Connectors

The J2EE Java Connector Architecture (JCA) provides a standard architecture for connecting J2EE Application Servers to enterprise information systems (EISs). An *enterprise information system* is any product that manages the information infrastructure of an enterprise. Examples of an EIS include Enterprise Resource Planning systems, mainframe Transaction Processing Monitors, and legacy databases.

The JCA defines a standard framework in which resource adapters can be developed for specific EIS products. A *resource adapter* plugs into an application server, offering all of the functionality needed to connect to and interact with the EIS. This integration extends to connection management, security, and transactions, providing a rich and robust way of interfacing with these external systems. J2EE components running on the application server then can interact with the resource adapter in a standard manner, and the resource adaptor in turn will interact with the EIS. Because the JCA is a requisite part of the J2EE platform, the EIS vendor can provide a single resource adapter that allows any J2EE application server to connect to the EIS.

The JCA framework deals with three important components:

System-level contracts
> The system-level contracts, implemented in WebLogic, define the interface between the application server and the resource adapter. This system-level interface deals with managing a pool of connections to the EIS, enabling the EIS resource manager to participate in local or distributed transactions, and providing secure access to EIS resources.

Common Client Interface (CCI)
> The CCI provides a generic interface to the resource adapter, allowing you to develop applications that work across heterogeneous EISs. J2EE components can use the CCI to interface with either the resource adapter or an EIS-specific interface. The resource adapter vendor is not required to implement the CCI.

Packaging and deployment

The JCA defines a standard way of packaging resource adapters and deploying them as part of an enterprise application.

In this chapter, we'll examine how WebLogic manages a pool of connections to the EIS and the various transaction levels and sign-on mechanisms supported by WebLogic. We'll cover how WebLogic lets you map credentials of a WebLogic user to valid user credentials on the EIS. We'll also look at the various deploy-time and runtime configuration settings that apply to any J2EE connector. Along the way, we'll cover how to configure and use a J2EE-compliant resource adapter.

 The terms *resource adapter* and *J2EE connector* will be used interchangeably.

Assembling and Deploying Resource Adapters

Resource adapters can be packaged and deployed in very much the same way as you would package and deploy web applications or EJB components. A resource adapter includes all the Java classes and interfaces that implement the required contracts and functionality. It also may use platform-specific libraries that enable it to talk to the EIS. All these files, along with any help files and documentation, are packaged into a JAR file, called the *resource adapter archive* (RAR). Just like a WAR file or an EJB JAR, a RAR file also packages XML deployment descriptors, which specify the deploy-time and runtime configuration settings for the resource adapter.

Packaging

A typical RAR includes the following components:

- One or more JARs that contain all the Java interfaces, implementation, and utility classes required by the resource adapter.
- Any platform-dependent libraries needed by the resource adapter.
- Help files and documentation.
- XML deployment descriptors (*ra.xml* and *weblogic-ra.xml*) that encapsulate metadata and various configuration settings for the resource adapter. The XML descriptor files must be placed in the *META-INF* directory.

Example 7-1 lists the contents of a typical RAR file.

Example 7-1. Contents of a resource adapter module (eis.rar)

```
/ra.jar
/cci.jar
```

Example 7-1. Contents of a resource adapter module (eis.rar) (continued)

```
/win.dll
/solaris.so
/Overview.html
/GettingStarted.html
/ReleaseNotes.html
/LICENSE.txt
/META-INF/ra.xml
/META-INF/weblogic-ra.xml
```

Here, *ra.jar* and *cci.jar* contain the Java classes and interfaces that implement the functionality and client contracts for the resource adapter, while *win.dll* and *solaris.so* hold the platform-dependent libraries. In addition, the RAR file includes the HTML documentation and licensing information.

The standard *ra.xml* descriptor file captures important metadata, licensing information, and configuration settings for the transaction levels and authentication levels supported by the resource adapter. The WebLogic-specific *weblogic-ra.xml* descriptor file captures information about the JNDI name to which the connection factory will be bound, and additional parameters for configuring the behavior of a pool of managed connections, detecting connection leaks, and logging.

A RAR file can be created very simply by placing the contents in a staging directory—say, *rardir*—and then using the jar tool that comes with your JDK to create the archive:

```
    jar cvf eis.rar -C rardir .
```

This creates a RAR file that then can be deployed to WebLogic. If you would like to deploy an existing RAR to WebLogic, you should update the Java archive to include the WebLogic-specific XML descriptor:

```
    jar uf eis.rar -C rardir META-INF/weblogic-ra.xml
```

If you don't include the WebLogic-specific deployment descriptor, WebLogic automatically will include one for you when you deploy the RAR. In that case, the descriptor file will hold just dummy values that you can edit. At the very least, you will need to supply the classname for the connection factory and the JNDI name to which the connector should be bound. Your RAR also may reference support classes, perhaps shared with other modules deployed together in an EAR, in which case the JAR should include the standard JAR manifest file */META-INF/MANIFEST.MF*, and it should use the Class-Path entry to point to any of the shared JARs used by the resource adapter.

Deployment

A resource adapter can be deployed directly to WebLogic Server by placing it under the *applications* folder in a WebLogic domain. In this case, the "standalone" resource adapter can be shared by multiple J2EE applications deployed to the server. Alternatively, the adapter can be bundled as part of a J2EE application alongside other J2EE modules such as web applications and EJB JARs. This is most appropriate if the resource adapter will be used only by the other J2EE modules within an enterprise application. WebLogic allows you to deploy a resource adapter in three ways:

- You can use WebLogic's deployer tool to deploy a resource adapter and target it to one or more servers:

```
java weblogic.Deployer -adminurl http://localhost:7001
    -username system -password mypassword -name eis.rar
    -activate -targets myserver -source myapps\eis.rar
```

Here, the resource adapter *eis.rar* is being deployed to the target server myserver. If the server has been started in development mode, in which the auto-deploy feature is enabled, you simply can drop the RAR file under the *applications* folder of your WebLogic domain and the resource adapter will be deployed as a standalone J2EE connector.

- You can use the Administration Console to configure a new J2EE connector for deployment. Start up the Administration Console and then select Deployments/ Connector Modules from the left pane. Then, select the "Deploy a New Connector Module" link from the right pane to deploy a new resource adapter. Choose a RAR file for deployment using the file browser at the bottom, then select the name for the J2EE connector, and target the component to one or more server instances. Once the component is deployed, you can use the Administration Console to redeploy or undeploy the resource adapter.

- You can bundle a resource adapter inside an EAR file that subsequently is deployed to WebLogic. To achieve this, you need to perform the following actions:

  a. Package the J2EE Connector archive inside the EAR file in the same way as you would package a web application, EJB component, or any other JAR.

  b. Modify the standard application-level deployment descriptor */META-INF/ application.xml* to include a reference to the RAR file:

```
<application>
  <display-name>My Application</display-name>
  <module>
    <web>
      <web-uri>mywebapp</web-uri>
      <context-root>/</context-root>
    </web>
  <module>
    <ejb>ejb_foo.jar</ejb>
  </module>
  <module>
    <connector>eis.rar</connector>
  </module>
    ...
</application>
```

Also ensure that the XML descriptor */META-INF/application.xml* includes the following DTD reference:

```
<!DOCTYPE application PUBLIC
            '-//Sun Microsystems, Inc.//DTD J2EE Application 1.3//EN'
            'http://java.sun.com/dtd/application_1_3.dtd'>
```

Once you've deployed the EAR file to WebLogic, the resource adapter will then be accessible to all web applications and EJB components within that J2EE application.

XML Deployment Descriptors

A resource adapter requires you to package the standard *ra.xml* descriptor file and the optional WebLogic-specific *weblogic-ra.xml* descriptor file. You can use these XML descriptors to specify metadata and adjust the runtime configuration settings for the resource adapter. The *ra.xml* descriptor file is defined in the JCA Specification from Sun Microsystems. It must be a valid XML document with the following DOCTYPE:

```
<!DOCTYPE connector PUBLIC
            '-//Sun Microsystems, Inc.//DTD Connector 1.0//EN'
            'http://java.sun.com/dtd/connector_1_0.dtd'>
```

The *ra.xml* descriptor lets you specify the following:

- A name and description for the resource adapter.
- The version of the J2EE connector and the JCA version with which it is compliant.
- The name of the EIS vendor that developed the resource adapter.
- The type of the EIS supported.
- Licensing information and whether a license is needed to use the J2EE connector.
- Fully qualified names for the `ConnectionFactory` and `Connection` classes and interfaces needed by the resource adapter.
- The level of transaction support provided by the J2EE connector.
- The authentication mechanism supported by the J2EE connector.

> WebLogic Server supports only resource adapters that implement the `BasicPassword` authentication mechanism. If the J2EE connector supports only the `Kerbv5` authentication mechanism or uses the `javax.resource.spi.security.GenericCredential` credential interface, you cannot deploy the resource adapter to WebLogic Server.

- Whether the resource adapter can reauthenticate existing managed connections.
- A set of configurable properties for the `ManagedConnectionFactory` instance. Each property is defined in terms of name, an optional description, type, and an optional default value.

A resource adapter can support one of three transaction levels: NoTransaction, LocalTransaction, or XATransaction. The JCA framework also provides for a set of well-defined configurable properties for a ManagedConnectionFactory, all of type java.lang.String:

```
<config-property-name>ServerName</config-property-name>
<config-property-name>PortNumber</config-property-name>
<config-property-name>UserName</config-property-name>
<config-property-name>Password</config-property-name>
<config-property-name>ConnectionURL</config-property-name>
```

These properties closely mimic the connection properties associated with a JDBC connection pool.

The *weblogic-ra.xml* descriptor file captures configuration settings specific to the runtime environment provided by WebLogic Server. As of WebLogic Server 8.1, the descriptor file must be a valid XML document conforming to the following DOCTYPE:

```
<!DOCTYPE weblogic-connection-factory-dd PUBLIC
        "-//BEA Systems, Inc.//DTD WebLogic 8.1.0 Connector//EN"
        "http://www.bea.com/servers/wls810/dtd/weblogic810-ra.dtd">
```

Using the *weblogic-ra.xml* descriptor file, you can specify the following:

- A logical name for the connection factory associated with the resource adapter.
- The JNDI name to which the connection factory is bound. EJBs and servlets can use this JNDI name to reference this resource adapter in their XML descriptors.
- The location of the folder where all native libraries will be copied during deployment.
- Configuration settings that describe the behavior of the pool of managed connections.
- Whether logging is enabled for the J2EE connector, and if so, the name of the log file to which log messages are written.
- Values for the configurable properties defined earlier in the config-entry element of the *ra.xml* descriptor file.

We'll take a closer look at the structure of this XML descriptor file in later sections. In the meantime, you can view and configure the important deployment descriptors using the Administration Console. Select the desired connector module from the left pane, and then choose the Configuration/Descriptor option. These options are available only if the connector is deployed in an exploded form. If it is deployed as a RAR file, you need to unpack and edit the XML files using either your favorite XML editor or WebLogic Builder.

Configuring Resource Adapters

We will use Sun's JDBC Connector to illustrate the various issues pertaining to the configuration of resource adapters. Sun's JDBC Connector lets you plug any JDBC-compliant driver into a J2EE Application Server. Its resource adapters serve as pluggable JCA wrappers around the JDBC driver and its connection factories. Please visit *http://java.sun.com/products/jdbc/related.html* for more information on Sun's JDBC Connector, and on how to download the product.

The downloaded ZIP packages resource adapters that implement the Service Provider Interface (SPI) contracts using the functionality of the `DriverManager`, the `DataSource`, the `ConnectionPoolDataSource`, and the `XADataSource` classes in a JDBC driver. It also contains resource adapters that implement the CCI contracts using the functionality of the `XADataSource`. Two versions of each resource adapter are included, one conforming to the Connector v1.0 specification and the other conforming to the more recent Connector v1.5 specification. You have to use the Version 1.0 files (for instance, *cci_10_xa.rar*) that are supported by WebLogic 8.1.

Generic Settings for the Resource Adapter

The standard *ra.xml* descriptor file captures general-purpose information about the J2EE connector. In the case of the XA-based JDBC Connector *cci_10_xa.rar*, the standard XML descriptor includes the following metadata:

```
<connector>
    <display-name>XADataSource Resource Adapter</display-name>
    <description>
      Resource adapter wrapping XADatasource implementation of driver
    </description>

    <!-- This is the name of the EIS vendor -->
    <vendor-name>Sun Microsystems</vendor-name>

    <!-- This is the version of the Connector specification -->
    <spec-version>1.0</spec-version>

    <!-- This is the type of the EIS resource supported -->
    <eis-type>Database</eis-type>

    <!-- This is the version of the resource adapter -->
    <version>1.0</version>

    <!-- This specifies licensing requirements for the resource adapter -->
    <license>
        <license-required>false</license-required>
    </license>

    <resourceadapter>
      ...
    </resourceadapter>
</connector>
```

In addition, the standard *ra.xml* descriptor specifies the fully qualified names of the Java interface and implementation class for the resource adapter's connection factory and the connection. The following portion from the *ra.xml* descriptor lists the Java interfaces and implementation classes used by Sun's XADataSource resource adapter:

```
<resourceadapter>
    <managedconnectionfactory-class>
      com.sun.gjc.cci.CciManagedConnectionFactory
    </managedconnectionfactory-class>
    <connectionfactory-interface>
      javax.resource.cci.ConnectionFactory
    </connectionfactory-interface>
    <connectionfactory-impl-class>
      com.sun.gjc.cci.CciConnectionFactory
    </connectionfactory-impl-class>
    <connection-interface>
      javax.resource.cci.Connection
    </connection-interface>
    <connection-impl-class>
      com.sun.gjc.cci.CciConnection
    </connection-impl-class>
    ...
</resourceadapter>
```

The transaction-support subelement specifies the level of transaction support provided by the resource adapter. As expected, Sun's XADataSource Connector supports distributed transactions, so the *ra.xml* descriptor includes the following transaction setting:

```
<transaction-support>XATransaction</transaction-support>
```

The *ra.xml* descriptor file also lists a number of configurable properties that apply to each ManagedConnectionFactory instance. The connection factory then uses these properties to establish managed connections to the underlying EIS resource. Sun's XADataSource resource adapter does support a number of configuration properties: ServerName, PortNumber, User, Password, DatabaseName, InitialPoolSize, MaxPoolSize, ClassName, and many more. These properties mimic the attributes of a JDBC connection pool that supports JTA transactions. For each property, the *ra.xml* descriptor file defines a name, type, and optional default value:

```
<config-property>
    <config-property-name>User</config-property-name>
    <config-property-type>java.lang.String</config-property-type>
    <config-property-value>scott</config-property-value>
</config-property>
<config-property>
    <config-property-name>Password</config-property-name>
    <config-property-type>java.lang.String</config-property-type>
    <config-property-value>tiger</config-property-value>
</config-property>
    ...
```

Finally, the *ra.xml* descriptor file includes information about the authentication mechanism supported by the resource adapter. Typically, a J2EE connector supports two kinds of authentication:

BasicPassword

Authentication based on username-password combinations.

Kerbv5

Authentication based on Kerberos v5 tickets. WebLogic doesn't support resource adapters that provide only Kerbv5-based authentication.

In addition, the *ra.xml* descriptor file specifies whether the resource adapter supports reauthentication of an existing physical connection. The following portion from the standard *ra.xml* descriptor file indicates that Sun's XADataSource connector does, in fact, support BasicPassword authentication, but doesn't support reauthentication of existing connections to the EIS resource:

```
<resourceadapter>
  ...
  <authentication-mechanism>
    <authentication-mechanism-type>BasicPassword</authentication-mechanism-type>
    <credential-interface>
       javax.resource.spi.security.PasswordCredential
    </credential-interface>
  </authentication-mechanism>
  <reauthentication-support>false</reauthentication-support>
  ...
</resourceadapter>
```

Support for Transaction Levels

The JCA framework works in coordination with WebLogic's transaction manager to provide robust support for distributed transactions. As mentioned earlier, WebLogic supports resource adapters that provide the following transaction levels:

XATransaction

This means the resource adapter can participate in a distributed transaction managed by WebLogic's transaction manager, external to the resource adapter. When a J2EE component uses a connection to the EIS in a distributed transaction, WebLogic ensures that the associated XA resource is enlisted with the transaction manager. Later, when the J2EE component closes the connection, WebLogic de-lists the XA resource from the transaction manager and cleans up the actual connection to the EIS when the transaction has completed successfully.

LocalTransaction

This setting enables the resource adapter to participate in local transactions only. Unlike the XATransaction setting, such a connection to the EIS cannot participate in the 2PC protocol. The local transaction is bound by the lifetime of the EIS connection. Thus, WebLogic initiates a local transaction when a client requests a connection to the EIS, and commits the local transaction when the client releases the connection. It also cleans up the actual connection to the EIS when the transaction completes successfully.

NoTransaction

This setting indicates that the resource adapter supports neither local nor distributed transactions. Any connection to the EIS obtained using the resource adapter should not be used within an existing transaction context.

Remember, a local transaction is limited in scope and managed by the single EIS resource manager itself. A distributed (XA) transaction can span multiple resource managers, and is coordinated by WebLogic's transaction manager using the 2PC protocol.

In fact, WebLogic does allow a *single* resource adapter configured for local transactions to participate in an XA transaction. In this case, when the resources in the XA transaction are called upon to prepare, the prepare is first invoked on the XA resources. Only if all XA resources vote to commit is the *local transaction* committed. If this local transaction successfully commits, all the other XA resources are instructed to commit. If the local transaction fails to commit, the XA transaction and all the other XA resources involved are asked to roll back. As you can see, this neat trick works only if no more than one local transaction resource adapter is involved in an XA transaction. If you attempt to enlist multiple resource adapters that are configured for local transactions, the XA transaction will fail with an exception. See Chapter 5 for another example of this two-phase commit emulation.

WebLogic-Specific Configuration Options

The *weblogic-ra.xml* descriptor file allows you to specify additional configurations for the resource adapter that are specific to the WebLogic platform. For instance, you must use the *weblogic-ra.xml* descriptor to specify a logical name for the connection factory associated with the J2EE connector, and the JNDI name to which the ConnectionFactory object will be bound:

```
<weblogic-connection-factory-dd>

    <connection-factory-name>XADsWithTx</connection-factory-name>
    <jndi-name>myapp.XADsWithTx</jndi-name>
    ...
```

If the resource adapter includes any native libraries needed for establishing a connection to the EIS, you can use the native-libdir element to specify the location of the folder where the native libraries will be copied. Sun's XADataSource connector doesn't require any native libraries, and therefore we can ignore this setting. The *weblogic-ra.xml* descriptor also holds values for configurable properties defined earlier in the standard *ra.xml* descriptor file. You need to define a map-config-property element for each property whose default value needs to be overridden.

The following XML fragment shows the values we've chosen when using Sun's
XADataSource resource adapter to wrap access to Microsoft's JDBC Driver for SQL
Server 2000:

```
...
<map-config-property>
  <map-config-property-name>ConnectionURL</map-config-property-name>
  <map-config-property-value>
    jdbc:microsoft:sqlserver://
  </map-config-property-value>
</map-config-property>
<map-config-property>
  <map-config-property-name>ServerName</map-config-property-name>
  <map-config-property-value>10.0.10.10</map-config-property-value>
</map-config-property>
<map-config-property>
  <map-config-property-name>PortNumber</map-config-property-name>
  <map-config-property-value>1433</map-config-property-value>
</map-config-property>
<map-config-property>
  <map-config-property-name>User</map-config-property-name>
  <map-config-property-value>sa</map-config-property-value>
</map-config-property>
<map-config-property>
  <map-config-property-name>Password</map-config-property-name>
  <map-config-property-value>tiger123</map-config-property-value>
</map-config-property>
<map-config-property>
  <map-config-property-name>DatabaseName</map-config-property-name>
  <map-config-property-value>MASTER</map-config-property-value>
</map-config-property>
<map-config-property>
  <map-config-property-name>ClassName</map-config-property-name>
  <map-config-property-value>
    com.microsoft.jdbcx.sqlserver.SQLServerDataSource
  </map-config-property-value>
</map-config-property>
<map-config-property>
  <map-config-property-name>DriverProperties</map-config-property-name>
  <map-config-property-value>
    setSelectMethod#cursor##
  </map-config-property-value>
</map-config-property>
...
```

The value for the DriverProperties setting is specified using some proprietary format for invoking methods on the XADataSource object, and is needed to set custom
properties not identified by the JDBC specification. In case of Microsoft's JDBC
Driver for SQL Server 2000, if the data source supports distributed transactions, you
need to enable server-side cursors by setting SelectMethod=cursor. Remember, all
these configurable properties are used by the ConnectionFactory instance when establishing managed connections with the target EIS—in this case, the master database
on SQL Server 2000.

Managing Connection Pools

The *weblogic-ra.xml* descriptor file also encapsulates optional settings to configure and automatically maintain the size of the connection pool. A ready pool of connections to the EIS can enhance the performance of your application, especially if creating a managed connection is a costly operation. The configuration settings for this connection pool are almost identical to those that apply to JDBC connection pools, as described earlier in Chapter 5. You need to use the pool-params element within the XML descriptor file to define the various configuration settings that control the behavior of the pool of managed connections. Table 7-1 lists the pool parameters available for the connection factory.

Table 7-1. Configuration settings for the pool of managed connections

Setting	Description	Default
initial-capacity	This option identifies the initial number of connections created when the resource adapter is deployed.	1
max-capacity	This option identifies the maximum number of connections created during the lifetime of the connection pool.	10
capacity-increment	This option identifies the number of connections created when the pool needs to be resized.	1
connection-reserve-timeout-seconds	This option determines the maximum amount of time WebLogic waits while trying to reserve a connection from a pool at maximum capacity. If this timeout is set to -1, WebLogic will not wait.	-1
highest-num-waiters	This option determines the maximum number of connection requests that may wait for an available connection once the pool has reached maximum capacity.	MAX-INT
connection-creation-retry-frequency-seconds	This option determines how often WebLogic should retry to create connections. This setting is used, for example, if a failure is detected while creating additional connections for a pool.	0
shrinking-enabled	If this option is set to false, unused managed connections are not reclaimed by WebLogic.	true
shrink-period-minutes	This option determines the amount of time (in minutes) that the pool manager waits before reclaiming unused connections.	15
inactive-connection-timeout-seconds	This option identifies the amount of time (in seconds) that a connection can remain idle. The setting detects and prevents connection leaks, in case managed connections have not been properly released once their use is complete.	0
connection-profiling-enabled	If this option is set to true, using the Administration Console you can view the call stacks of where each connection was allocated. The same information is available for idle and leaked connections. Typically, you will enable this feature for debugging purposes only.	false

All the configuration settings for controlling the behavior of the connection pool listed in Table 7-1 are *optional*. You need to set values for specific pool settings only if you need to override the default pool behavior. The following XML fragment shows how to configure the pool parameters for a resource adapter:

```
<!-- weblogic-ra.xml entry -->
...
<pool-params>
    <initial-capacity>5</initial-capacity>
    <max-capacity>15</max-capacity>
    <capacity-increment>2</capacity-increment>
    <shrinking-enabled>true</shrinking-enabled>
    <inactive-connection-timeout-seconds>120</ inactive-connection-timeout-seconds >
</pool-params>
...
```

Connection reservation

Let's examine how these pool parameters determine the way in which WebLogic services client requests for a managed connection from the resource adapter's pool of connections. Assume a client attempts to reserve a connection from the pool. If there is an available connection in the pool, it is simply returned to the client. If there are no available connections and the pool's size is not yet at max-capacity, WebLogic increases the size of the pool by capacity-increment new connections before returning a connection to the client.

If the pool's size is at max-capacity and cannot grow any further, WebLogic waits for, at most, connection-reserve-timeout-seconds in case a connection does become available. No more than highest-num-waiters requests may wait for a connection to become available. WebLogic will refuse further connection requests while the pool's size is at max-capacity and highest-num-waiters requests are already waiting for a connection to become available. While a client waits for an available connection, WebLogic attempts to reserve connections every connection-creation-retry-frequency-seconds, before the client's request times out.

Detecting connection leaks

Ideally, once a J2EE component (servlet, EJB, etc.) has completed using a connection to the EIS, it sends a close( ) connection request that enables WebLogic to perform any necessary cleanup and return the managed connection to the pool. However, a J2EE component may erroneously fail to close a connection. In this case, the configured pool will soon peak to its maximum capacity and run out of available connections to the EIS. WebLogic is able to avoid this situation by incorporating two mechanisms for detecting connection leaks:

Using the garbage collector

Suppose an EJB method fails to close a connection before completion. When the method completes, the connection object will no longer be referenced. The JVM will at some point invoke the garbage collector, which then invokes the object's finalize( ) method. If the connection object hasn't been closed, this method will automatically close the connection by simply invoking the cleanup( )

method on the actual ManagedConnection object, thereby releasing the object as if the user had closed it.

Using an idle timer

A JVM cannot guarantee when an unreferenced object will be garbage-collected, so WebLogic cannot efficiently manage the connection pool simply by relying on the garbage collector. For this reason, WebLogic also supports an *idle timer*, which tracks the last time a connection was used. The timer starts ticking when a client obtains a connection from the pool but doesn't actively use it. To minimize the chance that the connection is still being used, WebLogic will release only those connections that have exceeded their maximum time limit. Typically, this will happen when the connection pool is at maximum capacity and a client makes another connection request. You can specify the maximum idle time allowed for a managed connection using the inactive-connection-timeout-seconds subelement in the *weblogic-ra.xml* descriptor file.

By using a combination of these two approaches, the garbage collector and the idle timer, WebLogic is able to provide robust detection of connection leaks and thereby efficiently manage the pool of connections associated with the resource adapter.

Connection proxy wrappers

In order to implement the connection pool and transactional features, WebLogic augments the ordinary connection objects with proxy wrappers. Thus, when a client requests a managed connection associated with the resource adapter, WebLogic doesn't return the physical connection to the client, but instead returns the augmented proxy wrapper. Thus, if you cast the object returned from a connection pool to the actual Connection class, a ClassCastException will occur. This can happen either in your client code or in the resource adapter code itself. We recommend that you change your client code to avoid this situation.

When such an exception is thrown in the resource adapter code, or in client code that is using container-managed security, WebLogic tries to catch the exception and return the underlying Connection object instead of the proxy, thereby allowing the cast to succeed. WebLogic also logs a warning message when this happens. However, because the client is no longer using the proxy wrapper itself, WebLogic cannot detect connection leaks or enlist non-XA connectors in distributed transactions. Even though the Administration Console lets you monitor deployed resource adapters and associated connections, it provides no indication of which connections are proxy objects and which connections are unwrapped objects.

Error Logging and Tracing

Every ManagedConnectionFactory instance or ManagedConnection object supports the getLogWriter( ) and setLogWriter( ) methods, which provide error-logging and tracing facility for the resource adapter. The *weblogic-ra.xml* descriptor file provides two configuration settings that deal with error logging for a resource adapter deployed to WebLogic Server:

- A `logging-enabled` element that indicates whether logging is enabled for the connection factory.

- A `log-filename` element that specifies the location of the file to which all log messages generated by the resource adapter are written. This option needs to be supplied only if the `logging-enabled` element has been set to true.

The following XML fragment shows how to enable error logging for a resource adapter:

```
...
<logging-enabled>true</logging-enabled>
<log-filename>logs/eis.log</log-filename>
...
```

By default, error logging and tracing is disabled for the connection factory.

Secure Access

All resources within WebLogic can be protected by a security policy, as explained in Chapter 17. Resource adapters are no exception, and WebLogic insists that only authenticated and authorized users are permitted to use them. This security has to be applied at two levels. You need to define which calling principals are permitted to use the resource, and which principals the resource should run under when communicating with the EIS.

This section shows how WebLogic allows you to set up secure access to the underlying EIS using the resource adapter as the conduit. We look at the various sign-on and authentication mechanisms supported by WebLogic, and at how to map WebLogic users to credentials of a valid user on the remote EIS.

Sign-on mechanisms

WebLogic's JCA framework supports two sign-on mechanisms:

Application-managed sign-on
> Here, the client component is responsible for providing the credentials when it attempts to obtain a connection from the resource adapter. WebLogic simply passes these credentials on to the resource adapter.

Container-managed sign-on
> Here, the client component doesn't offer any security information. Instead, WebLogic provides the security information based on the client initiating the call, and a mapping between the calling and resource principals. This mapping is made using the Administration Console, and stored along with other security data in WebLogic's embedded LDAP server.

Once WebLogic has determined the resource principal information, it presents these credentials to the J2EE connector as a Java Authentication and Authorization Service (JAAS) Subject.

Mapping WebLogic users to resource principals

A security mapping is a mapping between WebLogic users (also known as *initiating principals*) and resource principals. For example, in a container-managed environment, a client will have been authenticated as a particular WebLogic user. Now this WebLogic user must be associated with a resource principal (i.e., a user and her credentials) that has access to the EIS. This security mapping can be configured only for resource adapters already deployed to WebLogic. To access these security mappings for a resource adapter, right-click the desired connector in the left frame of the Administration Console and choose the Define Credential Mappings option.

This lists all the current credential mappings, and also provides the "Configure a new Credential" option to create a new credential mapping. To set up this credential map, you will need to supply the names of the WebLogic user and the associated remote user. After you have created this credential mapping, you should return to the list of all credential maps. Here, you will be able to click the username of each remote user that you have defined and assign a password to the remote user.

For each credential map that you configure, you will need to also specify the password associated with the remote user. Your credential maps are persisted by the security realm implementation, and also will be available the next time you start WebLogic Server.

WebLogic reserves three special local usernames for any resource adapter:

`weblogic_ra_initial`
> If you map this user to a resource principal, the target credentials are used for setting up the initial connections for the connection pool when the resource adapter is deployed. If you haven't mapped this user to a resource principal, WebLogic uses the credentials associated with `weblogic_ra_default`.

`weblogic_ra_anonymous`
> If you map this user to a resource principal, the target credentials are used when no user is authenticated for the connection request to the resource adapter.

`weblogic_ra_default`
> If you map this user to a resource principal, the target credentials are used when the current runtime principal doesn't match any of the initiating principals defined, *or* when no user has been authenticated for the connection request and no anonymous credentials have been defined for the anonymous user.

Note that if initial capacity of the connection pool is greater than 0, you should map the `weblogic_ra_initial` user to a resource principal that is authorized to access the actual EIS.

Using the Resource Adapter

After configuring the *weblogic-ra.xml* descriptor file and deploying the resource adapter, client components (servlet, JSP, EJB, etc.) can look up the connection factory either using the global JNDI name or via a resource reference to the connection factory. For instance, if a JSP page were to request a connection from Sun's XADataSource Connector, it could look up the connection factory using the global JNDI name it was bound to:

```
javax.naming.InitialContext ic = new javax.naming.InitialContext ();
javax.resource.cci.ConnectionFactory cf =
    (javax.resource.cci.ConnectionFactory) ic.lookup("myapp.XADsWithTx");
```

Alternatively, you could define a reference to the resource adapter in the XML descriptors for the web application that holds the JSP:

```
<!-- web.xml entry -->
<webapp>
  ...
  <resource-ref>
    <res-ref-name>jca/xads</res-ref-name>
    <res-type>javax.resource.cci.ConnectionFactory</res-type>
    <res-auth>Container</res-auth>
    <res-sharing-scope>Shareable</res-sharing-scope>
  </resource-ref>
  ...
</webapp>

<!-- weblogic.xml entry -->
<reference-descriptor>
  <resource-description>
    <res-ref-name>jca/xads</res-ref-name>
    <jndi-name>myapp.XADsWithTx</jndi-name>
  </resource-description>
  ...
</reference-descriptor>
```

Here we've defined a resource reference *jca/xads* that points to the connection factory instance bound to the global JNDI name myapp.XADsWithTx. When you redeploy the web application, the connection factory will then be available to the JSP under the local ENC for the web application:

```
javax.naming.InitialContext ic = new javax.naming.InitialContext ();
javax.resource.cci.ConnectionFactory cf =
    (javax.resource.cci.ConnectionFactory) ic.lookup("java:comp/env/jca/xads");
```

In the same way, you can define a resource reference for an EJB component that is then available to all EJBs packaged within the EJB JAR file. Refer to Chapter 10 to see how you can set up references to J2EE resources.

Now you are ready to develop a client that uses the JDBC Connector to connect to the actual database. However, instead of using JDBC calls, the client will use the CCI contracts implemented by the XADataSource connector. Here's a summary of the steps that a client component needs to execute in order to interact with the underlying EIS (in this case, a database that lives on an SQL Server 2000 instance):

1. Request a connection from the resource adapter, and set up an interaction:

```
InitialContext ic = new InitialContext();
ConnectionFactory cf = (ConnectionFactory) ic.lookup("java:comp/env/jca/testds");
Connection con = (Connection) cf.getConnection();
Interaction i = (Interaction) con.createInteraction();
```

2. Describe the kind of interaction with the underlying resource. In this case, we will run a PreparedStatement SQL query that returns, at most, 10 rows in the result set:

```
// CciInteractionSpec implements java.resource.cci.InteractionSpec, and is one
// of the implementation classes provided by the resource adapter itself
CciInteractionSpec ispec = new CciInteractionSpec();
ispec.setFunctionName("EXECUTEQUERY");
ispec.setQuery("select firstname, lastname from tblEmployee
 where salary > ? and lastname like ?");
ispec.setPrepared(true);
ispec.setMaxRows(10);
ispec.setResultSetType(ResultSet.TYPE_SCROLL_INSENSITIVE);
```

3. Create an IndexedRecord instance that acts as a holder for any parameters that need to be provided for the interaction to succeed:

```
// CciIndexedRecord implements java.resource.cci.IndexedRecord, and is one
// of the implementation classes provided by the resource adapter itself
IndexedRecord rec = new CciIndexedRecord();
rec.add(new Integer(1000));
rec.add("mount%");
```

4. Execute the interaction using the InteractionSpec and IndexedRecord instances:

```
ResultSet rs = (ResultSet) i.execute(ispec, rec);
```

5. Iterate over the rows of the ResultSet and use the getXXX() methods to retrieve column values:

```
while (rs.next()) {
    out.println("First Name: " + rs.getString(1) + " Last Name: " + rs.
getString(2));
}
```

6. After completion, release any resources acquired during the interaction:

```
rs.close();
i.close();
con.close();
```

Make sure that you properly close the connection to the EIS before completion so that you avoid any connection leaks.

Clearly the exact nature of the interaction between the client and the EIS will depend on both the resource adapter and the EIS vendor itself. Thus, even though your code isn't portable across resource adapters, the JCA framework guarantees that your code remains portable across J2EE Application Servers.

Monitoring Connections

You can use the Administration Console to monitor the status of connections obtained via the resource adapter. Select Deployments/Connector Modules from the left pane of the Administration Console, and then select the Monitoring tab. This displays a list of all deployed resource adapters, together with their monitoring statistics.

For each resource adapter, you can view the number of active connections, the number of connections that have been created, the number of idle connections, and the number of connection leaks. You also can click some of the figures to view further details. For example, if you select the number of connections displayed below the Connections column, you can view the status of all active connections. If you also have enabled connection profiling on the resource adapter, then Connection Idle Profiles lets you view the profile of all idle connections, and Connection Leaked Connections lets you view the profile of all leaked connections. In both of these cases, the Administration Console provides a "delete" button that allows you to manually close the connection, provided WebLogic deems that it is safe to do so. In other words, the "delete" operation is allowed only if the connection has exceeded its maximum idle time limit and is not participating in any transaction.

CHAPTER 8

JMS

The Java Messaging Service (JMS) has become the de facto standard for accessing message-oriented middleware products. It equips the Java developer with a powerful programming model that facilitates asynchronous, decoupled communication. WebLogic provides both the point-to-point and publish-and-subscribe models, as well as message persistence, flow control, guaranteed delivery, message redelivery, expiry, paging, concurrent message handling, and more. By supporting all of these features and enhancements, WebLogic offers a rich and robust framework for creating portable JMS applications that can operate and scale in a clustered environment.

All of the messaging facilities are implemented by a JMS server, which is pinned to a particular WebLogic instance. The JMS server in turn hosts a number of destinations (either topics or queues) with which clients can interact. In order to connect to the JMS server, you need to set up one or more *connection factories*. A connection factory encapsulates a number of properties that typically apply to all connections (and sessions) manufactured by it. Both the connection factories and JMS destinations are available in the server's JNDI tree.

WebLogic provides a number of ways to tune the performance of the JMS server. You can set up quotas that limit the number of messages that can be held in the server's memory, and enable paging so that the messages held in memory can be swapped out to a persistent store under threshold conditions. A JMS server can also throttle the rate at which JMS clients produce messages when it reaches threshold conditions. In extreme situations, it can temporarily block producers from sending messages. WebLogic 8.1 lets you customize the manner in which expired messages are handled.

JMS stores are needed for facilities such as persistent messaging, paging, and durable subscriptions. WebLogic JMS supports two kinds of JMS stores: a file store and a JDBC store. In some ways, JDBC stores are more flexible and easier to manage when a JMS server fails. Nevertheless, file stores offer a large performance advantage, especially when combined with the various asynchronous write policies.

WebLogic provides several ways of adjusting how messages are delivered and handled. For instance, you can set a delay between when messages are sent and when they arrive at a destination. You can also set up a schedule that determines the exact time periods when messages are delivered. Of course, you can set a maximum age for the message, which determines how long the message will be retained by the system. And you can decide how JMS messages are redelivered, when a JMS session needs to recover, or when a transacted session needs to roll back. Messages intended for topics can be delivered to subscribers using the more optimal network multicasts, but at the expense of reliability. Producers can send (or broadcast) preacknowledged messages so that consumers need not acknowledge their receipt.

WebLogic JMS also introduces an additional message type for handling XML data. The message selector syntax has been augmented to allow XPath filters that can inspect the contents of the message body. Its support for a server-side pool of JMS sessions provides an alternative way to concurrently handle incoming messages, much like message-driven beans. Of course, WebLogic JMS is XA-enabled, which means that all activity within a JMS session can occur within the scope of a JTA transaction, alongside other XA-aware resources. In fact, WebLogic JMS neatly integrates with standard J2EE components so that your servlets and EJBs can automatically benefit from connection pooling, distributed transactions, and container-managed security.

WebLogic's JMS is designed to operate in a clustered environment. Connection factories deployed to a cluster can automatically route JMS requests to the pinned JMS server. Client requests for a JMS connection are automatically load-balanced among the available servers that host the connection factory. WebLogic JMS also introduces the notion of a distributed destination, which represents a number of physical destinations hosted on different JMS servers in the same cluster. Both consumers and producers are load-balanced among the members of this distributed destination. Unfortunately, WebLogic cannot automatically failover consumers when a member of the distributed destination becomes unavailable. Message producers can however, silently failover in certain situations, depending on how they are configured. Still, subsequent consumers and producers can be load-balanced among the remaining members of the distributed destination set. To better support availability, you can migrate a JMS server to another WebLogic instance, when required.

Finally, WebLogic provides two ways to integrate with other messaging systems. First, you can use a messaging bridge to connect WebLogic JMS with another JMS provider and thereby interoperate with a third-party enterprise messaging system. Alternatively, you can directly set up a foreign JMS server and make its connection factories and destinations available to JMS clients of WebLogic.

Configuring JMS Resources

This section looks at the major administered objects that constitute the configuration of WebLogic's JMS provider. To configure WebLogic JMS and related resources, you need to start up the Administration Console and then navigate to the Services/JMS node in the left pane. Here you can access and set up all the crucial JMS resources, such as the JMS servers, connection factories, physical destinations, JMS stores, and more.

Server

A JMS server implements the actual messaging facilities. Each JMS server lives on a *single* WebLogic instance and hosts a number of messaging destinations. Thus, the WebLogic instance that actually hosts the destination is determined only once you target its JMS server to a WebLogic instance. Distributed destinations, however, deviate from this rule. Because a distributed destination provides a transparent layer above an existing set of server-specific physical destinations, they aren't bound to any of the JMS servers. Note that multiple JMS servers may be hosted by the same WebLogic instance.

In order to configure a new JMS server, select the Servers node from the left pane of the Administration Console, and then click the "Configure a new JMS Server" link from the right pane. All the settings for the JMS server can be found under the Configuration tab. Here you must use the General tab to specify a logical name for the JMS server, to configure a JMS store for the persistent messages, to set the paging store for swapping in-memory messages to disk, and to configure a template that will be used to create any temporary destinations on the JMS server.

Then use the Target and Deploy tab to deploy the JMS server to a particular WebLogic instance. To enable support for high availability, you also can set up a *Migratable Target* list for the JMS server—i.e., a set of WebLogic instances within a cluster to which the JMS server and all its destinations can be migrated.

Whenever you do create a server such as this, it is often a good idea to also set the quotas and thresholds, and configure paging if it's needed.

Destinations

A JMS destination represents a delivery target for any message. It is a virtual channel that acts as an intermediary between the message producer and its consumers. The JMS server ensures that any messages delivered to a JMS destination are received by all who listen to (or poll) the destination. WebLogic supports both queue destinations, in which the delivered message is intended for a single consumer, and topic destinations, in which the message is intended for multiple subscribers. You can use the Administration Console to configure a predetermined set of JMS destinations that will be hosted by the JMS server. In order to set up a new JMS destination, choose a JMS server from under the Servers' node in the left pane, select its Destinations node, and then select either the "Configure a new JMS Queue" or "Configure a new JMS Topic" links.

Now use the General tab to specify a logical name for the destination, and the JNDI name to which the destination will be bound. In addition, you can assign a template to inherit (and possibly override) a set of configuration settings that are defined in the JMS template. You also can assign one or more destination keys to determine the sort order on any incoming messages.

The JMS destination will be available in the server's JNDI tree once the JMS server that owns the destination has been targeted to a WebLogic instance. In fact, if the JMS server is part of a cluster, the JMS destination can be made available to the cluster-wide JNDI tree, and therefore be accessible to all members of the cluster. Later, we examine how to programmatically create permanent destinations on a JMS server.

In addition, you should set the store characteristics of the destination on its Configuration/General tab. Here you can specify one of the following values for the Enable Store setting:

false
> By setting the value to false, you indicate to WebLogic that the destination will not support persistent messaging. Any persistent messages delivered to the destination will be downgraded to nonpersistent.

default
> The destination supports persistent messages, provided the JMS server has been configured with a JMS store. If a store has not been configured for the server, the behavior of the JMS destination is akin to "false."

true
> By setting this value to true, you indicate that the destination does support persistent messaging. Moreover, if the JMS server does not define a JMS store, the JMS server will not start.

Connection Factory

As noted earlier, a connection factory encapsulates a set of configuration properties for connections to the JMS server. A JMS client must use the connection factory to obtain a connection to a JMS server before it can perform any work. A JMS client can then use the connection to create JMS sessions. Each session defines a serial order for how messages are produced or consumed. Thus, a connection factory is an administered object that encapsulates a set of predefined characteristics that are shared by all connections it creates. A connection factory is independent of the JMS servers in the domain, and may be targeted to any number of WebLogic instances. A JMS server can be deployed to a single WebLogic instance only, while a JMS connection factory may be targeted to a WebLogic cluster. In this way, you can provide cluster-wide, transparent access to the destinations on a JMS server.

You can create multiple JMS connection factories that encapsulate predefined connection attributes. When a WebLogic instance starts up, any JMS connection factory targeted to the server is bound into the server's JNDI tree. A JMS client then can obtain a JMS connection factory from JNDI. In fact, WebLogic provides two JMS connection factories by default, which can be looked up using the following JNDI names:

`weblogic.jms.ConnectionFactory`
> A JMS connection factory that can be used to create connections to JMS servers.

`weblogic.jms.XAConnectionFactory`
> A JMS connection factory that creates JMS connections that can participate in distributed transactions, alongside other XA-aware resources.

These default JMS connection factories are available on all server instances in a domain. You have no control over which servers the default JMS connection factories ought to be deployed to. Moreover, applications that rely on a custom JMS connection factory are easier to port to an alternative J2EE environment. Once the application makes an explicit demand for a JMS resource, the Administrator can fulfill those needs, provided you steer away from WebLogic's default JMS factories. You can explicitly disable the default JMS factories on all JMS servers targeted to a server, using the Administration Console. Choose a server from the left pane, and navigate to the Services/JMS tab on the right. Use the Enable Default JMS Connection Factories option to toggle the default factories.

To configure a new JMS connection factory, select the Connection Factories node from the left pane of the Administration Console, and then click on the "Configure a new JMS Connection Factory" link in the right frame. Here you can configure the different aspects of the behavior of the connections returned by the JMS factory. Note that many of the attributes are dynamically configurable, so any configuration changes that are applied to a connection factory will automatically come into effect for subsequent connections made using the connection factory.

> JMS connection factories within a domain should be uniquely named, or else the server will not start up.

Use the General tab to specify a name for the connection factory and the JNDI name to which the JMS factory will be bound. You also can set the default message delivery attributes, the acknowledgment semantics, and the behavior of the close( ) method for any JMS clients of the factory. Then use the Targets and Deploy tab to target the connection factory to the desired servers or clusters. All remaining configuration issues are covered in later sections.

Imagine a JMS server, myJMSServer, that hosts a JMS queue, myQueue, targeted to a WebLogic instance named myServer. Furthermore, a JMS connection factory, myCF, is configured and also targeted to the same server. Given this scenario, the following code snippet shows how to create a JMS session that you can use to send or receive messages from the configured JMS queue:

```
// set up the initial JNDI context
javax.naming.Context ctx = new InitialContext(env);
// lookup the JMS factory from the server's JNDI tree
javax.jms.QueueConnectionFactory factory =
  (javax.jms.QueueConnectionFactory) ctx.lookup("myCF");

// use the factory to manufacture a QueueConnection
javax.jms.QueueConnection con = factory.createQueueConnection( );

// use the QueueConnection object to initiate a JMS session
javax.jms.QueueSession session = con.createQueueSession(false, DUPS_OK_ACKNOWLEDGE);

// use the createQueue( ) method to locate myQueue hosted on myJMSServer
javax.jms.Queue queue = session.createQueue("myJMSServer/myQueue");

// now send/receive messages using the queue
// ...
```

All this is standard JMS code. Because we wish to interact with a configured JMS queue, we have cast the connection factory object obtained from the JNDI lookup to java.jms.QueueConnectionFactory. This queue connection factory allows us to create a connection to the JMS server, and subsequently initiate a JMS session. A JMS connection factory is thread-safe, and so can be used concurrently by multiple threads. Notice how we've used the createQueue( ) method on the JMS session to locate the configured queue. Alternatively, we could have performed another JNDI lookup to access the JMS queue. Thus, if the queue were assigned the JNDI name oreilly.myQ at configuration time, you could access the destination as follows:

```
javax.jms.Queue queue = (javax.jms.Queue) ctx.lookup("oreilly.myQ");
```

If you need to interact with a configured JMS topic, then use the topic counterparts for the JMS factory, connection, and session.

As you can see, JMS servers, destinations, and connection factories are critical resources for any JMS-enabled application. We now look at other optional JMS resources that help you adjust other aspects of the JMS server configuration.

Templates

A *template* is a convenience mechanism that allows you to define a set of characteristics that then can be shared by multiple destinations. When you assign a template to a JMS destination, it inherits the values for any configuration settings defined by the template. Of course, a destination may override any values configured for its template. Thus, a template eases the configuration of multiple JMS destinations. Any changes to the values of configuration settings for the template are dynamically propagated to all destinations that use that template, provided the destination itself doesn't override those configuration settings. For instance, if all queues must share a particular threshold and quota policy, you can define a new template with the desired threshold and quota settings, and then assign this template to each queue.

To create a new template, expand the JMS/Templates node from the left pane and then select the "Configure a new JMS Template" link on the right pane. Here you can adjust the values for a subset of the usual configuration settings for any JMS destination. In particular, you can set the default threshold and quotas, expiration policy, and redelivery behavior for any destination that uses the template. You also must supply a logical name for the template. You will use this name to refer to the template when assigning it to a JMS destination.

In order to assign a template to a physical destination, you must set the Template option in the Configuration/General tab to the name of an existing destination. After this, the JMS destination automatically inherits any unchanged settings from the template. As you will see later, a template must also be configured for the JMS server if applications need to create temporary destinations.

Destination Keys

A destination key can be used to set the sort order for messages that have arrived at a physical destination. Messages are sorted in either the ascending or descending order of the values of some message header field or property. For example, if an application sets the message expiration times, you may sort the messages arriving at the destination on the JMSExpiration header field to bias the consumers toward processing messages that will expire the soonest. A destination key determines only a specific sort order. To actually implement the sort, you have to assign the key to a destination. You can assign multiple keys to a physical destination.

> Sorting occurs only if there are multiple messages waiting at a destination. If a queue is being used, and consumers are always available and constantly removing messages placed on the queue, the messages will not be sorted. Instead, the messages will be processed in the order in which they enter the queue. In such cases, using a destination key will yield no benefits. In fact, destination keys will always be ineffective unless multiple messages are waiting at a destination.

To create a new destination key, select the Destination Keys node from the left pane, and then the "Configure a new JMS Destination Key" link from the right pane. Here you must set the following values for a destination key:

Name
    Use this option to set the logical name for the key. The name of the key is used when assigning it to a physical destination.

Direction

Use this option to sort in either ascending or descending order. If ascending order is chosen, and the property is set to JMSMessageID, the messages arrive in a first-in, first-out (FIFO) fashion, which is the default ordering for messages arriving on a destination.

*Sort key**

Use this setting to determine the name of the property or header field on which to sort the incoming messages.

Key type

Use this setting to set the expected type of the key. The key type can take any one of the following values: String, Boolean, Byte, Short, Int, Long, Float, or Double. This setting is used only if the destination key defines a sort order on some message property field. If the destination key specifies a message header field instead, this setting is ignored.

If the key defines a sort order in terms of a message header field, then you may use any of the following names: JMSMessageID, JMSTimestamp, JMSCorrelationID, JMS-Priority, JMSExpiration, JMSType, JMSRedelivered, or JMSDeliveryTime.

Sorting on JMS header fields is more efficient than sorting on property names, and is recommended for better performance.

Once you have defined a number of destination keys, you can put them into action by selecting a destination from a JMS server. Then, in the Configuration/General tab, you can choose from the available destination keys and assign them to the particular destination.

Let's see how destination keys impact the way messages arrive on a JMS destination. First, let's create two destination keys:

- A destination key that defines an ascending sort on the JMSPriority header field.
- A second destination key that defines a descending sort on a message property field price of type Int.

After creating the two keys, assign both of these destination keys, in the same order, to an existing queue. Now imagine a queue receiver that does nothing much except listen to the queue and print out the values of the priority and price fields of any message delivered to the queue. In addition, we have a producer that sends a number of messages to the same queue in a loop, increasing the value of the price property field on each iteration. To make things interesting, our queue sender also delivers three messages of different priority on each iteration. The following code sample illustrates this:

---

* This is called Property in WebLogic 7.0.

```
for (int i=0;i<2;i++) {
    msg.setIntProperty("price", i);
    qsender.send(wlmsg, javax.jms.DeliveryMode.NON_PERSISTENT,
            2, 1800000);
    qsender.send(wlmsg, javax.jms.DeliveryMode.NON_PERSISTENT,
            3, 1800000);
    qsender.send(wlmsg, javax.jms.DeliveryMode.NON_PERSISTENT,
            1, 1800000);
    msg.clearProperties();
}
```

Remember that sorting occurs only if there are multiple messages waiting at the queue. If the queue receiver is listening at the time the messages are sent, no sorting will occur and the messages will arrive in the order in which they were sent. In that case, the queue receiver will generate the following output:

```
Got Message: Priority = 2 & Price = 0
Got Message: Priority = 3 & Price = 0
Got Message: Priority = 1 & Price = 0
Got Message: Priority = 2 & Price = 1
Got Message: Priority = 3 & Price = 1
Got Message: Priority = 1 & Price = 1
```

In order to ensure that sorting does occur on messages arriving on the queue, we must create a scenario in which multiple messages are waiting on the queue. One way to achieve this is by running the queue sender first, and then only later starting the queue receiver. With destination sorting enabled, the queue receiver will generate the following output:

```
Got Message: Priority = 1 & Price = 1
Got Message: Priority = 1 & Price = 0
Got Message: Priority = 2 & Price = 1
Got Message: Priority = 2 & Price = 0
Got Message: Priority = 3 & Price = 1
Got Message: Priority = 3 & Price = 0
```

As specified, the messages arriving on the destination are sorted first in ascending order of the priority field, and then in descending order of the property field price.

By default, messages received by a destination are sorted in ascending order of the JMSMessageID header field, which results in a FIFO ordering. If you want to impose a last-in, first-out (LIFO) ordering on the destination, simply assign a destination key that sorts on the JMSMessageID field in descending order. Note that sorting may degrade server performance because the JMS server must scan the destination to find the correct place to insert a received message.

Later in this chapter, in the section "Controlling Message Delivery," we shall see how WebLogic allows you to delay the delivery of JMS messages. In such cases, you must take care to sort on the JMSMessageID header field, as the delayed delivery times could mean that messages arrive at the JMS destination out of their message ID order, thereby defeating the purpose of the destination key altogether. In such situations, the better approach would be to sort on the JMSDeliveryTime header field.

JMS Stores

WebLogic lets you configure JMS stores for two reasons:

- For storing and paging persistent messages and durable subscribers to an external store, thereby guaranteeing their existence even if a JMS server fails
- For paging nonpersistent messages to an external store so that in-memory JMS messages can be swapped out when the JMS server is under heavy load

WebLogic lets you choose from two types of JMS stores: a file-based store and a JDBC-accessible database store. Both of these choices provide the same transaction semantics and guarantees, and so can be used interchangeably. A file store also is recommended for temporarily swapping out nonpersistent messages to disk when the JMS server is under load. Persistent messages don't need a dedicated paging store. If paging is enabled, they will simply use the persistent store. However, nonpersistent messages do need a dedicated paging store. If a JMS server must support both persistent and nonpersistent message paging, you will need to configure a persistent store and a paging store.

In order to configure a new file store, expand the JMS/Stores node from the left pane of the Administration Console, and then click the "Configure a new JMS File Store" link from the right pane. Use the General tab to specify a logical name for the file store and the location of the directory that will host the file store. Also, select the Synchronous Write Policy option to determine how the file store writes data to disk. In order to create a new JDBC store, select the JMS/Stores node from the left pane, and then click the "Configure a new JMS JDBC Store" link from the right pane. Once again, specify a logical name for the JDBC store, choose from one of the existing connection pools that will be used to access the database, and set the prefix name that will help identify the JMS-related tables in the database.

File stores generally are considerably faster than JDBC stores. Moreover, no network traffic is generated when you use a file-based store for the JMS server, whereas JDBC stores will generate network traffic if the database lives on a different machine. JDBC stores offer another significant advantage: they make it somewhat easier to recover from failures. If a machine hosting a JMS server fails, the JDBC store still can be accessed if you migrate the service to another machine. If you need the same functionality for a JMS file store, ensure that it resides on a shared disk.* This way, if a machine hosting the JMS server fails, the persistent messages are still accessible once the JMS server is migrated to another machine.

A JMS store for persistent messages invariably will slow down the application, so ensure that your JMS applications really need the persistent quality of service. Similarly, enabling message paging to a JMS store will be more expensive than disabling paging altogether.

---

* Preferably a SAN, or dual-ported SCSI—not NFS or even Windows network drives because these are not transactionally safe.

Distributed Destination

A *distributed destination* represents a collection of physical destinations that may be hosted on multiple JMS servers within a cluster. A distributed destination is accessible through a single JNDI name because it is bound to the cluster-wide JNDI tree. Just like physical destinations, it implements the javax.jms.Destination interface, and can be used just like them as well. Accessing a distributed queue is no different from accessing an ordinary queue:

```
javax.jms.QueueSession session = con.createQueueSession(false, DUPS_OK_ACKNOWLEDGE);
javax.jms.Queue queue = session.createQueue("myDistributedQueue");
```

The fact that the distributed queue represents multiple physical queues is transparent to the JMS client. Later, we shall see how you also can access the individual members of a distributed destination.

In order to configure a distributed destination, you must navigate to the Services/JMS/Distributed Destinations node within the left pane of the Administration Console, and then click the "Configure a new Distributed Topic/Queue" link. Here you must specify a logical name for the destination and the JNDI name to which the distributed queue or topic will be bound. Because a distributed destination includes multiple JMS destinations spread across different JMS servers in the cluster, you also must configure the distributed destination's load-balancing policy and its forward delay. After this, you must use the Configuration/Members tab to configure the physical destinations that belong to the distributed destination. As we shall see later, you can choose from preexisting destinations or from the existing set of JMS servers, and let WebLogic create the physical destinations on these servers for you.

JMS Session Pools

The JMS standard requires that JMS sessions be *single-threaded*. This means that a JMS listener cannot concurrently process multiple messages within a single JMS session. To circumvent this problem, the specification allows for a pool of server-side sessions, a feature that enables an application to process messages concurrently.

The server-side pool of JMS sessions is preloaded with a custom JMS consumer that is dedicated to processing the messages that arrive at the destination. In other words, each member of the JMS session pool loads an instance of a message listener class. When a message arrives on a JMS destination, the JMS server automatically dips into this session pool and invokes the onMessage() method supplied by your listener class. Because a separate instance of the message listener is assigned to each session in the pool, the JMS server is able to handle multiple incoming messages concurrently. Under heavy load, the JMS server may even dispense multiple messages to a session, thereby reducing context switching between the sessions (which is permitted by the JMS specification).

There are several key issues to resolve when configuring a server-side JMS session pool:

- You must specify the JNDI name of the connection factory that will be used to create the JMS sessions within the pool.

- You should specify the fully qualified name of the listener class that will consume the messages that arrive on the destination.

- You should set the JNDI name of the destination to which the JMS message listeners will be bound.

- You should configure the acknowledgment mode for the JMS sessions within the pool, and also indicate whether the sessions are transacted.

- Finally, of course, you must determine the size of the JMS session pool.

You wouldn't be completely wrong to think that JMS session pools were quite similar to message-driven beans. Both enable you to set up a pool of JMS consumers that concurrently process incoming messages on a configured destination. On the whole, message-driven beans are more powerful than JMS session pools. For instance, message-driven beans can participate in distributed transactions, whereas JMS session pools provide you with (local) transacted sessions only. In addition, message-driven beans are a part of the J2EE standard, whereas session pools are simply an optional feature of the JMS specification. If you want portability, use message-driven beans instead. For this reason, we recommend you use message-driven beans in any new development.

In order to "configure a JMS session pool," you must first select a JMS server from the left pane of the Administration Console and then expand the Session Pools node. Next, you must select the "Configure a new JMS Session Pool" link from the right pane to proceed. You can then attach one or more connection consumers to this session pool, and thereby concurrently handle messages arriving at multiple destinations. The actual setup is deferred until later in this chapter, in the section "Concurrent Messaging," where we also look at how to programmatically create a JMS session pool. For now, you must recognize the role of JMS session pools in concurrent message processing.

Foreign JMS Servers

WebLogic 8.1 provides direct support for accessing third-party JMS providers. Using the Administration Console, you can map the connection factories and destinations on the remote JMS server to the local JNDI tree. When a JMS client looks up the foreign JMS object from the server's JNDI tree, WebLogic automatically performs another lookup on the remote JMS connection factory or destination using its remote JNDI name and the supplied JNDI context factory for the remote JMS provider. In this way, WebLogic applications create seamless access to the foreign JMS server and its administered objects. You also can use this approach to reference JMS connection factories and objects on another WebLogic JMS server in another domain.

Note that this type of integration is slightly different from WebLogic's bridging between two JMS servers. Through the configured foreign JMS provider, your applications are direct clients of the remote JMS server. On the other hand, a message bridge creates a pipe between a destination on the local JMS server, and another on the remote JMS server, so that any messages that are sent to the source destination are automatically forwarded to the target destination. In other words, your applications can indirectly interact with the remote JMS server through the configured message bridge.

Foreign JMS providers provide an additional benefit. Because the foreign destinations are directly mapped to WebLogic's JNDI tree, any message-driven bean (MDB) that you deploy to the server can simply reference the remote destination using its local JNDI name. The MDB will continue to function as if it were bound to a destination on the local JMS server, except that now, of course, the MDB will be triggered whenever a message arrives on the foreign JMS destination.

Configuring a foreign JMS provider

In order to set up a foreign JMS provider, you must configure the following resources using the Administration Console:

- A foreign JMS server that provides WebLogic with the initial context factory
- A foreign JMS connection factory that is used to create connections to the remote JMS server
- Any number of foreign JMS destinations that live on the remote JMS server

To configure a foreign JMS server, select the JMS/Foreign JMS Servers node from the left pane, and then select the "Configure a new foreign JMS provider" option from the right pane. Here you must supply the following information:

JNDI Initial Context Factory
  Enter the fully qualified classname of the initial context factory that must be used to access the JNDI provider.

JNDI Connection URL
  Enter the URL that WebLogic should use to contact the JNDI provider. This URL will depend on the context factory that you have configured.

JNDI Properties
  Supply any additional JNDI properties that you want to be passed to the JNDI provider. Use the format "name=value" to specify each property.

This provides WebLogic with enough information to access the external JNDI provider. As an example, if you want to provide WebLogic applications with transparent access to JMS destinations on an IBM MQSeries installation, you could use the following settings to configure the foreign JMS server:

```
JNDI Initial Context Factory = "com.sun.jndi.fscontext.RefFSContextFactory"
JNDI Connection URL = "file:/MQJNDI/"
JNDI Properties = ""
```

Once you've created the foreign JMS server, you should use the Targets and Deploy tab to target the JMS server to multiple servers and/or clusters. After this, you must select the Foreign JMS Connection Factories node under your newly configured JMS server to configure a new JMS connection factory. Here, you will be asked to supply the following information:

Remote JNDI Name
> Use this attribute to specify the JNDI name of the connection factory on the remote JMS server. WebLogic then looks up the remote connection factory, using this JNDI name, and the JNDI initial context factory that you specified for the foreign JMS server.

Local JNDI Name
> Use this attribute to specify the JNDI name to which this foreign JMS connection factory will be bound.

Username and Password
> Use these attributes to specify a username and password that should be used to obtain a connection from the referenced JMS connection factory. These credentials are used only when the foreign JMS connection factory is referenced from within a resource-ref element in the deployment descriptors of the EJB or a web application, with a Container mode of authentication.

Use the Targets and Deploy tab to assign the connection factory to multiple WebLogic servers and/or clusters. When you assign the foreign JMS connection factory to multiple servers or a cluster, WebLogic binds a nonreplicated instance of the JMS connection factory to the local JNDI tree of each targeted server.

Once you have specified a foreign connection factory, you can configure one or more foreign destinations by choosing the "Foreign JMS destinations" node from under the new foreign JMS server node in the left pane. For each foreign destination, you must supply the remote JNDI name of the destination and the local JNDI name to which the foreign destination should be mapped. In this way, when an application looks up the foreign destination from the local server's JNDI tree, WebLogic transparently looks up the destination on the remote JMS server using its remote JNDI name. The foreign JMS destinations will be deployed to all servers and/or clusters to which the owning foreign JMS server has been targeted.

 Client applications must use the foreign connection factory to create producers and consumers that can interact with the configured foreign destinations. So, any MDBs that listen to a foreign destination also must be configured to use the foreign connection factory.

Optimizing JMS Performance

This section looks at how to optimize the performance of the JMS server. We examine how message quotas for the JMS server and/or the destinations can be used to limit the number of messages that can be stored in memory. We look at how to enable paging, and how to enable the JMS server to throttle the rate of message production under load. Both message paging and flow control rely on a set of threshold values that determine when the JMS server and/or destinations are considered to be under load.

After this, we devote our attention to improving the performance of JMS file stores and to achieving the ideal setup for the JDBC connection pool associated with a JDBC store. We also cover the active message expiration feature provided by WebLogic 8.1, and the various ways in which the JMS server can handle expired messages. Finally, we discuss the two important ways of implementing concurrent messaging, and in particular, probe the use of server session pools.

Message Quotas

Quotas allow you to restrict the number of messages that can be held in memory. These limits can be specified in terms of either the maximum number of messages or the maximum cumulative size of the messages (in bytes). WebLogic JMS lets you configure message quotas for both the JMS server and the destinations it hosts. The relevant settings, available within the Thresholds & Quotas tab for the chosen JMS server or destination, are as follows:

Messages Maximum
Use this setting to determine the maximum number of messages that can be retained in memory.

Bytes Maximum
Use this setting to set the upper limit on the cumulative size of all messages held in memory.

Do not confuse the Messages Maximum setting here with the Messages Maximum setting for a connection factory. The latter indicates the maximum number of messages that may be placed in an asynchronous session's pipeline.

 It is good practice to set a quota on your JMS servers or destinations. Otherwise, the server hosting the JMS server or destination could run out of memory.

Message quotas that are set for a destination determine the maximum number of bytes or messages that can be stored in the destination, while message quotas for a JMS server determine the maximum number of bytes or messages that can be stored in the JMS server. If a producer tries to send messages that exceed the quotas set for the JMS server or destination, a javax.jms.ResourceAllocationException exception is thrown, and the message will not be delivered. One possible action to take in these circumstances is to pause before resending the message.

Message Paging

Unless messaging paging has been enabled, all messages that arrive at the JMS server, regardless of whether they are persistent, are held in memory. This is an important aspect of the JMS server that you need to keep in mind when architecting a solution. Fortunately, WebLogic provides a message paging facility that allows the JMS server to move messages from memory to persistent storage during specified load conditions. The message header and property fields will continue to remain in memory, even though the body of the messages may be swapped out to the paging store. This ensures that more virtual memory is made available to the JMS server when it is under load. Message paging does not affect your JMS applications in any way. It occurs transparently on the JMS server. The only side effect of message paging is that it may slow down the server. Clearly, paging to a persistent store will be more expensive than not paging at all, so you should balance the paging thresholds to ensure that paging occurs only when you need it.

In order to support paging for nonpersistent messages, you must configure a paging store for the JMS server. Persistent messages, however, do not require a paging store. They will automatically use persistent JMS stores configured for the server or destination. Because paging is quite performance-intensive, we recommend that you use file stores for message paging, and not for JDBC stores. Moreover, if a JMS store serves as a paging store for a JMS server, it cannot be used for other purposes, such as for capturing persistent messages or durable subscriptions. Nor can paging stores be shared by multiple JMS servers. If your domain includes multiple JMS servers, you must create a separate paging store for each.

How paging works

WebLogic supports two forms of paging: bytes paging and message paging. Each form uses a different measurement for determining when paging occurs and for how long. *Bytes paging* uses the number of bytes consumed by the messages on the JMS server as its primary measurement, while *message paging* uses the number of messages that are stored on the JMS server. Let's examine how bytes paging works on the JMS server. The same discussion also holds true for message paging.

Paging occurs on the basis of two settings: a high and a low threshold. The high threshold is used to start the paging mechanism. If the cumulative size (in bytes) of all messages stored on the JMS server *exceeds* the high threshold, the JMS server starts swapping in-memory messages out to the store. This paging mechanism remains in place until the number of bytes consumed by the messages on the JMS server falls *below* the low threshold value. Thus, the high threshold value determines only when the paging starts, at which point the server is said to be *armed*. Once this point is reached, the JMS server ignores the high threshold, and the low threshold determines when the paging stops.

Configuring paging for servers and destinations

Message paging can be configured for a JMS server and/or individual destinations. For a JMS server, you can specify the paging store, enable bytes or message paging, and set the appropriate threshold values. Similarly, for a JMS destination, you can enable bytes and/or message paging, and set the appropriate threshold values. In this case, the destination uses the paging store configured for the JMS server. By default, message paging is not enabled for the JMS server or any of its destinations. However, if you enable either bytes or message paging on the JMS server or any of its destinations, WebLogic automatically will create a paging store for the JMS server, even if you didn't configure one manually.

You can set the paging store for a JMS server using the Administration Console. Simply navigate to the Configuration/General tab for the desired JMS server and then choose from one of the existing JMS file stores. Once you've configured the paging store, you must navigate to the Thresholds & Quotas tab and specify values for the following attributes:

Bytes Paging Enabled
> Check this option to enable bytes paging on the JMS server.

Bytes Threshold High
> Use this option to determine when bytes paging starts—i.e., when the cumulative size of the messages on the JMS server exceeds this threshold value.

Bytes Threshold Low
> Use this option to determine when bytes paging stops—i.e., when the cumulative size of the messages on the JMS server falls back below this threshold value.

Message Paging Enabled
> Check this option to enable message paging on the JMS server.

Messages Threshold High
> Use this option to determine when message paging starts—i.e., when the number of messages on the JMS server falls back below this threshold value.

Messages Threshold Low
> Use this option to determine when message paging stops—i.e., when the number of messages on the JMS server falls back below this threshold value.

Note that it is not enough that you simply enable the Bytes/Message Paging Enabled options. You also must specify positive values for the appropriate thresholds. Similarly, if you just configure the thresholds but do not enable either bytes or message paging, the JMS server will just log the threshold conditions when they occur, and take no action. Once paging has been enabled, it cannot be dynamically disabled by setting the paging thresholds to −1. Instead, you can set the high threshold to a very large number, to prevent paging from being triggered.

You can configure both message *and* bytes paging for the server. If the JMS server crosses either of the configured thresholds, the appropriate paging mechanism comes into effect.

You can set up message paging on an individual destination as well. The same paging thresholds can be configured for a destination from the Thresholds & Quotas tab.

You can also use the Thresholds & Quotas tab to adjust the paging behavior for a JMS template, in which case all destinations that use the selected template will inherit the settings. For this reason, the Bytes/Message Paging Enabled options for a destination accept an additional value, default, which implies that its value is inherited from the template assigned to the destination. In other words, paging is enabled on the destination, provided that the Bytes/Message Paging Enabled options have been set on the template associated with the destination. On the other hand, you can explicitly set the Bytes/Message Paging Enabled options on a destination to true or false to override the values inherited from the template.

Note that if message paging is enabled on a JMS server but not on a destination hosted by the JMS server, messages arriving at the destination still can be swapped to the store when paging is initiated on the server. In this case, if message paging is disabled on a destination, paging will not be triggered if the messages stored on the destination exceed the high threshold set for the destination.

Flow Control

In general, producers send messages at a much faster rate than consumers can handle them, and in some situations, overactive producers can swamp consumers. This in turn can degrade the performance of the JMS servers and further aggravate the situation. WebLogic provides a *flow control* feature that allows the JMS server or destination to throttle the producers by suppressing the rate at which the messages are produced. Flow control works by delaying the time it takes for calls to produce a message to return. The flow control mechanism kicks in when the JMS server or destination exceeds its specified bytes or message upper threshold. In fact, the flow control mechanism uses the same "paging" thresholds defined for the JMS server or destination to decide if the server is still armed.

The flow control mechanism can be enabled on a connection factory. The flow control settings on the connection factory then permeate through to the JMS connections created by the factory, and then to the JMS sessions created from those connections, and finally to the JMS producers that use the connection factory. The Configuration/Flow Control tab for a selected connection factory holds the configuration settings. Tick the Flow Control Enabled option to enable flow control for all message producers created using the factory. The other settings provide a way of tuning the flow control.

How flow control works

A connection factory defines settings that limit the rate of flow of messages of its producers within a minimum and maximum range. As conditions degrade, the producers will send messages at a rate that tends toward the flow minimum range; as conditions improve, the producers will send messages at a rate that will gradually tend toward the flow maximum range. Once flow control has come into effect, the producers check at configured intervals if the threshold conditions still apply and if the need for flow control still exists. This, along with the number of flow steps, defines the rate at which the production rate moves toward the flow minimum or flow maximum ranges.

The flow control mechanism ensures that the production rate degrades at a faster rate than it improves. The decay in message production follows a geometric progression, whereas the increase follows a linear algorithm. The following sequential steps outline the flow control mechanism in operation:

1. When a JMS server or destination exceeds its bytes or message upper threshold, it becomes armed and the flow control mechanism kicks in for all producers of a connection factory for which flow control has been enabled.

2. Once the server or destination is armed, the flow control settings on the connection factory kick in and work toward limiting the message flow of its producers. Under these conditions, the producers instantly will be limited to sending messages at a rate that never exceeds the configured flow maximum number of messages per second. In fact, when a producer is flow-controlled, the rate of message production will be bound by the flow minimum and flow maximum ranges.

3. Starting from the specified flow maximum value, a producer will then periodically determine whether the server or destination is still armed. In fact, it is the flow interval that determines the time period (in seconds) after which the producers check for threshold conditions. If, after the interval, the server or destination is still armed, the producer further throttles its production rate. This can continue until the rate of message production reaches the flow minimum number of messages per second.

4. As all of the producers slow down, the threshold condition in the server or destination gradually corrects itself until it becomes unarmed. A producer is then allowed to increase its production rate again, in a controlled way, until the rate eventually reaches the flow maximum range. Only after the message production reaches the flow maximum is the producer released from all flow control.

As you can see, once a server or destination is armed, flow control ensures that the rate of message production fluctuates between the flow minimum and flow maximum ranges. Once the server or destination is unarmed, the rate of message production is allowed to increase in a controlled way up to the flow maximum, after which the flow control mechanism is disengaged. Finally, in order to determine whether the server or destination is still armed, and thus whether the producers must still be controlled, WebLogic uses the bytes or message thresholds configured for the JMS server or destination.

Tuning the flow control mechanism

Now, let's revisit the configuration settings that impact the flow control mechanism on all producers of a JMS connection factory. From the Configuration/Flow Control tab for a selected connection factory, you can adjust the following attributes:

Flow Maximum

> This setting determines the maximum number of messages per second for producers when the server or destination is experiencing a threshold condition. During these conditions, the rate of message production will never exceed this limit.

Flow Minimum

> This setting determines the minimum number of messages per second for producers when the server or destination is experiencing a threshold condition. During these conditions, the rate of message production will never go below this limit.

Flow Interval

> This setting defines the adjustment time period (in seconds) for all producers experiencing flow control. Once the flow control is in effect, the producers check at regular intervals to see whether the server is still armed and determine whether producers still need to be throttled.

Flow Steps

> This setting defines the number of steps needed to move the production rate from the Flow Maximum down to the Flow Minimum (or vice versa). At each flow step, the producers adjust their flow, either upward or downward, depending on the current conditions.

In addition, you must set the appropriate flow control thresholds from the Thresholds & Quotas tab for the JMS server or destination:

Bytes/Messages Threshold High

> Flow control kicks in when the number/size of the messages stored on the JMS server or destination exceeds this threshold value.

Bytes/Messages Threshold Low

> The server or destination becomes unarmed when the number/size of the messages on the JMS server or destination falls below this threshold value. Flow control still remains in effect until the producers move their rate upward and go beyond the flow maximum.

Blocking message producers

WebLogic 8.1 supports additional flow control features for temporarily blocking message producers from sending messages when the JMS destination has exceeded its message quota limit:

Blocking Send Policy

This setting determines the blocking strategy that is adopted by the JMS server when multiple producers are competing for space on a JMS destination that has reached its maximum quota limit. For instance, you can choose a blocking strategy so that the JMS server allows smaller messages to be delivered to the destination when larger ones are still waiting for space.

Send Timeout

By setting a send timeout value on a connection factory, this setting lets you allow the producers to wait for a specific length of time until space becomes available on a JMS destination that has reached its maximum quota limit.

To determine how the JMS server blocks send requests when a destination has reached its maximum quota, you must navigate to the Configuration/Thresholds & Quotas tab for the desired JMS server. Here you can specify two values for the Blocking Send Policy setting:

FIFO

The FIFO policy ensures that all send requests for the destination are queued up until further space becomes available. A send request cannot complete until the send requests before it have been completed. This is the default policy.

Preemptive

The preemptive policy enables the JMS server to allow smaller send requests to proceed to the destination if there is space for them, preempting other send requests that also are blocked on the destination. The JMS server permits those send requests that can be accommodated by the destination as and when space becomes available, while remaining within the message quota limits.

The Send Timeout feature is an additional flow control mechanism that ensures that any send requests to a destination do not cause the destination to exceed its message quota limits. It provides message producers with the option of pausing for a specific length of time until enough space becomes available on the destination. Instead of just slowing down message production, you can block the producers completely for a specific period of time. The producer will then block until more space on the destination becomes available, or until the operation times out. In order to configure the send timeout, select a JMS connection factory from the left pane and then navigate to the Configuration/Flow Control tab. For the Send Timeout attribute, specify the maximum number of milliseconds that a sender should wait on a JMS destination that has reached its maximum quota. By default, JMS producers are blocked for 10 milliseconds when a destination has reached its maximum quota.

You can disable the Send Timeout feature altogether by setting this attribute to 0. In that case, a sender will instantly receive a "resource allocation" exception if the message quota on the JMS destination has been reached. If you specify a positive value for the Send Timeout attribute, a sender will receive this exception only after it has waited for the specified timeout period. If the producers are running on the server itself, it is best to keep the Send Timeout to a low value, so as to avoid blocking the sender for too long.

JMS Stores

Earlier we looked at how to configure both a file store and a JDBC store for a JMS server, and noted that the file store is considerably faster. In this section, we examine how you can improve the performance of JMS file stores. We also deal with how to manage the database tables for a JDBC store and the ideal settings for the JDBC connection pool that provides access to the backend database. Using a store invariably will slow down the application. For this reason, try to ensure that the persistent quality of service is used only when it is needed and should be used.

Tuning file stores

File I/O manifests in two forms. Asynchronous I/O usually involves accumulating the data that must be written in the OS buffers, and then writing the data periodically to the file. Synchronous I/O, on the other hand, typically involves blocking the application until the I/O operation completes, thereby ensuring that the data is written to disk. For this reason, synchronous I/O is typically far slower but more reliable than asynchronous I/O. Synchronous writes to a file store ensure that the data is written to the disk—it's what guarantees up-to-the-message integrity. Asynchronous writes to a file store possibly can result in lost information if the I/O buffer is lost during a machine crash. Note that the data in the I/O buffers will be lost only in the event of a severe crash. If you simply shut down an application server or the operating system itself, no data will be lost because the OS will flush all I/O buffers to disk. In fact, there are two I/O buffers to consider here: the I/O buffers of the OS itself, and an I/O buffer in the disk hardware. Appropriate disk hardware can reduce the risk of loss of data in the on-disk I/O cache.

By default, WebLogic's JMS guarantees up-to-the-message integrity via synchronous writes to a file store. In other words, transactions cannot complete until all writes to the JMS file store have been flushed to disk. You can, however, change the write policy to trade integrity for performance. This loss of integrity means that you may possibly lose sent messages or receive the same messages more than once (even if the messages are transactional) in the event of a severe crash.

You have to bear all of these considerations in mind when configuring the Synchronous Write Policy mode for a JMS file store. In fact, you can choose from the following three options:

Cache-Flush

> This ensures that transactions cannot complete until all writes have been flushed to disk. This is the default setting for a JMS store and the most reliable, though not the fastest.

Direct-Write

> This ensures that data is written directly to disk—implementing the synchronous I/O scheme. This policy is supported only on Sun Solaris, HP, and Windows systems (including 64-bit platforms). If you choose this policy for an unsupported OS, the cache-flush policy is used instead.

Disabled

> This disables the synchronous policy altogether, and thus enables both the OS cache and filesystem's on-disk cache to be used. Because both I/O caches are in operation, the I/O is no longer synchronous, and so its performance is dramatically increased.

The scalability, performance, and reliability of these schemes will vary depending on your OS and disks. In general, disabling the synchronous write policy leads to the fastest and most scalable option for a file store, although it presents some risk of loss. The default cache-flush policy offers high reliability and reasonably good performance. The direct-write policy with good hardware provides high reliability but lesser performance.

The performance and scalability of the direct-write policy also depend on whether an on-disk cache is enabled. For instance, direct writes on Solaris systems are transactionally safe because they don't rely on an on-disk cache. On the other hand, Windows systems do rely on an on-disk cache. Moreover, the direct-write policy on Windows systems may not directly write, since data may be left in the on-disk cache. To guarantee absolute integrity, you must either disable the on-disk cache or use a disk with a reliable, backed cache.

Further performance improvement can be gained by placing file stores on separate disks. In particular, try to avoid sharing the disk used by a JMS store with the disk used for the transaction logs or another JMS store. Utilizing high-performance disks is even better. All of this may seem like an overemphasis on the performance of JMS stores, but a well-tuned JMS store plays an important role in achieving good performance for the JMS server.

Managing the JMS tables for a JDBC store

WebLogic automatically creates the tables needed to represent a database-backed JMS store. When you configure a JDBC store, the JMS server creates two tables for private use: JMSStore and JMSState. These table names optionally can include a prefix to uniquely identify the tables associated with the JMS store. This prefix can take the form:

```
[[catalog.]schema.]prefix
```

A prefix must uniquely identify the JMS-related tables, and is generally needed only if multiple JMS stores have to be able to coexist in the same database, or to differentiate between the JMS tables of two different WebLogic instances that use the same database. It is important that all such tables are unique to each store and server. A table shared between multiple JMS stores will result in data corruption.

If these JMS-related tables become corrupted for some reason, you can use the utils.schema utility to regenerate them. The utility simply deletes all existing tables associated with the JMS store and re-creates them. For this reason, you should use this tool with caution.

As usual, you must set up your environment to include the *weblogic.jar* library. You can accomplish this by executing the *setEnv* batch file provided by WebLogic. In order to invoke the tool, you must supply the name of the DDL file that holds the SQL commands needed to re-create the JMS tables on the target database. The *weblogic/jms/ddl* directory within the *weblogic.jar* contains the DDL files for all the supported databases. Unpack the relevant DDL file from the JAR, and modify it suitably (for instance, if you must attach a prefix before all table names).

Then, you can run the tool by passing in the database URL, the driver class name, and the name of the DDL file:

```
java utils.Schema url JDBC_driver [-u username] [-p password] file.ddl
```

Running this command merely sends the SQL DDL commands to the database. Thus, in order to re-create the JMS tables on an MS SQL Server database, you can use the default DDL file supplied in the *weblogic.jar* library as follows:

```
java utils.Schema jdbc:microsoft:sqlserver://localhost:1433
                  com.microsoft.jdbc.sqlserver.SQLServerDriver
                  -u oracle -p rules weblogic/jms/ddl/jms_mssql.ddl
```

Configuring the JDBC pool for a JMS store

When configuring a JDBC store, you also must assign an existing JDBC connection pool to the JMS store. This connection pool has to be targeted to the WebLogic instance that hosts the JMS server because it enables the JMS server to access the backend database. If a JDBC connection pool is to be used by a JMS server to interact with a JDBC store, you also must follow certain guidelines when configuring the connection pool. First, you have to ensure that the JDBC connection pool uses a non-XA driver. In other words, the connection pool must not use an XA-aware JDBC driver, nor should you enable the "Emulate Two Phase Commit for non-XA Driver" option for the connection pool. Because WebLogic's JMS provider is its own resource manager in a distributed transaction, it handles all the support for distributed transactions without relying on any XA support from the JDBC connection pool.

So, as far as distributed transactions are concerned, an XA data source and a JMS server are considered two separate resources, even if the underlying connection pools may point to the same database. The cost of enforcing the two-phase commit protocol can be alleviated somewhat by collocating the connection pool being used for the

JMS store, with the JMS destination itself and the other XA resources participating in the transaction. In this way, WebLogic can optimize distributed transactions when both resources reside on the same server because it is able to avoid the network overhead.

Recall how JDBC stores offer the advantage of being easily accessible to multiple servers. As a result, if a WebLogic instance hosting a JMS server fails, it becomes easier to migrate the JMS server and related resources to another WebLogic instance. However, do note that a JDBC store presents its own point of failure as well. If the backend database goes down, the connections within the connection pool certainly will be broken, unless you've set the "Test Connections on Reserve" attribute on the pool. In this way, the JDBC connection pool can automatically reconnect to a failed database once it's brought back alive, without having to restart WebLogic Server. This mechanism allows the associated JDBC store to easily recover from database failures.

Message Expiration

Message expiration has been greatly enhanced in WebLogic 8.1. In previous WebLogic releases, the message expiration mechanism was *passive*. When a message expired, nothing happened. Of course, the expired messages were never delivered, but they were not actively cleaned up either. Rather, messages expired as and when they were encountered during the course of normal operations of the JMS server, after which they simply would be discarded. However, in WebLogic 8.1, the JMS server can be configured to actively scan for expired messages. How the JMS server treats these expired messages also can be adjusted differently for individual destinations. For instance, a destination could be configured so that the JMS server logs any expired messages discovered during the scan, or perhaps it sends them to a designated error destination.

Enabling active message expiration

By regularly scanning for expired messages, the JMS server can ensure that the expired messages do not accumulate on the destinations and hog server resources. To configure the active message expiration mechanism, you must select a JMS server from the Administration Console and then navigate to the Configuration/General tab. The value of the Expiration Scan Interval setting defines how often WebLogic will scan for expired messages. The default value is 30 seconds. If you set this interval to 0, WebLogic will never scan the destinations for expired messages. In other words, the messages will expire passively, which is the typical mode of expiry in WebLogic 7.0 and earlier.

Expired message handling

Previous releases of WebLogic simply would discard any expired messages, as and when they were discovered. In WebLogic 8.1, you can instruct the JMS server to take specific actions when expired messages are discovered. Expired messages now can be discarded, logged, or sent to an error destination. This expiration policy can be defined on a per-destination basis. You also can define the expiration policy on a JMS template, which is then common to all destinations that use that template. In order to adjust the expiration policy, you must select the Expiration Policy tab for a chosen destination or template, and then choose from one of the following options for the Expiration Policy attribute:

None

If a template has been assigned to the destination, this option is used to inherit the expiration policy configured for its template. Otherwise, this option is equivalent to "Discard."

Discard

This option causes expired messages to be removed from the system without logging or redirection.

Log

This option removes any expired messages that are discovered, and writes an entry to the server log file indicating that the messages were removed.

Redirect

This option moves all expired messages to the error destination configured for the destination.

If you decide to log all expired messages, you also can set the Expiration Logging Property attribute. This setting determines what information pertaining to the expired JMS message is actually written to the server's logs, over and above the JMSMessageID field. You can use %header% to indicate that all header fields should be logged, %properties% to indicate that all user properties should be logged, and the names of any JMS header fields (both standard and WebLogic-specific) or any user-defined properties. Here are a few examples:

```
%header%, Name, JMSPriority
%properties%, JMSCorrelationID
```

Concurrent Messaging

WebLogic JMS supports a pool of server-side sessions, a mechanism that allows an application to concurrently process messages arriving at various JMS destinations. MDBs provide another way to concurrently handle messages arriving on a destination. At deploy time, WebLogic creates a pool of EJB instances of the same MDB, dedicated to processing messages arriving at a preconfigured topic or queue. Conceptually, MDBs are quite similar to JMS session pools. Both provide a pool of resources that enable the application to process incoming messages concurrently. There are a few vital differences, though:

- MDBs can be attached to any JMS server, even to destinations on foreign JMS servers. However, session pools may be configured only for servers that use WebLogic's JMS provider.
- MDBs need not be deployed to the same WebLogic instance that hosts the JMS destination. On the other hand, session pools are configured on the JMS server itself, and hence always will reside on the same server that hosts the JMS destinations.
- MDBs can be transactional and can be used within the context of a two-phase commit transaction. JMS sessions within a session pool, however, do not support JTA transactions. They support only standard transacted sessions.
- You can attach multiple consumers to the same session pool. In this way, a single message listener can be used to handle messages arriving on multiple destinations. On the other hand, an MDB can be attached to a single JMS destination only.

MDBs are a standard requirement of any J2EE-compliant application server. Session pools are an optional feature of the JMS API, and thus may not be implemented by all vendors. For these reasons, we recommend that you always use MDBs instead of session pools. Chapter 10 explains how to build and deploy MDBs.

Using JMS session pools

You can associate a number of session pools with a JMS server, where each pool represents a collection of JMS sessions that can be invoked concurrently. Once again, you must use the Administration Console to configure a session pool, and then bind one or more connection consumers to the session pools. You can accomplish the same tasks programmatically using the public API provided by WebLogic JMS, which includes the classes and interfaces under the `weblogic.jms.extensions` package.

To create a new session pool using the Administration Console, expand a JMS server node from the left pane and then select the Session Pools node. Then choose the "Configure a new JMS Session Pool" option to proceed. Here, you must specify values for the following configuration settings:

Name
Use this option to specify a logical name for the server session pool.

Connection Factory
Use this setting to specify the JNDI name of the connection factory to be used for creating the JMS sessions in the pool.

Listener Class
Use this setting to determine the fully qualified name of the message listener class.

Transacted

Use this setting to indicate if the JMS sessions within the pool will be transacted.

Acknowledge Mode

Use this setting to determine the acknowledge mode employed by the nontransacted JMS sessions. If the sessions within the pool are transacted, this setting is ignored.

Sessions Maximum

Use this setting to set the maximum number of JMS sessions in the pool. A value of −1 indicates that there is no limit to the size of the session pool.

Once you hit the Create button, a new session pool appears under the Session Pools node in the left pane. Now we need to set up a number of consumers for the sessions. To accomplish this, you should expand the new server session node, select the Consumers child node from the left pane, and click the "Configure a new JMS Connection Consumer" option. The settings here are identical to the arguments that you would supply to the createConnectionConsumer( ) method, had you set up the consumer programmatically:

Messages Maximum

This attribute determines the maximum number of messages that may be loaded into a session at one time by the connection consumer.

Selector

This attribute lets you associate a message selector with the connection consumer.

Destination

This attribute specifies the JNDI name of the destination to be used.

You can attach multiple connection consumers to a server session pool. The session pool will be created when the JMS server starts up, and any consumers configured to the session pool immediately will be made ready for concurrent processing. Note that because the message listener class runs on the server, you must ensure that the class is available in the classpath of the particular WebLogic instance that hosts the JMS server with the server pool.

To create a session pool programmatically, you need to look up a WebLogic-specific ServerSessionPoolFactory object from the JNDI tree, which then can be used to generate a session pool. WebLogic automatically binds a session pool factory in the server's JNDI tree. The JNDI name for this factory can be determined by appending the name of the JMS server to the string weblogic.jms.ServerSessionPoolFactory:. So, you could look up the default server session pool factory from a WebLogic instance hosting a JMS server called MyJMSServer as follows:

```
ServerSessionPoolFactory factory = (ServerSessionPoolFactory)
  ctx.lookup("weblogic.jms.ServerSessionPoolFactory:MyJMSServer");
// use the factory to create a session pool
```

Now let's look at how to create a session pool on a JMS server called MyJMSServer, using the message listener class oreilly.wlguide.jms.PoolReceiver. First, you must retrieve a queue connection factory and obtain a reference to the queue:

```
QueueConnectionFactory qf =
  (QueueConnectionFactory) ctx.lookup("oreilly.myConnectionFactory");
QueueConnection qcon = qf.createQueueConnection();
Queue queue = (Queue) ctx.lookup("MyQ");
qcon.start();
```

All this is standard JMS code. The initial setup is similar to how you would create a queue receiver. But instead of explicitly creating a JMS session, you now will dip in to the newly created session pool. Here's how you can obtain the session pool factory from the JNDI namespace and then create a ServerSessionPool object:

```
ServerSessionPoolFactory sessionPoolFactory = (ServerSessionPoolFactory)
  ctx.lookup("weblogic.jms.ServerSessionPoolFactory:MyJMSServer");
ServerSessionPool sessionPool =
  sessionPoolFactory.getServerSessionPool(qcon, 8, false,
                     Session.AUTO_ACKNOWLEDGE,
                     "oreilly.wlguide.jms.PoolReceiver");
```

The getServerSessionPool() method lets you create a session pool. This method accepts the following arguments: a queue connection, the pool size, whether the sessions are transacted, the acknowledge mode for all transactions, and the message listener class. You then can attach a connection consumer to a server session pool by calling the createConnectionConsumer() method on the queue connection:

```
ConnectionConsumer cr = qcon.createConnectionConsumer(
                     queue, "TRUE", sessionPool, 10);
```

This method accepts the following arguments: the queue on which to listen, a message selector, the session pool that must be associated with the consumer, and the maximum number of messages that can be assigned to each session simultaneously. As messages are delivered to the queue, the connection consumer will dole them out to each session, ensuring in each case that no session is loaded with more than 10 messages at one time. In this way, you can assign a pool of JMS sessions to multiple consumers, and concurrently handle messages arriving at different destinations.

Controlling Message Delivery

WebLogic provides a number of features that can be used to control the different aspects of message delivery and handling. These features are critical in building a robust and scalable messaging system.

The timed message delivery feature lets you control exactly when messages are delivered. Using this mechanism, you can either configure a delay before the message is actually delivered, or set up a custom schedule for a destination that determines the permitted days and times during which the messages may be delivered. In this way, you can ensure that messages are delivered only when their consumers are ready to process them. The time-to-live attribute lets you adjust the maximum age of the outgoing messages—i.e., the maximum time period for which the messages will be retained by the system. After this time period, the messages will have expired and will no longer be tracked by the JMS server. The previous section showed how WebLogic can periodically reap expired messages from the JMS server.

WebLogic also provides enhanced support for redelivery by letting you limit the number of attempts at redelivery and configure a pause between redelivery attempts. WebLogic JMS makes two additional acknowledge modes available. The NO_ACKNOWLEDGE mode instructs the JMS server to not expect acknowledgment for the message. The MULTICAST_NO_ACKNOWLEDGE mode is similar, except that it enables the JMS client to use a more scalable multicast message distribution when delivering messages to a topic destination.

Delivery Modes

The delivery mode indicates whether the messages are stored in a persistent store. If a persistent delivery mode is used, the message will be stored so that the system can guarantee once-and-only-once message delivery. A nonpersistent delivery mode cannot offer this level of guarantee, as the JMS server may fail and lose a message. In this case, the best you can hope for is at-most-once message delivery. There are several ways to configure the delivery mode for outgoing messages:

- You can set the default delivery mode for a connection factory via the Administration Console. Choose a suitable value for the Default Delivery Mode attribute in the Configuration/General tab for the connection factory.

- You can set the delivery mode for a producer programmatically using the standard MessageProducer interface:

  ```
  QueueSender qsender = session.createSender(queue);
  qsender.setDeliveryMode(javax.jms.DeliveryMode.NON_PERSISTENT);
  ```

  This setting overrides the default delivery mode that may have been configured on its connection factory.

- You can use the send( ) method on a QueueSender or the publish( ) method on the TopicPublisher to set the delivery mode:

  ```
  // send nonpersistent message to a queue, using priority=2 and time-to-live=30min
  qsender.send(wlmsg, javax.jms.DeliveryMode.NON_PERSISTENT,
                  2, 1800000);
  // publish persistent message to a topic, using priority=3 and time-to-live=30min
  tpublisher.publish(wlmsg, javax.jms.DeliveryMode.PERSISTENT,
                  3, 1800000);
  ```

- A JMS destination also can override the delivery mode set for the connection factory, or any of the message producers. This can be done by choosing a suitable value for the Delivery Mode Override setting in the Configuration/Overrides tab for the selected JMS destination.

Remember, if you require support for persistent messages, you also must configure a persistent store for the JMS server. If no store has been configured for the JMS server, the persistent mode is downgraded to nonpersistent delivery. Similarly, if a topic doesn't have any durable subscribers, again the persistent mode is automatically lowered to nonpersistent delivery.

Timed Delivery

There are two ways in which to achieve finer control over *when* a message is delivered:

Delayed message delivery
> You can delay the delivery of a message by specifying a relative delivery time. The message will be made visible at the destination only after the delay has expired.

Scheduled message delivery
> You can configure a destination to schedule message delivery during particular time periods, using a flexible cron-like format.

Delayed message delivery

You can specify a delay between when a message is produced and when it is made visible on a destination. The delay value, specified in milliseconds, determines a relative delivery time, offset from the current time on the JMS server. The delay time period can be configured for a connection factory, or it can be set on an individual message producer using the proprietary API provided by WebLogic JMS. To set the delivery delay for a connection factory, select the factory from the Administration Console and change the value of the Default Time to Deliver attribute on the Configuration/General tab. This delay characteristic for the connection factory will be shared by all producers created using the connection factory. For instance, if a producer that has been created by a connection factory that has a time to deliver of 10000 sends a message to a queue, any queue receiver will not receive that message until at least 10 seconds after the message is sent.

Setting the delivery delay on the connection factory is useful because your code will remain largely portable. Alternatively, you could set the delay on an individual message producer using the setTimeToDeliver(long delay) method exposed by the weblogic.jms.extensions.WLMessageProducer interface. The following example illustrates this usage:

```
QueueSender qsender = session.createSender(queue);
WLMessageProducer mp = (WLMessageProducer) qsender;
mp.setTimeToDeliver(20000);
```

When you set the delivery delay on a message producer, this delay overrides the default time to deliver that has been configured for the connection factory.

There is another twist to the tale. A JMS destination can override the Time to Deliver attribute set on the connection factory or the message producer. If you specify a positive numeric value for the Time to Deliver Override setting in the Configuration/Overrides tab for a chosen destination, this value overrides the delivery delay you may have set for the connection factory or any message producer. If the setting has a value of −1 instead, no override occurs, and messages intended for that destination essentially will take on the delay characteristics of the connection factory or producer.

Scheduled delivery

The *same* Time to Deliver Override setting for a JMS destination can also be used to define a delivery schedule that overrides any delivery delays you may have configured for the connection factory or producers. Instead of a numeric value, you can specify a string value for the setting that represents the message delivery schedule.

The format of this delivery schedule is based on a cron-like syntax. A schedule is defined by specifying space-separated values for the millisecond, second, minute, hour, day of month, month, and day of the week fields. Figure 8-1 illustrates this format along with the minimum and maximum ranges for these fields.

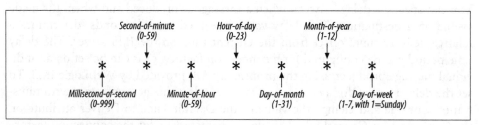

Figure 8-1. Fields and field values for a schedule

The order of the fields is important, and no field may be omitted. The values for each field can be specified in several different ways:

- A field may take a numeric value, in which case it must lie within the minimum and maximum range for the field. A numeric value indicates that the messages must be delivered at a date and time that match the field value. For example, a schedule whose day of the week field is set to 2 indicates that the messages must be delivered on Mondays. The value for the month field may exceed the maximum for a particular month—for instance, a value of 31 for the month of April. In this case, the messages will be scheduled for the last day of the month (in this case, 30).

- A field may take a range of numeric values. For example, a schedule whose day of the week field is set to 1–4 indicates that messages will be delivered on any day between Sunday and Wednesday, inclusive.

- A field may take a comma-separated list of values, including numeric values or a range of numeric values. For instance, a delivery schedule whose day of the week field is set to 1–4, 6, 7 indicates that the messages may be delivered on any day of the week except for Thursday.

- A value of * for a field indicates that the schedule places no restrictions on the field. For instance, a schedule whose day of the week field is set to * implies that the messages may be delivered on any day of the week.

- A special value of l or last may be used to indicate the maximum value for the particular field. For instance, you can set the day of the week field to 2–l to indicate all days from Monday through Saturday (the maximum).

- The millisecond value is rounded down to the nearest 50th of a second. The values are 0, 19, 39, 59, ... , 979. So, 42 will get rounded to 39, 63 to 59, and so on.

Together, the fields specify a scheduled time during which messages can be delivered to the destination. So, for example, the following schedule indicates that messages may be delivered every day between noon and 10 p.m.:

    * * * 12-22 * * *

Table 8-1 lists sample schedules and their meanings.

Table 8-1. Example schedules with their interpretation

Example	Description
* * 0 8 * * *	Every day at 8:00 a.m., until 8:01 a.m.
* * * 13 * * *	Every day at 13:00 p.m. until just before 14:00 p.m.
0 0 0 8 * * 2,4,6	Every Monday, Wednesday, and Friday at 8:00 a.m.
0 0 0,30 * * * *	The exact next nearest half hour
* * 0,30 * * * *	Anytime in the first minute of the half hours
* * 0-30 * * * 2-6	Anytime during the first half hour of any hour from Monday to Friday
* * * * 1-7 * 2	The first Monday of the month
* * * * 31 * *	The last day of the month
* * * * 13 * 6	The next time the 13th falls on a Friday
* * * * 31 12 *	Every Hogmanay (New Year's Eve)

Sometimes a single delivery schedule isn't sufficient. For instance, using the syntax explained previously, you cannot schedule delivery at a particular time on weekdays and some other time on weekends. To accomplish this sort of compound schedule, you need to specify multiple schedules. Do this by separating each schedule with a semicolon. In this case, the next scheduled time is determined by the schedule that returns the "soonest" value. The following schedule allows for message delivery between 9:00 a.m. to 5:00 p.m. on weekdays, and noon to 4:00 p.m. on weekends:

    * * * 9-17 * * 2-6; * * * 12-16 * * 1,7

Evaluating the next scheduled delivery time

WebLogic provides a programmatic interface to a schedule parser, which can be found in `weblogic.jms.extensions.Schedule`. This `Schedule` class lets you determine the next scheduled time for delivery that is permitted by a given schedule expression. The returned value can be either absolute, or relative to some specific date and time.

The `nextScheduledTimeInMillisRelative(String schedule)` method allows you to obtain the difference in milliseconds until the next scheduled time for delivery—it returns a `long` value. You can supply an additional time parameter, in which case it calculates the difference from the supplied time to the next scheduled time for delivery. The following example illustrates its usage:

```
long t = Schedule.nextScheduledTimeInMillisRelative(
        "0 0 30 11 * * * ", System.currentTimeMillis());
```

If this code is executed at 11:20 a.m., it will return the number of milliseconds equal to 10 minutes (10 * 1000 * 60).

The `nextScheduledTimeInMillis()` method takes a schedule as its parameter and determines the closest absolute time that fulfills the delivery schedule, returning a `long` value representing the time. If we run the following example at any time after 12:10 p.m. and before 12:05 p.m. the next day, it will return an absolute time of 12:05 for the following day:

```
long t = Schedule.nextScheduledTimeInMillis(
        "0 0 5-10 12 * * * ");
DateFormat df = DateFormat.getDateTimeInstance();
System.err.println(df.format(c.getTime()));
// Prints out 25-Oct-2002 12:05:00 when run on 24th at 12:12:22
// Prints out 24-Oct-2002 12:10:17 when run on 24th at 12:10:17
```

The final method, `nextScheduledTime()`, takes a delivery schedule as a parameter and returns a `Calendar` object, representing the next scheduled time for delivery after the current time. It can take a `Calendar` object as an additional parameter, in which case the method returns the next scheduled time after the given time. The following piece of code prints out the date of the first Monday in the next month, provided you don't run this code in the first week of the month:

```
DateFormat df = DateFormat.getDateTimeInstance();
Calendar c = Schedule.nextScheduledTime("* * * * 1-7 * 2");
System.err.println(df.format(c.getTime()));
```

Determining delivery time

Once a message has arrived at a destination, you can use the `weblogic.jms.extensions.WLMessage` interface to determine when the message was delivered. The `WLMessage` interface, which extends the standard `javax.jms.Message` interface, provides a `getJMSDeliveryTime()` method to return the actual delivery time for a message. If the delivery of the message was delayed, this value will be different from the timestamp returned by the standard `getJMSTimestamp()` method. The following example illustrates this difference:

```
public void onMessage(Message msg) {
    try {
        DateFormat timeFormatter = DateFormat.getDateTimeInstance( );
        //returns the time when the message was handed over to WebLogic JMS
        System.err.println("Msg Timestamp: " +
            timeFormatter.format(new Date(msg.getJMSTimestamp( ))));
        //returns the time when the message was actually delivered to the destination
        System.err.println("Msg Delivery Time: " +
            timeFormatter.format(new Date(((WLMessage)msg).getJMSDeliveryTime( ))));
    } catch (JMSException ehm) {
        System.err.println(ehm);
    }
}
```

If you are not using delayed message delivery, simply use the standard approach.

Time-to-Live

The delivery delay mechanisms also must take into account the expiry time set on the messages. If a message has an expiry value that is less than or equal to a delay, the message will be delivered and subsequently silently expire. The JMS API provides a standard approach to set the time-to-live attribute on a message, using the send( ) method on a QueueSender or the publish( ) method on a TopicPublisher. WebLogic JMS also lets you configure a default time-to-live attribute on the connection factory, which is then inherited by all messages sent using that factory. To configure this, choose the connection factory from the left pane of the Administration Console, and then enter the suitable value for the Default Time to Live attribute in the Configuration/General tab. A value of 0 indicates that any messages sent using the factory will not expire.

A message producer also can override the default expiry value set for the connection factory. For this, you must programmatically set the time-to-live attribute using the MessageProducer interface:

```
QueueSender qsender = session.createSender(queue);
qsender.setTimeToLive(20000);
```

If an expiry value is later specified in the send( ) or publish( ) methods, this value takes priority over any default expiry value set in the connection factory, or the time-to-live attribute set for the message producer itself. Finally, a JMS destination also can override the time-to-live attribute set on the connection factory or the message producer. To achieve this, simply specify a numeric value for the Time to Live Override setting in the Configuration/Overrides tab for a chosen destination.

Redelivery

Message redelivery occurs during a rollback or session recovery. WebLogic JMS defines a number of extensions to this standard mechanism giving you finer control over message delivery.

- You can delay the message redelivery by a certain period of time.

- You can limit the number of attempts that are made to redeliver a message to a particular destination.

- A JMS destination can override any of these settings individually, enabling you to customize the redelivery on a per-destination basis.

- A special error destination can be configured so that messages that could not be redelivered are automatically routed to the error definition.

In WebLogic 8.1, the JMS server can guarantee that the redelivered messages are sent in the same order in which they were produced. There are a few sensible qualifications, though:

- No ordering can be guaranteed if you have more than one consumer—for example, a pool of instances of a deployed MDB.

- If you have defined a sort order on a destination that differs from the order in which the messages are produced, no ordering can be guaranteed.

- If a JMS consumer uses a message selector, the redelivery order is preserved only between the message being redelivered and other messages that match the criteria for that selector.

Configuring redelivery

WebLogic lets you define a delay, in milliseconds, which is the length of time the server will wait before it tries to redeliver a message. This delay is especially useful in situations where external conditions affecting the delivery of messages are resolved only after a particular amount of time has passed, thus saving pointless attempts to redeliver the message.

You can use the Administration Console to configure the redelivery delay for a connection factory. Simply choose a suitable value for the Default Redelivery Delay attribute in the Configuration/General tab for the chosen connection factory. All JMS sessions created from the connection factory inherit this default redelivery delay. If a message is consumed by multiple sessions within the context of a user transaction, the message will receive different redelivery delays, depending on the settings of each JMS session. Of course, messages that are left unacknowledged or uncommitted by a client, either intentionally or as a result of a failure, are not assigned a redelivery delay.

An individual JMS session can override the default redelivery delay determined by its connection factory. You can set the redelivery delay for a JMS session using the proprietary weblogic.jms.extensions.WLSession interface. The following code example shows how to use the WLQueueSession subinterface to set the redelivery delay on a queue session:

```
QueueSession session =
    qcon.createQueueSession(false, Session.AUTO_ACKNOWLEDGE);
```

```
WLQueueSession qsession = (WLQueueSession) session;
qsession.setRedeliveryDelay(10000);
```

Any change to the session's redelivery delay will affect all subsequent messages that are consumed and later rolled back or recovered by the session. If no session-specific redelivery delay has been set, the session inherits its delay from its connection factory. In that case, you can use the getRedeliveryDelay( ) method to determine the redelivery delay inherited by the session.

A JMS destination can override the redelivery delay, specified for any connection factory or any JMS sessions. To set the redelivery delay for a destination, you must navigate to its Configuration/Redelivery tab. Here you additionally can specify a limit on the number of attempts that are made to redeliver a JMS message. If the message still can't be delivered after so many attempts, the message is considered to be undeliverable. Depending on whether an error destination has been configured, the undelivered message is either dropped or sent to the error destination. This applies to both persistent and nonpersistent messages.

Error destinations

Error destinations, if configured, receive messages that are deemed undeliverable. This includes those messages that have expired, and those that cannot be redelivered by the JMS server. An error destination is no different from any other destination, except that it must exist on the same JMS server that hosts the destination. To route undeliverable messages to this error destination, you must navigate to the Configuration/Redelivery tab for a chosen destination and specify the name of an existing queue or topic for the Error Destination attribute.

If the error destination supports persistent messaging, the undelivered messages will remain in the JMS store. In this way, WebLogic can ensure that the persistent messages eventually are delivered to the error destination, even if the JMS server fails for some reason.[*]

Extended Acknowledge Modes

The JMS standard provides three acknowledge modes for nontransacted JMS sessions:

AUTO_ACKNOWLEDGE
    This mode ensures that the consumer's runtime will acknowledge the message automatically, after it has finished processing the message.

---

[*] Prior to WebLogic 8.1, if an error destination reached its quota limit, undelivered messages simply were logged and deleted from the system.

CLIENT_ACKNOWLEDGE

> This mode requires consumers to explicitly invoke the acknowledge( ) method on a message, to acknowledge all messages received since the previous acknowledgment. This mode enables a JMS client to acknowledge a batch of messages via a single method call.

DUPS_OK_ACKNOWLEDGE

> The consumer's runtime will acknowledge the received message automatically once it has finished processing the message, although duplicate acknowledgments also may be permitted.

Together with persistent messaging, these acknowledge modes form the basis of reliable and guaranteed message delivery. Remember, the acknowledge modes are completely ignored for transacted JMS sessions, or when a nontransacted session is used within the context of a JTA transaction.

WebLogic JMS provides two additional acknowledge modes:

NO_ACKNOWLEDGE

> Unlike the standard modes where an acknowledgment always is expected and sent, a JMS server that delivers messages to a session created in the NO_ACKNOWLEDGE mode does not expect an acknowledgment.

MULTICAST_NO_ACKNOWLEDGE

> This mode supports multicasting for applications that can tolerate the quality of service offered by no acknowledgments. Messages sent to a session created in the MULTICAST_NO_ACKNOWLEDGE mode share the same characteristics as a JMS session created in the NO_ACKNOWLEDGE mode—both provide improved levels of performance.

In these no-acknowledge modes, the JMS server acknowledges the message itself before sending it! Thus, messages sent to JMS sessions created in either of these modes are deleted from the JMS server immediately. For this reason, there are a few consequences of using the no-acknowledge modes:

- A server, network, or client failure may result in a silent loss of the sent message. In addition, the JMS session cannot recover messages received in these modes as the consumer's runtime has no way of knowing which messages have not yet been acknowledged.

- Because a JMS session created in either of these modes cannot recover the received messages, a message may be lost or redelivered if the initial attempt to deliver the message failed.

- This mode saves the consumer from having to make the network call to acknowledge the received message(s). Through these extended acknowledge modes you can avoid this network overhead, and thereby increase the performance of your JMS applications as well as reduce network traffic during message delivery.

These extended acknowledge modes can be found in the proprietary WLSession class. The following code shows how to set up an asynchronous queue receiver within a JMS session that has been created in the NO_ACKNOWLEDGE mode:

```
QueueSession qsession =
    qcon.createQueueSession(false, WLSession.NO_ACKNOWLEDGE);
Queue queue = (Queue) ic.lookup(QUEUE_JNDI_NAME);
QueueReceiver qrec = qsession.createSubscriber(queue);
qrec.setMessageListener(this);
```

Multicasting

In general, a JMS topic will have subscribers running on different hosts within a domain. The more subscribers, the more network resources needed by the JMS server to deliver the messages to them. In such cases, you can set up multicasting on the JMS session. This enables the JMS server to deliver the messages to a select group of hosts that later can forward the messages to all subscribers running on that host. The benefits of multicasting are two-fold:

- A multicast consumes a constant amount of work and resources for the JMS server, regardless of whether the topic has one or multiple subscribers on different hosts. In other words, multicast delivery can easily scale as the number of topic subscribers increases.

- Another side effect of multicasting is that it decreases the amount of network traffic generated during message delivery, especially if the topic has many subscribers.

A potential risk of using multicasting is that the JMS messages are not guaranteed to be delivered to all subscribers within the host group. Messages may be lost (or duplicated) in a congested network, or if subscribers fall behind in their processing. If the subscribers cannot tolerate this quality of service, you should not enable multicasting on the topic.

 Multicasting is supported for nondurable subscribers that specify the MULTICAST_NO_ACKNOWLEDGE acknowledge mode. As a single destination can support both types of subscribers, durable subscribers will continue to get reliable replicas of the message via TCP/IP.

Enabling multicasting

In order to make use of multicast sessions, you must first configure the JMS connection factory and topics to support multicasting. Use the Administration Console to specify the multicast attributes for the connection factory and JMS topic. First, choose the desired JMS topic from the left pane and then navigate to the Configuration/Multicast tab. Here you can adjust the following multicast settings for the destination.

Multicast Address and Multicast Port

Use these attributes to specify a valid multicast address and port for your network. The JMS server will broadcast the messages intended for this topic, on this address, and the subscribers running on the different hosts will pick up the messages via this same address and port.

Multicast TTL

Use this attribute to specify the time-to-live for each multicast packet. Its value determines the number of routers that a multicast message can traverse. If this attribute is set to 1, the message will not be permitted to traverse any routers, and so all multicast packets will be restricted to the current subnet.

After this, you must navigate to the Configuration/General tab for the chosen connection factory to further refine the runtime multicast behavior. Here you can adjust the following two multicast attributes:

Messages Maximum

For a nonmulticast session, Messages Maximum determines the maximum number of messages that may exist on an asynchronous session but have not yet been passed to a listener. While a nonmulticast session will ensure that the JMS server retains messages if the pipeline is full, a multicast session will simply discard messages if the pipeline is full, and throw a DataOverrunException exception. The manner in which the messages are discarded is based on the overrun policy.

Overrun policy

You can choose from two overrun policies: Keep Old or Keep New. The default Keep Old value gives the older messages a higher priority so that the JMS server discards the most recent messages. The Keep New value ensures that the JMS server retains the most recent messages, but discards the older messages.

 The message age is determined by the order of receipt and not by the message timestamp.

The overrun policy and maximum messages threshold also can be set on an individual producer at runtime. To accomplish this, simply invoke the setMessagesMaximum( ) and setOverrunPolicy( ) methods on the WebLogic-specific WLTopicSession interface. In this case, the runtime values for the multicast session override the default values for the multicast attributes on the connection factory.

Using a multicast session

Once you've configured the multicast attributes on the JMS topic and the connection factory, you are ready to programmatically create multicast sessions. The following code sample shows how to create a JMS subscriber that handles multicast messages arriving at the topic:

```
TopicSession tsession =
    tcon.createTopicSession(false, WLSession.MULTICAST_NO_ACKNOWLEDGE);
Topic topic = (Topic) ctx.lookup(MULTICAST_TOPIC_JNDI_NAME);
TopicSubscriber tsub = tsession.createSubscriber(topic);
tsub.setMessageListener(this);
```

Notice how we've specified a WebLogic-specific acknowledgment mode to indicate that the JMS session would like to receive multicast messages. Except for this, we have adopted the standard approach to registering a topic subscriber.

 A topic subscriber can only receive multicast messages asynchronously. Any attempt to synchronously receive a message within a multicast session will result in a JMSException.

Sequence violations

WebLogic tracks received messages to correlate their order with the order in which the messages were produced. A multicast subscriber may receive a message out of sequence, which means that one or more messages may be skipped. If the JMS server determines that a message has been delivered out of sequence, WebLogic throws a SequenceGapException. This exception can be handled by an exception listener if you have registered one on the multicast session. If a skipped message is subsequently delivered, WebLogic will simply discard it.

JMS Programming Issues

We now examine the typical issues to consider when building JMS-enabled clients. In particular, you should understand the merits of synchronous versus asynchronous message consumptions, the impact of transacted sessions and distributed transactions on message redelivery and acknowledgment, and the benefits of integrating JMS resources with existing J2EE applications. We also look at how to create both temporary and permanent destinations at runtime. We will examine WebLogic's XML message type, and how the proprietary XPath message selector syntax can help filter out incoming XML messages by inspecting their payloads. (Other programming issues, such as concurrent message handling and multicast topics, were covered earlier.)

JMS Clients

In WebLogic 7.0, if an external JMS client has to interact with WebLogic JMS, you have to include the entire *weblogic.jar* in the client's classpath. WebLogic 8.1 provides a thin client-side library, *wljmsclient.jar*, which you can distribute with your application. This library contains all of the support for WebLogic JMS, and is available in addition to the general client JAR, *wlclient.jar*, which contains the standard client support for JNDI, clustering, and transactions. Together, these JARs are only about 700 KB in size. You can find these client JARs in the *WL_HOME/server/lib* directory of your installation. Any client that uses these smaller-footprint libraries must run on the Java 1.4 JRE.

Synchronous Versus Asynchronous Consumption

The JMS standard supports two ways in which a consumer may receive a message:

- A consumer could register a listener class to a JMS destination and *asynchronously* process incoming messages. In this case, the onMessage( ) method exposed by this listener class is invoked whenever a message arrives at the target destination.

- In the *synchronous* approach a consumer proactively asks for a destination for a message. In such a case, you must invoke one of the receive methods on the consumer.

It is useful to know how these two approaches perform, especially if you want to optimize your JMS clients. Asynchronous consumers generally perform and scale better than synchronous consumers for two reasons:

- A synchronous consumer consumes its thread for the duration of its receive call. This becomes even more significant if one of the blocking receive methods is invoked on the consumer:

```
/** call blocks indefinitely until a message arrives at the destination */
public Message receive( ) throws JMSException;
/** call blocks only until a message arrives within the specified time period;
    if the timeout expires, the call returns null */
public Message receive(long timeout) throws JMSException;
```

  On the other hand, asynchronous consumers do not consume a thread while they are inactive. This is especially crucial when the consumers run on the server because too many blocked synchronous consumers could mean that the JMS server runs out of available server-side threads.

- Asynchronous consumers create less network traffic because the incoming messages are pipelined to the consumer's session. This aggregation of multiple messages is often beneficial. Later in this section, we shall examine the role of pipelining when message selectors are used.

The size of the pipeline is, in fact, the maximum number of messages that may exist on an asynchronous session and have not yet been passed to a listener. To adjust the size of the session's pipeline, you should change the value of the Messages Maximum attribute on a connection factory. It defaults to a value of 10. A value of −1 indicates that the size of the session's pipeline is bound only by the amount of free memory available. Note that the behavior of the JMS session changes somewhat when it listens on a multicast topic.

Durable Subscribers

A *durable* subscription to a topic is one that can outlast the client's connection with the JMS server. By default, a subscription is not durable—i.e., a client's subscription lasts as long as it has an active session. Any messages that are sent after a client gets disconnected are lost. A durable subscription, on the other hand, ensures that the JMS consumer still can receive the messages destined for the topic, even after the connection to the JMS server has been severed. WebLogic will retain the messages in a JMS store for any subscriber that isn't active when the messages were published, and ensure that the unexpired messages are acknowledged by the subscriber when that client later reconnects.

A JMS client cannot create a durable subscription to a distributed topic.

Unique clients

In order to create a durable subscription, you must set up a JMS store for the topic. In addition, you must set a client identifier on the topic connection so as to uniquely identify the durable topic subscription. When a durable client reconnects to a topic, its client ID lets the JMS server know that it is the same client that was previously connected. This enables the JMS server to correctly determine those missed messages that should be sent to the topic subscriber. There are two ways to uniquely identify the client:

- A client can register its unique client ID with a topic connection.
- A client can use a connection factory that is specifically preconfigured for it. This ensures that any topic connection created using the factory is set with the correct client ID automatically.

The standard approach is to assign a client ID to a newly created topic connection:

```
connect = factory.createTopicConnection();
connect.setClientID(someUID);
```

Client IDs are supposed to be unique across connections. In fact, if a JMS client tries to set the client ID on two separate connections from a connection factory with no preset client ID, an `InvalidClientIDException` should be thrown.

It is your responsibility to ensure that the client ID remains unique for each subscriber. If your architecture can support this constraint easily, this scheme will suffice. If you cannot reliably guarantee uniqueness, you cannot always expect an exception to be thrown. For instance, there is a small risk that no exception is thrown when a duplicate client ID is assigned to two connections simultaneously. To avoid this problem, either restructure your clients or ensure that each durable subscriber uses its own connection factory with a preset client ID.

The Client ID attribute for a connection factory, if set, determines the client ID for any topic subscribers created using the factory. You can set the default client ID for any connection factory using the Administration Console. Of course, to use this scheme effectively, you must ensure that each unique client grabs its own connection factory, which is rather limiting. Note that you may not change a client ID on a JMS connection that has been obtained from a connection factory for which a default client ID has been set. You can use the getClientID( ) method on the connection to determine whether a client ID has been set already.

Creating and removing durable subscribers

Use the createDurableSubscriber( ) method on a topic session to create a durable subscriber. You must provide the topic to which to subscribe, and a unique name for the client's subscription:

```
tsession.createDurableSubscriber(theTopic, "someUniqueName");
```

You could use an alternative form of the same method that also lets you specify a message selector and whether the JMS client can receive messages published by itself.

It is important to remember to later unsubscribe from the topic. A common source of bugs in JMS programs is when durable subscribers do not properly unsubscribe from the topic. The server will continue to retain messages for durable subscriptions until they have expired, and therefore continue to unnecessarily eat server-side resources. To delete a durable subscription, use the unsubscribe( ) method on the topic session while passing the name of the client's subscription:

```
tsession.unsubscribe("someUniqueName");
```

Note that if the subscriber receives a message as part of an unresolved transaction, or if a message has not yet been acknowledged by the topic session, you will not be able to unsubscribe until these issues have been cleared.

Transactions and JMS

Using JMS in a transactional context enables you to treat a number of messages as an atomic unit. Any messages produced during a transaction will not be delivered to any consumers until a commit has been issued. A consumer, on the other hand, can receive a number of messages in a transaction. The JMS server will hold on to the messages until the consumer issues a commit. If the consumer instead rolls back the transaction, the server will attempt to redeliver the messages, in which case a redelivery flag is set on the messages. The redelivery behavior differs for topics and queues. If a topic subscriber rolls back a received message, the message is redelivered to that particular subscriber. If a queue receiver rolls back a received message, the message is redelivered to the queue so that another receiver has the opportunity to process the message.

The JMS standard supports two types of transactions: local and distributed. The concepts are analogous to those that exist in the JDBC world, as described earlier in Chapter 6. In the JMS world, local transactions manifest as *transacted sessions*, in which case the scope of the transaction spans the lifetime of the JMS session. A transacted session will influence only those send or receive operations that occur during the session. A transacted session will have no effect on, nor will it be affected by, JTA transactions that may be in scope. Conversely, a distributed transaction can include, for instance, EJB updates and nontransacted JMS sessions within the same scope. In this case, the two-phase commit protocol ensures the proper coordination among the multiple resources that are participating within the same transaction.

Transacted sessions

A transacted session ensures that all JMS send and receive operations occur as a single, atomic unit. To initiate a new transacted session, the createTopicSession( ) method on a TopicConnection object or the createQueueSession( ) method on a QueueConnection object to indicate whether the JMS session is transacted:

```
// create a transacted session for a topic
TopicSession tsession =
    tcon.createTopicSession(true, Session.AUTO_ACKNOWLEDGE);
// create a transacted session for a queue
QueueSession qsession =
    qcon.createQueueSession(true, Session.AUTO_ACKNOWLEDGE);
```

Note that in case of transacted JMS sessions, the acknowledge mode configured for the JMS session is ignored completely. All messages are acknowledged when a commit occurs during the session's lifetime. A local transaction is then started implicitly after the first JMS send or receive operation in the session, and will continue until a session is committed or rolled back. Another transaction is started automatically, as soon as the previous transaction commits or rolls back. This process also is called *transaction chaining*. The following piece of code shows how to produce multiple messages within a transacted session:

```
QueueSession qsession =
    qcon.createQueueSession(true, Session.AUTO_ACKNOWLEDGE);
QueueSender qSender = qsession.createSender(someQueue);
qsender.send(messageOne, java.jms.DeliveryMode.PERSISTENT,
                         javax.jms.Message.DEFAULT_PRIORITY,
                         2000000);
qsender.send(messageTwo, java.jms.DeliveryMode.PERSISTENT,
                         javax.jms.Message.DEFAULT_PRIORITY,
                         2000000);
if (noAwfulCondition)
  qsession.commit( );
else
  qsession.rollback( );
```

Depending on whether the session is committed or rolled back, the two messages either will be delivered as a single unit, or will not be delivered at all. After completing this segment of code, a new transaction will be started implicitly for any other local activity within the JMS session. This behavior is consistent with the JMS specification.

Note that transactional semantics still are guaranteed if the local transaction produces or consumes messages across multiple JMS servers within a cluster. In this sense, local transactions still can be "distributed" across multiple JMS servers.

Distributed transactions

A distributed transaction lets you coordinate updates to multiple resources that may be involved in the same transaction context. Create a JTA transaction in the usual way, by accessing the UserTransaction object bound to the server's JNDI tree:

```
UserTransaction tx = ctx.lookup("javax.transaction.UserTransaction");
tx.begin();
//a new transaction scope has been created...
```

In the JDBC world, you would need an XA-aware data source before it could participate in a JTA transaction. In the JMS world, you need to ensure that the JMS connection factory used to obtain JMS connections to the JMS server is XA-aware. One option is to use the default XA-enabled connection factory provided by WebLogic, which is bound to the server's JNDI tree under the name weblogic.jms. XAConnectionFactory.

To configure your own transactional JMS connection factory, you must modify the connection factory to produce XA-aware JMS connections. You can adjust the factory's transactional behavior using the Administration Console. Simply select a connection factory from the left pane and then navigate to the Configuration/ Transactions tab. Here, you must enable the XA Connection Factory Enabled setting for the connection factory.* So, for instance, the following code could participate in a JTA transaction:

```
qsession = qcon.createQueueSession(false, Session.CLIENT_ACKNOWLEDGE);

// Any JMS send/receive operations will honor the JTA transaction
// Any JDBC operations using an XA-aware datasource will honor the JTA transaction

if (noAwfulCondition)
  tx.commit();
else
  tx.rollback();
```

---

* In WebLogic 7.0, you also should enable the User Transactions Enabled setting for the JMS connection factory. If you need support for JTA transactions for server-side applications only, set the Server Side XA Enabled flag to true.

Note how we've created a nontransacted session to participate in a JTA transaction. This is essential because otherwise, the transacted JMS session will interfere with the scope of the global JTA transaction.

 WebLogic JMS ignores any acknowledge modes that may be configured for a JMS session participating in a JTA transaction.

WebLogic does not support JTA transactions with asynchronous message delivery, as their behavior is not defined in the JMS standard. If you need transactional capabilities in this situation, then you should consider using MDBs. An MDB provides concurrent handling of JMS messages arriving at a destination in an asynchronous fashion, while being able to automatically start a transaction just prior to message delivery.

MDBs

Duplicate messages, if not properly handled, can have undesirable effects: the same operation could be repeated several times, leading to an inconsistent application state. Typically, if an MDB receives a message but fails to acknowledge it, the JMS producer resends the message. To avoid the delivery of duplicate messages, you can configure the MDB to use container-managed transactions:

```
<!-- ejb-jar.xml entry: -->
<message-driven>
  <ejb-name>MyMDB</ejb-name>
  <ejb-class>org.foo.bar.MyMDBBean</ejb-class>
  <transaction-type>Container</transaction-type>
  <!-- ... -->
</message-driven>
```

In this way, both the message receipt and acknowledgment occur within the same transaction. If the MDB implements bean-managed transactions, you must explicitly code for duplicate messages because message acknowledgment will occur outside the scope of the transaction.

 Even with container transactions, there is the possibility that the MDB may receive duplicate messages—for instance, if the server crashes between the time the MDB's onMessage( ) method completes, and the container acknowledges the message.

Integrating JMS with Servlets and EJBs

WebLogic 8.1 provides a simplified way of using JMS resources from within a servlet or an EJB. These "JMS wrappers" provide a lot of additional support, including the items described next.

- Automatic pooling of JMS connections and sessions
- Automatically enrolling of the JMS session in a distributed transaction.*
- Testing the JMS connections and reestablishing the connection in the event of a failure
- Integrating JMS interactions with the security constraints on the EJB or servlet

To benefit from these enhanced features, you need only declare a reference to the JMS connection factory in the servlet's or EJB's deployment descriptor:

```
<!-- resource-ref declaration in the
        ejb-jar.xml or web.xml descriptor -->
<resource-ref>
  <res-ref-name>jms/mycf</res-ref-name>
  <res-type>javax.jms.QueueConnectionFactory</res-type>
  <res-auth>Container</res-auth>
  <res-sharing-scope>Shareable</res-sharing-scope>
</resource-ref>
...
<!-- matching resource-description in the
        weblogic-ejb-jar.xml or weblogic.xml descriptor -->
<resource-description>
  <res-ref-name>jms/mycf</res-ref-name>
  <jndi-name>weblogic.jms.ConnectionFactory</jndi-name>
</resource-description>
```

Here, the default JMS connection factory will be available to the servlet's or EJB's local JNDI context under the name *java:comp/env/jms/mycf*. The same approach can be used to reference a JMS connection factory on a foreign JMS server. In that case, you must map the reference by specifying the local JNDI name of the foreign JMS factory.

Similarly, you can declare a reference to a JMS destination using the resource-env-ref element in the servlet's or EJB's deployment descriptor. The following example shows how to set up a reference to a JMS queue:

```
<!-- declare the reference to the destination
        in the ejb-jar.xml or web.xml descriptor -->
<resource-env-ref>
  <resource-env-ref-name>jms/myQ</resource-env-ref-name>
  <resource-env-ref-type>javax.jms.Queue</resource-env-ref-type>
</resource-env-ref>
...
<!-- map the reference to a JMS destination
        in the weblogic-ejb-jar.xml or weblogic.xml descriptor -->
<resource-env-description>
  <res-env-ref-name>jms/myQ</res-env-ref-name>
  <jndi-name>com.oreilly.jms.someQueue</jndi-name>
</resource-env-description>
```

---

* Only JMS sessions created from foreign JMS connection factories require these wrappers for automatic enlist-ment in distributed transactions. Sessions created via connection factories hosted by WebLogic JMS do not.

The JMS queue then is accessible to the servlet or EJB from within its local JNDI context using the name *java:/comp/env/jms/myQ*. The next code sample shows how an EJB or servlet could use these configured resource references to send a JMS message:

```
InitialContext ctx = new InitialContext();
QueueConnectionFactory cf =
  (QueueConnectionFactory) ctx.lookup("java:comp/env/jms/mycf");
Queue queue =
  (Queue)ctx.lookup("java:comp/env/jms/myQ");
ctx.close();
QueueConnection con = cf.createQueueConnection();
try {
  QueueSession session = con.createQueueSession(0, false);
  QueueSender sender = session.createSender(queue);
  TextMessage msg = session.createTextMessage("Hello World");
  sender.send(msg);
} finally {
 con.close();
}
```

This piece of code is standard, and should run within any J2EE-compliant servlet or EJB container. WebLogic can offer additional benefits when a servlet or EJB uses JMS resources in this way via their references declared within the deployment descriptors.

Pooled connection objects and testing

Pooled JMS connection objects are an important benefit of references to preconfigured connection factories for servlets and EJBs. A pooled JMS connection means that WebLogic makes a pool of session objects available to a servlet or EJB when they utilize the reference to the JMS connection factory. In other words, the wrapped JMS connection factory, connection, and session objects can collaborate in such a way that the servlet or EJB merely retrieves a session object from the pool.

Another benefit of WebLogic's JMS wrapper objects is that they are able to monitor the JMS connections to the JMS provider. First, they register an exception listener on the JMS connection object. Second, the JMS connections are tested every two minutes, by sending a message to a temporary destination and then receiving it again.

Caching JNDI lookups and JMS objects

As the JMS connection factory and destination objects are thread-safe, it is sensible to look up these resources once when the servlet or EJB is initialized, and then to reuse these values whenever the servlet or EJB needs to send or receive a message to the destination. This becomes even more important when the servlet or EJB references a remote JMS provider. Typically, you would look up these objects from within the servlet's init( ) method or the EJB's ejbCreate( ) method, and then assign it to instance variables that can be used later, whenever the servlet or EJB needs to interact with the JMS destination.

Even though it may be tempting to cache other objects, such as the connection, session, or even producer objects, you should not. Your application code should create a JMS connection, set up a JMS session, and create JMS producers on demand, and later release these resources whenever you are done. Only then can the JMS wrapper objects properly pool these resources and ensure that they can be shared by other servlets or EJB instances. In addition, you lose the benefits of connection testing and re-creating the JMS connection and session objects if the servlet or EJB attempts to cache the session objects itself.

Automatic enlistment in transactions

If the actual foreign JMS provider supports XA transactions and the servlet, or if EJB uses a resource-reference wrapped JMS connection object to send or receive messages, then WebLogic can transparently enlist the JMS session in a transaction, if one exists. This occurs either when a transaction is implicitly started—for instance, if the EJB method supports container-managed transactions—or when the servlet or EJB explicitly creates a transaction context using the UserTransaction interface. At no point does the servlet or EJB need to rely on the XA extensions to the JMS API. If the JMS provider doesn't support XA, WebLogic throws an exception if the wrapped JMS connection object is used within a transaction context. In this case, you must either specify a transaction setting of NotSupported for the EJB method, or suspend the current transaction.

Enlisting a JMS session in a distributed transaction also is expensive. For example, if your application uses an XA-enabled connection factory to send or receive a JMS message outside the scope of a transaction, the container must still wrap the send or receive in a JTA transaction to ensure that your code works for any JMS provider. Even though it is a one-phase commit transaction, it still can slow down WebLogic. A more optimal approach would be to reference a non-XA connection factory when sending or receiving JMS messages outside the scope of a transaction.

J2EE compliance

The J2EE standard enforces certain constraints when using the JMS API within a servlet or EJB. WebLogic's JMS wrapper objects enforce these restrictions by raising exceptions when the methods listed in Table 8-2 are invoked.

Table 8-2. Restricted method calls from within a J2EE application

JMS class/interface	Restricted methods
Connection	createConnectionConsumer( )
	createDurableConnectionConsumer( )
	setClientID( )
	setExceptionListener( )
	stop( )

JMS class/interface	Restricted methods
Session	getMessageListener( )
QueueReceiver	setMessageListener( )
TopicSubscriber	

Also remember that WebLogic ignores the two parameters to the createSession( ) methods—the acknowledge mode and the transacted flag—when used from within an EJB. If a transaction context exists, the JMS session is enlisted in the transaction automatically. Otherwise, it is not enlisted in the transaction.

Container-managed security

By default, WebLogic JMS relies on the security credentials of the thread used to invoke the servlet or EJB method. In general, you should specify the res-auth subelement when setting up a resource-ref to a foreign JMS connection factory. The res-auth element can take one of the following two values:

Container
> Here the J2EE container handles the authentication when obtaining a JMS connection to the remote JMS provider. In this case, WebLogic relies on the username/password attributes configured for the foreign JMS connection factory.

Application
> Here the application code must supply the username and password when obtaining a connection from the foreign JMS connection factory. Any username/password set up for the foreign JMS factory is ignored by the servlet or EJB container.

If a reference to a JMS connection factory relies on container-managed security, it is illegal for the servlet or EJB to supply a username and password when obtaining a JMS connection.

Creating Destinations at Runtime

WebLogic allows JMS clients to create both temporary and permanent destinations at runtime. A temporary queue or topic is a transient destination, whose lifetime is bound to the JMS connection associated with the JMS session that spawned it. JMS provides a standard approach to creating temporary destinations. In addition, WebLogic's extensions let you dynamically create new destinations on the JMS server, which will live beyond the JMS connection that spawned them.

Temporary destinations

A JMS client can create a temporary destination on demand, without the administration overheads of a permanent queue or topic. Temporary destinations can be created dynamically by invoking either the createTemporaryQueue( ) method on a QueueSession object, or the createTemporaryTopic( ) method on a TopicSession object. A temporary destination can never live beyond the lifetime of the connection used to create it. In other words, if the JMS client is disconnected for whatever reason, the temporary destination can no longer be retrieved.

This implies that messages sent to a temporary destination cannot be made persistent. A JMS client has no way of reconnecting to a temporary destination once a connection has been severed—it can only create a new one. Hence, even if a JMS session uses a persistent delivery mode for messages to a temporary destination, they may still be lost if the intended recipients are disconnected from the temporary destination. For this reason, WebLogic JMS silently makes all such messages nonpersistent.

 Temporary destinations will not survive a server restart. JMS messages sent to a temporary destination are nonpersistent.

A JMS server must be configured properly before JMS clients can dynamically create temporary destinations. Select the particular JMS server in the Administration Console and choose from one of the predefined JMS templates from the Temporary Template option in the Configuration/General tab. Any temporary destination that is created on the JMS server will then use the settings supplied in the template.

Once a temporary destination has been created, a JMS client can publish the destination to its recipients using the JMSReplyTo header field. The next example shows how to create a temporary topic and then promote its existence to other applications using the reply-to header field:

```
TemporaryTopic tempTopic = session.createTemporaryTopic( );
message.setJMSReplyTo(tempTopic);
```

A JMS client may then subscribe to the temporary topic by retrieving this value from the message's header:

```
Topic myTempTopic = (Topic) message.getJMSReplyTo( );
publisher = session.createPublisher(myTempTopic);
```

After it serves its purpose, you can delete the destination using the delete( ) method on the TemporaryQueue or TemporaryTopic object.

Permanent destinations

A JMS client can use WebLogic's proprietary approach to dynamically create a *permanent* destination on the JMS server. These destinations are identical to those you create by using the Administration Console, except they are created dynamically.

The weblogic.jms.extensions.JMSHelper class provides the relevant methods:

```
public static void createPermanentQueueAsync(Context ctx,
    String jmsServerName, String queueName, String jndiName) throws JMSException;
```

```
public static void createPermanentTopicAsync(Context ctx,
    String jmsServerName, String topicName, String jndiName) throws JMSException;
```

These methods are asynchronous, and may incur a significant delay between when the request for a new destination is submitted and when the new destination is bound to the server's JNDI tree. They modify the domain's configuration to make the changes permanent, and do not support very good error handling. For instance, the call to the createPermanentQueueAsync( ) method can fail without throwing an exception. In addition, a thrown exception does not necessarily mean that the method call failed. For this reason, these methods should be used sparingly, if at all.

The following code shows how to create a JMS queue:

```
JMSHelper.createPermanentQueueAsync(
    ctx, "MyJMSServer","AnyQName", "MyPermanentQ");
```

The parameters include the JNDI context, the name of the JMS server that will host the queue, a name for the JMS destination, and finally, the JNDI name under which the queue will be bound.

 If you do not execute this code in the appropriate security context, you will get a NoAccessRuntimeException.

Because the method call is asynchronous, a client must regularly poll to determine whether the destination has been created. The next example shows how to implement a utility method that can locate a new queue on a JMS server:

```
private static Queue findQueue(
    QueueSession queueSession, String jmsServerName, String queueName,
    int retryCount, long retryInterval) throws JMSException {
  String wlsQueueName = jmsServerName + "/" + queueName;
  String command = "session.createQueue(" + wlsQueueName + ")";
  long startTimeMillis = System.currentTimeMillis();
  for (int i=retryCount; i>=0; i--) {
    try {
      System.out.println("Trying " + command);
      Queue queue = queueSession.createQueue(wlsQueueName);
      System.out.println("Obtained queue after " +
          (retryCount - i + 1) + " tries in " +
          (System.currentTimeMillis() - startTimeMillis) + " millis.");
      return queue;
    } catch (JMSException je) {
      if (retryCount == 0) throw je;
    }
    try {
      System.out.println(command + "> failed, pausing " + retryInterval + " millis.
");
      Thread.sleep(retryInterval);
    } catch (InterruptedException ignore) {}
  }
  throw new JMSException("out of retries");
}
```

Notice how instead of performing JNDI lookups on the new queue name, we have used the createQueue() method on a QueueSession object. If the method throws an exception, you can be reasonably sure that the destination hasn't been created yet, and you should wait a while before trying again. A JMS client can then invoke the findQueue() method, after a call to the JMSHelper class, to retrieve the dynamically created queue once it becomes available:

```
JMSHelper.createPermanentQueueAsync(ctx, "MyJMSServer","AnyQName", "MyPermanentQ");
Queue queue = findQueue(qsession, "MyJMSServer","AnyQName", 3, 5000);
```

JMS Messages and Selectors

WebLogic supports all the standard JMS message types, including JMS-defined header fields and user-defined properties. WebLogic also supports an XML message type, which lets you encapsulate XML data in a JMS message. A JMS consumer can use a *message selector* to filter unwanted messages arriving at a destination. A message selector defines a filtering criterion specified in terms of an SQL-like expression language using the message header and property fields. WebLogic extends this functionality with XPath selectors for XML messages.

Different message types have their own performance cost on the JMS server. Message selectors also can impact the server's performance and the efficiency with which a JMS consumer handles incoming messages. We look at these performance issues a little later in this chapter.

XML messages

The standard approach to exchanging XML data would be to wrap the XML text in a standard TextMessage object. Ideally, a JMS consumer should be able to easily identify the fact that the body of the JMS message is an XML document. WebLogic makes a new message type available through the weblogic.jms.extensions. XMLMessage class. In this way, JMS producers can exchange XML data more intuitively, and JMS consumers can correctly handle XML messages. To create an XML message, you must use WebLogic's extension WLSession interface. The following code shows how to create an XML message using a QueueSession object:

```
QueueSession qsession = /* ... */;
XMLMessage msg = ((WLQueueSession) qsession).createXMLMessage();
x1.setText("<a><b>yes</b></a>");
```

Here we've created an empty XML message with no body, and then invoked setText() to provide the XML data. The next code sample shows an alternative way of creating an XML message:

```
TopicSession tsession = /* ... */;
XMLMessage msg = ((WLTopicSession) tsession).createXMLMessage("<a><b>no</b></a>");
```

This version of the createXMLMessage() method creates an XMLMessage object and initializes it with the supplied XML text. An XML message can be treated like any other

JMS message. So, you can retrieve its header fields and create custom message properties. Its real utility, though, lies in the extended XPath selector syntax that lets you inspect the body of the XML message.

JMS selectors

Selectors allow a consumer to filter out messages that it does not want to consider. A message selector lets you define filtering criteria in terms of the message property and header fields. For example, a JMS producer could add relevant custom properties to a text message before sending it:

```
TextMessage message = qsession.createTextMessage();
message.setText(someText); // a text message contains text body
message.setStringProperty("category", "pets");
message.setIntProperty("price", somePrice);
qsender.send(message);
```

JMS consumers then may register their interest in the queue (or topic) while specifying a message selector for filtering out unwanted messages. So, a queue receiver could register its interest in expensive animals by using the following selector expression:

```
QueueReceiver qr = qsession.createReceiver(queue,
                    "price > 50 AND category = 'pets'");
```

A selector may be expressed only in terms of the message header and/or property fields—it can never use the body of the message itself. This restriction is lifted for XML messages.

XML message selectors

WebLogic extends the message selector syntax by providing for an XPath expression that is evaluated over the body of the incoming XML messages. The syntax provides for a built-in function, JMS_BEA_SELECT(), which wraps the XPath expression that you provide:

```
String JMS_BEA_SELECT(String type, String expression)
```

The type parameter must be set to the value xpath. The expression parameter may hold any valid XPath expression. The following code shows how to create a queue receiver using an XPath-based message selector:

```
String selector = "JMS_BEA_SELECT('xpath', '/a/b/text()') = 'yes'";
QueueReceiver qr = qsession.createReceiver(queue, selector);
```

The message selector indicates that the queue receiver will filter out any XML messages whose payload doesn't contain the word yes. For example, the following XML will be allowed by the selector:

```
<a><b>yes</b></a>
```

The following XML will be rejected:

```
<a><b>some arbitrary text</b></a>
```

Note the use of single quotes to denote string expressions within the XPath query. The new XPath syntax slots right in with the standard message selector syntax, and you can combine the two easily, as shown in the following code sample:

```
String selector = "price > 50 AND
                   JMS_BEA_SELECT('xpath', '/a/b/text()') = 'yes'";
TopicSubscriber ts = tsession.createSubscriber(topic, selector);
```

The JMS_BEA_SELECT( ) method returns null if the XML message does not parse, or if the specified elements in the XPath query are not present. This behavior is no different from the standard evaluation of the selector expression, where an identifier representing a property will be assigned the null value if the property does not exist.

Impact of messages on performance

The performance of a JMS server will vary depending on the type of messages that are being exchanged. You often need to balance the type of message, and the number of messages, with the following cost factors:

- The server must be equipped with enough memory to store all messages. Recall that all messages, including their property and header fields, are held in memory, unless paging has been enabled. In this case, the message bodies are swapped out and only the property and header fields are retained in memory.

- Message payloads must be serialized when they are sent and then deserialized before they are received by a consumer. For instance, an ObjectMessage must be serialized before it is delivered, and reconstructed at the consumer's end when it is received. Message header and property fields also must be serialized.

- Messages also will consume network resources when they are sent to their intended destinations and when they are acknowledged by their consumers. The same holds true when the JMS server must deliver messages to a number of topic subscribers that live on different machines.

- If the server or destination supports paging or persistent messages, you incur additional network and serialization costs when the message must be saved and retrieved from the JMS store.

Many of these cost factors are incurred when the message payload contains strings or large string properties. All of the Java string objects must be serialized and reconstructed, and they may place a significant burden on the server's memory. This cost is almost nonexistent when sending, for example, a ByteMessage object. To avoid these serialization costs, often it is preferable to use a ByteMessage or StreamMessage object, rather than a TextMessage or XMLMessage object. If large amounts of text need to be sent within a message, consider compressing the text so as to reduce the network and storage costs. Similarly, the default serialization for an ObjectMessage often can be improved by writing your own serialization logic, using the java.io. Externalizable interface.

The `StreamMessage`, `MapMessage`, `ObjectMessage`, and `ByteMessage` types are treated as simple byte buffers at the server's end. Serialization costs for these message types will occur only on the client's end.

Impact of message selectors on performance

Selectors incur additional processing cost, and it is important to know what kinds of costs are incurred and how they can be minimized. For example, WebLogic can access message header fields less expensively than message property fields. In addition, selector expressions are evaluated in a left-to-right order, together with short-circuit evaluation. Thus, for better performance, a selector expression should be written in such a way so that criteria using any header fields appear before the property fields.

All message filtering for a consumer takes place on the server, except for multicast topic subscribers, in which case the client filters the messages. Hence, selectors will not affect server performance if you are using multicast topic subscribers; they will affect only the client application's performance.

The message selector mechanism also works differently for queues and topics. For topics, the selector is evaluated when the message is published, once for each subscriber. The number of selector evaluations is then directly proportional to the number of subscribers. For queues, the selector is evaluated on every synchronous receive request. A synchronous receive request will force the server to scan each message in the queue until a matching message is found. Thus, the number of evaluations will vary depending on how fast a selector match is found. The situation is further exacerbated if the consumers are slow because this means that every time a consumer is ready for a message, the entire queue needs to be rescanned. In addition, if a message arrives at a queue and one or more synchronous receivers have been blocked, the message must be evaluated against each receiver's selector until a match is found.

Asynchronous receivers can alleviate the cost of queue selectors. Such receivers have a limit on the number of outstanding messages that may be held in the session's pipeline, as determined by the Maximum Messages attribute on the connection factory. By increasing the size of this pipeline, you allow asynchronous receivers to fall further behind without incurring the cost of the queue scans, as the messages will be delivered to the pipelines and then removed from the queue.

As you can see, selectors can be quite expensive. XPath selectors can be even more expensive. Accessing header fields and properties is always going to be cheaper than evaluating an XPath expression, so always place the XPath queries at the end of a selector expression to take advantage of short-circuit evaluation.

XPath selectors also can conflict with message paging for queues. When messages are paged, the bodies of the messages are paged out of memory, and the header and property fields are retained in memory, available for evaluating any message selectors. XPath selectors define filtering criteria using the body of a message. So, if the selector must be evaluated, the paged-out messages must be swapped back into memory. Recall that the topic selector is evaluated as soon as the message is published, before the message is paged out. Hence, topic selectors do not suffer from the same paging problems as queue selectors.

Clustered JMS

Even though a JMS server is pinned to a single WebLogic instance, WebLogic is able to provide a clustered implementation of JMS that offers scalability and load balancing at various levels of client access, as well as high-availability features to ensure that a pinned service such as the JMS server doesn't present a single point of failure to dependent JMS applications. WebLogic's JMS implementation is able to achieve this through a number of features:

- JMS clients can remain unaware of the exact locations of the JMS resources deployed to the cluster. The JNDI name of a JMS destination is made available to all servers in the cluster because it is bound in the cluster-wide JNDI tree. An external client need only use the JNDI name to look up the desired location, without consideration of which physical server hosts the destination. This provides cluster-wide, transparent access to the destinations.

- JMS connection factories can be targeted to all members of a cluster, even to those that do not host a JMS server. When a connection factory produces a connection, it automatically will target one of the servers hosting a connection factory using a load-balancing scheme. The servers that host these connections transparently route traffic through to the required destinations. This allows WebLogic to transparently load-balance remote JMS connections to the cluster, and also provide failover in the event of a server failure.

- WebLogic lets you configure multiple JMS destinations (queues and topics) as members of a distributed destination. What appears to be a single destination to a client actually is distributed across multiple JMS servers within a cluster. A producer or consumer is then able to send and receive messages using this distributed destination. WebLogic simply distributes the messaging load across the members of this distributed destination set. If a JMS destination becomes unavailable due to server failure, WebLogic diverts the traffic among the remaining available members of the distributed destination. Thus, distributed destinations contribute to load balancing and failover.

- WebLogic supports several load-balancing algorithms for distributing the load of incoming client JMS connections among the servers in the cluster, and also for distributing the messaging load between the members of a distributed destination. In addition, WebLogic is able to use various affinity-based heuristics to disable load balancing between the members of the distributed destination, and thus avoid extra network hops that may be needed to reach a member destination on another server in the cluster.

- Because WebLogic JMS is a "singleton" service in the cluster, it need not be enabled on all members of the cluster. Typically, it will be pinned to a single server in the cluster and then will be accessible to all JMS clients of that cluster. To ensure that the pinned JMS service is available even in the event of a failure, WebLogic lets you migrate a JMS server and all its destinations to another clustered server. For each JMS server, you can configure one or more migratable targets—i.e., a preferred list of servers in the cluster to which the JMS server can be migrated.

The next section explores these concepts, and how they combine to form a powerful platform for building scalable, highly available JMS solutions.

JMS Connections and Connection Factories

JMS clients use connection factories to obtain connections to a JMS server. There is an important interplay between connections and connection factories when these objects are used in a clustered environment. When a JMS connection factory is targeted to multiple servers in the cluster, the following occurs:

- For external clients, the connection factory can provide support for load balancing and failover.
- The servers that host the connection factory provide connection routing.

These features form the bedrock of WebLogic's clustered JMS implementation. Distributed destinations provide the next level of load-balancing and failover support for JMS producers and consumers. We will return to connections and connection factories again, after examining distributed destinations.

Load balancing

When an external client creates a JMS connection using a connection factory—for example, with the QueueConnectionFactory.createQueueConnection( ) method—the connection factory uses a load-balancing strategy to decide which server in the cluster should host the JMS connection. In fact, a choice is made between the available servers in the cluster whenever a connection factory is looked up *and* whenever a JMS connection is created. For example, if a remote JMS client uses a connection factory that is targeted to two servers in a cluster, Server1 and Server2, then the JMS connections created by the client (or any other client using the same connection factory) will alternate between the two servers.

On the other hand, if a server-side application uses its local JNDI context to look up a connection factory that is targeted to the same server that hosts the application, the context factory will *not* load-balance any of the connection requests from the application. Instead, the application will use a local connection that simply routes all JMS requests through the local server. This optimization helps minimize the cost of making remote network calls.

You can configure the default load-balancing scheme for a cluster using the Administration Console. Select the cluster from the left pane and then adjust the value of the Default Load Algorithm from the General tab. The default load algorithm impacts all clustered remote resources (e.g., stateless session EJBs) and not just JMS connections. By default, WebLogic uses a round-robin scheme.

Connection routing

It is surprising to note that connection load balancing does not involve the JMS servers at all. Connection factories can be targeted independently of the JMS servers. Furthermore, a JMS connection, which can route traffic to the appropriate JMS servers, will always be returned from a clustered server that hosts the connection factory, regardless of whether the server hosts a JMS server. All JMS traffic will be routed over this connection to the JMS server hosting the intended destinations. This routing is performed behind the scenes and is transparent to clients. However, it also may cause needless traffic.

Figure 8-2 shows an external client that (1) establishes a connection with a cluster, (2) looks up a connection factory, (3) creates a connection using the connection factory, and (4) then tries to access a destination Q1. Because the connection factory is targeted to the cluster, the connections it creates will be load-balanced over all the servers in the cluster. In the figure, the JMS connection has been created to Server 2. Because we want to interact with a destination that lives on Server 1, the connection will route all JMS traffic back to Server 1. Clearly, it would be far more efficient if the connection were returned from the same server that returned the connection factory. Later, we will see how your JMS traffic can avoid this unnecessary hop.

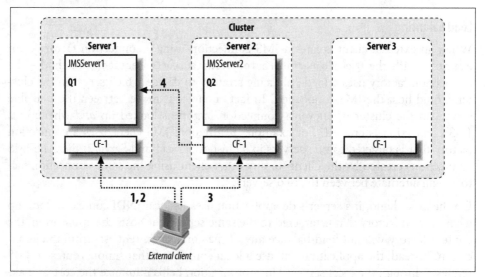

Figure 8-2. Unwanted connection routing

One advantage of the connection routing mechanism is that it provides scalability. If many hundreds of JMS clients are all trying to access the same destination and call on other server-side services, connection routing ensures that the work of maintaining the sockets to the clients is balanced between all of the members hosting connections, and not just the JMS server.

Failover

WebLogic's cluster-aware JMS connection factories enable JMS clients to fail over to another member of the cluster. Once a client has obtained a connection factory from one of the servers in the cluster, it will continue to work even if the server that hosts the client's JMS connection goes down. In other words, a JMS client can use the same connection factory instance to obtain a new JMS connection to another cluster member that also hosts the same factory. JMS clients can register an exception listener on the JMS connection to detect any connection failures, and then request a new connection from the connection factory. Because the connection factory maintains an internal list of available WebLogic instances that host the factory, it can dynamically select an alternative WebLogic instance for the JMS connection. All JMS requests are subsequently routed through this newly chosen server in the cluster.

Targeting for server-side applications

As we have just seen, the behavior of WebLogic's load-balancing and failover capabilities for a clustered JMS connection factory depends on whether the JMS application runs on a server within the cluster that hosts the JMS servers, or runs as an external JMS client. By judiciously targeting connection factories within a cluster, you can avoid unnecessary connection hops.

For a server-side application, you should ensure that the connection factory is targeted to all servers that host the JMS application, or more conveniently target the connection factory to the entire cluster. In this way, when the server-side application looks up a connection factory, it will be able to find one in its local JNDI tree. As a result, it will use a local connection factory and a local connection. This avoids any unnecessary routing of JMS requests through another server in the cluster.

The downside of not doing this is highlighted if you target the connection factory to only those servers in the cluster that host the JMS destinations needed by your server-side applications. The problem with this approach is that only these servers (the servers hosting the JMS servers) would handle all the connections and the work of routing JMS requests. Furthermore, if the JMS server were migrated to another server, you would have to target the connection factory to the new WebLogic instance.

Targeting for external applications

For external JMS clients, it is more optimal to target only the connection factory to the JMS server that hosts the desired destination. This avoids the unnecessary hops for JMS traffic, as illustrated earlier in Figure 8-2. If the client looks up a connection factory that is targeted to a server not hosting the desired destination, it may incur an extra network hop when it tries to interact with the JMS server. Note that if the connection factory is targeted to a subset of the servers in a cluster, external JMS clients still can use the cluster address to look up the JMS factory. All they need to know is the JNDI name of the connection factory. Later, we examine how server affinity can help JMS clients avoid extra network hops when clients need to interact with a distributed destination.

Affinity-based load-balancing algorithms

A round-robin-affinity strategy is useful in situations where external clients use a JMS connection factory that is targeted to multiple servers, and not just to the server that hosts the particular destination. If the external client already has established a JNDI context with a particular server in the cluster, the load balancer will favor the same server for the JMS connection factory, if it hosts the factory. In other words, the affinity-based schemes try to use existing connections, and create a new connection only if necessary. Clearly, it also reduces the number of sockets opened between the client and the cluster. Refer to Chapter 14 to learn how to enable affinity-based load balancing for the entire cluster.

Distributed Destinations

In a clustered environment, you would like to be able to distribute the messaging load across several physical destinations hosted on separate JMS servers. WebLogic provides this capability through *distributed destinations*. A distributed destination is a cluster-specific destination representing one or more physical destinations, typically residing on different JMS servers in the cluster. These physical destinations also are referred to as the *members* of the distributed destination. Any messages that are sent to this distributed destination are distributed over the actual member destinations. If a JMS server that hosts one of the members of the distributed destination fails, the messages are load-balanced automatically between the remaining JMS destinations that are still alive.

Thus, a distributed destination is a transparent proxy to a number of physical destinations located on JMS servers within a cluster. It is through this proxy that WebLogic is able to provide support for load balancing and failover at the destination level in a clustered environment. Before we examine how to configure a distributed destination, let's take a closer look at the behavior of distributed queues and topics.

Using distributed queues

A distributed queue represents a set of physical JMS queues. JMS applications can treat a distributed queue like any ordinary JMS queue, so they can send, receive, and even browse a distributed queue easily. The member queues that comprise the distributed queue can be hosted by any JMS server within the same cluster. When a message is sent to a distributed queue, it is sent to exactly *one* of its member queues.

A distributed queue provides a great way of distributing the messaging load across physical JMS queues, and so too across consumers of these queues. Any messages that are sent to the distributed queue will end up on exactly one of the member queues, and the choice of the physical queue can be load-balanced. You also can configure a Forward Delay on a member queue so that any messages that arrive at a queue with no consumers are forwarded automatically to another queue that does have consumers. The default forward delay for a queue member is -1, which means that no forwarding occurs if messages arrive at a queue with no consumers.

Whenever a message is sent to a distributed queue, a decision is made as to which queue member will receive the message. Messages are never replicated because each message is sent to exactly one member queue. If a member queue becomes unavailable before a message is received, the message is unavailable until that queue member comes back online. Whenever a consumer registers its interest with a distributed queue, it actually binds to one of its member queues. A load-balancing decision is made when choosing a member from the distributed queue. Once a queue has been selected, the consumer is pinned to that member queue until it subsequently loses access. For instance, a consumer will receive a JMSException if the physical queue to which it was bound becomes unavailable. For synchronous receivers, the exception is returned directly to the JMS client, whereas an asynchronous receiver can register an exception listener with the JMS session, and thereby handle a ConsumerClosed-Exception error. In this way, the consumers are always notified of a failure if the server hosting the queue member dies.

When a JMS client receives such an exception, it should close and re-create its queue receiver. The queue receiver then will be pinned to another available member of the distributed queue, if one exists. Here again, a load-balancing decision will help choose another available member from the distributed queue.

In the same way, if a JMS client attempts to browse a distributed queue, the queue browser is bound to one of the member queues at *creation time*. The queue browser then is pinned to that physical queue until it loses access. Any further calls to the queue browser will then raise a JMSException. A queue browser can browse only the physical queue to which it is pinned. Even though you've specified a distributed queue, the same queue browser cannot browse messages arriving from other queues in the distributed queue.

Figure 8-3 summarizes the behavior of distributed queues. Here, a distributed queue, DQ, consists of two member queues, Q1 and Q2. When a consumer is created for the distributed queue, WebLogic pins the consumer to a particular member queue, in this case, Q2. When a producer sends messages to the distributed queue, the messages are balanced across the member queues. Each message is sent to only a single queue member.

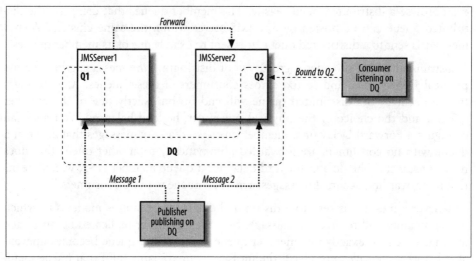

Figure 8-3. The behavior of publishers and consumers of a distributed queue

Using distributed topics

A distributed topic represents a set of physical topics. Overall, JMS applications can treat a distributed topic like any ordinary JMS topic, so they can publish and subscribe to a distributed topic. The fact that a distributed topic represents a number of physical topics on different JMS servers within a cluster remains transparent to your JMS applications. Any messages that are sent to a distributed topic are then sent to all members of that distributed topic, and hence to all its subscribers. So, unlike a distributed queue, any messages arriving at a distributed topic are copied multiple times, once for each subscriber. In addition, if a JMS application publishes a message to a member of a distributed topic, it is forwarded automatically to all of the other members of that distributed topic!

 We said that JMS applications can treat distributed topics like ordinary JMS topics. Well, not quite. You cannot create durable subscriptions to a distributed topic. This isn't really a drawback because you can still create durable subscriptions to a member of the distributed topic.

When a message is sent to a distributed topic, WebLogic tries to first forward the message to those member topics that use a persistent store, thereby minimizing potential message loss. If none of the member topics has a persistent messaging store, WebLogic still sends the message using the selected load-balancing algorithm. In fact, any message sent to a distributed topic is then sent to all member topics as follows:

- If the message is nonpersistent and some members of the distributed topic are not available, it is sent to only the available member topics.

- If the message is persistent and some members of the distributed topic are not available, it is stored and forwarded to those unavailable member topics when they become available. The message is persistently stored only if the available topic member(s) use a JMS store.

- Of course, if all the member topics are unreachable, the publisher receives a JMSException when it tries to send the message, regardless of the delivery mode.

In general, we recommend that all JMS servers participating in the distributed destination be configured to use persistent stores. As with distributed queues, a subscriber is pinned to a particular topic when it registers its interest with a distributed topic. A load-balancing decision is made to help choose the member topic to which the subscriber will be bound. The subscriber will remain pinned to the member topic until it loses access to the topic. Depending on whether the subscriber is synchronous or asynchronous, the JMS client can either handle the exception or register an exception listener with the JMS session.

Figure 8-4 summarizes the behavior of distributed topics. A consumer subscribed to the distributed topic, and was subsequently pinned to a member topic—in this case, T2. Messages published to the distributed topic then are delivered to all members of the distributed topic.

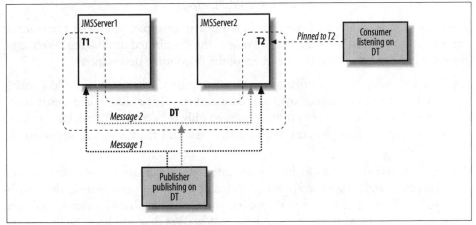

Figure 8-4. The behavior of publishers and consumers of a distributed topic

Creating a distributed destination

The configuration for a distributed destination takes place in the Services/JMS/ Distributed Destinations node within the Administration Console. Here you can select the "Configure a new Distributed Topic" link to create a new distributed topic, or the "Configure a new Distributed Queue" link to create a new distributed queue.

For each distributed destination, you should configure the following settings:

Name

> Use this setting to provide a unique name for the distributed topic/queue.

JNDI Name

> Use this setting to provide a JNDI name for the distributed queue/topic in the cluster-wide JNDI tree. If the destination hasn't been assigned a JNDI name, your JMS clients still can access the distributed queue or topic using the createQueue( ) method on a QueueSession object, or the createTopic( ) method on a TopicSession object.

Load Balancing Policy

> Use this setting to determine how producers will distribute their messages across the members of the distributed destination. The valid values for this setting are Round-Robin or Random.

Forward Delay

> This setting applies to a distributed queue. Use it to determine the amount of time that a member queue with messages but no consumers will wait before forwarding its messages to other member queues that do have consumers.

Now you can use the Thresholds & Quotas tab to set the message quota limits, and use threshold settings for message paging and flow control, on all members of the distributed queue/topic. Note that these settings will apply only to those physical queues or topics that don't already use a JMS template.

Now that you've configured the distributed queue or topic, you need to create or supply the queues or topics that will belong to the distributed destination. WebLogic provides two ways to set up the members of the distributed destination:

- You can select the Configuration/Members tab to manually include existing physical queues or topics that will be members of the distributed destination. For each member queue or topic, you need only to provide a name, choose from one of the existing physical JMS destinations, and then assign a weight to the member.

- You can use the Auto-Deploy tab to automatically *create* the physical destinations on selected JMS servers within a cluster that must participate in the distributed destination. If you use this option, you can either choose a cluster and then select the WebLogic instances and the JMS servers that will host the distributed destination, or directly choose the WebLogic instances and JMS servers that will host the distributed destination. Member destinations will then be generated automatically on the selected JMS servers and added to the distributed destination. The names of these destinations will be generated automatically as well. For instance, if a distributed queue MyDQ is targeted to a JMS server called MyJMSServer, then the name for the member queue on that JMS server will be MyDQ@MyJMSServer-1. Once the member destinations have been generated, you can view or edit the list of members from the Configuration/Members tab.

Note that the auto-deploy method is purely a convenience feature, allowing you to more easily generate the member destinations on various JMS servers.

Accessing a distributed destination

Suppose a distributed queue called MyDQ has two members, Queue1 and Queue2, each hosted by a separate JMS server within a cluster. You could access the distributed queue as follows:

```
Queue dQueue = myQueueSession.createQueue("MyDQ");
```

There is nothing special in this code—we simply have located the distributed queue using its logical name. If the distributed queue is assigned the JNDI name *jms/MyDQ*, you could easily perform a JNDI lookup:

```
Queue dQueue = (Queue) ctx.lookup("jms/MyDQ");
```

This emphasizes the fact that distributed destinations largely are transparent to JMS clients. The actual member that is returned depends on the load-balancing algorithm and various heuristics that may apply at that time.

Sometimes it is necessary to access a particular member of a distributed destination. You can do this in one of the following ways:

- If the member destination is assigned a JNDI name, you can look up the destination using this JNDI name.

- Alternatively, you can access a member destination if you know the name of the distributed destination and the name of the JMS server that hosts the member destination. So, to access the physical member Q1 of the distributed queue DQ residing on server JMSServer1, as shown in Figure 8-3, you can look up the member queue as follows:

  ```
  Queue queue = qSession.createQueue("JMSServer1/DQ");
  ```

  Similarly, to access the physical member topic T1 in Figure 8-4, which is targeted to a JMS server JMSServer1, you can access the member topic on that server as follows:

  ```
  Topic topic = tSession.createQueue("JMSServer1/DT");
  ```

An InvalidDestinationException is thrown if a member of the distributed destination does not exist on the requested server. Note that the second approach relies on a proprietary syntax for accessing a member of a distributed destination, and may not be supported by other JMS products.

Producer and consumer load balancing

Load balancing is somewhat different depending on whether the JMS client is a consumer or a producer. As a consumer, the choice of which member destination is used is made *only once* based on the load-balancing scheme set for the distributed destination. After the decision has been made, the consumer is bound to that physical member, and continues to receive messages from that member only, until the consumer or physical member fails. When the consumer subsequently reconnects to the distributed destination, a new physical member is chosen.

As a producer, however, the choice is made *each time* a message is sent to the distributed destination. However, if the message is to be delivered in a persistent mode, the producer will attempt to find a member destination that is equipped with a persistent JMS store. If none of the physical members has a persistent store, the message is sent to one of the member destinations chosen using the load-balancing scheme configured for the distributed destination. We recommend that you configure all member destinations with a persistent store.

In general, though, producers load-balance on every send( ) or publish( ) operation. You can prevent this behavior and instead configure the producers to make the choice only once, on the first call to send( ) or publish( ). To achieve this, select the connection factory that is being used by the producer from the Administration Console, and then disable the Load Balancing Enabled flag in the Configuration/General tab. Any producers created using this connection factory will be load-balanced only the first time a message is delivered to a distributed destination. All messages are then delivered to this member destination until the producer fails. When the producer subsequently reconnects and attempts to send a message to the distributed destination, a new physical member is chosen.

Load-balancing schemes

For any distributed destination, you can set the load-balancing algorithm to either round-robin or random distribution. Each physical destination within the distributed destination set can be assigned a weight. This weight is used as a measure of the destination's ability to handle the messaging load with respect to its peers within the distributed destination. The load-balancing algorithm, together with the destination weights, determine how the messaging load is distributed across the physical destinations.

A round-robin algorithm maintains an ordered list of the physical destinations, and the messaging load is distributed across these destinations one at a time. The list's order is determined by the order in which the destinations are defined within the domain's *config.xml* file. If the physical destinations have been assigned unequal weights, the member destinations will appear multiple times in the ordered list, depending on their weights. For example, if a distributed queue with two members, Q1 and Q2, have weights 2 and 3, respectively, the member queues will be ordered as follows: Q1, Q2, Q1, Q2, Q2. Effectively, WebLogic makes a number of passes over the same destination set, and then drops members as their weights fall below the number of passes. JMS clients who use the distributed queue will then be cycled through its member queues in this sequence.

A random distribution algorithm uses the weights of the physical destinations to create a weighted random distribution for the set of destinations. The messaging load is then distributed according to this weighted random distribution. Note that in the short term, the messaging load on each destination may not be proportionate to its weight, but in the long term, the load distribution will tend toward the ideal weighted random distribution. If all the destinations are assigned equal weights, a purely random distribution will result. The random distribution needs to be recalculated whenever a member destination is added or removed from the distributed destination set. This computation, however, is inexpensive and shouldn't affect performance.

Load-balancing heuristics

As we have already seen, if a producer sends a message to a distributed destination in persistent mode, WebLogic doesn't just blindly choose a member destination from the set. Instead, it tries to find one that has a persistent store to ensure that the message is persisted. In fact, WebLogic relies on three other load-balancing heuristics when choosing a member of a distributed destination:

Transaction affinity

Multiple messages sent within the scope of a transacted session are routed to the same WebLogic instance, if possible. For instance, if a JMS session sends multiple messages to the same distributed destination, all of the messages are routed to the same physical destination. Similarly, if a session sends multiple messages to different distributed destinations, WebLogic tries to choose a set of physical destinations that are all hosted by the same WebLogic instance.

Server affinity

When a connection factory has server affinity enabled, WebLogic first attempts to load-balance consumers and producers across those member destinations that are hosted on the same WebLogic instance a client first connects to. To configure this, select a connection factory from the Administration Console, and then change the value of the Server Affinity Enabled flag in the Configuration/ General tab. It is enabled by default on any connection factories that you create.

Queues with no consumers

When a producer sends messages to a distributed queue, member queues with no consumers are not considered in the load-balancing decision. In other words, only member queues with more than one consumer are considered for balancing the messaging load—unless, of course, all member queues have no consumers. For consumers, however, it is the physical queues without consumers that are first considered for balancing the load. Only when all member queues have a consumer does the configured load-balancing algorithm start to apply.

All of these heuristics help improve the performance of JMS in a clustered environment. Transaction affinity tries to minimize network traffic when multiple messages are sent in a transaction by routing all traffic to the same WebLogic instance. Server affinity gives you the opportunity to prefer destinations collocated with the connection factory. These affinity-based heuristics obviously will decrease network traffic, but at the expense of unbalancing the load distribution. Finally, it clearly makes sense for member queues with no consumers to be considered for balancing the load of consumers first, rather than producers.

Targeting connection factories

The previous look at targeting connection factories to prevent unnecessary network hops didn't take distributed destinations into account. If you have a server-side application *producing* messages to a distributed destination, you may incur a wasteful network hop. Publishing to a distributed destination generally causes a load balance between the physical members of the destination. You can disable this load balancing and instead force the server-side application to use only the physical destinations collocated with it. This changes the behavior of the distributed destination (it no longer publishes to all physical members), but in return you save many network calls. To disable load balancing in this scenario, ensure that the connection factory used by the application has the Server Affinity option enabled. This makes it prefer physical destinations that are collocated on the same server instance. If you have a server-side application *consuming* messages from a distributed destination, you should ensure that the application is deployed to the same servers as the members of the distributed destination and the connection factories. In other words, collocate the consumer of a distributed destination with the members of the distributed destination. If you don't do this, WebLogic may route messages to the consumer through other servers.

As stated previously, an external client should have the connection factory it uses targeted to the servers hosting the destinations. If a distributed destination is being used, the same applies—you should target the connection factory to each server hosting a member destination. For the same reasons as explained in the previous paragraph, an external client that *produces* to a distributed destination should usually enable Server Affinity to avoid unnecessary network hops.

Message-Driven Beans

Message-driven beans (MDBs) are the best way of concurrently handling messages arriving at a topic or queue. MDBs that listen to a nondistributed queue implement asynchronous, reliable delivery within a cluster. If the MDB becomes unavailable, the incoming messages collect at the queue and wait until the MDB comes up again. If the MDB listens to a nondistributed topic, any message arriving at the topic will be broadcast to all subscribers, including the MDB. If the MDB becomes unavailable, it will not receive the message, unless, of course, it has a durable subscription to the topic.

Some of the biggest issues surrounding MDBs include where to place them in the architecture and their interaction with distributed destinations.

Placement of MDBs

If the message bean responds to a physical JMS destination on a particular server in the cluster (i.e., *nondistributed* destination), you can deploy the associated MDB to the same WebLogic instance that hosts the destination. As a result, incoming messages can be delivered to the MDB without incurring any network traffic. Of course, if the application relies on a foreign JMS provider, it may not be possible to collocate the MDB with the foreign JMS server hosting the destination. Collocating MDBs and the destination will result in the best performance.

In a cluster scenario, you may have a distributed destination with its physical members distributed across the cluster. If you deploy an MDB to this cluster, which listens on the distributed destination, WebLogic will ensure that there is an MDB listening to each member of the distributed destination. So, in effect, you will have collocation of the destination and MDB, together with the load-balancing and failover capabilities of the distributed destination. This is ideal if there are high-performance and availability needs.

MDBs and distributed topics

MDBs that are configured to listen on a distributed topic will listen on each physical member of the topic. This may result in unnecessary processing if more than one physical member of the distributed topic is hosted on the same JMS server. If a message is sent to the distributed topic, it will be processed multiple times on the same server.

In essence, your applications will end up processing the same message twice! The better approach would be to simply set up the MDB to respond to one of the members of the distributed topic. That is, configure the MDB to listen to a particular physical member, and not to the distributed topic.

Delivery order

If an application uses an MDB to respond to messages arriving at a destination, it cannot assume that the MDB will receive the messages in the order in which they were produced. To receive messages in order, you need to limit the pool size to a single MDB, at the cost of concurrent handling:

```
<!-- MDB's weblogic-ejb-jar.xml entry: -->
<pool>
  <max-beans-in-free-pool>1</max-beans-in-free-pool>
  <initial-beans-in-free-pool>1</initial-beans-in-free-pool>
</pool>
```

Likewise, if the MDB is deployed in a clustered environment, you need to instead target it to only a single server within the cluster.

JMS Migration

Typically, your JMS servers will run on some subset of the servers in a cluster. To ensure that JMS servers can continue to service applications even after a failure, WebLogic provides a high-availability framework that lets you manually migrate a JMS server to another WebLogic instance in the cluster. All destinations hosted by the JMS server, including any members of distributed destination, also are migrated with the JMS server. This migration utilizes the same migration framework for pinned services in a clustered environment, as described in Chapter 14.

It may happen that a JMS server is migrated to a WebLogic instance that already hosts a JMS server. If both JMS servers host destinations that are members of the same distributed destination, that WebLogic instance must handle the messaging load of both physical destinations. This skews the results of load balancing configured for distributed destination by being less fair to that particular WebLogic instance. In such cases, you should migrate the failed JMS server back to its own WebLogic instance as soon as possible.

Before you can migrate a JMS server, you need to ensure the following:

- The JMS server is deployed on a WebLogic instance that belongs to a cluster.
- A migratable target has been assigned to the JMS server. To configure this, use the Targets/Migratable Targets tab to choose one or more preferred servers in the cluster to which the JMS server can be migrated.

Remember, a JMS server can only be migrated to another server in the same cluster to which it belongs.

Migrating a JMS server

A JMS server can be migrated either as a scheduled operation or in the event of a failure. Choose the server from which you want to migrate from the Administration Console. Then select a target server from the Control/JMS Migrate tab, and finally push the Migrate button. The JMS server, along with all of its destinations, will be migrated to the selected WebLogic instance.

Note that persistent stores are not migrated along with the JMS server. If the JMS server uses a persistent store, this store will need to be accessible to the JMS server in its new location. For JDBC stores, you simply need to ensure that the connection pool also is targeted to the new WebLogic instance. For file stores, you need to ensure that the JMS server at the new location also can access the file store. You can do this by employing either a hardware solution (e.g., a dual-ported SCSI disk), or a shared filesystem. Alternatively, you can copy the file store from the failed server to the new server at the same location under WebLogic's home directory.

To avoid any possible data consistencies, you also may have to migrate the transaction logs to the new server in the cluster. If the JMS server was migrated because of a server crash, it is important to make the transaction log files available at the new location before the server restarts. If you omit this step, any JMS operations invoked within the scope of the pending transaction may not complete as per expected semantics. Chapter 6 explains how to migrate the transaction recovery service onto another cluster member.

Migrating MDBs

Any MDBs configured to listen to a JMS destination can be migrated from a failed server to another server in the cluster. Even though an MDB doesn't have any migratable targets, it still can pick up the migratable targets configured for the JMS server to which it is deployed. So, to ensure proper migration of MDBs, you should ensure that the MDB is deployed to those JMS servers in the cluster that host the desired destinations. You can deploy the MDB either homogeneously to the entire cluster or to each migratable target configured for the JMS server hosting the destination. In other words, the list of target servers for the MDB should at least contain the JMS server's migratable target list. The migration is supported for both MDBs listening to JMS destinations, and for MDBs registered with distributed destinations.

WebLogic's Messaging Bridge

A *messaging bridge* provides interoperability between any two messaging systems. Messages arriving at one end of the bridge are forwarded automatically to other end, according to specified quality of service (QoS) and transaction semantics. You can set up a messaging bridge in the following scenarios:

- You can configure a bridge between two JMS servers running in your domain, or between two JMS servers running in separate domains, even on different versions of WebLogic.
- You can configure a bridge between WebLogic JMS and any other third-party JMS-compliant product—say, IBM MQSeries.

Clearly, it is up to the messaging bridge to handle all the forwarding and any necessary conversions, if it is interfacing with non-JMS products.

A messaging bridge runs between two destinations: a *source* destination from which messages are received, and a *target* destination to which the messages are sent. These *bridge destinations* can be either topics or queues. The bridge establishes a pipe between the source and target destinations, and ensures that messages received on the source destination are forwarded to the target destination. Applications that rely on WebLogic JMS can use bridges to integrate easily with other messaging products.

A messaging bridge provides additional facilities as well. In particular, a bridge can provide a certain QoS when forwarding messages from the source to the target destination. For instance, a bridge that provides an "exactly-once" guarantee ensures that a two-phase commit is used during the forwarding mechanism. A bridge also can make several attempts to reconnect to the source or target destinations if either becomes unavailable for some reason. This ensures that bridges provide a robust integration between two messaging systems.

Later in this chapter, we shall see how to temporarily suspend all traffic running through the bridge, and adjust the size of the execute thread pool.

Installing a Messaging Bridge

WebLogic's messaging bridges are supplied as resource adapters. Three different bridge adapters come shipped with your WebLogic distribution, one for bridging to a JMS server running on WebLogic 5.1, and two for bridging to any JMS-compliant products. The choice depends on the kind of transaction semantics you need. Table 8-3 describes the three adapters that are supplied with WebLogic Server.

Table 8-3. JMS bridges supplied with WebLogic Server

Adapter name	JNDI name	Bridge characteristics
jms-xa-adp.rar	eis.jms.WLSConnection FactoryJNDIXA	This bridge provides transaction semantics via an XAResource. It should be used when the QoS needs to be "exactly-once."
jms-notran-adp.rar	eis.jms.WLSConnection FactoryJNDINoTX	This bridge provides no transaction semantics, and so can be used when the QoS is "at most-once" or "duplicate-okay."
jms-notran-adp51.rar	eis.jms.WLS51Connection FactoryJNDINoTX	This bridge should be used when either the source or target destination is a WebLogic Server 5.1 server.

All of these adapters can be found in the *WL_HOME\server\lib* directory of your WebLogic installation. If you would like to bridge to a destination on a non-JMS messaging system, you can either create your own bridge or acquire one from the vendor. These resource adapters should be installed just like any other. Refer to Chapter 7 for more information on how to deploy resource adapters. The JNDI names listed in Table 8-3 will be needed later, when we use the adapter.

All of the configuration for a messaging bridge takes place under the Services/ Messaging Bridge node in the left pane of the Administration Console. Use the JMS Bridge Destinations node to configure the source and target destinations for the bridge. Use the General Bridge Destinations node if you intend to bridge to non-JMS destinations. Of course, you must create the bridge destinations first before you can create the messaging bridge itself. All of the messaging bridges can be found under the Bridges node. For now, we will look only at how to set up a bridge between WebLogic JMS and another JMS product (IBM MQSeries).

Configuring Bridge Destinations

To use a bridge, you will have to create a bridge destination for both the source and target destinations. Create each by selecting the JMS Bridge Destinations node and then selecting the "Configure a New JMS Bridge Destination" option. Table 8-4 lists the main configuration options that you need to set when creating a bridge.

Table 8-4. Configuration settings for a bridge destination

Setting	Description
Name	Use this attribute to specify a name for the destination. It should be unique across the domain.
Adapter JNDI Name	Use this attribute to set the JNDI name of the adapter that will be used to communicate with the destination. Refer to the adapter's documentation to find the JNDI name that should be used. Table 8-3 lists the JNDI names for the bridge adapters supplied by WebLogic.
Adapter Classpath	Use this option only if you are bridging to WebLogic Server 6.0 or earlier. If you are bridging to a third-party JMS provider, instead you must include the JMS provider's libraries in WebLogic's classpath.
Connection URL	Use this attribute to define the URL of the JNDI provider that will be used to look up the connection factory and the destination.
Initial Context Factory	Use this attribute to define the class name of the initial context factory for the destination.
Connection Factory JNDI Name	Use this attribute to hold the JNDI name of the connection factory that will be used to create connections. If the QoS is to be Exactly-once, an XAConnection Factory name must be supplied.
Destination JNDI Name	Use this attribute to determine the JNDI name of the JMS destination.
Destination Type	Use this setting to specify whether the destination is a queue or a topic.
User Name	Use this optional attribute to determine the username that enables the bridge to access the destination.
Password	Use this optional attribute to determines the password that enables the bridge to access the destination.

Example configuration of bridge destinations

Suppose we wish to create a bridge between IBM MQSeries and WebLogic JMS so that messages arriving on a queue on IBM MQSeries are forwarded automatically to another queue on WebLogic JMS. This means that we need to configure two bridge destinations: a source destination representing the queue on IBM MQSeries, and a target destination representing the queue on WebLogic JMS. Figure 8-5 illustrates the configuration of the destinations in our sample bridge MyBridge.

In this case, we're using a nontransactional bridge adapter, so the Adapter JNDI Name for both bridge destinations will be set to eis.jms.WLSConnectionFactory-JNDINoTX. You also must ensure that the required connection factories and JMS queues are set up on either JMS providers. Later in this chapter, we take a closer look at the configuration of this JMS bridge.

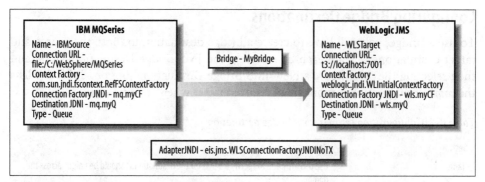

Figure 8-5. Configuring a non-XA JMS bridge between IBM MQSeries and WebLogic JMS

Configuring the Messaging Bridge

Now that you've set up the bridge destinations, you're ready to configure a messaging bridge and the manner in which it forwards messages from the source to the target destination. To create a bridge, click the Messaging Bridges/Bridges node in the left pane, and then select the Configure a New Messaging Bridge option. There are three sets of configuration tabs that we shall look at in turn.

General settings

Table 8-4 describes the configuration attributes that are provided in the General tab. Not surprisingly, the most important thing to do is to set the source and destination to the appropriate JMS Bridge Destinations that have been created. A bridge can provide one of three levels of QoS guarantees when forwarding messages:

Atmost-once
> Each message is sent, at most, once in this mode. It is possible that some messages may not be delivered to the target destination. Use the nontransactional bridge adapter for this mode, and do not use XA-enabled connection factories.

Duplicates-only
> Each message is sent at least once in this mode. All messages are delivered, though some may be delivered to the target destination more than once. Use the nontransactional bridge adapter for this mode, and do not use XA-enabled connection factories.

Exactly-once
> Each message will be sent exactly once in this mode. You can use this mode only if both the source and target destinations are XA-enabled—that is, both bridge destinations are configured to use XA-enabled connection factories. You must use the transactional bridge adapter for this mode, and so the Adapter JNDI name for both bridge destinations must be set to `eis.jms.WLSConnection-FactoryJNDIXA`. It is not recommended that you allow a QoS degradation in this mode.

Note that the Exactly-once mode requires a two-phase commit to be used by the bridge, and is hence the most expensive. If the Exactly-once guarantee is not required, use either of the other two modes for better performance.

The Asynchronous Mode Enabled flag determines whether the bridge may receive messages asynchronously. If the asynchronous mode is chosen, the messaging bridge listens for messages and forwards them as they arrive at the source destination. If the synchronous mode is chosen, the bridge will work in synchronous mode even if the source destination supports asynchronous receiving. In the synchronous mode, messages can forwarded in a batch. For an Exactly-once QoS guarantee, the synchronous mode can greatly improve the performance of the bridge. The asynchronous mode requires the bridge to start a new transaction for each message, performing the two-phase commit across both JMS servers involved in the transaction. If the synchronous mode is used, the two-phase commit will be used less often because the bridge can process multiple messages in each transaction. Thus, for a bridge with Exactly-once guarantees, it is more optimal to not set this flag. On the other hand, if the Exactly-once guarantee is not required, the bridge can forward messages more efficiently in the asynchronous mode—in which case, you should set the flag.

Table 8-5 explains the rest of the settings.

Table 8-5. General bridge configuration settings

Setting	Description
Name	This attribute specifies a name for the bridge.
Source Destination	This setting provides a drop-down list of all available JMS bridge destinations, and should be set to the destination that is to be the source for the bridge.
Target Destination	This setting provides a drop-down list of all available JMS bridge destinations, and should be set to the destination that is to be the target for the bridge.
Selector	This setting provides an optional message selector for the bridge. Only messages that pass the selector will be forwarded. Note that for queues, messages that do not match the selector accumulate in the queue. For topics, messages that do not match are dropped.
Quality of Service	This setting should be set to Duplicate-okay, Atmost-once, or Exactly-once, as explained earlier.
QoS Degradation Allowed	This setting indicates whether the quality of service can be downgraded if the configured QoS is not available.
Asynchronous Mode Enabled	This setting determines whether the bridge can be used in asynchronous mode.
Maximum Idle Time	If the bridge is in synchronous mode, this setting determines the maximum amount of time the bridge will block on a receive call if no transaction is involved. If the bridge is in asynchronous mode, this setting determines the maximum amount of time the bridge will remain idle before checking the health of the connection to the source destination.

Table 8-5. General bridge configuration settings (continued)

Setting	Description
Durability Enabled	This setting applies only to topics that are used as the source JMS destination. If enabled, the messaging bridge will create a durable subscription to the source destination. This means that if the bridge is down, the destination will retain messages sent to it, forwarding them to the target destination when it comes up again. If durability is not enabled, messages sent to the topic while the bridge is down will not be forwarded to the target destination. Note that if a bridge that had durability enabled is deleted, you must delete all durable subscriptions.
Started	This setting indicates the initial state of the bridge when the server is started. You also can use it during runtime to switch the bridge on or off.

Connection retry settings

The configuration options in the Connection Retry tab allow you to define how the bridge reconnects to a bridge destination if it fails. By doing this, you make your bridge far more robust, especially if durable sources are used, as the bridge will try and reconnect to destinations if the connections fail. There are three settings in this tab—minimum, maximum, and incremental delay—and all are specified in seconds. The bridge works as follows: if a connection needs to be reestablished, the bridge waits for at least "minimum delay" seconds before attempting to reconnect. Thus, if a connection is lost, or the server fails to reconnect, the minimum delay determines the delay between connection attempts. Each time a connection attempt fails, the incremental delay is added to the current delay before delaying and attempting to reconnect. The reconnect delays are increased by the specified increment, until the maximum delay is met, after which the delay is no longer increased and the bridge gives up.

Transaction settings

The configuration options in the Transactions tab tune the transaction characteristics of the bridge. If the bridge is configured to use transactions, use the Transaction Timeout setting to adjust the amount of time that the transaction manager will allow for a transaction to complete. The batch size and interval settings are used only if the bridge is operating in synchronous mode. In this case, the batch size determines the number of messages that will be batched together in a transaction. The batch interval defines the maximum time (in milliseconds) to wait before sending a batch, regardless of whether the batch size has been reached. Setting this attribute to –1 indicates that the bridge must always wait until the batch size is reached. You should experiment with both of these settings to arrive at an optimal configuration for your JMS bridge.

Example bridge configuration

Continuing with the earlier example of a bridge between MQSeries and WebLogic JMS, now that we have created two JMS bridge destinations, we need to create the messaging bridge itself. Set the source destination to IBMSource and set the target destination to WLSDest. Because we are using a nontransactional bridge, set the QoS to either Exactly-once or Duplicate-okay. Because durability is not supported for queues, deselect the Durability Enabled option. Ensure that the Started flag is selected, and hit the Apply button. Then restart the server, and you should have a fully operational bridge. Now if you send a message to the queue on the MQSeries, the bridge should forward the message to the queue at WebLogic's end automatically.

Monitoring a bridge

The state of a bridge can be determined from the Administration Console. Select the server hosting the bridge and choose the Services/Bridge tab. Clicking "Monitor all Messaging Bridge Runtimes" will show a list of messaging bridges, and their state.

Configuring the JMS thread pool

WebLogic has a default execute thread pool, as described in Chapter 15. The JMS bridge, by default, uses a separate thread pool, which is used when the bridge is operating in synchronous mode. You can change the number of threads in the pool by choosing the server hosting the bridge and then selecting the Services/Bridge tab. Next, use the Messaging Bridge Thread Pool Size attribute to adjust the size of this thread pool. Setting this to -1 will force the JMS server to use the default thread pool of the associated WebLogic instance.

Using the thread pool that is dedicated to messaging bridges avoids contention with the default execution pool. Clearly, its optimal size will depend on the characteristics of your bridge traffic and the server itself. As a rule of thumb, though, for best performance there should be at least as many threads in the pool as there are bridges that run in synchronous mode.

Monitoring JMS

The Administration Console lets you monitor just about everything: JMS servers, connections, pooled connections, destinations, messages producers and consumers, session pools, and durable subscribers. To monitor JMS servers, destinations, or pools, choose a JMS server from the left pane of the Administration Console and select the appropriate option from the Monitoring tab. The statistics gathered for each JMS server include the number of connections to a JMS server, the number of pending and received messages on all of its destinations, and so on. The JMS connection statistics provide a breakdown of these figures for a particular connection. This also includes important figures, such as the total number of messages stored in the destination, the number of bytes stored in the destination, the number of consumers, and the time since the threshold was last set. These figures are invaluable for tuning the threshold and quota mechanism. To monitor the number of JMS connections on a server, select the server in the left pane of the Administration Console and navigate to the Monitoring/JMS node. This same tab provides a link to monitoring all pooled JMS connections.

CHAPTER 9

JavaMail

The JavaMail API provides the necessary interfaces for adding electronic mail services to your J2EE applications. The API is extensible, permitting vendors to add support for various mail transport and store protocols such as Simple Mail Transport Protocol (SMTP), Post Office Protocol v3 (POP3), and Internet Message Access Protocol (IMAP). JavaMail does not support any mail server functionality—hence, in order to use JavaMail, you also must have access to a mail server. WebLogic includes the JavaMail API Version 1.1.3 reference implementation from Sun Microsystems. In this chapter, you will learn how to set up and use WebLogic's JavaMail integration.

Configuring a Mail Session

Very little needs to be configured to get JavaMail up and running. The basis of configuration is a *Mail Session*, which holds a global set of mail-related properties that define the behavior of the mail client and network. For instance, you could use the Mail Session to configure the transport protocol to be used, or the particular SMTP server or POP3 server to be used. Later, you can override these settings programmatically when you use the Mail Session.

WebLogic publishes the configured Mail Sessions in its JNDI tree. Each Mail Session must be associated with a JNDI name—once it's deployed, WebLogic makes the Mail Session available to all clients who need to interact with the JavaMail API. A client program simply performs a JNDI lookup to access the Mail Session, optionally overrides a few session properties, and then uses the Mail Session in a standard way according to the JavaMail API. The only WebLogic-specific configuration is for the Mail Session; for this, you must use the Administration Console.

To create a Mail Session, choose the Services/Mail node from the left pane of the Administration Console, and then select the "Configure a new Mail Session" option. Here you need to supply a name for the Mail Session, a JNDI name by which the Mail Session can be accessed, and a list of property/value mappings. These properties adhere to the JavaMail API specification and are listed in Table 9-1.

Table 9-1. JavaMail configuration properties

Property	Description	Default value
`mail.store.protocol`	This property defines the protocol that should be used to retrieve email.	`imap`
`mail.transport.protocol`	This property defines the protocol to be used when sending email.	`smtp`
`mail.host`	This property defines the address of the mail server.	`localhost`
`mail.<protocol>.host`	This property defines the mail host for a specific protocol. For instance, you can define the host addresses for SMTP and POP3 by creating an entry for `mail.smtp.host` and `mail.pop3.host`.	The value of the `mail.host` property
`mail.user`	This property defines the name of the default user that is used when retrieving email. Note that Java-Mail does not permit the storing of passwords as properties, so you have to specify this programmatically when contacting the mail host.	The value of the `user.name` Java system property
`mail.<protocol>.user`	The property defines the name of the default user used for the particular protocol.	The value of the `mail.user` property
`mail.from`	This property should be set to the return address of the email and is specified as an email address.	Required
`mail.debug`	This flag may be set to `true` to enable output of debugging information.	`false`

In general, you should set those properties for the Mail Session that you want all clients to inherit by default. For example, if your clients need to use JavaMail to send emails, the following list of property/value pairs should be sufficient for any client of the Mail Session:

```
mail.from=mountjoy@acme.org
mail.transport.protocol=smtp
mail.host=smtp.acme.org
```

Once the Mail Session has been created, you must target it to the server instances that need access to the session.

Using JavaMail

Once you have configured a Mail Session and targeted it to the relevant servers, a client can access it simply by performing a JNDI lookup using its JNDI name. The session then can be used to send or retrieve email according to the JavaMail API. Suppose we have created a Mail Session that is bound in the JNDI under the name *oreilly.mail*. The following code sample shows how to access the configured Mail Session:

```
import javax.activation.*;
import javax.mail.*;
import javax.mail.internet.*
```

```
// ...

InitialContext ctx = new InitialContext();
Session session = (Session) ctx.lookup("oreilly.mail");
```

If you need to change any of the default values assigned to the Mail Session, you can do so by populating a `Properties` object with the new property values, and then using that object to create a new Mail Session by calling the `getInstance()` method on the existing Session object:

```
Properties props = new Properties();

// Place any number of property overrides into props
props.put("mail.from", emailAddress);

// Create the new session from the old
Session otherSession = session.getInstance(props);
```

Of course, if you are happy with the default values for the Mail Session as specified in the Administration Console, there is no need to create a new session; just look up the preconfigured session.

Once you have obtained a session with the appropriate property values, you can use it to send and receive email. The following code sample shows how to use a Mail Session to send email:

```
Message msg = new MimeMessage(mysession);
msg.setFrom();
msg.setRecipients(Message.RecipientType.TO,
                   InternetAddress.parse("mountjoy@acme.org", false));
msg.setSubject("Subject of Message");
msg.setSentDate(new Date());
msg.setText("HELLO TEST TEST");
Transport.send(msg);
```

Here, we have made sure that the Mail Session is configured with appropriate values for the properties: `mail.from`, `mail.transport.protocol` and `mail.host`. MIME functionality can be added easily by using other parts of the standard JavaMail API.

In this next example, we look at how to retrieve mail messages from an existing POP3 account. Here, we first connect to a POP3 server, access the *INBOX* folder (it just so happens POP3 only supports the *INBOX* folder), and then list the Subject field of all email in that folder.

```
Store store = session.getStore();
store.connect("popd.acme.org","mountjoy","pssst123");
Folder folder = store.getDefaultFolder();
folder = folder.getFolder("INBOX");
folder.open(Folder.READ_ONLY);
Message[] messages = folder.getMessages();
for (int i =0; i< messages.length; i++)
  System.out.println(messages[i].getSubject());
```

There are two things that you should be aware of when using the JavaMail API:

- You must ensure that you catch and handle exceptions appropriately. For instance, you should handle exceptions thrown as a result of a malformed email address.

- You should avoid using the JavaMail API from within a transaction context. Connecting to mail servers can take an unpredictable amount of time, and you do not want to unnecessarily lengthen the duration of a transaction. In addition, JavaMail is not transactional, so any changes made using the JavaMail API cannot be undone if the current transaction later aborts and needs to roll back.

Using Other JavaMail Providers

All JavaMail implementations contain a Provider Registry that allows other providers to register their protocol implementations with the JavaMail framework. As WebLogic's JavaMail implementation is bundled in the *weblogic.jar* library, it is not particularly easy to change. If you need support for additional transports or protocols, you should prepend the location of the libraries for the JavaMail implementation to WebLogic's classpath. WebLogic's documentation states that the supplied JavaMail implementation supports only the IMAP and SMTP. We've found that WebLogic also contains Sun's optional support for the POP3 protocol.

You can find additional information on JavaMail and a list of suppliers for various protocol implementations on Sun's web site at *http://java.sun.com/products/javamail*.

CHAPTER 10

Using EJBs

Enterprise JavaBeans (EJBs) are reusable server-side Java components that encapsulate the business logic of a distributed application. All EJBs are created and managed at runtime by an EJB container, which provides essential system-level services such as support for transactions, security, persistence, and concurrency. WebLogic mediates all client invocations to the enterprise bean through the EJB container.

In this chapter, you will learn about building, deploying, and optimizing EJBs within WebLogic. To do this, you also will see how the XML deployment descriptors help configure the various services provided by the EJB container. In fact, the XML descriptors provide vital information on assembly and deployment, and also determine how the container manages the EJB instances at runtime. The standard XML descriptor contains information on deployment, the abstract schema model, security restrictions, and transaction settings for the EJB component. The WebLogic-specific deployment descriptors allow you to configure the main topics covered by this chapter—namely pooling, EJB concurrency, automatic EJB persistence, transaction, failover and clustering behavior, and life-cycle optimizations.

Any EJB implementation requires several Java classes and a number of XML descriptor files. Creating, synchronizing, and maintaining these configuration settings have traditionally been quite a burden on the developer. WebLogic provides several tools to remove this hardship. The primary tool is EJBGen, an EJB code generator. With this tool you need only maintain a single Java file—all the other source files and XML descriptors then can be generated automatically. WebLogic also provides several convenience classes that reduce the amount of boiler-plate code that you need to write when developing EJBs. Finally, many of these tasks are integrated with WebLogic Workshop, making EJB development very simple indeed.

WebLogic provides some great services for optimizing EJBs. The most important of these is the pool and caching behavior, which attempts to ensure that a ready instance of an EJB always is available. WebLogic also is able to limit unnecessary loading of data into an entity bean by storing the state across transactions. Of course, you can safely do this only if you can determine the circumstances under which the data will change. You also can minimize the writing of data by configuring read-only and read-mostly EJB types. The distributed invalidation framework is particularly powerful in these circumstances, allowing either the periodic or user-driven refresh of data stored in the read-only EJBs. Finally, WebLogic provides load-balancing and failover facilities for EJBs. EJBs can be clustered, allowing home retrieval and method invocation to be distributed across all members of the cluster.

Getting Started

Before we delve into the configuration of the various EJB types, it is useful to understand under which circumstances the different EJB types should be used. After this, we provide an overview of how to package your EJBs, and how to use the deployment descriptors to configure the runtime behavior of your EJBs. We also describe how you can use WebLogic's tools to generate and compile the classes needed to deploy your EJBs. Finally, we look at how to set up references to other EJBs and resources.

EJB Types

WebLogic provides full support for the different component models: session beans that model business processes, entity beans that model domain entities, and message-driven beans (MDBs) that represent asynchronous message consumers. Here's a quick summary of important characteristics of these three EJB types:

Session beans

- A session bean executes on behalf of a single client.
- It typically accesses or updates shared data in the underlying database.
- It supports both container-managed and bean-managed transactions.
- The EJB container supports a pool of stateless session EJB instances that can be shared across multiple clients. It also supports a cache of stateful session EJB instances, where each instance maintains the conversational state for a specific client.

Consider using a session bean when only one client can have access to an EJB instance, and session state is relatively short-lived and need not be persisted. Consider using a *stateful* bean if the EJB holds session information for a client across multiple method invocations, or the EJB mediates between the client and other EJB components. Consider using a *stateless* bean if the EJB doesn't need to hold any client-specific session data, or you require a pool of objects that implement a generic set of business tasks. Stateless session beans are often used to create façades to entity beans.

Entity beans

- An entity bean provides an object view of data in an enterprise store.
- Its object identity is defined by its primary key in the underlying database.
- Entity EJB instances can be shared across multiple clients—they represent long-lived, persistent data.
- It can participate only in container-managed transactions.
- WebLogic supports both *bean-managed persistence* (BMP)—i.e., when the EJB itself is responsible for keeping its in-memory state in sync with the underlying data, and *container-managed persistence* (CMP)—i.e., where the EJB container manages the EJB's persistent fields and relationships with other EJB instances.
- The EJB container maintains a pool and a cache of entity EJB instances that can be shared by multiple clients.

You should use entity beans to model business concepts (entities) and not business procedures. For instance, a Student (university applicant) should be modeled as an entity bean, whereas Registration (registering for university courses) should be modeled as a session bean.

Consider using entity beans when the EJB state needs to persist beyond the lifetime of the EJB container. Consider using automatic EJB persistence if you want to avoid JDBC code and just let the EJB container synchronize the EJB's in-memory state with the underlying database. In fact, WebLogic's EJB container also supports a powerful way to handle relationships with other EJB instances.

Message-Driven Beans

- A message-driven bean acts as a standard JMS consumer awaiting messages received on a particular JMS destination.
- It is a short-lived, stateless bean that is invoked asynchronously when a JMS message arrives at a JMS destination.
- It also may perform updates to the underlying database.
- It supports both bean-managed and container-managed transactions.

Consider using MDBs when you need a pool of listeners that can respond asynchronously to JMS messages received on a particular JMS destination.

There is a price to be paid for using an EJB component rather than an ordinary Java object to implement your business logic. The EJB container provides inherent support for pooling, transactions, concurrency, security, remote access, persistence, and state management. If your application doesn't require support for these enterprise services, ordinary Java objects should suffice, perhaps supplemented with an alternative persistence mechanism such as plain Java Data Objects, or JDBC. However, if your business processes do need support for these features, the EJB framework provides an ideal platform for building enterprise applications.

A detailed discussion of how to develop EJB components is beyond the scope of this book. You should refer to *Enterprise JavaBeans*, Third Edition, by Richard Monson-Haefel (O'Reilly), for an in-depth explanation of the EJB programming model. Instead, we cover WebLogic-specific issues of which you should be aware when developing and deploying your EJB components. We also look at how WebLogic's EJB container manages the life cycle of enterprise beans, as this is crucial to understanding how WebLogic lets you manipulate and optimize the behavior of the EJB container.

Building EJBs

To implement an EJB, you need to create the bean implementation class, together with the home and remote interfaces. Entity EJBs often require more, such as primary key classes and value objects. These are all standard J2EE requirements, and you should familiarize yourself with the EJB specification, and in particular the life cycle of EJB components, before starting your implementation. WebLogic eases the implementation burden by providing convenience classes, the EJBGen tool, and WebLogic Workshop. The latter items will be covered in later sections.

The EJB specification requires any bean class to implement a number of methods that are invoked at various stages in the life cycle of the bean. To help you on your way, WebLogic provides convenience classes that provide sensible default implementations of these methods. These classes can be found in the weblogic.ejb package, and are all abstract classes. The most relevant are the GenericSessionBean, GenericEntityBean, and GenericMessageDrivenBean classes. Here is an example demonstrating how easy it is to create a session bean implementation class:

```
import javax.ejb.*;
import weblogic.ejb.*;

public class EasySessionBean extends GenericSessionBean {
    public List getUsers() { /* ... */ };
    public List getGroups() { /* .. */ };
    ...
}
```

If you use EJBGen in addition to these convenience classes, you can construct complete EJBs, together with their metadata, using only a handful of lines.

EJBGen

EJBGen is a flexible code generator for EJBs. At one fell swoop it eliminates all the hassle associated with EJB development. The input to the tool is a bean implementation source file, annotated with JavaDoc tags. EJBGen parses this file, and generates the associated home and remote interfaces, as well as the accompanying XML descriptor files. The code generation is accomplished using templates, so you can modify these templates to enable the tool to generate code specific to your project.

EJBGen is supplied with WebLogic. Simply run the *setEnv* script to ensure that your classpath is set up appropriately before invoking the tool. The latest version of the tool, together with extensive documentation, is available at *http://www.beust.com/ejbgen*. There are many reasons why you should consider using EJBGen, instead of hand-coding all of the EJB source files and their subsidiary files:

- You no longer need to maintain several files when writing EJBs. In particular, the tool can generate all of the necessary EJB interfaces, primary keys, XML deployment descriptors, and even any value objects. This reduces maintenance and development life cycles.

- You no longer need to synchronize several files when changing an EJB. Adding an EJB method is now as simple as adding a method to a standard Java class, annotated with the proper JavaDoc tags.

- The JavaDoc tags required by EJBGen are readable and intuitive, and easily can form part of the source documentation. Clearly, better documentation of the EJB source code eases development and reduces the chance of errors.

- The JavaDoc tags can be generated automatically. For example, if you use WebLogic Workshop to create EJBs, its GUI property editor lets you directly specify EJB properties that get translated into EJBGen tags embedded in the source generated for the EJB.

The following sections provide an overview of how to use EJBGen, as well as a description of some of the additional features provided by the tool.

Using EJBGen

EJBGen is a command-line tool, implemented as a JavaDoc doclet. You can invoke it as follows:

```
javadoc -docletpath %WL_HOME%/server/lib/weblogic.jar
        -doclet weblogic.tools.ejbgen.EJBGen YourBean.java
```

Note that the -docletpath argument specified here must point to WebLogic Server's library, *weblogic.jar*. If you specify multiple Java files as arguments to the doclet, EJBGen will process each Java file. This will be necessary if you invoke the tool on entity EJBs that are involved in container-managed relationships. EJBGen also provides a standard Java class that you can invoke. In this case, you would invoke the tool as follows:

```
java weblogic.tools.ejbgen.EJBGen YourBean.java
```

Invoking this tool without any arguments lists all of the possible options.

Example 10-1 shows the source for a complete, annotated EJB that can be given to the tool as input. Notice how the EJB also makes use of the GenericSessionBean convenience class.

Example 10-1. An annotated session EJB file

```
package com.oreilly.wlguide.ejb;
import javax.ejb.*;
import weblogic.ejb.*;
/**
 * @ejbgen:session
 *    ejb-name = simpleSession
 *    max-beans-in-free-pool = 42
 *    enable-call-by-reference = true
 *    is-clusterable = true
 *    methods-are-idempotent = true
 *    trans-timeout-seconds = 20
 * @ejbgen:jndi-name
 *    remote = mySimpleSessionHome
 */
public class SimpleEJB extends GenericSessionBean {
  /**
   * Perform some business method.
   * @ejbgen:remote-method
   *    is-idempotent = true
   */
  public int calculate (int input) {
    return input*2;
  }
}
```

This example has two sets of JavaDoc tags—one annotating the entire class and which generally applies to the entire EJB, and the other specific for each EJB method. EJBGen provides a number of tags to take care of different deployment and configuration needs of the EJB. For example, you can use the @ejbgen:session tag to specify the general attributes of a session bean, the @ejbgen:jndi-name tag to specify its JNDI properties, and the @ejbgen:remote-method to indicate that the method must be exposed via the remote interface and to get additional information about its deploy-time and runtime behavior. Dozens of other tags can be used to specify everything from entity EJB finder methods and relationships to the details of a foreign JMS provider. Please refer to the tool documentation for a complete description of the supported JavaDoc tags.

Once you've properly annotated the EJB class file, you don't need to write anything else. Simply feed this source file to EJBGen, and it will produce the following items:

Simple.java

This file, representing the remote interface for the session bean, will look something like this:

```
public interface Simple extends EJBObject {
    public int calculate(int input) throws RemoteException;
}
```

SimpleHome.java

The home interface for the session bean also will be created. It will look like this:

```
public interface SimpleHome extends EJBHome {
  public Simple create() throws CreateException, RemoteException;
}
```

ejb-jar.xml

The standard EJB descriptor that is generated completely describes the EJB:

```
<ejb-jar>
  <enterprise-beans>
    <session>
      <ejb-name>simpleSession</ejb-name>
      <home>com.oreilly.weblogic.ejb.SimpleHome</home>
      <remote>com.oreilly.weblogic.ejb.Simple</remote>
      <ejb-class>com.oreilly.weblogic.ejb.SimpleEJB</ejb-class>
      <session-type>Stateless</session-type>
      <transaction-type>Container</transaction-type>
    </session>
  </enterprise-beans>
</ejb-jar>
```

weblogic-ejb-jar.xml

The WebLogic-specific descriptor file, which contains many of the tedious descriptor settings needed to configure the bean, is also generated:

```
<weblogic-ejb-jar>
  <weblogic-enterprise-bean>
    <ejb-name>simpleSession</ejb-name>
    <stateless-session-descriptor>
      <pool>
        <max-beans-in-free-pool>42</max-beans-in-free-pool>
      </pool>
      <stateless-clustering>
        <stateless-bean-is-clusterable>true</stateless-bean-is-clusterable>
        <stateless-bean-methods-are-idempotent>true</stateless-bean-methods-are-
idempotent>
      </stateless-clustering>
    </stateless-session-descriptor>
    <transaction-descriptor>
      <trans-timeout-seconds>20</trans-timeout-seconds>
    </transaction-descriptor>
    <enable-call-by-reference>true</enable-call-by-reference>
    <jndi-name>mySimpleSessionHome</jndi-name>
  </weblogic-enterprise-bean>
  <idempotent-methods>
    <method>
      <ejb-name>simpleSession</ejb-name>
      <method-name>calculate</method-name>
      <method-params>
        <method-param>int</method-param>
      </method-params>
    </method>
  </idempotent-methods>
</weblogic-ejb-jar>
```

As you can see, there is nothing more to do. Simply JAR up the source and descriptor files, compile the EJB using *weblogic.appc*, and deploy!

Tag inheritance

EJBGen fits nicely into the OO mold, letting you inherit tag and attribute values. For example, say that all of your session EJBs inherit from the following base class:

```
/**
 * @ejbgen:session
 *    trans-timeout-seconds = 20
 *    is-clusterable = true
 */
public class BaseSession extends GenericSessionBean {
  /* ... */
}
```

Classes that extend this BaseSession class will inherit the clusterable and timeout attributes automatically. Here is an example:

```
/**
 * @ejbgen:session
 *    ejb-name = concreteSession
 */
public class ConcreteSession extends BaseSession {
  /* ... */
}
```

These classes can, of course, also override the attribute values by specifying their own copies.

Templates

The latest version of EJBGen generates the source files from a set of templates. By modifying the templates that EJBGen uses, you can customize the generated files. If you want to modify the templates, then you first need to extract them:

```
java weblogic.tools.ejbgen.EJBGen –extractTemplates tempDirectory
```

After modifying the templates appropriately, use the -templateDir argument to instruct EJBGen to use the modified templates. For example, you could then invoke the tool as follows:

```
java weblogic.tools.ejbgen.EJBGen –templateDir tempDirectory SimpleEJB.java
```

Reverse engineering

EJBGen is accompanied by a tool that can be used to reverse-engineer an EJB JAR and produce an EJBGen-annotated source file. The tag information embedded in the generated file is gleaned from introspecting the class files in the EJB, as well as from the accompanying XML descriptor files. If you have existing EJB source files and you want to start using EJBGen, you should use this tool. You can run it like this:

```
java com.bea.wls.revejbgen.Main –d outputdirectory EJBJar.jar
```

The Java class generated by this command is an abstract class. You can either create a concrete class that implements all of its methods, or perhaps more simply use the generated class as the basis for a new source file.

Packaging EJBs

The EJB classes and XML deployment descriptors are packaged in a single, deployable unit called an *EJB JAR*. A typical EJB JAR file includes the following:

- Java class files for the EJB, which includes its home and component interfaces, the bean implementation class, and the primary key class (if it's a CMP entity bean)
- Container-specific classes generated by WebLogic's EJB compiler
- A standard XML descriptor (*ejb-jar.xml*) that provides information about the EJB structure, application assembly, security, and transaction settings
- A WebLogic-specific deployment descriptor (*weblogic-ejb-jar.xml*) that can be used to configure the entity cache, set limits on the size of the free pool of EJB instances, and adjust the runtime behavior of the EJB container
- A WebLogic-specific descriptor (*weblogic-cmp-rdbms-jar.xml*) that maps the EJB's persistent fields and relationships to the actual database schema

Container classes are not strictly necessary, as WebLogic can create them at deployment time. For instance, the contents of an EJB JAR that packages a Registration session EJB could include the following files:

```
org/foo/bar/Registration.class
org/foo/bar/RegistrationHome.class
org/foo/bar/RegistrationBean.class
meta-inf/Manifest.mf
meta-inf/ejb-jar.xml
meta-inf/weblogic-ejb-jar.xml
```

You also could package any dependent Java utility classes along with the EJB classes. Alternatively, you could set the Class-Path attribute in the JAR's manifest file, *META-INF/MANIFEST.MF,* to reference any dependent JAR files. However, this feature works only for EJB JARs that are deployed as part of an EAR file.

XML Deployment Descriptors

Every EJB JAR needs a standard *ejb-jar.xml* descriptor file. If your EJBs conform to the EJB 2.0 specification, this deployment descriptor must be a valid XML document that includes the following DTD reference:

```
<!DOCTYPE ejb-jar PUBLIC
        '-//Sun Microsystems, Inc.//DTD Enterprise JavaBeans 2.0//EN'
        'http://java.sun.com/dtd/ejb-jar_2_0.dtd'>
```

The standard *ejb-jar.xml* descriptor is used to specify (among other things) the EJB type, the transaction behavior, references to external resources, the security configuration of the bean, and in the case of CMP beans, the abstract persistence schema, relationships, and EJB QL statements.

EJB components also may require a WebLogic-specific *weblogic-ejb-jar.xml* descriptor file. This XML descriptor allows you to customize the behavior of the EJB container and map EJB references and environment entries to actual WebLogic Server resources. In WebLogic 8.1, the *weblogic-ejb-jar.xml* descriptor must be a valid XML document that should include the following DTD reference:*

```
<!DOCTYPE weblogic-ejb-jar PUBLIC
        '-//BEA Systems, Inc.//DTD WebLogic 8.1.0 EJB//EN'
        'http://www.bea.com/servers/wls810/dtd/weblogic-ejb-jar.dtd'>
```

As you will discover in this chapter, this deployment descriptor can be used to configure the pooling, caching, and concurrency behavior of beans, JNDI names of referenced resources, cluster behavior, security principal mappings, and method-level transaction isolation settings. An EJB JAR file also may include a *weblogic-cmp-rdbms-jar.xml* descriptor file that specifies how the EJB container handles both CMP and CMR fields with other entity beans. Chapter 11 covers WebLogic's brand of CMP in more detail. Refer to Chapter 12 for details on how to create and modify the deployment descriptors.

Compiling Your EJBs

Before you can introduce the EJB JAR to WebLogic, you need to generate the WebLogic-specific container classes for the EJB. In WebLogic 8.1, you can use the appc compiler to perform this task for you; in WebLogic 7.0, you can use the ejbc compiler. Once you've created the EJB JAR, you can deploy it to a server or cluster, either as a standalone EJB application or as an EJB module within an enterprise application.

You also can defer EJB compilation until deployment time. For instance, if you deploy a "raw" EJB JAR, WebLogic will automatically generate the container classes for the EJBs before deploying it. This approach is not recommended in a production environment because if something does go wrong, you will have to resolve compilation errors at deployment time. We recommend that you precompile your EJBs before you deploy the EJB JAR. This also will reduce the number of times that the EJB will be compiled. Deploying a raw EJB to several servers will result in the EJB being compiled on each server separately.

---

* In WebLogic 7.0, the *weblogic-ejb-jar.xml* descriptor file must use the following DTD reference:

```
<!DOCTYPE weblogic-ejb-jar PUBLIC
        '-//BEA Systems, Inc.//DTD WebLogic 7.0.0 EJB//EN'
        'http://www.bea.com/servers/wls700/dtd/weblogic-ejb-jar.dtd'>
```

The ejbc tool

In WebLogic 7.0, you can use the ejbc compiler to generate and compile the container classes needed by your EJBs. Container classes provide the underlying implementation for the EJBs and remote access between the client stubs and server-side skeleton classes. Here's a summary of what the ejbc tool does:

- It places the EJB classes, interfaces, and XML deployment descriptors in the target folder or JAR file.
- It ensures that all EJB classes and interfaces comply with the EJB specification.
- It generates the WebLogic-specific container classes for the EJBs.
- It runs the RMI compiler over each container class and generates client-side proxies and server-side classes.

Here's how you run the ejbc utility:

```
java weblogic.ejbc [options] <source directory or JAR file>
     <target directory or JAR file>
```

The ejbc command accepts the following two arguments:

source
> Use this argument to specify the name of the directory or JAR file that contains the compiled EJB classes and XML deployment descriptors.

target
> Use this argument to specify the name of the destination directory or JAR file. The original EJB classes and XML descriptors, and the newly generated container classes, will be written to this target.

The ejbc utility provides various options that let you alter the classpath, use a third-party Java compiler, and generate IDL for remote interfaces that are compliant with Orbix 2000 and Visibroker 4.5. The tool also is useful for identifying and correcting errors before you actually deploy the EJB JAR.

The appc tool

In WebLogic 8.1, the ejbc tool has been deprecated in favor of the appc tool. The appc compiler is a single tool for compiling and validating an EJB JAR, before it can be made ready for deployment. Not only does it ensure that the EJBs are packaged according to J2EE conventions, but it also validates the deployment descriptors of the EJB JAR and ensures that they conform to the specified DTDs. Use the following syntax to invoke the appc compiler:

```
java weblogic.appc [options] <source directory or JAR file>
```

The appc compiler accepts a single argument—i.e., the name of the directory or JAR file that holds the compiled EJB classes and deployment descriptors for the EJB module. You also can instruct the compiler to place the original EJB classes and XML descriptors as well as the newly generated container classes in another directory or

JAR file. For this, you must use the -output *<file>* option to specify the name of an alternative directory or JAR:

```
java weblogic.appc -output c:/myEjb.jar f:/ejb-staging-dir
```

Chapter 4 explains how to also use the appc tool to generate the IDL for the remote interfaces and to generate the necessary CORBA stubs for your EJBs. Refer to Chapter 12 for more information on how to use the appc compiler.

Generating an EJB client JAR

WebLogic can generate an EJB-specific client JAR, which packages all the necessary classes that a client needs to invoke the EJB. This includes the EJB's home and remote interfaces, the primary key class in the case of an entity bean with a composite primary key, and any other classes that may be referenced by these classes. In order to specify a client JAR, you must edit the *ejb-jar.xml* descriptor file and include the ejb-client-jar element:

```
<!-- portion from the ejb-jar.xml descriptor -->
<entity>
  <ejb-name>StudentEJB</ejb-name>
  ...
  <ejb-client-jar>ejb_studentclient.jar</ejb-client-jar>
  ...
</entity>
```

Place the compiled classes and XML descriptors in a staging folder or JAR file, and compile your EJBs for WebLogic Server as described earlier. External clients can then invoke the deployed EJBs, after they include the generated client JAR in their classpath. The EJBs also would be accessible to a web application, once the client JAR has been placed under the *WEB-INF/lib* folder.

Note that the additional classes are included in the EJB client JAR only if they are *not* already included in the system CLASSPATH. Thus, to ensure that a client does indeed have access to all the necessary classes, make sure any classes that may be referenced by the EJB's home and remote interfaces and by the primary key class are not specified in the system CLASSPATH when you compile your EJBs.

Referencing J2EE Resources

Earlier in Chapter 5, we saw how an application-specific JDBC data source factory can be made available to all modules within an enterprise application. For instance, an EJB could reference a data source factory from within its local Environment Naming Context (ENC) using the logical name of the JDBC factory:

```
DataSource ds = (DataSource) ctx.lookup("java:comp/env/mydsfactory");
Connection con = ds.getConnection();
```

An EJB can reference other EJBs and resource factories deployed to WebLogic in the same way. These references then are available to the EJB implementation code through its local ENC. The standard *ejb-jar.xml* descriptor file lets you declare references to other EJBs and resource factories. The *weblogic-ejb-jar.xml* descriptor file then maps these references to their configured JNDI names. The following portion from the *ejb-jar.xml* descriptor show how to set up a reference to another EJB:

```
<!-- ejb-jar.xml entry: -->
<session>
   <ejb-name>RegistrationEJB</ejb-name>
   ...
   <ejb-ref>
      <ejb-ref-name>ejb/studenthome</ejb-ref-name>
      <ejb-ref-type>Entity</ejb-ref-ype>
      <home>org.foo.bar.StudentHome</home>
      <remote>org.foo.bar.Student</remote>
   </ejb-ref>
   ...
</session>
```

For each EJB reference, you need to declare an `ejb-ref` element in the *ejb-jar.xml* file. It specifies the EJB's name, whether it's a session bean or an entity bean, and the names for the home and remote interfaces. Then, in the *weblogic-ejb-jar.xml* descriptor file, you must specify the JNDI name to which the EJB's home object has been bound:

```
<!-- weblogic-ejb-jar.xml entry: -->
<weblogic-enterprise-bean>
   <ejb-name>RegistrationEJB</ejb-name>
   ...
   <reference-descriptor>
      ...
      <ejb-reference-description>
         <ejb-ref-name>ejb/studenthome</ejb-ref-name>
         <jndi-name>org/foo/bar/StudentHome</jndi-name>
      </ejb-reference-description>
      ...
   </reference-descriptor>
</weblogic-enterprise-bean>
```

Similarly, if you need to provide a reference to a configured JDBC data source, you must declare a resource-ref element in the *ejb-jar.xml* descriptor file. The following portion from the *ejb-jar.xml* descriptor shows how to set up a reference to a data source:

```
<!-- ejb-jar.xml entry: -->
<session>
   <ejb-name>RegistrationEJB</ejb-name>
   ...
   <resource-ref>
      <res-ref-name>jdbc/myds</res-ref-name>
      <res-type>javax.sql.DataSource</res-type>
      <res-auth>Container</res-auth>
      <res-sharing-scope>Shareable</res-sharing-scope>
   </resource-ref>
   ...
</session>
```

The resource-ref element includes the resource name, the type of the resource, whether the application or the EJB container is responsible for authenticating access to the resource, and whether the resource is shareable. By default, the resource is considered shareable and the EJB container handles authentication on behalf of the application. After this, you must use the *weblogic-ejb-jar.xml* descriptor file to map the reference to the JNDI name of the configured JDBC data source:

```
<!-- weblogic-ejb-jar.xml entry: -->
<weblogic-enterprise-bean>
  <ejb-name>RegistrationEJB</ejb-name>
  ...
  <reference-descriptor>
    <resource-description>
      <res-ref-name>jdbc/myds</res-ref-name>
      <jndi-name>myds</jndi-name>
    </resource-description>
    ...
  </reference-descriptor>
</weblogic-enterprise-bean>
```

Given these settings for the Registration session EJB, any implementation code for the Registration EJB then can look up the Student EJB (or the data source) from its local ENC. For instance, in the case of our session bean, you could perform the lookups from within the ejbCreate method:

```
public void ejbCreate( ) throws CreateException {
  try {
    InitialContext ctx = new InitialContext( );
    ds = (DataSource) ctx.lookup("java:comp/env/jdbc/myds");
    Object home = ctx.lookup("java:comp/env/ejb/studenthome");
    ejbHome = (org.foo.bar.StudentHome) PortableRemoteObject.narrow(home, org.foo.
bar.StudentHome.class);
  } catch (NamingException ene) {
    throw new CreateException("Failed to look up referenced resource" + ene);
  }
}
```

Referencing application-scoped EJBs

Typically, you will deploy the EJB JARs as *modules* within an enterprise application. Whenever you deploy an EAR containing multiple EJB modules, WebLogic automatically makes the EJBs available to the local ENC through their EJB names. This means that instead of using the JNDI name, any code within the enterprise application can access the EJB's home object using its ejb-name:

```
Object home = ctx.lookup("java:comp/env/StudentEJB");
ejbHome = (org.foo.bar.StudentHome)
          PortableRemoteObject.narrow(home, org.foo.bar.StudentHome.class);
```

Alternatively, you can use the ejb-link subelement to directly reference another EJB bundled within the same EAR, without explicitly mapping it to the EJB's JNDI name. The following XML fragment shows how the Registration bean can reference the Student entity bean using the ejb-link subelement:

```
<!-- ejb-jar.xml entry: -->
<session>
  <ejb-name>RegistrationEJB</ejb-name>
  ...
  <ejb-ref>
    <ejb-ref-name>ejb/studenthome</ejb-ref-name>
    <ejb-ref-type>Entity</ejb-ref-ype>
    <home>org.foo.bar.StudentHome</home>
    <remote>org.foo.bar.StudentHome</remote>
    <ejb-link>ejb_student.jar#StudentEJB</ejb-link>
  </ejb-local-ref>
  ...
</session>
```

Here, we have defined an EJB reference to the Student EJB packaged in the same EAR, using its ejb-name. Notice how we've qualified the ejb-link with the name of the EJB JAR that contains the StudentEJB. This ensures that the reference is unique, especially when multiple EJBs in the EAR file could use the same EJB name. Once you've linked the EJB reference directly to the target EJB, you don't need to specify the target EJB's JNDI name in the *weblogic-ejb-jar.xml* descriptor. Any implementation code for the Registration EJB can now use the ejb-ref-name to access the StudentEJB home object.

Deploying EJB Components

An EJB component can be deployed either as a standalone EJB application or as a "module" bundled within an enterprise application. Typically, an enterprise application will be packaged as an EAR file, which is a JAR file that packages multiple EJB components and web applications in a single, deployable unit. Each EJB module has an entry in the standard *application.xml* descriptor file that specifies the associated EJB JAR:

```
<application>
  <module>
    <ejb>ejb_registration.jar</ejb>
  </module>
  ...
</application>
```

In development mode, you can automatically update an EJB application, simply by overwriting the existing EJB JAR file with a newer version. If the EJB JAR is deployed in exploded format, you can instead trigger its redeployment by "touching" a special empty file, which is named *REDEPLOY* and is located in the *META-INF* folder. If the EJB module contains uncompiled EJB classes and interfaces, WebLogic automatically picks up the changes, runs the configured Java compiler over the files, and then invokes the EJB compiler to generate the container classes.

Because the auto-deploy feature is disabled in production mode, you need to manually redeploy the EJB components. WebLogic allows you to refresh EJBs in two ways:

- You can use the Administration Console to redeploy an EJB component, regardless of whether the EJB JAR is deployed as a standalone EJB application or as a module in an EAR file. Select your EJB component from under the Deployments/EJB Modules node in the left pane of the Administration Console, and then select the Deploy tab in the right pane. Now use the righthand screen to redeploy the EJB component to individual servers or clusters. The new Deployment Assistants available in WebLogic 8.1 also provide a step-by-step approach to deploying an EJB module.

- You can use the `weblogic.Deployer` tool to update EJB modules already deployed to WebLogic. This tool offers the same functionality as the Administration Console—it allows you to reactivate (and undeploy) EJB applications to specific targets (note, *activate* is just a synonym for *deploy*). For instance, here's how you would update the Registration EJB in an EAR file that is targeted to myserver:

```
java weblogic.Deployer -adminurl http://adminserver:7001 -username system
    -password somepassword -name myapp.ear -activate
    -targets ejb_registration.jar@myserver -source /myapp.ear
```

Here we have passed the utility the following arguments: the URL of the Administration Server, the name of the EAR that needs to be redeployed, the name of the EJB module that needs to be updated, and the original location of the EAR file. In addition, you need to specify the credentials of a valid user with administrative privileges. Chapter 12 provides many more examples of using this tool.

Typically, you will invoke the tool from a shell script or an Ant script that automates the build/deployment process.

 You can use this feature to update only the EJB implementation classes—the public EJB interfaces and any support classes used by the public interfaces cannot be redeployed. If you do apply changes with modified public EJB interfaces, WebLogic Server flags an incompatible class change error the next time a client uses the EJB.

When you update an EJB component, WebLogic marks the classes associated with the EJB as unavailable. The EJB class loader and associated classes are abandoned, and a new EJB class loader is created that loads the modified EJB implementation classes. The next time a client obtains a reference to the EJB, the container uses the new EJB implementation classes. In Chapter 12, we look at how you can create a custom classloader hierarchy and thereby enable an EJB module to be redeployed independently of other components in an enterprise application.

Development Guidelines

Earlier, we looked at the various types of EJBs supported by WebLogic, and the different circumstances under which you should use them. In this section, we examine some of the important design principles you should adopt when building an enterprise application using EJBs. Careful choices can help you extract the best performance out of your EJBs in a WebLogic environment.

Collocation

The EJB 2.0 standard introduces the notion of local EJBs, which provide lightweight access from other EJBs and local clients running within the same server. An EJB, whose home interface extends EJBLocalHome and whose component interface extends EJBLocalObject, is accessible only to local clients running within the same JVM. Unlike remote EJBs where the client communicates with the EJB over RMI-IIOP, a client can communicate with a local EJB without incurring the overheads of marshalling and unmarshalling associated with remote method calls. Because both the client and the EJB reside within the same JVM, the EJB container is able to use *pass-by-reference* semantics, similar to an ordinary Java method call.

Consider using local EJBs when you want to ensure they are accessible only to other server-side components or local clients running within the same JVM. This means your local EJB interfaces will not be exposed to other remote clients—i.e., any client running on another JVM, or even another machine. EJBs that participate in container-managed relationships (CMR) with other EJBs are required to support local EJB interfaces. They may still expose a remote interface if they need to be accessible to remote clients. We will cover WebLogic's support for CMP and CMR in Chapter 11.

Clearly, a client running outside WebLogic Server cannot avoid the cost of marshalling and unmarshalling associated with method calls to a remote EJB. But you can avoid these overheads when the client and the remote EJB are collocated within the same JVM. The enable-call-by-reference element in the *weblogic-ejb-jar.xml* descriptor file lets you enable this optimization if the client and the EJBs run within the same VM. It indicates whether the EJB container should pass arguments by reference when a local client invokes a method on an EJB, instead of using traditional RMI "pass-by-value" semantics. When enabled, WebLogic is able to achieve better performance by using "pass-by-reference" semantics automatically, provided both the client and EJB are deployed as part of the same EAR:

```
<weblogic-enterprise-bean>
  <ejb-name>RegistrationEJB</ejb-name>
  ...
  <enable-call-by-reference>True</enable-call-by-reference>
  ...
</weblogic-enterprise-bean>
```

The default value of this setting is False.* This means that if a servlet invokes a method on a collocated EJB, WebLogic automatically will use pass-by-reference semantics for the method call (assuming the web application and the EJBs are deployed as part of the same enterprise application). You need to explicitly disable this setting if you do not want to use pass-by-reference semantics for local clients. In that case, arguments to EJB methods are always passed by value, regardless of whether the client is local or remote.

Network Latency

An enterprise application built on an n-tier architecture usually will involve an *EJB tier*—i.e., a layer of reusable business objects that mediates access to the underlying database. Typically, the EJB tier will manifest itself as a cluster of servers that host your EJB components. Unfortunately, this also introduces problems of network latency between the web tier (presentation), the EJB tiers (application), and the data-access tier (data). Network traffic between the web server and the EJB tier also contributes to the latency between the browser and the web server. The performance of your application depends on your ability to minimize the amount of network traffic between the web server, the EJB tier, and the underlying database.

At some point during development or performance testing, it is crucial that you monitor the strain on your network resources under high load. Let's examine some of the ways in which you can optimize use of network resources, especially when you've used EJBs to encapsulate your business logic.

A typical business process involves updates to multiple entity beans. If these updates occur directly from a JSP or a servlet, a number of method calls to remote EJBs means that you incur a performance cost because of the increased network traffic. Instead, you should use session beans to wrap access to your entity beans. By modeling your business processes using session beans in this way, you can limit the amount of network traffic between the client and remote EJBs. For instance, if a student needs to register for multiple university courses, you could create a Registration session bean that wraps updates to the Student and Course entity EJBs. A single remote call to the session bean now replaces multiple remote calls to all the entity beans involved. The session bean acts as a façade and hides access to the actual entity beans. In this scenario, where the remote clients always use the session beans to access the entity beans, you even could implement all the entity beans as local EJBs because only the session beans need to be accessible to remote clients.

On other occasions, you could perform JDBC access directly from within a session bean. For instance, if a JSP needs to render an HTML form that displays a list of all offered courses, you could implement an EJB method that returns a disconnected

---

* In WebLogic 7.0, the default value for the enable-call-by-reference element is True, which is not strictly compliant.

JDBC rowset with the necessary data. This approach limits the duration of the transaction and minimizes network traffic. Calling a find method on an entity bean that returns a list of EJB instances requires considerable network bandwidth. For each EJB reference, you need to fetch the actual data from the underlying database. This could result in unacceptable performance of your application.

Another way to restrict the network traffic is to simply limit the number of method calls to remote EJBs. For instance, bulk getter and setter methods minimize the number of round trips between the client and the underlying database. Suppose the Student EJB exposes the following remote interface:

```
public interface Student extends EJBObject {
...
    public String getHouseNo() throws RemoteException;
    public String getStreet() throws RemoteException;
    public String getCity() throws RemoteException;
    public String getPostCode() throws RemoteException;
    public void setHouseNo(String arg); throws RemoteException;
    public void setStreet(String arg); throws RemoteException;
    public void setCity(String arg); throws RemoteException;
    public void setPostCode(String arg); throws RemoteException;
...
}
```

Then you easily could simplify the EJB interface with remote methods that use a value object AddressVO instead:

```
public interface Student extends EJBObject {
...
    public AddressVO getAddress() throws RemoteException;
    public void setAddress(AddressVO vo) throws RemoteException;
...
}
```

A value object exists solely for the purpose of transporting data between the client and the remote EJB. Typically, it is implemented as an immutable, serializable Java object with getter methods for each attribute. Current literature is moving toward calling them *transfer* objects.

Using EJB Homes

In order to obtain a reference to the EJB instance, you need to first look up the name of the EJB's home in the JNDI tree. You should reuse the results of the first lookup and avoid subsequent JNDI lookups:

```
private EJBHome regHome;
...
public RegistrationHome getRegistrationHome() throws NamingExeption {
    if (regHome == null) {
        InitialContext ctx = new InitialContext();
        Object home = ctx.lookup("org.foo.bar.RegistrationHome")
        regHome = (EJBHome)
```

```
        PortableRemoteObject.narrow(home, org.foo.bar.RegistrationHome.class);
    }
    return (RegistrationHome) regHome;
}
```

A better approach would be to build a cache of EJB home objects, and then use the
cached values the next time you need to access the EJB home objects. For an external client, the only change is how you obtain a reference to the initial JNDI context:

```
try {
    Hashtable env = new Hashtable();
    env.put(Context.INITIAL_CONTEXT_FACTORY,
            "weblogic.jndi.WLInitialContextFactory");
    env.put(Context.PROVIDER_URL,
            "t3://server:port");  //URL of a running WebLogic instance

    InitialContext ctx = new InitialContext(env);
    Object home = ctx.lookup("org.foo.bar.RegistrationHome");
    RegistrationHome regHome = (RegistrationHome)
        PortableRemoteObject.narrow(o, org.foo.bar.RegistrationHome.class);
    //now create an instance of a session bean
}
catch (NamingException ene) {
    //handle naming exceptions
}
```

Note that because local EJBs do not follow RMI semantics, you do not need to use
the PortableRemoteObject.narrow() method. For instance, if the Registration bean is
designed as a local EJB, you simply need to cast the EJB home object to the desired
type:

```
Object home = ctx.lookup("org.foo.bar.RegistrationHome");
RegistrationHome regHome = (RegistrationHome) home;
```

You also can invoke the getHomeHandle() method on an EJB instance to obtain a
handle to the EJB's home object. This handle is an abstract network reference to the
EJB's home object, which can be passed to another client easily. The client can then
invoke the getEJBHome() method on the handle to access the EJB's home object. You
also can serialize the home handle to a file for later use.

By default, the home handle encapsulates the IP address of the server from which the
EJB home object was retrieved. This may result in unexpected behavior if your network configuration relies on firewall security. An EJB home handle that is sent
through a firewall may not be able to locate the home object. You can fix this problem by enabling reverse DNS lookups on the target server. In that case, WebLogic
stores the DNS name of the server in the EJB home handle instead of its IP address.
You can enable reverse DNS lookups for a chosen server from the Configuration/
Tuning tab in the Administration Console.*

---

* In WebLogic 7.0, use the Configuration/Network tab to enable reverse DNS lookups.

Conserving Transactions

Distributed transactions have a significant bearing on WebLogic's performance. You need to closely monitor the duration of your transactions at runtime because they impact the performance and scalability of your application. Typically, EJBs dip into a pool of JDBC connections to service their database requests. A connection that participates in a distributed transaction is in fact engaged for the duration of the transaction. So, short-lived transactions improve the efficiency of the connection pool because it can then serve more connection requests at a time. Short-lived transactions also limit the duration for which the transaction needs to hold on to any database locks on the underlying data. Thus, we find that the duration of distributed transactions affects both the efficiency of the connection pool and the database resources needed by your application.

WebLogic also lets you specify the transaction age for EJBs that support container-managed transactions. The trans-timeout-seconds element in the *weblogic-ejb-jar.xml* descriptor file determines the maximum time allowed for a transaction to complete:

```
<weblogic-enterprise-bean>
  <ejb-name>RegistrationEJB</ejb-name>
  ...
  <transaction-descriptor>
    <trans-timeout-seconds>120</trans-timeout-seconds>
  </transaction-descriptor>
  ...
</weblogic-enterprise-bean>
```

Alternatively, if the EJB supports bean-managed transactions, you can specify the maximum age for the transaction using the setTransactionTimeout( ) method on a UserTransaction object.

Whenever possible, we recommend that you rely on WebLogic's support for container-managed transactions. Container-managed transactions provide a standard, flexible way for using EJBs in a distributed transaction. When you let the EJB container manage the transaction boundaries, your EJB code then can focus on the application logic instead of ensuring that transactions are handled correctly. In addition, the new CMP 2.0 framework requires automatic container support for transactional access to entity EJBs and their related EJB instances. You also should remember that WebLogic demarcates transactions on a per-method basis. Container-managed transactions should be sufficient for your needs, unless you need to support multiple transactions within an EJB method, or the EJB method requires complex logic where transactions are committed under certain specific conditions.

You also should be careful about how you set the transaction attributes for the EJB methods. The following XML fragment from a typical *ejb-jar.xml* descriptor file may look very innocuous:

```
<enterprise-beans>
  <session>
    <ejb-name>RegistrationEJB</ejb-name>
    ...
```

```
      <transaction-type>Container</transaction-type>
    </session>
    ...
  </enterprise-beans>
  <assembly-descriptor>
    <container-transaction>
      <method>
        <ejb-name>RegistrationEJB</ejb-name>
        <method-name>*</method-name>
      </method>
      <trans-attribute>Required</trans-attribute>
    </container-transaction>
  </assembly-descriptor>
```

However, ask yourself whether you really need a transaction context for every EJB method. If the answer is no, you should modify the deployment descriptor and explicitly specify which methods require a transaction context when they are invoked by the EJB container. By default, all EJB methods can participate in a transaction context, if it exists.

Be careful when you explicitly specify a NotSupported setting for EJB methods that will not participate in a transaction context. It could actually impact the performance of your application. When a client invokes such an EJB method within a transaction context, WebLogic needs to temporarily suspend the existing transaction, then execute the EJB method, and finally resume the earlier transaction after the method completes execution. A transaction setting of Supports for an EJB method is preferable because it is easier for WebLogic to invoke the method as part of a transaction context, if it exists.

 If the EJB supports container-managed transactions, make sure that you use an XA-aware data source.

Clients participating in transactions should not hold on to valuable resources such as database connections, cursors, and locks for any longer than is required, and should always endeavor to complete a transaction before exiting.

Message-Driven Beans

An MDB is a standard JMS consumer that responds to messages delivered to a JMS destination. MDBs are invoked asynchronously when a JMS message arrives on a particular queue or topic. WebLogic creates a pool of MDB instances that can handle large volumes of messages sent to a JMS destination. Upon receiving a JMS message, WebLogic automatically picks up an EJB instance from the pool and invokes the onMessage( ) method on the instance. The MDB instance is returned to the pool once the JMS message has been processed. An MDB can be implemented without tying it to the actual JMS destination. It is only during deployment time that you configure the topic/queue that the MDB must listen to.

An MDB can handle only JMS messages received on a single topic or queue. If you need to handle multiple JMS destinations, you need to develop separate MDBs, one for each destination. Alternatively, you could build an ordinary Java client that consumes messages from the multiple destinations.

A client interacts with an MDB indirectly by sending a JMS message to its configured topic/queue. Because a client cannot invoke an MDB directly, it doesn't declare a home or any component interfaces. Furthermore, the only transaction settings that are allowed for MDBs are Required and NotSupported because no client can ever pass a transaction context to an MDB.

The destination-type element in the *ejb-jar.xml* descriptor file indicates whether the MDB is listening to a queue or a topic. The destination-jndi-name element in the *weblogic-ejb-jar.xml* descriptor associates the MDB with the actual JNDI name to which the JMS queue or topic has been bound. The following portions from the deployment descriptors show how to bind an MDB to a particular JMS queue:

```xml
<!-- ejb-jar.xml entry: -->
<message-driven>
   <ejb-name>EventsQEJB</ejb-name>
   <ejb-class>org.foo.bar.EventsQHandlerBean</ejb-class>
   <transaction-type>Container</transaction-type>
   <message-driven-destination>
      <destination-type>javax.jms.Queue</destination-type>
   </message-driven-destination>
   <!-- equip the MDB with a reference to a DataSource -->
   <resource-ref>
      <res-ref-name>jdbc/myds</res-ref-name>
      <res-type>javax.sql.DataSource</res-type>
   </resource-ref>
</message-driven>

<!-- weblogic-ejb-jar.xml entry: -->
<weblogic-enterprise-bean>
   <ejb-name>EventsQueueHandlerEJB</ejb-name>
   <message-driven-descriptor>
      <pool>
         <max-beans-in-free-pool>15</max-beans-in-free-pool>
         <initial-beans-in-free-pool>5</initial-beans-in-free-pool>
      </pool>
      <destination-jndi-name>org.foo.bar.MyQueue</destination-jndi-name>
   </message-driven-descriptor>
   <reference-descriptor>
      <resource-description>
         <res-ref-name>jdbc/myds</res-ref-name>
         <jndi-name>myds</jndi-name>
      </resource-description>
   </reference-descriptor>
</weblogic-enterprise-bean>
```

In addition, you can use the pool element to specify the initial and maximum size for the pool of MDB instances. The onMessage( ) method provides code for handling the JMS message. Whenever a message arrives on a JMS destination, WebLogic taps into the EJB pool and invokes the method automatically. The EJB instance is returned to the pool once the JMS message has been processed.

If an MDB supports container-managed transactions (i.e., the transaction attribute has been set to Required), the EJB container includes the receipt of the JMS message as part of the EJB's transaction. Otherwise, the receipt of the JMS message is always outside the scope of the transaction. Additionally, JMS messages are automatically acknowledged when the transaction commits. Otherwise, the message acknowledgment occurs outside the scope of the EJB's transaction. In this case, the EJB container uses the acknowledge-mode element in the *ejb-jar.xml* descriptor file to determine the acknowledgment semantics.

Chapter 8 is dedicated to how you can configure WebLogic JMS.

Using foreign JMS providers

MDBs also can be configured to work with foreign JMS providers. MDBs that utilize container-managed transactions can support Exactly-once semantics with foreign JMS providers. Furthermore, WebLogic will enlist the foreign JMS resource in a distributed transaction automatically. Of course, you need to ensure that both the foreign JMS provider and the JMS connection factory configured for it are XA-aware. The following portion from the *weblogic-ejb-jar.xml* descriptor file shows how to register an MDB with a queue hosted by an IBM MQSeries server:

```
<weblogic-enterprise-bean>
  <ejb-name>SomeMDB</ejb-name>
  <message-driven-descriptor>
   <!-- ... -->
    <initial-context-factory>com.sun.jndi.fscontext.RefFSContextFactory</initial-
context-factory>
    <provider-url>file:/MQJNDI/</provider-url>
     <connection-factory-jndi-name>mq.MyCF</connection-factory-jndi-name>
    <destination-jndi-name>mq.MyQueue</destination-jndi-name>
    <jms-polling-interval-seconds>30</jms-polling-interval-seconds>
  </message-driven-descriptor>
  <!-- ... -->
</weblogic-enterprise-bean>
```

As you can see, we've specified the initial context factory and the provider URL needed to connect to the foreign JMS provider. In addition, we've specified the JNDI names of the JMS connection factory and queue that reside on IBM MQSeries. The jms-polling-interval-seconds element specifies the time interval between attempts by the EJB container to reconnect to the foreign JMS server, in case the JMS destination it hosts becomes unavailable.

Managing WebLogic's EJB Container

WebLogic's EJB container controls the life cycle of an EJB object and provides the runtime environment for deployed EJB components. The EJB container allows a client to obtain the EJB's home object, either through a JNDI lookup, via an EJB reference defined during deployment, or by using the EJB home handle. It provides EJBs with access to a wide range of container-managed services such as the local ENC, transactions, security, persistence, concurrency, locking, caching, clustering, and session-state replication. These services can be configured for a particular EJB component through the deployment descriptors associated with it.

In this section, we examine the life cycle of session beans in WebLogic Server and the impact on the runtime behavior of the EJB container when you adjust the EJB deployment settings. In the next section, we examine the life cycle of entity beans and how you can configure the entity bean pool, caching behavior, and EJB concurrency.

Pool of Stateless Session EJB Instances

WebLogic Server maintains a *free pool* of stateless session EJB instances, which stores a number of inactive, "method-ready" EJB instances. You can prepare this pool of EJB instances during server startup by specifying an initial-beans-in-free-pool element in the *weblogic-ejb-jar.xml* descriptor file. When a client invokes a method on a stateless session EJB, WebLogic taps into this pool of method-ready EJB instances. The EJB instance then remains active for the duration of the method call, and is returned to the free pool once the method completes. Because stateless session EJB instances cannot carry any conversational state, they are all effectively identical to each other. Therefore, the actual EJB instance used may vary from one method call to the next because you have no guarantee as to which instance will be returned from the pool.

If a client requests a stateless session EJB, and the pool has not yet reached its maximum capacity, WebLogic simply returns an available instance from the pool. If all EJB instances in the pool are currently active, WebLogic adds a new instance to the pool before returning it. The capacity of the free pool is determined by the maximum available system memory, or by the value for the max-beans-in-free-pool element in the *weblogic-ejb-jar.xml* descriptor file (if it is specified):

```
<weblogic-enterprise-bean>
  <ejb-name>RegistrationEJB</ejb-name>
  <stateless-session-descriptor>
    <pool>
      <max-beans-in-free-pool>10</max-beans-in-free-pool>
      <initial-beans-in-free-pool>4</initial-beans-in-free-pool>
    </pool>
  </stateless-session-descriptor>
  <jndi-name>org.foo.bar.RegistrationHome</jndi-name>
</weblogic-enterprise-bean>
```

If all EJB instances in the pool are currently active and the pool has reached maximum capacity, the next client request for the EJB is blocked until one of the active EJB instances completes its method call and is returned to the pool, or until the transaction times out, in which case a RemoteException (EJBException, for local clients) is thrown.

In general, you should set a maximum limit on the size of the free pool only if you have very specific requirements for limiting its growth. By specifying no upper limit, you ensure WebLogic has more control over the resources and you do not unnecessarily restrict possible opportunities for greater concurrency.

Cache of Stateful Session Bean Instances

Unlike stateless session beans, stateful session beans need to maintain a one-to-one association with a client, and therefore WebLogic is unable to provide a pool of identical instances. Instead, WebLogic maintains a cache of stateful session EJB instances, which holds active EJB instances, including those EJBs that currently are in use and those that were used recently. The stateful bean cache is empty at server startup. The EJB instances get created and cached as clients obtain references to stateful EJB instances. The max-beans-in-cache element in the *weblogic-ejb-jar.xml* file lets you configure the size of the EJB cache.

Under certain circumstances, EJB instances in the cache become eligible for *passivation*. In other words, the EJB instance can be removed from the in-memory cache and persisted to disk while preserving its state, thereby freeing up valuable resources. The persistent-store-dir element in the *weblogic-ejb-jar.xml* descriptor file lets you choose a folder in the server's filesystem that will store all the passivated stateful session EJB instances.

 Active stateful session EJBs are passivated only when they are eligible for passivation and WebLogic is under pressure to conserve server resources, or when the server performs its regular cache maintenance.

By default, the EJB container regularly examines the cache. If the cache has reached its capacity and the EJBs in the cache are not being used, WebLogic passivates the *unused* EJB instances. If the cache has reached maximum capacity, but all the EJBs in the cache are currently in use, WebLogic throws a CacheFullException. In fact, you should use the cache-type element in the *weblogic-ejb-jar.xml* descriptor file to configure how WebLogic ought to passivate stateful session EJBs:

```
<weblogic-enterprise-bean>
  <ejb-name>ShoppingCartEJB</ejb-name>
  <stateful-session-descriptor>
    <stateful-session-cache>
      <max-beans-in-cache>15</max-beans-in-cache>
      <idle-timeout-seconds>300</idle-timeout-seconds>
```

```
    <cache-type>LRU</cache-type>
  </stateful-session-cache>
  <persistent-store-dir>temp</persistent-store-dir>
 </stateful-session-descriptor>
 <jndi-name>org.foo.bar.ShoppingCartHome</jndi-name>
</weblogic-enterprise-bean>
```

The cache-type setting accepts two possible values:

LRU (Least-Recently Used)

> The EJB container will passivate the stateful EJB instances after they have been idle for more than idle-timeout-seconds.

NRU (Not-Recently Used)

> The EJB container will passivate stateful EJB instances only when there is pressure on WebLogic. In this case, the idle-timeout-seconds setting determines how often WebLogic checks to see if the cache is near its maximum capacity.

By default, WebLogic adopts the NRU caching strategy for stateful session EJBs, which is less eager than the LRU scheme. The EJB container invokes the ejbPassivate( ) method on the EJB instance before it is actually passivated. You can use this method to ensure that the EJBs state can be serialized safely to disk. This means that any fields that need not be passivated should be declared as transient, and all nontransient fields should represent serializable objects.

The max-beans-in-cache and idle-timeout-seconds settings also influence how WebLogic removes stateful session EJBs from either the cache or the disk. If a client doesn't use a passivated stateful session EJB before the idle-timeout-seconds duration, WebLogic removes the passivated EJB instance from disk. When the cache is close to its maximum capacity, WebLogic removes EJB instances that have not been used for idle-timeout-seconds, instead of passivating them to disk. This ensures that inactive EJBs do not burden the cache or disk resources.

Moreover, you can prevent WebLogic from removing idle EJBs altogether by setting the idle-timeout-seconds to 0. However, the EJBs still may be passivated if cache resources become scarce.

Configuring Entity Beans

The life cycle of an entity bean is a hybrid of the life cycles of a stateless and a stateful session bean. WebLogic maintains a free pool of inactive entity EJB instances. Just like stateless session beans, you can set the initial and the maximum sizes for the EJB pool. If you do specify a value for the initial-beans-in-free-pool setting, WebLogic prepares the pool of EJB instances with this initial capacity when the server starts up. Each EJB instance is created using the newInstance( ) method, and the setEntityContext( ) method is invoked once it's added to the pool. At this point, each EJB instance has a reference to the EntityContext, which provides the entity EJB with access to various container-managed services. When an EJB instance is removed from the pool, the container invokes the unsetEntityContext( ) method. In general, an entity EJB instance will remain in this pooled state as long as clients continue to invoke methods on the home object, or when the EJB container invokes one of the query methods on the entity bean.

Just like stateful session beans, WebLogic also maintains a cache of active entity EJB instances. The max-beans-in-cache element in the *weblogic-ejb-jar.xml* descriptor determines the maximum size of the entity cache. When a client invokes a create( ) method on the entity bean, the EJB container dips into the free pool and automatically invokes the ejbCreate( ) method on the EJB instance obtained from the pool, before placing it in the entity cache. Typically, the ejbCreate( ) method inserts one or more rows in the database, initializes the state with the underlying data, and returns the primary key for the new EJB instance. Once the EJB instance has been placed in the entity cache, it calls the ejbPostCreate( ) method on the EJB instance.

The EJB container uses the ejbLoad( ) and ejbStore( ) methods to read and write the current state of persistent fields in an entity bean. Suppose a client invokes a method on an entity bean and a new transaction is initiated. A transaction context would exist either because the client has explicitly initiated a JTA transaction before the method call, or because the EJB container automatically has initiated a transaction before the method call. For instance, the EJB container would do this implicitly if the method has a transaction setting of, say, Required. The EJB container then invokes the ejbLoad( ) method on the EJB instance to ensure that it has the most recent version of EJB's persistent data. Upon successful completion of the transaction, the EJB container invokes the ejbStore( ) method so that it can save any changes to the persistent fields. Throughout this time, the entity bean remains in the active state, including when the container invokes one of the select methods on the entity bean.

The following XML stanza illustrates how you can configure the free pool and entity cache for an entity bean:

```
<!-- weblogic-ejb-jar.xml entry -->
<weblogic-enterprise-bean>
  <ejb-name>PatientEJB</ejb-name>
  <entity-descriptor>
    <pool>
      <max-beans-in-free-pool>15</max-beans-in-free-pool>
      <initial-beans-in-free-pool>5</initial-beans-in-free-pool>
    </pool>
    <entity-cache>
      <max-beans-in-cache>15</max-beans-in-cache>
      <idle-timeout-seconds>900</idle-timeout-seconds>
    </entity-cache>
  </entity-descriptor>
  <local-jndi-name>org.foo.bar.PatientHome</local-jndi-name>
</weblogic-enterprise-bean>
```

When the entity cache reaches its maximum capacity, the EJB instances are scrubbed from the cache after idle-timeout-seconds of inactivity. In this case, passivation involves removing the EJB instance from the entity cache and returning it to the free pool. The EJB container invokes the `ejbStore( )` method so that the current state of the EJB's persistent fields can be written to the database, and then calls the `ejbPassivate( )` method to return the EJB instance to the pooled state. A passivated EJB instance can be activated later, in which case the EJB container will invoke the `ejbActivate( )` method when it moves the EJB instance back into the entity cache.

Altering the Store Behavior

By default, WebLogic's EJB container calls the `ejbStore( )` method on an EJB 1.1–compliant entity bean whenever a transaction is committed, regardless of whether its persistent fields were modified. However, WebLogic also allows you to limit the number of calls to the `ejbStore( )` method by ensuring that it is invoked only when the persistent fields of the entity bean are dirty. You may use the is-modified-method-name element in the *weblogic-ejb-jar.xml* descriptor file to designate a method that the EJB container can use to determine whether the persistent fields of the EJB have been modified and should therefore be written to the database.

The following example shows how to use a dirty flag to track changes to the persistent fields of a bean-managed entity bean:

```
public class PatientBean implements EntityBean {

    /** serializable Java object that represents the home address of Patient */
    private AddressVO homeAddress;

    // other persistent fields of Patient

    /** flag that determines if entity bean is dirty */
    private boolean dirty;

    /** part of Patient's component interface */
    public void setAddress(AddressVO theAddress) {
      this.homeAddress = theAddress;
      dirty = true;
    }
    /** part of Patient's component interface */
    public AddressVO getAddress() {
      return this.homeAddress;
    }
    /** is-modified method */
    public boolean isModified() {
      return dirty;
    }
    /** ejbStore method */
    public void ejbStore() {
        //write changes to persistent fields to the db
        dirty = false;
    }
    /** ejbLoad method */
```

```
public void ejbLoad( ) {
    //refresh values of persistent fields from db
    dirty = false;
}

//provide implementation for other life-cycle methods
}
```

The isModified() method returns true to indicate one or more persistent fields have
been modified, and false otherwise. This allows the EJB container to decide whether
it needs to invoke the ejbStore() method and write those changes to the database.
The following XML stanza from the *weblogic-ejb-jar.xml* descriptor shows how you
can declare the isModified() method:

```
<weblogic-enterprise-bean>
  <ejb-name>PatientEJB</ejb-name>
  <entity-descriptor>
    <entity-cache>
      <max-beans-in-cache>10</max-beans-in-cache>
    </entity-cache>
    <persistence>
      <is-modified-method-name>isModified</is-modified-method-name>
    </persistence>
  </entity-descriptor>
  <jndi-name>org.foo.bar.PatientHome</jndi-name>
</weblogic-enterprise-bean>
```

Whenever the EJB container needs to write the EJB's persistent state to the database, it will first invoke the isModified() method to determine whether any changes
have been made to the EJB's persistent fields.

> The is-modified-method-name setting applies only to bean-managed
> entity beans, or entity beans that are compliant with the EJB 1.1 CMP
> standard. Entity beans that are compliant with the EJB 2.0 standard
> do not require this setting. The EJB container automatically detects
> any changes to the persistent fields of the EJB instance.

Even though the isModified() method can improve the performance of your entity
beans by avoiding unnecessary calls to the ejbStore() method, you need to properly
track the "dirty" flag throughout the life cycle of the entity bean to ensure that no
changes to any of the persistent fields are ever lost.

As we have seen, WebLogic calls the ejbStore() method just before the successful
completion of the transaction. Generally, this is quite optimal because you limit the
number of calls to the ejbStore() method during the transaction and avoid needless
database updates. However, you may need to alter this default behavior under certain conditions—for instance, if your database supports a READ_UNCOMMITTED isolation level, you can make the results of intermediate updates available to other
transactions by writing the data out sooner.

To perform this early writing, you can force the EJB container to call the ejbStore( ) method after the completion of each method call, instead of at the end of the transaction. The delay-updates-until-end-of-tx element in the *weblogic-ejb-jar.xml* descriptor lets you determine when the ejbStore( ) method is invoked. By setting the element to false, you ensure that the EJB container saves any changes to the EJB's persistent fields after every method call, rather than when the transaction completes successfully. Even though the ejbStore( ) method is invoked after every method call, the database updates are committed only when the transaction completes successfully.

EJB Concurrency

WebLogic provides a number of features that control how WebLogic's EJB container manages concurrent access to entity beans. The concurrency-strategy element in the *weblogic-ejb-jar.xml* descriptor file lets you choose from one of the following options:

Exclusive

> The EJB container places an exclusive lock on a cached entity EJB instance for the duration of the transaction. This means other clients are blocked from accessing the EJB's persistent fields until the current transaction completes. Clearly, exclusive locking doesn't provide optimal concurrency, especially because other clients are unable to even read the persistent fields while the EJB instance is involved in a transaction.

> *Exclusive locking* implies the EJB container must have exclusive update access to the underlying persistent data. You should use this feature only if you're deploying the entity bean component to a single-server configuration. You must *not* use this setting if your EJB component will be deployed to a cluster of servers.

Database

> By default, WebLogic allows concurrent access to entity beans and lets the database handle caching and locking issues. This option improves concurrent access to entity beans because now the database is responsible for obtaining the necessary locks on the EJB's persistent data, and for resolving deadlocks. WebLogic continues to maintain a cache of entity EJB instances; a separate EJB instance is allocated for each transaction.

> Because the container doesn't have exclusive access to the underlying data, it is unable to cache the state of the EJB instance between transactions, so you cannot enable the cache-between-transactions setting. At the start of a transaction, the EJB container will instead invoke the ejbLoad( ) method to obtain the latest values for the persistent fields of the EJB.

Optimistic

When the optimistic concurrency is used, no locks are held by the EJB container or the database during the transaction. Instead, the EJB container ensures that none of the data that was updated during the transaction has changed before the transaction is committed. If any of the data has changed, the transaction is rolled back.

To enable these "smart" updates and data checks for validity, you need to specify additional settings in the *weblogic-cmp-rdbms-jar.xml* descriptor file. We shall cover these settings in Chapter 11.

ReadOnly

WebLogic supports an additional cache of read-only entity beans. A read-only EJB instance is activated for each transaction, allowing multiple clients and transactions to proceed in parallel.

Most importantly, this scheme also can ensure that the state of the read-only bean accurately reflects the underlying data. You can persuade the EJB container to periodically refresh the state of the persistent fields of the entity bean by specifying the read-timeout-seconds element in the *weblogic-ejb-jar.xml* descriptor file. This setting determines the frequency with which WebLogic refreshes the cached EJB instances:

```
<!-- weblogic-ejb-jar.xml entry -->
<weblogic-enterprise-bean>
  <ejb-name>PatientEJB</ejb-name>
  <entity-descriptor>
    <entity-cache>
      <max-beans-in-cache>15</max-beans-in-cache>
      <read-timeout-seconds>300</read-timeout-seconds>
      <concurrency-strategy>ReadOnly</concurrency-strategy>
    </entity-cache>
  </entity-descriptor>
  <jndi-name>org.foo.bar.PatientHome</jndi-name>
</weblogic-enterprise-bean>
```

When an entity bean is invoked, WebLogic checks to see whether the cached data is older than read-timeout-seconds. If so, it invokes the ejbLoad( ) method on the entity bean. Otherwise, the client continues to use the cached values for the EJB's persistent fields. By default, cached EJB instances with read-only concurrency are reloaded every 600 seconds.

Read-only entity beans are bound by certain constraints as well:

- WebLogic never calls the ejbStore( ) method for a read-only entity bean because the EJB's persistent fields need not be written to the database.

- All methods of the entity bean must be idempotent—i.e., repeated calls to the same method with identical arguments must have exactly the same effect as a single method call.

Let's now look at two important refinements to the read-only concurrency model.

Read-only multicast invalidation

WebLogic allows the *client* to determine when cached instances of a read-only entity bean need to be refreshed, instead of relying on a periodic refresh. This makes the read-only beans a very flexible option because often you will know when the underlying data has been invalidated. In these circumstances, the client needs to simply trigger a multicast message that invalidates all EJB instances on the server, and perhaps cached copies on other servers in the cluster as well. When an entity bean is configured with a read-only concurrency strategy, WebLogic's EJB compiler generates an implementation class for the EJB's home, which implements the weblogic.ejb.CachingHome interface. If the entity bean has local interfaces, the home object also implements the weblogic.ejb.CachingLocalHome interface.

These interfaces provide additional methods that allow the client to invalidate cached EJB instances on the local server and/or cached EJB instances on other cluster members:

```
package weblogic.ejb;

public interface CachingHome extends javax.ejb.EJBHome {
    /**
     * invalidate cached EJB instances with supplied primary key
     */
    public void invalidate(Object pk) throws RemoteException;
    /**
     * invalidate cached EJB instances with supplied primary keys
     */
    public void invalidate(Collection pks) throws RemoteException;
    /**
     * invalidate cached EJB instances with supplied primary key
     * on local server only
     */
    public void invalidateLocalServer(Object pk) throws RemoteException;
    /**
     * invalidate cached EJB instances with supplied primary keys
     * on local server only
     */
    public void invalidateLocalServer(Collection pks) throws RemoteException;
    /**
     * invalidate all cached EJB instances
     */
    public void invalidateAll() throws RemoteException;
    /**
     * invalidate all cached EJB instances on the local server only
     */
    public void invalidateAllLocalServer() throws RemoteException;
}
```

Using the CachingHome interface, you then can invoke one of its invalidate() methods and force WebLogic to invalidate cached instances of the read-only entity bean:

```
/* use JNDI lookup to obtain reference to EJB home object */
InitialContext ctx = new InitialContext();
```

```
Object home = ctx.lookup("org.foo.bar.PatientHome")
PatientHome ejbHome = (EJBHome)
  PortableRemoteObject.narrow(home, org.foo.bar. PatientHome.class);

/* invalidate all cached EJB instances with the specified primary key */
((weblogic.ejb.CachingHome) ejbHome).invalidate(pk);
```

A subsequent call to an invalidated EJB causes the container to invoke the ejbLoad( ) method on the EJB, thereby allowing the values of the persistent fields to be reloaded from the database. If your read-only entity bean supports these multicast invalidations, you also may choose to disable the periodic reloading of EJB instances by setting the value of read-timeout-seconds in the *weblogic-ejb-jar.xml* descriptor to 0.

Read-mostly pattern

Let's look at how to implement a *read-mostly* pattern, which enables you to model entities that are *primarily* read-only, but perhaps also updated infrequently. WebLogic lets you employ a combination of *read-only* and *read-write* entity beans to model entities that are updated occasionally. In this scenario, both the read-only and read-write entity beans are mapped to the same data. Use the read-only EJB for read access to the underlying data, and use the read-write EJB when you need to persist changes to the CMP fields. The read-only EJB still can refresh its in-memory state at intervals specified by the read-timeout-seconds setting. The read-write EJB invalidates its read-only counterpart whenever any changes to its persistent fields are saved to the database.

This invalidation can be triggered in two ways:

- After updating the read-write EJB, the client can invalidate the read-only EJB explicitly by invoking the invalidate( ) method on the CachingHome interface. If the updates occur during a client-initiated transaction, you should ensure the invalidation occurs after the transaction has completed successfully.

- You can configure WebLogic's EJB container so that it automatically handles the invalidation whenever the ejbStore( ) method is invoked on the read-write EJB. The invalidation-target element in the *weblogic-ejb-jar.xml* descriptor file allows you to specify the name of the read-only EJB that ought to be invalidated when updates to the read-write EJB are committed.

So, for an entity object that needs to implement the read-mostly pattern, you require a combination of entity beans:

- A *read-only* bean that encapsulates read access to the underlying data and also may be periodically refreshed

- A *read-write* bean that invalidates the read-only bean whenever changes to the persistent fields are committed

The following XML fragment shows the deployment settings that enable you to implement this scenario:

```
<!-- settings for the read-only version of the Patient entity -->
<weblogic-enterprise-bean>
  <ejb-name>PatientReaderEJB</ejb-name>
  <entity-descriptor>
  <entity-cache>
    <read-timeout-seconds>0</read-timeout-seconds>
    <concurrency-strategy>ReadOnly</concurrency-strategy>
  </entity-cache>
  <persistence>
    <persistence-use>
      <type-identifier>WebLogic_CMP_RDBMS</type-identifier>
      <type-version>7.0</type-version>
      <type-storage>META-INF/weblogic-cmp-rdbms-jar.xml</type-storage>
    </persistence-use>
  </persistence>
  </entity-descriptor>
  <jndi-name>org.foo.bar.PatientReaderHome</jndi-name>
</weblogic-enterprise-bean>

<!-- settings for the read-write version of the Patient entity -->
<weblogic-enterprise-bean>
  <ejb-name>PatientEJB</ejb-name>
  <entity-descriptor>
  <persistence>
    <persistence-use>
      <type-identifier>WebLogic_CMP_RDBMS</type-identifier>
      <type-version>8.1</type-version>
      <type-storage>META-INF/weblogic-cmp-rdbms-jar.xml</type-storage>
    </persistence-use>
  </persistence>
  <invalidation-target>
    <ejb-name>PatientReaderEJB</ejb-name>
  </invalidation-target>
  </entity-descriptor>
  <jndi-name>org.foo.bar.PatientHome</jndi-name>
</weblogic-enterprise-bean>
```

By setting the read-timeout-seconds element to 0, you ensure the EJB data is loaded only when the EJB instance enters the cache and whenever the read-only entity bean is invalidated. Both of the entity beans involved in this configuration must use the same abstract persistence schema.

Entity Bean Caching

Earlier we looked at how to configure the entity cache for an entity EJB component—its size, caching strategy, and the idle-timeout after which a cached EJB instance may be passivated. In this section, we examine how to configure WebLogic so that it caches the EJB's persistent data across (between) transactions. We also look at how entity beans can share an application-level cache at runtime.

Caching between transactions

WebLogic's read-only and read-mostly schemes attempt to optimize EJB usage by minimizing unnecessary writes. Besides these concurrency strategies, WebLogic also supports caching between transactions, which attempts to minimize unnecessary reads. By default, WebLogic supports *short-term caching*, in which the EJB's persistent data is cached only for the duration of the transaction. In other words, WebLogic does not read the values of the EJB's persistent fields again until the next transaction. It does this by invoking the ejbLoad( ) method on the entity bean once, at the start of the transaction. This ensures that the transaction always uses the most current version of the EJB's persistent data. This approach is best suited when multiple applications may have update access to the underlying data.

Long-term caching occurs when the EJB container retains the state of the EJB's persistent fields across transactions, between the EJB's use in one transaction and its use in the next transaction. You can enable long-term caching by setting the cache-between-transactions element in the *weblogic-ejb-jar.xml* descriptor file to true.

 You can enable caching between transactions for an entity bean only if its concurrency strategy has been set to Exclusive, ReadOnly, or Optimistic.

Read-only entity beans always perform long-term caching of data, and refresh their data only if they are invalidated or during a periodic refresh. For this reason, read-only beans ignore the value of the cache-between-transactions setting.

If you enable long-term caching for an EJB that supports Exclusive concurrency, you also must guarantee that the EJB container has exclusive update access to the underlying data. Otherwise, your EJBs run the risk of working with stale data. Hence, no application outside the EJB container must be capable of updating the EJB's persistent data. This can be achieved by deploying the entity bean to a *single* WebLogic instance, in which case the state of any cached EJB instance since the last transaction always will be accurate. If you deploy such a bean to a cluster of servers, any member of the cluster would be able to update the EJB's persistent data, which violates the assumptions of the Exclusive concurrency strategy. In this case, WebLogic will automatically disable any caching between transactions to prevent any inconsistencies in the runtime state of the EJB's persistent fields.

If you enable long-tem caching for entity beans with Optimistic concurrency, the EJB container can reuse the cached values of the EJB's persistent fields from the previous transaction. The container checks for optimistic conflicts only at the end of the transaction, thereby ensuring that all changes to the EJB data are consistent. Finally, if an entity bean supports Database concurrency, the value of the cache-between-transactions setting is ignored. WebLogic continues to maintain a cache of entity EJB instances, but does not cache the EJB's persistent data between transactions. At the start of each transaction, the EJB container invokes the ejbLoad( ) method to obtain the latest copy of its persistent data. Therefore, you should not enable long-term caching if the entity bean is configured for Database concurrency.

Application-level cache

Different entity beans that are part of the same EAR may share a single cache. WebLogic lets you create these *application-scoped* entity caches by providing an entity-cache element in the *weblogic-application.xml* descriptor file. Individual entity beans within the EAR then can reference this entity cache using the entity-cache-ref element in the *weblogic-ejb-jar.xml* descriptor. The following XML stanza shows how you can declare an entity cache for an enterprise application:

```
<weblogic-application>
  <ejb>
    <entity-cache>
      <entity-cache-name>GlobalEntityCache</entity-cache-name>
      <max-cache-size>
        <megabytes>10</megabytes>
      </max-cache-size>
      <caching-strategy>Exclusive</caching-strategy>
    </entity-cache>
  </ejb>
</weblogic-application>
```

You can restrict the size of the entity cache in two ways:

- Using the max-cache-size subelement, you can specify a maximum limit on the amount of memory allocated for the entity cache, in terms of either bytes or megabytes.

- Using the max-beans-in-cache subelement, you can specify a maximum limit on the number of entity beans in the cache. If you set this to 0, there is no limit on the number of entity beans in the cache—it is restricted only by the available system memory.

If you do not explicitly restrict the cache size, by default WebLogic limits the entity cache to 1000 EJB instances, at most. Use the caching-strategy subelement to configure how the EJB container handles cached EJB instances. You can specify one of the following values for the caching-strategy setting:

Exclusive

Here, the entity cache maintains a single EJB instance in memory for each primary key value. The EJB container locks the EJB instance under the exclusive locking policy, which means only a single transaction can use an EJB instance at any given time.

MultiVersion *(default)*

Here, the entity cache can hold multiple EJB instances in memory for a primary key value. The EJB container ensures that each transaction gets a different cached EJB instance of the entity bean.

By default, WebLogic resorts to application-level caching whenever an entity bean does not specify an entity cache in its *weblogic-ejb-jar.xml* descriptor file. WebLogic also provides two application-scoped caches for each enterprise application—namely, ExclusiveCache and MultiVersionCache. An application deployed to Web-Logic Server can declare entity caches with these names, and then override the settings for these default caches. However, you cannot modify the caching strategy for these two entity caches.

An EJB component that is bundled within the enterprise application then can use the entity-cache-ref element to refer to the application-level entity cache:

```
<!-- weblogic-ejb-jar.xml entry: -->
<entity-cache-ref>
  <entity-cache-name>GlobalEntityCache</entity-cache-name>
  <concurrency-strategy>Exclusive</concurrency-strategy>
  <estimated-bean-size>20</estimated-bean-size>
</entity-cache-ref>
```

The entity-cache-name subelement indicates the application-scoped entity cache that will cache EJB instances of this entity bean. The estimated-bean-size element specifies the average size of the entity EJB instances (in bytes). You need this setting when the application-level cache has restrictions on its memory size because it allows WebLogic to determine the maximum number of instances of this entity bean that may be cached.

The concurrency-strategy subelement defines the concurrency model used for cached instances of the entity bean. Its value must be compatible with the caching strategy configured for the application-level entity cache. An Exclusive cache supports only entity EJB instances with Exclusive concurrency. A MultiVersion entity cache is compatible with entity beans configured for either Database, ReadOnly, or Optimistic concurrency strategy.

EJBs and Transactions

WebLogic's EJB container supports EJBs that can participate in distributed transactions. EJBs deployed to WebLogic Server can be involved in JTA transactions that may cover updates to multiple data stores. A single transaction can span multiple EJBs deployed to multiple WebLogic instances. The EJBs also can participate in the two-phase commit protocol, which coordinates transactional updates across two or more resource managers.

For entity beans, it is the EJB container that always manages the transaction boundaries. Session and message-driven beans support both bean-managed and container-managed transactions. In the case of bean-managed transactions, the EJB implementation must explicitly supervise the transaction boundaries. Typically, the EJB code will acquire a reference to the UserTransaction object from the EJBContext, and then make explicit calls to the begin, commit, and rollback methods to mark the start and completion of the transaction. For container-managed beans, the EJB container manages all transaction boundaries. You can specify the transaction attributes for the EJB methods in the *ejb-jar.xml* descriptor file for the EJB component. The default transaction setting for an EJB method is Supports. In other words, all EJB methods are capable of participating in a transaction, if one exists. Of course, you must *not* use the UserTransaction interface within an EJB method that supports container-managed transactions.

Distributed transactions

A client can explicitly wrap multiple EJB calls in a transaction, or invoke an EJB method that implicitly creates a transaction context around method calls to multiple EJBs. The following code snippet shows how you can wrap multiple EJB calls in a JTA transaction:

```
import javax.transaction.*;

UserTransaction tx = null;

...
try {
    tx = (UserTransaction) ctx.lookup("java:comp/UserTransaction");
    tx.begin();
    patient1.admit();
    patient2.release();
    patient3.doa();
    tx.commit();
}
catch (Exception e) {
    tx.rollback();
}
```

All the method calls to the Patient entity beans execute as a single, atomic unit, within the context of a client-initiated transaction. This assumes that the EJB methods can execute within a transaction context, so the EJB methods must have a transaction setting of either Required, Supports, or Mandatory. The EJBs involved in the transaction either commit or roll back together, regardless of whether the EJBs are targeted to a single server, multiple servers, or a WebLogic cluster.

Alternatively, you could implement a session bean that wraps calls to multiple entity beans. By assigning a Required transaction setting to the session bean method, you can guarantee that a transaction is available automatically when a client invokes the method. The EJBs involved in the wrapper method also should support transactions, so their transaction setting must be either Required, Supports, or Mandatory. If you have targeted an EJB to a WebLogic cluster, or deployed one across multiple server instances, WebLogic will try to use a copy of the EJB on the same server (if it exists) rather than choose a remote copy of the EJB on another server. Whenever multiple EJBs are involved in a transaction, WebLogic tries to minimize the network traffic for the transaction.

A transaction may need to use EJBs that reside on multiple servers in a WebLogic cluster. This could happen in a heterogeneous cluster, where the EJBs are not deployed uniformly across all members of the cluster. In such cases, WebLogic will create multi-tier JDBC connections to the underlying data source. For optimal performance, you should deploy EJBs uniformly to all members of a WebLogic cluster.

Transaction isolation levels

WebLogic extends the JTA by allowing you to set the isolation level for the transaction. The isolation levels determine how concurrent JTA transactions access the underlying data store. The following example shows how a Java application can specify the isolation level for new client-initiated transactions:

```
import java.sql.Connection
import javax.transaction.Transaction;
import weblogic.transaction.TxHelper:
import weblogic.transaction.Transaction;
import weblogic.transaction.TxConstants;

UserTransaction tx =
  (UserTransaction) ctx.lookup("java:comp/UserTransaction");
tx.begin();

//get transaction associated with this thread
Transaction tx = TxHelper.getTransaction();
//set isolation level to TRANSACTION_READ_COMMITTED
tx.setProperty (TxConstants.ISOLATION_LEVEL,
   new Integer(Connection.TRANSACTION_READ_COMMITTED));

//perform one or more transaction-aware updates
tx.commit();
```

In this example, we use a WebLogic-specific TxHelper class to obtain the transaction context associated with the current thread. WebLogic then will pass the isolation level to the underlying database (and to other data stores involved as well).

For container-managed transactions, you even can specify the isolation level for EJB methods using the transaction-isolation setting in the *weblogic-ejb-jar.xml* descriptor file. Once again, the EJB container passes the value of the isolation level to the underlying database. You can choose one of the following values for the isolation level of a transaction:

TRANSACTION_READ_UNCOMMITTED
  A transaction may view uncommitted changes made by other transactions.

TRANSACTION_READ_COMMITTED
  A transaction may view committed changes made only by other transactions.

TRANSACTION_REPEATABLE_READ
  Dirty and nonrepeatable reads are disallowed for any transaction.

`TRANSACTION_SERIALIZABLE`

This is the most restrictive isolation level, and emulates the serial execution of both transactions.

These values obey the same semantics as the isolation levels that apply to a JDBC connection. The following XML portion from the *weblogic-ejb-jar.xml* descriptor shows how to set the `TRANSACTION_READ_COMMITTED` isolation level for all of the EJB's database operations:

```
<!-- weblogic-ejb-jar.xml entry: -->
<weblogic-ejb-jar>
  <weblogic-enterprise-bean>
    <ejb-name>PatientEJB</ejb-name>
    ...
  </weblogic-enterprise-bean>
  ...
  <transaction-isolation>
    <isolation-level>TRANSACTION_READ_COMMITTED</isolation-level>
    <method>
      <ejb-name>PatientEJB</ejb-name>
      <method-intf>Remote</method-intf>
      <method-name>*</method-name>
    </method>
  </transaction-isolation>
</weblogic-ejb-jar>
```

Both the isolation level and concurrency strategy settings for an EJB component impact the behavior of EJBs when they participate in distributed transactions.

EJBs and Clustering

EJBs can be configured to operate in a clustered environment, leveraging WebLogic's support for load balancing and failover. In a single-server configuration, the client uses WebLogic-specific stubs corresponding to the `EJBHome` and `EJBObject` interfaces. When you deploy EJBs to a WebLogic cluster or to multiple Managed Servers, WebLogic supplies specialized versions of the EJB home and EJB object stubs. Both of these stubs provide load-balancing and failover support, first at the level of looking up a home object, and second at the level of invoking an EJB method. As discussed in Chapter 4, any of the features of WebLogic's clustered EJB support come directly from the operation of RMI objects in a clustered environment.

A cluster-aware `EJBHome` stub knows about the `EJBHome` objects on all WebLogic servers in the cluster. Client calls to the home stub are load-balanced between the servers to which the EJB has been deployed. The cluster-aware stub also provides failover for lookup requests by automatically routing requests to another available server in the cluster, when the original server hosting an EJB becomes unreachable. WebLogic supports clustered home stubs for all the EJB types—the `home-is-clusterable` element in the *weblogic-ejb-jar.xml* descriptor file determines whether the home object for an EJB is cluster-aware. If you specify true as the value of this setting, the EJB compiler ensures that the home stubs for the EJB are cluster-aware. By default, EJB home stubs are clusterable, which means an EJB can be deployed to a cluster.

The EJBObject stub provides similar functionality, but for method calls instead. These stubs can be made replica-aware, in which case they maintain a list of all copies of the EJBObject that reside on other servers within the cluster. A replica-aware EJBObject stub can distribute method calls across these available servers and automatically reroute method calls to an EJB instance on another available server. However, certain restrictions are imposed on the use of replica-aware stubs and failover, and we shall examine them shortly.

Failover and Replication

As mentioned earlier, WebLogic supports failover when you use a cluster-aware home object to look up an EJB object, and when you invoke an EJB method using a replica-aware EJB object. Clustered stubs are generated automatically during EJB compilation. In WebLogic 8.1, the appc compiler passes the EJB interfaces through to the RMI compiler, which then generates the cluster-aware stubs. The same process occurs in WebLogic 7.0 when using the ejbc compiler. A clustered stub essentially encapsulates logic that enables it to locate a home object or an EJB on any one of the available servers.

Whenever an EJB component is deployed to multiple Managed Servers, its EJB home object is bound to a cluster-wide naming service. Each server binds an instance of the home object under the same JNDI name. When a client asks the JNDI tree for the EJB's home object, it acquires a cluster-aware stub that can locate home objects on each server to which the EJB component is deployed. When a client invokes any of the create( ) or find( ) methods on the EJB's home object, the clustered home stub routes the request to one of the active members of the cluster. If one of the Managed Servers in the cluster becomes unreachable (perhaps because of an unexpected failure), the clustered home object is able to transparently redirect the request to another available server that hosts the same EJB.

Using a clustered home object, a client can obtain a replica-aware server-side EJBObject stub that can locate replicas on all available servers that host the EJB. The EJBObject stub can detect any attempts to invoke an EJB method on a failed replica, and can automatically reroute the method call to another available server.

WebLogic provides automatic failover when the failure occurs between method calls to the EJB—i.e., after a method completes, or if the EJB container is unable to contact a server in the first place. By default, if a failure occurs during an EJB method call, WebLogic will *not* automatically fail over to another available server that hosts the same EJB component. Automatic failover during a method call can occur only if the particular EJB method is marked as idempotent. By marking the methods as such, you are guaranteeing that repeated calls to the same method with identical arguments have the same effect as a single method call. This guarantee is needed to ensure that database updates performed by an EJB method aren't duplicated when the same method is retried on another EJB on another server.

You can use the idempotent-methods setting to indicate which EJB methods may be considered idempotent by the EJB container. The following XML stanza marks all EJB methods for the Patient entity bean as idempotent:

```
<!-- weblogic-ejb-jar.xml entry: -->
<weblogic-ejb-jar>
  <weblogic-enterprise-bean>
    <ejb-name>PatientEJB</ejb-name>
    ...
  </weblogic-enterprise-bean>
  ...
  <idempotent-methods>
    <method>
      <ejb-name>PatientEJB</ejb-name>
      <method-intf>Remote</method-intf>
      <method-name>*</method-name>
    </method>
  </idempotent-methods>
</weblogic-ejb-jar>
```

 Remember that WebLogic supports method failover only when you have declared the EJB methods as idempotent.

Stateless session beans

Stateless session EJBs support both cluster-aware home objects and replica-aware EJB objects. To enable cluster-aware home stubs to be generated, specify true for the home-is-clusterable element. To enable replica-aware EJB objects, specify true for the stateless-bean-is-clusterable element in the *weblogic-ejb-jar.xml* descriptor file. By default, an EJB method isn't considered idempotent. So, if you want method failover, you will need to include an XML stanza describing which methods are idempotent, as mentioned earlier.* The following XML fragment illustrates how to enable these settings for the Registration EJB, assuming that it will be deployed to a WebLogic cluster:

```
<!-- weblogic-ejb-jar.xml entry: -->
<weblogic-ejb-jar>
  <weblogic-enterprise-bean>
    <ejb-name>RegistrationEJB</ejb-name>
```

---

* In WebLogic 7.0, you also can use the stateless-beans-are-idempotent element in the *weblogic-ejb-jar.xml* descriptor file to indicate that the methods of the EJB are idempotent. This element is deprecated in WebLogic 8.1 in favor of the idempotent-methods element.

```
            <stateless-session-descriptor>
              <pool>
                <max-beans-in-free-pool>15</max-beans-in-free-pool>
                <initial-beans-in-free-pool>5</initial-beans-in-free-pool>
              </pool>
              <stateless-clustering>
                <home-is-clusterable>true</home-is-clusterable>
                <stateless-bean-is-clusterable>true</stateless-bean-is-clusterable>
              </stateless-clustering>
            </stateless-session-descriptor>
            <jndi-name>org.foo.bar.RegistrationHome</jndi-name>
          </weblogic-enterprise-bean>
          ...

        <!-- indicates that all methods of the stateless session EJB are idempotent -->
        <idempotent-methods>
          <method>
            <ejb-name>RegistrationEJB</ejb-name>
            <method-intf>Remote</method-intf>
            <method-name>*</method-name>
          </method>
        </idempotent-methods>
      </weblogic-ejb-jar>
```

Stateful session beans

Clustered stateful session EJBs also use cluster-aware home stubs. Failover for stateful session EJBs is rather different, though, and is based on in-memory replication. The EJB container transparently replicates the state of the EJB to another clustered WebLogic instance. In-memory replication for stateful session beans works along the same lines as HTTP session-state replication. When replicating HTTP session state, WebLogic uses the session-tracking cookie to keep track of the primary and secondary servers. In the case of stateful session EJBs, it is the replica-aware EJBObject stub that keeps track of the primary and secondary servers needed for replicating the state of the EJB.

As the EJBObject stub is replica-aware, it maintains a list of all available servers that host the EJB component. The *primary server* hosts the actual EJB instance (and its state) with which a client interacts. When a client obtains an EJB object, the target server automatically chooses a *secondary server* to host the replicated state of the stateful session EJB instance. Now, the EJBObject stub will keep track of the primary server that the client first connected to, and of the secondary server that is used for replicating the EJB's state. WebLogic keeps the replica on the secondary server in sync with any changes that the client makes to the EJB's state. If the EJB instance is involved in a transaction, its state is replicated once the transaction is committed.

It still is possible that the current state of a stateful session EJB can be lost. If the primary server fails before changes to the EJB state have been replicated successfully, the client will fail over to the previous state of the replica on the secondary server. If you need to ensure data is consistent under all possible failover scenarios, you should consider using entity beans.

Typically, WebLogic replicates the EJB's state to another member of the cluster, or chooses the secondary server from a replication group (if it exists). Whenever possible, WebLogic chooses a server that isn't collocated on the same machine that hosts the primary server. Chapter 14 covers replication groups in more detail.

If the primary server fails, the EJB stub automatically redirects the next method call to the replica hosted on the secondary server. The secondary server creates a new EJB instance using the replicated session data, and processing continues. The secondary server now becomes the primary server for the EJB instance, and a new server is chosen to replicate the EJB's state. The replica-aware EJBObject stub then will update its list of available servers that host the EJB, as well as the locations of the primary and secondary servers for the client.

In order to enable in-memory state replication for clustered stateful session EJBs, you need to do the following:

1. Ensure the stateful session EJB supports clustered home objects. You can enable this by specifying true for the home-is-clusterable element in the *weblogic-ejb-jar.xml* descriptor file.

2. Enable session-state replication by setting the replication-type element in the *weblogic-ejb-jar.xml* descriptor file to InMemory:

   ```
   <stateful-session-clustering>
      <home-is-clusterable>true</home-is-clusterable>
      <replication-type>InMemory</replication-type>
   </stateful-session-clustering>
   ```

3. Ensure the EJB component is deployed uniformly to all members of the cluster. In-memory replication doesn't work for heterogeneous deployments on a cluster.

In general, a client is guaranteed to have access to the last committed state of the stateful session EJB, even if the primary server fails. However, under certain rare conditions, a client will be unable to access the last committed state:

1. Suppose a client creates an EJB instance and commits the initial transaction, but the primary server fails before the state changes can be replicated to the secondary server. The next call to the EJB on the secondary server will fail because the initial state could not be replicated successfully to the secondary server.

2. If both the primary and secondary servers fail, the client needs to create another EJB instance and re-create its last committed state.

These are exceptional circumstances that shouldn't dissuade you from using stateful session beans in a clustered environment. The fact that WebLogic supports failover for stateful session beans is crucial in a production environment.

Entity beans

Clustered entity EJBs also support cluster-aware home stubs once you set the home-is-clusterable element in the *weblogic-ejb-jar.xml* descriptor. The clustering behavior is somewhat different, depending on whether the entity bean is a read-only or read-write bean.

For read-only entity beans, the home object returns a replica-aware stub that load-balances on every method call. However, it doesn't automatically fail over to a replica when a server becomes unavailable. For read-write entity beans, load balancing and failover occur only at the EJBHome level. The cluster-aware home object returns an EJBObject stub pinned to that server. Multiple instances of the entity bean may exist, each within its own server within the cluster. Because of this, each EJB instance needs to do the following:

- Invoke the ejbLoad( ) method at the start of the transaction so that it can acquire the latest version of the bean's persistent data. This occurs as long as you also have disabled long-term caching for the entity bean.

- Invoke the ejbStore( ) method at the successful completion of the transaction so that it can save any changes to the persistent fields.

Thus, read-write entity beans deployed to multiple servers behave in the same way as EJBs deployed to a single-server configuration.

Load Balancing

WebLogic supports several algorithms for load-balancing requests to clustered EJB objects: round-robin, weight-based, and random. WebLogic 8.1 supports additional affinity-based load-balancing algorithms, which attempt to minimize the number of connections clients make to a cluster. By default, WebLogic uses a round-robin policy for load balancing. You can use the Administration Console to change the default load-balancing scheme between replicas of an EJB home. Alternatively, you can declare a home-load-algorithm setting in the *weblogic-ejb-jar.xml* descriptor file. This setting can take one of the following values: RoundRobin, WeightBased, Random, RoundRobinAffinity, WeightBasedAffinity, or RandomAffinity. You even can implement a custom CallRouter class, which allows you to override the load-balancing behavior for EJB method calls. For stateless session EJBs instead, you must declare the stateless-bean-load-algorithm element, which accepts the same values.

Detailed explanations of the load-balancing algorithms are given in Chapter 14. The chapter also provides situations in which load balancing is avoided. For example, if two EJBs are deployed on the same server, and one makes a call on the other, no load balancing will occur. Instead, WebLogic will use its collocation optimization to avoid network calls, and simply call the local instance.

CHAPTER 11

Using CMP and EJB QL

WebLogic's EJB container supports container-managed EJB persistence based on the EJB 2.0 specification. When you deploy a CMP entity bean to WebLogic Server, the EJB container automatically handles updates to the EJB's persistent fields by concurrent transactions, synchronizes its state with the underlying database table(s), and manages its relationships with other EJB instances.

WebLogic provides a number of enhancements to the standard CMP requirements. These can be divided into two basic categories: those that provide additional architectural options and make EJB development more convenient, and those that can be used to tune an EJB's performance. In the first category, WebLogic lets you map container-managed fields to columns spread across multiple tables. During the development and prototyping stages, you can make WebLogic generate the necessary SQL tables for all entity beans and relationships defined in the EJB JAR. WebLogic does this by inspecting the information captured in the bean classes, as well as the abstract persistence schema and column mappings defined in the EJB deployment descriptors. In addition, you can ask WebLogic to validate the database schema expected by the EJB container at runtime.

WebLogic lets you defer certain tasks of the EJB container to the underlying database. For instance, if you've configured a remove operation on an entity bean to propagate to all related EJB instances, you can configure WebLogic so that it relies on the database to cascade the deletes to all related rows. Besides this, you can configure entity EJBs so that they rely on the underlying database to automatically generate a primary key when an entity bean is inserted into the table(s). For instance, you could rely on an Oracle sequence, or perhaps on an SQL server's IDENTITY column with AUTO-INCREMENT to automatically generate primary key values when the entity EJB instance is created. In addition, you can configure how the EJB container synchronizes updates to persistent fields with the underlying database.

In the performance category, WebLogic lets you specify precisely when the data associated with an entity bean is inserted into the database table. This is critical if you need to configure bulk inserts when a transaction is committed, or if a relationship field (also called a CMR field) maps to a foreign key column that doesn't allow null values. You also can optimize the performance of the EJB container by eagerly loading related entity beans when a finder query is executed using caching EJB relationships. Finally, field groups let you determine exactly which subset of fields in an EJB is populated as the result of a finder method call. These enhancements, together with the EJB container's support for optimistic concurrency and EJB caching, enable you to tune CMP entity beans effectively.

EJB QL is a portable SQL-like query language that defines the implementation for query (finder and select) methods associated with entity beans. It operates on the abstract persistence schema that you've defined for entity beans packaged in an EJB JAR. WebLogic supports the standard EJB QL features, but also incorporates some much-needed features. These include the support for the DISTINCT and ORDERBY keywords, aggregate functions, and SQL-like subqueries.

You also can define select methods that return the results of multicolumn queries. In this case, the collection is returned in the form of a java.sql.ResultSet, where the columns correspond to either CMP fields or aggregate functions applied to the CMP fields. Finally, WebLogic lets you dynamically construct and execute EJB QL queries in your application code, without requiring you to update and redeploy the EJB JAR.

Building CMP Entity Beans

When creating standard CMP entity beans, the standard *ejb-jar.xml* descriptor file is used to define the persistent fields for the CMP entity bean, its primary key class, and the nature of its relationships with other entity beans. The *weblogic-ejb-jar.xml* descriptor file hosts the WebLogic counterpart to this information. In addition, you need to create a *weblogic-cmp-rdbms-jar.xml* descriptor file that maps these "virtual fields" to actual table columns in the underlying database. The *weblogic-cmp-rdbms-jar.xml* file allows you to configure all aspects of WebLogic's RDBMS-based persistence services for CMP entity beans. It lets you specify the database columns associated with the persistent fields, the primary key columns that identify the EJB instances, and the foreign key columns that implement the EJB relationships.

Due to the sheer number of descriptor files and source files that need to be maintained, the easiest approach to developing entity beans is to use EJBGen, or IDEs such as WebLogic Workshop. The following sections show a working example of this approach, together with an outline of the descriptor files. If you don't want to use EJBGen, then you have to create, by hand, the same set of descriptor files described in the following sections.

A Simple EJB

Example 11-1 shows the complete code for a simple CMP entity bean. It uses WebLogic's GenericEntityBean class to simplify the development.

Example 11-1. The Department EJB abstract class

```
import javax.ejb.*;
import weblogic.ejb.*;

/**
 * @ejbgen:entity prim-key-class="java.lang.Integer"
 *    ejb-name = "DepartmentEJB"
 *    data-source-name = "MyDataSource"
 *    table-name = "tblDepartment"
 *    abstract-schema-name = DepartmentSchema
 * @ejbgen:jndi-name
 *    local  = "ejb.DepartmentEJBLocalHome"
 * @ejbgen:finder ejb-ql="SELECT OBJECT(o) from DepartmentSchema as o"
 *                generate-on="Local" signature="Collection findAll( )"
 */
abstract public class DepartmentEJB extends GenericEntityBean implements EntityBean {
    /**
     * @ejbgen:cmp-field primkey-field="true" column="Id"
     * @ejbgen:local-method
     */
    public abstract Integer getId( );

    /**
     * @ejbgen:local-method
     */
    public abstract void setId(Integer arg);

    /**
     * @ejbgen:cmp-field column="Name"
     * @ejbgen:local-method
     */
    public abstract String getName( );

    /**
     * @ejbgen:local-method
     */
    public abstract void setName(String arg);

    public java.lang.Integer ejbCreate(java.lang.Integer Id) {
      setId(Id);
      return null;
    }

    public void ejbPostCreate(java.lang.Integer Id) {}
}
```

The EJBGen tags capture a lot of additional metadata and deployment information about the Department EJB:

- The EJB has two CMP fields, Id and Name, both identified by the ejbgen:cmp-field tags. The primary-key field attribute also indicates that the Id field has been set as the EJB's primary key field.

- The EJB defines a findAll() finder method, which simply returns the collection of Department EJB instances.
- The EJB fields map to the columns of a table called tblDepartment.
- Other data, such as the EJB name, its JNDI name, and the data source name, are also are specified via the tags.

Associated Java Files

EJBGen now can generate a number of Java files using this code. For example, it can generate the EJB's local home and local interface files. Example 11-2 shows the local home interface generated for the Department EJB.

Example 11-2. Home interface for the Department EJB

```
public interface DepartmentLocalHome extends EJBLocalHome {
  public Collection findAll()  throws FinderException;
  public DepartmentLocal findByPrimaryKey(Integer primaryKey) throws FinderException;
  public DepartmentLocal create(Integer Id) throws CreateException;
}
```

Note how EJBGen is able to insert the findAll() method automatically, due to the presence of the ejbgen:finder tag in the Department EJB abstract class. More interestingly, EJBGen also will generate a transfer object. Example 11-3 shows the transfer object that is generated for the Department EJB.

Example 11-3. Transfer object for the Department EJB

```
public class DepartmentValue  implements Serializable  {
  public DepartmentValue() {}
  public DepartmentValue(java.lang.Integer id, java.lang.String name) {
    m_id = id;
    m_name = name;
  }
  private java.lang.Integer m_id;
  private java.lang.String m_name;

  public java.lang.Integer getId(){ return m_id; }
  public void setId(java.lang.Integer n){ m_id = n; }

  public java.lang.String getName(){return m_name;}
  public void setName(java.lang.String n){m_name = n;}

  public boolean equals(Object other) { /* ... */ }
  public int hashCode() { /* ... */ }
}
```

EJB Deployment Descriptor

EJBGen also generates the deployment descriptors needed to deploy the Department EJB successfully: *ejb-jar.xml*, *weblogic-ejb-jar.xml*, and *weblogic-cmp-rdbms-jar.xml*. *ejb-jar.xml* is the standard entity descriptor file, and we won't consider it any further. Example 11-4 shows the WebLogic-specific *weblogic-ejb-jar.xml* descriptor file that is generated for the Department EJB.

Example 11-4. The weblogic-ejb-jar.xml descriptor for the Department EJB

```
<!-- weblogic-ejb-jar.xml entry -->
  <weblogic-enterprise-bean>
    <ejb-name>DepartmentEJB</ejb-name>
    <entity-descriptor>
      <persistence>
        <persistence-use>
          <type-identifier>WebLogic_CMP_RDBMS</type-identifier>
          <type-version>8.1</type-version>
          <type-storage>META-INF/weblogic-cmp-rdbms-jar.xml</type-storage>
        </persistence-use>
      </persistence>
    </entity-descriptor>
    <local-jndi-name>ejb.DepartmentEJBLocalHome</local-jndi-name>
  </weblogic-enterprise-bean>
```

This file also can host other bean configuration properties, such as the cache and pool settings. The persistence-use tag in the *weblogic-ejb-jar.xml* file lets you specify an identifier for the type of persistence that is used by the entity EJB. It also lets you specify the location of the file that provides additional information about the abstract persistence model. Example 11-5 shows how the referenced *weblogic-cmp-rdbms-jar.xml* descriptor maps the EJB's persistent fields defined in the *ejb-jar.xml* file to the actual database columns.

Example 11-5. Configuring RDBMS-based EJB persistence

```
<weblogic-rdbms-bean>
  <ejb-name>DepartmentEJB</ejb-name>
  <data-source-name>MyDataSource</data-source-name>
  <table-map>
    <table-name>tblDepartment</table-name>
    <field-map>
      <cmp-field>id</cmp-field>
      <dbms-column>Id</dbms-column>
    </field-map>
    <field-map>
      <cmp-field>name</cmp-field>
      <dbms-column>Name</dbms-column>
    </field-map>
  </table-map>
</weblogic-rdbms-bean>
```

Let's take a closer look at the information captured in this deployment descriptor:

- The data-source-name element specifies the JNDI name of a configured data source that provides the EJB container with a pool of connections to the underlying database. Remember that if your entity bean supports transactions, you must specify the JNDI name of an XA-aware data source. You also could associate a separate data source (and therefore a separate connection pool) with each CMP entity EJB.

- The table-map element includes the name of a database table, and maps the CMP fields for the entity bean to its columns. You easily could map the same CMP fields for the entity bean to columns that are spread across multiple database tables. In that case, you need to ensure that the primary key CMP field is mapped to the primary key column(s) in each table involved. Also, you must ensure that there are no referential integrity constraints between the tables that map to the entity bean, or else you may encounter a runtime error when you attempt to remove an entity EJB instance.

- The database-type element indicates the type of the underlying DBMS; it can take one of the following values: DB2, Informix, Oracle, SQLServer, Sybase, and POINTBASE. WebLogic can use this element for various tasks, such as automatic table creation, caching EJB relationships, or any task that is specific to the actual database.

Creating the EJB JAR

Now you are ready to build the EJB JAR using a staging folder or JAR file. The content will include the compiled Java classes and the deployment descriptors:

```
/com/oreilly/ejbs/DepartmentLocalHome.class
/com/oreilly/ejbs/DepartmentLocal.class
/com/oreilly/ejbs/DepartmentEJB.class
/com/oreilly/ejbs/DepartmentValue.class
/META-INF/ejb-jar.xml
/META-INF/weblogic-ejb-jar.xml
/META-INF/weblogic-cmp-rdbms-jar.xml
```

In order to create the EJB JAR, use the appc compiler:

```
java weblogic.appc -output ejb_foo.jar staging-dir
```

In WebLogic 7.0, you need to use the ejbc compiler:

```
java weblogic.ejbc staging-dir ejb_foo.jar
```

Features of WebLogic's CMP

This section examines a number of WebLogic features that distinguish WebLogic's CMP implementation. These include convenience features such as automatic generation of primary keys for new EJB instances, automatic creation of DBMS tables that map to the abstract persistent model, and more performance-oriented features such as statement batching, optimistic concurrency, and fetching preconfigured groups of fields. Later in this chapter, we look at two optimizations for container-managed EJB relationships: enabling the DBMS to take charge of cascading an EJB remove to related EJB instances and relationship caching.

Automatic Primary Key Generation

WebLogic can generate primary key values automatically for noncompound primary key fields. To support this, the primary key class element in the *ejb-jar.xml* file must be either java.lang.Integer or java.lang.Long. The keys can be generated in two ways: WebLogic can either delegate the primary key generation to the DBMS, or it can use a named sequence table.

DBMS-generated primary keys

If you are using either Oracle or Microsoft's SQL Server, WebLogic can use the underlying DBMS to generate primary keys. In Oracle, the EJB container accomplishes this using Oracle's sequences. When a new primary key is needed, it calls on the sequence (or increments a cached sequence number). For SQL Server, it uses identity columns, which means that the primary key value is supplied automatically by the DBMS when the row is inserted.

Using Oracle, you can create a sequence together with an increment value via the following SQL:

```
create sequence seqEmployee start with 1 increment by 5;
```

By utilizing increment values, you can minimize the number of times that WebLogic has to interact with the sequence, which can in turn help performance. Once you have created the sequence, use the automatic-key-generation element in the *weblogic-cmp-rdbms-jar.xml* descriptor to specify the name of the sequence and a cache size:

```
<automatic-key-generation>
   <generator-type>ORACLE</generator-type>
   <generator-name>seqEmployee</generator-name>
   <key-cache-size>5</key-cache-size>
</automatic-key-generation>
```

Ensure that the cache size matches the sequence increment. If it does not, the EJB container may obtain duplicate values from the sequence or obtain unnecessary gaps in the primary keys generated for the actual rows. For SQL Server, simply ensure that the database column corresponding to the primary key field is an IDENTITY column with AUTO-INCREMENT enabled. Now set the generator-type to SQLServer in the *weblogic-cmp-rdbms-jar.xml* descriptor:

```
<automatic-key-generation>
    <generator-type>SQLServer</generator-type>
```

```
    </automatic-key-generation>
```

Sequence tables

An alternative approach that doesn't rely on any particular database is to provide a *table* that holds a monotonically increasing value. For this, you need a table with a single column and a single row. The row will hold the current key value. In Oracle, you can create and populate such a table as follows:

```
CREATE mySequenceTable (SEQUENCE int)
INSERT into mySequenceTable VALUES (1)
```

To ensure that no duplicate keys are generated under concurrent access, WebLogic uses the Serializable transaction isolation level when accessing the table. Hence, the DBMS must support this isolation level if the EJB container can generate primary keys using sequence tables. However, the Serializable isolation level also will slow down access to the sequence table. To minimize this degradation, you should create a unique sequence table for each entity bean type. Here are the changes you need to make to the *weblogic-cmp-rdbms-jar.xml* descriptor in order to use this form of key generation:

```
<automatic-key-generation>
  <generator-type>NamedSequenceTable</generator-type>
  <generator_name>mySequenceTable</generator-name>
</automatic-key-generation>
```

Automatic Table Creation and Validation

WebLogic can be configured to automatically generate the database tables that map to the EJB's persistence schema. WebLogic creates the database tables for all entity beans packaged in an EJB JAR during deployment. It uses the value of the database-type[*] element in the *weblogic-cmp-rdbms-jar.xml* descriptor to determine the SQL commands specific to the underlying DBMS that are needed to create the required database tables. The tables are generated based on the bean classes and the abstract persistence schema defined in the deployment descriptors. In WebLogic 7.0, you can enable automatic table creation when the EJB JAR is deployed by including the following element in the *weblogic-cmp-rdbms-jar.xml* descriptor:

```
<create-default-dbms-tables>True</create-default-dbms-tables>
```

The tables are created only if they do not already exist in the database. For this reason, you should delete the tables if the fields in the entity bean change and you use this flag in WebLogic 7.0. If an error occurs during table creation, WebLogic aborts

---

[*] WebLogic 8.1 can automatically detect the type to the DBMS being used to persist the EJBs. If the detected type conflicts with the value of the database-type element, WebLogic issues a warning and uses the specified type.

the process and continues with deployment. In that case, you need to set up the database schema manually.

WebLogic 8.1 can recreate the database tables automatically when the EJB's table schema changes—i.e., if any of the table columns that map to the CMP fields are modified. Thus, when you enable automatic table creation on an EJB JAR, the EJB container automatically changes the underlying database schema, to ensure that it remains in sync with the EJB's persistence schema. If any CMP field cannot be mapped properly to a database column, a Table Not Found error occurs indicating that the table could not be created and must be set up manually. Moreover, you must use the `create-default-dbms-tables` element to define precisely how WebLogic creates the database schema when the EJB module is deployed. You can choose from the following values for the `create-default-dbms-tables` element:

Disabled
: By default, the EJB container ignores any changes to the underlying table schema.

CreateOnly
: The EJB container creates the necessary database tables for each CMP bean in the JAR, provided they don't already exist.

DropAndCreate
: For each CMP bean in the JAR, the EJB container drops and creates the table if any of its columns have changed. All data held in the database table is lost.

DropAndCreateAlways
: For each CMP bean in the JAR, the EJB container drops and creates the table, even if none of its columns has changed.

AlterOrCreate
: For each CMP bean in the JAR, the EJB container attempts to alter the table schema, if it already exists. Otherwise, the EJB container creates the database table during deployment. Note that, if a new column (or a column with null values) is made the primary key, this table creation mode will fail.

 AlterOrCreate is disabled if the server is running in production mode. In general, the database tables generated will be a close approximation to the EJB's CMP fields and the EJB relationships defined in the deployment descriptors. For production environments, usually you will need to refine the database schema and provide a more precise schema definition.

WebLogic can validate whether the entity beans have been mapped correctly to the actual database schema during deployment. You can enable this validation by specifying a `validate-db-schema-with` element in the *weblogic-cmp-rdbms-jar.xml* descriptor file:

```
<weblogic-rdbms-jar>
```

```
<weblogic-rdbms-bean>
    <ejb-name>DepartmentEJB</ejb-name>
    ...
</weblogic-rdbms-bean>
...

<database-type>SQL_SERVER</database-type>
<validate-db-schema-with>TableQuery</validate-db-schema-with>
</weblogic-rdbms-jar>
```

You can specify two possible values for this setting:

MetaData

> This implies that the CMP runtime uses the JDBC metadata to validate the actual database schema.

TableQuery

> This means that the CMP runtime will query the database tables directly to determine whether they match the expected database schema.

If you don't want to rely on WebLogic's DBMS detection capability, make sure that you specify the database-type element when you enable automatic table creation or database schema validation.

Mapping CMP Fields Across Multiple DBMS Tables

Any entity bean in WebLogic can be partitioned across a number of tables. This means that you can store the different CMP and CMR fields of a single bean in several tables. You may want to do this for performance reasons, or simply because you need to support a legacy database schema. When using this feature, creating a new entity bean will result in a new row being inserted into each table to which the bean is mapped. Likewise, deleting a bean will delete a row from each table. The rows across the tables are correlated by their primary key values. This feature comes with a couple of sensible restrictions:

- Each table must contain the same primary key column data. The columns don't have to be identically named—they simply need to contain the same data to allow WebLogic to relate the rows.

- There should not be any referential integrity constraints on the primary keys involved in this mapping. If there are, bean deletion may be problematic.

To map the CMP fields to multiple database tables, simply include multiple table-map elements in the *weblogic-cmp-rdbms-jar.xml* descriptor file, one for each table involved, while ensuring that each table map includes the primary key column. Earlier, we saw in Example 11-5 how the CMP fields of the Department EJB were mapped to a single table. If you were to add an additional CMP field that mapped to a column in a separate table—say, tblHistory—you would modify the *weblogic-cmp-rdbms-jar.xml* descriptor file as described next.

```
<weblogic-rdbms-bean>
  <ejb-name>DepartmentEJB</ejb-name>
  <data-source-name>MyDataSource</data-source-name>
  <table-map>
    <table-name>tblDepartment</table-name>
    <field-map>
      <cmp-field>id</cmp-field>
      <dbms-column>Id</dbms-column>
    </field-map>
    <field-map>
      <cmp-field>name</cmp-field>
      <dbms-column>Name</dbms-column>
    </field-map>
  </table-map>
  <table-map>
    <table-name>tblHistory</table-name>
    <field-map>
      <cmp-field>id</cmp-field>          <!-- Primary key is necessary -->
      <dbms-column>Id</dbms-column>
    </field-map>
    <field-map>
      <cmp-field>history</cmp-field>     <!-- Here is the additional field -->
      <dbms-column>history</dbms-column>
    </field-map>
  </table-map>
</weblogic-rdbms-bean>
```

Adjusting the Insert Behavior

WebLogic lets you configure precisely when the EJB container inserts newly created
EJBs into the database. The delay-database-insert-element in the *weblogic-cmp-
rdbms-jar.xml* descriptor lets you adjust this setting. The default value for this setting is ejbPostCreate:

```
<delay-database-insert-until>ejbPostCreate</delay-database-insert-until>
```

This means that by default, WebLogic delays inserting the new bean until after the
call to the ejbPostCreate( ) method. If a CMR field is mapped to a foreign-key column, which doesn't allow null values, you must delay the actual database insert
until after the ejbPostCreate( ) method. In this way, you can initialize the CMR field
to a non-null value in the ejbPostCreate( ) method before the EJB instance is
inserted into the database, thereby avoiding a constraint exception. Remember, you
cannot initialize CMR fields in the ejbCreate( ) method before the primary key for
the entity bean is known. This setting generally yields better performance.

If you specify ejbCreate as the value for the delay-database-insert-until element,
WebLogic inserts the EJB immediately after the call to the ejbCreate( ) method. And
if you specify commit as the value for the previous setting, WebLogic performs a bulk
insert of EJBs when the transaction is committed. This improves the performance of
EJB creation because the EJB container then can execute a single batch command

that handles multiple database inserts for newly created EJB instances. In this case, the client must explicitly initiate a JTA transaction that wraps calls to multiple EJB create operations. The newly created EJB instances will be inserted only when the transaction completes successfully.

 WebLogic supports bulk inserts for entity beans only if the underlying JDBC driver also supports the addBatch( ) and executeBatch( ) methods on the JDBC Statement interface.

A client must ensure that a bulk insert does not create more EJBs than the max-beans-in-cache setting in the *weblogic-ejb-jar.xml* descriptor file.

Batch Operations

You often need to update multiple EJB instances of the same type within a transaction. For each update to an EJB instance, the EJB container needs to execute a corresponding database update. Clearly, this approach impedes performance when you need to update a large number of EJB instances because of the number of database trips that are involved. WebLogic lets you configure the EJB container to take advantage of JDBC 2.0 statement batching. By enabling batch operations, the EJB container is able to perform multiple database operations (inserts, updates, or deletes) using a single JDBC call, and can therefore limit the number of database trips to just one. The enable-batch-operations element within the *weblogic-cmp-rdbms-jar.xml* descriptor file toggles this behavior:

```
<enable-batch-operations>True</enable-batch-operations>
```

When batched operations are enabled, the EJB container delays all database updates on the EJB until the transaction is committed.

Delayed Existence Checking

By default, the EJB container in WebLogic 8.1 checks whether an entity EJB instance actually exists in the database before any EJB method call completes. If the EJB instance does not exist, it will notify the application with an exception. This is in keeping with the J2EE 1.3 standard. For instance, if a client gets the value of a CMP field and the entity bean no longer exists in the database, the EJB container will throw a NoSuchObjectException. (For local EJBs, it will throw a NoSuchLocalObjectException.)

For higher performance, you can instruct WebLogic to perform these checks only when a transaction commits. The check-exists-on-method element in the *weblogic-cmp-rdbms-jar.xml* descriptor file lets you enable this late checking:

```
<check-exists-on-method>False</check-exists-on-method>
```

Note that in WebLogic 7.0, the EJB container performs the late checking by default. You must explicitly enable this setting to force WebLogic 7.0 to perform strict checking for existence before an EJB method is invoked.

Optimistic Concurrency

In Chapter 10, we saw how the optimistic concurrency strategy ensures that no locks are held by the EJB container or the actual database. Instead, the EJB container does a "smart update" by ensuring that the data being modified hasn't changed since the start of the transaction. To configure optimistic concurrency for an entity bean, you need to use the concurrency-strategy element in the *weblogic-ejb-jar.xml* descriptor file:

```
<!-- weblogic-ejb-jar.xml entry -->
<entity-cache>
   <max-beans-in-cache>15</max-beans-in-cache>
   <concurrency-strategy>Optimistic</concurrency-strategy>
</entity-cache>
```

After this, you need to configure the EJB container so that it can check for data validity before it performs the updates. The verify-columns element in the *weblogic-cmp-rdbms-jar.xml* descriptor file lets you configure this checking:

```
<!-- weblogic-cmp-rdbms-jar.xml entry -->
<weblogic-rdbms-bean>
    <ejb-name>EmployeeEJB</ejb-name>
    <data-source-name>testds</data-source-name>
    <table-map>
        ...
        <verify-columns> ... </verify-columns>
    </table-map>
    ...
</weblogic-rdbms-bean>
```

You can specify one of the following values for the verify-columns element:

Read
> This implies that all database columns that have been read during the transaction are checked before the transaction is committed.

Modified
> This implies that only those columns that have been modified during the transaction are checked before the transaction is committed.

Version
> This implies that a version pseudocolumn exists in the table, and this column is used to determine whether database columns have been modified since the start of the transaction.

Timestamp

This implies that a `timestamp` pseudocolumn exists in the table, and this column is used to determine whether database columns have been modified since the start of the transaction.

If you choose either `Version` or `Timestamp` as the value for the setting, the database is responsible for keeping the version or timestamp columns in sync (typically via an update trigger). A `version` column should be an integer column whose value is incremented whenever a row is modified. A timestamp column should be set to the current system time whenever the row is modified. Finally, you need to designate a version or timestamp column that will be used to implement optimistic concurrency. For this, you should use the `optimistic-column` element in the *weblogic-cmp-rdbms-jar.xml* descriptor:

```
<table-map>
    ...
    <verify-columns>Timestamp</verify-columns>
    <optimistic-column>lastModified</optimistic-columns>
</table-map>
```

In this case, the EJB container uses the `lastModified` column in the underlying table to implement a timestamp-based optimistic concurrency strategy. Remember, if the EJB is mapped to multiple database tables, optimistic checking occurs only on those tables that are modified during the transaction.

In WebLogic 8.1, you can use the `verify-rows` element in the *weblogic-cmp-rdbms-jar.xml* descriptor to indicate which database rows are under the purview of optimistic checking:

```
<!-- weblogic-cmp-rdbms-jar.xml entry -->
<weblogic-rdbms-bean>
    <ejb-name>EmployeeEJB</ejb-name>
    <data-source-name>testds</data-source-name>
    <table-map>
        ...
        <verify-rows>Modified</verify-rows>
    </table-map>
    ...
</weblogic-rdbms-bean>
```

The default value for the `verify-rows` element is `Modified`—i.e., the EJB container checks only the rows that were updated or deleted during the transaction. If you set the `verify-rows` element to `Read`, the EJB container performs optimistic checks on *all* rows read during the transaction, regardless of whether they are updated later or deleted during the transaction. Clearly, this yields a higher level of data consistency, but at the cost of lower performance.

Clearly, if verify-rows is set to Read, verify-columns must not be set to Modified because otherwise, the EJB container will end up checking only the modified rows.

Field Groups and Finder Optimizations

The finders-load-bean element in the *weblogic-ejb-jar.xml* descriptor file determines whether the EJB fields are loaded eagerly or lazily. By default, this is set to true, which means that when a finder method is executed, the EJB container will eagerly load all of the EJB's data—the primary key as well as its CMP fields. This default strategy saves multiple round trips to the database if an application needs to access the EJBs returned by the finder method. However, if you set the finders-load-bean setting to false, the EJB instances returned by the finder method will not be loaded when it executes. Instead, the values of the CMP fields of the EJB will be loaded by the EJB container when a field is accessed by the application. Note that this behavior applies only to EJBs that are loaded explicitly by finder methods, or implicitly by navigating a CMR field.

Optimizing JDBC round trips by using eager loading is all very well, but what if this causes too much data to be transferred? For example, suppose the Department bean has a field containing a large amount of data—say, a "history" field. As an architect, you may know that the history field is used only rarely. In this case, the eager finder behavior may hurt performance. To compensate for this, you can use field groups.

A *field group* is a named subset of a bean's CMP and CMR fields. When a bean is loaded using a query or relationship that has been associated with a field group, only the fields specified in the field group are loaded. Example 11-6 shows a simple field group that contains only the identity and name CMP fields.

Example 11-6. A simple field group

```
<!-- weblogic-cmp-rdbms-jar.xml entry -->
<weblogic-rdbms-bean>
    <ejb-name>DepartmentEJB</ejb-name>
    <data-source-name>testds</data-source-name>
    ...
    <field-group>
        <group-name>noHistory</group-name>
        <cmp-field>id</cmp-field>
        <cmp-field>name</cmp-field>
    </field-group>
    ...
</weblogic-rdbms-bean>
```

If a field group is not specified, a special default field group is used that ensures that all of the bean's fields are loaded.

Once you have established a field group, simply associate it with a finder method to ensure that the finder loads only the desired EJB fields:

```
<weblogic-query>
  <query-method>
    <method-name>finderNoHistory</method-name>
    <method-params/>
  </query-method>
  <weblogic-ql>
    <![CDATA[SELECT OBJECT(o) from tblDepartment as o orderby o.id]]>
  </weblogic-ql>
  <group-name>noHistory</group-name>
</weblogic-query>
```

A CMP field may belong to multiple field groups, and the EJB may define many finder methods, each referring to a different field group. Because of these optimizations, you can implement precise control over how much data is loaded, as well as when it is loaded. Field groups also are used in optimizing relationship caching, discussed later.

Container-Managed Relationships

Container-managed EJB persistence lets you separate the entity beans from the actual data stored in the underlying database. The XML deployment descriptors allow you to map the abstract persistence model to the underlying database schema. In CMP 2.0 persistence, you also can let the EJB container handle relationships between entity beans. WebLogic's EJB container supports associations that can be navigated in either direction (bidirectional), or perhaps restricted to one direction (unidirectional).

A CMR field (or a relationship field) is defined between local interfaces of entity beans. If a bean is involved in a relationship, the bean may be aware of EJB instances at the other end. Thus, if you have defined CMR fields for EJBs at both "ends" of the relationship, the association between the two entity beans can be navigated in either direction. Typically, unidirectional associations are modeled with remote entity beans—i.e., when the entity bean does not reside in the same EJB JAR as the entity beans related to it. However, a bidirectional association may be defined only when both entity beans are packaged in the same EJB JAR. This means that you must use the same XML deployment descriptors to define their abstract persistence schema.

WebLogic's persistence framework supports one-to-one, one-to-many, and many-to-many associations. Suppose you've defined an association between two entity beans, A and B. The *ejb-jar.xml* descriptor file then will define the multiplicity and CMR fields for both ends (roles) of the EJB relationship. When you set the multiplicity for entity bean A to One, the type of the CMR field at B's end is implicitly the local interface of A. When you set the multiplicity for entity bean B to Many, the CMR field at A's end must be of type java.util.Collection (or java.util.Set if you want to ensure that duplicate EJB instances of B can never participate in the association).

Remember, CMR fields enable you to navigate an association from either end. You need to define CMR fields at both ends only if you want to ensure that EJB instances at both ends of the association are aware of each other.

Let's look at how you would define the underlying database schema for EJB relationships, and configure them using the *weblogic-cmp-rdbms-jar.xml* descriptor file.

One-to-One Association

In a one-to-one association between entity beans, you physically need to map the foreign key column from one EJB to the primary key column in the other EJB. For instance, if we were to store the login credentials for each employee separately, we could model a one-to-one relationship between the Employee and Login entity beans. The underlying database schema might look something like this:

```
create table tblLogin {
    id int(4) constraint pk_tblLogin primary key,
    username varchar2(15),
    password varchar2(15),
    lastlogin date
};
```

In order to accommodate the association between Employee and Login EJBs, a foreign key column userid will be added to tblEmployee:

```
create table tblEmployee (
    id number(4) constraint pk_tblEmployee primary key,
    lastname varchar2(30),
    ...
    userid number(4) constraint fk_userid references tblLogin(id)
);
```

Example 11-7 shows how you would define the one-to-one association between the two entity EJBs.

Example 11-7. WebLogic-specific settings for a one-to-one association

```
<!-- weblogic-cmp-rdbms-jar.xml entry -->
<weblogic-rdbms-bean>
    <ejb-name>LoginEJB</ejb-name>
    <data-source-name>myDS</data-source-name>
    <table-map>
        <table-name>tblLogin</table-name>
        <!-- primary key field for Login -->
        <field-map>
            <cmp-field>username</cmp-field>
            <dbms-column>username</dbms-column>
        </field-map>
        <!-- other cmp fields for Login EJB -->
    </table-map>
```

Example 11-7. WebLogic-specific settings for a one-to-one association (continued)

```
</weblogic-rdbms-bean>
<weblogic-rdbms-relation>
    <relation-name>Employee-Login</relation-name>
    <weblogic-relationship-role>
        <relationship-role-name>
            Login-for-an-Employee
        </relationship-role-name>
        <relationship-role-map>
            <column-map>
                <foreign-key-column>userid</foreign-key-column>
                <key-column>id</key-column>
            </column-map>
        </relationship-role-map>
    </weblogic-relationship-role>
</weblogic-rdbms-relation>
```

Here, the relationship-role-map element maps the foreign key column tblEmployee. userid to the key column associated with the Login EJB's primary key field id. Remember, if the bean on the foreign-key side is mapped to multiple tables, you should use the foreign-key-table subelement to specify the name of the table that holds the foreign key. Similarly, if the bean on the primary-key side is mapped to multiple tables, you should use the primary-key-table subelement to specify the name of the table that holds the primary key.

To express EJB relationships using EJBGen, you need to annotate your code using the ejbgen:relation tag. The following defines a one-to-one relationship between the Employee EJB and the Login EJB:

```
/**
 * @ejbgen:entity prim-key-class="java.lang.Integer"
 *    ejb-name="Employee"
 *    data-source-name = "MyDataSource"
 *    table-name="tblEmployee"
 * @ejbgen:relation role-name="Employee-has-Login" fk-column="userid"
 *                  cmr-field="login" target-ejb="Login"
 *                  multiplicity="One" name="Employee-Login"
 */
public abstract class EmployeeEJB extends GenericEntityBean implements EntityBean {
    /**
     * @ejbgen:cmr-field
     * @ejbgen:local-method
     */
    public abstract LoginLocal getLogin();

    /**
     * @ejbgen:local-method
     */
    public abstract void setLogin(LoginLocal arg);

    // other methods
}
```

Similarly, the Login EJB can be defined as follows:

```
/**
 * @ejbgen:entity prim-key-class="java.lang.Integer"
 *     ejb-name="Login"
 *     data-source-name = "MyDataSource"
 *     table-name="tblLogin"
 * @ejbgen:relation role-name="Login-has-Employee" cmr-field="employee"
 *                  target-ejb="Employee" multiplicity="One" name="Employee-Login"
 */
public abstract class LoginEJB extends GenericEntityBean implements EntityBean {
    /**
     * @ejbgen:cmr-field
     * @ejbgen:local-method
     */
    public abstract EmployeeLocal getEmployee();

    /**
     * @ejbgen:local-method
     */
    public abstract void setEmployee(EmployeeLocal arg);

    // other methods
}
```

Note that both classes have the multiplicity attributes set to one, and that the only difference between the two is that the Employee EJB contains the foreign-key definition.

One-to-Many Association

In a one-to-many association between entity beans, you physically need to map the foreign key column from one EJB to the primary key column of the other. The associating foreign key always is taken from the Many side of the EJB relationship—WebLogic does not permit you to create such an association using a third, intermediate, table. Let's consider a one-to-many association between a Department and Employee EJB, mapping a foreign key column deptid in tblEmployee (Many) to the primary key column id in tblDepartment (One).

In this relationship, each Department EJB owns a collection-based relationship field that holds references to multiple Employee EJBs, and each Employee EJB in turn holds a reference back to the aggregating Department EJB. We need to ensure that all Employee EJBs associated with the each Department EJB instance are unique. Thus, the Department EJB exposes a CMR field whose type is the collection interface java.util.Set.

The ejb-relation element in the *ejb-jar.xml* descriptor file lets you configure this association between the two entity EJBs. Example 11-8 shows how to define the one-to-many association between Department and Employee EJBs.

Example 11-8. The one-to-many bidirectional association

```
<!-- ejb-jar.xml entry -->
<enterprise-beans>
    <entity>
        <ejb-name>EmployeeEJB</ejb-name>
        <local-home>com.oreilly.ejbs.EmployeeHome</local-home>
        ...
    </entity>
    <entity>
        <ejb-name>DepartmentEJB</ejb-name>
        <local-home>com.oreilly.ejbs.DepartmentHome</local-home>
        ...
    </entity>
</enterprise-beans>
<relationships>
    <ejb-relation>
        <ejb-relation-name>Department-Employee</ejb-relation-name>
        <ejb-relationship-role>
            <ejb-relationship-role-name>
                Department-has-many-Employees
            </ejb-relationship-role-name>
            <multiplicity>One</multiplicity>
            <relationship-role-source>
                <ejb-name>DepartmentEJB</ejb-name>
            </relationship-role-source>
            <cmr-field>
                <cmr-field-name>employees</cmr-field-name>
                <cmr-field-type>java.util.Set</cmr-field-type>
            </cmr-field>
        </ejb-relationship-role>
        <ejb-relationship-role>
            <ejb-relationship-role-name>
                Employee-belongs-to-Department
            </ejb-relationship-role-name>
            <multiplicity>Many</multiplicity>
            <relationship-role-source>
                <ejb-name>EmployeeEJB</ejb-name>
            </relationship-role-source>
            <cmr-field>
                <cmr-field-name>department</cmr-field-name>
            </cmr-field>
        </ejb-relationship-role>
    </ejb-relation>
</relationships>
```

The ejb-relationship-role element lets you define metadata for each end of the association. At the Department end, we have set the multiplicity to One and declared a CMR field employees, whose type is java.util.Set. At the Employee end, we have set the multiplicity to Many and defined a CMR field department, whose type is implicitly com.oreilly.ejbs.Department.

The weblogic-rdbms-relation element in the *weblogic-cmp-rdbms-jar.xml* descriptor file lets you specify the table schema corresponding to all EJB relationships defined in the *ejb-jar.xml* descriptor. In this case, the foreign key column tblEmployee.deptid (on the "many" side) is associated with the primary key column tblDepartment.id (on the "one" side):

```
<!-- weblogic-cmp-rdbms-jar.xml entry -->
<weblogic-rdbms-relation>
    <relation-name>Department-Employee</relation-name>
    <weblogic-relationship-role>
        <relationship-role-name>
            Employee-belongs-to-Department
        </relationship-role-name>
        <relationship-role-map>
            <column-map>
                <foreign-key-column>deptid</foreign-key-column>
                <key-column>id</key-column>
            </column-map>
        </relationship-role-map>
    </weblogic-relationship-role>
</weblogic-rdbms-relation>
```

Here are the EJBGen-annotated EJBs that can create these mapping files. The Department EJB is quite straightforward. Note how the CMR field for the employees is defined in terms of a java.util.Set:

```
/**
 * @ejbgen:entity prim-key-class="java.lang.String"
 *    ejb-name = "Department"
 *    data-source-name = "MyDataSource"
 *    table-name = "tblDepartment"
 *
 * @ejbgen:relation role-name="Department-has-Employees" cmr-field="employees"
 *                  target-ejb="Employee" multiplicity="One"
 *                  name="Department-Employee"
 */
abstract public class DepartmentEJB extends GenericEntityBean implements EntityBean {
    /**
     * @ejbgen:cmr-field
     * @ejbgen:local-method
     */
    public abstract java.util.Set getEmployees( );

    /**
     * @ejbgen:local-method
     */
    public abstract void setEmployees(java.util.Set arg);

    // other methods
}
```

The Employee EJB source code will look similar to this:

```
/**
```

```
 * @ejbgen:entity prim-key-class="java.lang.Integer"
 *    ejb-name="Employee"
 *    data-source-name = "MyDataSource"
 *    table-name="tblEmployee"
 *
 * @ejbgen:relation role-name="Employees-have-Department"
 *                  fk-column="Department_DepartmentID" cmr-field="department"
 *                  target-ejb="Department"  multiplicity="Many"
 *                  name="Department-Employee"
 */
public abstract class EmployeeEJB extends GenericEntityBean implements EntityBean {
    /**
     * @ejbgen:cmr-field
     * @ejbgen:local-method
     */
    public abstract DepartmentLocal getDepartment();

    /**
     * @ejbgen:local-method
     */
    public abstract void setDepartment(DepartmentLocal arg);

    // other methods
}
```

Note how the CMR field is defined in terms of the local interface for the Department EJB.

Many-to-Many Association

In order to model a many-to-many relationship between EJBs, you physically need to map the association to a *join table*. In a join table, each row consists of two foreign keys, in which each foreign key maps to the primary keys of the entities involved in the relationship. For instance, suppose we need to model a concept of roles—i.e., each employee can assume multiple roles while she's working for company XYZ. Of course, we also may have multiple employees that can assume the same role at any given time. The SQL table corresponding to the Role entity EJB could be similar to this:

```
create table tblRole {
    id int(2) constraint pk_tblRole primary key,
    name varchar2(15),
    description varchar2(100),
};
```

In this scenario, we need to be able to model a many-to-many association between the two entity EJBs, Employee and Role.

An easy way to implement this relationship is through a join table tblRoleMembers, in which each row of the table holds two foreign keys, one that maps to tblEmployee and another that maps to tblRole.

```
create table tblRoleMembers (
  roleid number(4) constraint fk_roleid references tblRole(id),
  empid number(2) constraint fk_empid references tblEmployee(id)
);
```

Example 11-9 describes the EJB relationship in terms of the join table we just defined.

Example 11-9. WebLogic-specific settings for a many-to-many association

```
<!-- weblogic-cmp-rdbms-jar.xml entry -->
<weblogic-rdbms-relation>
    <relation-name>Employee-Role</relation-name>
    <table-name>tblRoleMembers<table-name>
    <weblogic-relationship-role>
        <relationship-role-name>
            Roles-have-Employees
        </relationship-role-name>
        <relationship-role-map>
            <column-map>
                <foreign-key-column>roleid</foreign-key-column>
                <key-column>id</key-column>
            </column-map>
        </relationship-role-map>
    </weblogic-relationship-role>
    <weblogic-relationship-role>
        <relationship-role-name>
            Employees-have-Roles
        </relationship-role-name>
        <relationship-role-map>
            <column-map>
                <foreign-key-column>empid</foreign-key-column>
                <key-column>id</key-column>
            </column-map>
        </relationship-role-map>
    </weblogic-relationship-role>
</weblogic-rdbms-relation>
```

Here, we see that the table-name subelement specifies the name of the join table. For each role involved in the EJB relationship, we define a weblogic-relationship-role element that maps a foreign key column to the primary key column of the EJB that occupies that end of the association. If this many-to-many association were bidirectional, we need to define CMR fields at both ends of the EJB relationship of type java.util.Collection, or of type java.util.Set if duplicate EJB instances must not be associated with the other EJB instance. For example, here are the EJBGen annotations for the Employee EJB:

```
/**
 * @ejbgen:entity prim-key-class="java.lang.Integer"
 *   ejb-name="Employee"
 *   data-source-name = "MyDataSource"
 *   table-name="tblEmployee"
 * @ejbgen:relation role-name="Employees-have-Roles"
```

```
 *                       fk-column="roleid" joint-table="tblRoleMembers "
 *                       cmr-field="roles" target-ejb="Role" multiplicity="Many"
 *                       name="Employee-Role"
 */
public abstract class Employee extends GenericEntityBean implements EntityBean
    /**
     * @ejbgen:cmr-field
     * @ejbgen:local-method
     */
    public abstract java.util.Set getRoles( );

    /**
     * @ejbgen:local-method
     */
    public abstract void setRoles(java.util.Set arg);

    // other methods
}
```

The Role EJB is similar:

```
/**
 * @ejbgen:entity prim-key-class="java.lang.Integer"
 *    ejb-name = "Role"
 *    data-source-name = "MyDataSource"
 *    table-name = "tblRole"
 * @ejbgen:relation role-name="Roles-have-Employees"
 *                       fk-column="empid" joint-table="tblRoleMembers "
 *                       cmr-field="employee" target-ejb="Employee" multiplicity="Many"
 *                       name="Employee-Role"
 */
abstract public class Role extends GenericEntityBean implements EntityBean {
    /**
     * @ejbgen:cmr-field
     * @ejbgen:local-method
     */
    public abstract java.util.Set getEmployee( );

    /**
     * @ejbgen:local-method
     */
    public abstract void setEmployee(java.util.Set arg);

    // other methods
}
```

Cascade Delete

Usually, when an entity EJB instance is removed, the EJB container automatically
purges its associations with other entity EJB instances. Sometimes, you want to
ensure that all EJB instances that are related to an entity EJB instance also are deleted
when the entity EJB is removed. That is, when an entity EJB is removed, the delete
operation should be cascaded to all related entity EJB instances. The *ejb-jar.xml*

descriptor file allows you to specify a `cascade-delete` element on one of the roles involved in the EJB relationship. For instance, given an association between two entity beans, A and B, if you specify `cascade-delete` at B's end of the EJB relationship, all related instances of B are deleted when an instance of A is removed.

However, cascade deletes may be enabled only for one-to-one or one-to-many associations. So, if A's end of an EJB relationship has multiplicity One, you may then specify `cascade-delete` at B's end of the association. Thus, the entity bean that triggers the cascade delete must have a multiplicity of One in the EJB relationship. In addition, the cascade-delete element affects only the EJB relationship in which it is defined, and has no effect on other EJB relationships. For instance, if you've enabled cascade delete on the association between EJBs A and B, but not on the association between EJBs A and C, only related instances of B will be removed when an instance of A is removed. All related instances of C still will remain; only their associations with the instance of A will be deleted.

Consider the situation in which all employees are fired when a Department is scrapped. We would like to automatically remove all related Employee EJB instances when a Department EJB instance is removed. The following XML fragment shows how you can configure the EJB container to automatically cascade a delete operation on any Department EJB instance:

```
<!-- ejb-jar.xml entry -->
<ejb-relation>
    <ejb-relation-name>Department-Employee</ejb-relation-name>
    <ejb-relationship-role>
        <ejb-relationship-role-name>
            Department-has-many-Employees
        </ejb-relationship-role-name>
        <multiplicity>One</multiplicity>
        ...
    </ejb-relationship-role>
    <ejb-relationship-role>
        <ejb-relationship-role-name>
            Employee-belongs-to-Department
        </ejb-relationship-role-name>
        <multiplicity>Many</multiplicity>
        <cascade-delete/>
        ...
    </ejb-relationship-role>
</ejb-relation>
```

WebLogic can improve the performance of cascade deletes by making the EJB container rely on the underlying database support for cascade deletes. When you specify a db-cascade-delete element in the *weblogic-cmp-rdbms-jar.xml* descriptor file, WebLogic's EJB container will implicitly use the cascade delete features of the underlying DBMS. By default, this feature is disabled, and the EJB container issues SQL DELETE commands when it needs to remove related EJB instances.

The following XML stanza shows how to configure database-driven cascade deletes for the Department EJB:

```
<!-- weblogic-cmp-rdbms-jar.xml entry -->
<weblogic-rdbms-relation>
    <relation-name>Department-Employee</relation-name>
    <weblogic-relationship-role>
        <relationship-role-name>
            Employee-belongs-to-Department
        </relationship-role-name>
        <relationship-role-map>
            <column-map>
                <foreign-key-column>deptid</foreign-key-column>
                <key-column>id</key-column>
            </column-map>
        </relationship-role-map>
        <db-cascade-delete/>
    </weblogic-relationship-role>
</weblogic-rdbms-relation>
```

You also need to modify the table schema in order to use database cascade deletes. In this instance, we have modified the foreign key constraint in tblEmployee so that any related rows in tblEmployee are deleted automatically when the parent row in tblDepartment is deleted:

```
create table tblEmployee (
  id number(4) constraint pk_tblEmployee primary key,
  ...
  deptid number(2) constraint
    fk_deptid references tblDepartment(id) on delete cascade
);

create table tblDepartment {
  id number(2) constraint pk_tblDepartment primary key,
  name varchar2(40),
};
```

Typically you will need to enforce cascade deletes when the association demands that the EJB instance "own" all related EJB instances—i.e., the lifetime of all related EJBs is bound by the lifetime of the aggregating bean. If the related EJB instances can be shared by multiple EJB instances or can survive without necessarily being associated with an EJB, you should not enable cascade deletes.

Use cascade deletes with great caution, because a single EJB remove could trigger a chain reaction. If you've configured your EJBs so that a delete on EJB A cascades to B, and a delete on EJB B cascades to C, then removing an instance of A will automatically remove all related instances of B and instances of C that are linked to those instances of B. The deletes will cascade through the associations to related EJB instances.

Avoiding deadlocks

Transactions that use EJB instances configured for exclusive concurrency sometimes can create a deadlock situation. For instance, in order to complete a cascade delete operation, a transaction may need access to an EJB instance locked by another transaction. A typical deadlock situation arises when a transaction holds a lock on an EJB that is required by another transaction, and vice versa. In fact, two transactions, T1 and T2, that need to operate upon (say) two EJB instances, E1 and E2, will be deadlocked if both of the following conditions hold simultaneously:

- T1 locks E1 and is waiting to lock E2.
- T2 locks E2 and is waiting to lock E1.

WebLogic lets you avoid this deadlock situation by setting a lock-order for the EJBs involved. In this case, whenever the two EJBs are involved in the same transaction, they are locked according to their lock-order value.

So, if you set the lock-order for E1 to 1, and the lock-order for E2 to 2, any transaction in which both EJB instances are involved locks E1 before E2. In this way, the EJB container can reduce the chance of deadlocks between transactions.

 The lock-order setting works only with the exclusive concurrency option, in a transactional scenario in which cascade delete operations are being used.

The following portion from the *weblogic-cmp-rdbms-jar.xml* descriptor shows how to set the lock order for entity EJBs:

```
<weblogic-rdbms-bean>
     <ejb-name>DepartmentEJB</ejb-name>
     <data-source-name>testds</data-source-name>
     <!-- table schema for the Department EJB -->
     <lock-order>1</lock-order>
</weblogic-rdbms-bean>
<weblogic-rdbms-bean>
     <ejb-name>EmployeeEJB</ejb-name>
     <data-source-name>testds</data-source-name>
     <!-- table schema for the Employee EJB -->
     <lock-order>2</lock-order>
</weblogic-rdbms-bean>
```

Assuming that both the Department and Employee EJBs are configured for exclusive concurrency, this means that transactions, which require a delete operation on a Department EJB instance to cascade to all related Employee EJB instances, will not deadlock with each other.

Caching EJB Relationships

In certain situations, it is more optimal to load related entity beans into the cache when a query method is executed so that later you can avoid multiple queries to retrieve related EJBs. The relationship-caching element in the *weblogic-cmp-rdbms-jar.xml* descriptor file allows the EJB container to eagerly load related EJB instances when a query method is executed. The following XML fragment illustrates how we can configure caching for EJB relationships:

```
<!-- weblogic-cmp-rdbms-jar.xml entry -->
<weblogic-rdbms-bean>
    <ejb-name>EmployeeEJB</ejb-name>
    <data-source-name>testds</data-source-name>
    ...
    <relationship-caching>
        <caching-name>cacheDept</caching-name>
        <caching-element>
            <cmr-field>department</cmr-field>
            <group-name>noHistory</group-name>
        </caching-element>
    </relationship-caching>
    ...
</weblogic-rdbms-bean>
```

Here, the caching-element tag instructs WebLogic to automatically load the related Department EJB when an Employee EJB is found. The caching-name element identifies the caching rule that we've defined. This element is important because it means that subsequent query methods can determine which of the caching rules WebLogic should apply. The cmr-field tag identifies the one-to-many relationship between the two EJBs, in this case from the Employee end.

The group-name element indicates that we would like to initialize only a subset of the CMP fields in the Department EJB when it's loaded. In this example, we are referring to the field group defined earlier in Example 11-7. If you don't specify the name of a field group in the caching-element tag, WebLogic uses the default field group that automatically initializes all CMP fields of the Department EJB when it is loaded. Now that you've set up how WebLogic should cache the EJB relationship, you can define a find method that utilizes this caching feature:

```
<!-- weblogic-cmp-rdbms-jar.xml entry -->
<weblogic-rdbms-bean>
    <ejb-name>EmployeeEJB</ejb-name>
    ...
    <weblogic-query>
        <query-method>
            <method-name>findByName</method-name>
            <method-params>
                <method-param>java.lang.String</method-param>
                <method-param>java.lang.String</method-param>
            </method-params>
        </query-method>
```

```
    <weblogic-ql>
        <![CDATA[
select object(e) from EmployeeEJB e where e.firstName = ?1 and e.lastName=?2
        ]]>
    </weblogic-ql>
    <caching-name>cacheDept</caching-name>
    <max-elements>10</max-elements>
    <include-updates>True</include-updates>
    <sql-select-distinct>True</sql-select-distinct>
    </weblogic-query>
    ...
</weblogic-rdbms-bean>
```

The caching-name subelement within the weblogic-query tag identifies the name of the relationship cache defined earlier. When a client invokes the findByName( ) query method on the Employee EJB home object, WebLogic will load the related Department EJB into the cache for all Employee EJBs returned by the find method. This load is quite optimal, as it is implemented under the hood using simple SQL join queries. In addition, it will initialize only the specified subset of CMP fields in the related Department EJB.

WebLogic also allows you to specify multiple levels of relationship caching. By nesting one caching-element tag within another, you can instruct WebLogic to load more than one level of related beans. The following XML stanza shows how to configure WebLogic to load the related Department EJB, and in turn all related Employee EJBs for that Department EJB:

```
<relationship-caching>
    <caching-name>cacheDept</caching-name>
        <caching-element>
        <cmr-field>department</cmr-field>
        <group-name>deptgroup</group-name>
        <caching-element>
            <cmr-field>employees</cmr-field>
            <group-name>empgroup</group-name>
        </caching-element>
        </caching-element>
    </caching-element>
</relationship-caching>
```

Here, department is a CMR field in the Employee EJB, and employees is a CMR field defined in the Department EJB. In general, too many levels of nesting for the cache-element tags will degrade the performance of your application. When you enable caching for EJB relationships, you also should be aware of certain key issues:

- You can configure relationship caching only for one-to-one and one-to-many relationships. Also, the feature works only for query methods that return instances of EJBObject or EJBLocalObject.

- You must ensure the finders-load-bean element in the *weblogic-ejb-jar.xml* descriptor isn't set to false.

- If you don't want to utilize WebLogic's DBMS detection capability, make sure that you specify the database-type element in the *weblogic-cmp-rdbms-jar.xml* descriptor. For example:

  ```
  <database-type>ORACLE</database-type>
  ```

  WebLogic maps relationship caching to outer joins in the underlying database. It needs the database-type element to determine the exact syntax for the join queries.

- A find or select query that is configured to cache related EJBs always will return a distinct set of results, even if the DISTINCT qualifier hasn't been used.

Clearly, WebLogic provides powerful support for caching EJB relationships, which allows you to optimize the performance of your EJB query methods.

EJB QL

EJB QL is the standard query language for defining the behavior of custom find and select methods. The EJB QL syntax is portable across databases, database schemas, and EJB containers because it is based on the abstract persistence schema defined for the entity beans and not the underlying data store. This allows you to specify the behavior of the query methods in an abstract, portable way. For each query method available to the entity bean, you must define a matching EJB QL statement that determines its runtime behavior.

WebLogic provides a number of extensions to the standard EJB QL. Some of these extensions also will be available in a future release of the EJB specification.

Using WebLogic Extensions to EJB QL

When using traditional EJB QL, you specify the EJB QL statement for each query method in the *ejb-jar.xml* descriptor file. However, if you intend to use any of the WebLogic extensions to EJB QL syntax, you also should define a weblogic-ql element in the *weblogic-cmp-rdbms-jar.xml* descriptor file. For instance, if you need to use the ORDERBY clause in your EJB QL statement, you must specify the EJB QL statement in the *weblogic-cmp-rdbms-jar.xml* file:

```
<!-- weblogic-cmp-rdbms-jar.xml entry -->
<weblogic-rdbms-bean>
    <ejb-name>EmployeeEJB</ejb-name>
    ...
    <weblogic-query>
        <query-method>
            <method-name>findByLastName</method-name>
            <method-params>
                <method-param>java.lang.String</method-param>
            </method-params>
        </query-method>
        <weblogic-ql>
            <![CDATA[
```

```
        select object(e) from EmployeeEJB e where
        e.lastName = ?1 orderby e.firstName
            ]]>
        </weblogic-ql>
        <max-elements>10</max-elements>
        <include-updates>True</include-updates>
        <sql-select-distinct>True</sql-select-distinct>
      </weblogic-query>
    </weblogic-rdbms-bean>
```

In this case, the findByLastName( ) method returns a list of Employee EJBs with matching last names, and in alphabetical order by their first names. The ORDERBY clause actually defers all sorting to the underlying DBMS; this means the order in which the results are returned depends on the actual database. As a result, the EJB no longer will be completely portable—the results of the find will be dependent on the DBMS to which it is deployed. Like the SQL ORDER BY clause, you can sort on multiple CMP fields, each in either ascending or descending order. Notice how we've configured additional properties for the query method:

- The max-elements element specifies the maximum number of EJB instances that will be returned by the find method. It resembles the setMaxRows( ) method on the JDBC Statement interface.

- The include-updates element lets you specify whether any updates made during the current transaction ought to be manifested in the results returned by the query. If you enable this option, the container flushes all changes for the cached transactions to the database before executing the find query. In WebLogic 8.1, this element is set to true by default, in order to maintain compliance with the J2EE 1.3 standard. In WebLogic 7.0, this option is set to false by default. Setting it to false yields the best performance. In this case, updates made by cached transactions are not reflected in the results of the query because the changes have not been written to the database yet.

- The sql-select-distinct* tag ensures that the database query generated from the EJB QL statement will include a DISTINCT qualifier automatically and thus return unique rows. If you enable this option, the find methods for the entity bean automatically will filter out any duplicate EJB instances. Once again, the EJB container defers the task of filtering out duplicated results to the underlying database.

Similarly, if the query method relies on other WebLogic extensions to the EJB QL syntax (such as aggregate functions or subqueries), you also should define them in the *weblogic-cmp-rdbms-jar.xml* descriptor—that is, until a future release of the EJB specification incorporates them into the standard.

---

* This element is deprecated in WebLogic 8.1. Instead, you should use the DISTINCT qualifier in the query itself.

Returning a ResultSet

In WebLogic, you can implement select methods that return the values of multiple CMP fields, in the form of a JDBC ResultSet. Just like SQL, WebLogic's QL extends the standard syntax by letting you specify a comma-separated list of CMP fields in the SELECT query. For instance, you could implement a select method that returns the first and last names of all employees in a department:

```
select e.firstName, e.lastName from DepartmentEJB d, in(d.employees) e
where d.id=?1
```

In this case, the corresponding select method would return a collection in the form of a java.sql.ResultSet:

```
public abstract class DepartmentBean implements javax.ejb.EntityBean {
  ...
  public abstract java.sql.ResultSet ejbSelectEmployeeNames()
    throws FinderException;
  ...
}
```

However, if a select method returns a ResultSet, the corresponding query may only return values of CMP fields or aggregates of CMP fields. It cannot return an EJB instance or a collection of EJB instances. For instance, the ejbSelectAll() method defined earlier for the Department EJB cannot return a ResultSet:

```
<!-- ejb-jar.xml fragment -->
<ejb-ql>
   select object(d) from DepartmentEJB d
</ejb-ql>

//disallowed: select method must return either Department, or a collection-type
public abstract java.sql.ResultSet ejbSelectAll() throws FinderException;
```

The select method ejbSelectAvgSalaries(), which returns the average salaries for all departments in company XYZ, could return a ResultSet:

```
select d.name, avg(e.salary) from DepartmentEJB d, in(d.employees) e
group by d.name orderby 2 desc
```

The ORDERBY 2 clause implies that the results should be sorted on the second field in the SELECT list. In other words, the list is returned in descending order of average department salaries.

Executing Dynamic Queries

The EJB specification forces all find and select methods to be declared statically for an entity bean in its XML deployment descriptors. WebLogic lets you construct EJB QL statements dynamically in your application code, and then execute these queries at runtime without having to redeploy the EJB JAR. You can enable dynamic EJB QL queries for an entity bean using the enable-dynamic-queries element in the *weblogic-ejb-jar.xml* descriptor file.

```
<!-- weblogic-ejb-jar.xml portion -->
<weblogic-enterprise-bean>
    <ejb-name>EmployeeEJB</ejb-name>
    <entity-descriptor>
        ...
        <enable-dynamic-queries>True</enable-dynamic-queries>
    </entity-descriptor>
    <local-jndi-name>EmployeeHome</local-jndi-name>
</weblogic-enterprise-bean>
```

This element ensures that the generated container class corresponding to the EJB's home interface also implements the weblogic.ejb.QueryLocalHome interface (or the QueryHome interface, if it is a remote entity bean).

Once you've compiled the EJB classes and redeployed the EJB JAR, you then can use the weblogic.ejb.Query interface to execute EJB QL statements. The following code fragment shows how you can dynamically create and then execute a custom find query:

```
Context ctx = new InitialContext( );
EmployeeHome home = (EmployeeHome) ctx.lookup("EmployeeHome");

//get all Employee(s) whose lastname is "Mountjoy"
QueryLocalHome qh = (QueryLocalHome) home;
Query query = qh.createQuery( );
query.setMaxElements(10);
Collection results = query.find(
  "select object(e) from EmployeeEJB e where e.lastName='Mountjoy'");

Employee e = null;
for (Iterator i=results.iterator( ); i.hasNext( ); ) {
  e = (Employee) i.next( );
  //process results any way you like
}
```

For a remote entity bean, you would look up the JNDI name for the remote bean, and use the weblogic.ejb.QueryHome interface instead. The Query interface allows you to assign properties that customize the behavior of the query:

- The setMaxElements( ) method sets the maximum number of results returned by the EJB query. By default, the EJB query will return all results that are matched.

- The setTransaction( ) method lets you specify the transaction setting for the EJB query. You can specify one of the following transaction settings for an EJB query: TX_REQUIRED, TX_REQUIRES_NEW, and TX_MANDATORY. These constants have the same meaning as the transaction attributes that can be applied to the methods of an EJB that supports container-managed transactions. For instance, the TX_REQUIRES_NEW constant implies that the EJB query will be executed in its own transaction context.

- The setIncludeUpdates( ) method lets you specify whether the EJB container should flush the changes of all cached transactions to the database before executing the query. By default, the changes of any cached transactions are not reflected in the results of the query.

- The setResultTypeRemote( ) method lets you specify whether the EJB query returns remote EJB instances.

The find( ) method suffers from the same limitations as any find EJB query. So, if you need to be able to create and execute a select method dynamically, you should use the execute( ) method. The execute( ) method returns a JDBC ResultSet, so you cannot execute an EJB query that returns just an EJB instance, or a collection of EJB instances. The following example shows how to dynamically execute an EJB query that returns the average salaries for all departments in company XYZ:

```
Context ctx = new InitialContext( );
EmployeeHome home = (EmployeeHome) ctx.lookup("EmployeeHome");

//get average salaries for all departments
QueryLocalHome qh = (QueryLocalHome) home;
Query query = qh.createQuery( );
query.setMaxElements(10);
ResultSet results = query.execute("select d.name, avg(e.salary)
    from DepartmentEJB d, in(d.employees) e group by d.name orderby 2 desc");

while (rs.next( )) {
  System.out.println("Name: " + rs.getString(1));
  System.out.println("Avg. Salary: " + rs.getDouble(2));
}
```

As with select methods, you can access the abstract persistence schema for other entity beans in the EJB JAR, and also return multiple CMP fields in the SELECT clause.

 You *cannot* dynamically execute a query that accepts input parameters. WebLogic doesn't provide a mechanism for supplying input values to parameters expected by a query.

Some purists may not like the idea of using EJB queries that return JDBC result sets because one of the goals of automatic EJB persistence is to minimize JDBC code in your applications. Nevertheless, it is important that you can build EJB queries where you can specify multiple CMP fields in your SELECT clause. In that case, the ResultSet is a convenient container for the collection of results returned by the EJB query.

WebLogic's EJB QL Extensions

Now we will examine various EJB queries that illustrate WebLogic's extensions to the EJB QL syntax. While discussing EJB QL, we'll continue to use examples from the Department-Employee scenario.

WebLogic lets you apply aggregate functions over a CMP field. Aggregate functions work like their SQL counterparts—these functions are evaluated over the entire range of EJB instances that match the WHERE clause. The following query returns the maximum and minimum salaries for any employee in a specific department:

```
select max(e.salary), min(e.salary) from DepartmentEJB d, in(d.employees) e
where d.id=?1
```

Aggregate functions may apply only to targets in the SELECT clause, and cannot appear in the WHERE clause. Other aggregate functions that can be used include SUM, COUNT, and AVG. The next query returns the average salaries for all departments in the company:

```
select d.name, avg(e.salary) from DepartmentEJB d, in(d.employees) e
group by d.name orderby 2 desc
```

We've already seen how WebLogic's ORDERBY clause closely mimics the SQL ORDER BY clause. In this case, the results are returned in descending order of average salaries. The GROUP BY clause is another WebLogic enhancement. The previous example implies that the average should be computed over all employees with matching department names.

As with SQL, WebLogic also allows you to implement complex query logic by embedding subqueries in the WHERE clause. The following query shows how you can use subqueries to return all employees in a given department:

```
select object(e) from EmployeeEJB e where e.department in (select object(d)
from DepartmentEJB d where d.id=?1)
```

Note that the subquery returns a collection of Department EJB instances (in this case, the collection will have only one element). Remember that a subquery may return EJB instances only if the EJBs returned don't use a compound primary key. Now, here's a query that returns all employees in a department who earn more than the average salary:

```
select object(e) from Department d, in(d.employees) e where d.id=?1 and
e.salary > (select avg(f.salary) from EmployeeEJB f)
```

In this case, the subquery returns the result of an aggregate function to the outer query. It also is called an *uncorrelated query* because the subquery can be evaluated independently of the outer query. WebLogic also supports *correlated queries*, in which the results from the outer query are involved in the evaluation of the sub-query. Here is an example that returns the names of all departments that have at least one employee in them:

```
select d.name from DepartmentEJB d where exists
(select e.id from EmployeeEJB e where e.department.id = d.id)
```

Subqueries allow you to build interesting and complex EJB queries—however, they also incur an overhead of additional processing. We easily could have written the previous query using the IS EMPTY clause:

```
select d.name from DepartmentEJB d where d.employees is not empty
```

For a more detailed understanding of EJB QL syntax and related issues, please refer to *Enterprise JavaBeans*, Third edition, by Richard Monson-Haefel (O'Reilly).

Reporting EJB-QL Compilation Errors

In WebLogic 8.1, error messages during EJB QL compilation visually indicate which parts of the query are erroneous. When an error is reported, the EJB QL compiler brackets the location of the problem with these symbols: =>> <<=. The following output shows how the EJB QL compiler indicates the nature of the problem:

```
ERROR: Error from appc: Error while reading 'META-INF/weblogic-cmp-rdbms-jar.xml'.
The error was:
Query:
EJB Name: DepartmentEJB
Method Name: findAvgDeptSalaries
Parameter Types: ()
Input EJB Query: SELECT f.name, avg(e.salary) FROM DepartmentEJB d, in(d.employees) e
GROUP BY d.name ORDER BY 2 DESC
SELECT =>> f.name <<=, avg(e.salary) FROM DepartmentEJB d, in(d.employees) e GROUP BY
d.name ORDER BY 2 DESC
Invalid Identifier in EJB QL expression:
Problem, the path expression/Identifier 'f.name' starts with an identifier: 'f'. The
identifier 'f', which can be either a range variable identifier or a collection
member identifier, is required to be declared in the FROM clause of its query or in
the FROM clause of a parent query.
'f' is not defined in the FROM clause of either its query or in any parent query.
Action, rewrite the query paying attention to the usage of 'f.name'.
```

In addition, the EJB QL compiler will report multiple errors during compilation, if they exist. In previous WebLogic releases, you would have to fix the first error in the query, and then recompile the EJB QL query to discover any subsequent problems.

CHAPTER 12

Packaging and Deployment

Now that we've looked at the different J2EE services supported by WebLogic and how your application components can take advantage of them, we turn our attention to how the different application components ought to be packaged and deployed. J2EE requires a number of different deployment descriptor files, and WebLogic adds its own set too. In this chapter, you will learn how WebLogic's tools help you to generate and edit the XML deployment descriptors needed for your J2EE modules. We also look at how to package enterprise applications, web applications, EJB modules, and any J2EE connectors your application may require.

Once your applications are packaged appropriately, you need to deploy them. WebLogic supports a two-phase deployment strategy wherein your application is first distributed to the servers. Your application then is checked during a prepare phase on each server, after which it is activated. You will learn about WebLogic's two-phase deployment, and the various staging modes that determine how an application is distributed to the different server instances in your domain. In addition, we look at how WebLogic's support for auto-deployment eases development and deployment during the development stages of your application. We also explore the various deployment tools that enable you to deploy an enterprise application (and its modules) to WebLogic, and how you can specify the order in which the different application modules ought to be deployed.

In order to correctly deploy the different J2EE modules within an enterprise application, you also need a good understanding of WebLogic's classloader hierarchy. We provide you with a firm grasp of WebLogic's classloading features and its impact on class visibility, the deployment of utility classes, and call-by-reference. We also discuss vital considerations for when you need to deploy applications in different situations—for example, application deployment in a single-server environment, a multi-server domain, and a clustered environment.

Finally, we illustrate WebLogic's split development directory approach, which eases the development and deployment of enterprise applications on a single WebLogic instance. It comes complete with Ant tasks for building, deploying, and packaging applications.

Packaging

The J2EE specification defines how a J2EE application and its components ought to be packaged. It also describes the structure and format of the different component types: web applications, EJB modules, enterprise applications, client applications, and resource adapters. For each component type, the specification describes the files needed and their locations within the directory structure. WebLogic requires that you adhere to the J2EE standard when packaging J2EE applications and modules.

A typical J2EE application includes the Java classes for the servlets and EJBs, their XML deployment descriptors, static web content (HTML files, images, etc.), and third-party utility libraries. Components that need to be deployed to WebLogic also may require WebLogic-specific XML descriptor files, and even container classes for any JSP pages, EJBs, and RMI objects. Except for connector modules, all J2EE modules also can be deployed in an exploded format. This means that although the deployment descriptors are still necessary, the module need not be bundled into a JAR. This is handy particularly during development, when you want to be able to easily change the contents of a module and its descriptor files.

The rest of this section outlines the traditional way of packaging and deploying J2EE applications. See the section "Split Directory Development" later in this chapter to learn about WebLogic's innovative directory structure, which eases the task of building and deploying J2EE applications during development.

Deployment Descriptors

As we've seen already, J2EE modules and applications use XML-formatted deployment descriptors to specify additional semantics on the contents of the JAR and deploy-time configuration settings. WebLogic defines its own set of deployment descriptors that supplement the default XML descriptors required by the J2EE standard. For example, you can use the *weblogic.xml* descriptor file in a web application to configure session handling (timeouts, persistence, and cookie names), JSP pages (the Java compiler, precompilation, JSP base class), references to other J2EE resources, and more.

Table 12-1 lists the standard deployment descriptors that are essential to the different J2EE component types, and their WebLogic-specific counterparts.

Table 12-1. Deployment descriptors for J2EE components

Component	J2EE	WebLogic
Web Application	WEB-INF/web.xml	WEB-INF/weblogic.xml
Enterprise JavaBean	META-INF/ejb-jar.xml	META-INF/weblogic-ejb-jar.xml
		META-INF/weblogic-cmp-rdbms-jar.xml
Resource Adapter	META-INF/ra.xml	META-INF/weblogic-ra.xml

Table 12-1. Deployment descriptors for J2EE components (continued)

Component	J2EE	WebLogic
Web Service	None	*WEB-INF/web-services.xml*
Enterprise Application	*META-INF/application.xml*	*META-INF/weblogic-application.xml*
Client Application	*application-client.xml*	*client-application.runtime.xml*

If you have purchased third-party J2EE components that do not include any WebLogic-specific deployment descriptors, you may have to modify the JARs to include the WebLogic-specific XML descriptor file(s) needed by that component.

Editing deployment descriptors

WebLogic provides several ways in which you can edit the XML deployment descriptors for an application/module:

WebLogic Builder
This is the preferred way to edit the deployment descriptors. It provides a convenient GUI for creating the XML descriptors for a J2EE component, while hiding all of the underlying XML and ensuring that only valid XML descriptor files are generated.

XML Editor
You can use a plain text editor or any XML editor that supports DTDs. For instance, you could use BEA's Java-based, standalone XML editor. It allows you to view the XML document either as a hierarchical XML tree or in raw XML form, and supports validation checks against the DTD.

DDInit
You can use the DDInit tool to generate skeleton deployment descriptors. For instance, you can run the following command to generate the *web.xml* and *weblogic.xml* deployment descriptors for an exploded WAR:

```
java weblogic.marathon.ddinit.WebInit exploded-war-staging-dir
```

Similarly, you can run the following command to generate the XML descriptors for an exploded EJB JAR:

```
java weblogic.marathon.ddinit.EJBInit exploded-ejb-staging-dir
```

In this case, DDInit will manufacture a valid *ejb-jar.xml* descriptor file for your EJBs that complies with the EJB 2.0 standard. If the *ejb-jar.xml* file already exists, this command will use it to generate the *weblogic-ejb-jar.xml* descriptor file.

These tools generate skeleton XML descriptors for the component by making a best guess for a number of configuration settings. Typically, you will need to modify the generated deployment descriptor files and supply the appropriate values for those settings.

DDInit also is available as the ddcreate Ant task.

Administration Console

You can use the Administration Console to edit deployment descriptors for a deployed J2EE application or module. If an application is deployed in an exploded format, the Configuration/Descriptor tab of most components provides you with a way to edit the most important descriptors.* Because the Administration Console can be used to modify only those deployment descriptors for J2EE components that already were deployed to WebLogic, you must ensure that the component is packaged properly and equipped with essential information in its deployment descriptors.

Besides this, you can use the EJBGen tool to generate the deployment descriptors and the home and interface files for an EJB module automatically. This utility generates the XML descriptors by inspecting your source code for predefined JavaDoc tags that provide additional semantic information. This approach is described in Chapter 10.

Web Applications

In order to package a web application for WebLogic, you need to execute the following sequence of steps:

1. Create a temporary staging folder on disk (say, *c:/war-staging*), and then copy all of your HTML files, JSP pages, images, and any other resources referenced by your web application into this folder. The staging folder serves as the document root for your web application. Therefore, the directory structure for the resources must be preserved under this folder.

2. Copy all compiled servlet classes and helper classes into the *WEB-INF/classes* folder under the staging directory. This includes the home and remote interfaces for EJBs referenced by your servlets and EJBs.

3. If you've packaged helper classes in a JAR, place these JARs into the *WEB-INF/lib* folder under the staging directory.

4. Place JSP tag libraries under the *WEB-INF* folder. The path to the TLD, or the tag library JAR, is then referenced either directly from within a JSP, or indirectly through the tag-lib-uri subelement in the *web.xml* descriptor.

5. Create the *web.xml* and *weblogic.xml* descriptor files for the web application, and place these in the *WEB-INF* folder under the staging directory.

6. Once you've organized the contents of the staging folder, package them into a JAR file:

```
jar cvf mywebapp.war -C c:/war-staging
```

---

* WebLogic 7.0 provides an Edit Descriptor option for most components instead. Choosing this option opens a new browser window with a GUI-based editor. This provides much of the same functionality as the WebLogic Builder tool.

A web archive always must have a *.war* file extension. It can be either packaged as a J2EE module within an enterprise application (EAR), or deployed independently using either the Administration Console or the deployer tool.

EJB Components

In order to package an EJB JAR for WebLogic, you need to execute the following tasks:

1. Create a temporary staging folder on disk (say, *c:/ejb-staging*), and then copy all of the EJB's compiled Java classes into this folder.

2. Create a *META-INF* folder under the staging directory, and generate the *ejb-jar.xml* and *weblogic-ejb-jar.xml* descriptor files for the EJB module. If the EJB module includes CMP entity beans, you also need to supply the *weblogic-cmp-rdbms-jar.xml* descriptor file, which captures the configuration settings for WebLogic's RDBMS-based persistence framework.

3. Once you've set up the contents of the staging folder, package them into a JAR file:

   ```
   jar cvf myjar.jar -C c:/ejb-staging
   ```

4. After this, pass the JAR file through the appc compiler, which generates the required container classes for the EJBs.

   ```
   java weblogic.appc -output myejbs.jar myjar.jar
   ```

An EJB JAR always must have a *.jar* file extension. The resulting EJB JAR then can be packaged as a J2EE module within an enterprise application (EAR), or deployed independently using either the Administration Console or the deployer tool.

Resource Adapters

In order to package J2EE connectors, you need to perform the following tasks:

1. Create a temporary staging folder on disk (say, *c:/rar-staging*), and then copy all of the compiled Java classes for the resource adapter into this folder.

2. Package the contents of this staging directory into a JAR:

   ```
   jar cvf myrar.jar -C c:/rar-staging
   ```

   Place the resulting JAR back in the staging folder, and remove the exploded contents of the JAR from the staging directory.

3. Create a *META-INF* folder under the staging directory, and place the XML descriptor files *ra.xml* and *weblogic-ra.xml* into this folder. You may have to generate only the *weblogic-ra.xml* descriptor if you've purchased a third-party resource adapter.

4. Once you've set up the structure of the staging folder, package them into a JAR:

   ```
   jar cvf myconnector.rar -C c:/rar-staging
   ```

The resulting RAR file can then either be packaged as a J2EE module within an enterprise application (EAR), or deployed independently using the Administration Console or the deployer tool. Resource adapter archive files always must end with a *.rar* file extension.

Enterprise Applications

Example 12-1 depicts the structure of a typical enterprise application (EAR).

Example 12-1. Internal structure of an enterprise application (EAR)

```
META-INF\application.xml
META-INF\weblogic-application.xml
ejb_jar1.jar
ejb_jar2.jar
...
my_webapp1.war
my_webapp2.war
...
shared-lib.jar
```

In order to bundle the J2EE modules within an EAR file, you need to perform the following tasks:

1. Create a temporary staging directory—say, *c:/staging*.
2. Copy the necessary web applications (WAR files), EJB components (EJB JARs), J2EE connectors (RAR files), and any shared libraries into the staging folder.
3. Create a *META-INF* directory under the staging folder *c:/staging*. Place the standard *application.xml* descriptor and the optional *weblogic-application.xml* descriptor into the *META-INF* folder.
4. Package the contents of this staging folder into an EAR file (*myapp.ear*):

   ```
   jar cvf myear.ear -C c:/staging
   ```

An enterprise application archive always must end with a *.ear* file extension. The *application.xml* descriptor file must adhere to the J2EE standard. Example 12-2 reveals the contents of the standard *application.xml* descriptor for the sample EAR, as depicted earlier in Example 12-1.

Example 12-2. Sample application.xml descriptor for an EAR

```
<!DOCTYPE application
        PUBLIC "-//Sun Microsystems, Inc.//DTD J2EE Application 1.3//EN"
        "http://java.sun.com/dtd/application_1_3.dtd">

<application>
  <display-name>My Application</display-name>
  <module>
    <web>
      <web-uri>my_webapp1.war</web-uri>
```

Example 12-2. Sample application.xml descriptor for an EAR (continued)

```
      <context-root>/</context-root>
    </web>
  </module>
  <module>
    <web>
      <web-uri>my_webapp2.war</web-uri>
      <context-root>/admin</context-root>
    </web>
  </module>
  <module>
    <ejb>ejb_jar1.jar</ejb>
  </module>
  <module>
    <ejb>ejb_jar2.jar</ejb>
  </module>
  <!-- other J2EE modules -->
</application>
```

Here, the enterprise application includes the web application *my_webapp1.war*, which is made available under the default context root */*, and another, *my_webapp2.war*, which is available under the */admin* context. In other words, if a WebLogic instance hosts both the web applications in the EAR, the HTTP request *http://server:7001/foo.jsp* fetches *foo.jsp* from the *my_webapp1.war* module, while the HTTP request *http://server:7001/admin/login.jsp* fetches *login.jsp* from the *my_webapp2.war* module.

You also can deploy enterprise applications in the exploded directory format. In this case, if the exploded EAR contains a web application that also exists in exploded format, then the web-uri element in the *application.xml* descriptor file must refer to the folder that holds the resources of the web application. Thus, if the *mywebapp* folder is the document root for a web application in the EAR, the web-uri element should be specified as follows:

```
    <module>
      <web>
        <web-uri>mywebapp</web-uri>
        <context-root>/mywebapp</context-root>
      </web>
    </module>
    ...
```

Later, we discuss how to include shared libraries and utility classes and make them visible to other J2EE modules within an enterprise application.

The *weblogic-application.xml* descriptor lets you configure application-wide resources and WebLogic-specific tuning information. These resources include application-scoped JDBC pools, XML parsers, and entity-EJB caches—resources that are available only to the enterprise application, and not to the entire WebLogic configuration. Example 12-3 shows the sample structure of the *weblogic-application.xml* descriptor file for an enterprise application.

Example 12-3. Sample weblogic-application.xml descriptor for an EAR

```
<weblogic-application>
  <ejb>
    <entity-cache>
      <entity-cache-name>GlobalEntityCache</entity-cache-name>
      <max-cache-size>
        <megabytes>10</megabytes>
      </max-cache-size>
      <caching-strategy>Exclusive</caching-strategy>
    </entity-cache>
  </ejb>
  <xml>
    <parser-factory>
      <saxparser-factory>
        weblogic.xml.babel.jaxp.SAXParserFactoryImpl
      </saxparser-factory>
      <document-builder-factory>
        weblogic.apache.xerces.jaxp.DocumentBuilderFactoryImpl
      </document-builder-factory>
      <transformer-factory>
        weblogic.apache.xalan.processor.TransformerFactoryImpl
      </transformer-factory>
    </parser-factory>
    <entity-mapping>
      <entity-mapping-name>My Mapping</entity-mapping-name>
      <public-id>-//OReilly and Associates//DTD WL//EN</public-id>
      <system-id>http://www.oreilly.com/dtds/wl.dtd</system-id>
      <entity-uri>dtds/wl.dtd</entity-uri>
      <when-to-cache>cache-at-initialization</when-to-cache>
      <cache-timeout-interval>300</cache-timeout-interval>
    </entity-mapping>
  </xml>
</weblogic-application>
```

Application-scoped pools are covered in Chapter 5, whereas application-scoped entity caches are discussed in Chapter 10. Chapter 18 explains how to configure application-scoped parser factories and entity resolution mappings.

Client Applications

The J2EE specification also defines a standard way to package client J2EE applications. A client application module is packaged as a JAR, which includes the compiled Java classes that run in the client's VM. It also encapsulates deployment descriptors that specify the EJBs and other WebLogic resources needed by the client application. For each client application module, you need to supply the standard *application-client.xml* descriptor and an optional WebLogic-specific deployment descriptor. In fact, you can package the client application modules within an EAR, along with other server-side J2EE modules that comprise the enterprise application. By doing this, both client-side and server-side modules can be distributed as a single unit.

In order to package a client application module, you need to execute the following sequence of steps:

1. Create a temporary staging folder—say, *c:/client-staging*—and then copy all of the required files of the client into this folder. You also may place a batch file or script under the staging folder to start the client application.

2. Create a *classes* subfolder that holds the Java classes and JAR files, and modify the startup script so that the client's classpath includes the locations of these classes.

3. Modify the client JAR's manifest file */META-INF/MANIFEST.MF* to include an entry for the Main-Class attribute.

4. Now that you've packaged the client-application JAR into an EAR, you can use the ClientDeployer tool to extract the client module from the EAR:

   ```
   java weblogic.ClientDeployer myapp.ear myclient
   ```

   Here *myclient.jar* is a J2EE client module packaged within the EAR *myapp.ear*. The ClientDeployer tool generates a *client.properties* file and then adds it to the client-application JAR.

5. Once the client-application JAR has been extracted from the EAR, you must use the weblogic.j2eeclient.Main utility to bootstrap the J2EE client and point it to a running WebLogic instance:

   ```
   java weblogic.j2eeclient.Main helloWorld.jar t3://localhost:7001 Greetings
   ```

The j2eeclient.Main utility establishes the client's local JNDI context using the T3 URL of a running WebLogic instance, before invoking the client from the entry-point specified by the client JAR's manifest file. The client's deployment descriptor may reference any resource that is bound to the global JNDI tree: EJB home objects, JMS connection factories and destinations, JDBC data sources, and Mail Sessions. All of these references are resolved and bound to the client's local ENC, available under the *java:comp/env/* context. In addition, the j2eeclient.Main utility makes a UserTransaction object available to the client's local JNDI tree under *java:comp/UserTransaction*.

Deployment Tools

WebLogic provides several tools to configure and deploy J2EE applications and modules. WebLogic Builder is one such graphical tool that allows you to generate and modify the deployment descriptors of J2EE applications. It can even deploy applications to a single WebLogic instance. However, its primary role is in packaging J2EE applications because its deployment options are rudimentary. For this reason, we won't consider WebLogic Builder any further. Instead, we look at how to use the Administration Console to deploy J2EE components to multiple WebLogic instances and/or clusters. In addition, WebLogic provides a command-line deployer tool, which mimics the deployment capabilities of the Administration Console and more.

Administration Console

The Administration Console lets you deploy, redeploy, and undeploy J2EE applications and modules. Expand the Deployments node from the left pane of the Administration Console. Here, you can select from one of the following nodes: Applications, EJB Modules, Web Application Modules, Connector Modules, and Startup & Shutdown. If you click one of these nodes, you'll find the "Deploy a new ..." option on the right pane, which enables you to deploy a new application or module. For instance, if you've chosen the Web Applications node, then from the right pane you can select the "Deploy a new Web Application Module" option to deploy a new web application.

Subsequent deployment screens let you choose an EAR (enterprise application), EJB JAR (EJB module), RAR (resource adapter), or WAR (web application) from the filesystem for deployment. You even can upload the application component through your web browser. You also can select a directory from the filesystem instead of a packaged module, in which case WebLogic expects the directory to hold an exploded form of the same module. After choosing the component, you need to target the module to the WebLogic instances in your domain to which the component ought to be deployed. The component may be targeted to an individual server, cluster, or virtual host configured for the domain. Remember, when you target the enterprise application (EAR) to a server or cluster, it is the individual modules within the EAR that are targeted, and not the EAR itself.

After this, you must indicate how the module will be staged—i.e., how the application files will be copied over to the different servers. You will be presented with two choices:

"Copy this application onto every target for me"
> This option instructs WebLogic to copy the module onto every targeted server. Each server will then deploy the application using its own copies of the module. This is a deployment in a *staged* mode.

"I will make the application accessible from the following location"
> This option requires you to supply the path of the directory that holds the application. Each targeted server must then access the source from the given directory; therefore, the directory must be shared among all of the targeted servers. This corresponds to a deployment in a *nostage* mode.

We look at the different application staging modes later in the "Application Staging" section. For now, you must note that the Administration Console doesn't allow you to create a deployment in the externally staged mode.

Once the application has been deployed, you can modify the deployment by selecting the relevant node from under the Deployments node in the left pane of the Administration Console, and then navigating to either the Deploy or the Targets tabs. The Targets tab lists the servers or clusters to which the component has been targeted. Changing the targets of a deployed application usually will come into effect only when the server subsequently is restarted, or in some cases if you undeploy and redeploy the application. The Deploy tab lists the deployment status of the component for each target. Choose the Stop option to undeploy the application component from the particular target, and the Redeploy option to initiate a fresh deployment for the component on the particular target.

WebLogic's Deployer Tool

The Deployer tool is a powerful tool to manage the deployment and redeployment of applications on WebLogic. It even allows you to deploy specific modules within an EAR—for instance, you can use the Deployer tool to deploy a WAR that has just been added to an EAR. Your understanding of the Deployer tool won't be complete until we've looked at WebLogic's two-phase deployment strategy and its support for different application staging modes. We begin by examining the syntax and a few examples of how to use the Deployer tool.

Here is the general syntax for invoking the Deployer tool:

```
java weblogic.Deployer [options]
    -user user -password password -adminurl url
    [-start|-stop|-remove|-cancel|-list | -deploy | -undeploy | -redeploy|
        -distribute]
    [files/directories/jars]
```

-user, -password, and -adminurl are command-line options that must be supplied at all times. They allow you to specify the username/password of the WebLogic user that is executing the deployment operation, and the URL of the Administration Server. The following example shows how to use the deployer tool to list the status of current deployment tasks:

```
java weblogic.Deployer -user system -password pst
                    -adminurl t3://10.0.10.10:8001/ -list
```

Don't be surprised if we omit these options from further examples of the Deployer tool. We'll assume you understand that these options need to be passed to the Deployer tool on every invocation.

Any task initiated using the Deployer tool is executed synchronously by default. You can execute a task asynchronously by supplying the -nowait command-line option. You can view this list of all deployment tasks by specifying the -list option. By selecting the Tasks node from the left pane of the Administration Console, you can view the same list of tasks. You also can abort a task that hasn't completed yet by using the -cancel option. In WebLogic 8.1, the Deployer tool supports two additional options: the -listtask option for listing all deployment tasks that are currently in progress, and the -listapps option for listing all modules that are currently deployed.

Any deployment task that needs to operate on one or more modules must refer to the module by its name. For example, you can undeploy an application named *myapp* using the following command:

```
java weblogic.Deployer -undeploy -name myapp
```

Here, the -name option lets you specify the name of the application or module that must be undeployed. The -listapps option lets you list the names of all deployed modules. Use the -deploy option to deploy or redeploy an application or its modules. The -deploy option usually is followed by the -targets option, which specifies the servers or clusters to which the application or module ought to be deployed. The following example shows how to deploy a WAR:

```
java weblogic.Deployer -targets server1, server2 -name myWar
                       -source oo.war -deploy oo.war
```

In this case, the -source option specifies the location of the web archive or directory that holds the web application. In WebLogic 8.1, you don't need to use the -source option and can write something like this instead:

```
java weblogic.Deployer -targets server1, server2 -name myWar
                       -deploy oo.war
```

If you are not on the Administration Server, you can use the -upload option to first upload the application to the Administration Server, and then subsequently deploy it to all targeted servers. The following command shows how to deploy a web application to a cluster from a machine that doesn't host the Administration Server:

```
java weblogic.Deployer -targets mycluster -name oo
                       -deploy -stage -upload oo.war
```

The web application will be deployed once the WAR file has been copied to the upload directory on the Administration Server.

You can refine the targets even further by referring to individual modules within the application that ought to be deployed. For example, assume that you have added a new web application to a deployed EAR, and updated the EAR's deployment descriptors to reflect this change. You then can deploy the new web application *only*, without having to redeploy the entire EAR, as follows:

```
java weblogic.Deployer -targets myNewWar@server1
                       -name myEar -deploy myEar.ear
```

Note that the @target suffix used to specify target servers is not required if the targets of the new module are the same as those of the already deployed EAR. This feature can be used to deploy different parts of an EAR to different servers by qualifying each target server with the name of the module that should be deployed to that server. The following example shows how to deploy a WAR and EJB JAR to different servers, even though they are both modules within the same EAR:

```
java weblogic.Deployer -name myEar -targets myWar@webserver,myEJB@ejbserver
  -deploy myEar.ear
```

Exploded (unarchived) web applications also support partial redeployment; we saw an example of this in Chapter 2:

```
java weblogic.Deployer -name mywebapp -targets server1,server2 -redeploy help/*.jsp
```

Here, the file list is specified relative to the root of the deployed application. So, for example, if the JSPs were part of a web application, *mywebapp*, packaged within an EAR, the file list would have to be specified as *mywebapp/help/*.jsp*. If you supply a -targets option, the files will be refreshed on all of the targeted servers. If you remove the -targets option, the specified files would be redeployed on all servers to which the web application is deployed. We will look at many more examples of the Deployer tool when we turn our attention to two-phase deployment and application staging.

Application Deployment

WebLogic uses a two-phase deployment strategy. When you initiate a deployment task for an application, it first *prepares* the application on all target servers and then *activates* the application in a separate phase. This two-phase approach reduces the likelihood of inconsistent deployment states across a cluster because the application is deployed on target servers only after acknowledging the success of the prepare phase.

During the prepare phase of deployment, copies of the application and its components are distributed to all target servers. In addition, certain validation checks are performed to ensure that the application and its components can be deployed reliably. A deployment enters the activation phase only if the prepare phase completes successfully. The actual deployment occurs during the activation phase—that is, when the application and its components are deployed to each target server. The application is available to clients only after the completion of the activation phase.

By adopting this two-phase deployment strategy, WebLogic can perform intermediate checks that ensure subsequent activation will succeed on all of the target servers. This greatly helps to reduce the risk of an inconsistent and potentially unstable deployment across the domain. In a clustered environment, if deployment fails on any of the target servers during either the prepare or activation phases, the deployment task is rolled back as a whole from all targets. For example, if an application targeted to a cluster fails on any of the cluster members during either the prepare or activation phases, the application will not be deployed on any of the servers in the cluster. This helps to ensure the cluster deployment is kept homogenous.

Note that if the prepare phase does succeed on all servers in the cluster, the activation will occur regardless of any subsequent errors that may occur during activation. The prepare phase is designed to minimize the likelihood of activation errors, but if they do occur, the deployment will not be rolled back and you will have a nonhomogenous deployment. In this case, you may have to undeploy the application, fix the error causing the activation problem, and redeploy.

Application Staging

The prepare phase is particularly important in a WebLogic domain composed of multiple managed servers. During the prepare phase, the application that is being deployed has to be distributed somehow to all of the managed servers participating in the deployment. *Staging* refers to this process of copying application files to locations from where they can be deployed to target servers. Generally, you can make the application files available to the Administration Server, which will organize the distribution of these files. However, if you have a shared directory setup, you may not want this behavior. Alternatively, you may want to take on the responsibility of ensuring that the components are distributed yourself.

WebLogic provides various staging modes that control the way in which an application can be distributed:

stage

> Application files are copied automatically to a staging directory on the target server. Once the server boots up, it will run the application from this staging folder.

external_stage

> An external user or process (and not WebLogic) ensures that the application is available on the server's staging folder before initiating deployment.

nostage

> Application files are not copied to another location during deployment, so all targeted servers deploy from the same file or directory.

The staging mode can be specified for each server in the domain, and later overridden by individual applications on the server. However, once an application is deployed, its staging mode cannot be changed.

 For managed servers in a domain, the default staging mode is stage, which means application files are copied to the target servers automatically. For the Administration Server, however, the default staging mode is nostage, which means the application is deployed from the source location provided.

Staging

When you enable application staging for a managed server, WebLogic is responsible for distributing the components to the targeted servers before the actual deployment is initiated. During the prepare phase, the application files are copied automatically to a staging directory on the targeted server and subsequently activated from there. This is the default deployment behavior for a managed server in the domain. It is perhaps the most robust because each managed server has its own local copy of the application module. In doing so, it can avoid problems caused by network outages during deployment. For example, if the shared directory used in nostage mode becomes unavailable, it can cripple the servers in the domain that rely on the shared directory.

The name of the application's staging directory on a managed server is a combination of the server's name and the name of the application. For instance, if you deploy a web application, *MyWebApp*, packaged within *oo.war* to ServerA, the WAR file is copied to *ServerA\MyWebApp\oo.war* located on ServerA. The same behavior is observed on each targeted server on which the default staging mode is configured. Staging ensures that each server has its own copy of the application. The naming scheme for the application's staging folder works nicely to avoid any conflicts if you are running multiple servers on a single machine (or a shared filesystem).

The following example shows how to deploy a web application to a WebLogic cluster:

```
java weblogic.Deployer -targets mycluster -name oo -source oo.war -deploy -stage
```

Note that the command is run from the machine hosting the Administration Server. The -stage option instructs the Deployer tool to stage the web application, and the -deploy action instructs the members of the cluster to deploy the web application. This will ensure that the WAR is copied to each server in the cluster, and then activated on each cluster member. Once the web application is deployed successfully on all members of the cluster, a request such as *http://mycluster:7001/oo/index.jsp* then can be directed to any server in the cluster. You subsequently can stop the application on all servers in the cluster by invoking the Deployer tool as follows:

```
java weblogic.Deployer -name oo -stop
```

If you want to stop the application on just a subset of the servers, use the -targets option to specify those servers:

```
java weblogic.Deployer -targets someserver -name oo -stop
```

The application will no longer be available on any member of the cluster. This means that any HTTP requests for a resource hosted by the web application will return an HTTP 503 error response (Service Unavailable). In general, you should specify the -targets option only if you must stop the application on a subset of the servers to which it is deployed. Unless otherwise specified, the -targets option always defaults to the existing targets that have been configured for the application. Stopping an application doesn't change its staging mode, however—a copy of the WAR still is available on each server and can be restarted quickly using the following command:

```
java weblogic.Deployer -name oo -start
```

In this case, no staging needs to occur—the web application (WAR) already had been copied to all servers in the cluster. We are merely reactivating the web application using the previously staged copy of the WAR on each cluster member.

Use a combination of the -deploy and -stage options when you need to deploy a new copy of the application on all target servers.

Stopping an application simply makes the application unavailable to clients, and avoids the need for any further preparation (and staging) if the application needs to be restarted. If you really need to undeploy the application, use the -undeploy option. This stops the application and removes the staged files. If you want to redeploy the application, you must distribute and prepare the application again. The following command shows how to undeploy a web application from all the servers to which it is deployed:

```
java weblogic.Deployer -name oo -undeploy
```

Now any HTTP requests for a resource hosted by the web application will return an HTTP 404 error response (Not found). Be careful when you use the -undeploy option because the Deployer tool physically removes all staged files from all targeted servers.

If you simply want to redeploy an application, perhaps because you have changed the code in some way, run the Deployer tool as follows:

```
java weblogic.Deployer -name oo -redeploy
```

Because WebLogic Server adopts a two-phase deployment strategy, you can instruct the Deployer tool to only distribute an application component, and not start it. The following command shows how to distribute a web application module:

```
java weblogic.Deployer -targets myserver -name myapp -source oo.war
                        -stage -distribute
```

At this point, the web application will be distributed and is ready to be activated. Once the application module has been distributed, you can activate (or start) the application module in the usual way:

```
java weblogic.Deployer -name myapp -start
```

External staging

External staging is quite similar to WebLogic's support for staging, except that WebLogic isn't responsible for distributing copies of the application to each targeted server. Instead, the user (or an external process) is in charge of distributing the application files before initiating actual deployment. The application files need to be placed in the same staging directory as WebLogic would use were you using the default staging mode. For instance, if you need to deploy the application *MyWebApp* located in the file *oo.war* to a cluster containing the servers, ServerA and ServerB, you must copy *oo.war* to the *ServerA\MyWebApp* folder located on ServerA, and to the *ServerB\MyWebApp* folder located on ServerB. In addition, the application files being deployed also must be available to the Administration Server. You typically will use this staging mode if you have external tools that can handle the distribution of your application files.

Let's assume that you've copied the web application (*oo.war*) to staging directories on all managed servers in the cluster `mycluster`. Then you can activate the web application on `mycluster` using the Deployer tool on the Administration Server:

```
java weblogic.Deployer -targets mycluster -name mywebapp -source oo.war
                -deploy -external_stage
```

All other deployment operations such as stopping, starting, and unpreparing work exactly as described before. The -undeploy option behaves differently when it operates on an externally staged application. In this case, the Deployer tool undeploys only the application from all servers in the cluster, but doesn't remove the application files from the staging directory.

No staging

By disabling application staging, you ensure that WebLogic does *not* distribute the application files during the prepare phase of deployment. Instead, the staging directory is ignored completely and the applications are deployed to the target server directly from their source directories. This is the default staging mode for the Administration Server.

No staging is ideal for incremental development on a single-server domain. Because the application is deployed from the target files directly, this mode allows the web container to detect changes to servlets and JSPs and reload them as necessary. It also can be used if you have multiple application servers running on the same machine, where the servers share the same disk.

The following command shows how to deploy and activate a web application to a cluster using the no staging mode:

```
java weblogic.Deployer -targets mycluster -name goo
                -deploy -nostage goo.war
```

Just like the external staging mode, the application files being deployed also must be available to the Administration Server.

Configuring the Staging Mode

To set the default staging mode for a server, start up the Administration Console, select the server from the left pane, and navigate to the Configuration/Deployment tab. Here you will find options to modify the server's staging mode and the default staging directory for the server. If your domain consists of servers that use a shared disk, you even can specify a shared staging directory for each server. In the case of the Administration Server, you also can specify the default directory that should be used to store the uploaded files for deployment.

In WebLogic 8.1, you can set the staging mode for an application when you choose between the following two options during deployment: "Copy this application onto every target for me," which enables the staging mode, and "I will make the application accessible from the following location," which disables staging altogether. If you want to deploy an application with external staging, the Administration Console cannot help you. You must use the Deployer tool to deploy an application in the externally staged mode. WebLogic 8.1 also lets you set the staging mode for individual applications, in which case they override the default staging mode for the server. For example, you can set the staging mode for a web application by choosing the application from the left pane of the Administration Console and then navigating to the Configuration/General tab.

Remember, you cannot alter the staging mode of an application once it has been deployed. Instead, you need to use the Deployer tool to set the application's staging mode the first time it is deployed.

Auto-Deployment

WebLogic also supports an auto-deployment feature that typically should be used only during the development stages of a single-server deployment. In the *development* mode, applications are deployed to the Administration Server automatically as soon as they are copied into the *domain\applications* folder. By default, WebLogic Server runs in the development mode, which means that the auto-deployment feature is enabled by default. By placing the server in *production* mode, you can disable this auto-deployment feature. In this situation, you explicitly need to deploy your applications using either the Deployer tool or the Administration Console. Developers on WebLogic 8.1 instead can use the split-directory development methodology, detailed later in this chapter.

In order to enable the auto-deployment feature for a server, you need to ensure that the following command-line option is set when you start up WebLogic Server:

```
java -Dweblogic.ProductionModeEnabled=false
    ... weblogic.Server
```

The startup script *startWebLogic* uses a shell variable PRODUCTION_MODE for this purpose. When the server runs in development mode, you can deploy any J2EE component automatically by simply placing the JAR (or directory, if the component exists in exploded format) under the *applications* directory of the domain. This support extends to enterprise applications, web applications, EJB modules, and resource adapters. If the J2EE application is copied to the directory when the server is not running, it is deployed the next time the server starts. Similarly, you can undeploy the application by simply deleting the JAR (or directory, if it exists in exploded format) from the domain's *applications* directory.

In auto-deployment mode, applications are deployed to the Administration Server. For this reason, you should just enable the auto-deployment feature in a single-server development environment only.

You may notice occasional file-locking errors on Windows platforms when using the auto-deployment feature. These errors occur when WebLogic attempts to read the file (say, a JAR) while you still are copying the file to the *applications* directory. For instance, when you redeploy an EJB JAR within an exploded EAR, you may find the deployment aborts because of ZIP errors due to file-locking. One way to get around this issue is to avoid JARs in the first place and simply deploy all J2EE modules within the application in exploded format. Alternatively, you can minimize the occurrence of file-locking errors by lengthening the time period that WebLogic uses to poll the filesystem for application changes.

WebLogic also provides a cute mechanism for redeploying applications already deployed on a server running in development mode. Suppose you have deployed an enterprise application in exploded format, and it includes a large number of application files. It would be impractical for WebLogic to poll every application file continuously for any changes. Instead, WebLogic polls a single file *REDEPLOY* located in the *WEB-INF* or *META-INF* directory of your exploded component. For instance, if you have an exploded EAR, you simply need to copy a blank file called *REDEPLOY* into its *META-INF* directory. Now if you want to redeploy the application, just "touch" the file to alter its timestamp. WebLogic will detect the modified timestamp and redeploy the application. This redeploy feature works only for applications and components placed directly under the domain's *applications* folder.

Alternative Descriptors

You also can use the Deployer tool to deploy an enterprise application with an alternative set of deployment descriptors. Instead of the default *application.xml* and *weblogic-application.xml* descriptor files, you can instruct the Deployer tool to use an alternative set without actually modifying the packaged EAR that must be deployed. Use the –altappdd option to set an alternative J2EE deployment descriptor (*application.xml*) for the enterprise application, and use the –altwlsappdd option to set an alternative WebLogic-specific deployment descriptor (*weblogic-application.xml*). The following example shows how to deploy an EAR file *myApp.ear* using alternative descriptor files:

```
java weblogic.Deployer -targets mycluster -name myApp -deploy –nostage
    -altappdd f:\myapp.xml -altwlsappdd f:\mywlsapp.xml myApp.ear
```

If the application is deployed in the staged mode, the alternative descriptor files are copied to the top level of the application's subdirectory under the staging folder of each target server.

This feature is quite handy during development time because it lets you easily experiment with different runtime configurations of your application. For example, you could deploy the EAR with a different set of descriptors in order to experiment with different context properties, or even a different set of EJB and WAR modules. This mechanism works for any enterprise application, regardless of whether it has been packaged in an archived format (EAR) or in exploded directory format.

There are a few caveats when specifying alternative deployment descriptors. If you've already deployed an application with an alternative set of descriptors, you cannot change the location of the descriptor files when you later redeploy the application. Thus, you cannot specify different locations for the alternative descriptors when you subsequently invoke the Deployer tool with the -redeploy option. Likewise, if you've deployed an enterprise application using the default deployment descriptors, then you cannot redeploy the same application with an alternative set. In both cases, you need to first undeploy the enterprise application and then deploy it again with the alternative descriptor files.

Deployment Order

It is important to understand the order in which WebLogic deploys J2EE applications and components. In general, WebLogic first deploys the managed resources such as JDBC connection pools, data sources, JMS connection factories and destinations, and Mail Sessions. After this, WebLogic deploys the application components in the following sequence: J2EE connectors, EJB modules, and finally web applications. For enterprise applications, WebLogic loads the individual components in the order in which they are declared in the *application.xml* descriptor file. So, for instance, the EJBs packaged within an EAR will be loaded in the order in which they're declared in the *application.xml* descriptor file.

WebLogic also lets you adjust the order in which separate applications are deployed. For each application, you can specify a numeric value for the Load Order attribute. WebLogic then will deploy applications in increasing order of their Load Order values. By default, all applications deployed to WebLogic are assigned a Load Order of 100. So, in order to change the sequence in which your applications are deployed, you need to change their Load Order attributes. Once the application is deployed, you can use the Administration Console to locate the J2EE component from the left pane and then change its Load Order setting from the right pane. These changes will come into effect the next time the server is started. You even can make this change programmatically by modifying the value of the LoadOrder attribute of an ApplicationMBean instance. Chapter 20 explains how to use WebLogic's MBeans to effect this change.

WebLogic's Classloading Framework

A classloader is used by the JVM to locate and load Java classes into memory at runtime. Java classloaders define a hierarchy, a tree-like collection of parent and child classloaders. The root of this classloader hierarchy is the bootstrap classloader, which is created by the JVM for loading its internal classes and the java.* packages included within the JVM. An extensions classloader, which is a child of the bootstrap class-loader, is used to load any JARs placed in the extensions directory of the JDK. This means that any JAR in the JDK's extensions directory may refer only to other classes in that directory, or to the JDK classes. Finally, the system classpath classloader, which is a child of the extensions classloader, is responsible for loading classes from the JVM's classpath. Any custom classloader created by an application, including WebLogic's classloaders, are all descendants of this system classpath classloader.

This classloader hierarchy plays an important role when locating and loading classes into memory. In general, classloaders try to reuse a preloaded version of a class. The hierarchy of classloaders intrinsically determines the scope from where the pre-loaded version of the class may be fetched. By default, child classloaders and classes loaded by these classloaders have direct access to their parent classloader and any classes loaded by it. This means that any classes loaded by a classloader are visible directly or indirectly, to all its descendants. Conversely, a parent classloader cannot see any class loaded by any of its child classloaders. In the same way, a classloader cannot access any classes loaded by a sibling classloader.

Given these visibility constraints, we can infer the *general* sequence of actions that occur when a classloader needs to load a particular class. First, the classloader checks to see whether the class isn't loaded already. If so, the in-memory version of the class is used. If the class hasn't been loaded already, the classloader delegates the request to its parent classloader. The parent classloader performs the same checks. If it hasn't loaded the class already, the request again is forwarded to its parent. In this way, each classloader may potentially delegate the request to its parent until it reaches the root of the hierarchy.

Only when a parent fails to load the class does the child classloader attempt to do so. This is an important point to remember: a child classloader loads a class only if its parent fails to load it. This means that even if both parent and child classloaders have access to a particular class, and the child classloader receives a request to load the class, it is the parent that actually loads the class. The application that triggered the request to load a class receives a ClassNotFoundException if neither the classloader nor any of its ancestors can locate the class. For this reason, you could say classload-ers follow the *delegation model* when loading classes.

Let's reinforce this classloading mechanism with an example from WebLogic. Sup-pose you've included a library JAR in WebLogic's classpath, and also bundled it within a deployed EAR. WebLogic provides a separate classloader for the EAR, which is a child of the system classpath classloader. This means that the library JAR and all of the Java classes bundled with it are visible to both the system classpath classloader and the EAR's classloader. Now if a Java class within the EAR attempts to create an instance of the class located within the JAR (or invokes a static method on the class), then the class is loaded by its parent classloader—i.e., the system class-path classloader, and not the EAR's classloader. Even though the class is visible to the EAR's classloader, it is the parent's version of the class that is always used. If you remove the library JAR from the system classpath, the parent classloader will fail to load the particular class, and in this case, the EAR classloader will locate and load the class.

Remember, we've just described the general behavior for Java classloaders. You can build custom Java classloaders that deviate from this default classloading scheme.

The Need for Custom Classloaders

In fact, WebLogic relies on a number of classloaders to support auto-deployment, dynamic class updates, and application redeployment. WebLogic needs to depend on custom classloaders because Java classloaders don't support any standard mechanism for *unloading* or replacing a set of classes. This makes it a little more awkward to build an application server that also must support dynamic updates of compiled classes, drop-in replacements for EJBs, and other modules, without redeploying the entire application server! The only way to get around this problem is to throw away the entire classloader and effectively dispense with all the Java classes it has loaded.

For this reason, WebLogic creates a number of classloaders for effective deployment. For instance, WebLogic creates a child classloader for each EAR that is deployed to the server. By doing this, it needs only to throw away the EAR's classloader when it has to reload and update the application classes in the EAR. In fact, depending on the structure of the enterprise application, WebLogic establishes a hierarchy of classloaders for each EAR. WebLogic can then prune (and rebuild) an entire branch of the classloader hierarchy rooted at the EAR's classloader when it needs to redeploy the EAR or parts of it. Of course, the EAR's redeployment doesn't affect any of the sibling classloaders of other deployed applications.

Let's now put all of this theory into practice and see how WebLogic implements its classloader hierarchy.

WebLogic's Classloaders

WebLogic's standard classloading framework needs to support two objectives:

- It must be able to isolate multiple applications deployed on a single server. This means that classes used by application A must never come in conflict with any classes used by application B. Furthermore, redeploying application A must have no effect on classes used by application B.
- Within an application, it must allow you to redeploy web applications without having to redeploy the EJBs.

WebLogic achieves these goals by creating a separate classloader hierarchy for each application deployed to the server. The parent of this hierarchy is the system classpath classloader, which is used to load the classes specified in WebLogic's classpath.

An application generally is packaged in an EAR file, and everything within the EAR (servlets, JSPs, EJBs, etc.) is treated as being part of the same application. However, you also can deploy web applications (WARs), EJB modules (EJB JARs), and resource adapters (RARs) directly to WebLogic. In this case, if you deploy a web application (WAR) and EJB module (EJB JAR) independently, they both are considered to be two separate applications, so WebLogic establishes separate classloaders for both the WAR and the EJB module. If you deploy two EARs independently, again WebLogic creates separate classloaders for both applications.

By creating a separate classloader hierarchy for each application, classloaders associated with one application cannot see the classloaders or classes of another application, and because sibling classloaders are isolated from each other, this also isolates the applications.

WebLogic constructs a hierarchy of classloaders for each deployed application (EAR). The base application classloader loads all of the EJB JARs within the EAR. In addition, a child classloader is created for each web application (WAR) within the EAR. Figure 12-1 illustrates this classloading hierarchy.

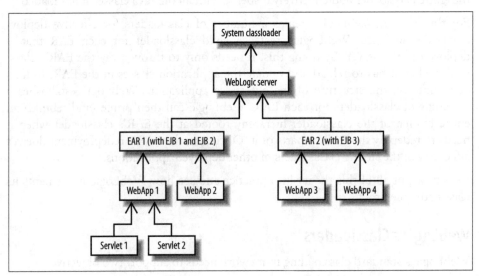

Figure 12-1. WebLogic's classloader hierarchy

Thus, the base application classloader is a child of the system classloader. All EJBs within an EAR share the same classloader, whereas each web application acquires its own classloader. Moreover, the EJB classloader is the parent for all web application classloaders. This classloader hierarchy has the following consequences:

- Any classes and libraries referenced in WebLogic's classpath at startup are loaded by the system classpath classloader, so you cannot unload (or refresh) any of the classes referenced in WebLogic's system classpath while the server is running. For this reason, redeploying an application or any of its modules has no effect on any class referenced in WebLogic's classpath.

- Within the same EAR, each web application is isolated from every other web application. This allows you to redeploy a web application without affecting other web applications. In addition, you can redeploy a web application without affecting any of the deployed EJBs.

- All EJB modules share the same classloader, so in order to refresh a particular EJB module, you must redeploy all EJB JARs within the application. This means that WebLogic must effectively redeploy the whole EAR.

- JSP pages and servlets can access the EJB interfaces in their parent classloader. Because the EJB classloader is the parent for all web classloaders, you need not package EJB interfaces in any of the web applications. The delegation model ensures that if the class in the web application needs to invoke an EJB method, it can load the required EJB interfaces by passing the call to the parent EJB classloader.

- Each web application creates a separate classloader for each servlet and JSP page (actually, the compiled implementation class for the JSP). This servlet-specific classloader is a child of the web application classloader. This allows you to reload individual servlets and JSPs easily, without the need for redeploying the web application or affecting any of the EJBs.

We've just looked at the standard classloading scheme supported by WebLogic. Later, we shall see how you can override this and set up your own classloading hierarchy.

Overriding the parent delegation model

There is another twist in this tale. As explained in Chapter 2, you can configure a web application classloader so that it doesn't use the default parent delegation scheme by setting the prefer-web-inf-classes element to true in the *weblogic.xml* descriptor file. When this flag is enabled, the web application classloader instead tries to load classes from its *WEB-INF/* directory *before* asking its parent classloader. For example, if you need to ensure that your web application uses its own version of an XML parser, you can package the parser classes in the WAR and enable the prefer-web-inf-classes option. In this case, any code within your web application will always use the version of the XML parser in your WAR.

You must be careful, though. If you try to pass an XML Document object, say, to an EJB, a ClassCastException will be thrown because the EJB classloader will load a different version of the Document class.

EJB redeployment

WebLogic 8.1 provides an additional redeployment capability for EJBs, which can be useful during development. If you set the enable-bean-class-redeploy element to true in the *weblogic-ejb-jar.xml* descriptor file, the bean implementation class is loaded in a child classloader of the EJB classloader. In other words, the EJB classloader loads all the classes (such as the interface files) except for the implementation class, which is loaded by a new child classloader. As a result, you will be able to redeploy the bean's implementation without redeploying the entire bean. For example, to refresh the implementation class, you need only execute something like the following:

```
weblogic.Deployer -name appname -redeploy com/oreilly/ejb/EJB.class
```

Deploying EJB modules and web applications as separate applications

If your application includes servlets and JSPs that make use of EJBs, we recommend deploying the web application and EJB components as part of the same application (EAR). If you instead deploy your web applications and EJB modules independently (i.e., not as part of an EAR), then they are treated as separate applications. This means that all web applications and EJB applications are assigned their own classloaders. As a result, your EJB classes are not visible to the servlets and JSPs because they are bound within the scope of their own classloaders. In this instance, if you want to provide servlets and JSPs with access to the EJBs, you need to package the EJB interfaces in the web application (WAR).

Earlier we saw how WebLogic optimizes the performance of method calls to "remote" objects if the objects are located in the same JVM, using pass-by-reference instead of the marshalling and unmarshalling that usually would occur. This same difference in the behavior of method calls is observed when packaging web applications and EJBs in the same EAR, as well as when deploying web applications and EJBs separately as independent applications. In the former case, if a servlet invokes an EJB method, WebLogic uses pass-by-reference semantics just like an ordinary Java method call. In the latter case, WebLogic uses traditional RMI semantics even though the web application and the EJB component live in the same JVM. The same behavior occurs when an EJB invokes a method on another EJB deployed as a separate application.

Thus, WebLogic's pass-by-reference optimization occurs only if the caller and callee belong to the same application. If WebLogic were to support pass-by-reference semantics, a ClassCastException would be generated when a parameter bound to a version of the class loaded in one classloader is assigned to another version of the same class in another classloader. To avoid this problem, WebLogic must use the traditional call-by-value semantics when making RMI calls between applications. For this reason, WebLogic cannot support pass-by-reference semantics when web applications and EJB components are deployed as separate applications.

 Packaging your web applications and EJB modules within the same application results in much better performance than if they were deployed as separate applications.

Customizing the classloader hierarchy

WebLogic 8.1 lets you customize the default classloading scheme. You can determine your own classloading hierarchy, arranging the classloaders for the EJB and web application modules in any way you like. A custom classloading scheme gives you better control over which modules are reloadable and which classes are visible between modules. However, this flexibility is useful in limited cases for the following reasons:

- Any custom classloading scheme may not have more than three levels of nesting. This includes the base application classloader.
- Only web applications and EJB modules may participate in this custom classloading scheme.
- Servlet reloading is disabled for web application modules participating in a custom classloading scheme.
- If you set up a classloader for each EJB module, you lose WebLogic's call-by-reference RMI optimization, and the call-by-value semantics are used instead.
- Other application servers may not support custom classloader hierarchies. Thus, your application may break compatibility with other J2EE application servers by choosing to avoid the default classloading scheme.
- You may need to package your application in such a way that it can take advantage of the new classloading scheme.

Given these caveats, let's look at how you can create your own classloader hierarchy. The key lies in specifying a collection of nestable XML elements within the *weblogic-application.xml* descriptor file. These elements are, of course, optional, and if you don't specify them, the default classloader scheme is used. As an example, let's create the classloader hierarchy depicted in Figure 12-2.

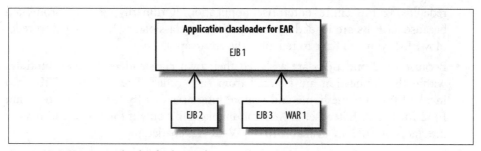

Figure 12-2. A custom classloader hierarchy

As the figure illustrates, the top-level application classloader loads an EJB module and has two child classloaders. The first child classloader loads an EJB module, while the second classloader loads an EJB and web application module. This nonstandard hierarchy for the enterprise application can be accomplished with the following XML definition:

```
<!--
    The classloader-structure element nesting indicates the classloader hierarchy.
    Each can contain any number of module-ref elements, indicating the modules
```

```
    at that level.
    -->
<classloader-structure>
 <!-- Each module-ref element contains a module-uri, which points
  to a module within the enterprise application -->

 <!-- load EJB1.jar within the base application classloader -->
 <module-ref>
  <module-uri>EJB1.jar</module-uri>
 </module-ref>
 <classloader-structure>
   <!-- load EJB2.jar in a child of the base application classloader -->
   <module-ref>
    <module-uri>EJB2.jar</module-uri>
   </module-ref>
 </classloader-structure>
 <!-- load EJB3.jar and WAR1.war in a child of the base application classloader -->
 <classloader-structure>
  <module-ref>
   <module-uri>EJB3.jar</module-uri>
  </module-ref>
  <module-ref>
   <module-uri>WAR1.war</module-uri>
  </module-ref>
 </classloader-structure>
</classloader-structure>
```

This classloader structure has several implications, all of which follow from the earlier description of classloading:

- Because EJB2 is assigned its own classloader, you can redeploy EJB2 without redeploying the entire enterprise application. Ordinarily, this is prohibited because all EJBs are loaded by the application classloader. If you need to redeploy EJB1, you will have to redeploy the entire application.

- Because EJB2 and EJB3 are assigned their own classloaders, the two modules within the application are isolated from each other. The only way EJB2 can invoke EJB3 is if the home and remote interfaces of EJB3 are packaged within EJB2 (or EJB1). Likewise, WAR1 can invoke EJB2 only if the home and remote interfaces of EJB2 are available to the WAR classloader.

You can use standard techniques to overcome these visibility problems. For instance, our sample classloader hierarchy ensures that WAR1 can, by default, see and make use of EJB1. If WAR1 must be able to use EJB2, you must make its home and remote interfaces available to WAR1. An easy way to achieve this is to place the home and remote interfaces of the EJB within the *WEB-INF/classes* directory in WAR2 itself.

Deployment Considerations

In this section, we consider some of the implications of deploying applications to a single-server development environment, as well as the changes to your deployment strategy when migrating to a multiserver domain or clustered domain. We examine how you can partially redeploy files within web applications and EJB modules, and also examine class visibility restrictions on resource adapters. In addition, we cover how to effectively package shared utility classes within an enterprise application. Finally, we look at how to register server-specific startup and shutdown classes, and how to register application-specific listener classes that respond to specific events during the deployment life cycle of the application.

Single-Server Deployment

Suppose your domain consists of a single WebLogic server—a setup that is typical during the development stages of your application. This means that you're deploying applications directly to the Administration Server itself for development purposes. This setup is ideal for iterative development environments, where your IDE in combination with build scripts can deploy to WebLogic Server as you develop your applications.

Setting up this scenario is quite simple—you need to create a WebLogic domain that consists of the Administration Server alone. As we saw earlier, this single-server setup automatically defaults to the development mode. This means you can immediately begin deploying your application components by placing them under the *applications* folder of your domain. Things are even simpler if you deploy application components in exploded format. Because the Administration Server starts up in no-staging mode by default, this allows you to make in-place updates to static files and JSPs within any exploded WAR. Likewise, you can update servlets in place by simply overwriting the older class files in the *WEB-INF/classes* directory of your exploded application. In fact, as we shall see later, you can perform in-place updates on any class that's loaded by the web container! This includes the tag-implementation classes for any JSP tags you may use.

In many instances you will need to redeploy an application. For example, when you add a new servlet to a WAR deployed in exploded format, even though the new class files have been copied to *WEB-INF/classes*, your changes to the *web.xml* descriptor file will not be picked up by WebLogic until you redeploy the WAR. Of course, you can redeploy the web application using either the Administration Console or the Deployer tool. Alternatively, you could trigger the redeployment of the exploded WAR by "touching" a *REDEPLOY* file placed under the *WEB-INF* directory.

Likewise, if you need to incorporate any changes made to EJBs deployed directly under the *applications* directory, you need to simply "touch" the *REDEPLOY* file located under the *META-INF* directory, in which case the EJB module or resource adapter is redeployed. If the EJBs and resource adapters are packaged within an exploded EAR, you must redeploy the entire EAR. Again, this can be done by simply touching a *REDEPLOY* file placed under the *META-INF* folder of the exploded EAR. It is a harsh world—to have to redeploy the entire EAR in order to refresh the EJBs within the exploded EAR. But, as we've already seen, the reason for enforcing this constraint lies within WebLogic's classloading hierarchy.

Multiserver Deployment

If your development environment spans beyond a single WebLogic instance, the auto-deployment features are ineffectual because the auto-deploy feature supports deployment only to the Administration Server. In these situations, you should consider using the Deployer tool, which lets you target applications to particular servers within the domain. Alternatively, you can use the Administration Console to handle multiserver deployments. We already have seen how the Deployer tool lets you deploy, redeploy, and undeploy an application across multiple target servers. Typically, you need to redeploy static files or JSPs within a web application:

```
java weblogic.Deployer -name mywebapp -targets server1,server2 -redeploy help/*.jsp
```

Or you need to refresh EJB modules used by your web applications:

```
java weblogic.Deployer -name myEJB -targets server1,server2 -redeploy
```

Alternatively, you could rely on external staging for your application. In this case, if you need to redeploy the application on multiple servers, you need to manually copy the application to the staging directory of each target server. Then you need to use the Deployer tool along with its -external_stage option to activate your application on all target servers. Clearly, it becomes easier to distribute the application files if the Administration Server and the managed servers use a shared disk.

Cluster Deployment

You should be careful when deploying applications to a WebLogic cluster. By default, WebLogic allows you to deploy applications to a partial cluster.* In other words, the two-phase deployment strategy ensures that the deployment succeeds on those clustered servers that can be reached by the Administration Server at the time of deployment. If it detects an unavailable clustered server during the prepare phase, a warning message is written to the console log, and the deployment proceeds on all available members of the cluster. Deployment on the unavailable server is initiated the next time the server starts and joins the cluster.

Alternatively, you can configure the domain so that the two-phase deployment strategy succeeds only if *all* members of the cluster are reachable when deploying an application to a WebLogic cluster. If a clustered server instance is not available during the prepare phase, the deployment is terminated with an error message written to the console log. You can either start the failed server or remove it from the cluster, before

---

* In WebLogic 7.0, deployment to a partial cluster is available only once you've applied Service Pack 1 or higher.

reinitiating the deployment. In order to configure this strict deployment strategy, you can select the domain from the left pane of the Administration Console, and then navigate to the Configuration/General tab. By enabling the Enable Cluster Constraints option, you ensure that an application is deployed to a cluster only if *all* members of the cluster also are available at the time of deployment. Another way to enforce the same constraint is to enable the -DClusterConstraintsEnabled=true command-line option when starting up the Administration Server.* We recommend you ensure that all servers in the cluster are running and available before you deploy applications to the cluster. You should not modify a cluster's membership during deployment—i.e., add, remove, or shut down managed servers when one or more deployment tasks on the cluster are in progress.

WebLogic also allows you to deploy a pinned service to multiple managed servers in a cluster.† However, this approach isn't recommended because it affects the load balancing and scalability of your solution. If you target a pinned service to multiple servers within a cluster, a warning message is written to the logs, but the deployment still succeeds.

Remember, if you shut down the Administration Server for a domain, you cancel all pending deployments. This means you could potentially end up with an inconsistent deployment across the cluster. For instance, you could deploy an application to a partial cluster where one or more of the clustered servers are unavailable, then shut down the Administration Server and later restart the unavailable server in the cluster. Because the Administration Server is unavailable, the target server is incapable of receiving the pending deployment task for that particular application. In this way, your cluster reaches a state where the application is not available on all members of the cluster. Of course, this inconsistent state will remain only until the Administration Server is brought back up. Thus, the availability of the Administration Server is vital to ensuring homogenous deployments across the cluster.

Web Applications

Let's revisit some of the issues concerning deploying web applications to WebLogic. As mentioned earlier, you can run WebLogic in two modes:

- In development mode, where the auto-deployment feature is enabled
- In production mode, where the WebLogic instance participates in a live deployment

Each mode has a very different impact on how web applications are deployed.

---

* In WebLogic 7.0, you can enforce this strict deployment strategy by invoking the Deployer tool with the -enforceClusterConstraints flag.

† WebLogic 7.0 prevents you from deploying a pinned service to multiple servers in the cluster, unless you have applied Service Pack 1 or higher.

Using auto-deployment

You'll find that auto-deployment works differently, depending on whether the web application is deployed as a WAR (in archived format) or as a directory (in exploded format). If the web application has been deployed in archived format, you can trigger redeployment automatically, simply by modifying the WAR file or by overwriting it with a new version. If the web application is targeted to other managed servers, it also will be redeployed on those server instances.

If the web application has been deployed in exploded format, many of the changes to the resources within the web application are reflected automatically, without the need for redeployment. For instance, changes to static files (HTML pages, images, etc.) and JSP pages are reflected automatically. You also can refresh compiled Java classes used by the web application. More accurately, we mean Java classes loaded by the web application classloader. This means you can overwrite compiled classes for the servlets, JSP tag implementation classes, and any Java classes located under the *WEB-INF/classes* folder without the need for redeployment. You even can copy new classes into the *WEB-INF/classes* folder, and they will be loaded automatically by the web container on demand. Of course, if you've created new servlets or JSP tags, you will need to register those changes in the appropriate descriptors and redeploy the web application. The only annoying side effect of this hot-deploy feature is that by replacing any Java class with a later timestamp, you force the web container to reload everything under the *WEB-INF/classes* folder using a new classloader.

As we saw earlier, you can trigger the redeployment for the web application by simply touching a *REDEPLOY* file in the *WEB-INF* directory. Alternatively, you can use the Administration Console. Select the web application from the left pane and then click the Redeploy button. You also can adjust the frequency with which WebLogic looks at the filesystem for changes. Simply navigate to the Deployments/Web Application Modules node in the left pane of the Administration Console, select the desired web application, and then go to the right pane to change the value of the Servlet Reload Check Secs setting in the Configuration/Descriptor tab.

Using production mode

If the web application has been deployed as a WAR, you need to redeploy the entire WAR to reflect any changes to JSP pages, static files, or compiled Java classes. However, if the web application has been deployed as an exploded directory, you can use the Deployer tool to reflect any changes you've made to JSPs or static files:

```
java weblogic.Deployer -name myapp -redeploy mywar/index.jsp
```

So, WebLogic permits partial redeployment only for web applications that are deployed in an exploded form. If you've overwritten or created new Java classes, or modified the XML descriptors for the web application, you must redeploy the entire web application for those changes to take effect.

You also need to be aware of serious consequences when redeploying a web application on a production WebLogic environment. If a web application has been deployed using the default staging mode, the entire web application may need to be distributed over the network to all the targeted servers. This increased administration traffic may have performance implications on your network.

By default, WebLogic destroys all current HTTP user sessions when you redeploy a web application. You could work around this limitation by initiating the redeployment when no one is using your web application. Alternatively, you could instruct WebLogic to preserve all active user sessions when the web application is redeployed. To preserve user sessions across redeployment, you must enable the save-sessions-enabled flag in the container-descriptor element of the *weblogic.xml* descriptor file for the web application:

```
<!-- weblogic.xml descriptor entry -->
<container-descriptor>
  <container-param>
    <param-name>save-sessions-enabled</param-name>
    <param-value>true</param-value>
  </container-param>
</container-descriptor>
```

EJB Modules

WebLogic 8.1 lets you organize the application's classloaders in a way that lets you reload individual EJB modules. By assigning a separate classloader to each EJB module, you can ensure that an EJB module may be redeployed independently of others. The following portion from the *weblogic-application.xml* descriptor file shows how to set up this classloading scheme:

```
<classloader-structure>
  <classloader-structure>
    <module-ref>
      <module-uri>EJB1.jar</module-uri>
    </module-ref>
  </classloader-structure>
  <classloader-structure>
    <module-ref>
      <module-uri>EJB2.jar</module-uri>
    </module-ref>
  </classloader-structure>
  <!-- load other EJB JARs in their own classloaders -->
</classloader-structure>
```

In addition, WebLogic lets you reload the EJB implementation classes, without having to reload the entire EJB module. We recommend that you utilize this EJB reload feature only in a development setting. Because EJBs are accessed via their interfaces, WebLogic is able to load the EJB implementation classes in their own classloaders, thereby allowing you to reload these classes without having to redeploy the entire module. The following example shows how to partially update the files within an application:

```
java weblogic.Deployer -name myapp -redeploy myejb/FooImpl.class yourejb
```

After the -redeploy option, you must specify a list of files that need to be refreshed. The paths must be relative to the root of the application, and must refer to either a specific element (e.g., FooImpl.class) or a module within the application (e.g., yourejb). This approach is similar to how you would partially update individual JSP pages within a web application.

If you have specified the EJB implementation class, WebLogic is able to refresh the class without having to redeploy the EJB module. However, if you've specified an EJB interface or an EJB module, the whole EJB module must be redeployed. Depending on the classloader hierarchy, this may result in other modules being redeployed as well. For instance, if the modules myejb and yourejb are assigned the same classloader, any request to redeploy myejb also triggers a redeployment on yourejb (and vice versa). Moreover, if a module (say, mywar) is loaded into the child of the myejb classloader, any request to redeploy myejb also triggers a redeployment on mywar.

Utility Classes

There are several ways to make shared libraries and utility classes available to various application components. If the utility classes need to be shared by multiple applications, you can include them in WebLogic's classpath so that they can be picked up by the system classloader. This also holds true for any classes that are used by WebLogic during the startup sequence—for instance, JDBC driver classes, XML parser factories, and RMI implementation classes. However, if you need to replace any of these libraries with newer versions, these changes are reflected only after you reboot the server. You should consider this approach only if you want to explicitly share the libraries across multiple deployed applications, and these libraries are not likely to change very often.

If the utility classes will be used only by a specific web application, you can either place them in the *WEB-INF/classes* folder, or package them into a JAR and then place the JAR in the *WEB-INF/lib* folder. If you update or overwrite any of these utility classes, you need only to redeploy the web application for those changes to take effect.

If the utility classes must be accessible to an EJB module, you can either bundle them directly into the EJB JAR, or use the standard Class-Path entry in the EJB's *META-INF/MANIFEST.MF* manifest file to reference the shared libraries:

```
Manifest-Version: 1.0
Class-Path: shared_library1.jar shared_libary2.jar
```

Because all EJB modules are loaded into the same classloader, this implies that the libraries are visible to all EJBs within the enterprise application. Furthermore, because the web application classloader is a child of the EJB classloader, this means that the shared libraries will also be visible to all web applications. In this way, you can make the shared libraries accessible to all EJB modules and web applications within the enterprise application.

A downside of using the manifest file to extend the EJB classloader is that you must create an EJB JAR or web application WAR. Hence, shared libraries referenced from within the manifest file have *no* effect in exploded applications.

WebLogic 8.1 provides a less portable but simpler approach to sharing libraries and utility classes between the modules of an enterprise application. Simply place the utility classes in the *APP-INF/classes* folder and the libraries in the *APP-INF/lib* folder of your enterprise application. The following example illustrates the internal structure of an EAR that allows you to make utility libraries accessible to all modules within the EAR:

```
APP-INF\lib\log4j.jar
APP-INF\lib\dom4j.jar
APP-INF\lib\jdbc-ra_tx.jar
...
APP-INF\classes\com\oreilly\wlguide\utils\MyUtils.class
...
META-INF\application.xml
META-INF\weblogic-application.xml
ejb_jar1.jar
ejb_jar2.jar
...
my_webapp1.war
my_webapp2.war
...
```

One advantage of this approach is that it will work with exploded applications as well. All of the utility libraries that are deployed in this way are loaded by the application classloader, and hence can be shared by all modules.

In addition, classes placed under the application's *APP-INF* folder are accessible to all EJBs and web applications, *regardless* of the classloader hierarchy you specify. Any module-specific classloader is a descendant of the base application classloader. On the other hand, the visibility of any libraries declared in the EJB JAR's manifest file is limited only by the scope of its classloader and any of its child classloaders. So, under the default classloading scheme, classes referenced in the EJB JAR's manifest file are available to all EJBs and web applications. If you have defined a custom classloader hierarchy for the enterprise application, the libraries referenced in the EJB JAR's manifest file are accessible either to the EJB module itself or to other modules as well, depending on how you have set up the classloader hierarchy.

By sharing the same copy of utility classes and library JARs, you maintain consistency among the various applications and their modules, and also ease the task of managing the overall deployment.

Resource Adapters

In WebLogic 8.1, a resource adapter packaged within an enterprise application is assigned its own classloader. This means that the other web applications and EJB modules within the application cannot access the classes implementing the resource adapter. To make the resource adapter implementation classes visible to EJB modules and web applications, you should treat them as utility classes and libraries. In other words, you can either place the resource adapter classes in the *APP-INF/classes* folder, or package them in a JAR and then place the JAR in the *APP-INF/lib* folder. Also ensure that you don't include any resource adapter classes in WebLogic's system classpath.

Startup and Shutdown Classes

Startup and shutdown classes provide you with the opportunity to execute Java code during the server's startup or shutdown sequence. A *startup class* is any Java class that implements the weblogic.common.T3StartupDef interface. Similarly, a *shutdown class* is any Java class that implements the weblogic.common.T3ShutdownDef interface. Example 4-6 shows how to create a startup class that registers a custom RMI object. Note that startup classes are not packaged like J2EE components—they are distributed simply as class files, or perhaps bundled in a JAR. To deploy a startup or shutdown class, you need to make the class available to the server's classpath. If your domain is configured to use Node Managers, you also must add it to the classpath attribute in the Remote Start tab for the Managed Server.

Once the classes are placed in the server's classpath, you can then deploy the class from the Administration Console. Navigate to the Deployments/Startup & Shutdown node from the left pane, and then choose one of the "Configure a new ..." options to set up a startup or shutdown class. You will need to supply the fully qualified class name and values for any arguments that are expected by the class. Startup classes support two additional configuration options:

"Failure is Fatal"
  This option determines whether a failure in the startup class should prevent the server from starting. By default, the server proceeds with its boot sequence even if a startup class fails.

"Run before Application Deployments"
  This option determines whether the startup class should be run before (or after) all services have been instantiated and all applications have been deployed. By default, startup classes are run after applications are deployed, at which stage all the services, including JMS and JDBC, are also in place.

The ServerMBean interface provides an additional Run Before Application Activation attribute, which ensures the startup classes are invoked just after the services have been initialized, but before any of the applications are deployed. Figure 12-3 illustrates these stages during the server's startup sequence.

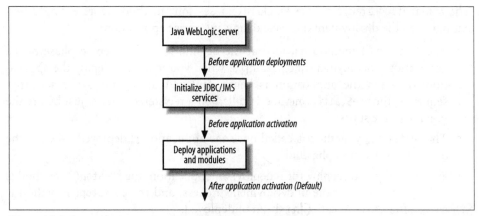

Figure 12-3. Stages during server startup sequence

Application Deployment Life Cycle Listeners

In WebLogic 8.1, you can associate a listener class with an enterprise application, which is invoked at specific times during the deployment life cycle of the enterprise application. This provides you with the opportunity to execute specific actions either before or after the enterprise application is deployed or undeployed. A common use for the life cycle listener class is to initialize (or destroy) singleton objects, such as an application-wide cache of EJB home objects. An application life cycle listener class must extend the weblogic.application.ApplicationLifecycleListener abstract base class. Example 12-4 shows a simple implementation of such a listener class.

Example 12-4. A simple deployment life cycle listener

```
package com.oreilly.wlguide.pkg;

import weblogic.application.ApplicationLifecycleListener;
import weblogic.application.ApplicationLifecycleEvent;

public class MyAppLifecycleListener extends ApplicationLifecycleListener {
    public void preStart(ApplicationLifecycleEvent evt) {
        System.out.println(evt.getApplicationContext().getApplicationName());
    }
    public void postStart(ApplicationLifecycleEvent evt) {
        //initialize some app-specific cache of service objects...
        com.oreilly.wlguide.pkg.MyObjCache.initialize();
    }
    public void preStop(ApplicationLifecycleEvent evt) {
    }
    public void postStop(ApplicationLifecycleEvent evt) {
    }
}
```

The ApplicationLifecycleListener class exposes four methods representing different points in the deployment life cycle of any enterprise application:

- The preStart() method is called at the beginning of the prepare phase of the application's deployment. For example, when you manually deploy the application, or when the application is being deployed during the server's startup sequence, the preStart() method is called on a registered listener just before the prepare phase starts.

- The postStart() method is called once the application is deployed—i.e., at the end of the activation phase.

- Similarly, if you undeploy (or redeploy) an application, the preStop() method is called at the start of the undeployment process, and the postStop() method is called after the application has been undeployed.

So, for example, if you redeploy an application, the methods will be invoked on each registered application life cycle listener class in the following order: preStop(), postStop(), preStart(), postStart(). In the case of a multiserver deployment, the registered application life cycle listeners will be invoked on each server to which the enterprise application is targeted.

Once you've created the application life cycle listener class, you simply need to register it with the enterprise application. To achieve this, you can specify the listener element in the *weblogic-application.xml* deployment descriptor of an enterprise application. The following example shows how to register our simple listener class with an enterprise application:

```
<weblogic-application>
<!-- -->
<listener>
  <listener-class>com.oreilly.wlguide.pkg.MyAppLifecycleListener</listener-class>
</listener>
<!-- possible startup and shutdown class registration -->
</weblogic-application>
```

The listener class must be made available to all servers that will host the enterprise application. You can either include the listener class in the server's classpath, or place it in the *APP-INF/classes* directory within the application itself. Alternatively, you can bundle the class into a JAR, and later package the JAR within the EAR. In this case, you also need to specify the listener-uri element to indicate the path to the JAR within the EAR file. For instance, if the sample listener class is packaged within *utils.jar* in the enterprise application, you must register the listener class as follows:

```
<listener>
  <listener-class>com.oreilly.wlguide.pkg.LifecycleListener</listener-class>
  <listener-uri>utils.jar</listener-uri>
</listener>
```

Instead of registering a listener class that responds to all of these events during the application's deployment, you can create simple application-specific startup or shutdown classes. A startup class will get executed at the same point as the listener's preStart( ) method, and the shutdown class will be invoked at the same point as the listener's postStop( ) method. A startup or shutdown class extends the same abstract listener class, but simply implements a static main( ) method. Here is an example of a shutdown class:

```
public class MyShutdown extends ApplicationLifecycleListener  {
    public static void main(String argp[]) {
        System.err.println("Just shut down the application!");
    }
}
```

Startup and shutdown classes are registered in a similar way to the listener classes, using the startup and shutdown elements in the *weblogic-application.xml* descriptor for the application:

```
<weblogic-application>
 <!-- -->
  <startup>
   <startup-class>com.oreilly.wlguide.pkg.MyStartup</startup-class>
   <!-- Use startup-uri if packaged in JAR -->
  </startup>
  <shutdown>
   <shutdown-class>com.oreilly.wlguide.pkg.MyShutdown</shutdown-class>
   <!-- Use shutdown-uri if packaged in JAR -->
  </shutdown>
</weblogic-application>
```

You may register any number of startup and shutdown classes with an application. Startup and shutdown classes are invoked in the order in which they are declared in the *weblogic-application.xml* descriptor file.

We recommend that you use life cycle listeners instead of the startup and shutdown classes. The latter approach may be deprecated in future releases.

Split Directory Development

WebLogic 8.1 introduces a split development directory structure to facilitate the iterative development of applications on a single WebLogic instance. This development methodology allows you to very quickly create, build, and deploy applications to WebLogic Server. The essence of the methodology, as the name suggests, is a split development directory. In other words, the files within the enterprise application are spread across two directories:

- A *source* directory that contains the source for the enterprise application and all its modules, including the deployment descriptor files

- A *build* directory that contains the compiled classes generated by the build process.

Even though it is the build directory that is deployed, WebLogic can recognize the split directory deployment and automatically locate information from both the source and build directories.

The split development directory structure is applicable only to enterprise applications that exist in exploded form. If you are developing web applications or EJB modules only, you easily can organize them in an enterprise application and still benefit from the split development directory approach. The best way to illustrate the technique is by example, and the following sections look at all aspects of the development. We also examine the directory layout, and the various Ant tasks (wlcompile, wlappc, wldeploy, wlpackage) used to support this scheme.

You don't have to use the split development directory scheme if you already have established a build process that prepares the enterprise application and all the necessary modules. However, the split directory layout does let you set up an easily manageable and quickly deployable development environment.

Directory Layout

The most important part of the split directory development approach is the structure of the source and build directories. Example 12-5 illustrates the layout of a sample split development directory.

Example 12-5. A split development directory structure

```
myappdev/build.xml
myappdev/src
myappdev/src/myappEar/APP-INF/lib/log4j-1.2.6.jar
myappdev/src/myappEar/META-INF/application.xml
myappdev/src/myappEar/META-INF/weblogic-application.xml
myappdev/src/myappEar/myEJB/META-INF/ejb-jar.xml
myappdev/src/myappEar/myEJB/META-INF/weblogic-ejb-jar.xml
myappdev/src/myappEar/myEJB/src/com/oreilly/wlguide/MyEJB/MyEJB.java
myappdev/src/myappEar/myEJB/src/com/oreilly/wlguide/MyEJB/MyEJBBean.java
myappdev/src/myappEar/myEJB/src/com/oreilly/wlguide/MyEJB/MyEJBHome.java
myappdev/src/myappEar/www/index.jsp
myappdev/src/myappEar/www/WEB-INF/lib/dom4j.jar
myappdev/src/myappEar/www/WEB-INF/src/com/oreilly/wlguide/MyServlet.java
myappdev/src/myappEar/www/WEB-INF/lib/somelib.jar
myappdev/src/myappEar/www/WEB-INF/web.xml
myappdev/src/myappEar/www/WEB-INF/weblogic.xml
myappdev/build
```

As you can see, the files within the enterprise application have been split across two directories:

src

> The *src* directory holds the source files for the application and all its modules, including their deployment descriptors. In the example, the *src* folder includes the web resources for a web application, the source Java files for any servlets and JSP pages, the source Java files for an EJB, and their deployment descriptors. In fact, the *src* directory also contains any support libraries that may be required by the enterprise application or the web application. In the example, we have placed a dom4j library in the *WEB-INF/lib* folder, and a log4j library in *APP-INF/lib* folder.

build

> The *build* directory holds the compiled classes generated by the supplied Ant tasks during the build process. You must refer to this directory when deploying the enterprise application. In the example, we've placed the *build* directory right next to the *src* folder. It could be placed anywhere so long as it's accessible to the WebLogic server on which you are going to eventually deploy the application.

WebLogic's split development directory layout provides you with a number of benefits:

- As far as WebLogic Server is concerned, the enterprise application is split across two directories. Hence, the source files never need to be copied over to the deployment directory. WebLogic will automatically locate the required source files, such as the deployment descriptors, JSP pages, and third-party libraries, from their source locations.

- The output generated as a result of compiling the EJBs, servlets, and JSPs is placed in the separate build directory. This clean separation makes for a neater development environment, and lends itself to a more intuitive integration with existing source code version control systems.

- You continue to develop your enterprise application using the exploded directory format. This means that you can make any changes to the source files, without having to synchronize these changes. WebLogic will pick up these changes automatically, and avoid a full redeployment of the application or module. This behavior is similar to the auto-deploy feature we discussed earlier.

Building an Application

To compile the source Java files within an application that uses the split development directory layout, you should use the `wlcompile` Ant task. Here is an excerpt from an Ant build file that can be used with our example directory layout:

```
<property name="tmp.dir" value="build" />
<property name="app.name" value="myappEar" />
<property name="src.dir" value="src/${app.name}" />
<property name="dest.dir" value="${tmp.dir}/${app.name}" />
<target name="compile" description="Only compiles myappEar application, no appc">
  <wlcompile srcdir="${src.dir}" destdir="${dest.dir}" />
</target>
```

Running this Ant target will compile all the Java files located under the application's *src* directory, including the source code for the web application under *WEB-INF/src* and all the EJB modules. The compiled classes will be placed in the *build* directory. Thus, if you invoke this Ant target on our example application, the following class files are generated in the build directory:

```
myappdev/build/myappEar/.beabuild.txt
myappdev/build/myappEar/myEJB/com/oreilly/wlguide/MyEJB/MyEJB.class
myappdev/build/myappEar/myEJB/com/oreilly/wlguide/MyEJB/MyEJBBean.class
myappdev/build/myappEar/myEJB/com/oreilly/wlguide/MyEJB/MyEJBHome.class
myappdev/build/myappEar/www/WEB-INF/classes/com/oreilly/wlguide/MyServlet.class
```

The *.beabuild.txt* file shouldn't be removed because it points back to the source directory and allows WebLogic's deployment machinery to access the source files and deployment descriptors. You can further refine which modules get compiled using the includes and excludes attributes. These attributes should be set to a comma-separated list of modules that you want to explicitly include (or exclude) during the compile. For example, to only compile the EJB module, invoke the wlcompile task as follows:

```
<wlcompile srcdir="${src.dir}" destdir="${dest.dir}" includes="myEJB" />
```

Similarly, to compile all application source files except for certain modules, you could invoke the wlcompile task like this:

```
<wlcompile srcdir="${src.dir}" destdir="${dest.dir}"
           excludes="myEJB, someOtherModule" />
```

The wlcompile task simply compiles the source Java files within the application. You also can run the appc compiler over the modules, which goes a step further and compiles the JSP pages and generates the container classes for all EJB modules. If you omit this step, this compilation would otherwise occur at runtime or deploy time. In order to invoke the appc compiler, we've used the wlappc Ant task from within the build script as follows:

```
<target name="appc" description="Runs weblogic.appc on your application">
    <wlappc source="${dest.dir}" />
</target>
```

In our example, the following additional files will be generated:

```
myappdev/build/myappEar/myEJB/com/oreilly/wlguide/MyEJB/stateless_7ismqx_EOImpl.class
myappdev/build/myappEar/myEJB/com/oreilly/wlguide/MyEJB/stateless_7ismqx_EOImplRTD.
xml
myappdev/build/myappEar/myEJB/com/oreilly/wlguide/MyEJB/stateless_7ismqx_HomeImpl.
class
myappdev/build/myappEar/myEJB/com/oreilly/wlguide/MyEJB/stateless_7ismqx_HomeImplRTD.
xml
myappdev/build/myappEar/myEJB/com/oreilly/wlguide/MyEJB/stateless_7ismqx_Impl.class
myappdev/build/myappEar/myEJB/com/oreilly/wlguide/MyEJB/stateless_7ismqx_Intf.class
myappdev/build/myappEar/www/WEB-INF/classes/jsp_servlet/__index.class
myappdev/build/myappEar/www/WEB-INF/classes/jsp_servlet/__new.class
```

Deploying an Application

Once you have compiled the enterprise application, you are ready to deploy it to WebLogic Server. Once again, you can either use the Administration Console or invoke the wldeploy Ant task, which functions much like the Deployer tool. The following snippet from an Ant script shows how to deploy the application in the example:

```
<property name="adminurl" value="t3://10.0.10.10:7001/" />
<target name="deploy" description="Deploys (and redeploys) the entire application">
    <wldeploy adminurl="${adminurl}" user="${user}" password="${password}"
            action="deploy" source="${dest.dir}" name="myappEar" />
</target>
```

Notice how we've specified the build directory as the source for the application. Similarly, if you use the Administration Console to deploy the application, again you must refer to the build directory so that WebLogic can detect the split development directory layout. Use the action attribute to specify a particular deployment action. The wldeploy task can perform the same actions as the Deployer tool, so you can specify all of the following values for the action attribute: deploy, undeploy, redeploy, cancel, start, stop, and distribute. The wldeploy task supports other attributes that have the same semantics as the Deployer tool, including the Boolean-valued attributes debug, verbose, failonerror, nowait, nostage, and remote attributes, and the string-valued attributes id, name, and targets. The next example shows how to verbosely redeploy just the web application to a particular server:

```
<target name="redeploy.www" description="Redeploys just the www module only">
    <wldeploy adminurl="${adminurl}" user="${user}" password="${password}"
            action="redeploy"  targets="www@${servername}" name="myappEar"
            verbose="yes" debug="yes" />
</target>
```

Packaging an Application

You also can generate a more traditional EAR from the split development directory layout of your application. The wlpackage task extracts the relevant application files from the source and build directories and packages these into an EAR, either in archived form or exploded directory form. The following two targets show how to package an application that uses the split development directory scheme:

```
<property name="ear" value="${dist.dir}/${app.name}.ear"/>
<target name="ear" depends="build" description="Create std. J2EE EAR file">
    <wlpackage srcdir="${src.dir}" destdir="${dest.dir}" toFile="${ear}" />
</target>
<target name="explodedEar" depends="build" description="Create exploded EAR">
    <wlpackage srcdir="${src.dir}" destdir="${dest.dir}"
            toDir="${dist.dir}/${app.name}" />
</target>
```

Strictly speaking, you don't need to invoke the wlpackage task during the development life cycle. Still, it provides a useful way to package the application, perhaps when it needs to be delivered for testing or used in a production environment.

Generating the Build File

To ease the creation of the build script, WebLogic provides a utility that can automatically generate a build file for compiling, building, deploying, and redeploying the application. All you need to do is simply point the utility to an application's split development directory layout. Here is how we created the build file for the example directory layout:

```
java weblogic.BuildXMLGen -projectName myappEar -d . -user system -password psst123
src\myappEar
```

The user, system, and projectName arguments are made into Ant properties, which subsequently are used in the wlpackage, wldeploy, and wlcompile Ant tasks. The -d argument simply tells the utility where to place the generated *build.xml* file. The build script is equipped with all the tasks that you could wish for. Here is a list of targets captured by the resulting build file for the example directory structure:

```
Main targets:
  appc            Runs weblogic.appc on your application
  build           Compiles myappEar application and runs appc
  build.myEJB     Builds just the myEJB module of the application
  build.www       Builds just the www module of the application
  clean           Deletes the build and distribution directories
  compile         Only compiles myappEar application, no appc
  deploy          Deploys (and redeploys) the entire myappEar application
  descriptors     Generates application and module descriptors
  ear             Packages a standard J2EE EAR for distribution
  redeploy.myEJB  Redeploys just the myEJB module of the application
  redeploy.www    Redeploys just the www module of the application
  undeploy        UnDeploys the entire myappEar application
```

Some of these targets, such as the redeploy.myEJB target, will work only if the application's classloader scheme permits it.

Managing Domains

Imagine deploying an enterprise application to several instances of WebLogic Server (some of which may be clustered) spread across a handful of machines with different physical and network characteristics. How can you easily manage the disparate deployments on the different server instances, the different cluster configurations, the heterogeneous machines, and the multiple networks? The J2EE specification prescribes the environment and architecture for building Java applications using standard enterprise APIs. However, it does not deal with the issues of managing deployment across multiple servers and heterogeneous machines, configuring a cluster of servers for high availability and failover, or administering services and resources across multiple servers on different machines. The J2EE standard lets application server vendors implement these features using any proprietary approach. WebLogic supports the concept of domains, which satisfies these very requirements.

Domains lie at the heart of WebLogic administration, and you need to create a domain before you can use any of the resources described in this book. This chapter explains what domains are, how to create a domain, how to back up the data in a domain, and how to configure the network characteristics of a domain. It also looks at how to create and use node managers, which provide a way of monitoring and controlling the life cycle of managed servers within a domain.

Structure of a Domain

A *domain* represents a logical collection of one or more WebLogic server instances and the resources associated with them. It consists of a single *Administration Server* that allows you to centrally manage a number of other WebLogic servers, called *Managed Servers*, which may be distributed over several machines. The domain encompasses all of the configuration data for the various machines—the deployments, clusters, physical network characteristics, and health statistics—into a single unit that can be centrally monitored and managed. The Administration Server is responsible for the domain configuration, and maintains the domain configuration data in a configuration file called *config.xml*. It also hosts the Administration Console, a tool that allows you to manage all Managed Servers, domain resources, application services, and deployed applications.

When a Managed Server starts up, it contacts the Administration Server during its configuration. The Managed Servers are the workhorses of the system—they host the various applications and associated resources and services that are needed. A Managed Server will own resources such as application components (EJBs, servlets, tag libraries), resource adapters, and startup classes. It will host services such as JDBC connection pools, JMS connection factories, JTA transaction services, XML registries, etc., that will be utilized by deployed applications.

Orthogonal to the notion of domains is the concept of a *Node Manager*. The Node Manager is a single, dedicated process on a physical machine that is responsible for the availability of *all* servers running on that machine. The Node Manager acts as one of the many agents that can monitor server health, and helps you start, stop, and automatically restart remote Managed Servers in a WebLogic domain. The Node Manager can kill managed servers that have become unstable and automatically restart servers on machines that have shut down unexpectedly. The Node Managers cooperate with the Administration Server via a secure channel. Using the Administration Console, the Node Managers provide complete control over the availability and health of all Managed Servers in the domain.

A WebLogic domain also allows you to configure different network cards and/or port numbers and adapt to the network and performance characteristics of your setup. WebLogic Server allows you to assign multiple IP addresses and ports to a Managed Server, customize the protocols supported on individual ports, and even separate external, client-based traffic from internal, server-based traffic. *Network channels* allow you to tailor the network configuration for a domain; network access points (NAPs) allow you to adjust the configuration for individual Managed Servers. For instance, you can ensure that all client-facing traffic arrives on a particular network interface card (NIC), while all internal traffic uses a different NIC. You can also use these facilities to segment application traffic from administration control traffic and elegantly handle NIC failures.

It is vital that you back up the configuration and security data associated with a WebLogic domain. We shall see how you can restore a failed Administration Server and how you can restart Managed Servers in the absence of the Administration Server. We also will examine how you can configure the behavior of the Node Manager when it needs to restart a failed server automatically or kill a server with "poor health."

A domain is WebLogic's way of simplifying management, administration, and monitoring of multiple server instances and their resources. Even though the notion of domains may seem alien to a J2EE developer, WebLogic Server provides seamless integration between the J2EE world and the administration of servers and their resources. Whenever possible, WebLogic relies on standard Java APIs to implement many of the administration and management tasks. For instance, WebLogic Server provides a JMX interface for introspecting the configuration data and monitoring runtime server statistics.

We begin by looking more closely at the structure of a domain, and at how to use the Configuration Wizard to prepare a domain. We then examine how to configure domain network resources, how to back up and restore domain information, and how to use the Node Managers to keep the domain up and running. Finally, we examine various states of a server's life cycle, and how WebLogic allows you to transition between the various states.

Designing a Domain

A WebLogic domain consists of an Administration Server together with any number of Managed Servers. The Administration Server allows you to configure all Managed Servers and resources within the domain. Every Managed Server needs to contact the Administration Server during startup so that it can obtain its configuration. For this reason, the Administration Server always should be started before any Managed Servers. The default startup script for a Managed Server takes the URL of the Administration Server as another command-line argument. For instance, you could start a Managed Server manually as follows:

```
startManagedWeblogic server-name http://localhost:7001
```

 Even though the Administration Server is critical for administering all domain resources, it is possible in certain cases to start a Managed Server in the absence of the Administration Server.

Subsets of the Managed Servers within a domain may be placed in a cluster. Thus, a domain can consist of an Administration Server, any number of Managed Servers, and multiple clusters of these Managed Servers.

WebLogic allows you to create a domain that consists of a standalone Administration Server. Typically, this configuration will be used only in development environments. In this case, your applications will be deployed (and targeted) to the single WebLogic Server instance—effectively, you are hosting applications on the Administration Server.

In general, you should deploy your applications to Managed Servers only, and leave the Administration Server to focus on the management tasks. In a typical production environment, the Administration Server will reside on a different physical machine for improved security and failover. You should take special care to ensure the availability of the Administration Server because a domain cannot be managed without it. Later, we shall see how to back up the domain's configuration data, and how to use the backup to restore the Administration Server on a different machine while still retaining control of the Managed Servers.

Managed Servers within a domain are assigned to machines. A *machine* (in WebLogic terminology) is a logical entity within a domain that represents the physical machine that hosts a Managed Server in the domain. A machine may have more than one WebLogic instance installed and running. The machine definition allows the Administration Server to connect to the Node Manager and use it to monitor, start, stop, and restart Managed Servers that belong to the domain. In addition, a WebLogic cluster uses the machine definitions to determine locality information and decide how best to replicate session data on separate hardware.

Figure 13-1 illustrates all of these concepts via a diagram of a WebLogic domain with multiple Managed Servers.

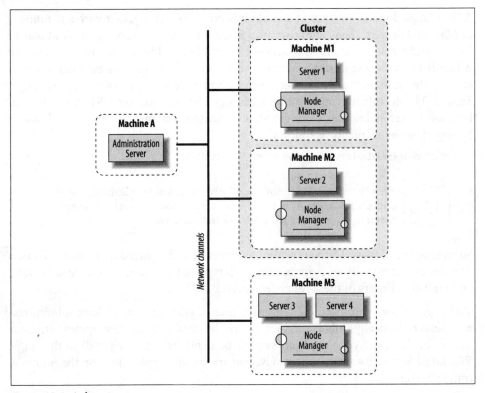

Figure 13-1. A domain

The figure shows a WebLogic domain consisting of a single Administration Server running on Machine A, and multiple Managed Servers running on machines M1-M3. Machine M3 hosts more than one Managed Server, both part of the same domain. The domain also includes a WebLogic cluster, whose members are the Managed Servers Server1 and Server2. Each machine running a Managed Server hosts a single

Node Manager that monitors the health of all of the servers on the machine and controls restarting of failed servers. Finally, network channels control the various aspects of communication between all servers and machines. This includes the listen addresses, port numbers, protocols, and NICs for each server in the domain.

A domain additionally can define a number of J2EE resources. For instance, the JDBC connection pool and JMS servers are components made available to applications within a domain. A WebLogic installation can define multiple domains, but there are certain restrictions as well. Because a domain "owns" the resources and services configured for it, domain resources cannot be shared across domains. For instance, multiple domains cannot share a resource such as a JDBC connection pool. Instead, you need to define a connection pool for each domain. A WebLogic cluster is a domain resource as well. Hence, a cluster cannot contain Managed Servers straddling different domains; they must all belong to the same domain. This means that application failover within a cluster can occur only among the Managed Servers in the same domain.

When you're setting up multiple domains, it is important that you are aware of these restrictions and keep all of these aspects in mind. A domain is a WebLogic administrative unit, a mechanism for describing your WebLogic environment. This includes the Managed Servers, the machine configuration, the network resources, and the services needed by the applications. There are no hard and fast rules for how you set up a domain, but a good design eases administration, considers the security requirements of your applications, and provides for performance and scalability. A domain should be designed to ease your management tasks while providing the required configuration of machines and level of service. Therefore, you might need to create multiple domains depending on the geographical location of your servers, or depending on the boundaries of your application.

Creating Domains

A WebLogic domain maintains a domain configuration file, called *config.xml*, along with security settings, domain and transaction logs, and startup scripts for the Administration Server and Managed Servers on the different machines. WebLogic eases the creation of all of these by providing a tool, the Configuration Wizard, which you can run as part of WebLogic Server installation or after installation. The Configuration Wizard presents a series of templates that you can use to create or extend domains. You can use the tool to create a domain with either a standalone Administration Server, a domain with multiple Managed Servers, or a domain with multiple clustered Managed Servers. In addition, the tool lets you create domains that are preconfigured with example applications.

Directory Layout

All settings for a domain are stored within the domain's root directory. Under the root directory, you will find the configuration file *config.xml*, startup scripts for Windows and Unix platforms, and subdirectories for the domain-level logs, the security data, and the applications themselves. The root directory always will contain at least the following files:

- The *config.xml* file holding the domain configuration.
- An *applications* directory that can be used to deploy J2EE applications if you configure auto-deployment.
- A *logs* directory that holds the domain logs.
- A subdirectory for the Administration Server and each Managed Server in the domain. This contains log files and LDAP data for each server.
- Scripts with which to start the servers.

When WebLogic Server runs in development mode (see Chapter 12 for details), an application poller looks at the *applications* folder under the domain, picks up any updates to a deployed application, and automatically redeploys the application. So, even though an application can be hosted from anywhere in the filesystem, you should place it under the *applications* folder if you want to take advantage of automatic redeployment.

The root directory can be placed anywhere on your filesystem, so long as the scripts and applications have access to the WebLogic Server installation and the JDK. You can configure a server to use a particular directory as its root directory by passing in the weblogic.RootDirectory command-line argument. Here is an example:

```
java -Dweblogic.RootDirectory=/shared/myRoot weblogic.Server
```

If this argument is not supplied, WebLogic examines the directory from which it was started for a *config.xml* file. If it finds this file, it assumes that this directory is the root directory. The root directory information also needs to be supplied to the Node Managers using the Remote Start tab. If it is not supplied, each Node Manager will create its own root directory (in *BEA_HOME\WL_HOME\common\nodemanager*) for each server, as explained later.

Each WebLogic server has a root directory. This does not stop you from sharing a root directory among a number of servers. For example, you may have a shared disk system. In this case, you can configure a number of server instances, possibly on different physical machines, each sharing the same root directory. No conflict will arise, though you must take extra care to ensure that the shared directory remains available at all times.

The Configuration Wizard

The Configuration Wizard is a standalone Java tool that you can use to easily create WebLogic domains from a set of prepared templates. The templates let you choose between creating a domain for the Avitek* Medical Records application, a domain for the WebLogic examples, a WebLogic domain with no preconfigured applications, and a domain for WebLogic Workshop. You then can create a domain with either a standalone Administration Server or multiple (clustered) Managed Servers. After creating the domain, you can use the Administration Console later to further modify its configuration as per your needs.

 Select the Avitek Medical Records domain or the Examples domain if you are keen to explore the application development environment on WebLogic Server. The Examples Domain creates a set of applications that demonstrate how to use the various features of WebLogic Server.

We will focus on the "Basic WebLogic Server Domain"—a domain with no preconfigured applications. The same discussion holds for the other options as well, except they create WebLogic domains with a default set of applications.

Starting the Configuration Wizard

The Configuration Wizard can be found in the *WL_HOME/common/bin/* directory. In WebLogic 8.1, run the *config* script; in WebLogic 7.0, run the *dmwiz* script. Depending on your operating system, you also may find a shortcut to this script placed in your launch bar. By default, the Wizard starts up in a GUI mode—to start a text-based version of the Wizard, run it in Console Mode by supplying a mode argument:

```
config -mode=console
```

The Configuration Wizard automatically starts up in Console Mode if your platform doesn't support a graphical display environment.

Typical configurations

When creating a basic domain, the most important configuration options are those that determine the structure of the domain:

- You can create a domain with a standalone Administration Server that hosts your applications. This single-server domain is the simplest domain possible, and often is used for development purposes.

- You can set up a domain with an Administration Server and multiple Managed Servers. The Managed Servers also could be members of a WebLogic cluster.

---

* This is available only in WebLogic 8.1. In WebLogic 7.0, you can choose the PetStore template for a sample domain.

In all cases, you at least must have configured the Administration Server. Let's examine each option in more detail.

Single server

A single-server domain consists of a standalone Administration Server only. This configuration is ideal for development or testing environments when you need to be able to rapidly deploy applications to the domain. While you can deploy applications to the Administration Server, this approach should not be used for production environments. Once you have created the domain, you still can use the Administration Console to adjust the configuration. For instance, you could add one or more Managed Servers, and perhaps organize them in WebLogic clusters.

After selecting this option, you must supply the location of the root directory for the domain. The domain can reside anywhere on your filesystem so long as the WebLogic installation and JDK are accessible to it. After this, you will be prompted for a name for the server, a listen address, a listen port, and an SSL listen port. Finally, you must supply a system username and password needed for the various administration tasks.

Domain with Managed Servers

You also can use the Configuration Wizard to create a WebLogic domain with multiple Managed Servers under the control of an Administration Server. In this case, you must supply the name, address, and port details of the Administration Server, and of each Managed Server in the domain.

Domain with clustered Managed Servers

The Configuration Wizard can be used to create a domain that has Managed Servers in a cluster. The means that you must supply a name for the cluster, the multicast address, and a selection of which Managed Servers will belong to the cluster. You can learn more about these configuration settings in Chapter 14.

By exploring the Clusters node in the left pane of the Administration Console, you will find an entry for the newly created cluster, along with all of the Managed Servers that are members of the cluster.

Using the Configuration Wizard in WebLogic 8.1

The simplest way to create a single-server domain using the Configuration Wizard is to choose the Basic WebLogic Server Domain option, followed by the Express setup. Supply the username and password of the administrative user, choose a location for the domain on your filesystem, and hit Create. The domain will consist of just the Administration Server called *myserver*, and by default it will bind to all IP addresses on port 7001.

If you choose the Custom setup, you can configure just about every aspect of a domain, right from Managed Servers and clusters up to JDBC and JMS resources. After choosing the Custom setup, your first task will be to define the settings for the Administration Server: the IP address and listen port, the server name, and an SSL port if SSL is enabled.

The rest of the setup is fairly intuitive, and the GUI comes with instructions on how to configure the various domain resources. For example, the Configuration Wizard lets you modify how the domain is distributed across servers, clusters, and physical machines. You can create a number of Managed Servers and clusters, as well as add managed servers to these clusters. You also can create machines and assign WebLogic instances to these machines.

In addition, the Configuration Wizard lets you create any JDBC connection pools and data sources; configure JMS servers, destinations, and connection factories; and set up security. You don't have to perform all of these aspects of your domain from the Configuration Wizard. If you like, you can use the Administration Console later. Finally, you must supply the username and password of an administrative user. Remember these details, as you will need them to access the Administration Console.

The Configuration Wizard is a powerful tool that also supports the creation of custom templates. For example, you can create a standard template for a WebLogic domain that can be used consistently to establish the base configuration for a new domain. Refer to the WebLogic documentation for more information on how to use the template builder.

Using the Configuration Wizard in WebLogic 7.0

After starting the Configuration Wizard, choose from the available templates to create a domain. We recommend you select the WLS Domain template because it defines a new domain with no preconfigured applications. You then can choose between Single Server, Admin Server with Managed Servers, and Admin Server with Clustered Managed Servers to create the three types of domains discussed earlier. Note that the Configuration Wizard lets you create only a single cluster, and all managed servers will become members of that cluster automatically. After creating the Managed Servers (if any), you must supply the name and address of the Administration Server, and then the username and password of the administrative user. You will need these details in order to log in to the Administration Console.

Using weblogic.Server

An easy way to create a very basic domain is to use the weblogic.Server command, which is normally used to start a server. You first need to add the relevant libraries to your classpath, which you accomplish by executing the *setWLSEnv* script located in the *WL_HOME\server\bin* directory. You then need to execute the following command in a clean directory:

```
java -Dserver.name=myservername weblogic.Server
```

We have used the `server.name` property to assign a name to the Administration Server. You then will be prompted for a username and password, and you will be asked whether you wish to create a new domain. This creates a fully functional basic domain, just as if you had used the Configuration Wizard to create a single-server domain. The Administration Server will be bound to all IP addresses, on port 7001.

Starting the Servers

Once you have created a domain, you then can run the Administration Server. Execute the *startWeblogic* script from the domain's root directory. Once the server has started, you can access the Administration Console using the URL *http://hostname:port/console*. Here *hostname* and *port* must be the listen address and port configured using the Configuration Wizard.

Under the Servers node in the left pane of the Administration Console, you will find entries for each Managed Server created for the domain. You can start each Managed Server from the command line using the *startManagedWebLogic* script created for your domain. The startup script takes two parameters: the name of the Managed Server to start, and the URL for the Administration Server. A typical invocation looks like this:

```
startManagedWebLogic servername http://adminaddress:adminport/
```

Here `servername` is the name of one of the Managed Servers in the domain, and `adminaddress` and `adminport` represent the address and port for the Administration Server. You must execute several such commands, one for each Managed Server in the domain. Later, we will see how you can start a Managed Server remotely from the Administration Console, after setting up a Node Manager on the machine hosting the Managed Server.

Domain Backups

Now that you have created a domain, it is important to understand how to back up critical domain data in case of a failure. You can archive domain configurations in various ways—by using periodic backups to tape or fault-tolerant disks, or by manually copying files to another machine. Having a backup allows you to restart the Administration Server on a different machine in case of failure, or restart a Managed Server in the absence of the Administration Server.

The three resources to back up are the configuration data for the domain, the security data for the domain, and, of course, any deployed applications.

Configuration Data

The most critical aspect of a domain configuration is the *config.xml* file that holds the configuration for the entire domain. The *config.xml* file usually is stored in the

---

root directory of the domain. Although you can start a Managed Server without it in certain circumstances, it is necessary for the overall administration of the domain.

The file usually is accompanied by a useful secondary backup, *config.xml.booted*. This file is created only after the Administration Server has successfully started up. So, for instance, if you have made severe changes to the configuration for a domain, and the Administration Server no longer starts up, you can overwrite the *config.xml* file with the *config.xml.booted* file, and thereby restore the domain to its last known successful startup configuration. This is very useful while you are experimenting with the various domain options. We recommend that you back up both versions of the *config.xml* file.

WebLogic 8.1 also maintains a number of backups of the *config.xml.booted* file. For example, whenever you make a change to the domain, the current *config.xml.booted* file is archived to *config.xml#2*. When you make another change, the same thing happens after renaming *config.xml#2* to *config.xml#3*, and so on. You can use the Administration Console to set the maximum number of archived versions to keep. Select the domain node in the left pane, and change the value of the Archive Configuration Count parameter in the Configuration/General tab. By default, WebLogic maintains five archived versions, all kept in the *configArchive* subdirectory of your domain.

WebLogic 8.1 also creates a *config.xml.original* file. Whereas the *config.xml.booted* file is created after the server has successfully started up, the *config.xml.original* file represents the *config.xml* file before the system has fully started. Some subsystems add information to the configuration file (for example, the security system adds serialized security information) when the Administration Server starts up, and the *config.xml.original* file captures the state before any of these changes take place.

Security Data

The Administration Server holds all of the security data for a domain. The domain's security data is spread across WebLogic's LDAP repository, the *config.xml* file, the *SerializedSystemIni.dat* file, the Security Configuration Data, and the keystores for the servers' identity and trusted certificate authority (CA) certificates. It also includes the *boot.properties* file, if it is being used to store the username and password for server startup.

Security data is as crucial as the domain's configuration file. Without a running Administration Server, the domain's security data cannot even be modified; without security data, you cannot start the Administration Server. For these reasons, it is important to maintain backups of the security data. Having a backup copy of the domain's configuration and security data allows you to restart the Administration Server on another machine, and subsequently regain control of the Managed Servers in case the Administration Server fails.

The LDAP repository

If you are using the default security realm and settings of WebLogic Server, the configuration data is stored in the embedded LDAP server within WebLogic Server. Chapter 17 explains more about how WebLogic uses an internal LDAP repository to persist its security settings. For a domain called *mydomain*, the Administration Server *adminServer* serializes this data into the *mydomain\adminServer\ldap* folder. Note that WebLogic makes a backup of this data once a day, and then places the backup in the *mydomain\adminServer\ldap\backup* directory in the form of a ZIP file. Any changes to the security data made after the backup is created are reflected only on the next day's backup—so, be aware that the ZIP may not always contain the latest security information.

Take care when backing up the *ldap* directory yourself. If anybody is modifying the security data during the time of the backup, the files may be copied while still in an inconsistent state. The ZIP backups created by WebLogic, albeit not always up to date, are always consistent.

The LDAP data is also replicated to all Managed Servers whenever changes are made to security settings using the Administration Console. Thus, it is not necessary to back up this data on the Managed Servers. You need to back up only the master LDAP data on the Administration Server.

Every server needs access to the security realm before it can start. If your WebLogic servers use the default security realm, all the necessary information will be stored in the LDAP repository, which gets replicated automatically to all Managed Servers. If, however, the domain uses a custom security realm, ensure that all of the servers can access the necessary information for this realm. Its configuration and repository should be added to your backup list as well.

The serialized security datafile

The *SerialiazedSystemIni.dat* file is located in the root directory of each server and contains encrypted security data necessary to start the server. This file also should be backed up.

Certificates

If the server has been configured to use SSL, the security certificates, keys, and keystores also need to be backed up. See Chapter 16 for more details on SSL configuration.

Security configuration data in WebLogic 7.0

For WebLogic 7.0, you also must back up the security configuration data, stored in the *domain_name\userConfig\Security* directory. WebLogic persists the security provider information here, and this data is used as the basis of a runtime cache.[*]

---

[*] WebLogic 8.1 stores this information in the domain's *config.xml* file.

To remove all of the changes to the domain's security configuration and return the domain to its factory settings, you can remove this directory and restart the Administration Server. WebLogic then will populate the domain with default security data.

Note that you can manipulate this security data in several ways. WebLogic lets you dump the security configuration data into an XML file. The data is actually a serialization of the security provider MBeans. You then can make changes to the contents of this XML document and reload the XML data into the MBean repository. WebLogic provides tools to do this mapping, which we describe later in Chapter 20. The following command maps the security information to an XML output file:

```
java weblogic.management.commo.WebLogicMBeanDumper
    -includeDefaults -name Security:* XML-file
```

This command will map the XML file back into WebLogic:

```
java weblogic.management.commo.WebLogicMBeanLoader XML-file
```

Handling System Failure

The backup data will help recover from a system failure. As we shall see, the Administration Server and Managed Servers have different backup considerations. In particular, you can set up the Managed Servers to start without the Administration Server.

Restarting the Administration Server

By default, the Administration Server can discover the presence of any of the Managed Servers running in the domain. Therefore, when the Administration Server shuts down while the Managed Servers continue to run, you don't need to restart the Managed Servers to ensure the Administration Server can regain control of the domain. The Administration Server maintains the current state of all Managed Servers that are under its control in a file called *running-managed-servers.xml*, which resides under the domain's root directory. The Administration Server uses this file to discover those Managed Servers under its control. You also can disable this discovery of running Managed Servers in the domain by setting the property -Dweblogic. management.discover=false in the startup script for the Administration Server. We do not recommend that you do this.

However, if a system crash has corrupted your WebLogic installation or prevents you from restarting the Administration Server on the same machine, you need to restore the Administration Server on another machine and let it regain control over the Managed Servers. Typically, you will need to take the following series of steps:

1. Install WebLogic on the new machine.
2. Make the application files available to the Administration Server again. The applications must be available in the same relative locations on the new machine as on the filesystem on which they were originally deployed.

3. Copy the backed-up configuration and security data to the new machine, and make sure you place the data in the same folders as the backup.

An Administration Server that is started in this way should rediscover all of the Managed Servers that were under its control before it shut down. When the Administration Server starts, it communicates its new IP address to all of the Managed Servers under its control. In this way, you can continue to administer the Managed Servers, even after the Administration Server is restarted on a different machine.

 The Administration Server will not discover Managed Servers that were started while it was down.

Restarting Managed Servers

During startup, a Managed Server retrieves its configuration data from the Administration Server. If the Administration Server is running, the Managed Server will boot with the configuration data that it is sent. However, if the Administration Server is down, the Managed Server must read its configuration and security settings from the filesystem. In this case, a server will start in *Managed Server Independence* mode—i.e., in the absence of the Administration Server. Note that you cannot modify the configuration of a Managed Server that is started in this mode, until it reestablishes contact with the Administration Server.

If a Managed Server needs to start in the absence of the Administration Server, it needs access to the configuration data and security files. Normally, only the Administration Server needs access to the domain's *config.xml* file. However, because we are booting in Managed Server Independence mode, the Managed Server also must have access to this file. In WebLogic 8.1, the *config.xml* file must be renamed to the *msi-config.xml* file for the Managed Server. You must not rename it in WebLogic 7.0.

The root directory for a Managed Server defaults to the directory from which the startup script was executed. If a Managed Server runs on the same machine as the Administration Server and shares the same root directory, the Managed Server will locate these files automatically. Otherwise, these files can be made available in a number of ways:

- The easiest way is to just copy the files from a backup store. They have to be placed in the root directory of the server being started.
- An alternative is to point the server to a different root directory that does contain these files, using the -Dweblogic.RootDirectory=*path* startup option.
- Finally, if you have enabled replication of domain configuration files, all the necessary configuration files already will be present in the root directory. However, if you are using a *boot.properties* file during startup, this must be copied over to the right location. The boot identity file is not considered part of the domain configuration, and is therefore ignored during replication. In the next section, we look at how to enable replication of the domain configuration data.

A Managed Server started in this way will first attempt to communicate with the Administration Server. Because the Administration Server is shut down, a connection exception will occur, which you can safely ignore. After this, it will try to read the configuration files from its root directory, and then boot itself up.

 You cannot use the Node Manager to start a server in Managed Server Independence mode. The Node Manager can monitor only Managed Servers under the control of the Administration Server.

Managed Server Independence mode

By default, a Managed Server can start in Managed Server Independence mode. You can use the Administration Console to disable this mode. Select the server from the left pane, and then under the Advanced options in the Configuration/Tuning tab, deselect the Managed Server Independence Enabled option. When this option is disabled, the server will not start in the absence of the Administration Server, even if the necessary configuration and security files are present.

This tab includes another option, MSI File Replication Enabled, which determines whether the domain configuration files will be replicated to all Managed Servers. By default, this setting is not enabled. When activated, the domain configuration file and *SerializedSystemIni.dat* file are replicated to all Managed Servers every 5 minutes. In WebLogic 8.1, the *config.xml* file is replicated under a new name, *msi-config.xml*. So, if the file replication has been enabled, each Managed Server should create its own *msi-config.xml* file, which will be used only to reboot in Managed Server Independence mode.

 Be careful of increased administration traffic when replicating potentially large configuration files across servers. In addition, do not enable the replication of domain configuration files if a server shares its installation or root directory with another server. It could result in unpredictable errors for both servers.

A Node Manager cannot be used to remotely start a Managed Server in the absence of the Administration Server, even if the Managed Server Independence mode has been enabled. If you cannot get the Administration Server up but still want to start a Managed Server, you must start it manually from the command line.

Domain Network Configuration

In a simple server setup, you usually would assign a single network address and port number to a WebLogic instance and use this address and port for all communication with the server. Each different protocol supported by WebLogic is then multiplexed onto the same host address and port. You can tune the setup by specifying various connection and messaging timeouts and enabling tunneling. This default network configuration for a server is called the *default network channel* (although not explicitly in the Administration Console). You can further refine this basic setup by creating an *administration channel*, which provides an additional port exclusively for administration traffic. In this way, all administration traffic will use the dedicated administration port, while all other traffic will use the default network channel. This separation provides many benefits, including increased reliability and security of administration traffic.

Finally, WebLogic lets you exploit a far more complex network configuration that assigns different protocols to different addresses and ports on the same server. You can achieve this by creating custom network channels. Each network channel can be tuned independently and even be assigned different NICs on a multihomed machine.

The Default Network Channel

The most important connection settings for a Managed Server are its listen address and port. These settings form the basis of all communication with the server, using any of the permitted connection protocols. You also can adjust other network characteristics by enabling SSL ports and refining individual protocol settings through timeout values and tunneling. All these network settings can be configured individually for each server in the domain.

Use the Administration Console to adjust the network configuration for a particular server. Select the server node from the left pane, and then choose the Configuration/General tab. If you want to view or modify the more advanced network settings, choose the Protocols* tab. All of these settings come under the scope of the default network channel. Its significance in creating custom network channels will become clearer a bit later.

General settings

The most general settings are available under the Configuration/General tab. This tab lets you configure the listen address and ports:

Listen Address
> This is perhaps the most important of all—the IP address or DNS name of the server used to listen for incoming connections. If you leave this field blank or specify a localhost address, you implicitly bind the Listen Port and SSL Listen Port to all IP addresses available for the machine hosting the server.

Listen Port and Listen Port Enabled
> If the listen port is enabled, plain-text connections are allowed on the specified port. Otherwise, no plain-text connections are allowed.

---

* In WebLogic 7.0, use the Connections tab instead.

SSL Listen Port and SSL Listen Port Enabled

If the SSL port is enabled, SSL traffic is allowed on the specified port. Otherwise, no SSL traffic is allowed.

If you disable the plain-text listen port, make sure that you enable an SSL port for secure traffic—otherwise, the server instance will be isolated. To properly configure SSL, you need to configure the server's identity and a list of certificates of trust CAs. SSL setup is covered in more detail in Chapter 16.

Protocols

WebLogic supports a number of different protocols, listed in Table 13-1. To configure these protocols using the Administration Console in WebLogic 8.1, select a server from the left pane, and then choose from one of the tabs under the Protocols tab. The General tab provides the configuration for all types of connections, whereas the HTTP, COM, and IIOP tabs cover the individual protocols. In WebLogic 7.0, the tabs under the Connections tab for the selected server provide similar functionality.

Table 13-1. Supported network protocols

Protocol	Description
HTTP and HTTPS	These protocols are used primarily for HTTP communication between the browser and the web server.
IIOP and IIOPS	These protocols are used for IIOP traffic between WebLogic and Java clients.
T3 and T3S	WebLogic uses the T3 protocols for internal and external connections to the servers. The T3 protocol often is used in WebLogic's implementation of RMI.
COM	This allows Windows-based COM objects to talk to WebLogic. You can enable COM traffic on the plain-text port, but not on the SSL port.

By default, COM is not enabled for a server. You can customize each protocol individually by clicking the appropriate tab.

All of these protocols are, by default, multiplexed over the same connection to the server's address and port. So you can access a web page hosted by the server using a URL such as *http://host:port/page.jsp*. An external client can set up an initial JNDI context to a server using the URL *t3://host:port/*. All that has changed is the protocol over which the client must communicate with the server.

Tuning

There are a number of places where you can tune network characteristics. Use the Tuning tab to adjust the more general network characteristics. In particular, you can tune the following parameters:

Accept Backlog

This parameter determines the maximum number of connection requests on the listen port(s) that may be queued. It defaults to 50.

Login Timeout and SSL Login Timeout
> Use these timeouts to set the maximum amount of time allowed for a new plain-text or SSL connection to be established. The default timeout for plain-text connections is 5000 ms, and for SSL connections it is 25000 ms.

Maximum Open Sockets
> This setting determines the maximum number of open sockets allowed by the server at any given time. If this value is exceeded, the server will stop accepting any new requests until the number of active sockets drops below this threshold. The default value for this setting is 2147483647.

The Protocols/General tab in WebLogic 8.1 lets you tune the default network channel. These settings are relevant particularly to withstanding denial-of-service attacks:

Complete Message Timeout
> Use this parameter to set the maximum amount of time that WebLogic will wait for a complete message to be received. It defaults to 60 seconds.

Idle Connection Timeout
> Use this parameter to set the maximum duration (in seconds) that a connection may be idle before WebLogic closes it. It defaults to 65 seconds.

Maximum Message Size
> Use this parameter to set the maximum size allowed for the message header. It defaults to 10000000 bytes.

The final set of tuning parameters is protocol-specific. Simply select the appropriate tab: HTTP, COM, or IIOP (in WebLogic 7.0, use the additional attributes found in the Protocols tab itself). For example, you can specify the maximum size allowed for an HTTP POST message (to help prevent denial-of-service attacks).

Tunneling

You can configure WebLogic to tunnel various protocols from the Protocols/General tab. When tunneling is enabled, a client can connect to WebLogic in a way that allows requests using one protocol to be sent over another protocol. For example, an RMI client typically would use a T3 URL to connect to a WebLogic instance. By default, WebLogic uses its proprietary T3 protocol for all RMI interaction. However, your network may not allow you to always use T3—for instance, this is the case if all client requests must pass through a protocol-filtering firewall that permits only HTTP connections. In such a situation, you may need to tunnel T3 requests over HTTP connections. To enable this setup, the server must be explicitly configured to support tunneling, as well as the HTTP and T3 protocols and either plain-text or secure connections (or both).

> Tunneling generally is quite expensive. A remote client can communicate much faster and more efficiently if it creates connections using the correct protocol, and does not tunnel requests over another protocol. So, for example, T3 calls are far more efficient than if they were tunneled over HTTP.

RMI tends to be a common source of confusion. RMI is an API for building remote clients and servers, and it can use any number of communication protocols. By default, WebLogic implements RMI using the T3 protocol. It also can use the IIOP protocol. RMI clients can indicate their preference by selecting the protocol when constructing the URL. T3 tends to be the fastest. Other application servers may use a different protocol—for example, JRMP. Things are a little different for WebLogic JMS. By default, most communication takes place using RMI implemented over T3. However, JMS thin clients will communicate using RMI over IIOP, even if you specify a T3 URL!

You always should be aware of which protocols are in effect in a given situation, as well as whether tunneling is being used. Besides the performance implications, there also are behavioral consequences. For example, a remote JMS thin client will use the IIOP protocol and therefore be subjected to IIOP timeouts.

Two other options are relevant to tunneling on the Protocols/General tab, and are needed only if tunneling is enabled:

Tunneling Client Ping
> This setting determines how often WebLogic pings a tunneling client to see if it is still alive. This defaults to 45 seconds.

Tunneling Client Timeout
> This setting determines the duration after which an unreachable tunneled client is considered dead. This defaults to 40 seconds.

The Administration Channel

Usually all administration traffic flows through the same channels as application traffic. That is, the administration traffic uses the same address and port as the default channel. By creating a separate channel for all administration traffic, you get the following benefits:

- The administration and application traffic are *physically* separated. This ensures that you always can send administration operations to a server regardless of the volume of application traffic. For instance, you would be assured of having enough network capacity to deploy an application or optimize a server setting.

- A Managed Server can be started in standby mode if you use an Administration Channel. When a server starts in standby mode, only its Administration Channel is active; all other network channels are unavailable to its clients. Additionally, all applications and services are initialized. This is essentially a hot standby mode, ready for a signal to activate to the "running" state.

- Servers that have an Administration Channel support the shutdown and thread_ dump administrative commands in case the server is deadlocked. Without an Administration Channel, these commands may not work on a deadlocked server.

When you enable the "Enabling the domain wide administration port" setting for a domain, you implicitly create an Administrator channel, much like the default network channel that is available to each server. When this is enabled, all of the Managed Servers in the domain are required to use the secure administration port for all administration traffic.

Consequences on domain configuration

Once the administration port has been enabled, all administration traffic flows through it. All Managed Servers will communicate with the Administration Server on this channel, and all administration tasks must be routed through the Administration Channel to any of the Managed Servers. Administration channels impose some demands on the design of the domain. The primary requirement is that SSL is enabled on the Administration Server and *all* of the Managed Servers. When starting a Managed Server, you always specify the URL of the Administration Server:

```
-Dweblogic.management.server=http://10.0.10.10:7001
```

Here 7001 is the listen port for the Administration Server. Because the Administration Channel operates in SSL mode, the URL of the Administration Server now must use the HTTPS protocol:

```
-Dweblogic.management.server=https://10.0.10.10:9002
```

In this case, 9002 is the default domain-wide administration port. Furthermore, the Administration Console now will be accessible via an HTTPS URL—e.g., *https://10.0.10.10:9002/console*.

All Managed Servers are required to support SSL and use the secure administration port to talk to the Administration Server. For this reason, the administration port is a domain-specific setting that cannot be configured separately for each Managed Server.

Configuration changes

You can use the Administration Console to enable the administration port. Select the domain from the lefthand pane and then tick the "Enable the domain-wide administration port" setting from the Configuration/General tab. You must specify a port number that should be used (by default, it is 9002). You also must configure SSL on all the servers in the domain. SSL setup is described in detail in Chapter 16. The administration port number can be customized for each Managed Server. Select a server and choose the Configuration/General tab.* Under the advanced section, change the Local Administration Port Override setting. All servers, including the Administration Server, will need to be restarted for these changes to take effect.

---

* In WebLogic 7.0, this setting is in the Connections/SSL Ports tab.

If you need to further refine the Administration Channel, perhaps by binding it to a different IP address, you must create a custom network channel that uses the admin protocol.

Custom Network Channels in WebLogic 8.1

We've just seen how you can use the Administration Console to define the network characteristics for each server in the domain. The configuration options are rather limited, though, because each protocol is multiplexed onto the same host and port. To build on the server's setup for the default channel, you need to create one or more custom network channels. As explained earlier, a network channel is a combination of host, port, and protocol. It lets you assign a protocol to a particular host and port combination. You can create a number of network channels for every server, each capturing the configuration for a particular protocol. This lets you accomplish a number of things:

- Because a channel assigns a specific protocol to a particular host and port, you can designate different NICs to different protocols.
- A network channel can be configured independently, allowing you to change the connection settings such as timeout values and message size limits on a per-protocol basis.
- A network channel can be configured to support outbound connections (to an external client). By creating two separate channels, one for outbound traffic only and another for local server-to-server traffic only, you can segregate client traffic from interserver traffic.

All of these options provide you with a richer network configuration with which to design the physical architecture of your system.

Without any custom network channels, a server uses the settings for the default channel supplied in the Configuration/General tab. When you create additional network channels for the server, you can choose to not set certain connection attributes of the channel, such as the host address. In these cases, the custom network channel inherits its settings from the default channel. For this reason, whenever you set up custom channels, keep an eye on the default channel configuration as well.

Creating network channels

Network channels are created on a per-server basis. If a number of servers must share the same network configuration, you need to create network channels with identical settings on each server. Select the server from the left pane of the Administration Console and then select the Protocols/Channels tab. You can use this same tab to list previously created network channels.

For a new network channel, you should supply the listen address, listen port, and a network protocol for the channel. The protocol can take any one of following values: t3, t3s, iiop, iiops, com, http, https, or admin. Each channel for the server must have a unique combination of host, port, and protocol. If you create two channels with the same host, port, and protocol combination, it may result in a network configuration error during startup. Once you create a network channel, you can tune its configuration independently of other channels. Note that new network channels come into effect only after you restart the server.

Use the admin protocol to create a custom administration channel. A custom channel for administration traffic provides you with just a little more flexibility and security. For example, on a multihomed machine, you can bind the administration channel to the IP address of a NIC that is used only in internal communications, and that is hidden from external clients.

Note that for a T3 network channel, you also can enable tunneling of T3 requests over HTTP by setting the Tunneling Enabled flag to true. If you do this, remember also to enable HTTP on the same channel—set the HTTP Enabled for this Protocol flag to true.

Enabling interserver communication

Network channels let you tune an important network attribute—the Outbound Enabled setting. When this attribute is set to true, a network channel will support internal server-to-server communication. WebLogic then can use the channel to initiate outbound connections to other WebLogic servers. For example, if the server needs to make an EJB call to a remote server, it will use a channel that supports server-to-server communication. By default, a network channel will support internal, server-to-server communication. If this setting is disabled, the channel will not be used for interserver communication.

You can use this feature if the machine hosting the server was equipped with multiple NICs. In such a case, you could set up a channel dedicated for client traffic on one NIC (by disabling server-to-server traffic), and another channel to support interserver communication on the other NIC. In this way, you can separate external, client traffic from internal server-based communication. Later, we shall examine various network configurations that make use of this feature.

Network Channels and Access Points in WebLogic 7.0

Network channels were introduced in WebLogic 7.0 and also are available in WebLogic 8.1. There is one crucial difference, though. In WebLogic 8.1, network channels are server-specific and cannot be shared. In WebLogic 7.0, however, network channels can be shared across servers—i.e., you could assign a channel to multiple servers in the domain. So, for instance, you could assign a channel to all members of a cluster to ensure that they all use the same multicast address.

Because the same network channel could be targeted to multiple servers, WebLogic 7.0 also provides a mechanism for adjusting the behavior of the channel for any of the targeted servers. WebLogic 7.0 supports this through a NAP. A NAP allows you to adapt the behavior of a network channel for individual servers. Thus, a NAP is a server-specific customization of a network channel. You can use a NAP only in conjunction with a network channel—for instance, to override the listen address and ports, to adjust the tuning properties, and to override the protocol settings. Clearly, because network channels cannot be shared in WebLogic 8.1, it does not need to support NAPs. If you want to ease future migration to WebLogic 8.1, avoid using NAPs and avoid sharing network channels.

The Administration Console does not explicitly list the NAPs for the network channels for a server. Instead, you have to choose a server from the left pane and select the Connections tab. Then select the Channel Overrides link at the bottom, from either the Tuning Protocols or the SSL Ports tabs, to view the network channels associated with the server. When you select a particular channel, you implicitly view the details of the associated NAP.

Because a NAP customizes the network channel for a particular server, you can specify, at most, one NAP for each network channel for each server in the domain. Remember that a NAP is optional—set up a NAP only if the default configuration provided by the network channel isn't adequate. However, if you do specify a NAP, only the changed values override the network settings for the channel. The NAP will inherit all settings from the channel that are left unaltered.

Other than NAPs, the configuration of network channels and their use follows that of WebLogic 8.1.

Getting a summary

Earlier, we looked at how to configure the various characteristics of the default channel. In general, a network resource has a listen address, listen ports for plain-text and SSL connections, support for one or more allowed protocols, and finer adjustments on connection settings. The Connections/Summary tab for a server provides a snapshot of all these settings. Here's an overview of a sample network configuration for a server:

```
Cluster Participant:        false
Native Socket IO Enabled:   true
Reverse DNS Allowed:        false
Network Channel:     Default
Listen Address:      not configured
Listen Port:         7001
SSL Listen Port:     7002
External DNS Name:   not configured
Cluster Address:     not configured
Protocol(s):         T3,T3S,HTTP,HTTPS,IIOP,IIOPS
Tunneling Enabled:   false
```

```
Outgoing Enabled:        true
Admin Traffic Only:      false
Admin Traffic OK:        true
Channel Weight:          50
Accept Backlog:          50
Login Timeout:           5000 ms
Login Timeout SSL:       25000 ms
Message Timeout HTTP:    60000 ms
Message Timeout T3:      60000 ms
Message Timeout IIOP:    60000 ms
Idle Timeout IIOP:       60000 ms
Max Message Size HTTP:   10000000
Max Message Size T3:     10000000
Max Message Size IIOP:   10000000
```

Viewing network configurations

The easiest way to view the domain's network configuration is to use the Administration Console and then select the Network Channels node on the left pane. If you choose the "View network summary table (all servers, without channels)" option, it will show the default channels for the servers. This includes the Default and Administrator channels for the Administration Server and all of the Managed Servers. The information includes a list of all listen addresses, listen ports, SSL listen ports, and allowed protocols.

If you choose the "View network summary table (all servers and all channels)" option, you additionally can view the configuration settings for all network channels targeted to each server. However, in order to view all the NAPs for a server, you must select the Channel Override option for that server. Even though it returns a list of network channels targeted to the server, when you click a network channel, you actually view the server-specific overrides for that channel.

Channel priority for outgoing connections

WebLogic can have multiple network channels associated with it, some of which may support internal, server-based communication. WebLogic lets you prioritize network channels used for interserver communication. Each channel has an associated *channel weight*, which is an integer value between 1 and 100. When a server needs to initiate a connection to another server, it first determines all outbound-enabled channels that support the required protocol. Then, from this list it picks the network channel with the higher-weighted value over channels with a lower weight.

If the server runs on a system with multiple NICs, you can create multiple network channels, one corresponding to each NIC, and assign weights to each NIC based on known speeds of the network cards (so, the faster the NIC, the higher the weight). This way you can ensure all interserver communication has a guaranteed level of throughput because the server always will try to use the higher-priority channels.

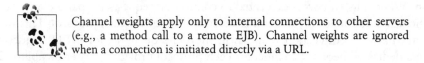

Channel weights apply only to internal connections to other servers (e.g., a method call to a remote EJB). Channel weights are ignored when a connection is initiated directly via a URL.

Sometimes WebLogic may upgrade the service level needed for an outgoing connection. For instance, if the server needs to perform an RMI lookup using a T3 connection, and the server can resolve only to a network channel that support T3S connections, the server will initiate an outgoing T3S connection.

WebLogic also is capable of handling channel failures—usually it will pick the higher-weighted channel before the lower-weighted ones. However, if a channel becomes unavailable because of a network failure, it automatically tries the channel with the next-highest weight. WebLogic returns a connection failure only when all available channels for a requested outgoing connection are exhausted.

Channel weights are no longer available in WebLogic 8.1. Instead, WebLogic 8.1 relies on the operating system to handle NIC failover. Most modern operating systems do support some sort of NIC failover and QoS levels. You comfortably can use this support instead of channel weights in WebLogic 7.0 as well.

Best Practices for Configuring Networks

Earlier we saw how the network configuration for a server is spread across its default configuration and across any network channels. A well-designed network configuration facilitates ease of management, adaptability, and optimization. You should be able to incorporate future changes to the physical network easily, and continue to get the best performance out of your network resources. This means that you need to be aware of the relative benefits and limitations of using the default network configuration and network channels.

If your domain has multiple Managed Servers that are running on separate machines or on a multihomed machine with multiple NICs, or if the domain caters to clients that communicate via different protocols, you should consider using network channels. Let's look at how a judicious setup of network channels can help you achieve interesting network configurations.

Segmenting network traffic by port number

Task: You can use channels to segment network traffic by port numbers, typically assigning different protocols to different ports. For instance, you could demand that HTTP traffic arrive on port 8001 only, while T3 traffic arrives on port 9001. You don't have to force each different server to use the same port number either—any server can use different port numbers of the same protocol, something that you will need to do if you run more than one server on a single machine.

Reason: When a listen port is dedicated to connection requests for particular protocols, the server automatically maintains a separate queue for each protocol. This way you don't have T3 connection requests in the same queue as for HTTP requests. Having a dedicated network channel for each protocol provides greater flexibility. If you ever add another NIC to the machine, you can create a channel that assigns the HTTP traffic to the faster NIC, while the T3 channel still can be targeted to the existing NIC. It also provides additional flexibility when designing the security aspects of the hardware setup. If external clients use only HTTP, you should only expose a port that runs the HTTP protocol.

Sample Configuration: Figure 13-2 illustrates a network configuration that places HTTP traffic on its own port.

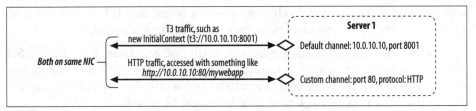

Figure 13-2. Segmenting traffic by port numbers

Here we create a network channel dedicated to HTTP traffic. This channel should listen on port 80, while the other channel, which handles traffic on all other protocols, listens on port 8001.

To create such a configuration, you must perform the following tasks:

1. Set up the default network configuration on the server. In the example, the default channel is set for the address 10.0.10.10 and for port 8001.

2. Create a custom network channel on the server, using the HTTP protocol and setting the port to 80.

If you want to duplicate this network setup on several servers, you need to create the same network channel on each server. In WebLogic 7.0, you simply can create one network channel and assign it to each machine.

Even though this example creates two ports for the different types of traffic, they are still on the same physical network. That is, both ports are configured to run on the same NIC, and so there is no physical separation of traffic.

Physically segmenting network traffic

Task: To physically separate network traffic by assigning different protocols to different NICs.

Reason: A physical separation of network traffic could be useful for both security and performance reasons. If the server traffic is network-bound, for instance, it may be useful to add an additional NIC and network, and configure WebLogic to use this NIC as well.

Sample Configuration: Figure 13-3 illustrates how you can physically separate network traffic.

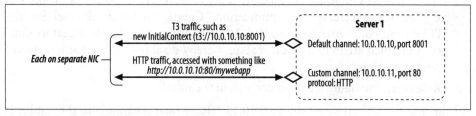

Figure 13-3. Physically segmenting network traffic

Here we have a server with two NICs. The first is assigned the IP address 10.0.10.10, and the second is assigned 10.0.10.11. The intention is to get HTML traffic to flow through one NIC, while other traffic is to flow on the other NIC.

To create this setup, ensure that the default channel is configured for the NIC hosting the 10.0.10.10 IP address, and create a custom channel for the HTTP protocol, making sure that it is assigned the 10.0.10.11 IP address. All HTTP traffic will use the 10.0.10.11 NIC, while all T3 and other traffic will use the 10.0.10.10 NIC.

Separating internal and external traffic

Task: To physically separate internal server-to-server traffic from external client traffic. Server-to-server traffic occurs when one server communicates with another—e.g., when a servlet needs to invoke a remote EJB method. Client-facing servers also are called *edge servers*, and typically use HTTP-based traffic in their communication with the clients.

Reason: A physical separation between client and server traffic improves the security of your domain. In addition, because the traffic flows on different NICs, you can guarantee different levels of throughput for the client and server traffic, if desired.

Sample Configuration: Figure 13-4 shows how we want to separate the client traffic from the internal server traffic.

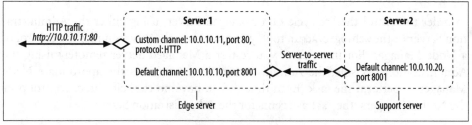

Figure 13-4. Separating internal and external traffic

Here we have installed two NICs on the edge server, with IP addresses 10.0.10.10 and 10.0.10.11 assigned to the NICs. The 10.0.10.11 address will be exposed to the client. Now you need to perform the following tasks:

1. On Server1, configure the default channel to use the 10.0.10.10 IP address. Ensure that its Outgoing Enabled attribute is set to true, thereby allowing it to be used for interserver communication. Create a custom channel for the HTTP protocol to listen on the 10.0.10.11 IP address, and ensure that its Outgoing Enabled attribute is set to false, thereby disabling its use for interserver communication.

2. On Server2, configure a default channel in the usual way.

All client traffic will arrive on the 10.0.10.11 NIC, which is exposed to the public. If the edge server needs to call a method on a remote EJB, it will try and find a channel that supports outgoing connections. Because the custom channel is the only channel available that supports interserver communication, it will use the 10.0.10.10 NIC.

Node Manager

WebLogic provides a standalone Java tool called the Node Manager, which is responsible for managing the availability of all Managed Servers running on a machine. It runs as a dedicated process on a machine, either as a daemon on a Unix machine or as a service on the Windows platform. It provides a way to automatically restart Managed Servers in the case of failure, and even handles servers that are in a "failed" state. A Node Manager also lets the Administration Server remotely start, kill, and monitor Managed Server instances. A *single* Node Manager process should run on every machine that hosts Managed Servers. When the Node Manager boots a server, it creates a separate process for that server, just as if you had run the *startManagedWebLogic* script on that machine.

 A Node Manager does not control the starting and stopping of the Administration Server. The machine that hosts the Administration Server doesn't need a Node Manager, unless it also hosts one or more Managed Servers.

Figure 13-5 illustrates the role of Node Managers in a domain.

In order to control the life cycle of a Managed Server, using either the Administration Server or the weblogic.Admin tool, you must start the servers under the control of a Node Manager. For instance, if you restart a Managed Server remotely using the Administration Console, the Administration Server contacts the appropriate Node Manager to perform the task. Even though you have no explicit, direct control over the Node Managers, they act as agents for the Administration Server.

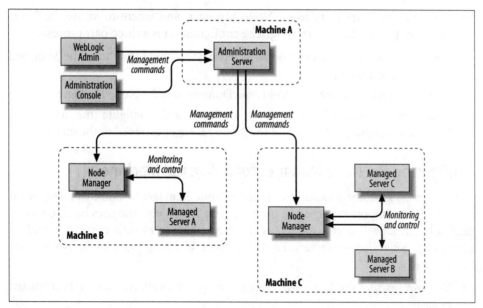

Figure 13-5. Node Managers act as agents to the Administration Server

Even though the Administration Server works closely with the Node Managers running on the different machines that host the Managed Servers in the domain, a Node Manager is still outside the scope of a WebLogic domain. The same Node Manager monitors all Managed Servers on a machine, regardless of the domains to which they belong.

> The Node Manager will not perform health monitoring and automatic restarts on servers that were not started using the Node Manager.

It is important to note that when Node Managers are used, each server is started up through the Node Manager running on the machine, using either the Administration Console or a JMX application, and not through your own startup scripts.

Finally, Node Managers use SSL in their communication. The Administration Server talks to the Node Managers using (short-lived) two-way SSL-protected messages, ensuring that only authorized Administration Servers can control the Node Managers. In addition, the Node Manager itself uses an SSL connection with each of the Managed Servers under its control. This connection remains alive for the entire duration that a Managed Server is up, and is used to monitor the server.

Configuring the Node Managers can be a little tricky, but once you have set them up, you can leave them humming away by themselves without any further intervention. The following sections look at how to configure a machine to use a Node Manager, how to configure a server to use a Node Manager, and where to locate the Node Manager logs in case things go wrong. The configuration is a three-part process:

1. Configure the Node Manager on each physical machine that hosts the Managed Servers of the domain.

2. Configure each machine in a WebLogic Domain to use a Node Manager.

3. Assign each Managed Server to a machine, and configure the interaction between the Managed Server and the Node Manager assigned to the machine.

Configuring the Node Manager for a Physical Machine

Every physical machine should have a single Node Manager instance running. Security is the most important aspect of the configuration. WebLogic tries hard to ensure that only authorized users can access the Node Manager—otherwise, it could be used to tamper with your servers. For this reason, WebLogic secures the Node Managers in two ways:

- You can instruct the Node Manager to accept connections from certain trusted hosts only.

- The Node Manager and the Administration Server communicate with each other through SSL. So, both the Administration Server and the Node Managers must be configured to use SSL.

Trusted hosts

In order to configure a list of trusted hosts for a Node Manager, you must create a text file with the addresses of all Administration Servers that are allowed to contact the Node Manager. Each line specifies either the IP address or the DNS host name of an Administration Server. By default, a Node Manager uses the *nodemanager.hosts* file located under the *WL_HOME\common\nodemanager* folder.* For example, you could have the following entries in the file:

```
wladmin.oreilly.com
10.0.10.10
```

The default entries allow access from the local host only. You can create a different trusted hosts file, and modify the Node Manager's startup script so that it specifies the location of this file:

```
java -Dbea.home=%BEA_HOME%
  -Dweblogic.nodemanager.javaHome=%JAVA_HOME%
  -Dweblogic.nodemanager.trustedHosts=nodemanager.myhosts
  ...
  -Dweblogic.ListenAddress=10.0.10.10
  weblogic.nodemanager.NodeManager
```

* In WebLogic 7.0, it's in the *config* subdirectory of this folder.

If you specify DNS names, you also must enable a reverse DNS lookup for the Node Manager (by default, it is not enabled). To do this, simply specify an additional system property in the startup script:

```
-Dweblogic.nodemanager.reverseDnsEnabled=true
```

The Node Manager then will accept connections only from an Administration Server running on one of the addresses specified in the trusted hosts file.

SSL configuration

Because all communication between the Administration Server and the Node Manager uses SSL, both the server and Node Manager must have SSL configured. Refer to Chapter 16 for the necessary SSL background. A Node Manager uses the same public key infrastructure as WebLogic Server itself, and the default installation uses the *DemoIdentity.jks* and *DemoTrust.jks* stores. So, if you just want to get everything going, you can use the default configuration and ignore the rest of this setup.

The best way to modify the default setup is to edit the *nodemanager.properties* file in the *WL_HOME\common\nodemanager* directory. Alternatively, you can specify any of the system properties from the command line when starting up the Node Manager. The default *nodemanager.properties* file also provides the syntax for most properties. For example, depending on which keystores you wish to use, the KeyStores property can take any of the following values:

```
#Possible values for the Keystores property
#KeyStores = [DemoIdentityAndDemoTrust|
CustomIdentityAndJavaStandardTrust|CustomIdentityAndCustomTrust]
```

Here is an example property file:

```
KeyStores=CustomIdentityAndCustomTrust
CustomIdentityKeyStoreFileName=y:\mystores\myIdentityStore.jks
CustomIdentityKeyStorePassPhrase=mykeystorepass
CustomIdentityKeyStoreType=JKS
CustomIdentityAlias=myalias
CustomIdentityPrivateKeyPassPhrase=mypassword

CustomTrustKeyStoreFileName=y:\server\lib\DemoTrust.jks
#These are commented out as the default trust store doesn't need them
#CustomTrustKeyStorePassPhrase=mypassphrase
#CustomTrustKeyStoreType=JKS
#CustomTrustKeyPassPhrase=mykeypass
```

This file sets up a custom identity and trust store for the Node Manager, which is typical of most production deployments. It references the demonstration trust store and an example identity store that is described in Chapter 16. After restarting the Node Manager, all of the pass phrases will be encrypted.

SSL for WebLogic 7.0

SSL configuration for a Node Manager in WebLogic 7.0 is slightly different. You can either use your own key and certificate files, or in a test setup, use the sample key and certificate files that are supplied with WebLogic's installation. The demonstration SSL certificate and key files are located in the *WL_HOME\common\nodemanager\config* directory, as well as in the root directory of any domain created using the Configuration Wizard.

Once you have the required SSL certificate and key files, you need only to specify additional system properties in the Node Manager's startup script:

weblogic.nodemanager.keyFile
> This property identifies the path to the key file.

weblogic.nodemanager.keyPassword
> This property specifies the password to use if the key file is encrypted.

weblogic.nodemanager.certificateFile
> This property identifies the path to the certificate file.

weblogic.security.SSL.trustedCAKeyStore
> This property identifies the path to the keystore that holds the trusted CA certificates.

weblogic.nodemanager.sslHostNameVerificationEnabled
> This property causes the Node Manager to perform hostname verification of the Administration Server that is communicating with it.

Chapter 16 provides a more detailed explanation of SSL configuration for WebLogic.

Additional configuration properties

Table 13-2 provides a list of additional system properties that you may need to specify. For instance, you may wish to modify the listen address for the Node Manager. All of these properties can simply be placed in the *nodemanager.properties* file. In WebLogic 7.0, you must specify them from the command line.

Table 13-2. Node Manager properties

Property name	Description	Default
JavaHome	This property specifies the Java home that should be used to start the managed servers. Otherwise, it uses the Java home defined in the Remote Start tab for the server. If that is not defined, it uses the Java home used to start the Node Manager itself.	None
WeblogicHome	This property sets the WebLogic home directory. You also can specify it on a per-server basis on a server's Remote Start tab.	None
ListenAddress	This property sets the address on which the Node Manager should listen.	All IP addresses assigned to the machine

Table 13-2. Node Manager properties (continued)

Property name	Description	Default
ListenPort	This property determines the port number on which the node manager should listen.	5555
NativeVersionEnabled	This property defines whether the Node Manager will run in a native mode.	true
ReverseDnsEnabled	This property defines whether reverse DNS may be used to resolve addresses in the trusted host file.	false
SavedLogsDirectory	This property determines where the log files will be written.	./NodeManagerLogs
TrustedHosts	This property determines the file containing the list of all trusted hosts.	./nodemanager.hosts
ScavengerDelaySeconds	This property is used if a server is started using the Node Manager. It will wait for this number of seconds before expecting a response from the server. Otherwise, it considers the task to have failed.	60 seconds
StartTemplate	This property is used by Unix systems to specify the path to a script file that will be used to start Managed Servers.	./nodemanager.sh

If you change any of these properties, you must stop and restart the Node Manager for the changes to take effect.

Starting a Node Manager

In a production environment, it is very important that the Node Manager is running at all times. Without the Node Manager, there is no way to automatically start, restart, or kill Managed Servers. The simplest way to accomplish this is to ensure that it runs as a Unix daemon or Windows Service. The default installation process provides you with an option to install the Node Manager in this way. For the Windows platform, you can use two scripts located in the *WL_HOME\server\bin* directory to install and uninstall the service:

installNodeMgrSvc.cmd
This script installs the Node Manager as a Windows Service.

uninstallNodeMgrSvc.cmd
This script stops and uninstalls the Node Manager service.

Make sure that you first modify these scripts to include the system properties we described earlier. The WebLogic documentation provides additional information on more advanced configurations of the Node Manager and Windows Services.

In addition, you can start the Node Manager using the *startNodeManager* script, which is also located in the *WL_HOME\server\bin* directory. To check on the status of a Node Manager, select a machine node from the left pane of the Administration Console and then choose the Monitoring/Node Manager Status tab.

Configuring a Machine to Use a Node Manager

After installing, configuring, and running a Node Manager on each physical machine, you must configure the machines for the domain and assign server instances to these machines. This information tells WebLogic which Managed Servers run on which physical machines, and hence which servers are under the control of the Node Manager on that machine. This is a two-part process. First you have to define the machines and configure them to use the Node Manager, and then you have to assign Managed Servers to the machines.

Using the Administration Console, select the Machines node in the left pane to view all of the machines in the domain. Each machine entry should encapsulate the settings for a physical machine. Use the righthand pane to create a new machine or modify an existing machine entry. For each machine, select the Node Manager tab and enter the listen address and port used by the Node Manager on that machine.

Finally, you need to assign the machine to the Managed Servers. Use the Servers tab to select those servers that run on the chosen machine. You also can assign a machine to a server from the Configuration/General tab of that server. This assignment is used in other situations as well. For instance, in a clustered environment WebLogic will try to replicate session data onto a server that runs on separate hardware. It does this by treating the different machines in the domain as physically different pieces of hardware. The servers assigned to a machine then determine which servers in the cluster are collocated (and which aren't).

Configuring the Node Manager for a Managed Server

The final task is to configure each Managed Server so that the Node Manager can control it. Because the Node Manager does not rely on external scripts to remotely start and kill a Managed Server, the information found in the startup scripts needs to be configured for each server using the Administration Console. The information is then saved as part of the domain configuration. Select a Managed Server from the left pane, and then choose the Configuration/Remote Start tab to specify the following parameters:

- The home directory of your JDK
- The home directory of your BEA installation
- The root directory of the domain
- The classpath that should be used to start the server
- Any additional JVM arguments to use
- The security policy file to use
- The username and the password of a WebLogic user with administrative privileges

All of these settings mirror the environment variables used in the *startWebLogic* scripts; we already saw that some of them can take on default values assigned to the Node Manager. Note that the directory paths used in the preceding settings must be valid on the machine that hosts the Managed Server, and not the Administration Server. This data is sent to the Node Manager on that machine, which then starts up the Managed Server in a separate process.

Configuring Node Manager Behavior

By default, the Node Manager will automatically restart servers that fail, or when it cannot determine the server's state. Once a Managed Server has failed, it will try to restart it no more than twice within the next hour.

Table 13-3 lists the configuration settings available for monitoring the health of a Managed Server. You can modify these settings from the Administration Console. Select a Managed Server from the left pane, then select the Configuration/Health Monitoring tab.

Table 13-3. Configuring server health monitoring

Setting	Description	Default
Auto Restart	If you disable this option, the Node Manager will not attempt to restart a failed server.	true
Auto Kill if Failed	If this is set to true, the Node Manager may kill the server process if the server's health is in the failed state, or when it cannot query the server for its health state.	false
Restart Interval ; Max Restarts within Interval	The Node Manager will try to restart the server only within the specified restart interval period. If this time period is exceeded, no further attempts will be made. During the time period, the Node Manager will try no more than Max Restarts to restart the server. By default, the Node Manager makes no more than two attempts within an hour to restart a failed server.	3600; 2
Health Check Interval	This setting determines the interval (in seconds) at which the Node Manager polls the server for its health state.	180
Health Check Timeout	This setting determines the number of seconds to wait for a response from a health check. By default, if the timeout is reached, the Node Manager will kill the server process and attempt to restart the server.	60
Restart Delay Seconds	This setting determines the number of seconds that the Node Manager will wait before trying to restart the server after killing it. This may be needed on some systems where killing the process does not immediately release all resources before the restart.	0

Default Operation of the Node Manager

Once a Node Manager has been installed and configured on a machine and the Managed Servers have been configured, the Node Manager is finally ready for use. You interact with the Node Manager indirectly using the Administration Console or the weblogic.Admin tool. To use the Administration Console, select a Managed Server from the left pane and then choose the Control tab. You then will be able to start, suspend, resume, and shut down a server. We discuss the various shutdown options and the use of the weblogic.Admin tool in a later section.

Starting managed servers

Imagine that you try to start a Managed Server remotely. Let's say that you want to start ServerA in Figure 13-5. The Administration Server will receive the instruction and forward it to the Node Manager on the machine that is configured to host ServerA—i.e., MachineB. The Node Manager running on MachineB then will start the server. By default, if the Managed Server doesn't respond within 60 seconds (the Scavenger Delay), the Node Manager will set the server's state to UNKNOWN. If the server does start after this delay, the Node Manager will change this state to RUNNING.

Suspending and stopping managed servers

Requests to suspend or stop managed servers don't proceed quite in the same fashion. The commands are issued directly to the Managed Servers from the Administration Server. Only if the Administration Server cannot reach a Managed Server does it dispatch the command to the appropriate Node Manager, which then forwards it to the Managed Server. Likewise, if a Managed Server does not respond to a shutdown request, the Node Manager can shut down the process forcibly (it records the process ID for this purpose).

Health monitoring

By default, the Node Manager checks the health status of each Managed Server every 180 seconds. If a Managed Server is in the failed state and its Auto Kill If Failed attribute is set to true, the Node Manager will kill and restart the process. By default, this attribute is set to false. The same occurs if a server fails to respond to three consecutive health queries.

By default, the Node Manager will not restart a Managed Server more than twice within an hour. The frequency of restarts is governed by the Restart Interval and Max Restarts within Interval attributes.

It is worth stressing the following points on the use of a Node Manager:

- Managed Servers can be started, monitored, and shut down by a Node Manager only if it started the server. If you start a Managed Server manually, the Node Manager will not interact with the server at all.
- If a Node Manager itself fails, this won't affect servers running on that machine. However, you won't be able to monitor the heath of the servers and automatically restart if a server is in poor health. For this reason, you should run the Node Manager as a service or daemon on your operating system.

- If you haven't enabled the Managed Server Independence mode for a Managed Server, you cannot restart a Managed Server without the Administration Server, even if the Node Manager is running on that machine already. For this reason, you should take whatever measures are necessary to ensure that the Administration Server is always available, and that it can be restarted if it ever fails.

Node Manager Logs

Two sets of logs are associated with the Node Manager. Both sets are useful when you need to debug any problems with the Node Manager or when you need to set up a more comprehensive monitoring environment. A subset of the logs is available from the Administration Console. Choose a Managed Server from the left pane, and then select the Control/Remote Start Output tab.[*]

Three sets of logs are maintained for each Node Manager:

Node Manager client logs
> The Administration Server maintains Node Manager log files in the *NodeManagerClientLogs* directory of the domain. These logs hold information about the commands directed to the Node Manager via the Administration Console (or the `weblogic.Admin` tool).

Node Manager logs
> The Node Manager itself generates log messages when it starts up or shuts down. These logs are located in the *WL_HOME/common/nodemanager/NodeManagerLogs/NodeManagerInternal* directory on the particular machine. Use these log files to diagnose whether a Node Manager is not starting up properly. These logs essentially correspond to the View Node Manager Output option in the Administration Console.

Managed Server logs
> The Node Manager maintains a subdirectory under the *NodeManagerLogs* directory, for each Managed Server that it controls. These log files hold the full output of the server that was started. These logs correspond to the View Server Output option in the Administration Console.

You may need to clean these directories periodically as the number and size of log files continue to grow.

Node Manager client logs

The client logs record all *actions* executed by a Node Manager on behalf of a JMX-based client, such as the Administration Console or the `weblogic.Admin` tool. A separate directory created within the domain log directory for each server within the

---

[*] In WebLogic 7.0, it's the Monitoring/Process Output tab.

domain. All of the recorded actions are timestamped and usually include a notification of the success or failure of the action. Here's a typical example of the client logs:

```
<05-Jul-2003 14:07:05 BST> <Info> <NodeManager> <Starting Node Manager...>
<10-Jul-2003 13:12:38 BST> <Info> <NodeManager@*.*:5555> <Server mydomain::ServerA
started, process id = 1,468>
<10-Jul-2003 13:14:50 BST> <Info> <NodeManager@*.*:5555> <__COMMAND_DONE__>
```

These logs contain *only* actions that were submitted through the Administration Console or any JMX-based client. For instance, if the Node Manager automatically restarts a failed server, this action is not recorded in the logs. Instead, it will be recorded in the machine logs for the Node Manager in charge of that server.

Managed Server logs

The server logs also are organized into subfolders, one for each server running on the machine. Each directory contains the following files:

servername_pid
> This file contains, in text, the process ID of the Managed Server. If a Managed Server on a machine is using all of the CPU for some reason, you can trace the error to the actual server by grepping through these files. The Node Manager in turn uses this data to kill the process.

servername_output.log
> This file records startup messages saved by the Node Manager when it starts a server.

servername_error.log
> This file records any error messages that are generated when the Node Manager starts a server.

config.xml
> This file contains any configuration information passed to the Node Manager by the Administration Server and can be safely ignored.

Except for the configuration file, all of the Managed Server log files are renamed by appending *_prev* to the filename whenever a server is restarted.

The Server Life Cycle

A server can cycle through a number of different states during its lifetime. It is useful to know how and when WebLogic transitions between these various states. You can explicitly move WebLogic Server to a new state, using either the Administration Console or the weblogic.Admin tool. Figure 13-6 illustrates the different states that a server goes through during its lifetime.

Let's take a closer look at the various states of the server's life cycle:

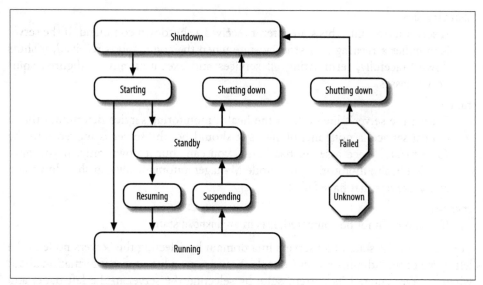

Figure 13-6. Life cycle of WebLogic Server

shutdown

> A server that is not running is considered to be in the shutdown state. The only thing that you can do with such a server is to start it!

starting

> A server that has been started from the command line or by a Node Manager moves into the starting mode. During this state, the server contacts the Administration Server, retrieves its configuration, starts all services, deploys all applications, and executes any startup classes.

standby

> If an administration port has been configured, the server is capable of moving into the standby state after it has started. Otherwise, the server moves directly from the starting to the running state. In the standby state, all services are initialized and all applications are deployed. Except for the administration port, however, all ports are closed. Therefore, the server is effectively in hot standby and ready to go.

running

> A server in the running state is fully operational and participating as a regular member of the domain.

suspending

> A server moves into the suspending state during a graceful shutdown. This allows the server to complete any in-flight work to enable a clean shutdown without loss of important state information. This state is skipped during a forced shutdown.

`shutting down`

A server moves into this state after it receives a shutdown command. If the server is in either a running or a standby state when the command is received, it shuts down gracefully, terminating all services and executing any configured shutdown classes.

`failed`

During the server's life cycle, if the health monitoring service determines that a critical service is not functioning as it should be, the server is moved into the failed state. Once a server has failed, you can shut it down only. If you have enabled health monitoring, the Node Manager automatically can shut down and restart servers that have failed.

`unknown`

If a server cannot be contacted, it is in an unknown state.

You can view the state of all servers in a domain by selecting the Servers node in the left frame of the Administration Console. You can get a little more information about when a server entered its current state by selecting the server in the left pane, and then navigating to the Server/Monitoring tab from the right. You also can use the `weblogic.Admin` tool to fetch the state of a server. Here is an example:

```
java weblogic.Admin -adminurl t3://10.0.10.10:7001 -username system -password pssst
GETSTATE
```

Graceful Shutdown

WebLogic supports two forms of shutdown. A graceful shutdown causes the server to transition through the following sequence of states: running, suspending, standby, shutting down, and shutdown. A forced shutdown simply moves the server from its current state into standby and then shutdown.

During a graceful shutdown, the server attempts to complete any in-flight work and tries to suspend the servers in an order that minimizes disruption to your applications. A graceful shutdown begins by rejecting further nontransactional remote RMI requests. After this, the web container rejects any new requests and sessions and cleans up any current sessions. The server then waits for pending client transactions to complete, after which all remote RMI requests are rejected. The timer service cancels all triggers, after which all pending work on the execute queues is completed. Any active message-driven beans then are suspended, followed by the JMS service after all pending requests are handled. Finally, all idle connections in the JDBC connection pools are closed, and the transaction service waits for all pending transactions to complete.

When the web container shuts down, it handles existing sessions (at this point, new sessions are rejected), depending on the type of persistence used for the sessions:

- If the sessions do not have persistence configured, the sessions are "allowed to complete."

- If the sessions are configured for in-memory replication, WebLogic tries to transparently move the clients across to other machines that hold the secondary session state. All the sessions that have replicated their state to a secondary server are suspended immediately. If no secondary session state is available, the container waits until a secondary session is created, or until the session times out, whichever comes first.

- If the sessions are configured for JDBC or file persistence, the sessions that are replicated are suspended immediately.

You may not want WebLogic to handle active sessions in such a graceful way because it may take some time for the sessions to complete or time out. For example, the default timeout for HTTP sessions is one hour. You can instruct WebLogic to ignore sessions during shutdown. From the Administration Console, enable the "Ignore Sessions during Shutdown" option from the shutdown panel, or use the -ignoreSessions option when invoking the weblogic.Admin tool. This forces WebLogic to drop all sessions immediately, which may result in a loss of session information.

As a compromise, it is useful to set a Graceful Shutdown Timeout period. If the timeout is set, the server waits for this duration to complete a graceful shutdown. If the period is exceeded, and the server still is not completely shut down (for example, some sessions haven't yet completed), WebLogic forces the shutdown on the server, dropping the remaining sessions. You also may want this behavior for pending transactions. Depending on the transaction timeout, completing pending transactions can take some time. The transaction service waits for all pending transactions to complete before allowing the server to shut down. To cap this time period, specify a shutdown timeout so that all pending transactional work will be suspended after the timeout expires.

Starting a Server

Earlier, we saw how to start a Managed Server remotely using the Administration Console (and the Node Manager). The weblogic.Admin utility also can be used to start a Managed Server remotely. Just like the Administration Console, it requires a Node Manager on the machine that hosts the target server. In fact, the tool lets you start up a server in normal or standby mode, resume a server from standby mode, or force a server to shut down. For instance, if you need to start a Managed Server in the domain remotely, you can run the tool with the START parameter:

```
java weblogic.Admin -url t3://10.0.10.10:7001/
    -username system -password yourpassword
    START managedServer1
```

Here the Administration Server is running on port 7001, and managedServer1 is the name of a Managed Server in the domain. If you've configured a domain administration port, you must supply additional system properties in order to use the SSL-enabled administration port. The following command starts a Managed Server in a domain that uses a secure administration port:

```
java -Dweblogic.security.TrustKeyStore=DemoTrust weblogic.Admin
    -url t3s://10.0.10.10:9002/
    -username system -password yourpassword
      START managedServer1
```

If you have tweaked the SSL setup, you probably will have your own trust file and want to use something like the following:

```
java -Dweblogic.security.TrustKeyStore=CustomTrust
    -Dweblogic.security.CustomTrustKeyStoreFileName=myTrust.jks
    -Dweblogic.security.CustomTrustKeyStorePassPhrase=passphrase
    weblogic.Admin
    -url t3s://10.0.10.10:9002/
    -username system -password yourpassword
      START managedServer1
```

In WebLogic 7.0, you may run the command as follows:

```
java -Dweblogic.security.SSL.trustedCAKeyStore=X:\cacerts
    -Dweblogic.security.SSL.ignoreHostnameVerification=true
    weblogic.Admin
    -url t3s://10.0.10.10:9002/
    -username system -password yourpassword
      START managedServer1
```

In all these cases, the URL uses the default Administration Port 9002. Because it is a secure channel, the URL must use the T3S protocol. In addition, if you are using the demonstration certificates, you also must disable hostname verification (as we have done).

A Managed Server may be started in standby mode only if you have configured a domain-wide administration port. If a Managed Server is configured to start in standby mode, the earlier commands with the START parameter will ensure the server moves into the standby mode.

You can conveniently start, stop, and resume all of the Managed Servers in a domain at once. Choose the domain node from the Administration Console and navigate to the Control tab to use this functionality.

Standby Mode

In the standby state, a Managed Server is ready to become an active member of the domain. All services are initialized and all applications are deployed. No network channels are available to the client, and only the Administration Channel is active. Here are the steps to follow:

1. Ensure that the domain-wide administration port has been configured and enabled.

2. Using the Administration Console, select the server from the left pane and then set the "Startup mode" attribute in the Configuration/General tab to STANDBY. This means that whenever the Managed Server is started, it will move into the standby state.

Alternatively, you can explicitly start the server in standby mode with an additional system property in the *startManagedWeblogic* script:

```
-Dweblogic.management.startupMode=STANDBY
```

Note that this setting will override the Startup Mode specified for the Managed Server using the Administration Console.

If the Node Manager is set up on the machine that hosts the server, you also can start the server in standby mode remotely by issuing the following command:

```
java weblogic.Admin
      -url t3s://10.0.10.10:9002/
      -username system -password yourpassword
      STARTINSTANDBY managedServer1
```

Once you have started a server in standby mode, it will stop and wait for a signal to be activated. Only then will it move to the running state. To determine which servers are in the standby state, click the Servers node from the left pane of the Administration Console. The State column indicates STANDBY for those servers that are in this state.

You can move a server from a standby state into a running state from the Administration Console or by using the weblogic.Admin tool. To use the console, right-click the server's node and choose the "Start/Stop this server" option. Then select the "Resume this server" option from the right pane. To use the administration tool, you can issue the RESUME command:

```
java weblogic.Admin
      -url t3s://10.0.10.10:9002/
      -username system -password yourpassword
      RESUME managedServer1
```

Shutting Down

A server can be shut down from anywhere in its life cycle. To shut down a server from the Administration Console, right-click the server's node in the left pane and choose the "Start/Stop this server" option. Then select the "Shutdown this server" option from the right pane. To use the administration tool, you can issue the SHUTDOWN command:

```
java weblogic.Admin
      -url t3s://10.0.10.10:9002/
      -username system -password yourpassword
      SHUTDOWN mangedServer1
```

The preceding command shuts down the server gracefully, and can be issued only if the server is in the running or standby state.

You can supply two additional arguments in WebLogic 8.1. Use the -timeout argument to determine the maximum number of seconds that WebLogic should wait for a graceful shutdown to complete. This effectively sets a limit on the completion of pending in-flight tasks. Without this argument, WebLogic uses the timeout value set for the server from the Administration Console. By default, this timeout value is set to 0, which means that the server will wait indefinitely. Use the -ignoreExistingSessions flag to drop all HTTP sessions immediately. Without this argument, WebLogic uses the setting defined in the Administration Console, which waits for HTTP sessions to complete or time out. Here is an example:

```
java weblogic.Admin  -url t3s://10.0.10.10:9002/
    -username system -password yourpassword
    SHUTDOWN -ignoreExistingSessions -timeout 10 managedServer1
```

In some circumstances, you may need to force a server to shut down. You can do this by issuing the FORCESHUTDOWN command:

```
java weblogic.Admin
    -url t3s://10.0.10.10:9002/
    -username system -password yourpassword
    FORCESHUTDOWN servernameToStart
```

Note that a forced shutdown could result in a loss of session-state information or could cause currently active transactions to roll back. If a server was started with the Node Manager and later does not respond to a forced shutdown command, the Node Manager is asked to kill the process entirely.

Node Manager

If a Managed Server is under the control of a Node Manager, it can be in three additional states:

FAILED_RESTARTING
>	This indicates that the Node Manager currently is restarting a failed server.

ACTIVATE_LATER
>	This indicates that the Node Manager has tried to restart the server a number of times, and has reached its limit within the current restart interval (as described in Table 13-3). The Node Manager will attempt to restart the server later, in the next restart interval.

FAILED_NOT_RESTARTABLE
>	This indicates that the server has failed (or was killed), but because it isn't configured to Auto Restart, the Node Manager did not restart the server.

Monitoring a WebLogic Domain

You should give serious consideration to monitoring a WebLogic domain in a production environment. Here's a summary of the various options available to you:

- You can use the Administration Console to actively monitor the domain. The Administration Console provides exhaustive monitoring information about virtually all aspects of the domain. For instance, you can use it to monitor the health of all servers and access their log files. In addition, you can use it to monitor other domain resources such as clusters, JDBC connection pools, and JMS destinations. Chapter 15 gives a good overview of how to monitor the various domain resources. Refer to individual chapters for additional material on monitoring that particular resource. For instance, Chapter 6 provides information on how to monitor both active and pending in-flight transactions.

- You can use the JMX framework, as described in Chapter 20, to access the same information as the Administration Console.

- You can use the logging framework to monitor the domain. This chapter described the various logs that are maintained by WebLogic: the domain logs, the server logs, and the log files created by the Node Manager for itself and for the servers under its control. In addition, you can access logs for different subsystems such as the HTTP server, JTA, and JDBC. You also can alter the logging behavior in a more proactive way, as described in Chapter 21. For example, you can write log listeners that actively notify you when a server's health fails.

- You can use the SNMP framework, as described in Chapter 22, to extend the monitoring capabilities that you may have in place already in order to include your WebLogic domain.

CHAPTER 14
Clustering

Clustering creates an illusion—it permits the deployment of application components and services to several machines while presenting only a single face to the client. There are good reasons to support this illusion. When a client requests a service, it should make no difference if the service runs on a single server or across a number of servers. The clustering abstraction provides you with a clear route to improving the performance and scalability of your applications, albeit with increased administration of hardware and network resources. WebLogic's clustering offers three important benefits:

Scalability
    A solution that allows you to create additional capacity by introducing more servers to the cluster, thereby reducing the load on existing servers.

Load balancing
    The ability to distribute requests across all members of the cluster, according to the workload on each server.

High availability
    A mix of features that ensure applications and services are available even if a server or machine fails. Clients can continue to work with little or no disruption in a highly available environment. WebLogic achieves high availability using a combination of features: replication, failover, and migratable services.

Clearly, WebLogic's support for clustering impacts all aspects of J2EE development, deployment, and application security. In previous chapters, we encountered several instances in which WebLogic allows you to improve the scalability and availability of your applications: HTTP session state replication, load balancing HTTP requests across web servers, JMS distributed destinations, JDBC multipools, load balancing and failover for calls to EJB homes and EJB objects, and more. These all fall under the broad umbrella of WebLogic clustering. This chapter aims to put all of these WebLogic features into perspective, and looks at their impact on a clustered solution.

Architecting a clustered solution requires you to understand three concepts: the clustering features that WebLogic provides for the various J2EE resources, the communication infrastructure that is imposed by WebLogic on any clustered solution, and the different ways to logically and physically partition the various WebLogic server instances and applications. This chapter examines all of these aspects of WebLogic clustering by using a running example of a multi-tiered architecture. We begin by taking a closer look at clusters and tiers, consolidating the facts and examining the two most important benefits of WebLogic clustering: load balancing and failover. We then cover the various configuration issues involved in setting up a WebLogic cluster and how to physically construct the various application tiers. We also examine important issues affecting the front tier, including replication of HTTP session state and the use of a load balancer. Next, we see the impact of adding an object tier, the role of JNDI and replicated stubs in the communication between the two tiers, and how EJBs, RMI objects, and JMS resources behave in a WebLogic cluster.

Finally, we look at how to protect your cluster configuration, how to set up replication groups, and how to configure the underlying communication infrastructure according to the needs of your cluster. By the end of this chapter, you will be able to architect a multi-tiered framework for your J2EE applications, and understand the implications of this framework in terms of network, server, and application resources.

There is no best way to architect a clustered solution—a good solution will adapt to the design of your application and meet your requirements regarding scalability, availability, and security. The goal of this chapter is to emphasize the framework options that WebLogic provides so that you can better architect your clustered solutions to take advantage of them.

An Overview of Clustering

A WebLogic domain can be extended to incorporate a cluster of servers, typically spread across different physical machines in a network. Usually, a cluster will host a well-defined set of services and J2EE components that form part of a larger application framework. Multiple clusters of server instances, called *tiers*, are often used to set up the application architecture. These tiers provide both a logical and a physical partitioning of application components that offers greater security, scalability, and fault tolerance. Once you set up the servers that belong to the cluster, you can use the Administration Console to manage its configuration and to monitor its runtime health.

Domains, Machines, and Clusters

As described in Chapter 13, a WebLogic domain can be composed of a number of WebLogic instances, and several of these servers may be grouped into clusters. For instance, you could set up a cluster of WebLogic servers, all of which host your web application and related resources. This cluster of servers could be fronted by a load balancer that distributes requests evenly across all the members of the cluster. The load balancer could itself be another WebLogic instance. All server instances must belong to the same WebLogic domain. Thus, a *WebLogic cluster* is a group of servers working together with services, such as clustered JNDI, to provide support for failover and load balancing. A domain may in turn have a number of WebLogic instances, several groups of which can be placed into different clusters.

Note that we refer to WebLogic instances as being part of a cluster, and not the machines hosting the WebLogic instances. This is because a physical machine may host multiple copies of WebLogic, and each such instance is considered a separate entity. When you define a WebLogic cluster, the servers participating in the cluster can be distributed across multiple machines or may reside on the same machine. The only caveat is that if a machine fails, all of the WebLogic instances running on the machine will become unavailable. If the cluster includes server instances that live on different machines, the clusterable services will still be available if one of the machines dies, even though the cluster may now operate with reduced capacity. For nonclusterable services, WebLogic provides a migration strategy, allowing you to migrate a service from a failed machine to another member of the cluster.

For components that need to replicate their state onto a secondary server instance, you can minimize the damage due to a machine failure by ensuring that the secondary server instance is chosen from a different physical machine. WebLogic implements this notion by introducing the concept of a Machine and replication groups. As explained in Chapter 13, a Machine is simply a tag that can be assigned to a WebLogic instance, which indicates the physical machine that hosts the server. WebLogic can then use this tag to select a clustered server on a different physical machine for holding the replicated state. Later in the section "Replication Groups," we will see how *replication groups* let you specify the preferred servers for holding the backup state of a server.

Tiers

Layered architecture is a common design methodology used in software engineering. The software is decomposed logically into a number of layers (tiers), each layer providing a well-defined set of services. J2EE applications can be partitioned in the same way. A typical J2EE application includes multiple web components (servlets, JSPs, and filters), a number of EJBs that implement the business logic, and data access classes or EJBs that interface with the underlying data store. WebLogic's support for clustering enables you to physically partition these services across well-defined application tiers. In this context, a *tier* represents a number of WebLogic instances that behave in a similar way, each hosting the same set of applications and services. Clearly, it makes sense to map each tier to a different WebLogic cluster. A typical application setup would define at least one of the following tiers:

Web tier

Refers to the bank of servers that provide static content, such as HTML and images, to clients. The web tier is usually the first point of contact for clients, although client requests also may be directed transparently through firewalls and then distributed to these servers via a load balancer. The web tier usually is composed of a number of web servers.

Presentation tier

Refers to WebLogic instances that provide dynamic content. In our context, this applies to servers hosting the JSP pages and servlets. The presentation tier often is combined with the web tier, though this isn't necessary.

Object tier

Refers to WebLogic servers that host the RMI and EJB objects, which encapsulate the business logic of your application. If your application is a pure web application not utilizing any EJB or RMI objects, the object tier may not even be needed.

Data tier

Refers to the servers that provide access to the actual data store(s). This includes servers hosting your DBMS, LDAP store, and more.

Figure 14-1 illustrates an architecture composed of multiple tiers. Each tier is implemented as a separate cluster. We've combined the web and presentation tiers by creating a single WebLogic cluster that hosts all the servlets, JSPs, and HTTP servers. On the other hand, the object tier is mapped to a cluster of WebLogic instances that host the EJB and RMI objects, JMS servers, and JDBC resources. Both clusters can live on their own hardware and have their own set of WebLogic instances.

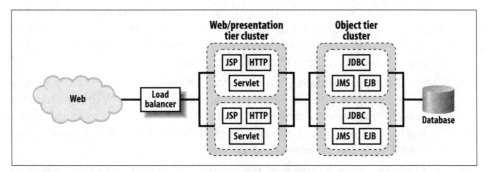

Figure 14-1. A multi-tier application setup using WebLogic clusters

This multi-tier architecture opens up the opportunity to load-balance EJB method calls. A method call from a server in the presentation tier to a remote EJB on the object tier can be directed to any of the servers in that object tier. There is a trade-off, though—although the calls to remote EJBs can be load-balanced, they always will involve network traffic because the servlets and EJBs live on separate tiers (clusters). As a result, EJB calls will be slower than if you collocated the EJBs with the web tier.

The multi-tier scenario opens up other opportunities for enhanced scalability as well. For instance, if you find that most of your resources are being spent servicing EJBs, you can improve the capacity of the object tier by simply adding another server to it. You could even move a server from the presentation tier to the object tier. Later when we look at the section "Combined-Tier Architecture," you'll find that this flexibility is absent. The multi-tier application setup just shown also improves availability. Servers in the presentation tier are shielded from server crashes in the object tier (and vice versa). If a server hosting EJB objects fails, the servers in the presentation tier are unaffected because subsequent requests are simply routed to other available servers in the object tier.

Partitioning your application setup into various tiers also has security implications. The multi-tier architecture shown in Figure 14-1 allows you to protect the physical servers in the object tier from direct access by external clients. Other scenarios, in which all of the separate tiers are collapsed into a single tier, may not permit this.

Load Balancing

Load balancing is about distributing work across multiple servers within a cluster. Ideally you want this work to be distributed evenly, to the capabilities and load on each server within the cluster. WebLogic is able to load-balance requests to members within a cluster when certain conditions are satisfied:

- First, WebLogic requires that (most) components be deployed homogeneously to each server in the cluster. In the multi-tier application setup illustrated in Figure 14-1, the web application is targeted to all servers that belong to the presentation tier cluster. Because of this, incoming requests can be distributed evenly across the different members of the presentation tier. Similarly, the EJB components are available on all members of the object tier cluster. Because of this, incoming EJB calls from the presentation tier (or any external client) can be distributed across the different servers in the object tier.

- When a component is deployed to a cluster, multiple copies of the component will be sitting on the different servers comprising the cluster. WebLogic uses the cluster-wide JNDI tree to record the availability of these replicas in the object tier, whereas a proxy plug-in typically holds the information about the availability of servers hosting the servlets and JSP pages.

- WebLogic also must be aware of the status of the components that have been deployed to the cluster. This information forms the basis on which a load balancer can decide which server instances should be used when a request is made to the cluster. WebLogic uses a variety of methods to determine the health status of servers, including multicast heartbeats. By knowing when a server instance is under heavy load while the others aren't, a load balancer is able to direct new requests to the other members of the cluster. Hardware load balancers often have this capability.

It also is important to understand when WebLogic avoids load balancing. In many cases, WebLogic simply locates a resource that resides on the same instance, instead of locating another replica of the same resource on other servers within the cluster. By doing this, WebLogic can optimize network traffic and transaction times, and serve requests in less time—even if this means compromising on failover and scalability. You will see more examples of this optimization in later sections.

The ultimate goal of load balancing is to evenly distribute the load on all of the servers that host the various components of your enterprise application. A good load-balancing scheme can then provide the ideal opportunity for your application to scale. For instance, suppose you find that under heavy load the servers in the object tier all run at maximum capacity because of the intensive processing involved in your EJB methods. Now if you add another WebLogic instance to the object tier cluster, your application setup can take advantage of the additional resources automatically. The new server can participate in the overall load balancing and hopefully diminish the load on the original set of servers. Most importantly, this change can occur transparently without affecting any clients of the cluster.

Failover

High availability is another important benefit of a WebLogic cluster. By deploying components and installing services homogeneously across all members of a cluster, you incorporate a certain degree of redundancy into your application setup. This ensures that you can continue servicing users, even if one of the servers in the cluster goes down. WebLogic supports a number of clusterable services and provides high availability by including failover features in many of these services. For nonclusterable services, WebLogic still can support high availability by enabling you (the Administrator) to migrate the service onto another running instance within the cluster.

Central to WebLogic's support for failover is knowing where duplicate components are located, and also maintaining the operational state of these components. For instance, a hardware load balancer constantly can monitor the operational state of the servers in the presentation tier cluster. If one of the servers in the cluster becomes unavailable for some reason, the load balancer can avoid distributing requests to it. Likewise, a replica-aware EJB stub can load-balance a method call from a servlet or JSP (or any external client) across all server instances in the object tier that host the EJB component. If one of these servers fails, this change in the operational status of the cluster is communicated to all of the replica-aware stubs. Subsequent calls to the EJB then will be redirected to a running server instance.

Typically your clients will need to maintain conversational state on the server side when interacting with your application. The J2EE framework offers several mechanisms for managing client-specific session information on the server side, such as HTTP sessions and stateful session beans. In such cases, simply knowing which servers have failed is not enough. For high availability, you need to be able to preserve the user's conversational state, even in the event of a server failure. WebLogic can preserve the client's session-state information by duplicating the state—for example, onto a secondary server. In the presentation tier cluster, the HTTP session state held on a primary server can be replicated to a secondary server within the cluster. If the primary server maintaining the HTTP session fails, subsequent requests to the cluster automatically are directed to the secondary server, which then can use the backup of the session-state information. This form of in-memory replication was explained in Chapter 2. WebLogic implements a similar mechanism for other stateful components that live in the object tier.

A Closer Look at the Frontend Tier

The frontend of our demonstration multi-tier cluster architecture consists of two managed servers that host the JSPs, servlets, and HTML pages. If your application doesn't use any EJB or RMI objects, the web/presentation tier cluster should be sufficient for your "pure" web application. To this end, the server instances that live in this frontend cluster host a servlet/JSP container and an HTTP server. Typically, this tier sits in front of a DBMS server—you may need to configure one or more data sources that provide JDBC access to the cluster. In this section, you will learn how to set up this frontend tier, and how to deploy web and presentation tier components to such a cluster.

Our web/presentation tier consists of two servers in a WebLogic cluster. External to this cluster is the Administration Server, which hosts the Administration Console and the domain configuration. So, our application setup requires a WebLogic domain with an Administration Server and two Managed Servers that belong to a cluster. We'll expand on the load balancer later.

Figure 14-2 depicts the structure of the web/presentation tier within a domain. Here, we have zoomed in on the configuration of the frontend cluster of the multi-tier application setup illustrated earlier in Figure 14-1.

As the figure shows, each server instance has its own name, listen address, and port, just as you would expect in a nonclustered scenario. The Managed Servers belong to a WebLogic cluster named FECluster. Here, 237.0.0.1:7777 is the address/port combination that each cluster member uses for multicast broadcasts. Finally, the cluster itself has an address, whose value identifies all of the server instances that participate in the cluster. An important constraint of this cluster configuration, and of any other WebLogic cluster you may design, is that the Administration Server must be accessible to all the Managed Servers in your domain.

Working with Clusters

Before examining the frontend tier, let's cover some aspects of configuring a WebLogic cluster. The most important aspect is how to address the cluster. The

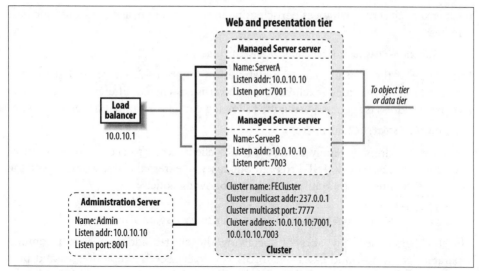

Figure 14-2. A simple web/presentation tier

cluster address needs to be set up both for internal use (e.g., EJB handles need the cluster address when load balancing method calls), and external use (e.g., a Java client needs the cluster address to access the various resources available to the object tier cluster).

Addressing a cluster

A cluster is composed of a number of individual WebLogic instances. In previous chapters, if you needed to address a server, you simply supplied the hostname and port of the server instance. This still will work if the server instance is part of a cluster, but it usually is not what you want. For example, if a servlet needs to make a call to an EJB that is hosted on a separate cluster, the servlet should not need to know which server it should contact. Clearly, a more generalized addressing scheme is required that will allow you to point to a cluster (all servers within the cluster, really), and not just to a single server. We will call this address the *cluster address*. WebLogic lets you specify the cluster address either as a list of IP addresses, or as a DNS name that is mapped externally to the addresses of all servers that belong to the WebLogic cluster.

You can specify the cluster address using a comma-separated list of hostnames and port numbers. Both of these are valid examples of the cluster address for a WebLogic cluster:

```
10.0.10.10:7001,10.0.10.10:7002,10.0.10.11:7001
oreilly1:7001,oreilly2:7001
```

Remember that any address/port combination in the cluster address must be unique. This means that if you need to run a WebLogic cluster on a single machine, you must ensure all server instances participating in the cluster are assigned a unique port number:

```
dnsofmachine:7001,dnsofmachine:7002,dnsofmachine:7003
```

In the case of the web tier cluster illustrated in Figure 14-2, we've configured two servers to run on the same machine. Each server is assigned a different listen port, so its cluster address is specified using the following comma-separated list of addresses:

```
10.0.10.10:7001,10.0.10.10:7003
```

The cluster address generally is used when a client needs to access some resource bound in the cluster-wide JNDI tree. In our case, an external client would create the initial JNDI context to this cluster using the following code:

```
InitialContext ctx =
        new InitialContext("t3://10.0.10.10:7001,10.0.10.10:7003");
```

This highlights the drawbacks of specifying the cluster address using a comma-separated list of host addresses—it forces you to hardcode the addresses and port numbers of the servers that belong to the cluster. That is, your code is no longer immune from changes in the configuration of your cluster. For instance, if you add or remove physical hardware or alter the IP addresses assigned to your NICs, those same changes need to be applied to your WebLogic configuration and then to your code source. Clearly, this is not pretty.

For this reason, we recommend that in production environments you configure the cluster address using a DNS name. Your DNS server would then be configured to map the DNS name to all of the servers that belong to the WebLogic cluster. By specifying a DNS name for the cluster address, you establish a naming abstraction that shields your source code and cluster configuration from any changes in the hardware configuration.

There are disadvantages to using DNS names. They do not capture port information, so if the DNS name assigned to the WebLogic cluster is mapped to multiple IP addresses, you must assign the same listen port to all Managed Servers in the cluster. For instance, if we configure a WebLogic cluster with two Managed Servers running on separate machines—say, 10.0.10.10 and 10.0.10.11 on port 7001—you could modify the DNS server for the participating machines to map a DNS name—say, mycluster—to both of these addresses. You then can set the cluster address for the WebLogic cluster to mycluster:7001. If a client needs to interact with the cluster-wide JNDI tree, it would set up the initial JNDI context as follows:

```
InitialContext ctx = new InitialContext("t3://mycluster:7001");
```

WebLogic will expand the DNS name to the list of IP addresses mapped to the DNS name—in this case, 10.0.10.10 and 10.0.10.11—and then proceed as before.

You also can specify a cluster address from the Administration Console. Select a cluster from the left pane and then navigate to the Configuration/General tab. The cluster address that you specify is used internally when constructing EJB home handle references.

This entry does not define the cluster address for the WebLogic cluster. It simply informs WebLogic of the cluster address that it should embed in its EJB home handles returned to clients so that the EJB handles can locate the cluster when their homes are reconstructed.

Creating a cluster

The easiest way to create a WebLogic cluster is to use the Domain Configuration Wizard. This lets you create a WebLogic domain composed of an Administration Server and a cluster of Managed Servers. Start up the Domain Configuration Wizard as described in Chapter 13. In WebLogic 8.1, you need to choose the Custom setup. Remember to indicate that your WebLogic configuration should be distributed across a cluster. In WebLogic 7.0, after choosing the WLS Domain template and a name for the WebLogic domain, select the Admin Server with Clustered Managed Servers option. On the Configure Clustered Servers panel, you then can create an entry for each server instance that will participate in the cluster.

For each Managed Server, you must specify the name of the server, and the listen address and listen port on which the server will be available. Each member of the cluster also uses a particular address and port that it needs to send multicast broadcasts. This address/port combination will apply to all of the servers in the cluster. The Domain Configuration Wizard supplies default values for the multicast address and port: 237.0.0.1:7777. All of these settings are independent of the Administration Server, which needs its own name, listen address, and port number.

If you've already created a WebLogic domain, you can simply use the Administration Console to configure a new WebLogic cluster, or to modify the configuration settings of an existing WebLogic cluster. In order to create a new cluster, you need to first configure one or more Managed Servers that will participate in the new cluster. After this, choose the Clusters node from the left pane of the Administration Console and then select the Configure a New Cluster link. Here you should supply values for various configuration settings for the new WebLogic cluster, such as its name and cluster address. Then select the Configuration/Servers tab to add or remove Managed Servers that should belong to the cluster.

Starting and monitoring the domain

Starting a WebLogic domain that is clustered is no different from starting one that isn't. You first need to start the Administration Server, followed by the Managed Servers that belong to the domain. Each Managed Server notifies the Administration Server when it's up and running, and automatically enlists itself with the cluster. The cluster is alive and healthy when all of its servers are up and running. You can start the Administration Server by running the startWebLogic command. You then can start each Managed Server by using the startManagedWeblogic command:

```
startManagedWebLogic ServerA http://10.0.10.10:8001/
startManagedWebLogic ServerB http://10.0.10.10:8001/
```

Here, 10.0.10.10:8001 refers to the listen address and port of the Administration Server, and ServerA refers to the name of a Managed Server. Once a Managed Server completes its boot sequence, you may notice an additional log message at the bottom of the console log, similar to the following:

```
<13-Jan-2003 23:01:31 GMT> <Notice> <Cluster> <000102>
                    <Joining cluster MyCluster on 237.0.0.1:7777>
```

This indicates that the Managed Server has located the cluster and has joined it successfully.

You also can use the Administration Console to monitor the status of the cluster. Select the cluster from under the Clusters node in the left pane. Then, if you select the Monitoring tab from the right pane, you can view the number of servers configured for the cluster, and the number of servers currently participating in the cluster. For the example setup, once both servers have completed their boot sequence successfully, you should expect a value of 2 for both settings.

Deploying to a cluster

In a multi-tier application setup in which each tier is mapped physically to a WebLogic cluster, you need to deploy only those components that must live on that tier. So, in our sample web tier cluster, only the web applications should be deployed. If the application is available as a WAR file, you can deploy and target the WAR to the cluster. If the web application is part of an EAR file, only the web applications ought to be deployed to the web tier cluster. Remember to also deploy any shared classes that may be referenced from the servlets and JSP pages within the web application. You can achieve this via the Administration Console itself. Simply choose the Targets tab for a selected web application, and then choose the name of the cluster that will host the web application.

As explained in Chapter 12, you need to be particularly vigilant when deploying to a cluster. The last thing that you want is a partially deployed application in which the web application has failed to deploy on some servers in the cluster. You always should try to deploy components when all of the members of the cluster are available. In addition, you must not change, add, or remove members of the cluster during deployment.

Furthermore, in a WebLogic 7.0 domain where no service packs have been applied, you cannot deploy to a partial cluster. This means that you will not be able to deploy a component to a cluster successfully if the Administration Console detects an unavailable cluster member. If you must deploy under these circumstances, you can either bring up all the Managed Servers in the cluster, or remove those members that you are unable to start. WebLogic 7.0 SP 1 and WebLogic 8.1 lift this restriction, and allow you to deploy to a partial cluster. In this case, the application component (web application, EJB module, resource adapter) is deployed only to those servers in the cluster that are alive at that time. Deployment on those members that are not available at that time will be deferred until they come back up.

Servlets and JSPs in a Cluster

The major components that typically are deployed to the presentation tier are servlets and JSP pages. You also could deploy JDBC connection pools and data sources to this cluster, though in our multi-tier application framework, we will make these available to the object tier cluster only. Let's review the load-balancing and failover features WebLogic provides for the servlets and JSPs.

WebLogic can load-balance the requests to servlets and JSP pages deployed to a cluster. It can distribute the requests across all of the servers in the cluster that host the web application. There is one important caveat. This load balancing occurs only for those requests that are not bound to an HTTP session. As soon as a client is involved in an HTTP session on the server side, session-aware requests to servlets and JSPs are directed to that server while it's available. WebLogic provides various session persistence mechanisms that ensure the HTTP session can be re-created on another member of the cluster in case the primary server fails.

If you choose in-memory session replication for persisting the HTTP session state, WebLogic maintains on a secondary server a copy of the session-state information that is held on the primary server. This means that all web requests to the cluster that are involved in a session are directed to the same server instance holding the primary session state. Only when the primary server fails are the requests redirected to the secondary server holding the replicated session-state information. For this reason, we refer to sessions as "sticky." In this case, failover is provided by replicating the session state onto a secondary server within the cluster.

If you want to deploy JSPs and servlets to a cluster and benefit from WebLogic's load-balancing and failover features, you also should enable session-state persistence for the web application. We've already looked at the various session persistence mechanisms provided by WebLogic in Chapter 2. In our case, we chose in-memory session-state replication for handling session-state failover in the presentation tier cluster. To enable in-memory session-state replication, you need to ensure that the *weblogic.xml* descriptor file for the deployed web application incorporates the following XML fragment:

```
<!-- weblogic.xml entry -->
<session-descriptor>
  <session-param>
    <param-name>PersistentStoreType</param-name>
```

```
      <param-value>replicated</param-value>
   </session-param>
   <!-- other session param's -->
</session-descriptor>
```

In addition, you should target your web application to the cluster, and not to each server in the cluster individually.

Configuring a Load Balancer

A frontend cluster cannot work effectively without a load balancer. The load balancer provides a single unified address that clients can use (ignoring firewalls), and it serves as the main entry point into the cluster. The role of the load balancer is two-fold. First, it should balance the load across the available members of the cluster while remaining faithful to the sticky sessions. Second, the load balancer should detect and avoid failed servers in the cluster. WebLogic provides a rudimentary software load balancer, the HttpClusterServlet, which round-robins HTTP requests through all the available servers in the cluster. A hardware solution typically includes additional logic to monitor the load on individual machines and distribute the requests accordingly. You also can use web server plug-ins, described in Chapter 3.

In our example multi-tier application framework depicted in Figure 14-1, we included a single load balancer that distributes requests across all members in the web/presentation tier. This means that we can use either the HttpClusterServlet running on a single WebLogic instance or a hardware load balancer. Later, we vary the frontend tier setup using proxy plug-ins in tandem with popular HTTP servers.

If we use the HttpClusterServlet, the load balancer in Figure 14-2 represents an additional WebLogic instance that hosts the HttpClusterServlet. This server instance is not part of the cluster—it simply forwards requests to the members of the cluster. The servlet maintains a list of WebLogic instances that host the clustered servlets and JSP pages, and forwards HTTP requests to these servers using a round-robin strategy. If a client has created an HTTP session, the HttpClusterServlet forwards the request to the WebLogic instance that holds the primary state, and fails over to a secondary server in case of a failure. In general, it can do this by creating a cookie that holds the locations of the primary and secondary servers specific to the client's session. This cookie is then passed between the browser and the server on subsequent requests to the cluster. The HttpClusterServlet examines the cookie sent by the client on subsequent session-aware requests, and determines the cluster member it should forward the request to.

Chapter 2 shows how to configure the HttpClusterServlet in more detail. The two important aspects of its setup include the set of URL requests that ought to be forwarded and the cluster address for the frontend tier cluster. In our case, we want all HTTP requests to be forwarded to the front tier. The cluster address would be specified as an initialization parameter for the HttpClusterServlet in the *web.xml* descriptor file:

```
<!-- web.xml entry -->
<init-param>
  <param-name>WebLogicCluster</param-name>
  <param-value>
    10.0.10.10:7001:7002|10.0.10.10:7003:7004
  </param-value>
</init-param>
```

Alternatively, if you require more sophisticated load-balancing logic, you can use a hardware load balancer. You need to ensure the load balancer is configured to work with WebLogic. For instance, if the load balancer supports passive cookie persistence, you must configure the load balancer to recognize WebLogic's cookie format. Only then can the load balancer extract the locations of the primary and secondary servers from the cookie, which is vital to preserving sticky sessions.

Using the Front Tier

Once you've set up the web/presentation tier cluster, you are in a position to test its load-balancing and failover features. You can access the various web applications deployed to the cluster by using the address of the load balancer. A request to a resource within the web application then will be directed to all available servers in the cluster. In the example, a web request such as *http://10.0.10.1/index.jsp* will be routed by the load balancer to either ServerA or ServerB. If *index.jsp* initiated an HTTP session, further requests from the same client will be directed to the same server.

Moreover, because we've already configured session replication for the web application and targeted the application to FECluster, we can comfortably take the primary server down and watch WebLogic automatically redirect further web requests from the client to the other available server, re-creating the primary session state on that server.

Other Frontend Architectures

In the previous multi-tier application architecture, the web and presentation tiers were combined into a single WebLogic cluster. Sometimes, a more elaborate setup is necessary—say, when your application needs to be integrated with an already established bank of web servers. In this case, the existing web servers can be used to serve up the static content, while WebLogic can be used to serve up the rest. That is, the web tier maps to a bank of web servers that handle requests for all the static content, and the presentation tier maps to a WebLogic cluster that handles requests for all the dynamic content.

By doing this, you can take advantage of the existing hardware and resources for serving requests for static content, and let the WebLogic cluster focus on serving requests for dynamic content only. This does, however, increase the complexity of your application setup, and places extra demands on its proper configuration and administration. This physical split between the web and presentation tiers is depicted in Figure 14-3.

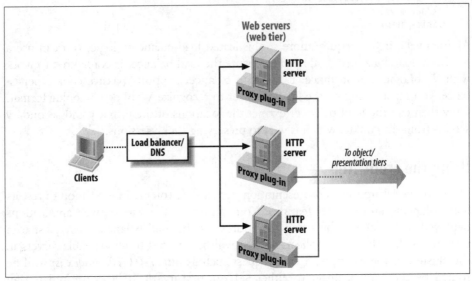

Figure 14-3. A two-tier frontend architecture

Here we have used a bank of web servers, each configured identically with a proxy plug-in. The plug-ins work in the same way as the HttpClusterServlet, each maintaining the operational state in the sibling tier and routing requests to the appropriate server. Chapter 3 shows how to install and configure these plug-ins. The web tier could even consist of a single HTTP server/proxy plug-in combination. A bank of web servers merely ensures that your web tier can survive even if one of the web servers fails. There are two ways in which you can distribute web requests across the bank of web servers:

- Using a hardware load balancer to distribute incoming requests across the bank of web servers. A good load balancer will ensure web requests are always forwarded to the available HTTP servers. So, in this case, the load balancer provides the failover at the web tier. It also can monitor the workload on the machines participating in the web tier. This is the recommended approach.

- Using DNS round-robining, where the DNS server is configured to map a DNS name to the addresses of all web servers in the web tier. Clients then use this DNS name to access the web tier as well as servlets and JSPs that are available on the presentation tier cluster. A downside of this approach is that the client still may resolve the DNS name to a failed web server. In that case, it is up to the client to issue another request to the web tier and avoid the failed server. For this reason, we do not recommend this approach.

The bank of web servers also could be implemented by a cluster of WebLogic instances that serve static content only, each hosting the HttpClusterServlet. In all cases, the web servers in the web tier should serve requests for static content while forwarding requests for JSPs and servlets to the presentation tier.

Note that in the situation depicted in Figure 14-3, the load balancer doesn't handle sticky sessions. Unlike the load balancer in Figure 14-2, this one is distributing requests to a bank of web servers that do not hold any session-state information. The load balancer still may hold some (internal) client session information for its own load-balancing purposes, but this is WebLogic-independent. The plug-in, on the other hand, will look at the client's cookie to determine which server to choose from in the presentation tier.

Load-Balancing Schemes

The heart of WebLogic's load-balancing schemes lies in its clustered JNDI and RMI implementation, described in Chapter 4. As the overview pointed out, the replica-aware stubs maintained by the cluster allow calls to the RMI object to be routed to any of the servers in the cluster hosting that object. This scheme underlies WebLogic's support of load balancing for JDBC data sources, EJBs, and distributed JMS destinations, as all of these are implemented using RMI. The rest of this section describes these load-balancing schemes and some of the general conditions under which they will and won't be used.

Server-to-Server Routing

Both WebLogic 8.1 and 7.0 support several algorithms for balancing requests to clustered objects: *round-robin*, *weight-based*, *random*, and *parameter-based routing*. By default, WebLogic uses a round-robin policy for load balancing. An example of a server-to-server scenario was illustrated in Figure 14-1, where a JSP deployed to a presentation tier makes a call to an EJB or RMI object deployed to a separate object tier cluster. The algorithm used to choose between the servers in the object tier cluster depends on two factors:

- If the RMI object was compiled with a particular load-balancing scheme, that scheme will be used.
- If no scheme was explicitly configured, the default load-balancing scheme for the cluster will be used.

You can configure the default load-balancing scheme for the cluster by selecting the cluster in the Administration Console and picking a suitable load balancing scheme for the Default Load Algorithm setting in the Configuration/General tab. Let's look at these schemes in more detail.

Round-robin

When the round-robin algorithm is used, requests from a clustered stub are cycled through a list of WebLogic instances hosting the object. A specific order is chosen, and then each server is used in this order until the end of the list is reached, after which the cycle is repeated. A round-robin scheme is simple and predictable. However, this strategy does not react according to the varying loads on the servers. For example, if one server in the cluster is under heavy load, it still will continue to participate in the round-robining scheme like the other members in the cluster, so work may pile up on this server.

Figure 14-4 illustrates the round-robin scheme. A server in the presentation tier cluster makes a number of calls on some clusterable component c1 deployed to another cluster. Each method call is directed to one of the servers hosting the component, according to the load-balancing scheme that applies in the situation. Under the round-robin scheme, the method calls simply will alternate between the two servers, ServerA and ServerB.

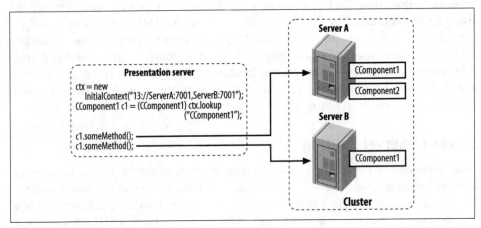

Figure 14-4. Round-robin routing

Weight-based

When using the weight-based load-balancing scheme, the replica-aware stub distributes the requests based on a preassigned numeric weight for each server. You can choose a number between 1 and 100 for the Cluster Weight setting for each clustered server under the Configuration/Cluster tab in the right pane. The *cluster weight* determines what portion of the load a server will bear, relative to other members in the cluster. So, a server with weight 25 will take half as much load as the rest of the servers whose weights are 50. If all members of the cluster are assigned the same weights, they all bear an equal share of the load.

This load-balancing scheme is best suited for clusters with heterogeneous deployments, in which different EJBs are deployed to different sets of servers, or when the processing power of the machines in the cluster varies. You should consider several factors before assigning a weight for the server:

- The number of CPUs dedicated to the particular server
- The speed of the network cards that are used by the machine hosting the clustered server
- The number of nonclustered (pinned) objects or services running on a server

Remember, cluster weights provide only an indication of the "expected" load on a server. A weight-based scheme does not react and respond to the current loads on the cluster servers.

Random

The random load-balancing scheme distributes requests randomly across all members of the cluster. This scheme is recommended for homogenous clusters, in which components are deployed uniformly to all members of the cluster and the servers run on machines with similar configurations. A random load-balancing strategy can distribute loads evenly to all members of the cluster. The longer a WebLogic cluster remains alive, the closer the distribution is to the "mean." However, each request must incur a slight processing cost of generating a random number. In addition, a random distribution does not account for the differences in the configuration of the machines that are participating in the cluster, and so does not react to different loads on the cluster servers.

Parameter-based

Parameter-based routing lets you programmatically determine which server should be chosen to handle a method call on a clusterable RMI object. Unlike the other load-balancing schemes, this is not a general scheme that can be applied to any clusterable component. Rather, it is needed only when you want extreme control in routing RMI objects. This scheme is described in Chapter 4.

Client-Server Routing

Both WebLogic 8.1 and 7.0 support the round-robin, weight-based, and random load-balancing schemes for *external client applications* that make connections into a cluster. External clients are at a disadvantage because the client eventually makes IP connections to each server in the cluster, as all of these schemes distribute the load across all available servers in the cluster.

WebLogic 8.1 can limit this promiscuous connection behavior for clients. A load-balancing scheme with *server affinity* attempts to always use connections to servers that are already established, instead of creating new ones. The three load-balancing schemes each have an affinity-based counterpart: round-robin affinity, weight-based affinity, and random affinity. If you set the default load algorithm for a cluster to round-robin affinity, for example, the round-robin scheme will still be used for load balancing server-to-server requests. However, server affinity will cause external clients to simply use servers to which they are already connected. This minimizes the number of IP sockets opened between clients and the clustered servers, but at the cost of eliminating load balancing.

Note that server affinity also affects the failover behavior. If a client is already connected to a server in a cluster and the server eventually fails, the client will either use an alternative connection to the cluster (if it exists) or create a new connection to another cluster member.

Figure 14-5 illustrates the impact of server affinity on client-server interactions. For instance, if the client has already set up a JNDI context with ServerA, server affinity ensures that subsequent calls to the clustered component are routed to the same server. Ultimately, the goal of server affinity is to reuse existing client connections to the cluster, whenever possible.

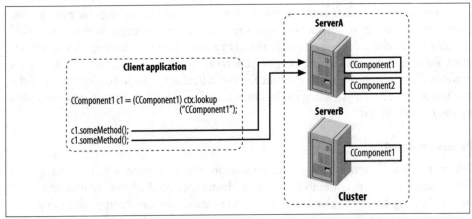

Figure 14-5. Client-server communication with server affinity load balancing

Server affinity for JNDI contexts

If a client or server creates a new context using a cluster address, by default the contexts are distributed on a round-robin basis among the available servers determined by the address. WebLogic lets you disable this round-robining by inducing the client to create the JNDI context on a server to which it is already connected. In other words, you can enable server affinity for client requests for a JNDI context. You need to supply the ENABLE_SERVER_AFFINITY property when creating the initial JNDI context:

```
Hashtable h = new Hashtable( );
h.put(Context.INITIAL_CONTEXT_FACTORY, "weblogic.jndi.WLInitialContextFactory");
```

```
h.put(Context.PROVIDER_URL, "t3://server1:7001,server2:7001");
h.put(weblogic.jndi.WLContext.ENABLE_SERVER_AFFINITY, "true");
Context ctx = new InitialContext(h);
```

This, combined with one of the affinity-based load-balancing schemes, ensures that all interaction between the client and the cluster is routed to the first server in the cluster to which the client connects.

Scenarios in Which Load Balancing Is Avoided

You should be aware of the optimizations that WebLogic uses to *avoid* load balancing. WebLogic employs two schemes:

- Collocation of objects
- Collocation of transactions

Suppose an EJB object makes a call to another EJB. If the second EJB is collocated on the same server as the first, then WebLogic automatically avoids the load-balancing logic—even if both EJB objects have been deployed to the cluster. WebLogic decides it is more optimal to make the method call on a local replica of the second EJB object rather than forward the call to a remote replica on another server in the cluster.

Figure 14-6 illustrates this collocation strategy. We have two clustered components (EJBs)—CComponent1 and CComponent2—deployed to two members of a cluster—ServerA and ServerB. Suppose a remote client creates a JNDI context and looks up an instance of CComponent1, and WebLogic returns a stub that defaults to ServerA. Suppose also that the method on CComponent1 looks up CComponent2. In this case, both of the JNDI contexts that are created (one on the client and one on the server) will use the address of the *cluster*. The collocation strategy then will ensure that the CComponent2 instance that is used will be returned from ServerA and not ServerB.

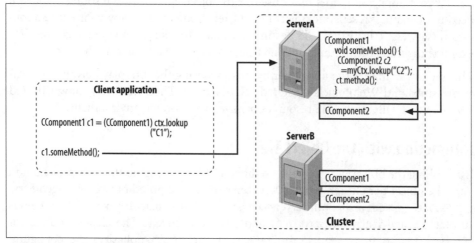

Figure 14-6. Collocation of objects

Of course, if another remote client comes along and creates a JNDI context using the same cluster address, the JNDI context would round-robin to ServerB and the same behavior is repeated there. The key point to remember is that WebLogic always tries to avoid load balancing. There is no way you can avoid this optimization, nor do you want to. Clearly, it always is cheaper to invoke a method on a local object than it is to make the same invocation on a remote object.

The same optimizations motivate WebLogic to use transaction collocation. The cost of managing a distributed transaction in which all of the enlisted resources live on different machines is higher than if those objects were collocated on the server on which the transaction was initiated. By avoiding the overhead of network traffic, WebLogic is able to reduce the duration of distributed transactions. This effect also filters through to the objects enlisted in the distributed transaction because they too are locked for the duration of the transaction. Hence, if multiple cluster-aware objects are engaged in a distributed transaction, WebLogic tries to collocate the objects on the server on which the transaction was begun.

Using J2EE Services on the Object Tier

The object tier usually maps to a WebLogic cluster that houses the heavier J2EE services such as EJB and RMI objects, as well as the JMS resources. Because the EJB objects typically need JDBC access to the backend DBMS (data tier), the object tier in our multi-tier application setup also hosts the JDBC resources. Remember, a clustered architecture need not have an object tier. If your application doesn't use EJBs to encapsulate the business logic or doesn't require any asynchronous message handling, you easily can bypass the object tier. In that case, you could deploy the JDBC resources to the presentation tier directly.

Even if your application does make use of EJB objects and/or JMS resources, you still need not construct a separate object tier cluster. You could deploy your entire application (servlets, JSPs, EJBs, JMS destinations, etc.) to a single WebLogic cluster. We examine the trade-offs of this combined-tier architecture later in this chapter.

This section examines the object tier by first exploring the interplay between replica-aware stubs and WebLogic's clustered JNDI service. Then we review how EJB and RMI objects, JDBC, and JMS resources behave in a clustered environment.

Interacting with the Object Tier

Establishing the object tier cluster is no different from setting up the web/presentation tier. The object tier cluster, named OCluster here, is composed of two Managed Servers, ServerF and ServerG. Both servers coexist on another machine whose IP address is 10.0.10.12, and listen on ports 7001 and 7003 respectively. The cluster address for OCluster is 10.0.10.12:7001,10.010.12:7003. Figure 14-7 emphasizes the configuration of the object tier, as depicted earlier in Figure 14-1.

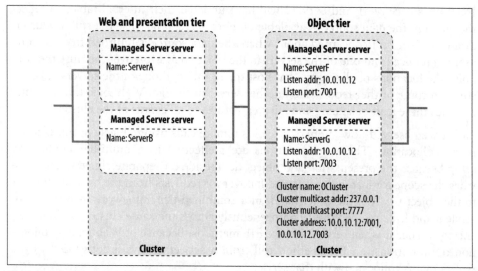

Figure 14-7. The object tier configuration

Objects that live in the presentation tier will need to reach resources deployed on the object tier. For instance, a servlet may need to access EJB objects or JDBC resources deployed to the object tier. Moreover, requests to these resources should be load-balanced across those various members of the object tier cluster. Clustered JNDI and replica-aware RMI stubs provide us with these capabilities.

Suppose you were to deploy a data source to OCluster. If a servlet in the presentation tier needs to use the data source, it should establish an initial context to OCluster, not an individual server within the cluster. In this case, the servlet would set up the JNDI context as follows:

```
// code running on the presentation tier, which establishes
// a context to the object tier using the object tier's cluster address
InitialContext ctx = new InitialContext("t3://10.0.10.12:7001,10.0.10.12:7003");
```

Remember that although we've specified the cluster address, the context eventually will be associated with a particular server in the list, round-robining between the servers each time we set up the initial JNDI context. By specifying the addresses of all the servers in the cluster, we allow for the Context object itself to fail over. Even though the JNDI context is initially bound to a particular server, because it is aware of the addresses of other servers in the list, it automatically can fail over to the next available server if the original server becomes unavailable.

Since we established a context on a member of the object tier, we now can look up resources bound to the cluster-wide JNDI tree, such as our JDBC data source:

```
DataSource ds = (DataSource) ctx.lookup("oreilly.DS")
```

This returns a cluster-aware data source stub. Because we've deployed the data source to the object tier cluster, the cluster-aware stubs that are bound to the local

JNDI trees of ServerF and ServerG will have updated their internal tables to reflect the fact that the data source is available on both servers. Because the stub is cluster-aware, a client isn't concerned about where the data source is returned from, so long as it is a replica from one of the servers in the object tier. Moreover, because the stub holds the locations of all servers that host the resource, if one of the servers fails, the stub can route further requests to another server in the list. WebLogic transparently provides these load-balancing and failover features to all clients of the cluster.

Earlier we observed how WebLogic avoids remote calls using object- or transaction-based collocation. These optimizations are ineffectual in a multi-tier application setup because the presentation and object tiers reside on separate clusters. This provides the scope for load balancing and failover for requests from the presentation tier to the object tier. On the other hand, in a combined-tier framework in which both servlets and EJBs are deployed homogeneously across the same cluster, no load balancing can occur when servlets invoke EJB methods. Because of WebLogic's collocation optimizations, an EJB method call from a servlet always is forwarded to the replica that is collocated with that servlet.

Clustering EJB and RMI

WebLogic's load-balancing and failover support for EJB and RMI objects stems from the replica-aware stubs that it uses. This section summarizes the load-balancing and failover features WebLogic provided for EJB and RMI objects. Chapters 4 and 10 cover this in more depth and explain how to configure your EJBs appropriately.

Load balancing and failover

Load balancing for EJBs occurs at both the EJB home and EJB object level. When a client looks up the JNDI tree for an EJB home object, it acquires a cluster-aware stub that can locate home objects on each server to which the EJB component was deployed. Likewise, the EJB object itself is represented by a replica-aware stub that automatically can fail over between method calls. Failover during method calls occurs only if the EJB methods are marked as being idempotent.

WebLogic 8.1 and 7.0 support several load-balancing schemes for EJB and RMI objects: round-robin, weight-based, random, and parameter-based routing. The round-robin algorithm is the default load-balancing strategy. WebLogic 8.1 supports three additional schemes: round-robin affinity, weight-based affinity, and random affinity.

EJB load balancing

WebLogic lets you adjust the default load-balancing strategy for a cluster. This default strategy applies to all clusterable services running on the cluster. Aall clusterable services use a round-robin algorithm as their default load-balancing strategy. The default strategy can be overridden on a per-service basis. For instance, when you compile a clusterable RMI object, you can explicitly select a load-balancing strategy for the generated RMI stub.

Every EJB component type supports load balancing at the home level. In order to enable cluster-aware EJB home stubs, specify true for the home-is-clusterable element in the EJB's *weblogic-ejb-jar.xml* descriptor file. The load-balancing scheme for the EJB home object will default to the load-balancing strategy you've configured for the cluster to which the EJB component is subsequently deployed. You also can change the load-balancing scheme for a particular EJB by specifying a value for the home-load-algorithm element in the *weblogic-ejb-jar.xml* descriptor file. Its value can be set to either RoundRobin, WeightBased, Random, RoundRobinAffinity, WeightBased-Affinity, or RandomAffinity. In addition, you can use the home-call-router-class-name element to specify a custom call router class for the home stub of a stateful session EJB or an entity EJB.

Here is a breakdown of other features particular to the different EJB types:

Stateless session beans

> Stateless session EJBs support replica-aware EJB objects. To enable replica-aware EJB objects, specify true for the stateless-bean-is-clusterable element in the *weblogic-ejb-jar.xml* descriptor. To set the load-balancing strategy at the EJB object level, use the stateless-bean-load-algorithm element in the *weblogic-ejb-jar.xml* descriptor file. You also may use the stateless-bean-call-router-class-name element to specify a custom call router class for a stateless session EJB.

Stateful session beans

> Because of the sticky nature of stateful session EJBs, method calls to a stateful session bean always are routed to the same EJB instance.

Entity beans

> For read-only entity EJBs, WebLogic supports load balancing and failover on every method call, while read-write entity EJBs are pinned to a particular member of the cluster.

Failover for EJB and RMI objects

If an RMI stub makes a call to a service on one of the servers hosting the object and the call fails, the stub will detect the failure and retry the call on a different server.

As explained earlier in Chapter 10, automatic failover occurs only if WebLogic knows that the method call is idempotent. If a method is not marked as idempotent, WebLogic cannot be sure that by retrying the method on a different server it won't duplicate any changes made during the previous call. To avoid this potential mistake, WebLogic errs on the safe side and refuses to automatically failover on non-idempotent EJB methods. By default, all methods of stateless session EJB home objects and read-only entity beans are marked as idempotent.

WebLogic still can failover on nonidempotent methods, but only in two exceptional cases. If a ConnectException or a MarshalException is thrown when a stub attempts to reach the object on the server side, the stub will fail over to a different server. Both of these exceptions can be thrown only before the EJB method begins its execution, and therefore no changes could have been initiated.

Failover manifests in different ways when it comes to EJB and RMI objects. Depending on the EJB type, an EJB may have replica-aware EJBHome and EJBObject stubs. As a result, failover and load balancing can occur when a client looks up the EJB's home object, or when it invokes an EJB method using its EJBObject stub. The varying types of failover are here:

Stateless session EJBs

As stateless session EJBs do not maintain any server-side state, the EJBObject stub returned by the EJB home object can route a method call to any server hosting the object. Failover occurs only on idempotent methods.

Stateful session EJBs

The EJBObject stub for a clustered stateful session EJB maintains the locations of the servers that hold the EJB's primary and secondary states. The EJB instance exists only on the server hosting the primary state, while its state may be replicated to a secondary server. Calls to the EJB object are routed to the server hosting the primary state. If the primary server fails for some reason, subsequent calls are then routed to the server hosting the secondary state. In this case, the EJB instance is re-created on the secondary server using the replicated session state, and a new server is chosen as the secondary server. Changes to the stateful session EJB instance are replicated either when a transaction commits, or after each method invocation if the client hasn't initiated a transaction.

Entity EJBs

For read-only entity beans, the EJBObject stub load-balances on every method call, and supports failover for idempotent methods. WebLogic avoids database reads by caching read-only beans on every server to which they've been deployed. For read-write entity beans, when an EJB home object finds or creates such an EJB instance, it obtains an instance from the same server and returns an EJBObject stub pinned to that server. Hence, for read-write entity beans, WebLogic supports load balancing and failover only at the home level, and not at the method call level (the EJBObject level).

Pinned objects and migration

In certain scenarios, it makes sense to maintain only a single copy of an object within a cluster. That is, the object is not replicated among all of the servers in the cluster. This can be achieved for RMI objects, and for certain J2EE services such as JMS servers and the JTA transaction recovery service. At any time, these *pinned services* are active on only a single server within the cluster.

Pinned services can be manually migrated from one server to another member of the *same* cluster. This migration cannot occur automatically; instead it has to be initiated by the administrator. WebLogic supports the migration of JMS servers and the JTA transaction recovery services; these services are called *migratable services*. Chapter 8 explains how to migrate a JMS server from one WebLogic instance to another.

Instead of replica-aware stubs, migratable services rely on migration-aware stubs. These stubs keep track of which server hosts the pinned service, and redirect all requests to that server. If the service is migrated to another clustered server, the stub transparently redirects further requests to the new server hosting the service.

You also can specify the list of servers to which a service may migrate by establishing a migratable target list. If you do not configure one or more migratable targets, the service may be migrated to any server in the cluster. Otherwise, it may migrate only to those specified in the target list.

Using JDBC Resources in a Cluster

WebLogic provides failover and high-availability features through JDBC multipools and cluster-aware data sources. Note that a JDBC connection established with the backend DBMS relies on state tied to the physical connection between the JDBC driver and the DBMS. This implies that WebLogic cannot offer failover for JDBC connections. If a client has acquired a JDBC connection and the DBMS to which it is attached or the server from where the connection was obtained fails, the connection is terminated and the client no longer is able to use that connection object.

WebLogic provides high-availability and load-balancing features at the connection pool level through the use of a multipool. A multipool is simply a pool of connection pools, each connection pool potentially drawing its connections from a different DBMS instance. A multipool may be used if the DBMS supports multiple replicated, synchronized database instances. If the multipool is configured for failover, then a connection always is drawn from the first connection pool until failure, after which the connection is drawn from the next pool in the list. If the multipool is configured for load balancing, requests for JDBC connections are distributed through the connection pools in a round-robin fashion.

Finally, JDBC DataSource objects deployed to a WebLogic cluster are replica-aware. In order to use connection pools and data sources in a clustered environment so that you can take advantage of these features, ensure that you deploy both the connection pool and the data source to the cluster, and not to individual servers within the cluster.

Clustering JMS

WebLogic's support for load balancing and failover for JMS resources is fundamentally different from the support offered for servlets, EJBs, and RMI objects. Because

JMS is a pinned service, it can be associated only with a single WebLogic instance. We now look at WebLogic's load-balancing and failover features for various JMS resources: connection factories, JMS servers, destinations, and distributed destinations.

JMS servers and destinations

JMS servers are pinned services and can be targeted only to a single WebLogic instance. A JMS server may host multiple queues and topics; therefore, these destinations are bound to the JMS server in which they are defined. Failover at the JMS server level occurs when the administrator manually migrates the JMS service to another WebLogic instance. If the JMS server isn't migrated to another cluster member, the JMS server and the destinations it hosts become unreachable. If a JMS server goes down, any client connected to that JMS server or using a destination that resides on that JMS server also fails.

Thus, WebLogic doesn't provide automatic failover for JMS servers and destinations. You may consider these resources as being "highly available" because of the migration facility. Distributed destinations, as we shall see later in the section "Distributed destinations," do provide room for failover and load balancing.

Connection factories

JMS connection factories are used to manufacture connections to a JMS server. Even though a JMS server is pinned to a single WebLogic instance, you can deploy the connection factory to a WebLogic cluster. By assigning the JMS connection factory to a WebLogic cluster, you enable cluster-wide access to the JMS servers for all clients of the cluster. Each replica of the connection factory on any cluster member automatically can route the call to an appropriate WebLogic instance that does host the JMS server and required destination. So, it is the combination of two things that enable cluster-wide, transparent access to any client of the pinned JMS destination: deploying the connection factory to the cluster, and automatic routing of requests to the WebLogic instance that hosts the desired JMS destination. WebLogic lets you configure two flags for JMS connection factories—Load Balancing and Server Affinity—that further influence the behavior of distributed destinations.

Distributed destinations

WebLogic supports distributed destinations that also provide failover and load balancing for JMS queues and topics. A distributed destination is a named collection of physical destinations, all taken from the same cluster. For instance, you can define a distributed queue using several JMS queues, each of which may be hosted on different JMS servers within the same cluster.

If a producer sends a message to a distributed queue, a single physical queue is chosen to receive the message. The queue may be selected randomly or by using a weight-based, round-robin algorithm. Load balancing occurs because each physical queue may reside on a different JMS server. Every time a message is sent to a distributed queue, the message will be distributed across the various JMS servers hosting the physical queues.

If a producer sends a message to a distributed topic, the message is delivered to all physical topics that form the distributed topic. If the message is nonpersistent, it will be sent only to available JMS servers that host the physical topics. If the message is persistent, it is additionally stored and forwarded to other JMS destinations as and when their JMS servers become available. Remember, JMS messages can be stored only if you've configured a JMS store for the physical topic. For this reason, WebLogic always attempts to first forward the message to distributed members that utilize persistent stores.

When a queue receiver or topic subscriber is created on a distributed destination, a single physical member is chosen and the receiver is pinned to that member for the duration of its lifetime. This choice is made only once, at creation time. If the physical member fails, the receiver/subscriber receives an exception, at which time the application should *re-create* the receiver/subscriber. If other physical members are available, another member from the distributed destination is chosen and assigned to the client. The client then can continue to proceed as before. So, even though WebLogic doesn't provide automatic failover for distributed queue receivers and topic subscribers, it does offer clients the opportunity to re-create their session on a different member of the distributed destination.

Several other factors influence the behavior of distributed destinations:

- The Load Balancing setting on a JMS connection factory determines whether producers created by the connection factory will load-balance on every send( ) or publish( ). If this flag isn't enabled, load balancing occurs only on the first call to send( ) or publish( )—thereafter, all messages are sent to the same member destination.

- The Server Affinity flag affects how clients of a distributed destination behave when they run on the same server as the connection factory. If the flag is enabled, WebLogic first will attempt to load-balance consumers and producers across physical destinations that are running on the same server. So, for instance, if the client was sending to a distributed queue and a physical queue member was hosted on the same WebLogic instance, the local queue member will be chosen over any other.

- Transaction affinity also plays a role here. When producing multiple messages to a distributed destination within a transacted session, WebLogic sends all messages to the same physical destination. Likewise, if a transacted session sends multiple messages to multiple distributed destinations, WebLogic will try to choose a set of member destinations, all served by the same WebLogic instance.

- When a client produces a message to a distributed queue, WebLogic will load-balance using only those physical members of the distributed queue that do have consumers. Physical members of a distributed queue that don't have any consumers are not considered for message production (unless all queues have no consumers). In addition, when you create a consumer on a distributed queue, WebLogic will attempt to create the consumer on physical queues that don't yet have any consumers.

All of these load-balancing and failover optimizations provided by WebLogic operate transparently to client code. However, a good understanding of these features enables you to properly assess the performance implications of your JMS setup within your object tier cluster.

Maintaining State in a Cluster

It is useful to think about how state is maintained in a cluster. There are essentially three types of state in a J2EE environment: stateless services, nonpersistent stateful services, and persistent state.

A *stateless service* doesn't capture any server-side state during its interactions with clients. Examples of stateless services include a JDBC connection factory, an EJB home object, a stateless session EJB, or a message-driven EJB. If you deploy a stateless service to a number of WebLogic instances, client requests can be forwarded to any of these servers, as it doesn't matter which one is chosen. In this case, clustering for a stateless service is just a matter of load-balancing requests among the servers hosting the service. Failover is possible only if the service fails before the request has been handled, or if the service is guaranteed to be idempotent. Although stateless services are easily clusterable, WebLogic doesn't simply hop around between all server instances hosting the service. As we have seen, WebLogic favors optimizations such as transaction collocation, which ensures that once a client has initiated a distributed transaction, all resources used during the lifetime of the transaction are collocated on the same server on which transaction was initiated. No persistence is needed, and load balancing is easy because any hosting server in the cluster can be chosen.

Nonpersistent stateful services are those in which the client-specific, server-side state information is not fundamentally persistent. For example, HTTP sessions do not have to be backed up to disk or to a database. Stateful session EJB instances are another example of nonpersistence state. In both of these cases, WebLogic lets you employ in-memory replication of the state, thereby avoiding persistence to disk. This offers you a speed advantage because the session-state information doesn't need to be kept in sync with a persistent store.

One consequence of session-state replication is that the locations of the primary and secondary servers need to be tracked. An arbitrary server can no longer be chosen, as it could for stateless services. We already have seen how WebLogic handles this additional complexity. In the case of HTTP sessions, WebLogic uses session cookies to ensure client requests stick to the HTTP session on the correct server in the presentation tier. For the object tier, it is the replica-aware stubs that hold the locations of the server hosting the primary and secondary state. In this case, persistence based on in-memory replication is relatively cheap. However, the load balancing is now confined to those servers that host the session-state information and its backup.

Persistent services, such as CMP entity beans and persistent JMS messaging, need to be backed up to some kind of store. Here WebLogic provides you with a number of features that effectively trade-off data consistency for scalability. For instance, read-only entity beans scale extremely well. Each cluster member can create instances of a read-only entity EJB independently and leave them cached. Read-only beans need not be persisted, and load balancing is inexpensive because any client request for the EJB can simply choose from one of the cached EJB instances without having to refresh the state from the persistent store. If there is a concern that the cached data may not be in sync with the underlying store, WebLogic lets you configure a refresh timeout interval or send multicast invalidations to other cached read-only entity EJB instances. To optimize data consistency checks, you may choose to enforce optimistic concurrency in your entity beans, whereby WebLogic defers all checks for data consistency until the point of transaction commit. Right at the other scale is the serialized entity bean. Here persistence is expensive (locking in order to maintain strict data consistency), as is replication.

Combined-Tier Architecture

The multi-tier architecture illustrated earlier in Figure 14-2 provides many benefits, such as the opportunity to load-balance at the EJB level, and the freedom to add further WebLogic instances at either the presentation or object tier. Simpler cluster architectures can be designed by combining the web/presentation and object tiers into a single WebLogic cluster. This means deploying the entire application (including servlets, JSPs, EJBs, RMI objects, JDBC, and JMS resources) homogeneously across all members of the WebLogic cluster. Figure 14-8 depicts the layout of the combined-tier architecture. Here, each server instance in the tier hosts all of the aforementioned services, including the HTTP server.

An obvious benefit of such an architecture is the ease with which it can be constructed and administered. You can deploy your application and its components to all members of the cluster. The network configuration of this setup also is simplified, as are your security considerations. By placing a firewall before the load balancer, you can set up a DMZ for your application quite simply. If you need to disable direct access to your EJB objects, you also can configure WebLogic to disable all external T3/IIOP requests to the cluster.

The combined-tier architecture also performs quite well. Because servlets and EJBs are deployed homogeneously across the cluster, all EJB objects are collocated with

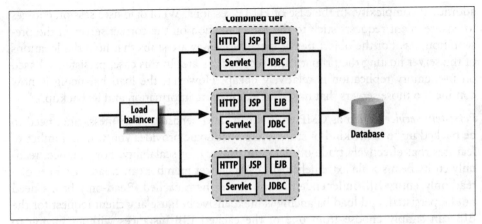

Figure 14-8. Combined-tier architecture

servlets. This means any call from a servlet to an EJB object is forwarded automatically to a local replica of the EJB, and not to a remote replica of the same EJB. The same optimization occurs when an EJB invokes a method on another EJB.

However, this performance gain also comes with certain trade-offs in terms of limiting the flexibility of your architecture. The combined-tier framework limits the load-balancing and failover capabilities of the cluster. Load balancing cannot occur on EJB method calls because the local copy of the EJB object always will be preferred over a remote EJB instance on another cluster member. In addition, all of your eggs are in one basket. If a server instance fails, all services on that instance will become unavailable. Likewise, if you find that most of your processing occurs at the EJB level, the additional server instance must host the same services as the other cluster members. It can't be used solely to boost the capacity of your EJBs.

In general, WebLogic supports load balancing at the interfaces between the tiers. The multi-tier architecture maintains physical separation between the presentation tier and the object tier, thereby providing load-balancing and failover opportunities. The combined architecture, however, offers load balancing and failover only at the interface to the web tier. It is ideal for web applications, and even suited to small-scale enterprise applications where load balancing and failover at the object tier is not an essential requirement. In addition, you need to evaluate the cost of administering a multi-tier setup—if this outweighs the cost of maintaining the application, a combined-tier setup may be an affordable option. If the network overhead incurred due to invocations between the presentation and object tiers yields unacceptable performance, a combined-tier setup with its collocation of services may offer better performance than a multi-tier architecture.

Securing a Clustered Solution

When you design the physical architecture for your enterprise application using clusters of WebLogic instances, you need to determine which resources are directly exposed to external clients, and which resources need not be on the front line but instead require extra defenses. This means you need to outline a demilitarized zone (DMZ), a conceptual area of hardware and software resources that is directly exposed to the outside world. All resources that live behind the DMZ are protected. A DMZ is often created by employing a firewall, which can deny access to specific ports and IP addresses (and hence physical machines) participating in a WebLogic domain. The firewall lets you clearly define which services on which machines ought to be accessible to external clients. Generally, the smaller the extent of your DMZ, the safer your architecture is from malicious attacks.

Your application setup also impacts the scope of your DMZ. For instance, if you adopt the combined-tier architecture as illustrated earlier in Figure 14-6, you are forced to include all of the servers in the DMZ, even though you may wish to grant clients direct access only to the servlets, JSPs, and static web resources, and not to the EJBs and RMI objects deployed to the cluster. Instead, if you adopt the more complex multi-tier application setup, you have the option of physically denying access to the object tier machines, thereby excluding them from the DMZ.

Firewalls can provide network address translation (NAT) services as well, which let you hide internal IP addresses and make them inaccessible to clients on the other side of the firewall. We shall look at configuration implications of using a firewall, especially if it's configured for NAT.

Firewall Placement and Address Translation

Firewalls generally are placed before the web tier, presentation tier, and data tier. Figure 14-9 depicts how you can position a firewall before a bank of web servers (web tier). In this situation, the DMZ includes only the HTTP servers running on the web tier itself. That is, you can configure the firewall to permit access only to the servers in the web tier. If your application demands it, you also may configure the firewall to grant access only to the HTTP and HTTPS ports.

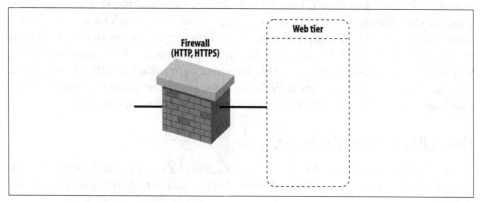

Figure 14-9. Firewall before the web tier

Figure 14-10 illustrates how you can place a firewall between the web and presentation tiers.

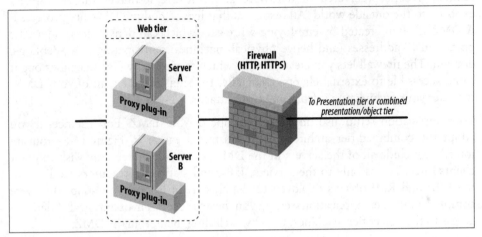

Figure 14-10. Firewall between the web and presentation tiers

A firewall between the web and presentation tiers creates a slight configuration problem if your firewall also performs NAT. Imagine that an external client performs a JNDI lookup for an RMI object. The stub returned to the client holds the addresses of the servers that host the RMI object. Because these addresses are behind the NAT layer, an external client will fail if it uses the stub to invoke a method on the RMI object. The same problem will manifest for proxy plug-ins that try to forward requests for servlets and JSPs to the presentation tier, or when WebLogic creates a session cookie that records the locations of the primary and secondary servers that maintain the client's HTTP session-state information.

To avoid these issues, you should not bind a WebLogic instance to an IP address. If you do, the internal, untranslated IP address is sent back to the external client, which is useless. Instead, you should bind your WebLogic instances to DNS names. In this way, the client can resolve the DNS name to an IP address, which then can be translated by the firewall to the internal IP address of the server that provides the required service. If your internal DNS names differ from their external DNS names, again you will have same naming problems. This issue can be resolved as well by setting the External Listen Address* for each WebLogic instance. This setting is located in the Configuration/General tab for each server in the Administration Console.

Firewalls and Load Balancers

You may position a firewall before a load balancer. This setup greatly simplifies the firewall configuration, as the firewall needs to limit access to only the load balancer.

---

* This option is called External DNS Name in WebLogic 7.0.

That is, the DMZ consists of the load balancer only. Figure 14-11 depicts this configuration.

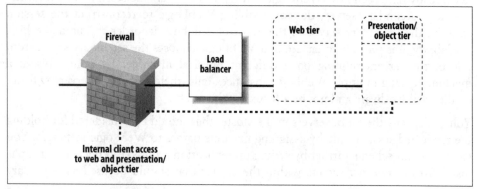

Figure 14-11. Firewall with both external and internal client access

You easily can expand this setup to support internal clients of the web and presentation/object tiers. This scenario is indicated by the dotted lines in Figure 14-11. In this case, the firewall would be configured to permit HTTP and HTTPS requests from external clients, and HTTP, HTTPS, and RMI requests from internal clients that live behind the firewall.

Databases

Databases also can be protected by a firewall. This provides additional security in case the frontend firewalls have been breached somehow. In this case, you could simply configure the database firewall with an application-level policy that permits only servers in the object tier (if it exists) to connect to the database. Figure 14-12 illustrates this configuration.

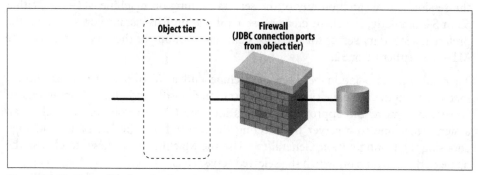

Figure 14-12. Firewall before the data tier

Machines, Replication Groups, and Failover

We already have seen how WebLogic can replicate server-side session-state information to a secondary server, thereby enabling WebLogic to reconstruct the session state on the secondary server in the event of a failure. In order to guarantee high availability, it is sensible to ensure that WebLogic chooses the secondary server from one of the servers running on a different physical machine. By doing this, if a machine hosting multiple WebLogic instances fails, their secondary servers will run on different hardware and not be affected by the crash.

You can specify the set of servers in the cluster that should be considered for holding the replicated session state by assigning machine names to WebLogic instances. You can refine this scheme further by setting up replication groups. A replication group is just a list of preferred servers within the cluster that should be used as secondary servers.

Machine Names

To set up a new machine, click the Machines node in the left pane of the Administration Console, and select the "Configure a new Machine" option. Chapter 13 shows how the Node Manager configuration uses these machine definitions.

A machine name is a tag that can be associated with a number of WebLogic instances. By making these associations, you indicate which servers are running on which machines. WebLogic's clustering framework can use this information to determine the preferred secondary server. By default, the secondary server is chosen from a WebLogic instance running on a different machine. Suppose you've configured a cluster with four Managed Servers (S1...S4), and assigned machine names M1 to servers S1 and S2, and M2 to servers S3 and S4. If an HTTP session is initiated on server S1, and assuming you haven't configured any replication groups, by default the session is replicated on any of the servers running on machine M2—i.e., either S3 or S4. Similarly, if a client creates a stateful session EJB instance on server S4, the preferred secondary server for the EJB is chosen from one of the servers on machine M1—i.e., either S1 or S2.

To make this association between a machine and a WebLogic instance, select a machine from the left pane of the Administration Console and, in the Configuration/ Servers tab, move the appropriate servers into the Chosen column. You also can assign a machine to a server by selecting the server from the left pane, and then choosing the Configuration/General tab. Use the Machine drop-down to choose the name of the machine on which the selected server runs.

If you run each WebLogic instance on its own hardware, you do not need to create machine names other than for the purposes of the Node Manager. Servers that are not associated with machines are treated as if they reside on different physical machines, which is exactly the behavior you want in these circumstances.

Replication Groups

Replication groups let you specify which servers in the cluster should be preferred to act as the secondary server. You need replication groups only if the default strategy for choosing a secondary server from a different machine doesn't meet your requirements.

This mechanism works by assigning a group name to each server. All of the servers that share the same group name are considered to be in the same replication group. For each server in the cluster, you can specify two group names: the replication group the server belongs to, and the replication group from which the secondary server preferably should be chosen. You can adjust these configuration settings from the Administration Console. Select a server from the left pane, and then choose the Configuration/Cluster tab to find the following options for setting up replication groups:

Replication Group
> Use this attribute to specify the replication group to which this server belongs.

Preferred Secondary Group
> Use this attribute to specify the name of the replication group that identifies the set of clustered instances that should be preferred for hosting replicas of the primary state created on this server.

In this way, you can precisely configure for each server the set of servers in the cluster from where its secondary server preferably should be chosen, and the set of servers for which this server is the preferred secondary server.

Suppose you've configured replication groups for all members of a WebLogic cluster. How, then, does WebLogic choose the secondary server for replicating the session state held on a server instance? Quite simply, WebLogic ranks the other servers in the cluster, and then chooses among the best-ranked servers. The rank is determined by giving priority first to members of the preferred replication group, and then to servers running on a different machine. Table 14-1 illustrates this ranking strategy.

Table 14-1. Ranking cluster members when choosing a secondary server

Rank	Server on different machine?	Server member of preferred replication group?
1	Yes	Yes
2	No	Yes
3	Yes	No
4	No	No

Figure 14-13 shows this ranking mechanism in action. Consider a cluster with six servers. Within this cluster, we defined two replication groups, Group 1 and Group 2. Servers A, B, and C are members of the replication group Group 1 and have their preferred secondary replication group set to Group 2. Servers X, Y, and Z are members of the replication group Group 2 and have their preferred secondary replication group set to Group 1. Furthermore, assume that the server instances A, B, and X are all running on the same physical machine, StarFire.

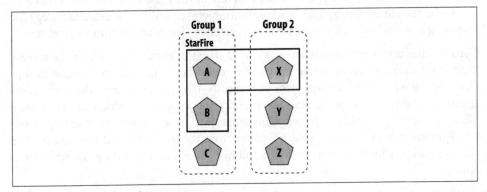

Figure 14-13. Example replication groups

Now suppose that a client connects to Server A and creates its primary session state on that server. Then, based on the ranking strategy described earlier, we can deduce the following:

- The secondary server most likely will be chosen from servers Y or Z, as they are members of Server A's preferred secondary group (Group 2) and also reside on a different physical machine.
- Server X is the next most likely to be chosen as the secondary server because it too is a member of Server A's preferred replication group, even though it runs on the same physical machine.
- Server C is the next most likely to be chosen as the secondary server, as it resides on a different machine.
- Server B is the least likely to be chosen as the secondary server for Server A because it is neither a member of the preferred replication group, nor does it live on another machine.

This means that for Server B to be chosen as the secondary server, servers X, Y, Z, and C must be unavailable. Thus, you should remember that replication groups determine only which servers ought to be preferred over others when determining which server should act as the secondary. If there no members are available in the preferred replication group that can act as the secondary, WebLogic has no choice but to look outside the preferred group.

Network Configuration

Now that you know how the various J2EE services operate in a clustered environment and understand different cluster architectures, let's turn our attention to the network infrastructure needed to support WebLogic clustering. By understanding

---

how WebLogic clusters interact with this infrastructure, you are in a better position to configure and optimize the cluster configuration. WebLogic uses two forms of network communication within a cluster:

- WebLogic instances within a cluster use multicast communication to broadcast heartbeats. These heartbeats verify the server's availability to other members of the cluster. The clustered JNDI service also relies on multicast communication to broadcast the availability of cluster-aware objects and services. Thus, multicast communication is vital for both high availability and load balancing.

- Socket communication is used in peer-to-peer communication between members of a cluster. This can occur when server-side objects access objects on a peer server, or when session-state information is replicated to a secondary server.

Each server listens for heartbeats broadcast by other servers in the cluster. This enables the server to detect any failure among its peers. In fact, each server broadcasts a unique heartbeat message every 10 seconds. If a server in the cluster misses three heartbeats of a peer, it marks that peer server as failed. Likewise, if a socket is closed unexpectedly by a peer server, the server that initiated the communication with the peer marks it as failed. So, both multicast heartbeats and peer-to-peer sockets can be used to detect the operational status of members within a cluster. In both cases, the server marks the peer server as failed and then updates its local JNDI tree to remove all services published by that peer. This ensures that peer services will no longer take part in any failover and load-balancing considerations.

This behavior stresses the importance of a stable and properly configured network communication infrastructure. In order to set up a WebLogic cluster successfully, you need to configure the cluster and its members so that both forms of communication can take place reliably.

Multicast Communication

WebLogic uses IP multicasts for one-to-many communication among server instances of a cluster. IP multicast communication manifests in various ways:

- Broadcast of cluster heartbeats relies on multicasts. Each server instance in a cluster uses a multicast to broadcast a heartbeat message indicating its availability. Each server in the cluster monitors the heartbeats of fellow servers, and marks a fellow server as failed when that server cannot detect any heartbeats.

- WebLogic's clustered JNDI service also uses multicast messaging. For example, when a clusterable EJB component is deployed to a server, the server advertises its availability to other members of the cluster by issuing a multicast broadcast to update their local JNDI trees.

- The implementation of WebLogic's multicast delivery to a JMS topic also depends on IP multicast. Here, each topic subscriber listens for a multicast broadcast of the JMS message.

Multicast addresses are IP addresses in the range 224.0.0.0 to 239.255.255.255. Messages sent as a multicast broadcast are not guaranteed to be delivered, or to be delivered in order. For this reason, the cluster infrastructure must allow for the possibility of missed messages. Multicast communication is sometimes difficult to set up, especially in older networks. If it isn't configured properly, and heartbeat messages are not being received in a timely fashion, clustered servers may erroneously mark each other as unavailable. You should adhere to the following guidelines when designing the network configuration for your clustered architecture:

Be careful when using network equipment within a WebLogic cluster
> For instance, we recommend that you don't split a cluster across a firewall. This includes any other network equipment that may interrupt IP traffic and disrupt cluster communication by delaying or removing critical multicast messages, such as cluster heartbeats.

Ensure that other applications do not use the same multicast address and port
> Other applications should not use the multicast address and port assigned to a WebLogic cluster. If other services within the cluster need to use multicast communication, assign a different multicast address and port for these services. Introducing external applications can cause the multicast buffer to overrun, resulting in lost messages. Multiple clusters may share the same multicast address and port without any problems.

Take care when configuring multicast across subnets
> If a WebLogic cluster is distributed across multiple subnets, you need to ensure that the network is configured to do this properly and efficiently. This means configuring all routers and other equipment to propagate multicast packets properly. In these circumstances, the network latency also should be kept as low as possible, ensuring that multicast packets reach their destinations in no more than 200 to 300 milliseconds. In addition, the time-to-live (TTL) value for multicast packets should be set at the appropriate level for the subnets, ensuring that routers do not discard the packets prematurely. The TTL value for multicast packets indicates the number of subnets that a multicast packet can traverse before it will be discarded.

Avoid long-running garbage collection cycles
> Ensure that your servers aren't busy with long-running garbage collection cycles. If your garbage collector runs for more than 10 seconds, for instance, a WebLogic instance may not get the opportunity to send a heartbeat. A change in your heap allocation and/or garbage collection strategy can help avoid this problem.

Multicast setup

In order to establish a cluster, you need to decide on a multicast cluster address and port. Using the Administration Console, you'll find that the Configuration/Multicast tab for a cluster holds all of the configuration settings for multicast setup. The address, port, and TTL values are absolutely essential settings for proper cluster configuration:

Multicast address
> This address is used for all multicast communication within the cluster.

Multicast port
> This port number is used for all multicast communication within the cluster.

Multicast TTL
> The TTL value indicates the number of subnets that a multicast packet may traverse before it will be discarded.

Specifying a multicast address and port may not be enough. On a multihomed machine, it won't be obvious which network card WebLogic should use to handle all the multicast traffic. To resolve this problem, you need to set the Interface Address for each *server*. This is available in each server's Configuration/Cluster tab. Use this setting to specify the IP address of the NIC that will be used for all multicast traffic on that server.

Two additional low-level configuration options can help optimize multicast traffic:

Multicast Send Delay
> This setting defines a delay (in milliseconds) before sending message fragments. This delay helps avoid buffer overflow at the OS level.

Multicast Buffer Size
> This setting determines the size of the multicast socket send/receive buffers. Its value defaults to 64 KB.

You also may need to tune the behavior of your OS before multicast communication for the cluster is functioning properly. In certain situations, your cluster setup may be devastated by "multicast storms," whereby servers within the cluster are unable to process incoming messages fast enough, thereby leading to a large increase in network traffic. Here, you may need to modify the behavior of UDP socket buffers at the OS level.

Peer-to-Peer Communication

WebLogic supports IP-based socket communication when accessing remote objects deployed on another machine, and for replicating HTTP session state and stateful session EJB instances from a primary server to a secondary server. All remote RMI communication also occurs using sockets. For optimal performance in a cluster, be sure to follow the guidelines described in Chapter 15.

Administration Server Considerations

The Administration Server hosts the configuration for the entire domain, including all clusters that belong to the domain. For this reason, the Administration Server should be accessible to all Managed Servers within the domain. In addition, it should not participate in any of the clusters. A WebLogic cluster usually maps to an application tier and hosts a number of application components and services. The Administration Server should not be dedicated to application-specific tasks, but should rather focus on completing domain administration tasks.

Remember to exclude from the cluster-wide DNS name the listen address and port that is assigned to the Administration Server. For security reasons, you also may wish to place the Administration Server behind a DMZ.

Monitoring Clusters

The Administration Console can be used to monitor the status of servers and clusters. Choose the Servers node in the left pane to view a list of servers and their status. To monitor a cluster, choose the cluster in the left pane and navigate to the Monitoring tab. This will display all of the servers that are configured for the cluster, and whether they are participating in the cluster. The Deployments tab, available on any cluster, is useful for determining which applications, EJB modules, web modules, or connectors have been deployed to that cluster.

Performance, Monitoring, and Tuning

So, you've now reached a stage where your application has acquired a certain level of maturity. You understand how to apply and benefit from WebLogic's support for various J2EE services. You've set up a working domain, perhaps even several WebLogic clusters that model the various application tiers. You've deployed your application components and ensured that all necessary WebLogic resources and services are available and configured properly. You've also deliberated on the network and hardware infrastructure needs of your production environment. Now you must determine how your application performs under live conditions, monitor its execution, and tune the entire system.

Somehow, you need to verify that your application setup is optimal, and that it performs to its maximum capacity. As this chapter shows, this is as much an art as it is a science. It is beyond the scope of this book to look at all performance-related aspects of your application setup. We would require several books to do justice to tuning your operating system, your hardware resources, and your network infrastructure. Far too many variables are involved, not the least of which include the different platforms, vendors, and architectures we'd need to consider. Instead, we focus on how to improve the performance of WebLogic and the most important WebLogic features your application may use. We do this by examining three topics. First, we examine how to monitor and tune the major J2EE components that your application most likely will use. This includes the HTTP sessions, JDBC pools, JMS server, and EJBs. We then look at how to tune WebLogic itself, which chiefly entails the configuration and monitoring of the execute queues and server threads. Finally, we look at a few optimizations that can be made at the JVM level.

Tuning WebLogic Applications

Many aspects of WebLogic's performance were already covered in earlier chapters. We examined the impact of various features on the flexibility of your application setup and discussed the trade-offs involved. We've looked at various session persistence mechanisms, proxy web servers, the benefits of JDBC connection pools and data sources, the collocation and transaction optimizations that occur when using EJBs, the load-balancing and failover features in a WebLogic cluster, the different ways to reduce the overheads of network traffic, the issues involved when JMS connection factories are used in a transacted session, and the various packaging and deployment options that also make a difference in application performance. Many of these performance enhancements are the outcome of adjusting either the configuration settings supported by WebLogic-specific deployment descriptors or those configuration options that can be viewed and modified from the Administration Console.

We won't revisit all of these issues here. We presume that you have read (or browsed through) the previous chapters and now have a good understanding of how to build applications on WebLogic Server, making effective use of the supported J2EE services.

Instead, we discuss specific bottlenecks that can impede the performance of WebLogic applications. After all, WebLogic can run only as well as the applications deployed to it. Before you consider allocating blame for missing performance targets on other aspects of your configuration, it is wise to first scrutinize your application setup and try to resolve any glaring performance hitches. This chapter hopefully adds to your existing arsenal of weapons for improving application performance. Along the way, we provide details on how to monitor the application resources you may use and how to interpret these performance figures.

Managing Sessions

HTTP session management is very important in determining the performance of your web applications. In general, you should consider using HTTP sessions only when the session-state information cannot reliably be held on the client. You shouldn't use the server-side HTTP session to share objects between different parts of the web application. Whenever possible, you should place frequently used values in local variables. The best performance usually can be extracted by using sessions only when necessary, and then holding as little data as necessary.

If your web application is deployed to a cluster and you've enabled session persistence, in-memory replication is almost 10 times faster than JDBC-based persistence. Whenever possible, you should place fewer, coarse-grained objects into the HTTP session, rather than multiple, fine-grained objects. In case of in-memory replication, every "put" operation on the session means that the update needs to be propagated to the secondary server that holds a replica of the HTTP session. In case of JDBC-based session persistence, every "put" operation triggers a database write of the entire object. Fewer coarse-grained objects means you are able to minimize the number of "put" operations on the HTTP session. If the objects in your session are too large—say, an object tree—a single change still requires you to update the entire tree, and hence replicate the entire tree. Clearly, this is less efficient than if your session data had been split across a number of variables, in which case changes to individual variables would require less replication. Thus, your decisions on the size of the objects in the HTTP session will depend on the volume of changes to the session data and the structure of the session data. Ultimately, you need to strike a balance between the volume of data replicated and the number of replications.

Chapter 2 explains the various session persistence mechanisms WebLogic provides for a web application.

Monitoring servlets and sessions

To monitor servlets, select a web application in the Administration Console and select the Monitoring tab. From here you can monitor the web application of which the servlet is a part, the servlet runtimes, and active sessions. When monitoring servlets, you will be able to view deployed servlets and JSPs, together with an indication of the number of times the page or servlet has been accessed, the number of times the servlet has been reloaded, the URL pattern mapped to the servlet, and statistics on how much time was spent in each servlet. This may help determine potential bottlenecks. As the current trend is to use an MVC architecture, in which a controller servlet delegates incoming requests to appropriate action handlers, the statistic is less useful. In this case, it is far more useful to employ a profiler to determine the time spent in each handler.

When monitoring a web application, you will find a list containing the context root for the web application, together with the number of active sessions, the number of total sessions, and the highest number of active sessions that you have had. To optimally tune your application, you must know not only the average number of sessions, but also the average session size—information that WebLogic does not provide. One way to do this is to use memory profiling tools and examine the relevant objects and their sizes.

You can make WebLogic gather additional session statistics by selecting the Session Monitoring Enabled option. You then will need to reboot your server for session monitoring to take effect. This provides access to the Time Last Accessed attribute of a servlet, which may be useful to determine the behavior of your clients on the server. For example, you can use this to tune the default session timeout.

Optimizing JDBC Pools

WebLogic's support for JDBC connection pools minimizes the cost of opening and closing connections to the database. The connection pool can grow and shrink between the configured minimum and maximum number of open connections. In addition, you can specify an initial capacity for the pool that defines the initial number of physical database connections that are set up for the pool.

During development stages, you can set the initial capacity to a low number to help WebLogic start up faster. However, in a production environment you should consider setting the pool's initial capacity equal to its maximum capacity. All database connections should preferably be acquired before WebLogic becomes available. If the pool's initial capacity is lower than its maximum capacity, WebLogic needs to create additional connections when there is increased load on the JDBC pool. When the server is under load, it is preferable that all of its resources are used to serve requests as fast as possible, rather than spending time creating database connections.

The pool's maximum capacity defines the maximum number of database connections that the pool holds at any time. You need to set the pool's maximum capacity to a sensible number, taking into account any limitations of the DBMS. The ideal setting for the maximum pool size depends on your application. A good place to start is to set the pool's maximum capacity to the size of your execution thread count (discussed later). This makes sense, as you don't want an execution thread waiting to obtain a connection. However, as usual in performance tuning, the details may vary. If much of the work involved in entering the server will not require any JDBC connections, you could set the maximum pool size to a value less than the number of execute threads. On the other hand, the connection pool size may need to be greater than the number of execute threads if your application requires more than one connection for each thread. This situation arises, for example, when an EJB method that is using a connection calls another EJB method that has the "Requires New transaction" setting, before committing its own transaction. The method marked as Requires New will get its own connection from the connection pool.

Statement caching can offer a performance boost to JDBC access as well. By caching the compiled prepared (or callable) statements used most often, WebLogic can avoid recompiling a prepared statement the next time it is used. By default, WebLogic caches 10 prepared statements per pooled connection. The size of the statement cache may be limited by the number of open cursors allowed by the database. Chapter 5 discusses the advantages and limitations of enabling statement caching.

You should spend some time investigating the interaction between your application and JDBC resources, as often the performance of many applications is constrained by the database. A good indicator that the database is possibly the culprit is when you have low CPU utilization on a server, no matter how much load you apply.

Monitoring the connection pool and transactions

Connection pools can be monitored on each server by choosing the pool from the Administration Console and selecting the Monitoring tab. This will give you a good indication of the number of current connections using the pool, the highest number of connections, and the total number of connections. It also provides information on connection requests that have been made but could not be serviced because all of the connections were being used. This list, called the Waiters list, gives a good indication of potential bottlenecks in your database. The Wait Seconds High setting indicates the highest number of seconds that a request had to wait for a free connection, while Waiters High indicates the highest number of requests that had to be kept waiting for a connection. If this value is greater than zero, it indicates a shortage of JDBC resources. If client requests to the connection pool have to wait, consider increasing the size of the pool.

To monitor transactions, select the Monitoring/JTA tab for a server in the Administration Console. The statistics that are displayed here can give you an indication of the transactional behavior of your system. These are described in Table 15-1. Depending on your application, unusually high levels of rolled-back or heuristic completions of transactions could provide further information in tracking down performance problems. Likewise, excessive timeouts may indicate an overutilization of participating resources.

Table 15-1. Transaction monitoring attributes

Attribute	Description
Total Transactions	The total number of transactions processed. This includes those that were committed, heuristically committed, and rolled back.
Total Committed	The number of transactions that were committed.
Total Rolled Back	The number of transactions that were rolled back.
Timeout Rollbacks	The number of transactions that were rolled back due to a timeout expiration.
Resource Rollbacks	The number of transactions that were rolled back due to a resource error.
Application Rollbacks	The number of transactions that were rolled back due to an application error.
System Rollbacks	The number of transactions that were rolled back due to an internal system error.
Total Heuristics	The number of transactions that completed heuristically.
Total Transactions Abandoned	The number of transactions that were abandoned.
Average Commit Time	The average amount of time, in milliseconds, that the server has taken to commit a transaction.

An important figure here is the ratio of rolled-back transactions to the total transactions. Rolled-back transactions, especially those that roll back due to a timeout, are unfortunate—not only has the effort taken to roll back the transaction and all participating resources been wasted, but also the work hasn't been completed. Even worse, this same work probably will be retried later. You should always examine the reasons for a high ratio of rolled-back transactions—it probably will lie in your code somewhere, usually as a result of poor transaction management or resource utilization.

The Monitoring/JTA tab also provides further links:

Monitor all transactions by name
> This option allows you to monitor statistics about named transactions coordinated by the server. For example, if you have an EJB method that has a Requires transaction attribute, transactions due to calls to this method will appear here.

Monitor all transactions by resource
> This option lets you monitor statistics for transaction resources accessed by the server. For example, it will include aggregates for your transactional connection pools and JMS file stores.

Monitor inflight transactions

This option shows inflight transactions—those that have started, but which have not yet committed or rolled back.

If you are using EJBs in your application, you may want to examine these statistics together with the transaction and locking statistics that are available for EJBs.

Tuning the JMS Server

WebLogic provides a whole host of performance-related settings that can be configured for the JMS service. For each server or JMS destination, you can adjust the message/byte thresholds and quotas. You also can configure an upper limit for the number of JMS sessions that may be retrieved from a session pool. In addition, you can set the maximum number of messages that can be accumulated at a JMS consumer. All of these configuration aspects are explained in Chapter 8.

Optimizing paging and flow control

WebLogic's message paging feature lets you free up virtual memory during peak message loads. When the message loads reach (or go beyond) a configured threshold, WebLogic swaps out messages from the virtual memory to a persistent store. This prevents the JMS service from impeding the performance of other WebLogic services. In addition, WebLogic supports flow control features whereby the JMS server (or JMS destination) can instruct its message producers to limit their message flow when it's overloaded.

Optimizing persistence

In order to support persistent messaging, WebLogic allows you to configure a file or JDBC store. In general, file stores perform much better than JDBC stores. The scalability, performance, and reliability of the disk persistence are governed by the synchronous write policy that you choose for the file store. Choose the most appropriate for your application. Note that hardware and OS play a role here too, in the sense that the speed of the synchronous write may be determined by whether the system you use has a direct-write capability, and whether the disk cache can survive a power outage. Chapter 8 goes into more detail describing the pros and cons of the various synchronous write policies.

Monitoring the JMS servers

Finally, WebLogic captures a gamut of statistics for various JMS objects: JMS servers, connections, sessions, server session pools, destinations, durable subscribers, message producers, and consumers. By monitoring these statistics, you have enough information to properly tune the various resources available on JMS. To monitor JMS resources, choose a JMS server in the Administration Console and then select the Monitoring tab.

EJB Tuning

The WebLogic-specific deployment descriptors for an EJB describe the configuration settings for EJB pools, caching, concurrency strategy, clustering, and transaction isolation levels. Here, we examine the various performance-related settings that may be configured using the *weblogic-ejb-jar.xml* descriptor file.

Optimizing the EJB pool size

WebLogic establishes a free pool of EJBs for each stateless session bean, message-driven bean, or entity bean deployed to the server. The `max-beans-in-free-pool` element in the *weblogic-ejb-jar.xml* descriptor lets you specify the size of the free pool. By default, the `max-beans-in-free-pool` element has no upper limit, which means that the size of the free pool is limited only by the server's available memory. For best performance, you should use the default value for the `max-beans-in-free-pool` parameter, which lets the server run as many EJBs concurrently as possible, maximizing thread usage.

For stateless session and message-driven beans, you need to specify a value only if you need to limit the number of concurrent EJBs running on the server. If your application invokes a lot of finder and home methods or frequently creates entity EJB instances, you may wish to tune this parameter to ensure that the pool has enough anonymous entity EJB instances. If the cost of frequently creating and removing EJBs is quite significant, a fixed pool of EJBs also may improve application performance. If you find that your EJBs are quite database-intensive, it is best to let the size of the free pool be bound only by the server's available memory. Remember, even though you may have specified the maximum number of EJB instances held in the free pool, it still can be overridden by a WebLogic instance at runtime depending on the state of its memory resources.

Moreover, you can use the `initial-beans-in-free-pool` element in the *weblogic-ejb-jar.xml* descriptor file to specify the initial number of EJB instances that are created for the pool when the server boots up. By default, the free pool is empty when the server starts. This setting applies only to stateless session beans, message-driven beans, and entity beans. By establishing a ready pool of EJB instances, you can improve the initial response times for the server, as this will eliminate the delay of creating new EJB instances.

Optimizing the EJB cache size

The `max-beans-in-cache` element in the *weblogic-ejb-jar.xml* descriptor allows you to specify a maximum size for the EJB cache—i.e., the cache of active EJB instances that are held in memory. When an EJB cache reaches its capacity, WebLogic passivates one or more EJB instances not currently used by any client. This behavior holds true for stateful session EJBs and entity beans. You should choose a suitable value for the size of the EJB cache so that excessive passivation of EJBs can be avoided—otherwise, these actions negate any of the benefits of using an in-memory EJB cache. This is even more important when WebLogic needs to handle a large number of stateful session or entity EJBs.

Chapter 10 describes how you also can configure an application-level entity cache that is shared among all the EJBs that are packaged with the application.

EJB concurrency

WebLogic supports exclusive EJB locks, optimistic locks, and database locking. In general, WebLogic can provide better support for concurrent EJB access when it defers locking services to the underlying database. The underlying DBMS can offer finer granularity for locking data, and avoid deadlocks. The optimistic locking strategy often offers the best performance, as it minimizes the amount of locking that needs to occur. You can specify the locking mechanism for the EJB using the concurrency-strategy element in the *weblogic-ejb-jar.xml* descriptor. By default, WebLogic uses database locking.

Transaction isolation levels

The transaction isolation level for an EJB decides the extent to which multiple, interleaved transactions can interfere with each other. Thus, the transaction isolation level setting also affects the performance of your EJBs. In general, lower isolation levels result in better database concurrency but at the cost of reduced transaction isolation. Chapter 10 explains how to set the transaction isolation level for an EJB using the isolation-level element in the *weblogic-ejb-jar.xml* descriptor.

Optimizing CMP

EJB relationship caching can help improve the performance of accessing entity beans. WebLogic can automatically load related EJB instances into the cache by running a single join query to fetch the related EJBs and thereby avoid multiple queries. In addition, WebLogic allows you to defer cascade delete operations to the underlying database. In this way, the DBMS automatically handles the deletion of related EJB instances when the parent EJB instance has been removed. WebLogic also supports optimistic locking, which allows the EJB container to defer all database checks until the point of transaction commit. Fetch groups can also provide you with control over exactly which fields of an EJB are populated from the database.

In addition, batch inserts, updates, and deletes enable the EJB container to combine multiple database operations into a single JDBC operation. This helps reduce the number of network round trips for the EJB container and enhances the performance of your CMP entity beans. These and many other CMP optimizations are explained in Chapter 11. By carefully enabling these optimizations, you can improve the performance of an application that relies heavily on CMP entity beans.

Monitoring EJBs

However much you enhance your EJB's, you won't know if you are doing the right thing unless you monitor the statistics of your EJBs in action. WebLogic gathers a wealth of information to help guide you. To access this information, select an EJB module that is already deployed and then choose the Monitoring tab. Next, you must choose which types of beans in the JAR you wish to monitor—either stateless, stateful, entity, or message-driven beans. WebLogic 8.1 provides a richer set of statistics than is available in WebLogic 7.0. We will mark each statistic that is available only in WebLogic 8.1 with the § symbol. All of the ratios quoted in the following list are made available to you in WebLogic 8.1's Administration Console. In WebLogic 7.0, you have to calculate the ratios yourself.

The first set of statistics relates to the free pool. These statistics are relevant to all bean types except stateful session beans because they don't have an associated pool.

Pool Beans Current Count *
This value indicates the number of bean instances available in the free pool.

Beans in Use Current Count
This value indicates the total number of bean instances currently in use.

Pool Waiter Total Count
This value indicates the total number of threads currently waiting for an available bean instance from the free pool.

Pool Timeout Total Count
This value indicates the total number of threads that have timed out waiting for an available bean instance from the free pool.

Access Total Count §
This value indicates the total number of times an attempt was made to get an instance from the free pool.

Miss Total Count §
This value indicates the total number of failures to get an instance from the free pool. For example, if the pool is empty, a failure will occur.

Pool Miss Ratio §
The pool miss ratio is calculated by dividing the Miss Total Count by the Access Total Count.

Pool Timeout Ratio §
This ratio is calculated by dividing the Pool Timeout Total Count by the Access Total Count.

Ideally, you never should get pool timeouts. By raising the value of the max-beans-in-free-pool element, you provide additional EJB instances for servicing requests; therefore, you reduce the number of pool timeouts. The transaction timeout configured

---

* This is called Pool Idle Beans Count in WebLogic 7.0.

for the EJBs also may contribute to a high number of pool timeouts. The amount of time a thread waits for an EJB from the pool is bound by the EJB's current transaction timeout. By increasing the transaction timeout setting for the EJB, threads wait longer for an EJB from the free pool.

If you limit the size of the free pool for stateless session beans, the miss ratio will indicate the ratio of calls that have had to wait for a bean to become available. Entity and message-driven beans do not wait for an instance to become available. If a pool miss occurs for these bean types, a new bean is created to service the request. Ideally, requests never should have to wait due to the pool being full, nor should they have to wait for a bean to be created. The pool timeout ratio provides an indication of the proportion of requests that timed out while waiting for a bean instance. If this value is high, you may need to increase the size of the pool.

Entity beans and stateful session beans have associated caches that hold active bean instances. At WebLogic's discretion, the beans in the cache can be passivated and activated again later. The following statistics are held for these bean types:

Cached Beans Current Count
>   This value indicates the total number of beans currently cached.

Cache Access Count
>   This value indicates the number of times that the cache has been accessed.

Cache Hit Count
>   This value indicates the number of times that a bean has been looked up and successfully found in the cache.

Activation Count
>   This value indicates the total number of beans that have been made active.

Passivation Count
>   This value indicates the total number of beans that have been passivated.

Cache Miss Ratio
>   This ratio can be calculated by dividing the cache hit count by the cache access count. This indicates the effectiveness of the cache.

The cache miss ratio is particularly useful. A high reading for the cache miss ratio may indicate that you need to resize the EJB cache. The amount of time saved by getting a bean from the cache depends on the cost of the bean's ejbActivate( ) method, as well as the bean's cache-between-transactions setting. Whenever a cache miss occurs, a bean will be obtained from the pool and its ejbActivate( ) method called. Obviously, the more expensive this method is to execute, the higher the penalty for a cache miss. If the EJB is configured with the cache-between-transactions set to true, a cache miss will also force the EJB container to make an extra call to the database to load the bean.

If certain EJB instances (primary keys) are used more frequently than others, you can resize the EJB cache to ensure that frequently used EJB instances remain in the cache, while less frequently used EJBs can enter or leave the cache on demand. By increasing the cache size, you could reduce the cache miss ratio. If a subset of EJB instances is not used more frequently than others, test your application setup against different EJB cache sizes to determine which gives you the lowest cache miss ratio. The server's memory is a valuable resource, so you need to balance the cache miss ratio against the memory requirements of the EJB cache.

Stateful and entity beans also have locking statistics associated with them:

Lock Entries Current Count
    This value indicates the total number of beans that are currently locked.

Lock Manager Access Count
    This value indicates the total number of attempts to obtain a lock on a bean, which includes attempts to obtain a lock on a bean that is locked already.

Lock Manager Waiter Total Count
    This value indicates the total number of threads waiting for a lock on a bean.

Lock Manager Timeout Total Count
    This value indicates the total number of transactions that have timed out while waiting for a lock on a bean.

Lock Waiter Ratio
    This ratio is calculated by dividing the Lock Manager Waiter Total Count by the Lock Manager Access Count.

Lock Timeout Ratio
    This ratio is calculated by dividing the Lock Manager Timeout Total Count by the Lock Manager Access Count.

There are a few caveats here. For entity beans, if you choose the optimistic concurrency strategy, no locks are held by the EJB container. Similarly, if you use the ReadOnly strategy, WebLogic activates a new instance for each transaction so that the requests can proceed in parallel and so that no locking occurs here. Finally, if you use the database concurrency strategy, locking is deferred to the underlying database. So, the only time an entity bean will be locked by the container is if you use the Exclusive locking strategy. The default concurrency strategy for entity beans is the database strategy.

The waiter ratio gives a good indication of how often a thread had to wait for a locked bean. A high reading for this ratio may indicate a less-than-optimal setting for the EJB's concurrency strategy. Choosing the database or optimistic locking guarantees greater EJB concurrency and eliminates the need for locking EJBs at the container level. Moreover, by reducing transaction times you can reduce the duration for which locks are held and improve EJB concurrency.

The timeout ratio gauges the number of times a thread timed out while waiting for a lock on an EJB. These timeouts are particularly harmful as they will result in an exception that will roll back the current transaction. A high timeout ratio may indicate an improperly configured transaction timeout, as the amount of time a thread waits for a lock is bound by the EJB's current transaction timeout. Ensure that the transaction timeout isn't set to a low value—otherwise, a thread may not wait long enough for locks to be released and may prematurely time out. On the other hand, raising the transaction timeout value means your valuable server threads wait longer than usual for locks. Moreover, you may increase the request times because requests wait longer before timing out.

The final set of statistics that are gathered are those for transactions:

Transactions Committed Total Count
This value indicates the total number of transactions that have been committed for this EJB.

Transactions Rolled Back Total Count
This value indicates the total number of transactions that have been rolled back for this EJB.

Transactions Timed Out Total Count
This value indicates the total number of transactions that have timed out for this EJB.

Transaction Timeout Ratio
This ratio can be calculated by dividing the Transactions Timed Out Total Count by the Transactions Committed Total Count.

Transaction Rollback Ratio
This ratio can be calculated by dividing the Transactions Rolled Back Total Count by the Transactions Committed Total Count.

A high reading for the transaction timeout ratio could again indicate an improperly configured transaction timeout. Too low a value for the transaction timeout means your threads are timing out prematurely before the transaction can complete its work. Raising the transaction timeout value may reduce the number of transaction timeouts. Again, you need to exercise caution when raising the transaction timeout value, as this may generate additional bottlenecks for your server.

Before investigating a high transaction rollback ratio, first sort out any high transaction timeout ratios. Because timeouts cause rollbacks, it also will affect the rollback statistics. Otherwise, you should investigate which resources are causing the transactions to time out.

These statistics play a vital role in determining the ideal settings for an EJB's transaction timeout, concurrency strategy, and the size of the free pool and EJB cache. The complex interplay between these configuration settings determines the average request times, the degree of concurrency, and the efficiency of the server's threads. What's more, you can effectively determine the most appropriate settings only by running your application under its expected load and monitoring these performance figures.

Monitoring with JMX

Using the Administration Console to monitor your application can be somewhat tedious, especially because the performance of the system hinges on so many different variables. A nicer way to obtain the desired performance data is to directly access the runtime MBeans that capture the data. This process is described in Chapter 20.

Although you can inspect the runtime MBeans programmatically, you also can use WebLogic's administration tool to reach the data. The following example extracts the current count for the lock entries from all of the EJB locking runtime MBeans:

```
java weblogic.Admin -url t3://hostname:port -username system -password psst
              GET -pretty -type EJBLockingRuntime
              -property LockEntriesCurrentCount
```

For the full list of MBeans that are available to you, see the API documentation for the `weblogic.management.runtime` package.

Tuning the Application Server

WebLogic provides many server-specific performance-related configuration settings. For instance, enabling native I/O on specific platforms greatly improves the efficiency with which WebLogic can carry out I/O operations. WebLogic provides various execute queues that serve as a pool of ready threads operating on a first-come-first-served fashion. You can adjust the Thread Count attribute of an execute queue to set the number of execute threads that can operate concurrently. An execute queue then can be shared by multiple applications deployed to WebLogic. Alternatively, you can create custom execute queues and assign them to specific applications. In this way, you can guarantee that critical applications always can rely on a fixed number of threads.

WebLogic lets you specify when an execute queue is considered to be overwhelmed. This threshold is specified in terms of a user-defined percentage of the maximum length of the execute queue. The server detects an overflow condition when the execute queue exceeds this threshold value, and changes its health status to "warning." You can configure the server to allocate additional threads to complete the outstanding work in the queue under these conditions.

WebLogic also can detect when threads in the execute queue are "stuck"—i.e., when a thread is unable to complete its current task or accept new tasks. Depending on the execute queue, the server's health state is changed to either "warning" or "critical." You can adjust the thread detection behavior by varying the time interval after which WebLogic periodically scans the queue for stuck threads. In addition, you can specify the allowed backlog of connections for any server. This restricts the number of TCP connections that WebLogic accepts into its wait queue, before refusing additional requests.

The combination of these settings plays an important role in enhancing the server's performance.

Execute Queues

In WebLogic, an *execute queue* represents a named collection of worker threads for a server. Dedicated execute queues can be made available to servlets, JSPs, EJBs, and RMI objects deployed to the server. Any task that is assigned to a WebLogic instance is first placed into an execute queue and then assigned to an available server thread on a first-come-first-served basis.

The default execute queue, `weblogic.kernel.default`, is preconfigured for each WebLogic instance. If a server is in development mode, this queue defaults to 15 threads. If the server is in production mode, it defaults to 25 threads.* Unless you create additional execute queues and assign them to specific applications, all web applications and RMI objects rely on this default execute queue.

WebLogic also depends on two queues reserved for administration purposes only. The `weblogic.admin.HTTP` execute queue belongs to the Administration Server and is dedicated to the Administration Console. The `weblogic.admin.RMI` execute queue is available on the Administration Server and all Managed Servers. It too is reserved for administration traffic only. Neither of these execute queues can be reconfigured in any way.

Creating an execute queue

You can use the Administration Console to configure a new execute queue for a server. Choose the desired server instance from the left pane. Right-click the server's name and choose View Execute Queues to view the execute queues for the server. The resulting page also provides a "Configure a new Execute Queue" option. Table 15-2 provides a description of the configuration settings available on this tab.

Table 15-2. Configuration settings for an execute queue

Setting	Description	Default
Queue Length	This setting defines the maximum number of simultaneous requests that can be held in the queue. WebLogic automatically doubles the queue size when the maximum queue length is reached.	65536
Queue Length Threshold Percent	This setting determines the threshold beyond which the server indicates an overflow condition for the queue. It is specified in terms of a percentage of the queue length (1–99). When the actual queue length exceeds this threshold value, this indicates an overflow condition. WebLogic logs an error message and provides additional threads to reduce the workload on the execute queue.	90

* In WebLogic 7.0, the default size of the execute queue in production mode is 15.

Table 15-2. Configuration settings for an execute queue (continued)

Setting	Description	Default
Thread Count	This setting defines the number of threads assigned to this queue.	15
Threads Increase	This setting determines the number of worker threads WebLogic may create to resolve an overflow condition on the execute queue. By default, WebLogic merely changes the health status of the server to "warning" without providing any additional threads to handle the overflow. Note that once WebLogic creates the additional threads to handle the queue overflow, the new threads remain in the execute queue until the server reboots. In general, you should examine application setup to determine the reasons for the overflow and modify the thread count to avoid the overflow condition in the future.	0
Threads Minimum	This setting determines the minimum number of threads WebLogic should maintain in its execute queue to prevent unnecessary overflow conditions.	5
Threads Maximum	This setting determines the maximum number of threads in the execute queue. It prevents WebLogic from continually adding more threads to the queue in response to overflow conditions.	400
Thread Priority	This setting specifies the priority for threads in the execute queue.	5

Once you've applied your changes to the settings for the new execute queue, you need to reboot the associated server in order for the changes to take effect.

Assigning execute queues to J2EE applications

By default, all applications deployed to WebLogic (except JMS producers and consumers) use the server's default execute queue. After creating a new execute queue on a server, you still need to ensure that the applications you run on the server can use this execute queue. Fortunately, WebLogic lets you assign an execute queue to servlets, JSPs, EJBs, and RMI objects. In order to associate the execute queue with a servlet (or JSP), you need to specify the wl-dispatch-policy initialization parameter for the servlet (or JSP) in the *web.xml* descriptor file. The following code sample shows how to assign the execute queue mySpecialQueue to a particular JSP page:

```
<!-- web.xml entry -->
<servlet>
        <servlet-name>MyServlet</servlet-name>
        <jsp-file>/critical.jsp</jsp-file>
        <init-param>
                <param-name>wl-dispatch-policy</param-name>
                <param-value>mySpecialQueue</param-value>
        </init-param>
</servlet>
```

In order to assign an execute queue to an RMI object, you must specify the -dispatchPolicy option when using WebLogic's RMI compiler (rmic). Here's how you would assign the execute queue mySpecialQueue to an RMI object:

```
java weblogic.rmic -dispatchPolicy mySpecialQueue ...
```

In the same way, use the -dispatchPolicy option when invoking WebLogic's EJB compiler to assign the execute queue to an EJB. WebLogic's EJB compiler implicitly passes the -dispatchPolicy argument to the underlying RMI compiler. In WebLogic 8.1, use the dispatch-policy element in the EJB's *weblogic-ejb-jar.xml* descriptor to set the execute queue:

```
<!-- weblogic-ejb-jar.xml descriptor -->
<weblogic-enterprise-bean>
  <ejb-name>MyEJB</ejb-name>
  ...
  <dispatch-policy>myEJBQueue</dispatch-policy>
</weblogic-enterprise-bean>
```

Custom execute queues are supported for all EJB types—session beans, entity beans, and MDBs.

> The dispatch policy for an MDB may be ignored if the MDB is attached to a foreign JMS destination.

At runtime, WebLogic allocates worker threads for your servlets, JSPs, EJBs, and RMI objects from their configured execute queues, thereby guaranteeing that selected objects in your application have access to a fixed number of server threads. For those objects for which no execute queue is assigned, the threads will be allocated from the server's default execute queue.

Monitoring active queues

To monitor the active queues using the Administration Console, right-click a server and select View Execute Queues, then navigate to the Monitoring tab. Alternatively, select the Monitoring/General tab and then choose the "Monitor all Active Queues" link. This will provide an indication of each execution queue, including the queue length, the number of idle threads, and the throughput. Clicking any queue will let you monitor the threads on that queue. You also can determine the queue length graphically, along with throughput and memory usage indicators, by selecting the Monitoring/Performance tab for any server.

Monitoring the queue length is particularly important. For instance, if your queue length increases over time while your throughput stays the same, any new incoming requests will have to wait longer and longer for the next available thread. Some kind of tuning undoubtedly will be needed in these circumstances. If this situation persists even after tuning and reconfiguration, your server setup may have simply reached the limit on the amount of traffic that it can handle.

Server Threads

The runtime behavior of an execute queue is influenced by a number of parameters, and optimal server performance depends on the optimal configuration of these parameters:

- The thread count for an execute queue
- The percentage of execute threads that will act as socket readers
- How execute queues react to overflow conditions
- How often WebLogic detects "stuck" threads in the queue
- The size of the wait queue, or the number of TCP connections that are accepted before WebLogic refuses additional requests

Let's look more closely at the implications of these parameters on the performance of WebLogic's server threads.

Configuring the thread count

The *thread count* for an execute queue determines the number of allocated threads that can be used concurrently to serve application tasks that utilize the execute queue. You can use the Administration Console to modify the thread count for the default execute queue on any WebLogic instance. Choose the desired server from the left pane, right-click it, and select the View Execute Queues option to display all available execute queues for the chosen server. From the Name column, click the name of the default execute queue, `weblogic.kernel.default`, to view or modify its configuration settings. You now can raise or lower the default Thread Count value for the execute queue. Once you've applied your changes to the execute queue, you need to reboot the particular server for those changes to take effect.

You must be careful when allocating more server threads to the default execute queue. Threads are valuable resources and they consume memory. You may degrade server performance by increasing the thread count to an unnecessarily high value. Too many execute threads means more memory consumption, and thus more context switching among the available threads. The ideal value for the number of execute threads will depend on the nature of your application. In general, you need more execute threads if the client relies on RMI method calls for a significant amount of its work, or if the application relies on a number of database calls for processing client requests. On the other hand, if your application makes short calls with rapid turnover, a small number of execute threads may also improve server performance.

The ideal value for the queue's thread count can best be determined through trial and error—more accurately through observation under test conditions in which all applications in the execute queue are operating under high load. You need to continually raise the number of threads in the execute queue and repeat the same load test, until you've attained peak throughput for the queue. At some stage during the repeated executions of the load test, the thread count for the execute queue will exceed a threshold, beyond which the memory consumption of the threads and excessive context switching actually degrade server performance.

Threads as socket readers

Ideally, a WebLogic instance should rely on the native I/O implementation provided for the server's OS. If you must rely on WebLogic's pure-Java socket reader implementation, you still can improve the performance of socket communication by configuring the appropriate number of execute threads that will act as socket readers for each server (and client). You can use the ThreadPoolPercentSocketReaders attribute to specify the maximum percentage of execute threads that are used to read incoming requests to a socket. By default, WebLogic allocates 33% of server threads to act as socket readers—its optimal value is again application-specific.

By ensuring that you've configured an adequate number of threads to act as socket readers, you enhance the server's ability to accept client requests. However, finding the right balance between server threads that are devoted to reading requests received on a socket and those threads that actually perform the required tasks is a matter of trial and error. Again, you need to use the Administration Console to set the maximum percentage of server threads that will act as socket readers. Choose the particular server from the left pane, and then select the Configuration/Tuning tab from the right pane. You now can specify a number (between 1 and 99) for the Socket Readers attribute. The number of Java socket readers is defined by the percentage of the total number of execute threads. The Execute Threads attribute represents the total number of execute threads.

You even can configure the number of socket reader threads for the JVM on which the client runs. Use the -Dweblogic.ThreadPoolSize option to specify the size of the client's thread pool—i.e., the number of execute threads available to the client. The number of socket readers then can be expressed as a percentage of the size of the thread pool.

The following example illustrates how to specify the number of socket reader threads for the client's JVM, through the -Dweblogic.ThreadPoolPercentSocketReaders option from the command line:

```
java -Dweblogic.ThreadPoolSize=6
     -Dweblogic.ThreadPoolPercentSocketReaders=33 ...
```

Queue overflow conditions

We have seen how WebLogic can detect and resolve potential overflow conditions in an execute queue. An overflow occurs when the current size of the execute queue exceeds a certain threshold. This threshold is specified in terms of a certain percentage of the maximum length of the execute queue. When this threshold value is exceeded, WebLogic changes the server's health status to "warning" and optionally allocates additional worker threads to reduce the workload on the execute queue. These additional threads are introduced to bring the execute queue back to its normal operating size.

Thus, in order to configure overflow detection and resolution, you need to configure the following parameters for an execute queue:

- The threshold percentage that indicates an overflow for the server's execute queue.
- The number of additional server threads that must be allocated to resolve the queue's overflow condition.
- The minimum number of threads that always should be available to the execute queue, and the maximum number of threads that may be assigned to the queue at any time. The upper limit ensures that WebLogic doesn't continually assign new server threads in order to handle repeated occurrences of queue overflow.

Table 15-2 lists the configuration settings that determine how queue overflow conditions ought to be handled. Remember, additional server threads assigned to the execute queue for the purposes of resolving the overflow remain in the execute queue until the server shuts down.

Detecting stuck threads

WebLogic automatically detects when a thread assigned to an execute queue becomes "stuck." A thread becomes stuck when it cannot complete its current task or accept new tasks. The server logs a message every time it detects a stuck thread. When all threads in the execute queue become stuck, WebLogic changes the server's health status to "warning" or "critical," depending on the execute queue. If all threads allocated to the server's default execute queue become stuck, WebLogic changes the server health status to "critical." For all other execute queues, WebLogic changes the health status to "warning." This includes any user-defined queues and the `weblogic.admin.HTTP` and `weblogic.admin.RMI` execute queues. Recall that the Node Manager can be configured to automatically restart a Managed Server whose health status is "critical." In addition, you can write log listeners that can alert you if this condition arises.

At regular intervals, WebLogic inspects the server threads assigned to the execute queue to determine whether any of these threads are stuck. You can adjust the frequency with which WebLogic checks for stuck threads, and the elapsed time after which WebLogic marks a thread as stuck.

 WebLogic lets you configure thread detection behavior only on a per-server basis rather than on a per-execute-queue basis.

Select the desired server from the left pane of the Administration Console and then choose the Configuration/Tuning tab from the right pane. Here you can adjust the following configuration settings:

Stuck Thread Max Time
> This setting determines the duration (in seconds) for which a server thread must continually be busy before WebLogic marks the execute thread as stuck. By default, WebLogic marks a thread as stuck if it has been busy for 600 seconds.

Stuck Thread Timer Interval
> This setting determines the frequency with which WebLogic periodically scans execute queues for stuck threads. By default, WebLogic scans for stuck threads every 600 seconds.

Once you've applied your changes to these settings, you need to reboot the particular server for these changes to take effect.

Monitoring active server threads

To monitor the active server threads using the Administration Console, right-click a server and select View Execute Threads. This will provide an indication of each server thread, the execute queue that is associated with the thread, and further information such as the total number of requests that have been handled by the thread. Alternatively, you can select the Monitoring/General tab and then the "Monitor all Active Queues" option. This enables you to view server threads on a per-queue basis.

Socket Connections

WebLogic supports IP-based socket communication in many scenarios. For example, all remote RMI communication uses sockets, as does internal cluster communication such as state replication.

WebLogic supports two socket configurations: a pure-Java implementation and a native socket reader implementation. If you can, always use the native implementation because it improves the performance of socket-based communication considerably. The pure-Java implementation uses threads that must actively poll all open sockets to determine whether they contain data that needs to be read. The same problem is faced by developers who build applications using sockets on the JDK 1.3 platform. The threads reading from the sockets are always polling the sockets, even if there is no data to be read. This severely reduces the performance of these applications.

JDK 1.4 introduces a mechanism whereby a socket reader can be asynchronously notified when there is data, and hence the socket readers do not have to waste CPU cycles polling. A similar technique is used in WebLogic's native socket implementation. This makes the native socket reader implementation much faster than the pure-Java implementation. As applets don't have access to the native code implementation, they cannot use it, so the efficiency with which they can perform socket I/O is still limited. BEA's web site lists all of the supported platforms for WebLogic, together with availability information regarding the native service pack.

In order to enable the native socket implementation for a server, choose the server from the left pane of the Administration Console and move to the Configuration/ Tuning tab. The Enable Native IO option already should be selected; this option is enabled by default.

Optimizing the pure-Java socket implementation

The pure-Java socket implementation can be optimized somewhat by ensuring that there are always enough reader threads available on a WebLogic instance. Too few reader threads may degrade performance because of unnecessary waits while the reader threads eventually get around to polling a socket that does have data. Of course, too many reader threads will unnecessarily consume more resources.

The number of reader threads necessary for a WebLogic instance is highly contextual. If the server belongs to a combined-tier cluster, each server potentially will open a maximum of two sockets, which it needs to replicate any session state. Both web applications and EJB components will be deployed homogeneously to the cluster. The collocation optimizations mean that method calls from servlets and JSPs to EJBs always will be directed to local replicas of the EJB objects. Therefore, no additional socket reader threads will be needed.

If a cluster has a pinned object, you will need an additional socket reader on each member of the cluster, which can be used to reach that pinned object. If you've designed a multi-tier application setup, such as that depicted in Figure 14-1, each member of the web/presentation tier will potentially communicate with each member of the object tier. A clustered object may be fetched from any member of the object tier, depending on how the load balancing occurs. In addition, a server in the web tier will need to communicate with other members for state replication. This means that each server in Figure 14-1 needs three sockets for this communication. If a cluster also will be accessed by external Java clients, you need to take these into consideration as well.

To adjust the number of socket readers on platforms on which there are no available performance packs (or native socket reader implementations), choose the server from the left pane of the Administration Console and modify the Socket Reader setting from the Configuration/Tuning tab. This number determines the percentage of the total execute threads that will be dedicated to socket readers.

Client socket readers

External Java clients that communicate with a server or cluster generally will use the pure-Java implementation of sockets. You can configure the number of socket readers on a client using two command-line options that specify the thread pool size and the percentage of the thread pool that may be used for the socket readers. The following example shows how to specify the number of socket readers at the client's end:

```
java -Dweblogic.ThreadPoolSize=20
     -Dweblogic.ThreadPoolPercentSocketReaders=40 ...
```

Managing TCP connections

For each WebLogic instance, you can use the Accept Backlog parameter to set the number of TCP connections WebLogic accepts before refusing additional connections. This parameter determines the maximum number of TCP connections that may be buffered in the wait queue. By default, WebLogic accepts 50 TCP connections before refusing additional connection requests. The Accept Backlog configuration setting can be located from the Administration Console by navigating to the Connections/Tuning tab for the selected server. The maximum value for this setting is OS-dependent.

WebLogic must queue up client requests for socket connections when the deployed applications aren't accepting those connections fast enough. For example, this might occur during excessive server load or during lengthy garbage collection cycles. If clients keep getting "connection refused" messages when trying to access the server, it may be because your accept backlog is not large enough. In this case, keep increasing the value until your clients no longer get the messages.

Tuning a Clustered Setup

As we saw earlier in Chapter 14, a WebLogic cluster represents a group of servers working together to provide scalability and high availability for all kinds of applications and services deployed to the cluster.

WebLogic offers scalability to J2EE applications in a way that is transparent to both end users and developers. *Scalability* refers to the system's capacity to grow in specified dimensions, as more demands are placed on the system. Typical dimensions include the number of concurrent users at any time, the number of transactions that can be handled in a unit of time, the average response times, and many more. In case of a well-designed application, you can improve performance by simply adding another server to the cluster. WebLogic automatically balances the load between the available members of the cluster. Thus, a WebLogic cluster allows you to add more capacity to the middle tiers, without affecting any existing clients of the application.

In addition, the cluster provides high availability by including multiple redundant servers that host duplicate copies of applications and services. This way, a client is insulated from individual server failures. In case of stateful or pinned services, WebLogic provides replication services that enable a peer server to take control of the service in case the primary server fails. This too enhances the availability of applications and services to clients.

A cluster configuration that provides (near) linear scalability for your J2EE applications is ideal. This means you should tune your setup to ensure that the system can grow along specified dimensions proportionately as more servers are added to the cluster. In general, you should isolate any application-specific performance issues before optimizing your application setup in a clustered environment.

Chapter 14 provides an in-depth discussion of the performance implications of adopting combined-tier architectures in favor of the multi-tier application setup. It presents several scenarios in which you need to balance the flexibility of your application setup against the performance of your applications. It also covers the impact of IP multicast and socket-based communication on the overall traffic flowing through your network infrastructure.

Multi-CPU machines

A multi-CPU machine may host a cluster of WebLogic instances, or perhaps even multiple clusters. In this scenario, the ratio of the number of WebLogic instances to the number of CPUs becomes a critical factor. In order to determine the ideal ratio for a CPU-bound application, you should first set up performance tests for your application using a ratio of 1:1—that is, one WebLogic instance for each CPU. If you discover that CPU utilization is at (or very near) 100%, repeat the same tests using a higher ratio of number of CPUs to servers—say, one WebLogic instance for every two CPUs. Remember that in a production environment, a server is sporadically involved in administration tasks as well. Thus, you should set aside a limited CPU capacity for handling the administration tasks under load. BEA holds the view that 1:2 is the optimal server-to-CPU ratio—i.e., one WebLogic instance for every two CPUs, ignoring the individual processing needs of a particular application. Your mileage may vary, though.

Of course, before you determine the optimal ratio of the number of servers to the number of CPUs, ensure that your application is truly CPU-bound. For network I/O-bound applications, you may in fact improve performance by replacing the existing NIC with a faster one, rather than bolting on additional CPUs. For disk I/O-bound applications, you may improve application performance by upgrading the number of disks or controllers, or simply by installing faster disks. Thus, you should consider the ratio of the number of servers to CPUs only after verifying that your application is indeed CPU-bound.

Tuning the JVM

Clearly, the JVM's performance also affects WebLogic's performance. Most aspects of JVM tuning relate to the efficient management of the memory heap, an efficient garbage collection scheme, and the choice between two Unix threading models: green and native threads.

Choosing a JVM

WebLogic publishes a list of certified JVM and operating system combinations on its web site; we recommend that you only use one of these certified combinations. This list also indicates what JVM version can be used. For example, WebLogic 8.1 supports JDK 1.4.1, whereas WebLogic 7.0 supports JDK 1.3.1.

SunSoft's JVM and BEA's JRockit are the two most commonly used JVMs. JRockit is a production VM optimized for server-side applications on Intel platforms. WebLogic 8.1 installs with a version of JRockit 8. You can download a version of JRockit 7 for WebLogic 7.0 from BEA's dev2dev web site.

The right JVM will strike a balance between several constraints, such as operating system, hardware and JVM stability, and performance. You can reference third-party documents for an overview of the general performance characteristics of the various JVMs.

Heap Size and Garbage Collection

The Java heap represents the memory space for all runtime objects. At any time, the heap consists of live objects, dead objects, and free memory. When an object is no longer referenced by anyone, it is considered "garbage" and is ready to be reclaimed as free memory. Garbage collection is the JVM's way of managing the JVM heap—it refers to the process of reclaiming unused Java objects from the heap. JVM heap size impacts the frequency and duration that a JVM spends on garbage collection.

Ultimately, you need to tune the JVM's heap size to ensure that the VM spends as little time on garbage collection as possible while still maximizing the number of clients that WebLogic supports. We look at how to adjust the heap size for a WebLogic instance, and how to automatically log low memory conditions for the server. In order to understand Java's heap size options, we also look at the generational garbage collection scheme used by Sun's Java 1.4 Hotspot VM. There are many other garbage collection schemes, and you will need to read your JVM's documentation to familiarize yourself with them.

Configuring the heap size

You must specify Java heap size values each time you start WebLogic. You can do this either from the Java command line or by modifying heap size values used by WebLogic's startup scripts. For instance, here's how you can specify the minimum and maximum heap sizes from the Java command line:

```
$ java -Xms512m -Xmx512m
        -Dweblogic.Name=%SERVER_NAME% -Dbea.home="C:\bea"
```

```
-Dweblogic.management.username=%WLS_USER%
-Dweblogic.management.password=%WLS_PW%
-Dweblogic.management.server=%ADMIN_URL%
-Dweblogic.ProductionModeEnabled=%STARTMODE%
-Djava.security.policy="%WL_HOME%\server\lib\weblogic.policy"
    weblogic.Server
```

The -Xms and -Xmx options enable you to set the minimum and maximum sizes for the JVM heap, respectively. In this case, the JVM heap size is set to 512 MB of the system's memory. In general, you can minimize the number of garbage collections if you set the minimum heap size (-Xms) equal to the maximum heap size (-Xmx).

In WebLogic 7.1, you can modify WebLogic's startup script, *startWLS*, located in the *WL_HOME\server\bin* directory. This script specifies default arguments for the JVM's heap size using environment variables, which are then used to start WebLogic Server.

You also should consider the following guidelines when configuring the JVM's heap size:

- Ensure that the heap's size is not larger than the available free RAM on the machine. You should allocate as much of the free RAM as possible without causing your machine to unnecessarily swap pages to disk.
- You may discover that the JVM is spending too much time on garbage collection. In that case, consider lowering the JVM's heap size. In general, you may allocate up to 80% of the available free memory for your JVM while still monitoring the time the server spends on garbage collections.

Generational garbage collection

Both the Java 1.3 and 1.4 VMs rely on a generational collector that significantly improves the overall speed of object allocation and the efficiency of the garbage collection. It works on the principle that most objects created during the lifetime of a program are short-lived. By creating separate spaces for different generations of objects, the JVM can limit the scope of its garbage collection. A *generation* refers to the set of objects in the heap that survive an iteration of the JVM's garbage collection. Older generations survive more iterations than their younger counterparts. *Infant mortality* refers to those objects that become garbage very shortly after being allocated in the heap.

The JVM's heap is divided into two areas: *young* and *old*. The young generation area is further subdivided into Eden and two survivor spaces (of equal size). *Eden* refers to the area where new objects are allocated. After a pass of the JVM's garbage collector, all surviving live objects are copied into either one of the two survivor spaces. On successive iterations of garbage collection, objects are copied between these survivor spaces until they exceed a maximum heap size threshold value, in which case they are transferred to the old generation area.

By setting aside separate memory pools to hold objects of different generations, the garbage collector needs to run in each generation only when it fills up. You can therefore fine-tune the JVM's garbage collection by relying on the fact that the majority of the objects die young, thereby optimizing the garbage collection cycles. However, improperly configured sizes for different generations also can degrade the performance of garbage collection.

In order to specify the sizes for the Eden and survivor spaces for WebLogic, you need to run the following command:

```
java -Xms768m -Xmx768m -XX:NewSize=192m -XX:MaxNewSize=192m -XX:SurvivorRatio=8
    -Dweblogic.Name=%SERVER_NAME% -Dbea.home="C:\bea"
    -Dweblogic.management.username=%WLS_USER%
    -Dweblogic.management.password=%WLS_PW%
    -Dweblogic.management.server=%ADMIN_URL%
    -Dweblogic.ProductionModeEnabled=%STARTMODE%
    -Djava.security.policy="%WL_HOME%\server\lib\weblogic.policy"
    weblogic.Server
```

The -XX:NewSize and -XX:MaxNewSize options let you specify the minimum and maximum sizes of the new generation area, respectively. As a general rule, you should ensure the size of the new generation area is one-fourth of the maximum heap size. If you have a larger number of short-lived objects, you also may consider increasing the size of the new generation area. As mentioned earlier, the new generation area is further subdivided into Eden and two survivor spaces of equal size. Use the -XX:SurviverRatio=Y option to set the ratio of the Eden/survivor spaces—8 is a good starting point for the Eden/survivor ratio. You then can monitor the frequency and the duration of garbage collection during the lifetime of the server and adjust this setting accordingly.

These additional JVM heap size configuration options may differ depending on the platform or operating system on which the JVM runs. In that case, you need to consult the vendor documentation to learn more about the platform-specific equivalents for these JVM heap tuning options.

In order to enable the HotSpot VM, you may need to explicitly pass additional options to the Java command line. On Windows platforms, use the -hotspot or -client option to select the HotSpot VM for client-side applications, and use the -server option to enable the HotSpot VM for server-side applications. For an in-depth discussion on the Java HotSpot VM, refer to *http://java.sun.com/docs/hotspot/*.

In some cases, the generational garbage collector may not give you optimal performance. For example, if you have deployed a WebLogic server to a multi-CPU machine, using WebLogic's JRockit and its parallel garbage collector could be more optimal.

Automatically logging low memory conditions

WebLogic can log low memory conditions automatically. It samples the available free memory a set number of times during a fixed time interval. At the end of each interval, it computes the average free memory for that interval. If the average drops by a user-configured amount after any sample interval, WebLogic logs a warning message indicating the low memory and changes the server's health status to "warning." In addition, WebLogic logs a warning message if at any time the average free memory after any interval drops below 5% of the initial free memory.

Use the Administration Console to adjust the low memory detection behavior for a particular server. Select the desired server from the left pane of the Administration Console and then choose the Configuration/Tuning tab from the right pane. Table 15-3 lists the parameters that determine how the server detects low memory conditions.

Table 15-3. Detecting low memory conditions on a server

Setting	Description	Default
Low Memory Sample Size	This setting specifies the number of times the server samples free memory during the interval. A higher sample size can increase the accuracy of the average free memory computed for the interval.	10
Low Memory Time Interval	This setting specifies the duration (in seconds) of the time interval over which the average free memory is calculated.	3600
Low Memory GC Threshold	This setting specifies a threshold below which WebLogic logs a low memory warning. This threshold is specified as a percentage (0–99) of the initial free memory when the server boots up.	5
Low Memory Granularity Level	This setting specifies the minimum extent of the drop in free memory between two intervals, before WebLogic logs a low memory warning and changes the server's health status to "warning." This drop is specified as a percentage value (1–99) of the free memory calculated in previous intervals.	5

Once you've applied your changes, you need to restart the server for them to take effect.

Explicit request for garbage collection

You can use the Administration Console to explicitly request garbage collection on a particular WebLogic instance. Choose the desired server from the left pane of the Administration Console and then select the Monitoring/Performance tab. Examine the Memory Usage graph to verify high memory utilization on a server. You then can click the "Force garbage collection" button to explicitly invoke System.gc( ) on the particular JVM. This call's behavior will differ between different JVMs. If you must go to these lengths, your application's memory allocation needs probably suffer from a more fundamental problem.

Green Versus Native Threads

On many Unix platforms, the JVM has a choice between two threading models: green threads and native threads. *Green threads* are Java threads provided by the JVM itself. *Native threads* are kernel-based threads provided by the OS on which the JVM runs.

Green threads are lightweight and have a smaller memory footprint than native threads. A JVM typically runs multiple green threads within a single OS thread. Therefore, green threads enable the JVM to optimize thread-management tasks such as scheduling, switching, and synchronization. Alternatively, a JVM can rely on native threads directly, in which case each JVM thread maps to a single OS thread. Native threads have a larger memory footprint and also incur a higher overhead during creation and context switching. It also means that the number of concurrent JVM threads is limited by the number of processes/threads built into the kernel.

Native threads offer better performance on multi-CPU machines because they can benefit from the OS support for thread scheduling and load balancing across multiple CPUs. On a single-CPU machine, green threads probably offer better performance for most applications.

Most JVMs for Unix platforms provide a –native or –green option that lets you choose the threading model for your application.

Monitoring the JVM's Performance

It is a good idea to occasionally monitor the performance of the JVM, especially the garbage collection behavior. Most JVMs have a –Xverbosegc switch that can help trace the garbage collection behavior, and additional tools that can be used to analyze these traces. Some JVMs, such as BEA's JRockit, have management consoles that provide real-time information about the JVM and the application running in the JVM.

SSL

The Secure Sockets Layer (SSL) is an important component of WebLogic's security framework. J2EE applications deployed to WebLogic can rely on SSL to maintain data integrity and confidentiality of communications at the socket level. SSL-enabled clients also can rely on SSL to verify the identity of the server. In fact, if the server is configured for two-way SSL, it also may verify the client's identity. SSL can be used to secure communications between the Administration Server and the various Managed Servers in a WebLogic domain. Node Managers that monitor the health of all Managed Servers running on a single machine must communicate over the SSL port.

Let's consider some typical scenarios in which SSL can protect network communication between two parties:

- A web browser could connect to a WebLogic instance over an HTTP over SSL (HTTPS) port. This would then secure all communication between the web browser and the server, and at the very least require the server to present a digital certificate to the browser as proof of its identity. The SSL mode typically would be used to protect transmission of sensitive data such as login credentials, credit card information, details of bank transactions, etc.

- A Java client could establish a JNDI context with a server using the T3S protocol. All subsequent actions—for instance, looking up an EJB object and invoking one of its methods—occur in SSL mode. If the server is configured for two-way SSL, the client also needs to submit a certificate. If one or more security policies were applied to the EJB's method, WebLogic's security could be augmented so that it can map the client's certificate to a valid user and then use this identity to evaluate whether the client is authorized to invoke the EJB method.

- Within a domain, you can configure an SSL administration channel that effectively secures all administration traffic between the Administration Server and all of the Managed Servers. In a production environment, it is ideal for the Administration Server and the Managed Servers to use an SSL administration port for all traffic.

All of these scenarios require you to properly configure SSL on the particular WebLogic instance. WebLogic supports SSL on a dedicated listen port, which defaults to 7002. Thus, a web browser (or any client) can securely interact with a configured WebLogic instance via a URL connection to *https://server:7002/*.

SSL configuration requires a little more effort than just enabling HTTPS traffic on port 7002. As we shall see, SSL relies on a public-key encryption technology that uses a combination of two keys: a private key that is known only to the owner, and a public key that is embedded in a digital certificate. In fact, WebLogic comes equipped with demonstration keys and certificates that are used to verify the server's identity when a client establishes an SSL connection with the server. While these may be sufficient for development purposes, you should configure WebLogic with a production-quality private key and digital certificate. Later, we explain how to generate the server's private key and a request for a digital certificate to be issued by a certificate authority (CA).

For added security, WebLogic lets you store the server's private key, public certificate, and certificates of all trusted CAs in a keystore. We examine how you can create and configure these keystores. Trusted CA certificates are an essential requirement of SSL setup because they allow a party to trust the other party's certificate presented during the initial SSL handshake. We also look at how to extend two-way SSL configuration by mapping the client certificate to a WebLogic user, which effectively lets you use certificates as a form of user identity.

Finally, we look at how to build Java clients that use WebLogic's SSL implementation to access SSL-protected resources. For instance, a client can establish an SSL session by making a URL connection to a JSP page deployed on another WebLogic instance. A web browser may be required to present a valid certificate as proof of its identity when attempting to access a protected web resource over the SSL port. A Java client that needs to establish an initial JNDI context with a WebLogic instance can do so securely using the T3S protocol, optionally sending a digital certificate to prove its identity. These are just some of the ways in which SSL can protect network communication in a WebLogic environment.

WebLogic supports the Java Authentication and Authorization Service (JAAS), Java Secure Sockets Extensions (JSSE), and Java Cryptography Extensions (JCE). It recognizes digital certificates in the X.509 v3 format, and its SSL implementation conforms to the SSL 3.0 and TLS 1.0 standards.

Besides SSL, WebLogic provides a modular security infrastructure that controls many other aspects of security. These features include connection-level filtering, server-side authentication and authorization, and interdomain trust. We cover these issues in the next chapter—however, we touch on one or two here.

An Overview of SSL

This section provides a quick primer on SSL and a useful background to concepts and interactions that you need to understand in order to configure WebLogic's SSL.

If you feel confident about the terms and concepts involved in the world of SSL, you can skip to the next section, which dives into WebLogic's SSL configuration.

WebLogic's SSL implementation fulfills three important goals of secure communication: confidentiality, data integrity, and authentication. SSL is now often found under the name of Transport Layer Security (TLS), the new protocol based on SSL and currently being developed by the Internet Engineering Task Force (IETF). As the name indicates, TLS offers security at the transport layer, somewhere between the network layer (e.g., TCP/IP) and application layer (e.g., HTTP) protocols. A thorough description of SSL and its use within Java security services deserves a book of its own. We recommend *Java Security,* Second Edition, by Scott Oaks (O'Reilly) for a deeper understanding of SSL and related concepts. In this section, we give an overview of the key concepts that are relevant to configuring WebLogic's SSL implementation.

Suppose a client, such as a browser, needs to securely communicate with a WebLogic server. SSL can ensure that this communication remains secure in the following ways:

Confidentiality
> SSL maintains the privacy of the conversation between the client and server. By encrypting the data sent between both parties, SSL makes it difficult for a third party to discover the true contents of the conversation. SSL supports a number of different cryptographic routines from which you can choose.

Integrity
> SSL can help ensure that the data has not been tampered with. Integrity checks based on encrypted checksums called digests allow both parties to ensure that the data was not tampered with en route.

Authentication
> SSL can help establish the identity of both parties involved in the secure communication. In general, the client verifies the server's identity before initiating a conversation, but the server also may wish to verify the client's identity. This verification is possible only when each party provides a certificate as proof of its identity. This certificate is signed by a CA that can vouch for the authenticity of the certificate.

Let's take a closer look at how SSL supports these features of secure communication.

Encryption

Encryption is a time-tested way of maintaining the confidentiality of the conversation between two parties. A strong encryption algorithm makes it hard for an external party to decipher the message. This means that both parties can be reasonably sure that no one else can interpret the transmitted message. Encryption involves the use of keys—numerical values that are used to encrypt the message before it is sent or decipher the message after it has been received. Depending on how the keys are managed, there are two flavors of cryptography to choose from:

Symmetric cryptography
> Both parties use the same key to encrypt and decrypt the message. Symmetric cryptography is reasonably fast and provides a safe and reliable way to send an encrypted message. An outside party cannot interpret the message unless it has access to the shared private key. It also means that both parties need to have prior knowledge of the key. Thus, the difficult problem lies in securely transferring the key to the intended recipient.

Asymmetric cryptography
> Also called *public-key cryptography*, this removes the need for using the same key for encryption and decryption. Instead, it uses a pair of keys: a *public key* that is openly distributed, and a *private key* that is kept secret with the owner. If one key is used to encrypt a message, the other key must be used to decrypt it. For instance, a client can use the public key to encrypt a message, and the server can then decrypt the same message using its private key. No longer do we have the problem of distributing a private key. Only the public key is needed as the message can be decrypted only using the recipient's private key. Still, public-key cryptography is much slower than symmetric cryptography.

SSL strikes a compromise and uses both. It uses the slower asymmetric cryptography during the initial connection handshake when it needs to securely agree on a symmetric key to use for subsequent communication. Once both parties reach an agreement, the symmetric key is used to encrypt all subsequent communication.

WebLogic supports the RSA algorithm for asymmetric cryptography, and DES-CBC, two-key triple-DES, and RC4 for symmetric cryptography.

Message Digests

Message encryption is not enough. There is still the small probability that a malevolent hacker could tamper with the encrypted message so that when it is decrypted the recipient gets a corrupted version. SSL solves this integrity problem by introducing the notion of a *message digest*. A digest is a fixed-length representation of a message generated by applying a hash function to the original message. A good hash algorithm makes it computationally infeasible to generate two messages that would yield the same digest. With this kind of guarantee, a digest acts as a "fingerprint" for the message.

By sending the message digest along with the encrypted message, SSL enhances the integrity of the data. When the recipient decrypts the message, it computes its own digest and compares it with the received digest. If the two versions do not match, the recipient knows that the message was almost certainly was tampered with.

WebLogic supports the MD5 and SHA algorithms for creating message digests. SHA generates 160-bit message digests, while MD5 generates 128-bit message digests. Even though SHA is slower than MD5, the larger digest size makes it more secure.

Certificates

Even encryption and message digests together are not enough to completely guarantee secure communications. Both parties involved in the communication must be able to trust each other. Usually, the client needs to be able to verify the server's identity and guarantee the authenticity of the server's public key. This is called *one-way SSL*. The server accepts connections from any client because the client is not required to provide a certificate. In addition, WebLogic can be configured for *two-way SSL*, also called mutual SSL, in which the client also needs to present a certificate to the server.

Thus, SSL uses certificates to establish this trust between both parties. For instance, if the server needs to authenticate itself to the client, it sends back a signed copy of its digital certificate. The server's public key will be embedded in the digital certificate. The server is authenticated only when the client validates and accepts the server's digital certificate. These validation checks may include verifying whether the certificate has expired, whether the certificate has been signed by a trusted certificate authority, and more. The client may choose to abort the SSL connection if any of these validation checks fail.

WebLogic recognizes only those digital certificates that adhere to the X.509 v3 standard. It requires that the certificates hold at least the following information:

- The real identity of the certificate's owner, also known as the *subject*. This could be the domain name of a server or the email address of an individual.
- The name of a CA that issued the certificate, and the period for which the certificate is valid.
- The subject's public key that can be used by the recipient to encrypt the actual data before sending it back to the subject.

An SSL-enabled application, such as a web browser, typically accepts any valid certificates signed by a trusted CA. A digital certificate can be invalidated if it has expired or if the digital certificate of the trusted CA (used to sign the certificate) has expired. A server certificate can also be invalidated if the server's URL doesn't match the domain name embedded in the certificate.

Certificate Authorities

Digital certificates are issued by a trusted third party, called a *certificate authority* (CA). A CA signs the certificates with its own private key before it issues them. Given the server's certificate, a client now can verify the certificate by using the public key of the certificate authority. As a matter of caution, the client does not trust just any certificate authority. When a CA publishes its public key, it is signed with a certificate issued by a higher-level CA. Of course, the higher-level CA can do the same. This *certificate chain* stops with a *self-signed* certificate, whereby the issuer of the certificate is the same as the subject of the certificate. This also is referred to as the *root key*. Hopefully somewhere along the chain, the client will recognize a CA that it can trust. Only then can the client trust the original CA that issued the server's certificate.

You should be careful about trusting self-signed certificates. Certificate chains can't go on forever and must stop at some point. The certificate chain ends once you've reached a self-signed certificate. Root certificates are hard to forge because they are so widely published, making it harder for a server (or client) to palm you an invalid root certificate. For instance, your browser will already be populated with a number of root keys from various trusted CAs. If WebLogic is configured for mutual authentication, the server must be equipped with a list of trusted CAs so that it can validate incoming client certificates. Thus, WebLogic must have access to a number of root certificates of CAs that it trusts.

A CA issues a certificate after receiving a Certificate Signature Request (CSR); WebLogic provides tools to generate such a request.

Cipher Suites

During an SSL handshake, the two parties have to agree on a number of issues:

- A key exchange mechanism, which determines the asymmetric algorithm that is used to exchange the symmetric key
- A cipher for the data transfer, which determines the symmetric algorithm that is used to encrypt the data
- A message digest algorithm, which determines the hash algorithm that is used to generate the digest

The combination of these three schemes provides a certain level of encryption. The exact set of ciphers that you are allowed to use is controlled by the WebLogic license file. You also can programmatically limit the set of ciphers that are accepted on an SSLSocket by calling the setEnabledCipherSuites( ) method. WebLogic supports only RSA for exchanging keys. The message digest algorithm can be either SHA or MD5. The cipher for the bulk of the data transfer must be one of CBC-DES, triple-DES, or RC4.

The length of the keys adds another dimension to the level of encryption. The larger the key length, the more secure the data is likely to be and the more resistant it is to brute-force attacks. WebLogic is available with exportable and domestic-strength SSL:

- Exportable SSL supports 512-bit certificates and 40- and 50-bit bulk data encryption.

- Domestic-strength SSL supports 768- and 1024-bit certificates and 128-bit bulk data encryption.

Clearly, domestic-strength SSL is more secure. The particular SSL strength that you can use depends on your local and U.S. government restrictions. In fact, your WebLogic license determines the SSL strength supported by your servers. If the license permits only exportable-strength SSL, and you configure WebLogic to use domestic-strength SSL, the server defaults to the exportable-strength SSL instead.

Table 16-1 lists the various cipher suites supported by WebLogic.

Table 16-1. Cipher suites supported by WebLogic Server

Cipher suite	Symmetric key strength (bits)
TLS_RSA_WITH_RC4_128_SHA	128
TLS_RSA_WITH_RC4_128_MD5	128
TLS_RSA_WITH_DES_CBC_SHA	56
TLS_RSA_EXPORT_WITH_RC4_40_MD5	40
TLS_RSA_EXPORT_WITH_DES40_CBC_SHA	40
TLS_RSA_WITH_3DES_EDE_CBC_SHA	112
TLS_RSA_WITH_NULL_SHA	0
TLS_RSA_WITH_NULL_MD5	0
TLS_RSA_EXPORT1024_WITH_DES_CBC_SHA	56
TLS_RSA_EXPORT124_WITH_RC4_56_SHA	56

The name of the cipher suite captures all of the information about the cipher suite itself. For instance, the TLS_RSA_WITH_DES_CBC_SHA suite indicates that the RSA algorithm will be used for the exchanging the symmetric key, the DES-CBC algorithm will be used for bulk data encryption, and the SHA algorithm will be used for generating the message digests.

Keystores

A *Java Keystore* (JKS) is a standard mechanism for protecting and storing private keys and certificate chains, and for managing the list of certificates of all trusted CAs. You can choose from various tools to insert, remove, or list the items stored in the keystore.

A keystore can hold two kinds of entries: a *key* entry that holds the private key and the associated certificate chain, or a *certificate* entry that holds a trusted CA certificate. Each keystore entry may be accessed via a unique, case-insensitive alias. The entire keystore is protected with its own password. Each entry in the keystore is protected by its own password. In this way, the keystore provides a secure, tamper-proof repository for private keys, certificate chains, and trusted CA certificates.

WebLogic doesn't always use the configured aliases. For example, if you store private keys in a keystore, you need to supply an alias so that WebLogic can determine the private key to be retrieved from the keystore. On the other hand, a keystore may contain a number of trusted CA certificates. In this case, WebLogic retrieves all of the entries within the keystore and therefore doesn't require an alias for each keystore entry. Note that some tools require you to supply an alias when you add an item, even if you are not going to use it.

 In WebLogic 7.0, you could set up only those keystores that held the server's private key and list of trusted CA certificates. The server's public certificate had to be stored in a plain file. SSL configuration in WebLogic 8.1, however, makes it obligatory for you to use keystores— one that holds the server's private key and digital certificate, and another that holds a list of trusted CA certificates.

Configuring WebLogic's SSL

There are three steps to configuring WebLogic's SSL:

1. You need to establish the server's identity, by acquiring a private key and digital certificate for the server. You can either use demonstration keys and certificates supplied with WebLogic or generate your own. Alternatively, you can contact a reputed CA for production-quality certificates. You also need to establish trust for the server. This requires you to configure WebLogic with a keystore that holds the certificates of all the CAs that the server is willing to trust.

2. Once you obtain the server's key and certificate, you need to store them in a keystore* before they can be made available to WebLogic.

3. Finally, you need to fire up the Administration Console and point the server to the appropriate keystore files.

Once you configure the required SSL resources for WebLogic, you need to enable the SSL port. By default, SSL is not enabled for WebLogic because it consumes additional CPU resources when it has to service SSL connection requests. Thus, before you connect to the SSL-enabled port, you must weigh the benefits of secure TCP connections over the overhead of additional CPU processing. Yet secure SSL communication is mandatory in many scenarios. For instance, as we saw in Chapter 13, the Administration Channel requires you to configure SSL support for all servers in the

* WebLogic 7.0 requires that the digital certificate remain in a text file.

WebLogic domain. In a production environment, SSL connections are essential to protecting access to sensitive application services.

Most SSL configuration takes place on a per-server basis. The Configuration/General and Configuration/Keystores & SSL tabs are the most important when configuring SSL in WebLogic 8.1. WebLogic 7.0 users should use the Connections/SSL and Connections/SSL Ports tabs. After configuring the SSL resources needed by the server, you must ensure that the SSL Listen Port Enabled flag is selected and a suitable port number is specified.

To help assimilate these concepts, we will end this section with examples on how to set up one-way and two-way SSL configurations.

Obtaining Keys and Certificates

Your WebLogic distribution comes shipped with a set of "demonstration" keys and certificates. These can be used while you explore WebLogic's SSL configuration options, but should not be used in a production setting. The demonstration keys and certificates are not signed by a well-known CA. In fact, WebLogic provides you with a self-signed CA certificate that you can use to produce your own keys and certificates. Any demonstration certificate generated in this way is signed by a CA called CertGenCAB.

For production-quality SSL, you should use a certificate signed by a well-known CA, such as Entrust.net or Verisign. For this, you need to send a formal CSR to the CA. WebLogic supplies tools with which to create your own certificates and generate these CSRs.

Demonstration keys and certificates

The demonstration keys and certificates are distributed differently in WebLogic 7.0 and WebLogic 8.1. In WebLogic 7.0, they are located in the *WL_HOME\server\lib* directory. When you create a WebLogic domain using the Domain Configuration Wizard, they are copied into the root directory of the new domain. The files *democert.pem* and *demokey.pem* provide the export-strength certificate and private key, while the files *democert1024.pem* and *demokey1024.pem* provide the domestic-strength certificate and private key. In WebLogic 8.1, the demonstration key and certificate already are deposited in a keystore located in the *WL_HOME\server\lib* directory, called *DemoIdentity.jks*. This doesn't mean that you won't need to manipulate key and certificate files, though.

WebLogic 7.0 is also configured with a default keystore, the *cacerts* file, which holds the PEM-encoded certificates of all trusted CAs. This keystore is located in the *WL_HOME\server\lib* directory. In WebLogic 8.1, the default keystore that holds the list of trusted CA certificates is now called *DemoTrust.jks* and is located in the same directory. In fact, this keystore, which we will call the *trust* keystore, holds the certificate for the CA called CertGenCAB, which is the same CA that signs the demonstration certificate. Thus, the default trust keystore and the demonstration certificate/key work together. For instance, if a Node Manager needs to communicate with a WebLogic instance using a demonstration certificate, WebLogic can validate only the Node Manager's certificate, provided it can trust the CA that signed the demonstration certificate. This will be possible only if you set up WebLogic SSL using the default trust keystore.

Refer to the sidebar "keytool—Managing Keystores" in this chapter for more information on how to use the keytool utility to manipulate a keystore.

The CertGen utility

You can use WebLogic's CertGen utility to generate your own demonstration private keys and certificates, signed by CertGenCAB. The *CertgenCA.der* and *CertGenCAKey.der* files, located in the *WL_HOME\server\lib* directory, represent the digital certificate and the private key, respectively, of the demonstration CA trusted by WebLogic. You can issue the following command to generate a new private key and certificate:

```
java utils.CertGen keypass certfile keyfile [export] [hostname]
```

Here, keypass is used to specify a password for the private key, while the certfile and keyfile arguments let you specify the names of the files used to store the digital certificate and private key. The CertGen utility generates domestic-strength certificates by default. If the optional export flag is supplied, the tool will generate export-strength certificates. The hostname argument lets you specify the name of the machine for which the certificate will be generated. If the certificate undergoes host-name verification, the hostname attributed to the certificate will be extracted from this field.

 If you wish to enable hostname verification, you must generate a separate private key and digital certificate for each server instance that needs to accept SSL connections.

Note that if you do not specify a hostname, the CertGen utility invokes the InetAddress.getLocalHost().getHostname() method to determine the subject's common name for the certificate. The getHostName() method is somewhat platform-dependent because it may return a fully qualified domain name on some platforms, and return a short hostname on other platforms. You need to ensure that the hostname returned by this method matches the subject's common name in the certificate. Otherwise, the certificate will be invalidated because the URL doesn't match the domain name used in the certificate's subject. Later, we'll see how you can configure WebLogic to bypass the server name check and utilize your own hostname verifiers.

CertGen generates two versions of the certificate and private key. It creates two *.der* files (*certfile.der* and *keyfile.der*) and two *.pem* files (*certfile.pem* and *keyfile.pem*). You can use either pair when configuring SSL for WebLogic Server. You also can view the contents of the *.der* files in your browser and inspect the details of the new certificate. Refer to the sidebar "Certificate Formats" in this chapter for more information about the certificate formats recognized by WebLogic.

Certificate Formats

WebLogic groks certificates that are in either the *.pem* or *.der* format. The *.der* format is binary and is used to hold only a single certificate. The *.pem* format is textual; you can recognize a certificate in this format because it looks something like this:

```
----BEGIN CERTIFICATE----
...
----END CERTIFICATE----
```

The PEM format lets you store multiple certificates in the same file. This is ideal for a certificate chain in which a list of certificates needs to be stored in the same file. This list is organized so that each certificate is followed by its CA's public certificate. The last certificate in the list is a self-signed certificate from the root CA. Each certificate in this chain then can be stored in a single *.pem* file, in this particular order.

Note that private keys must be stored in the PKCS#5/PKCS#8 PEM format. Some tools such as OpenSSL generate certificates with additional text before the "----BEGIN CERTIFICATE----" line. In such cases, you need to remove the text before this line to obtain a valid certificate.

If you have a *.der* certificate and you need a *.pem*-style equivalent—for example, because you need to add it to a certificate chain—you can use WebLogic's der2pem utility. Here's how you would invoke the der2pem tool to handle the conversion:

```
java utils.der2pem derFile [headerFile] [footerFile]
```

By default, the certificate header and footer adhere to the standard *.pem* format. However, if you are creating a key, you need to specify the locations of two separate files that hold the certificate header and footer:

```
### contents of mypemheader:
-----BEGIN RSA PRIVATE KEY-----
### contents of mypemfooter:
-----END RSA PRIVATE KEY-----
```

Make sure to append a newline character at the end of the line in the header and footer files.

Microsoft also can act as a CA, but issues its certificates in a different format: *p7b*. Certificates issued by Microsoft can be recognized by WebLogic provided you first convert them to the *.pem* format. You can accomplish this by double-clicking the certificate file in Windows Explorer, and then selecting the Certificates/Certificate Export option from the pop-up window to export the certificate as a Base 64–encoded certificate. This resulting certificate file then can be used as a PEM certificate.

The Certificate Request Generator tool

Until now, you've had to persevere with private keys and digital certificates that are not fit for a production environment. Fortunately, WebLogic's Certificate Request Generator tool eases the task of obtaining a production-quality certificate for the private key. It lets you generate a CSR that can be submitted to any trusted CA. A trusted CA then will authenticate the CSR (usually offline) before issuing a signed digital certificate.

The Certificate Request Generator tool, which runs as a servlet on the Administration Server, collects all the necessary data and then generates a private key and certificate request file. Once the trusted CA has authenticated your details, it will return a signed certificate verifying your public key. In some instances, the CA may return a certificate chain, whereby each certificate in the chain authenticates the public key of the signer of the previous certificate in the chain.

 You don't necessarily need to use the private key generated by the request generator tool. You can use any other private key as well, so long as it adheres to the PKCS#5/PKCS#8 PEM format.

Because the Certificate Request Generator tool runs as a servlet on WebLogic, you need to first deploy the web application that packages the servlet. You can accomplish this by copying the *certificate.war* file located in the *WL_HOME\server\lib* directory to the *applications* directory under the domain's root directory. The web application will be deployed successfully once you target the web application to the Administration Server.

Now you can invoke the Certificate Request Generator tool from your browser by navigating to the following URL: *http://adminserver:port/certificate/*. Use the login credentials of WebLogic's administration user account to gain entry. You then need to fill out a form with all the necessary information required by the digital certificate. Most importantly, you must specify the fully qualified hostname that clients will use to access the server. The tool then generates three files:

hostname-key.der
> This represents the Base 64–encoded server's private key. Retain this private key for subsequent SSL configuration.

hostname-request.dem
> This represents the CSR in binary format.

hostname-request.pem
> This represents a *.pem*-formatted CSR file that must be submitted to a CA. It holds the same data as the *.der* file but is encoded in ASCII. You can copy and paste the contents of this CSR file into an HTML form or an email.

The servlet can also submit the request file to a CA—either VeriSign or Baltimore Technologies. You don't have to use these CAs—you could quite easily email the .*pem* file to any preferred CA. If you do submit the CSR manually, make sure that you select BEA WebLogic Server as the Server type. The trusted CA can then ensure that the signed certificate is compatible with WebLogic Server.

Storing Private Keys and Certificates

At this point, we assume that you have obtained the server's identity (private key and digital certificate) and the certificates of a number of CAs that you trust. The final task before you can configure WebLogic's SSL is to place these items in the appropriate keystores. For this, you need to understand how to create and populate a keystore with private keys and trusted CA certificates. WebLogic's ImportPrivateKey utility can be used to import private keys and trusted CA certificates into a keystore. For instance, the following command shows how to import an existing public/private key pair into the default keystore:

```
java utils.ImportPrivateKey myIdentity.jks mykeystorepass \
        myalias mykeypass mycert.pem mykey.pem
```

In this case, we've imported the .*pem*-encoded private key and digital certificate into the keystore named *myIdentity.jks*, and created an alias, myalias, that references the new entry in the keystore. You could have easily imported .*der* files holding the private key and digital certificate. Remember, you need to specify a password both for the keystore itself and for the key entry within the keystore. Refer to the sidebar "keytool—Managing Keystores" in this chapter for more information on the structure of a keystore.

Trusted CA certificates are essential when WebLogic needs to validate any incoming certificates. The following command shows how to use the keytool utility to load a trusted CA certificate into a keystore:

```
keytool -import -trustcacerts -alias arbuniquealias
        -file y:\server\lib\certgenca.der
        -keystore myTrust.jks -storepass 12341234
```

Remember, all private key entries in a keystore are accessed via their unique alias. Even though WebLogic never uses the alias to access a trusted CA certificate from the keystore, you still need to specify the alias when using keytool to import a trusted CA certificate into a keystore.

Configuring SSL for WebLogic 8.1

WebLogic 8.1 requires you to set up a keystore to hold the server's identity (private key and public certificate), as well as a keystore to hold all the trusted CA certificates. Once you prepare the identity and trust keystores, you simply need to point WebLogic to the location of these keystores, specify the alias for the private key, and then enable SSL.

keytool — Managing Keystores

Your JDK installation comes equipped with the keytool utility for managing a keystore of private keys, digital certificates, and trusted CA certificates. The *WL_HOME\server\lib\cacerts* file is an example of a JKS keystore that holds the certificates of all root CAs trusted by WebLogic.

A keystore can hold two kinds of entries: a *key* entry that holds the private key and the associated certificate, or a *certificate* entry that holds a trusted CA certificate. Each keystore entry may be accessed via a unique, case-insensitive alias. The entire keystore is protected with its own password, and each entry in the keystore is protected by its own password. In this way, the keystore provides a secure, tamper-proof repository for private keys, certificate chains, and trusted CA certificates.

The keytool utility is the standard way to manipulate entries within a keystore. For instance, the keytool utility can generate a private key and a self-signed certificate, and then create a keystore entry using this public/private key pair. Here a single-element certificate chain consisting of a self-signed certificate is linked to the private key. The keytool utility can also create a CSR, which then can be submitted to any trusted CA. The new certificate you procure can replace the existing self-signed certificate in the keystore. If you use the keytool utility to load any trusted CA certificates into the keystore, ensure that the trusted CA certificates are genuine.

To list all the entries in a keystore, use the following command:

```
keytool -list -keystore mykeystore.jks
```

If you run this command on the *cacerts* file, it lists all the trusted CA certificates, including certificates of the demonstration CAs. To create a new keystore, use the following command:

```
keytool -genkey -keystore mykeystore.jks -storepass mykeystorepass
```

To generate a new private key and a matching self-signed certificate, use the following command:

```
keytool -alias myalias -genkey -keypass mykeypass -keystore mykeystore.jks
  -storepass mykeystorepass
```

To replace a self-signed certificate with a production-quality certificate or to import a trusted CA certificate into a keystore, run the following command:

```
keytool -import -alias myalias -file mycert.pem -keypass mykeypss -keystore
mykeystore.jks -storepass mykeystorepass
```

If you intend to import a trusted CA certificate, no existing entry for myalias should be in the keystore. Otherwise, the keytool utility simply replaces the self-signed certificate for the private key with the specified certificate file. Refer to your JDK documentation for more information on how to use the keytool utility to manage keystores.

Configuring the identity and trust keystores

You can set up the keystores for a server by selecting the server node from the left frame of the Administration Console and then navigating to the Configuration/ Keystores & SSL tab. Here, you can select the Change option next to the Keystore Configuration title to specify the locations of the keystores. You will be presented with four options for the identity and trust keystores:

Demo Identity and Demo Trust
> Instructs WebLogic to use the demonstration identity and trust keystores, *DemoIdentity.jks* and *DemoTrust.jks*, which are installed in the *WL_HOME\ server\lib* directory. In addition, the server uses the alias DemoIdentity to access the private key and digital certificate stored in the identity keystore.

Custom Identity and Java Standard Trust
> Lets you configure the server to use your own identity keystore, and the standard list of trusted CA certificates that are provided by your JDK—i.e., *JAVA_ HOME\jre\lib\security\cacerts*. When you configure a custom identity keystore for the server, you must supply the name of the keystore file, the type of the keystore (for example, jks), and the pass phrase that should be used to access the keystore.

Custom Identity and Custom Trust
> Lets you configure the server to use your own identity and trust keystores. For each keystore, you will have to supply the name of the keystore file, the type of the keystore (for example, jks), and the pass phrase that should be used to access the keystore.

Custom Identity and Command Line Trust
> Lets you set up the server to use your own identity keystore only, and assumes that you will specify the location of the trust keystore from the command line.

Use the -Dweblogic.security.SSL.trustedCAKeyStore option to set up the server's trust keystore from the command line:

```
java -Dweblogic.security.SSL.trustedCAKeyStore=c:\trustedStore.jks \
    ... weblogic.Server
```

Setting up the server identity

Once you've configured the identity keystore for WebLogic, you still need to associate the server with its private key and digital certificate. By default, when you configure WebLogic with the demonstration identity keystore (*DemoIdentity.jks*), it uses the alias DemoIdentity to access the private key and public certificate. For a custom identity keystore, however, you must supply the alias and pass phrase assigned to the key entry within the keystore. Only then can WebLogic access the private key and certificate from the identity keystore.

Although the server's identity is established when you configure the keystores for the server, you can change the server's identity from the Configuration/Keystores & SSL tab as well. Simply choose the Change option next to the SSL Configuration title to specify a new alias and pass phrase for an entry within the keystore.

 For backward-compatibility, this option also lets you configure a file-based server identity, whereby you can supply the names of the files that hold the private key and public certificate.

Enabling SSL

The final step in the server's SSL configuration is to enable SSL. Select the Configuration/General tab and tick the SSL Listen Port Enabled option. In addition, choose a suitable value for the SSL Listen Port option to determine the server's SSL port. After a server restart, you should have a fully operational SSL listen port.

Configuring SSL for WebLogic 7.0

Once you've obtained the server's identity (private key and public certificate) and a keystore that holds all trusted CA certificates, you need to point the server to the location of the private key, the public certificate, and the trust keystore, and then enable SSL on the desired ports. As mentioned earlier, any public certificate used to configure SSL on WebLogic 7.0 always must be stored in a file. However, the server's private key and trusted CA certificates can be stored either in a file or in a JKS keystore. In the following section, we look at how to configure WebLogic with keystores that hold the private keys and trusted CA certificates (which we recommend you do). If you need to store the private key and trusted CA certificates in plain files instead, you should skip ahead to the section, "Using plain files for the private key and trusted CA certificates."

Configuring a Keystore Provider

Most of the SSL configuration options are available on the Connections/SSL tab for the selected server. Select the Configure Keystore Providers link to equip WebLogic with keystores that hold the server's private key and trusted CA certificates.

A Keystore Provider provides domain-wide access to JKS keystores for the private keys and trusted CA certificates. You can access the Keystore Provider either from the Configure Keystore Providers option on the SSL tab or from under the Security/Realms/Providers/Keystores node in the left frame of the Administration Console. By default, a WebLogic domain is configured with a Keystore Provider called *DefaultKeyStore*. On the General tab, you then can adjust the following SSL attributes to allow WebLogic to access the keystores holding the private keys and trusted CA certificates:

Private Key Store Location
Use this option to specify the location of the keystore that holds the private key. You may specify a location relative to the domain's root directory. By default, the Keystore Provider is configured to use a keystore named *wlDefaultKeyStore.jks*.

Private Key Store Pass Phrase
Use this option to specify the password you assigned to the keystore.

Root CA Key Store Location
Use this option to specify the location of the keystore that holds the certificates of CAs trusted by WebLogic. You don't need to configure this attribute if the same keystore is used to store both the private keys and trusted CA certificates.

Root CA Key Store Pass Phrase
Use this option to specify the password (if any) assigned to the keystore holding the trusted CA certificates.

 Because the Keystore Provider is configured for the entire domain, the keystore file(s) must be placed in the same location for all servers in the domain. Otherwise, the server instance will be unable to locate the configured keystore.

You can use the -Dweblogic.security.SSL.trustedCAKeyStore option to configure the trust keystore from the command line when starting up the server:

```
java -Dweblogic.security.SSL.trustedCAKeyStore=c:\trustedStore.jks \
    ... weblogic.Server
```

Here, *c:\trustedStore.jks* refers to the location of the keystore holding your trusted CA certificates. In fact, if you create a WebLogic domain using the Domain Configuration Wizard, the *startWebLogic* scripts also configures WebLogic to use the default keystore for the trusted CA certificates:

```
-Dweblogic.security.SSL.trustedCAKeyStore=\WL_HOME\server\lib\cacerts
```

Remember, you need to configure the Keystore Provider only if you do *not* intend to store the private keys and trusted CA certificates in ordinary files.

A keystore for trusted CA certificates is particularly important if you intend to configure two-way SSL for the server. Because you can specify the keystore for the trusted CA certificates in several ways, WebLogic adopts the following sequence when looking for a trusted CA that can vouch for the authenticity of a client's certificate:

- If you used the weblogic.security.SSL.trustedCAKeyStore option from the command line when starting up WebLogic Server, it looks in the keystore specified by this option. By default, WebLogic's startup scripts use the trusted CA certificates in the *WL_HOME\server\lib\cacerts* keystore.

- If you didn't use this command-line option to specify the keystore location, WebLogic uses the Root CA Key Store Location and Root CA Key Store Pass Phrase attributes of the configured Keystore Provider to access the keystore for the trusted CA certificates. If both private keys and trusted CA certificates are stored in the same keystore, WebLogic uses the Primary Key Store Location and Primary Key Store Pass Phrase attributes to access the keystore.

- If you haven't configured a Keystore Provider for the domain, WebLogic has no choice but to inspect the default keystore file that is shipped with your JDK—i.e., the *JAVA_HOME\jre\lib\security\cacerts* keystore.

Remember, a Keystore Provider offers domain-wide access to keystores that hold the private keys and trusted CA certificates. A keystore, on the other hand, is configured on a per-machine basis. Thus, if your domain has multiple security realms or multiple servers running on the same machine, they all can be configured to use the same keystore.

Setting up the server identity

Once you configure the Keystore Provider, you need to return to the Connections/ SSL tab for the selected server. Here you must supply values for the following SSL attributes in order to complete the SSL configuration for the server's identity:

Server Private Key Alias
 Use this option to specify the alias for the server's private key in the keystore.

Server Private Key Passphrase
 Use this option to specify the password that was used to protect the server's private key.

Server Certificate File Name
 Use this attribute to configure the location of the server's digital certificate (e.g., *democert.pem*). Remember, WebLogic insists that you store the server's digital certificate in an ordinary file (and not in a keystore).

WebLogic then can use the configured Keystore Provider to access the keystore holding the server's private key. It can also use the configured alias and pass phrase to look up the private key from the keystore.

Using plain files for the private key and trusted CA certificates

If you intend to store the private key and trusted CA certificates in ordinary files, you need to configure the following SSL attributes:

Server Key File Name
 Use this setting to specify the location of the server's private key (e.g., *democert1024.pem*). If the private key has been protected via a password, you also must specify the weblogic.management.pkpassword argument from the command line when starting up WebLogic.

Trusted CA File Name

Use this attribute to specify the name of the file that holds the PEM-encoded certificates of all trusted CAs. (e.g., *trusted-ca.pem*).

Once again, these SSL attributes are available from within the Connections/SSL tab, after selecting the desired server from the left pane of the Administration Console.

> These SSL options, which let you refer to keys and certificates stored in ordinary files, are deprecated and exist only for compatibility with previous versions. Even though they provide a quick and easy way to set up WebLogic SSL—for instance, when you need to use demonstration keys and certificates during development/testing—we recommend that you store the private keys and trusted CA certificates in keystores.

Enabling SSL

The final step in the configuration is to enable SSL. Select the Connections/SSL Ports tab and tick the Enable SSL Listen Port option. In addition, choose a suitable value for the SSL Listen Port option to determine the server's SSL port. After a server restart, you should have a fully operational SSL listen port.

Other SSL Configuration Issues

This section looks at other issues of WebLogic's SSL setup, including how to configure two-way SSL, disable hostname verification, and choose the appropriate level of certificate validation. These configuration issues are available from the Administration Console for the selected server, under the Advanced options of the Keystores & SSL tab in WebLogic 8.1, and in the Connections/SSL tab in WebLogic 7.0.

Two-way SSL

In WebLogic 8.1, you can use the "Two way client Certificate behavior" option[*] under the Advanced options in the Keystores & SSL tab, to configure two-way SSL for the server. The default value for this setting is "Client Certificates not requested," which means that by default, two-way SSL is not enabled for the server. Thus, WebLogic does not request a client to present a certificate when it establishes an SSL connection. However, you can enable two-way SSL by choosing from two other possible values for the "Two way client Certificate behavior" setting.

---

[*] In WebLogic 7.0, the Connection/ SSL tab provides analogous settings for configuring two-way SSL—i.e., the Client Certificate Enforced and Client Certificate Requested But Not Enforced flags. By default, both flags are disabled, which means that two-way SSL is disabled for the server.

Client Certificates requested and enforced

If you select this option, all clients are forced to authenticate themselves to the server. This means that the client must also present its public certificate to the server when initiating an SSL connection. If the client fails to do so, the SSL connection request is refused.

Client Certificates requested but not enforced

If you select this option, WebLogic still requests the client for its digital certificate. However, unlike the previous case, WebLogic does *not* terminate the connection if the client fails to furnish a certificate and decides to remain anonymous. However, if the client does submit a certificate as proof of its identity, and the server is unable to validate the certificate for some reason, the SSL connection request is refused.

Remember, if you do enable two-way SSL for the server, you must also equip the server with a trust keystore.

Hostname verification

WebLogic performs hostname verification whenever it needs to validate a certificate. A hostname verifier compares the hostname within the certificate's SubjectDN with the hostname of the other party that is involved in the SSL connection. If the two hostnames do not match, the SSL connection is aborted. This is the behavior of the default hostname verifier installed with WebLogic. A WebLogic server will need to validate a certificate whenever it is acting as an SSL client during an SSL handshake. This will happen, for example, whenever one WebLogic instance communicates with another using two-way SSL.

In WebLogic 8.1, you can use the Hostname Verification setting within the Advanced options of the Keystores & SSL tab to adjust the hostname verification behavior. The default value for this setting is BEA Hostname Verifier, which means that the hostname verifier works in the way that we've just described. If you choose None as the value for this setting, you disable hostname verification altogether. This means WebLogic does not verify whether the hostname URL matches the hostname embedded within the SubjectDN field of the digital certificate sent back by the other party. Hostname verification should be disabled only during development and testing—for instance, when clients access your server using its internal IP address instead of its URL in the certificate. You can disable hostname verification from the command line as well, by setting the following property when you run an SSL client:

```
java -Dweblogic.security.SSL.ignoreHostnameVerification=true \
    ... com.oreilly.wlguide.sslclients.MyClientA
```

If you need to replace the default hostname verifier with your own custom hostname verifier, choose the Custom Hostname Verifier option as the value of the Hostname

Verifier setting.* In this case, you must specify the fully qualified name of a Java class that implements the `weblogic.security.SSL.HostnameVerifier` interface. You can specify the custom hostname verifier from the command line as well, by setting the following option when running an SSL client:

```
java  -Dweblogic.security.SSL.HostnameVerifier=classname \
    ... com.oreilly.wlguide.sslclients.MyClientA
```

A custom hostname verifier is ideal if you need to modify the default behavior in any way. To prevent man-in-the-middle attacks, we recommend that you do not disable hostname verification in a production environment. When enabling hostname verification, you should ensure that all certificates use the correct hostnames and not IP addresses, and that all URLs use hostnames rather than IP addresses.

Certificate validation options

A trusted CA may issue a certificate chain, starting with the digital certificate that holds the public key, followed by the public certificate of the CA that signed the certificate before it, and so on, ending with a self-signed certificate from a trusted CA. Previous versions of WebLogic did not properly validate whether a CA issued each certificate in the chain. As a result, WebLogic was unable to detect certificates in a chain that potentially were signed by parties using their own personal certificate. The current WebLogic release requires that each certificate in the chain have its Basic Constraint property set to CA, thereby ensuring that all certificates in the chain are issued by a CA. By default, any certificate in the chain that doesn't meet this criterion is rejected. In fact, the IETF RFC 2459 standard that the industry is converging on goes a step further and asks that the extension be marked "critical" as well.

You can choose from several certificate validation levels. You can adjust the level of certificate validation via the command-line option specified when starting up WebLogic Server:

```
java -Dweblogic.security.SSL.enforceConstraints=option  \
    ... weblogic.Server
```

WebLogic supports the following levels of certificate validation:

strong *or* true

> Use this option to ensure that each certificate in the chain has its Basic Constraint property set to CA. WebLogic uses this level of certificate validation by default.

strict

> Use this option to enforce the IETF RFC 2459 standard. This level provides the most secure certificate validation strategy, and ensures that the Basic Constraint extension is set to CA and marked as "critical." This option isn't configured to be the default because many CA certificates currently don't adhere to the standard.

---

* In WebLogic 7.0, the Connections/SSL tab provides settings that let you turn off hostname verification for the selected server, and also override the default behavior with a custom hostname verifier.

off

Use this option to disable all certificate validation. We don't recommend that you turn off certificate validations in a production environment.

If possible, set the certificate validation level to strict, as it offers maximum security. WebLogic also provides a utility for checking whether a certificate chain will be rejected by the server. The utility can take as an argument either a Java keystore or a PEM-encoded file:

```
java utils.ValidateCertChain -pem mycertfile.pem
```

The tool will notify you of any CA certificates in the chain that are not valid. In case the certificate chain is invalid, you can either adjust the validation constraints, or more beneficially, apply for CA certificates that do adhere to the standard.

SSL debugging

SSL debugging provides you with more detailed information about the events that transpire during an SSL handshake. You can enable SSL debug tracing for applications involved in SSL communication. These debugging options can be supplied from the command line before starting WebLogic Server:

```
-Dssl.debug=true -Dweblogic.StdoutDebugEnabled=true
```

You can configure the same command-line options for a Java client using WebLogic's SSL implementation.

Export key lifespan and SSL login timeout

WebLogic lets you adjust the values of several other miscellaneous SSL configuration options. These options assume default values that you don't generally need to change.

Export Key Lifespan
Use this attribute to specify the number of times the server can use an exportable key between a domestic server and an exportable client before generating a new key. The more secure you want the server to be, the fewer times the key should be used before generating a new key.

SSL Login Timeout
Use this attribute to set the maximum duration allowed for a login sequence. The login sequence times out when its duration exceeds the value of this setting. By default, the SSL login sequence times out after 25 seconds. A value of 0 disables the SSL login timeout.

If your clients have a high network latency, perhaps due to a congested pipe leading into your server, you may want to raise this timeout value. The timeout option is available in the Advanced section of the network channel Configuration screen in WebLogic 8.1. In WebLogic 7.0, use the Connections/Tuning tab.

Using SSL in a cluster

Because SSL configuration takes place on a server-by-server basis, you must ensure that each server has its own copy of the private key and digital certificate. Likewise, if you've configured a Keystore Provider, you must ensure the keystores are placed in the same locations on each server. If you've configured Node Managers to run on the different machines in the domain, you also must ensure that each Node Manager has access to the relevant SSL resources.

SSL Configuration Scenarios

As an example, we will use CertGen to create our own private key and digital certificate, and then use these SSL resources to configure the Administration Server to use a domain-wide administration port. As explained in Chapter 13, this creates a dedicated administration channel, which always requires the use of SSL. Then, we extend this setup by configuring two-way SSL. To access the Administration Console under these conditions, you will have to configure your browser with a certificate that it can present to WebLogic.

One-way SSL

Let's start by creating the digital certificate and private key. You can accomplish this by invoking the CertGen utility:

```
java utils.CertGen mypassword mycertfile mykeyfile export
```

This generates an export-strength digital certificate *mycertfile.pem*, and a private key *mykeyfile.pem*. Of course, if you received your certificate and private key from a proper CA, you can skip this step and use your production items instead. Now, import the private key into a JKS keystore. The following command shows how to load the private key in a new keystore file *myIdentityStore.jks*:

```
java utils.ImportPrivateKey myIdentityStore.jks mykeystorepass
                myalias mypassword mycertfile.pem mykeyfile.pem
```

Notice how we've assigned a pass phrase to the keystore, the alias myalias for the private key, and a pass phrase to protect the key entry.

Now you need to configure WebLogic to use this keystore. Select the server from the left pane of the Administration Console, and then select the Configuration/Keystores & SSL tab. Select the Change option under the Keystore Configuration. Here you can simply choose the "Custom Identity and Java Standard Trust" option. Set the keystore filename to *myIdentityStore.jks*, the keystore type to jks, and the pass phrase to mykeystorepass. Finally, set the private key alias to myalias, and the key pass phrase to mypassword.

Now, in order to enable the domain wide administration port, click the top-level Domain node in the left pane of the Administration Console and then tick the Enable

Administration Port option. The domain-wide administration port defaults to port 9002.

This completes the SSL configuration for the Administration Server, so you can reboot the Administration Server after applying all the changes to the server's setup. Once the Administration Server is up and running, you can access the Administration Console by pointing a browser to the following URL: *https://hostname:9002/console*. Because you've forced all the administration traffic over the SSL-enabled administration channel, the Administration Console is no longer available over the plain HTTP port.

The first time you access the site, your browser will pop up a message indicating that a certificate has been sent from the server (i.e., the server has presented its digital certificate to prove its identity). Because we've configured a digital certificate signed by a dummy CA, the browser warns that this is the case and gives you the opportunity to view the certificate. If you do view the certificate, notice that the certificate has been issued by a demonstration CA called CertGenCAB. At this stage, you can be assured that the one-way SSL configuration for the Administration Server is well and operational.

If a Java client needs to communicate with the Administration Server over SSL port 9002, the client must be able to validate the digital certificate sent back by the Administration Server. As you have learned already, this is possible if you configure a keystore that holds a list of trusted CA certificates. For instance, if you intend to use the weblogic.Admin tool to update the domain's configuration, the SSL connection to the Administration Server succeeds only if you also set the list of trusted CA certificates for the tool:

```
java -Dweblogic.security.TrustKeyStore=DemoTrust
    weblogic.Admin -url t3s://10.0.10.10:9002/
    -username system -password pssst VERSION
```

In WebLogic 7.0, use the following options:

```
java -Dweblogic.security.SSL.trustedCAKeyStore=x:/server/lib/cacerts
    weblogic.Admin -url t3s://10.0.10.10:9002/
    -username system -password pssst VERSION
```

Two-way SSL

Setting up two-way SSL for the server should not be a problem. Because you are using demonstration certificates, you simply need to configure WebLogic to use the demonstration trust keystore. Choose the Configuration/Keystores & SSL tab again. Select the Change option under Keystore Configuration, and this time select the "Custom Identity and Custom Trust" option. Leave the details of the custom identity keystore unchanged, and modify only the details for the custom trust keystore. Enter the absolute path to the *DemoTrust.jks* keystore (or copy it into the domain directory and use a relative path). This keystore isn't protected by any password, so you can leave the pass phrase field blank.

In the Advanced options of the Configuration/Keystores & SSL tab, set the two-way SSL behavior to "Client Certs Requested and Enforced." By enabling two-way SSL for the server, any client that needs to create an SSL connection must present a certificate to the server as proof of its identity. This requirement is especially crucial to the Node Manager because it relies on two-way SSL to protect communications with the Administration Server and all Managed Servers running on its machine. Restart the Administration Server for the changes to take effect.

If you now try to access the Administration Console using a browser, you will fail unless your browser has been populated with a certificate that it can present to the server. As a test, you can populate your browser with the certificate you created earlier. The only hitch is that most browsers want the certificate in the PKCS/12 format. To achieve this, we can use the freely available openssl tool to convert the certificate into a format understood by Mozilla and IE:

```
openssl pkcs12 -inkey mykeyfile.pem -in mycertfile.pem
              -out myCert.p12 -export
```

Now simply import the generated certificate *myCert.p12* into your browser. The next time you access the Administration Console, your browser will send its certificate to WebLogic, and you should successfully reach the login page.

Programmatic SSL

SSL clients are Java programs that use SSL-enabled connections to communicate with WebLogic Server. These clients could be running within WebLogic itself—for instance, as a servlet. WebLogic uses the Certicom JSSE extensions in its implementation of the JSSE, and provides APIs that ease the task of communicating over an SSL channel. In fact, the APIs let you create SSL-enabled socket connections, URL connections over SSL, and JNDI contexts using certificate-based authentication. You don't have to use WebLogic's implementation of the JSSE in Java clients, though what follows in this section assumes that you are. For server-side code, you have to use WebLogic's JSSE.

 At the time of publishing this book, WebLogic 7.0 is certified only for JKD 1.3 and not for JDK 1.4. You will experience SSL problems if you use JDK 1.4 to run your clients and/or the server. An unofficial way around some of these problems is to delete the file *jre\lib\jsse.jar* that is shipped with your JDK 1.4 distribution. You do *not* need to do this if you are using WebLogic 8.1.

Whenever you run an SSL-enabled Java client, it is very important that you supply the correct values for the environment settings. Without these system properties, your Java clients surely will fail. For instance, any Java client that needs to use WebLogic's SSL implementation must set the following system property:

```
-Djava.protocol.handler.pkgs=com.certicom.net.ssl
```

Otherwise, the client may be using an alternative SSL implementation; therefore, you may get the following exception when creating an HTTPS URL connection:

```
Exception in thread "main" java.net.MalformedURLException: unknown protocol: https
```

If the client is intended to run within WebLogic itself, it implicitly relies on WebLogic's SSL implementation and you do not need to set this system property. Also, if the client needs to validate an incoming certificate, you must ensure that the client is configured with the location of a keystore that holds a number of root CA certificates:

```
-Dweblogic.security.SSL.trustedCAKeyStore=x:\server\lib\cacerts
```

Otherwise, the Java client will experience handshake errors similar to this:

```
java.io.IOException: Write Channel Closed, possible SSL handshaking
or trust failure
```

Similarly, if the Java client attempts to make an SSL connection to a server that requires two-way SSL, and the client fails to present a digital certificate as proof of its identity, the client will experience a fatal handshake error indicating the reason for dropping the connection:

```
javax.net.ssl.SSLHandshakeException: FATAL Alert:HANDSHAKE_FAILURE - The handshake
handler was unable to negotiate an acceptable set of security parameters.
```

URL Connections

The `weblogic.net.http` package contains two useful classes for establishing URL connections. Use an `HttpURLConnection` object to establish plain-text URL connections and an `HttpsURLConnection` object to set up SSL-protected URL connections. The following example illustrates how to create a plain URL connection to a resource on a remote server:

```
URL url = new URL("http", host, portnumber, "/index.html");
weblogic.net.http.HttpURLConnection connection =
        new weblogic.net.http.HttpURLConnection(url);
connection.connect();
// ... Work with the connection, open inputstream, etc.  ...
System.err.println(con.getResponseCode());
InputStream in = con.getInputStream();
byte buf[] = new byte[256];
int numRead ;
while ( (numRead  = in.read(buf)) != -1 ) {
  System.out.write(buf, 0, numRead);
}
connection.disconnect();
```

Once the client has connected to the specified URL, it obtains the response code and uses the input stream from the `HttpURLConnection` object to read and print the contents of the HTML page. In order to make an SSL connection to a resource on a server, you need to create an `HttpsURLConnection` object that connects to the specified

URL. The following example shows how to create an SSL connection to the same HTML page, but this time uses the *https* protocol:

```
URL url = new URL("https", host, port, "/index.html");
weblogic.net.http.HttpsURLConnection sconnection =
        new weblogic.net.http.HttpsURLConnection(url);
sconnection.connect();
// ... Work with the connection, open inputstream, etc. ...
sconnection.disconnect();
```

However, if the server was configured for two-way SSL authentication, you need to use the HttpsURLConnection object to supply additional SSL resources from the client's end. The following code sample shows how to connect to an SSL-protected resource on a server configured for two-way SSL:

```
URL url = new URL("https", host, port, "/index.html");
weblogic.net.http.HttpsURLConnection con =
        new weblogic.net.http.HttpsURLConnection(url);
// Now we create inputstreams to the key and certificate
FileInputStream keyFile = new FileInputStream(KEYFILE);
FileInputStream certFile = new FileInputStream(CERTFILE);
con.loadLocalIdentity(certFile, keyFile, KEYPASSWORD.toCharArray());
con.connect();
// ... Work with the connection, open inputstream, etc. ...
con.disconnect();
```

In this case, we used the loadLocalIdentity() method to furnish the HttpsURLConnection object with the files that hold the client's digital certificate and private key. Of course, you also must specify the password used to protect the client's private key. For instance, you easily could use the PEM-encoded digital certificate and private key for the client:

```
//...
FileInputStream keyFile = new FileInputStream("mykeyfile.pem");
FileInputStream certFile = new FileInputStream("mycertfile.pem");
con.loadLocalIdentity(certFile, keyFile, ("mypassword").toCharArray());
//...
```

The loadLocalIdentity() method on an HttpsURLConnection object also can extract the client's private key from within a JKS keystore. In this case, use the standard java.security package to access and manipulate the keystore:

```
URL url = new URL("https", host, port, "/index.html");
weblogic.net.http.HttpsURLConnection con =
        new weblogic.net.http.HttpsURLConnection(url);

// Load key and certificate from the keystore
KeyStore ks = KeyStore.getInstance("jks");
ks.load(new FileInputStream(KEYSTORE_NAME), KEYSTORE_PASSWORD.toCharArray());
PrivateKey key =
    (PrivateKey) ks.getKey(KEY_ALIAS, KEY_PASSWORD.toCharArray());
Certificate[] certChain = ks.getCertificateChain(KEY_ALIAS);
con.loadLocalIdentity(certChain, key);
con.connect();
```

```
// ... Work with the connection, open inputstream, etc.  ...
con.disconnect( );
```

Clearly, you need to specify the keystore location and the pass phrase used to protect the keystore in order to create a KeyStore object. Using this KeyStore instance, you can do the following:

- Extract the client's private key using the alias for the key entry, and the password used to protect the key entry

- Extract the certificate chain associated with the client's private key (using the same alias)

You then can use this combination of the private key and the matching certificate chain to set up the client's identity. When a client invokes the connect( ) method on the HttpsURLConnection object, the server can use the key and certificate chain to authenticate the client and later negotiate an acceptable set of parameters for the SSL connection. Later, we shall see how to use the setHostnameVerifierJSSE( ) method on the HttpsURLConnection object to configure a custom hostname verifier for the client.

SSL Sockets

SSL sockets are the equivalent of TCP sockets—they allow you to connect to an SSL-enabled port and then use one of the configured protocols to invoke a service available on the port. SSL sockets provide a low-level API for interacting with SSL-protected services. You need to be familiar with the underlying protocol before you can access any resource. Nevertheless, SSL sockets are extremely versatile and allow you to build powerful clients that can do more than just ordinary HTTPS connections.

The JSSE API plays a major role in setting up SSL socket connections. In particular, a client must create a javax.net.ssl.SSLSocket object to connect to the SSL port on a running server. Using WebLogic's SSL implementation, all of the client's SSL configuration revolves around the weblogic.security.SSL.SSLContext class. An SSLContext instance provides the context for any SSL socket connections you create:

- It helps you configure the client's identity—i.e., you can initialize the context with the client's private key and matching certificate chain.

- You can assign a custom trust manager, an instance of the TrustManagerJSSE interface, to the SSLContext object and supply your own validation logic for the server's certificate chain.

- You can assign a custom hostname verifier—for example, a HostnameVerifierJSSE instance—to the SSLContext object.

- You may choose to register one or more handshake listeners that can automatically react to notifications indicating that the SSL handshake sequence has completed.

Most importantly, once you've initialized the SSLContext object, you can use it to obtain an SSL socket factory. This SSLSocketFactory instance will allow you to establish socket connections to an SSL-enabled port on a running WebLogic instance.

Using SSLSocket

Let's look at how to use SSLContext to set up an SSL socket connection to the web server over HTTPS, and then interact with the port. In this case, the Java client will use a mixture of WebLogic's SSL implementation classes and the standard JSSE interfaces:

```
import java.security.KeyStore;
import java.security.PrivateKey;
import java.security.cert.Certificate;
import javax.net.ssl.HandshakeCompletedEvent;
import javax.net.ssl.HandshakeCompletedListener;
import javax.net.ssl.SSLSocket;
import javax.security.cert.X509Certificate;
import weblogic.security.SSL.HostnameVerifierJSSE;
import weblogic.security.SSL.SSLContext;
import weblogic.security.SSL.SSLSocketFactory;
import weblogic.security.SSL.TrustManagerJSSE;
```

The SSLContext class provides a getInstance() factory method for creating an SSLContext object. In our case, we intend to set up an SSLContext object for socket connections to an HTTPS port:

```
SSLContext ctx = SSLContext.getInstance("https");
```

Using a custom hostname verifier

The next step is to assign a custom hostname verifier to the SSLContext object. A hostname verifier assures the client that the server's hostname to which the client connects matches the server name in the SubjectDN field of the server's digital certificate. WebLogic requires that any custom hostname verifier class implement the weblogic.security.SSL.HostnameVerifierJSSE interface. This interface exposes a single method, verify(), which conveniently accepts two arguments: the server's hostname URL and the hostname embedded in the server's certificate. Here is a sample implementation for the hostname verifier:

```
HostnameVerifierJSSE myVerifier = new HostnameVerifierJSSE() {
  public boolean verify(String urlHostname, String certHostname) {
   return urlHostname.equals(certHostname);
  }
};
ctx.setHostnameVerifierJSSE(myVerifier);
```

Notice how we've invoked the setHostnameVerifierJSSE() method to register our hostname verifier with the SSLContext object. Clearly, if the verify() method always returns true, you are programmatically mimicking what happens when you actually disable hostname verification from the command line:

```
-Dweblogic.security.SSL.ignoreHostnameVerification=false
```

Using a custom trust manager

For the next step, we assign a custom trust manager. A trust manager is invoked when an SSL peer presents a certificate chain to your client during the initial SSL connection handshake. Typically, you will implement this method so that the client can ignore certain errors in the certificate chain, thereby allowing the SSL handshake to continue in spite of these validation errors. WebLogic requires that any custom manager implement the `weblogic.security.SSL.TrustManagerJSSE` interface. This interface exposes a single callback method, `certificateCallback( )` (which gets supplied with the server's chain of X.509-compliant certificates), and an indication of any validation errors. Here is our sample implementation for a trust manager, which ensures that the certificate validation always succeeds, but nevertheless prints out the subject and issuer of each certificate in the chain:

```
TrustManagerJSSE dumpTManager = new TrustManagerJSSE( ) {
  public boolean certificateCallback(X509Certificate[] chain, int validateErr) {
    for (int i = 0; i < chain.length; i++) {
      System.err.println("Issuer: " + chain[i].getIssuerDN( ).getName( ));
      System.err.println("Subject: " + chain[i].getSubjectDN( ).getName( ));
    }
    return true;
  }};
ctx.setTrustManagerJSSE(dumpTManager);
```

The `TrustManagerJSSE` interface defines the possible errors that can occur during certificate validation. For example, `ERR_NONE` indicates that no error occurred during certificate validation, while `ERR_CERT_EXPIRED` indicates that one of the certificates in the chain has expired.

When an SSL client connects to an SSL server, the SSL server presents its digital certificate chain to the client for authentication. That chain could contain an invalid digital certificate. The SSL specification says that the client should drop the SSL connection upon discovery of an invalid certificate. Web browsers, however, ask the user whether to ignore the invalid certificate and continue up the chain to determine whether it is possible to authenticate the SSL server with any of the remaining certificates in the certificate chain.

The trust manager eliminates this inconsistent practice by allowing you to control when to continue or discontinue an SSL connection. Using a trust manager, you can perform custom checks before continuing an SSL connection. For example, you can use the trust manager to specify that only users from specific localities (such as towns, states, or countries) or users with other special attributes can gain access via the SSL connection.

Setting up the client's identity

Finally, use the `SSLContext` object to establish the client's local identity, something that is needed only if the server is configured for two-way SSL. The following code sample shows how to equip the SSLContext object with the client's private key and certificate chain from a JKS keystore:

```
KeyStore ks = KeyStore.getInstance("jks");
ks.load(new FileInputStream(KEYSTORE_NAME), KEYSTORE_PASSWORD.toCharArray());
PrivateKey key = (PrivateKey) ks.getKey(KEY_ALIAS, KEY_PASSWORD.toCharArray());
Certificate[] certChain = ks.getCertificateChain(KEY_ALIAS);
ctx.loadLocalIdentity(certChain, key);
```

Once again, we extract the private key and certificate chain from the JKS keystore and pass these to the loadLocalIdentity( ) method on the SSLContext object. Now that you've established an SSL context, you can ask for an SSL socket factory and use it to create SSL socket connections. The following code sample shows how to obtain an SSLSocketFactory instance and then use it to create an SSL socket:

```
SSLSocketFactory sf = (SSLSocketFactory) ctx.getSocketFactoryJSSE();
SSLSocket sslSocket = (SSLSocket) sf.createSocket(hostname, portNumber);
OutputStream out = sslSocket.getOutputStream();
// Send a request
String req = "GET /index.html HTTP/1.0\r\n\r\n";
out.write(req.getBytes());
InputStream in = sslSock.getInputStream();
// Read any reply
sslSock.close();
```

Once you've successfully established an SSL socket, you can use the HTTP protocol to retrieve an HTML page from the web server. This is essentially how you'd program against the standard JSSE interfaces.

Using an SSL handshake listener

Another handy addition you can make to the SSLContext object is to register an SSL handshake listener, which enables the client to receive notifications when an SSL handshake sequence completes. A handshake listener provides the client with the ideal opportunity to access to the cipher suite negotiated between the two parties, the client's certificates, the server's certificates, and the SSL session and socket that triggered the event. You typically would register a handshake listener just after creating the SSL socket connection:

```
HandshakeCompletedListener hcl = new HandshakeCompletedListener() {
  public void handshakeCompleted(HandshakeCompletedEvent evt) {
    // React to event
  }
};
sslSocket.addHandshakeCompletedListener(hcl);
```

JNDI Clients

Earlier, we encountered several instances of JNDI clients that set up a JNDI context while providing the login credentials of a valid WebLogic user. The following shows a simple variation to our typical JNDI client.

```
Hashtable env = new Hashtable( );
env.put(Context.INITIAL_CONTEXT_FACTORY, "weblogic.jndi.WLInitialContextFactory");
env.put(Context.PROVIDER_URL, "t3s://10.0.10.10:9002");
env.put(Context.SECURITY_PRINCIPAL, "system");
env.put(Context.SECURITY_CREDENTIALS, "12341234");
Context ctx = new InitialContext(env);
```

In this case, we've used the T3S protocol to create an SSL-secure JNDI context. This means WebLogic will send its public certificate back to the client, which the client will validate before successfully establishing the JNDI context. As usual, this server-side authentication will occur automatically, so long as you have configured a list of trusted CA certificates for the client.

If the server is configured for two-way SSL, we can build Java clients that rely on certificate-based JNDI authentication. In this case, the client needs to use its private key and digital certificate. WebLogic lets you wrap the private key and digital certificate in a weblogic.security.PEMInputStream. Example 16-1 shows how you can use the weblogic.jndi.Environment class to establish the JNDI context.

Example 16-1. Certificate-based JNDI authentication

```
Environment env = new Environment( );
env.setProviderUrl("t3s://10.0.10.10:7002");
// Set the username and password
env.setSecurityPrincipal("system");
env.setSecurityCredentials("12341234");
// Create PEMInputStreams around our key and certificate
InputStream key = new PEMInputStream(new FileInputStream(CERT_KEYFILE));
InputStream cert = new PEMInputStream(new FileInputStream(CERT_CERTFILE));
// Configure this as our local identity in the environment
env.setSSLClientCertificate(new InputStream[] { key, cert});
env.setSSLClientKeyPassword(CERT_KEYPASSWORD);
// Now proceed as usual
env.setInitialContextFactory(Environment.DEFAULT_INITIAL_CONTEXT_FACTORY);
context = env.getInitialContext( );
// Use the context
UserTransaction ut = (UserTransaction)
                     context.lookup("javax.transaction.UserTransaction");
//...
```

As you can see, we've invoked setSSLClientCertificate( ) to assign the PEMInput-Stream objects that wrap the client's private key and digital certificate. The order in which the elements of the PEMInputStream array are filled also is predefined:

- The first element of the array must refer to a PEMInputStream built from the client's private key file.
- The second element of the array must refer to a PEMInputStream opened from the client's digital certificate.
- Additional elements of the array may contain PEMInputStream objects built from other certificates in the chain.

In addition, we've invoked the setSSLClientKeyPassword( ) method to specify the pass phrase used to protect the client's private key. There is a small caveat—you must create a new Environment object each time you need to invoke the getIntitialContext( ) method with new user and security credentials. Once you specify the user's login and security (i.e., private key and digital certificate), this security context remains set within the Environment object and cannot be modified during its lifetime.

JCE

JDK 1.4.1 supports the Java Connector Architecture (JCA) and Java Cryptography Extensions (JCE) APIs. Together, these APIs provide Java clients with access to cryptographic functionality. The framework is pluggable, allowing you to install a third-party provider that overrides the default provider that is supplied with the JDK. Different providers, for example, could supply additional cryptographic algorithms or engines. Although WebLogic does not supply a JCE provider, it does support the JCE implementation shipped with Sun's JDK 1.4.1 and nCipher's JCE provider. nCipher's JCE provider allows you to offload (and optimize) the usual server-side SSL processing to additional hardware, thereby freeing up more resources for WebLogic. Please visit *http://www.ncipher.com* for more details about the nCipher product.

Mapping Certificates to WebLogic Users

As we saw earlier in Example 16-1, when a Java client creates a JNDI context bound to a server configured for two-way SSL, the server authenticates the client on two levels:

- At the socket level, where the client's certificate is validated at the server's end. A server configured for two-way SSL needs to trust the client's certificate before it can successfully negotiate the SSL connection. A similar situation arises when you use a browser to access a web application that enforces authentication using client certificates.
- At the application-level, where WebLogic takes the user's credentials to populate the client's subject with valid WebLogic principals. WebLogic subsequently uses this subject to perform authorization checks on protected server-side resources.

If the client needs to interact with an SSL server configured for two-way SSL, the client will be requested to present its digital certificate to prove its identity. The client's certificate can perform the dual role of identifying the WebLogic principals that map to the client. After all, a client's certificate does affirm its identity. WebLogic lets you configure the server so that it can map the client's certificate to the username of a valid WebLogic user. In this way, a Java client can securely establish a JNDI context that is bound to an SSL server by supplying only its private key and digital certificate, and WebLogic will map the client's certificate to a username.

Typically, a client (e.g., the JNDI client) supplies a username and password to authenticate itself to WebLogic. At the server end, WebLogic determines the client's principals—i.e., the corresponding user and the groups it belongs to—and uses these to populate the client's subject. In Chapter 17, you'll learn how WebLogic's authorization framework works with these principals populated in the client's subject to evaluate whether the client is permitted to access a server-side resource. However, if an SSL-enabled client connects to a server configured for two-way SSL, and the client doesn't supply a username, the server still can use the client's certificate to determine the user and its associated groups and roles.

This mapping is executed by the configured *Identity Asserter*, one of the modules of the Authentication Provider, which allows you to determine the client's identity using some client-supplied token such as an X.509-compliant certificate or a CSIv2-compliant certificate. An Identity Asserter validates these tokens and maps each to a particular WebLogic user. If you haven't configured an Identity Assertion Provider that can handle these tokens, the client must authenticate itself using some alternative mechanism—e.g., supplying a username/password combination in addition to its client-side certificate. Without an Identity Assertion Provider set up for the security realm, our SSL-enabled JNDI client must also supply the login credentials of a valid WebLogic user:

```
Environment env = new Environment();
env.setProviderUrl("t3s://10.0.10.10:7002");
// Set the username and password
env.setSecurityPrincipal("system");
env.setSecurityCredentials("12341234");
// As in Example 16-1, obtain the client's private key and certificate
// ...
env.setSSLClientCertificate(new InputStream[] { key, cert});
// ...
context = env.getInitialContext();
```

When you configure an Identity Assertion Provider for a security realm to handle certificate-based tokens, WebLogic passes the digital certificate received from the Java client to a user mapper class. As the name suggests, this class maps the client-supplied token (digital certificate) to a WebLogic username. The client should not supply the additional login credentials of a WebLogic user because that is now evaluated by the configured user mapper class.

Once again, you must use the Administration Console in order to configure an Identity Asserter. You need to navigate to the Security/Realms/myrealm/Providers/Authentication/Default Identity Asserter node from the left pane of the Administration Console to view and modify its configuration. The Active Types field lets you select the type of tokens that clients may supply in order to establish their identity. By default, the Identity Asserter supports AuthenticatedUser—i.e., traditional username/password authentication. If you need to support identity assertion based on X.509 certificates required by two-way SSL, you also must add X.509 to the list on a separate line.

The Identity Asserter setup is complete once you specify the fully qualified name of the user mapper class in the User Name Mapper Class Name field. The username mapper class must be available in WebLogic's classpath. It also must implement the `weblogic.security.providers.authentication.UserNameMapper` interface. The `UserNameMapper` interface lets you execute the mapping using X.509 certificates received during an SSL handshake or through CSIv2, or on the basis of distinguished names passed via CSIv2. Example 16-2 provides a sample implementation of the `UserNameMapper` interface:

Example 16-2. Custom username mapper class

```
package com.oreilly.wlguide.ssl;
import java.security.cert.X509Certificate;
public class UserNameMapper implements
        weblogic.security.providers.authentication.UserNameMapper {
  /**
    * Maps a certificate to a username based on the certificate chain presented
    */
  public String mapCertificateToUserName(X509Certificate[] certs, boolean ssl){
    if (certs.length > 0)
        String subjectDN = certs[0].getSubjectDN( ).getName( );
        if (subjectDN.equals("xena"))   // Whatever logic you want
          return "system";
        else
          return "jon";
  }
  /*
    * Map an X.501 distinguised name to a username based on the
    * distinguished name attributes and values.
    */
  public String mapDistinguishedNameToUserName(byte[] distinguishedName) {
    // Not used for X.509 certificates
    return null;
  }
}
```

In order to map X.509 certificates to a username, you need to implement only the mapCertificateToUsername( ) method. This method accepts two parameters: an array of X509Certificate objects that represents the client's certificate chain presented to WebLogic; and a Boolean flag that is set to true if the certificates were received from an SSL handshake, or set to false otherwise. For instance, if the certificates were obtained from using CSIv2 tokens, the ssl flag would be set to false. Use this method to examine the incoming certificates and, based on the information embedded in these certificates, return the username that ought to be associated with the client. In the preceding example, we simply associate any incoming certificate whose SubjectDN field is set to xena, or to the user system, and associate all other certificates to the user jon. You could imagine other scenarios in which the username is embedded within the client's certificate, thereby allowing you to set up a one-to-one mapping between the client's certificates and WebLogic users.

There is an unfortunate consequence to using X.509 certificates as the basis for your identity assertion. A Java client whose identity is determined using client-side tokens cannot change its identity. The client's certificate is validated only once, during the SSL handshake between the client and WebLogic. If you did not configure an Identity Assertion Provider for the security realm, the client may simply establish another JNDI context and supply the new username/password combination. In this case, the client's certificate that was originally passed to the server isn't used to assert the client's identity, and the original parameters negotiated during the SSL handshake are cached for subsequent SSL connections to WebLogic.

Two-Way SSL Authentication for Web Applications

In Chapter 2, we learned how to apply declarative security constraints to a collection of web resources within a web application. The deployment descriptors for the web application allow you to restrict access to a URL pattern to one or more WebLogic security roles. Consequently, when a user accesses the particular resource from a web browser, she is required to authenticate herself. Typically, if you've configured BASIC or FORM authentication for the web application, the user is required to supply the login credentials of a valid WebLogic user within the security realm. WebLogic then will authenticate the user and determine whether the browser has sufficient access privileges to invoke the web resource.

This authentication mechanism can operate even when a web browser connects to an HTTPS port. However, if WebLogic is configured for two-way SSL, any browser that interacts over the HTTPS port also must present a digital certificate as proof of its identity. In this way, two-way SSL provides the avenue for client certificate-based web authentication. This means that a browser is required to present a digital certificate as proof of its identity when it attempts to access a protected web resource. WebLogic then will authenticate the browser by mapping its certificate to a valid user within the security realm. Based on this identity assertion, WebLogic can determine whether the browser is permitted to access the web resource.

In order to set up this certificate-based authentication scheme for resources in a web application, you need to execute the following tasks:

1. In the standard *web.xml* descriptor file, define the collection of web resources that require the browser (or any web client) to authenticate itself:

```
<security-constraint>
  <display-name>MySecurity Constraint</display-name>
  <web-resource-collection>
    <web-resource-name>MyWeb Resource Collection</web-resource-name>
    <url-pattern>/*</url-pattern>
    <http-method>PUT</http-method>
    <http-method>GET</http-method>
  </web-resource-collection>
  <!--... -->
</security-constraint>
```

2. In the *web.xml* descriptor, define the security role that is permitted to access the collection of web resources:

```
<security-constraint>
  <display-name>MySecurity Constraint</display-name>
  <web-resource-collection>
    <!-- ... -->
  </web-resource-collection>
  <!--... -->
  <auth-constraint>
    <description>web app only accessible to users in mysecrole</description>
    <role-name>mysecrole</role-name>
  </auth-constraint>
</security-constraint>

<login-config>
  <auth-method>CLIENT-CERT</auth-method>
  <realm-name>myrealm</realm-name>
</login-config>

<security-role>
  <description>security role with access to web app</description>
  <role-name>mysecrole</role-name>
</security-role>
```

Notice how we've used the login-config element to indicate the authentication mechanism supported by the web application.

3. In the *weblogic.xml* descriptor file, list the principals that belong to the security role defined earlier in the standard *web.xml* descriptor:

```
<security-role-assignment>
  <role-name>mysecrole</role-name>
  <principal-name>system,jon</principal-name>
</security-role-assignment>
```

This completes the list of changes you need to make to the web application (its deployment descriptors, really) in order to enable certificate-based web authentication.

As you can imagine, this setup is no different from configuring BASIC- or FORM-based web authentication. However, certificate-based web authentication requires additional setup on the servers to which the web application will be deployed. In fact, you need to ensure the following:

- Each server to which the web application will be deployed is set up for two-way SSL authentication.

- The client must use the HTTPS port to access the protected web resources.

- An Identity Assertion Provider must be configured for the security realm.

- Browsers must be equipped with a digital certificate. If you need a one-to-one mapping between the client certificates and WebLogic users in the security realm, you could consider embedding the actual username of the WebLogic user within the SubjectDN field of the browser's certificate.

Only after all these instances are true can your web application support certificate-based web authentication for a collection of web resources.

Security

WebLogic provides a comprehensive suite of security services that can be used to protect all aspects of a domain and its deployments. These security services affect all aspects of your domain: from the lowest level provided by the Java Security Manager, to connection-level security, to application-level security in which you can protect your administered and deployed objects (such as EJBs, web services, and JDBC pools), and finally to domain-level security in which you can establish trust between two domains. These security services target three distinct sets of users: application developers who can use the services to secure their applications; administrators who need to configure security for the system and deployments; and security vendors or customers who can change and extend the facilities provided by WebLogic.

Let's begin at the JVM level. Here, the Java Security Manager uses a security policy file to restrict access to specific runtime operations. This ensures that programs running on the JVM, including WebLogic Server itself, can access protected resources in permitted ways only. For instance, you can configure the Java Security Manager so that all Java threads have write-access only to specific directories in the filesystem. WebLogic enhances the Security Manager by allowing you to define additional security policies for resource adapters and EJBs, thereby ensuring that these components have access to defined resources only. There are also other global, higher-level security permissions that apply to these resources and application code.

WebLogic can filter connection requests from clients. A *connection filter* defines rules that determine what basis the server accepts or denies client connections. These rules are based on several parameters: typically, the client's IP address and port; the protocol used to establish the connection; and the server's listen address and port. You can assign multiple connection filters to a server, or perhaps even write your own connection filter class that implements custom filtering logic. Using connection filters, you can easily ensure that the server accepts only T3 connections from within your intranet, for example. SSL security is another mechanism available at the socket level, which we encountered in Chapter 16. SSL protects network communication provided through its support for data integrity, confidentiality, and authentication.

WebLogic provides partial support for standard JAAS. The JAAS framework is a standard extension to J2SE v1.3 and is now part of the J2SE v1.4 platform. *Authentication* enables the server to verify the identity of the user who is running the Java code, whether it is an applet, servlet, EJB, or application. *Authorization* is the server's ability to enforce access control based on the user's identity, security privileges, and policies. WebLogic allows Java clients to use JAAS authentication, and login modules are implemented using JAAS. If you need to use JAAS authorization, you will have to code your own schema above WebLogic's infrastructure.

WebLogic's security infrastructure is founded on a set of modular, extensible security service provider interfaces (SSPIs). This architecture allows you to plug in new security providers, swap out old ones, and run WebLogic's default providers alongside your own. Your WebLogic distribution is equipped with a set of security providers that provide the default implementations for the SSPIs. WebLogic's security providers implement the underlying security framework for your J2EE applications. That is, the standard J2EE-defined security mechanisms are implemented (and extended) through the SSPIs. Often, WebLogic's security providers will refine the existing security constraints. For instance, the standard *ejb-jar.xml* deployment descriptor allows you to restrict access to an EJB method to authenticated users in a specific role. WebLogic allows you to refine this constraint by ensuring that the user has access only during certain times of the day. In fact, the SSPIs are an open architecture, and you can easily plug in a third-party security provider from a security vendor. Alternatively, you can build new security services by implementing your own security providers.

WebLogic's default security providers are quite versatile. A *security realm* is a logical grouping of users, groups, roles, and security policies, along with the complete set of security providers. Security policies assigned to server resources can be used to determine who is authorized to access the resource. WebLogic lets you protect a whole range of resources: individual EJB methods, a web application, a collection of web pages, connection pools, data sources, or any administered object. You even can protect a branch within the JNDI tree, thereby preventing unauthorized clients from looking up objects in the JNDI tree. All this security data is stored in an embedded LDAP server. WebLogic also can be configured to use an external LDAP repository, such as Open LDAP, Active Directory, or Novell NDS. These external repositories can be used for authentication only, not authorization.

Finally, WebLogic allows you to set up a trust mechanism between two domains. This ensures that authenticated users from one domain can then access resources in another domain.

This chapter examines all of these security mechanisms. Although they are all quite different from each other, they complement each other quite well. We begin with a look at the Java Security Manager and how WebLogic is able to filter connection requests. We then examine WebLogic's authentication and authorization framework and learn how it supports the standard J2EE security services. We also cover the various security providers available within a security realm and their default implementations. Finally, we end with a look at how to authenticate using JAAS, and examples of Authentication and Identity Assertion providers.

The Java Security Manager

At the JVM level, WebLogic can use the standard Java Security Manager to prevent untrusted code from performing unwanted actions. Using a security policy file, you can configure the JVM so that all threads running on the JVM have restricted access to sensitive runtime operations. The security policy file encapsulates a set of permissions that are granted to (or revoked from) all classes loaded within the current instance of the JVM. You can define a whole range of security permissions to control access to particular resources—e.g., "write" access to certain folders on the filesystem, "connect" access to a particular host and range of ports, "read" access to environment variables, "get" access to the current class loader, and more. Refer to your JDK documentation for more information on the Security Manager and security policy files.

Java's Security Manager ensures that any code running within WebLogic accesses these critical resources only in the permitted ways. This low level of access control may be useful for third-party untrusted code. The Java Security Manager also can interact with J2EE deployment settings. For instance, you can use the standard *ra.xml* deployment descriptor to define security permissions that apply to the resource adapter. WebLogic also provides similar access control for web applications and EJBs.

Note that WebLogic itself requires a policy file to be in place before it can run. The *startWebLogic* scripts load the policy file located at *WL_HOME/server/lib/weblogic. policy* by default.

Configuring the Security Manager

In order to use the Java Security Manager, you need to supply two options from the command line when starting WebLogic Server:

- You must use the -Djava.security.manager option to ensure that the default security manager is installed, and that the JVM is subjected to policy checks.
- You must use the -Djava.security.policy option to specify the location of a security policy file.

By default, the JVM uses security policies defined in the *java.security* and *java.policy* files located under the *JAVA_HOME/jre/lib/security* folder. Here is the syntax for starting WebLogic Server using a custom security policy file:

```
java -Djava.security.manager -Djava.security.policy==c:\oreilly.policy
   ... weblogic.Server
```

The default startup scripts created by WebLogic refer to the sample security policy file located at *WL_HOME/server/lib/weblogic.policy*. Notice how we've used the == (double equal sign) when specifying the java.security.policy argument. This persuades the Security Manager to use *c:\oreilly.policy* as its only source of policies. If we had used a single equal sign instead, the policy file would be used in conjunction with default security policy files provided by your JDK installation.

Usually the JVM will use the security policy file to enforce access control over any code running within WebLogic. The only deviation from this rule is when WebLogic Server starts up. When a server boots up, WebLogic partially disables the Java Security Manager and replaces it with a variation that disables the checkRead( ) method. While this approach improves the performance of the startup sequence, it also reduces the security of the JVM during startup. In addition, it means that the startup classes for WebLogic will run using this modified security manager. You will need to ensure that these classes cause no security breaches.

 Because the policy file determines access privileges for all classes running within WebLogic's JVM, we recommend that only the Administrator has read and write access to the security policy file. No other users should be allowed to access the policy file.

Global Security Policies

WebLogic allows you to define security policies for EJBs, resource adapters, and web applications in the *weblogic.policy* file. Table 17-1 lists the codebases under which the default permissions for these component types may be defined.

Table 17-1. Default codebases for access permissions that apply to J2EE components

Application type	Codebase
EJBs	*file:/weblogic/application/defaults/EJB*
Resource adapters	*file:/weblogic/application/defaults/Connector*
Servlets	*file:/weblogic/application/defaults/Web*

You can use these codebases to grant special privileges to particular J2EE component types. Note that any security policies defined under these codebases apply to all EJBs, resource adapters, and web applications deployed to that particular server instance.

Application-Specific Security Policies

You also can define security policies that are specific to an EJB component or resource adapter, and thereby ensure that only particular components are targeted. To achieve this, you must modify their deployment descriptors, and not the policy file itself. Resource adapters support this mechanism as part of the J2EE standard, and you need only modify the standard *ra.xml* descriptor file. For EJBs, you need to modify the *weblogic-ejb-jar.xml* descriptor file. In both cases, it is the security-permission element that allows you to define additional security policies.

Let's look at specifying permissions for EJBs. The security-permission element in the *weblogic-ejb-jar.xml* descriptor specifies security privileges that apply to all EJBs packaged in the EJB JAR. The following example grants read and write access to a temporary directory on the server's filesystem for the EJBs:

```
<weblogic-enterprise-bean>
 <!-- weblogic enterprise bean statements go here -->
</weblogic-enterprise-bean>
<security-role-assignment>
  <!-- the optional security role assignments go here -->
</security-role-assignment>
<security-permission>
  <description>
    grant permission to special folder
  </description>
  <security-permission-spec>
    grant {
      permission java.io.FilePermission
        "f:${/}tmp${/}-", "read,write";
    }
  </security-permission-spec>
<security-permission>
```

Notice how the security-permission-spec element defines a grant permission using the same syntax for security policy files. The only restriction to this syntax is that you cannot use the codebase or signedBy clauses.

Tracing the Security Manager

BEA provides a Recording Security Manager that can be used to trace any permission problems caused by the Java Security Manager. When installed, the tool detects and records all access control exceptions that occur at runtime. In this way, you can easily pinpoint problems in your access control policy and later reconfigure the security policy to remove these errors. The tool is not distributed with WebLogic Server. However, it can be downloaded from BEA's dev2dev web site (*http://www.dev2dev. bea.com*).

Connection Filtering

At the connection level, WebLogic provides two security features: filtering and SSL. Chapter 16 provides a detailed look at SSL. Let's take a look at connection filtering here. A connection filter allows the server to reject unwanted connections based on some criteria. For example, a connection filter would allow you to configure

WebLogic to permit T3 or IIOP connections only from within your intranet, and reject any T3 or IIOP connection request from outside the intranet. So, connection filtering provides network-level access control.

WebLogic comes equipped with a default connection filter that examines one or more connection filter rules defined in the Administration Console. Alternatively, you can create your own custom connection filter that evaluates the basis that incoming connections are accepted by the server. A custom connection filter is a Java class that implements WebLogic's ConnectionFilter interface. The interface is dead simple—the class must implement the accept() method, which simply throws a FilterException to indicate that an incoming connection request should not be allowed through. Here is an example of a connection filter that refuses T3 connections from hosts unless their IP address matches 10.*.*.*:

```
import weblogic.security.net.*;

public class MyConnectionFilter implements ConnectionFilter {
    public void accept(ConnectionEvent evt) throws FilterException {
        if ( evt.getProtocol().equals("t3") ) {
            byte [] addr = evt.getRemoteAddress().getAddress();
            if ( !(addr[0]==10))
                throw new FilterException();
        }
    };
}
```

This filter simply throws a FilterException whenever the filter criteria have been violated. If the method completes without throwing any exceptions, the connection is allowed through. The method receives a single parameter, a ConnectionEvent object, that encapsulates vital information about the connection request. Typically, you will use this information to implement the acceptance criteria for the filter. The ConnectionEvent class provides various methods to access this information:

getProtocol()
> Retrieves a string value that represents the protocol used to establish the connection.

getRemoteAddress()
> Retrieves a java.net.InetAddress object that represents the client's address.

getRemotePort()
> Returns the client's port number used to establish the connection.

getLocalAddress()
> Retrieves a java.net.InetAddress object that represents the server's listen address.

getLocalPort()
> Obtains the server's port number to which the connection is being made.

Once you have compiled the filter class, you need to install it. First, you need to ensure the class can be located from the server's classpath. Then, using the Administration Console, expand the topmost node indicating your domain and choose the View Domain-Wide Security Settings option. The Configuration/Filter tab contains the settings for connection filters. WebLogic 7.0 users should select the Security/Filter tab after expanding the domain node from the left pane.

Enter the name of your connection filter class in the Connection Filter setting. You will also notice the Connection Filter Rules setting. Use this option if your filter class also implements the optional ConnectionFilterRulesListener interface. In this case, the connection filter will be able to receive and process filter rules defined in the Administration Console.

The Default Connection Filter

WebLogic comes preconfigured with a useful connection filter that can process a number of filter rules defined using the Administration Console in the Connection Filter Rules setting. The connection filter attempts to match an incoming connection against all the rules, beginning from the first rule in the list. If a matching rule is found, the connection is allowed (or disallowed) depending on the rule's action. If no matching rule is found, the incoming connection is permitted.

You can specify any number of rules; each rule should be on a single line. The syntax for a connection filter rule is shown here:

```
target localAddress localPort action protocolList
```

Here are the definitions for the parameters of a connection filter rule:

- The target parameter specifies the client hosts that the rule must examine. We discuss its syntax later.

- The localAddress parameter refers to the server's host address to which the client connects. If you specify an asterisk (*), this matches all local IP addresses.

- The localPort parameter indicates the server port to which the client connects. If you specify an asterisk (*), this matches all available ports.

- The action parameter indicates whether the rule should allow or reject the incoming connection request. It can take two possible values: allow or deny.

- Use the protocolList parameter to define a space-separated list of protocol names that should be matched. The protocol names can be: http, https, t3, t3s, giop, giops, dcom, or ftp. If no protocols are listed, the rule checks for all protocols. Versions of WebLogic 7.0 and WebLogic 8.1 also permit the ldap protocol to be specified.

You also can include a # character anywhere on the line. Any text after this character until the end of the line is treated as a comment.

A filter rule can define the target parameter in two forms:

- It can be a "fast" rule if the value for the target parameter is either a hostname or an IP address.
- It can be a "slow" rule if the value for the target parameter is a domain name.

For fast rules, you can specify either the client's hostname or IP address. The IP address can be followed by an optional netmask, the two being separated by a / character. If you supply a hostname that resolves to a list of IP addresses, the server automatically generates multiple versions of the same rule for each IP address when it boots up. These rules are called "fast" because the server eventually has a list of rules that use static IP addresses; therefore, no connect-time DNS lookups are required once the server is up and running. All hostnames are resolved to their IP addresses when the server boots and goes through all the filter rules. Here are a few examples of fast rules:

```
www.oreilly.com 127.0.0.1 7001 allow t3  # allow t3 requests from www.oreilly.com
10.0.20.30/255.255.0.0 127.0.0.1 7001 allow t3 t3s http https
```

Notice how the second filter rule uses a netmask.

For slow rules, the value for the target parameter is a domain name beginning with an asterisk (*). An asterisk may be used only at the head of the domain name. Here is an example of a slow rule:

```
*.oreilly.com 127.0.0.1 7001 allow t3
```

This rule allows incoming T3 connections on port 7001 from any client that runs on a host within the oreilly.com domain. It's called a "slow" rule because it requires a connect-time DNS lookup in order to execute the match, so it is literally slower than the fast rules.

The following rule is very handy for denying all access to your server:

```
0.0.0.0/0 deny   # refuse the connection request
```

You can define this rule at the *end* of the list of filter rules, and thereby deny access to all connections that fail to match any of the previous rules in the list. In this way, you can ensure that an incoming connection request is allowed only if it matches one of the preceding filter rules.

The Security Provider Architecture

Let's now turn our attention to WebLogic's infrastructure for application-level security. WebLogic defines a standard set of SSPIs that provide high-level security services. WebLogic also supplies a default set of security providers that implement these SSPIs. These default security providers support and enhance the standard J2EE role-based security framework. In fact, they also allow you to programmatically control its behavior. There are two important characteristics of this security framework:

Modular

> The SSPIs are split into discrete modules so that each security provider can deal with different but specific aspects of WebLogic's security (e.g., authentication, authorization, auditing, and more).

Pluggable

> Because these security providers live behind a layer of SSPIs, WebLogic makes it easier to replace or enhance the default implementation with your own or a third-party implementation.

The SSPIs hide the actual implementation of the security providers, thereby enabling you to plug in and play your own modules and modify selected aspects of the security. For instance, the default Authentication Provider can be replaced with one that supports some form of biometric recognition, or the Auditing Provider can be replaced with one that notifies interested parties after a user has made a certain number of failed attempts to log in.

A security realm is a logical grouping of users, groups, roles, and security policies, along with a complete set of security providers. By default, WebLogic Server comes equipped with two such realms: the legacy compatibility realm that provides support for WebLogic 6.x–type security configurations, and the new default realm. The *default realm*, which is often referred to by its default name myrealm, is WebLogic's standard implementation of the security providers. Although you can configure multiple realms for a domain, *one* realm can be active only; this active realm controls all aspects of the domain's security.

You can determine which realm your domain is set up to use by selecting the domain from the left frame of the Administration Console and then choosing the View Domain-Wide Security Settings option. The Configuration/General tab displays a Default Realm field that indicates the security realm currently being used by your domain. The Administration Console lets you configure virtually all aspects of the security realm. You can view and modify the realm's configuration by selecting the realm from under the Security/Realms node in the left pane of the Administration Console. Here, you will find subnodes for all the security providers within the realm, together with access to the realm's users, groups, and roles.

To understand how WebLogic's default security realm works, you need to understand the authentication and authorization structure that WebLogic imposes on its resources and how it integrates with the standard J2EE role-based security. The remainder of this section is dedicated to exploring these concepts. The following section examines the security providers in more detail.

Overview

WebLogic's authentication and authorization providers, part of the default implementation of the SSPIs, rely on the important concepts shown in the following list.

- A *user*, which represents a person, system, or Java client
- A *group*, which represents a static collection of users
- A *role*, which represents a dynamic collection of users
- A *security policy*, which defines which users are granted access to a WebLogic resource

You can use WebLogic to configure these entities and thereby protect any resource within a domain, right from the call to an EJB method all the way through to a particular operation from the Administration Console. This framework prohibits unauthorized access both from within (e.g., a servlet invoking an EJB method) and from without (e.g., a Java client attempting to use a JDBC data source).

To place these concepts in context, let's refer back to the "Security Configuration" section in Chapter 2, where we examined how to protect the web resources in the */admin* directory of a web application. In the standard *web.xml* deployment descriptor, we defined a security constraint that granted access to a security role named webadmin:

```
<!-- web.xml entry: -->
<security-constraint>
  <web-resource-collection>
  <web-resource-name>Admin Resources</web-resource-name>
    <description>security constraints for admin stuff</description>
    <url-pattern>/admin/*</url-pattern>
    <http-method>POST</http-method>
    <http-method>GET</http-method>
  </web-resource-collection>
  <auth-constraint>
    <role-name>webadmin</role-name>
  </auth-constraint>
  <user-data-constraint>
    <transport-guarantee>NONE</transport-guarantee>
  </user-data-constraint>
</security-constraint>
```

Of course, this setup relies on a security role that we also defined in the descriptor file:

```
<!-- web.xml entry: -->
<security-role>
  <role-name>webadmin</role-name>
</security-role>
```

Up until this point, we have utilized the standard J2EE security features found in the deployment descriptors. Now we have to assign the virtual security role defined in the *web.xml* file to an actual physical entity in WebLogic Server. This is achieved by associating the role name to a number of principals already configured in WebLogic Server. The *weblogic.xml* descriptor file for the web application holds this mapping:

```
<!-- weblogic.xml fragment -->
<security-role-assignment>
  <role-name>webadmin</role-name>
```

```
        <principal-name>jmountjoy</principal-name>
        <principal-name>achugh</principal-name>
    </security-role-assignment>
```

This XML fragment correlates the webadmin role defined and used within the web application with the actual WebLogic users jmountjoy and achugh. In this way, we are able to prohibit users who are not in the webadmin role from accessing web content under the /admin folder. Let's now look at just how this setup protects the web resources in the web application.

A *protected resource* restricts access to only a subset of users. Any user that satisfies the access constraints laid down on the protected resource is then authorized to access the resource. WebLogic lets you protect a variety of resources: web applications, URLs (as in the earlier example), individual EJB methods, web services, connection pools, and even branches of the JNDI tree. For instance, you could ensure that only certain users are allowed to access a connection pool or invoke a method on a protected EJB. In the case of our sample web application, the set of URLs matching the pattern /admin/* represents a protected resource. This means that you can easily set up a secure environment in which applications are forced to obey the security constraints that you've laid out. WebLogic also makes it easy to adapt the configuration according to your needs with minimal code changes. In the case of our sample web application, the security constraints are defined declaratively in the deployment descriptors. Thus, you can adjust the security settings with no code changes.

The access control mechanism relies on the notion of an authenticated user. The user represents an authenticated entity—it could be a person (as in this case) or an external, client program. A user may authenticate itself in different ways. Over the Web, a user may be required to fill in a login form. A Java client application, on the other hand, may rely on JAAS authentication to establish trust with WebLogic Server. In our example, the user is determined from the username and password (login credentials) supplied over the Web. In general, a user has a number of principals (identities) associated with it as a result of an authentication. For instance, the principals associated with the system user after successful authentication include the system user itself and the group to which it belongs—i.e., the Administrators group. Some users may not authenticate at all, in which case they will remain *anonymous*.

When the domain holds an overwhelming number of WebLogic users, it becomes cumbersome to manage the security needs of each individual user. For this reason, WebLogic lets you configure static collections of users, called *groups*. From a security point of view, if a role or policy statement is applied to a group, the role or policy is assigned to all members of the group. From an administration point of view, it is easier to manage a handful of groups rather than (say) several hundred users. Remember, a group is a *static* collection of users. An administrator explicitly defines the members of a group at configuration time. As we saw earlier, a group can also act as a security principal. So, for instance, our *weblogic.xml* descriptor file could easily map the security role to the name of an existing group:

```
<!-- weblogic.xml fragment -->
<security-role-assignment>
  <role-name>webadmin</role-name>
  <principal-name>someAdminGroup</principal-name>
</security-role-assignment>
```

In this case, access to the web content would be restricted only to all users within someAdminGroup.

A security role represents a *dynamic* collection of users whose membership is evaluated at runtime based on the subject's principals and other membership criteria. Whether a user is in a role depends on whether the user satisfies the *membership conditions* of the role at runtime. You can specify a number of membership conditions for the role. These include a logical mix of usernames, group names, and times of access during the day. For instance, you may define the membership condition for the DayShopper role as being "any user who belongs to the Shopper group and the time of access is between 8:00 a.m. and 5:00 p.m.". You may assign a number of roles to a resource in order to help specify the authorization conditions of the resource. Note that the roles themselves do not guarantee access control, they just facilitate in the definition of a policy statement that ultimately protects access to the target resource. In terms of the earlier example, we created a role called webadmin. The membership conditions for the role are simple: the client has to be authenticated as either jmountjoy or achugh before the web application considers it in the webadmin role.

You can protect a WebLogic resource by defining a policy statement for it. A *security policy* is a statement about access—it determines which users will have access to the resource. Just as you can with roles, you can define a policy in terms of a logical combination of a number of conditions: usernames, group names, the time of access during the day, and role names. For instance, you could assign the following policy to a JDBC pool: "the caller must belong to the DayShopper role or the Administrator group." This means that only authenticated users who belong to the Administrator group or pass the membership criteria of the DayShopper role may access the pool. If any user fails these access control checks defined for the JDBC pool, WebLogic will raise an authorization exception.

Now let's revisit the earlier security constraints on our web application in terms of these concepts. The *weblogic.xml* descriptor file defines a webadmin role. At deploy time, WebLogic reads this descriptor file and creates a webadmin role within its internal security configuration. This internal security role is configured to ensure that only the users achugh and jmountjoy can qualify for membership to this role. Thus, the J2EE role gets mapped to a WebLogic role, whereas the role-to-principal(s) assignment defines the membership criteria for the internal role.

In addition, WebLogic creates and assigns a policy statement to the web application that protects all web resources that match the URL pattern /admin/*. The policy statement will grant access to any caller satisfying the following condition: "the caller is in the webadmin role." Through this policy statement, WebLogic can ensure that any user who isn't a member of the webadmin role is unable to access the web content under the /admin folder. Thus, WebLogic relies on a behind-the-scenes policy statement to enforce the security constraints defined by the deployment descriptors. Later, we see how you can explicitly create your own policy statements.

Users and Groups

To list the users that belong to a realm, select the realm from the Administration Console and choose the Users node. You then can use the righthand frame to view all the users or filter the list. The System user account also will be part of the list— this is the Administration user account that was defined when you used the Configuration Wizard to create the domain. Select the "Configure a new User" option to create a new user. For each user, you need to specify a name, a short description, and a password. Note that all usernames within a realm must be unique. The default provider uses case-insensitive usernames. The user may belong to one or more groups.

To list and edit all the groups that belong to a security realm, select the realm from the Administration Console and then choose the Groups node. You can also create a new group here. The Membership tab for a group is a little misleading, as it does not let you view the members of the group. To see if a user is a member of a group, you have to select the user and view its Groups tab. WebLogic allows you to add groups to other existing groups, and the Membership tab lists all subgroups that are contained within the selected group. You can also use this tab to add another group to the current group.

Group membership places two important implications on your security configuration. Imagine you've defined two groups, A and B, in your domain, where group B is a member of group A. This means that:

- Every user that belongs to group B also belongs to group A.
- If you assign a role or policy to group A, all members of group A as well as all members of group B will be assigned the same role or policy.

When you view the Groups tab for a user, the Administration Console lists only the groups that the user belongs to directly. So, if a user belongs to group B, the Administration Console lists only group B under the Groups tab, even though the user actually belongs to both groups A and B.

When you create a new domain using the Configuration Wizard, the following groups are created automatically and are ready for use: Administrators, Deployers, Operators, and Monitors. Initially, the System user is the only user created, and it is also the only member of the Administrators group in the domain.

Remember, groups simply ease the task of administration. If a user is a member of a group, he is not automatically guaranteed any special privileges. A group inherits access privileges only when it participates in a policy statement (either directly or through a role). For example, the initial System user account acquires Administrative access rights only because it is a member of the Administrators group, which in turn is a member of a (global) Admin role, and a policy statement is in place that grants access to all areas of the domain to the Admin role.

Two groups are not listed on the Groups page, but are automatically made available to the security realm:

users
> This group represents the set of all authenticated users. Any user that successfully authenticates itself is a member of the users group.

everyone
> This group represents the set of all WebLogic users, including anonymous users. Any user, whether authenticated or anonymous, is a member of the group everyone.

These groups provide a convenient way for setting up the default access control. For instance, a resource can be made accessible to all users through the policy statement "User is a member of the group everyone." Alternatively, you can restrict access to only authenticated users by defining the following policy on a resource: "User is a member of the users group." You can also programmatically check for group membership on the server side. The following example checks whether the current user is a member of the users or everyone group:

```
/** returns false if executed without any security context */
weblogic.security.SubjectUtils.isUserInGroup(
                    weblogic.security.Security.getCurrentSubject(),"users");
/** returns true regardless of whether the user authenticates */
weblogic.security.SubjectUtils.isUserInGroup(
                    weblogic.security.Security.getCurrentSubject(),"everyone");
```

Protecting User Accounts

WebLogic provides a user lockout facility to prevent abuse of user accounts. A user is locked out when a set threshold number of failed login attempts are made. When this happens, the user account is locked for a configurable period of time, or until an Administrator unlocks the user account. During this period, the user is prohibited from using those credentials to access the server. In order to configure user lockout, select the realm from under Security/Realms node in the left frame of the Administration Console. You then can use the User Lockout tab to adjust the lockout features and view lockout statistics.

Table 17-2 lists the various configuration options available under the User Lockout tab. By default, these settings are configured for maximum security.

Table 17-2. *Configuring user lockout*

Setting	Description	Default
Lockout Enabled	This setting indicates whether the lockout facility is enabled. You will need to disable this feature if you use an alternative Authentication Provider that supports its own mechanism for protecting user accounts.	true
Lockout Threshold	This setting determines the maximum number of failed login attempts that are permitted before the user is locked out.	5
Lockout Reset Duration	Suppose the Lockout Threshold is 5 minutes and the Lockout Reset Duration is 3 minutes. If a user makes five failed login attempts within 3 minutes, the user account will be locked out. If the five failed attempts do not occur within 3 minutes, the account still will remain alive.	5 minutes
Lockout Duration	This setting determines the duration (in minutes) that a user will not be able to access his account after being locked out.	30 minutes
Lockout Cache Size	This setting specifies the size of the cache that holds the invalid login attempts.	5
Lockout GC Threshold	This setting determines the maximum number of invalid login attempts that are held in memory. When the number of invalid login records exceeds this value, WebLogic's garbage collector removes all records that have expired — i.e., when the associated user has been locked out.	400

While a user is locked out, a Details link appears under the Locked column in the user list (under the Users node). If you select this link for any user in the list, you can view the number of failed login attempts for the user and the time when the last login attempt failed. You also can choose the Unlock option to manually reactivate the user's account.

Roles

Unlike a group, a role represents a dynamic collection of users. Role membership can be defined in terms of the following criteria:

Username

You can specify a number of usernames. If the authenticated user matches one of the names in the list, and it satisfies all other criteria, it automatically becomes a member of the role.

Group names

You can specify a number of group names. If the authenticated user is a member of any of the groups in the list, and it satisfies all other criteria, it automatically becomes a member of the role.

Hours of access

You can define a number of time periods during which users are allowed access. If the user tries to access a resource during one of the time periods specified and satisfies all other criteria, it automatically becomes a member of the role.

You can combine these rules in various ways, using logical AND and OR relationships. For instance, you could create RoleA based on the criteria that the user belongs to the group UKSeller and hours of access are between 8:00 a.m. and 9:00 p.m. Any user who then tries to access a resource between these hours and also is a member of the UKSeller group will be a member of RoleA. Alternatively, you could create RoleB based on the criteria that the user belongs to the group UKSeller or the hours of access are between 8:00 a.m and 9:00 p.m. In this case, any member of UKSeller will always be in the role, and any user who tries to access a resource between 8:00 a.m and 9:00 p.m also will be a member of the role, regardless of the groups it belongs to. The membership conditions for the role are evaluated at runtime when a user attempts to access a resource that is protected by a policy statement defined in terms of that role. Thus, the membership conditions help evaluate whether the user is in the role at a point in time.

In general, WebLogic's default Role Mapping Provider manages the information about all the roles defined in a security realm. In fact, two kinds of roles can be defined: global and scoped roles.

Global Roles

Global roles are available to all resources within a security domain. A default set of global roles is created automatically when you create a new domain; it is used to grant access to various operations. These prefabricated global roles are associated with default security policies that implement the factory-set security configuration for your WebLogic domain:

Admin

> Users that belong to this role have complete access to all areas of the domain. This includes the ability to view and edit the domain configuration, start and stop servers, deploy applications (EJBs, JMS factories, web applications), and more. Any user that belongs to the Administrators group automatically inherits the Admin role. That is, the membership condition for the Admin role is that the user must belong to the Administrators group.

Deployer

> Users in this role are allowed to view the domain configuration, view and edit deployment descriptors, and deploy applications, EJBs, startup and shutdown classes, J2EE connectors, and web service components. The membership condition for the Deployer role is that the user must belong to the Deployers group.

Operator

> Users in this role can view the server configuration, as well as start, stop and resume server instances. The membership condition for the Operator role is that the user must belong to the Operators group.

```
Monitor
```
> Users in this role are allowed only to view the server's configuration. The membership condition for the Monitor role is that the user must belong to the Monitors group.

In order to create or modify existing global roles, select the realm from the left frame of the Administration Console and then select the Global Roles node.

WebLogic also provides a global role called anonymous. Its membership is defined to include all users in the everyone group. Even though the anonymous role does not appear in the roles listed in the Administration Console, you still can use it to define policies on resources.

Scoped Roles

Most roles are *scoped*, meaning that they apply to a particular resource or branch of a JNDI tree. Unlike global roles that are independent of any resource and can be managed centrally via the Administration Console, scoped roles are distributed across various resources. You have to select a particular resource in order to view the associated scoped roles. Regardless of the actual resource, the underlying principle for creating a scoped role is the same. Locate the resource from the left pane of the Administration Console, then right-click and select Define Scoped Role. In some cases, you can define scoped roles and their brethren, scoped policies, on even finer aspects. For example, you can define a scoped role and policy on a per-method basis for EJBs, on a per-operation basis for web services, and on an HTTP method type (POST, GET, HEAD, etc.) basis for web resources within a web application. Let's now look at how to create scoped roles for particular resources, and at some precautions you need to take during setup.

Connection pools and multipools

JDBC resources are located under the Services/JDBC subtree. You can right-click a chosen resource (e.g., connection pool) and select Define Scoped Role to define a role for the resource. You also can delete or modify previously assigned roles.

JDBC roles are hierarchical. If you right-click the JDBC/Connection Pools node, you can follow the same procedure to create a scoped role that is applicable to all connection pools.

JNDI branches

You can assign a role to a specific node or branch of the JNDI tree for a server. Select the server from the left frame of the Administration Console, then right-click and select the "View JNDI tree" option. This launches a new browser window that lets you explore the JNDI tree for the chosen server. You then can select any node in the tree, right-click, and select the Define Scoped Role option.

Web applications

The role and policy assignment for web applications is slightly different, in the sense that the roles and policies are scoped to particular URLs within the web application. Choose the web application from the left pane of the Administration Console and then select the Define Scoped Role option. You then will be asked to supply a URL pattern and a role that will be used to restrict access to the URL pattern. Later, you can apply a policy statement to the web application using the same URL pattern and scoped role. For example, you may wish to scope a role and policy to a particular servlet only, in which case you can use a URL pattern such as */servletname*. If you want the role to apply to all resources in the web application, use the URL pattern /*.

Web services

Web service components are typically packaged in an EAR. You can locate the web service by expanding the node representing the application under the Deployments/ Applications node. In WebLogic 7.0, you can locate the web service from under the Deployments/Web Services node.

Right-click a service and select the Define Scoped Role option. This will let you define a role for all of the services in the selected web service module. You also can select the Define Policies and Roles for Individual Services option, which provides you with a table listing all web services. For each web service, you can choose the Define Scoped Role option to create a scoped role for that web service alone. When you define a scoped policy in this way, you also will be able to choose to which operations the policy should be applied.

The web service roles and policies are hierarchical. In essence, if you set up a role or policy on a web service module using the Define Roles option, all services within the module inherit the role and policy. You also can set a policy on the application that bundles the web service module. In this case, all web service modules and all web services within the modules will inherit the role and policy.

EJBs

The assignment of scoped roles to EJBs is very similar to that for web services. If you select the EJB Modules node, any role or policy you define will be inherited by all EJBs. If you select a particular EJB module and choose the Define Scoped Role option, any roles you define will be scoped to all EJBs within that module. Finally, if you select the Define Policies and Roles for Individual Beans option, you will be presented with a list of EJBs, thus allowing you to assign the scoped role or policy individually to each EJB. If you define a policy for a particular EJB in this manner, you also can specify to which EJB methods the policy should be applied. An alternative approach to defining scoped roles for all the EJBs in an application is to simply define a global role instead.

JMS destinations

To assign a scoped role to a JMS destination, select the JMS destination under the JMS server node that hosts it, right-click, and select the Define Scoped Role option.

Using the deployment descriptors

For a J2EE component (e.g., EJB, web application), the role information also can be obtained from the deployment descriptors, as demonstrated earlier in the web application example. When you deploy a J2EE component, the roles are automatically created and populated with the data held in the deployment descriptors. If you subsequently make changes to the new security roles, these changes are *not* persisted back to the deployment descriptors. Ideally, once the J2EE component is deployed, you need to reconfigure WebLogic so that it doesn't refresh the roles when the component is redeployed. Later, we'll see how to alter this default behavior of the security providers by instructing them to ignore the security constraints in the deployment descriptors.

The externally-defined Element

Recall how we used the *weblogic.xml* descriptor file for a web application to map the security roles defined earlier in the standard *web.xml* descriptor file to actual principals in WebLogic's security realm. For example, the following portion from the *weblogic.xml* descriptor file shows how to list the principals associated with the role mysecrole:

```
<security-role-assignment>
   <role-name>mysecrole</role-name>
   <principal-name>jon</principal-name>
   <principal-name>system</principal-name>
</security-role-assignment>
```

Alternatively, you could use the externally-defined* element to indicate to WebLogic that the security role defined in the *web.xml* descriptor file actually points to a role in the security realm created manually using the Administration Console. This approach means that you don't need to explicitly map the security role to existing WebLogic users and groups. Instead, you can defer the membership conditions for the security role until after the web application is deployed. For instance, suppose the *weblogic.xml* descriptor file for our web application includes the following security information:

```
<security-role-assignment>
   <role-name>mysecrole</role-name>
   <externally-defined/>
</security-role-assignment>
```

---

* This element is called global-role in WebLogic 7.0.

This indicates that the security constraints for the web application's descriptor rely on a role called mysecrole that already has been configured for the realm. When you deploy the web application, WebLogic will look for mysecrole within its security realm and use this security role to configure a policy statement on the web application. In this case, the policy statement will specify the following condition: "Caller is a member of the role mysecrole." In this way, WebLogic can ensure that only users who are members of the security role mysecrole may invoke the protected resource. Of course, mysecrole now must be configured for the realm using the Administration Console, either as a global role or as a scoped role for this particular web application. A similar technique can be used for EJBs.

An important benefit of the externally-defined element is that you don't need to modify the way in which WebLogic handles security information in the deployment descriptors (see the section "Ignoring the Deployment Descriptors" later in this chapter). Because the security constraints are implemented through a policy statement defined in terms of a security role that only can be populated using the Administration Console, there is no chance of overwriting this role and policy assignment. The major difference between this element and the traditional J2EE role assignment is that any security role assignment that lists the principals in the *weblogic.xml* descriptor file will create a role whose membership conditions are defined in terms of these principals. If you use the externally-defined element, the security role assignment must refer to a role that you've configured for the realm using the Administration Console.

Policies

Security policies let you protect a wide variety of server resources. For instance, you can decide who has access to the Administration Console, who can start and stop the servers, and who can access the connection pools, web applications, EJBs, enterprise applications, J2EE connectors, a particular branch of the JNDI tree, and more. Security policies offer very tight control over the authorization settings within the WebLogic domain. Although scoped roles look very similar to policies, policies define access control while roles do not. In summary:

- A policy statement is used to protect a resource.
- A policy statement lets you specify a number of conditions under which users may access the resource.

A security policy uses a superset of the conditions that are available to a role. You can define a policy in terms of a logical combination of usernames, group names, time-of-day settings, and roles. The roles used in a policy can be either global roles, or those scoped to the resource for which you are defining the policy.

A WebLogic resource is protected only when it has been assigned a security policy. Some WebLogic resources come with a set of default policies applied to them.

Whereas role information is stored by the Role Mapping Provider, policy information is stored by the Authorization Provider. Even though you may configure the security policies in the same way as the roles, we recommend that you set up roles to identify user responsibilities and create policies to specify access restrictions using these roles. That is, you should define roles in terms of existing users, groups, and time-of-day settings, and then you can use these roles to configure a policy statement for the resource. This scheme fits nicely with the J2EE role-based security model covered earlier in the section "Overview."

A policy can be assigned in a number of ways:

- WebLogic can assign policies to web applications and EJBs automatically, after it has read their deployment descriptors.
- The Administrator can assign policies to WebLogic resources manually and tweak their configuration.
- WebLogic provides default security policies that are applied to many resources.

Using the Administration Console

An Administrator can explicitly define security policies that help protect WebLogic resources. You can assign a security policy in the same way that you define a scoped role for a resource. Simply select the resource from the left pane of the Administration Console, then right-click and choose the Define Security Policy option instead. EJBs offer an additional option, "Define Security Policies and Roles for Individual beans," that allows you to define a policy for a particular EJB and to further limit this policy to selected EJB methods. Web service modules offer similar functionality, allowing you to define a policy for a particular web service within a module and to further limit the policy to selected web service operations. This same functionality exists for JMS destinations, whereby the policy can be limited to either a send, receive, or browse operation on a queue, or to a send or receive operation on a topic.

Enabling user-defined policies

In WebLogic 8.1, *new* policies that you create using the Administration Console will, by default, *not* be applied. Instead, only those policies that were defined using deployment descriptors will be in operation. For example, if you add a new scoped policy for all *.html* files in a web application, and assuming that you had no such security constraint defined in the deployment descriptors, your new scoped policy will not be operational. To toggle this behavior, you need to select the security realm from the left pane of the Administration Console and then select the General tab. The Check Roles and Policies setting can assume two possible values.

Web Applications and EJBs Protected by DD

This option ensures that WebLogic honors only those security constraints defined in the deployment descriptors of web applications and EJB modules. This is the default behavior of the security realm.

All Web Applications and EJBs

This option ensures that WebLogic honors any security policies that are configured for the web applications and EJB modules using the Administration Console.

Thus, you must change the value of the Check Roles and Policies setting to the latter option if you need to enable the policies defined using the Administration Console.

Using the deployment descriptors

WebLogic supports the J2EE security model, which relies on the security roles defined in the descriptor files to determine access privileges. WebLogic's Authorization Provider examines the deployment descriptors when the EAR or WAR is deployed and creates internal security roles based on the configuration settings. In addition, the provider defines a security policy that grants access to all principals that belong to these roles. Later, we'll see how to alter the default behavior of the providers by instructing them to ignore the security data held in the deployment descriptors.

Default policies

WebLogic comes equipped with a number of default security policies—for example, WebLogic supports a default policy that restricts access to the Administration Console. The following security policies are based on role membership:

Administrative resources

The Administration Console and other administrative resources are protected by a security policy that demands that the caller be in one of the following roles: Admin, Deployer, Operator, or Monitor.

Server resources

Resources under the Server node in the Administration Console are protected by a security policy that demands that the caller be either in the Admin or Operator roles.

COM resources

Resources under the Services/jCOM node in the left pane of the Administration Console are protected by a policy that demands that the caller be in the JCOM role.

By default, all application-specific resources, such as those related to JDBC, JMS, EJB, EIS, MBean, and Web Services, are accessible to all users. This is possible because these resources are protected by the default policy, which demands that the caller be in the everyone group. You can always view the default security policy that applies to a WebLogic resource. For instance, if you right-click the Connection Pool node under the Services/JDBC node and then choose the Define Security Policy option, you can view the default policy for all connection pools.

When you configure a new resource—for example, a new JDBC pool or a web services component—it automatically inherits the default security policy. Any new security policy associated with a resource also uses the inherited policy conditions. However, if you define a new security policy for a resource with new policy conditions, these settings override the inherited policy conditions. That is, if you define a policy for a resource, the inherited policy conditions are ignored. For instance, if you define a policy constraint for a JDBC pool that requires that the caller be in the role MyRole, it overrides the default policy constraint that the caller be a member of the group everyone.

Ignoring the Deployment Descriptors

When an application is deployed, WebLogic inspects the security constraints defined in the deployment descriptors and sets up the appropriate role and policy statements in the various providers. Because these roles and policy statements are not persisted to the deployment descriptors (but rather to an internal store), reading this information from the descriptor files the next time the application is deployed means that WebLogic may overwrite any changes that you make to the role and policy information. You can prevent this overwriting behavior by instructing WebLogic to ignore the security constraints in the deployment descriptors the next time the application is deployed. To configure this, navigate to the security realm using the left pane of the Administration Console, and then in the General tab change the value of the On Future Re-Deploys* attribute. The default value for this setting—i.e., initialize roles and "policies" from DD—ensures that WebLogic does create the roles and policies based on the security information held in the deployment descriptors. If you set the attribute to "ignore roles and policies from DD," you can prevent WebLogic from reading the security information held within the deployment descriptors.

Because the providers manage all the information about the roles and policy statements, you have greater control over this access control information now that you can decide *when* WebLogic should ignore the security data in the deployment descriptors. You have two basic options, each with their own security implications:

- If you choose to ignore the deployment descriptors before actually deploying an application, the security constraints for the application need to be configured manually from the Administration Console. The providers will persist the access control information in their own stores, and the security data in the deployment descriptors will be ignored completely.

---

* WebLogic 7.0 users should enable the Ignore Security Data in Deployment Descriptors flag instead.

- If you choose to ignore the deployment descriptors after deploying the application, the providers already will be populated with the security constraints in the descriptor files, which you can later further refine from the Administration Console. Once again, the providers will store this information in their own stores. However, because the security settings in the descriptor files have been ignored, they can no longer override any changes you've made to the roles and policy statements.

Summary

Figure 17-1 summarizes the security architecture that we have just described.

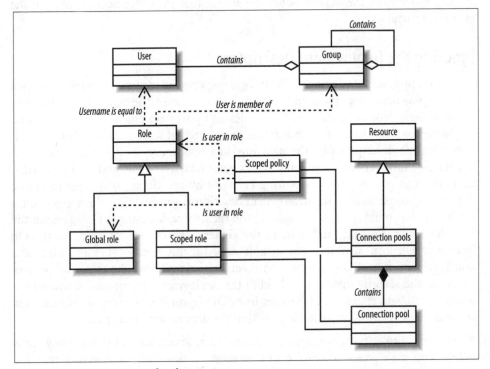

Figure 17-1. Static structure of authentication components

As you can see from the figure, users may belong to groups, and groups may contain other groups. Roles may be defined in terms of users and/or groups. Roles can either be global or scoped to a particular kind of resource. Here we haven't shown all resources—just the hierarchical connection pool resources. A particular connection pool is contained in the Connection Pools resource.

Strictly speaking, policies are applied to a ResourceMBean. At runtime, a ResourceMBean will exist that represents each actual JDBC Connection Pool, all of which extend to another MBean that represents the "container" holding all of the connection pools. Inheritance of policies works because the ResourceMBeans extend each other in this way.

Scoped roles and policies may be associated either with the Connection Pools container (in which case it is inherited by all its instances), or with a particular JDBC Pool itself. All policies are scoped because they are always associated with a particular resource.

The Providers

Now we'll take a closer look at the different SSPIs that constitute a security realm. We'll learn about WebLogic's default implementation of these security providers and how to configure them. The default implementation provides the authentication architecture (and much more) that we have just seen. You can replace one or more of the providers with your own code if you want to change its behavior. Once again, the Administration Console lets you view and modify the configuration of these security providers. All of the security providers available to your realm can be found under the Security/Realms/myrealm/Providers node in the left pane of the Administration Console, where "myrealm" refers to the name of the security realm. Finally, we'll learn about the embedded LDAP server that holds all of the security data for the domain on behalf of the default security providers.

Authentication Providers

Authentication refers to the server's ability to reliably verify the identity of a user or system. We generally refer to a user or system being authenticated as simply a user. A user requires some proof of identity before it can establish trust with the server. WebLogic supports Authentication Providers that can validate user credentials based on a username-password combination or a digital certificate. The *security provider repository*, which stores the user and group information, can be implemented in the following ways:

- As an embedded LDAP server, which is the default used by WebLogic's security providers
- As an external LDAP store, such as Open LDAP, Active Directory, Novell, or NDS
- As a DBMS, which you may already be using to host the data for your enterprise applications
- As a text file, which is used by WebLogic's sample security providers

WeblLogic's authentication provider architecture closely follows the authentication part of the standard JAAS. Following the JAAS terminology, a *subject* represents the source of a security request—it represents a user or system that is trying to be authenticated. The point of authentication is to assign *principals* to a subject. Principals are identities that represent the result of a successful authorization. As we have seen, when the system user authenticates successfully, the subject representing this user is assigned a principal recording the fact that he is in the Administrators group, and another recording that he is a WebLogic user with the name system. Therefore, a subject is a standard container for authentication information, including principals. A client can use a subject to query its identity and other attributes. Figure 17-2 illustrates this client authentication process.

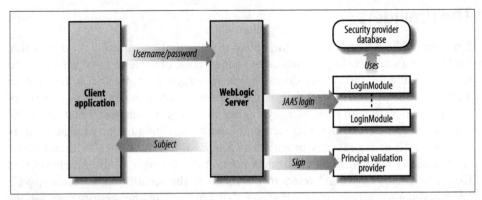

Figure 17-2. The client authentication process

The Authentication Provider adheres to the standard JAAS framework by structuring the authentication sequence on top of a number of configurable JAAS LoginModules. *LoginModules* are critical components of an Authentication Provider, as they are responsible for authenticating users within a security realm and populating the subject with the required principals (existing users and groups).

WebLogic demands that you have at least one authentication provider configured in your security realm.

Principal Validation Providers

Once a (possibly remote) client has established trust with WebLogic, the authenticated subject is retained on the client between server invocations. The Principal Validation Provider ensures that no hanky-panky has taken place with the subject's principals at any time between these invocations. It does this by signing and verifying the authenticity of the principals held by the subject. Once the principals have been validated, they can be used by an Authorization Provider for access control checks or by the Role Mapping Provider for role-mapping decisions. A security realm must define a Principal Validation Provider for each Authentication Provider.

Identity Assertion Providers

Identity Assertion Providers help secure access to the entry points of a WebLogic deployment. Instead of using usernames and passwords, an external client may use tokens to establish trust with a WebLogic Server. The Identity Assertion Provider verifies a token and, if successful, maps it to a valid WebLogic user. Once the token is mapped to a valid user, an Authentication Provider can then generate the principals for the user. This mechanism is called *perimeter authentication*, so you can consider an Identity Assertion Provider a special type of Authentication Provider. The key point here is that an external agent is responsible for authenticating the user, and then for conveying the user data to WebLogic.

As a side effect, perimeter authentication also enables single sign-on. For instance, an Identity Assertion Provider could supply an X.509 digital certificate as an identity token, and these credentials then could be used across multiple systems. WebLogic supports Identity Assertion Providers that can handle different token types (X.509, IIOP-CSIv2). Alternatively, you can create an Identity Assertion Provider that supports custom token types (e.g. Kerberos tickets). An Identity Assertion Provider can have multiple active token types. However, a token type can be active only in a single provider. Of course, a security realm may support multiple Identity Assertion Providers, though none is required. Figure 17-3 illustrates perimeter authentication.

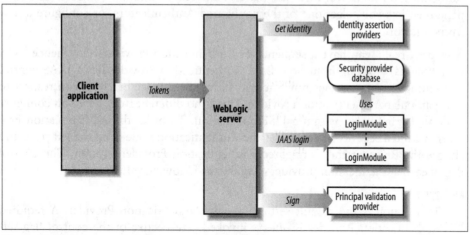

Figure 17-3. Identity assertion during perimeter authentication

The Default Authentication Providers

WebLogic supports authentication based on username-password combinations, authentication using digital certificates transmitted either directly to WebLogic or via an HTTP server, and perimeter-based authentication based on security tokens. WebLogic lets you use the Authentication Providers described next.

Default Authenticator
> This is WebLogic's default Authentication Provider, which relies on the embedded LDAP server to persist all security information.

Realm Adapter Authentication Provider
> This provides backward compatibility with user and group information held in old WebLogic 6.x realms.

Default Identity Asserter
> This is WebLogic's default Identity Assertion Provider, which verifies the authenticity of X.509 and IIOP-CSIv2 tokens and maps them to valid WebLogic users.

LDAP Authentication Providers
> These providers use external LDAP stores to persist all security information about users and groups. WebLogic lets you configure Authenticators that can access various LDAP stores, including Open LDAP, Sun's iPlanet, Microsoft's Active Directory, and Novell NDS.

In addition, you may assign custom-built Authenticators and Identity Asserters to the security realm.

In order to access the Authentication Providers assigned to a realm, select the Authentication node from the left pane of the Administration Console. The right pane then lets you select one of the configured Authenticators, or configure a new Authenticator.

A security realm can have a sequence of Authentication Providers (and hence JAAS LoginModules) working in unison. Each Authentication Provider has a JAAS control flag setting that determines how the overall login sequence behaves with respect to that particular Authentication Provider. This is no different from how you configure multiple LoginModules within a J2SE application. To order the Authentication Providers within a security realm, select the Authentication node from the left pane and choose the Re-order the Configured Authentication Providers option. The control flag of each authentication provider can take the following values:

REQUIRED
> This option is the default setting for any Authentication Provider. A required Authentication Provider is *always* invoked, irrespective of the control flag settings on other providers. The overall authentication cannot succeed if any REQUIRED provider fails. Thus, REQUIRED providers are always invoked, and overall authentication fails if any one of them fails.

REQUISITE
> This option also requires the Authentication Provider to succeed during the login sequence. However, all of the REQUISITE providers need not be invoked for the overall authentication to succeed. If a REQUISITE provider succeeds, the authentication proceeds as normal to other providers in the sequence. However,

if it fails, the overall authentication cannot succeed, and control is immediately passed back to the application once all REQUIRED providers in the login sequence have been invoked.

SUFFICIENT

This option does not require the Authentication Provider to succeed during the login sequence. If a SUFFICIENT provider does succeed, the overall authentication proceeds to ensure that only the remaining REQUIRED providers in the login sequence are executed. However, if it fails, the overall authentication proceeds as normal to the other providers in the login sequence.

OPTIONAL

This option does not require the Authentication Provider to succeed during the login sequence. Regardless of whether an OPTIONAL provider succeeds, the authentication proceeds to other providers that have been configured as part of the login sequence.

When multiple LoginModules are used to authenticate a user, the authentication occurs in two phases. During the first phase, the modules are asked to attempt to authenticate the user. Only if the modules pass this phase is the second phase invoked. During the second phase, each module commits the login and assigns the relevant principals to the subject. The control flags influence how this two-phase commit occurs. Thus, for the overall authentication to succeed, the following rules must be met:

- All REQUIRED modules must be invoked, and each must successfully validate the user.
- Any REQUISITE module that gets invoked must successfully validate the user.
- If a SUFFICIENT module successfully validates the user, the overall success depends on the success of all REQUIRED modules, and any REQUISITE modules invoked before the SUFFICIENT module.
- If the login sequence consists only of OPTIONAL modules, at least one module must successfully validate the user.

Though you can write your own Authenticators, WebLogic's default implementation of the SSPIs comes with a number of built-in authenticators that you can use. Let's look at these authenticators in more detail.

The Default Authenticator

The Default Authenticator authenticates against the embedded LDAP repository. It provides the notion of a user and group and stores user and group information in its own repository, allowing you to manipulate this information. The only configurable option provided by this Authenticator is the Minimum Password Length setting. By default, all WebLogic users must specify a password that is at least eight characters in length; the password length is validated when the user is created. When you log on to the Administration Server using the console or through a JNDI context, it is generally *this* authenticator that validates the username and passwords you supply. Of course, the control flag will determine exactly which providers are called.

Configuring an LDAP authenticator

WebLogic also lets you configure an Authentication Provider that can use existing external LDAP directories such as iPlanet LDAP, Active Directory, Open LDAP, and Novell NDS. In fact, WebLogic's LDAP Authenticators can interface with any LDAP v3–compliant directory servers. In this section, we look at how you can set up an iPlanet Authenticator for your security realm. Other LDAP Authenticators can be configured along the same lines. By using one of the LDAP Authenticators, you can configure WebLogic to recognize users and groups defined in the LDAP repositories and authenticate against this information.

First, select the Authentication node under the realm from the left frame of the Administration Console. If you're using the default security realm myrealm, then the node will be under Security/Realms/myrealm/Providers. Then, select the "Configure a new iPlanet Authenticator" option, either by right-clicking the node or from the right frame itself. Now under the General tab on the right, you'll see the overall details of the new Authenticator. Choose a name for the Authenticator and make sure that the value of the JAAS Control Flag is Required, and then hit the Create button.

 When starting out, it may be useful to set the Control Flag to Optional. In this way, even if your LDAP authentication fails, you still can authenticate using WebLogic's default authenticator and gain access to the Administration Console.

Now select the iPlanet LDAP tab, and enter the values for the host, port, and principal as they apply to your LDAP server. Here, the principal refers to the distinguished name (DN) of the LDAP user that WebLogic will use to connect to the LDAP Server. Typically, you'll use the DN associated with some administrative user account on the LDAP server. For iPlanet LDAP, this is usually uid=admin, ou=Administrators, ou=TopologyManagement, o=NetscapeRoot. If the LDAP server is listening on an SSL port, tick the SSL Enabled option and ensure that you've specified the SSL port. Now hit the Apply button to save changes to the form. Next, change the Credential attribute for the LDAP Principal. In the new screen, you must enter the password that will be used to authenticate the LDAP user defined in the Principal attribute.

Now, select the Users tab and make sure the fields in this form match the configuration of your LDAP repository. In most cases, you will need to modify only the value of the User Base DN attribute to ou=people, o=mydomain.com. This attribute defines the base DN of the branch within the LDAP tree that holds the actual users. Table 17-3 lists the other configuration settings under the Users tab.

Table 17-3. Configuring the Users tab for an LDAP Authenticator

Setting	Description	Default
User Object Class	This attribute indicates the LDAP object class that holds user information	`person`
User Name Attribute	This setting specifies the name of the attribute within the LDAP user object that holds the username.	`uid`
User Search Scope	This setting determines how the users are organized in a multilevel hierarchy or a flat, single-level tree. It affects how deep in the hierarchy to search for users. You can choose from the following values: `subtree/onelevel`.	`subtree`
User From Name Filter	This attribute specifies a search filter for finding a user given the username.	`"(&(uid=%u)(objectclass =person))"`

WebLogic populates these fields with sensible default values, so in most cases you won't have to alter them. Hit the Apply button and move on to the Groups tab. Again, you need to ensure the settings accurately reflect the structure of your LDAP repository. In most cases, you will need to modify only the Group Base DN setting to (say) `ou=groups, o=mydomain.com`. Table 17-4 lists the other configuration settings available under the Groups tab.

Table 17-4. Configuring the Groups tab for an LDAP Authenticator

Setting	Default
Static Group Object Class	`groupofuniquenames`
Static Group Name Attribute	`cn`
Group Search Scope	`subtree`
Group From Name Filter	`"(|(&(cn=%g)(objectclass=groupofUniqueNames))(&(cn=%g)(object-class=groupOfURLs)))  "`

These settings are pretty straightforward, and they have the same semantics as the attributes under the Users tab, just applied to groups.

The Membership tab determines how group members are stored and located in the LDAP directory. WebLogic specifies default values for all fields in the form. Table 17-5 lists two important attributes under the Membership tab.

Table 17-5. Configuring the Membership tab for an LDAP Authenticator

Setting	Description	Default
Static Member DN Attribute	This setting specifies the name of the attribute within the LDAP group object that holds the DNs of members of the group.	`member`
Static Group DNs from Member DN Filter	This attribute specifies a search filter for finding all groups that contain the member, given the name of the group member.	`(&(uniquemember=%M)(o bjectclass=groupofuni quenames))`

Unlike the other authentication providers, the iPlanet provider also supports dynamic groups for which there are additional options.

Now that you have configured the LDAP Authenticator, you are almost ready to reboot the Administration Server. However, you need to ensure that the server's boot identity (i.e., the WebLogic user account used to start the server) corresponds to an LDAP user with the necessary Admin privileges. This means you need to use the iPlanet Console (or any management tool specific to the LDAP server) and complete the following steps:

1. Create an Administrators group in the LDAP repository and place the LDAP user, which is associated with WebLogic's boot identity, in this group.

2. If you are unable to create an Administrators group, create a new group in the LDAP Repository—say, MyAdministrators. Make the LDAP user, which is associated with WebLogic's boot identity, a member of the MyAdministrators group. Then using WebLogic's Administration Console, assign the MyAdministrators group to the default global role Admin.

By doing this, you guarantee that WebLogic's boot identity has the required Admin privileges. The next time you restart the server, go into the Administration Console and remove the Default Authenticator from the list of Authentication Providers. Once you've applied these changes, restart the server—hopefully, you should be able to boot without any authentication errors and set up your WebLogic domain to use the LDAP repository for its user and group information base.

The Default Identity Asserter

The Default Identity Asserter supports perimeter authentication using either X.509 certificates or IIOP CORBA Common Secure Interoperability Version 2 (CSIv2) tokens. A good example of perimeter authentication is when you configure a web application to use CLIENT-CERT authentication. In this case, WebLogic can perform identity assertion based on values from request headers and cookies. If the header name or cookie name matches the active token type for the provider, the value is passed to the provider.

This provider requires you to configure the following attributes:

User Name Mapper Class Name
This attribute specifies the name of a Java class that maps the X.509 certificates or X.501 DNS to WebLogic users, according to some scheme. The User Name Mapping class must implement the weblogic.security.providers.authentication. UserNameMapper interface, and also must be available in WebLogic's CLASSPATH during startup.

Trusted Client Principals
This attribute specifies a list of client principals that may rely on CSIv2 identity assertion. You can use the wildcard character (*) to indicate that all client principals are trusted. If a client principal isn't included in this list, the CSIv2 identity assertion fails and access is denied.

Note that Identity Assertion Providers do not verify proof material. A user can forge a CSIv2 token, for instance, and assume a false identity. Because WebLogic cannot trust such tokens, the Trusted Client Principals setting offers a way to restrict the set of client principals that can use identity assertion. We saw a good example of using X.509 certificates as perimeter authentication in the previous chapter, where we also supplied a custom username mapper class for mapping digital certificates to WebLogic users. When using two-way SSL and X.509 certificates for identity assertion, the SSL protocol ensures that the certificate is not forged. So, the Trusted Client Principals setting applies only to CSIv2 identity tokens.

WebLogic 8.1 comes with a default username mapper that you can enable from the Details tab. This is a general username mapper that can be configured to extract a username from a given attribute of the subject DN field in a certificate. So, for example, if the client's certificate has an email attribute (E), then you can set the Default User Name Mapper Attribute Type to E. You also can specify a delimiter, in which case WebLogic will use that part of the attribute up to but not including the delimiter. For instance, if you need to extract a username from the email attribute, you will want to use the delimiter @. Other attribute types that can be used are the C, CN, L, O, OU, S, and ST types. If you need anything more complex than this, you will have to create your own username mapper class. See Example 17-2 later in this chapter to learn how you can write a custom username mapper.

Authorization Providers

Authorization is synonymous with access control—it determines whether a subject has access to a resource. Whenever an application requests an operation on a protected resource, the resource container that receives the request calls the WebLogic Security framework to determine whether the user is authorized to access the resource. In making this call, any relevant request parameters, such as the subject making the request, are passed to the framework. A few things need to happen before an access decision can be made, as illustrated in Figure 17-4.

First, the configured Role Mapping Providers are invoked. These providers use the request parameters to determine a set of roles that are valid for the subject. After this, the Authorization Providers are asked to decide whether access should be allowed. The Adjudication Provider has the final say in the matter. It looks at the different access decisions returned by the Authorization Providers and reconciles any potential conflicts. The Adjudication Provider generates a final verdict based on these individual access decisions.

A realm may include one or more Authorization Providers. For instance, you could define Authorization Providers that separately control access to JNDI branches, web applications, JMS connection factories, and more.

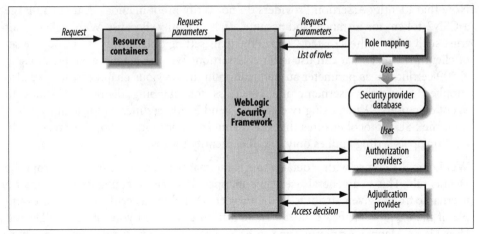

Figure 17-4. The authorization process

The Default Authorization Provider

WebLogic's Authorization Provider performs the aforementioned tasks by using a policy-based authorization engine. This means that WebLogic's resources are protected via security policies assigned at deployment time. Earlier, in the section "The Security Provider Architecture," we looked at how your security policy statements can help protect server-side resources.

Security policies may be assigned manually through the Administration Console, or automatically via the role settings specified in deployment descriptors. The Default Authorizer lets you specify whether the authorizer will store policies that are created when EJBs and web applications are deployed. The Policy Deployment Enabled option indicates whether the provider will evaluate security policies while EJBs and web applications are being deployed. By default, this setting is enabled. This option is quite similar to the Role Deployment Enabled flag in the Role Mapping Provider.

Role Mapping Providers

A Role Mapping Provider determines dynamically at call time the set of roles that are valid for a particular subject when it tries to access a protected resource. An Authorization Provider can then use this information to determine whether a user is allowed access to the resource by evaluating the policy and role information.

The role information is generally based on the role settings defined in J2EE and WebLogic-specific deployment descriptors, the requested operation on the resource, and any custom business logic. You can configure these roles at deployment time, either using the deployment descriptors or via the Administration Console. Because the Authorization Provider makes calls to the Role Mapping Provider just before calculating an authorization decision, and because the role binding occurs dynamically, this gives you the ideal opportunity to embed your own logic for role allocation into a custom provider.

A security realm can define one or more Role Mapping Providers. You could configure a Role Mapping Provider that handles role associations for resources bound to the JNDI tree, or another that handles role associations for web applications.

The Default Role Mapper

Given a protected resource and a user, WebLogic's default Role Mapping Provider will determine all the roles that are valid for user for the resource using the role information stored in its repository. In order to configure the Default Role Mapper, select the Default Role Mapper node from under the Role Mapping node in the left pane of the Administration Console.

The Default Role Mapper has one configuration setting only: the Role Deployment Enabled option. This indicates whether the provider stores roles that are created while deploying a web application or EJB. This setting is similar to the Ignore Security Data in Deployment Descriptors setting that we encountered earlier, except that it is specific to role information. If the Role Deployment Enabled option is set, WebLogic automatically creates roles based on security data in the deployment descriptors and stores them in the embedded LDAP server. This means that if you subsequently ignore the security data in the deployment descriptors, the deployment descriptors won't be processed the next time the EJB or web application is deployed. By default, the Role Deployment Enabled setting is enabled, and you need at least one role mapper with this setting enabled in order to deploy web applications and EJBs.

Adjudication Providers

A subject may access a protected resource in a way that requires multiple Authorization Providers to decide whether the subject has access to the protected resource. Each Authorization Provider may pass one of the following access decisions: PERMIT, ABSTAIN, or DENY. The Adjudication Provider needs to arbitrate between potentially conflicting decisions made by the different Authorization Providers involved. Typically, the Adjudication Provider resolves potential authorization conflicts among the Authorization Providers by carefully weighing the access decisions of each provider.

Thus, you must define an Adjudication Provider if the security realm supports multiple Authorization Providers. Clearly, a security realm may have only a single Adjudication Provider!

The Default Adjudicator

In order to configure the Default Adjudicator, select the Default Adjudicator node from under the Adjudication node in the left frame of the Administration Console.

Here you can adjust the Requires Unanimous Permit setting, which determines the basis on which the Adjudicator grants access to a resource when multiple Authorization Providers are concerned.

If this setting is enabled, the Adjudicator grants access to the resource only if *all* participating Authorization Providers return a result of PERMIT. That is, the decision must be a unanimous PERMIT decision. If any provider returns a DENY or ABSTAIN, the overall decision must be to refuse access.

If the setting is disabled, the Adjudicator grants access to the resource only if no Authorization Provider returns a DENY. This means that the Adjudicator will grant access to the resource even though a unanimous decision could not be reached. So long as all Authorization Providers vote to PERMIT or ABSTAIN, the subject will be allowed to access the resource. Of course, at least one Authorization Provider must vote to PERMIT access to the resource.

Credential Mapping Providers

When a WebLogic user needs to access some external systems, the credentials of the user need to be mapped to valid credentials on the external system. Only then can a subject already authenticated by WebLogic log into the external system. A Credential Mapping Provider is responsible for associating users authenticated by WebLogic to appropriate credentials in an external system. Typically, the Credential Mapping Provider is invoked by WebLogic on behalf of another component—in particular, the container that hosts a resource adapter that needs to connect to a remote resource.

A Credential Mapping Provider can handle different kinds of user credentials—e.g., a username-password combination, a digital certificate, and more. For instance, you could implement a credential map between WebLogic users and credentials of valid users on a remote legacy DBMS. This could be the username-password combination of a valid user on the remote system who is authorized to perform the necessary operations. You can define these credential mappings either in the deployment descriptors or via the Administration Console. A security realm must define at least one Credential Mapping Provider. If you've defined multiple providers, WebLogic queries all providers and returns a list of credentials that may be associated with the WebLogic user.

The Default Credential Mapper

WebLogic's Credential Mapper associates WebLogic users to appropriate credentials in an external system when a user makes use of a resource adapter. So, the Credential Mapping Provider holds a map of WebLogic users and groups to external identities that can be used to authenticate to a remote system. A good example of this is the use of J2EE connectors. Here you typically need to map a WebLogic user to a remote user that has access to the target EIS. Chapter 7 shows how to configure credential maps for deployed J2EE connectors.

In order to configure the provider itself select the Default Credential Mapper node from under Providers/Credential Mapping in your security realm. The Default Credential Mapper provides only one configuration setting, the Credential Mapping Deployment Enabled option, which indicates whether the provider processes the credential maps from the descriptor files of a resource adapter when it is deployed. By default, the Credential Mapping Deployment Enabled flag is set to true. Like the other Deployment Enabled settings, if you disable this setting, the credential maps specified in the deployment descriptor for the resource adapter won't overwrite the credential maps you may have created via the Administration Console.

Auditing Providers

Auditing is another important feature of WebLogic's security framework. Nonrepudiation requires that you maintain a log of security events that provides an electronic trace of how the data has been accessed. WebLogic's Auditing Provider can be configured to log information about security requests and their outcomes. Usually, the Auditing Provider is invoked by WebLogic's Auditor on behalf of other security providers, both before and after a security operation has been executed. In this way, the Auditor is able to capture detailed information about any security requests and responses.

Typically, the Auditing Provider will decide whether to audit the security request based on several criteria. For instance, you could configure a security level for the Auditing Provider that automatically filters out audit requests that do not reach the desired security level. An Auditing Provider also supports channels that can record the information to a variety of sinks, such as an LDAP store, database table, or plain file. WebLogic's Auditor can interact with multiple Auditing Providers. However, you may choose not to define any Auditing Provider for a security realm.

The Default Auditor

By default, there are *no* Auditing Providers configured for a security realm. In order to configure a new Auditing Provider, expand the Auditing node from the left frame of the Administration Console and then choose the "Configure a new Default Auditor" option. In the new screen, assign a severity level for the audit log and hit the Create button.

The severity level determines the kind of events that are logged by WebLogic's Default Auditor. The lower the severity level, the more verbose the auditing. The severity level can be chosen from the following (in increasing order of verbosity): FAILURE, SUCCESS, ERROR, WARNING, and INFORMATION. For example, a severity level of FAILURE ensures that the Auditor logs only security requests that have failed (e.g., failed authentication), while a severity level of INFORMATION ensures that the Auditor logs all authentication activity. The default severity level is ERROR.

 The lower the severity level, the more verbose the output. This can impact server performance because the Auditor is potentially a lot busier. You should set a sensible severity level and carefully monitor your setup to ensure it doesn't yield unacceptable performance levels.

The audit information is written to the *mydomain\myserver\DefaultAuditRecorder.log* file, where mydomain is the name of the WebLogic domain. For example, if an authenticated user attempts to dip into a connection pool and is denied access, the Default Auditor logs the following information:

```
#### Audit Record Begin <05-Sep-02 22:24:46>  <Severity =FAILURE>
<<<Event Type = Authorization Audit Event ><Subject: 1
   Principal = class weblogic.security.principal.WLSUserImpl("A")>
<ONCE><<jdbc>><type=<jdbc>, application=, module=, resourceType=ConnectionPool,
resource=MyPool, action=reserve>>> Audit Record End ####
```

The Embedded LDAP Server

Any implementation of the SSPIs requires some kind of security provider database that can act as a repository for the domain's security data. WebLogic relies on an embedded LDAP server to persist all of its information about users, groups, policies, roles, and user credentials. The embedded LDAP server is accessible to all of WebLogic's security providers that need to store and manipulate such data: the Authentication, Authorization, Role Mapping, and Credential Mapping Providers. In the default setup, the Administration Server holds a master LDAP repository, and this repository is then replicated to all Managed Servers. Any changes made by WebLogic's providers are sent to the master LDAP server, which then sends the appropriate changes to each replicated server. Managed Servers in the domain are synchronized as soon as the data is changed on the Administration Server's LDAP repository. There is, however, a small window between the write to the Administration Server and the replication due to network traffic.

To configure the embedded LDAP server, select your domain from the left frame of the Administration Console. Choose the View Domain-Wide Security Settings* option and select the Configuration/Embedded LDAP tab. Table 17-6 lists the various settings that can be configured from the Embedded LDAP tab.

---

* WebLogic 7.0 users should just choose the Security/Embedded LDAP tab after selecting the domain node.

Table 17-6. Configuring the embedded LDAP server

Setting	Description	Default
Credential	This setting specifies a password that allows you to connect to the LDAP server.	none
Backup Hour/Minute	This setting determines the hour/minute when the backups are supposed to occur.	23;5
Backup Copies	This setting determines the number of backup copies of the LDAP data that should be made.	7
Cache Enabled	This option indicates whether caching is enabled for the LDAP server.	true
Cache Size	This setting determines the size of the cache used by the LDAP server.	32KB
Cache TTL	This setting determines the duration for which items are held in the cache.	60s
Replica Refresh	By default, changes are sent periodically to the Managed Servers. If you've made a number of changes while a Managed Server has been down, then sending a large number of changes may be expensive. To optimize this, enabling this parameter ensures all of the replicated data will be refreshed as a whole at boot time.	false
Master First	In extreme cases, you can enable this flag so that any Managed Server must contact the master LDAP server instead of its local LDAP server.	false

Note how the LDAP server can be configured to back itself up. The backup files are written to a directory called *mydomain\servername\ldap\backup* and can be used to replace those files in the *ldapfiles* directory.

External access to the LDAP server

You can use your favorite LDAP browser to gain access to WebLogic's embedded LDAP server. This may be useful for integration purposes, or perhaps more usefully as providing a way of importing and exporting user data. Before accessing the server, you need to set up its security credential. Select the Embedded LDAP tab as described in the previous section. Then select the Credential option and enter a credential (password) for the LDAP server. WebLogic will use this password to authenticate any LDAP clients.

Now start up your favorite LDAP browser and point it to the following URL:

```
ldap://hostname:port/dc=mydomain
```

Here, mydomain refers to the name of the WebLogic domain. The LDAP server isn't set up for anonymous access, so you must specify the username cn=Admin. For the password, you need to supply the same credentials you configured earlier for WebLogic's embedded LDAP server. You then can browse the LDAP data, which includes information about the users, groups, security roles, policy statements, and more.

Some LDAP browsers also let you import and export the LDAP data in the LDIF format. This provides you with an easy way to migrate some data, such as the information on users and groups located under the DNs ou=people,ou=myrealm,dc=mydomain and ou=groups,ou=myrealm,dc=mydomain, respectively. Once again, myrealm refers to the name of the security realm, while mydomain refers to the name of the WebLogic domain. Experienced administrators can further restrict access to the embedded LDAP server. Because WebLogic's LDAP server also supports the IETF LDAP Access Control Model, you can implement fine-grained access to the LDAP server if the need arises.

In WebLogic 8.1, many security providers also permit the export and import of their data. You can find this facility on the Migration tab of the Authentication, Authorization, Credential Mapper, and Role Mapper Providers.

Configuring Trust Between Two Domains

Two or more WebLogic domains can be configured so that they *trust* each other. When you've set up trust between two different WebLogic domains, you enable authenticated WebLogic users in one domain to access protected resources in another domain. For instance, an authenticated user in one domain may invoke a protected web service or an EJB in another domain without requiring any additional authentication. Let's say that we have two WebLogic domains, A and B. Trust between the domains means that the subject's principals in one domain—say, A—are accepted by the other domain, B (and vice versa) and are treated as if they were local principals of domain B. The Authorization Providers within domain B remain unaware of the fact that the subject's principals belong to domain A.

Two WebLogic domains will trust each other only if they both have the same Credential attribute. The Credential attribute represents a string value that is assigned to a domain and then is used to sign principals that belong to subjects created in that domain. Ordinarily, if you haven't explicitly set the domain credential, it is assigned a random value when the Administration Server is first booted. All Managed Servers in the domain subsequently import this credential when they are booted as well. In order to set the Credential attribute for a WebLogic domain, select your domain from the left pane of the Administration Console, choose the View Domain-Wide Security Settings[*] option, and select the Configuration/Advanced tab. If two domains share the same Credential attribute value, the signatures of the principals will match and be recognized by both domains. Thus, in order to establish trust between several domains, you need to simply ensure they are assigned the same value for the Credential attribute.

JAAS Authentication in a Client

We already have seen many examples of how a Java client authenticates itself to WebLogic Server. In most cases, the client submits a username-password combination as its credentials when setting up the JNDI context:

---

[*] WebLogic 7.0 users should simply select the Security/Advanced tab after selecting the domain node.

```
Hashtable env = new Hashtable( );
env.put(Context.INITIAL_CONTEXT_FACTORY,
                  "weblogic.jndi.WLInitialContextFactory");
env.put(Context.PROVIDER_URL, "t3://10.0.10.10:7001");
env.put(Context.SECURITY_PRINCIPAL, "system");
env.put(Context.SECURITY_CREDENTIALS, "12341234");
Context ctx = new InitialContext(env);
// use the JNDI context as "system" user ...
```

WebLogic also lets you build Java clients that can use the more standard approach to authentication using JAAS. Even though JAAS authentication is somewhat more long-winded than traditional JNDI-based authentication, your clients will be more portable. Because of the pluggable nature of the JAAS framework, it should enable you to benefit from future changes to the authentication technology without changes to the client code.

Anatomy of a JAAS Client

A JAAS client involves the interplay among a number of classes and interfaces, as shown in Figure 17-5. Let's examine how these different objects interact during JAAS-style authentication:

Subject

> This represents the goal of the authentication sequence. Once a client has been authenticated, it obtains a Subject instance that is populated with all of the principals that map to the client.

LoginContext

> This is responsible for populating the Subject with its principals. Its all-important login( ) method delivers an authenticated Subject back to the client. To construct a LoginContext instance, you need to supply objects of two subsidiary classes: a CallBackHandler and LoginModule instance.

CallBackHandler

> This is responsible for retrieving the username and password of the client being authenticated. In the case of a Swing-based application, the CallBackHandler instance could conceivably pop up a dialog box requesting the data from the end user. In fact, the CallBackHandler instance is invoked by the LoginModule.

LoginModule

> This is any entity capable of authenticating the user's credentials. A separate JAAS configuration file settles how the LoginModule is implemented. In general, you can implement your own login modules. However, WebLogic also provides you with a convenient LoginModule that can authenticate the client via the supplied username and password against a WebLogic instance whose URL is also supplied. On successful authentication, the LoginModule populates the subject with its principals. Using this authenticated subject, the JAAS client can now perform one or more privileged actions.

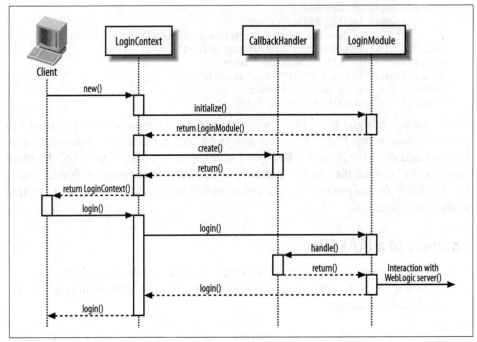

Figure 17-5. Typical interaction when authenticating a JAAS client

PrivilegedAction

Any class that implements the PrivilegedAction interface encapsulates the code that a Java client can run within the security context defined by the populated Subject. The weblogic.security.Security.runAs() method allows the client to associate a Subject with the current thread, before invoking the privileged action under this security context.

A Sample JAAS Client

Let's look at how to build a JAAS client that can authenticate itself to WebLogic. We'll cover this example using a top-down approach, starting with what the JAAS client needs to accomplish and then breaking it down into the individual components of its implementation. Let's begin with the main class, SimpleJAASClient, which takes the following steps:

1. It reads the username, password, and URL as input arguments from the command line.
2. It attempts to connect to the specified URL and then authenticates the client using the supplied username and password.
3. It executes a privileged action under the newly acquired authenticated subject.

Example 17-1 lists the source code for our JAAS client.

Example 17-1. A sample JAAS client

```
package com.oreilly.wlguide.security.jaas;

import javax.security.auth.Subject;
import javax.security.auth.login.LoginContext;

public class SimpleJAASClient {
  public static void main(String[] args) {
    String username = args[0];
    String password = args[1];
    String url = args[2];
    LoginContext loginContext = null;
    // Create a LoginContext using our own CallBackHander
    try {
      loginContext = new LoginContext("Simple",
             new SimpleCallbackHandler(username, password, url));
    } catch (Exception e) {
      // Can get a SecurityException or a LoginException
      e.printStackTrace();
      System.exit(-1);
    }
    // Now authenticate.  If we don't get an exception, we succeeded
    try {
      loginContext.login();
    } catch (Exception e) {
      // Can get FailedLoginException, AccountExpiredException,
      // or CredentialExpiredException
      e.printStackTrace();
      System.exit(-1);
    }
    // Retrieve authenticated subject and perform action using it
    Subject subject = loginContext.getSubject();
    SimpleAction simpleAction = new SimpleAction(url);
    weblogic.security.Security.runAs(subject, simpleAction);
  }
}
```

Notice how we've highlighted the important bits of the JAAS client. Our first critical step is to establish a LoginContext object:

```
loginContext = new LoginContext("Simple",
             new SimpleCallbackHandler(username, password, url));
```

The LoginContext object initializes the client with the CallBackHandler and LoginModule instances that will be used during JAAS authentication. The second argument to the constructor is our own CallBackHandler instance that will be used by the LoginModule to retrieve the user's credentials, and the URL of the WebLogic instance that will authenticate our client.

The first argument to the constructor, Simple, is used to look up the appropriate LoginModule for the client. JAAS clients rely on a configuration file that maps the names of JAAS login modules to their implementation, and also may specify additional parameters. Example 17-2 lists the JAAS configuration file that we used.

Example 17-2. Login configuration file, jaas.config

```
Simple {
    weblogic.security.auth.login.UsernamePasswordLoginModule
    required
};
```

Our configuration file contains a single entry for Simple that specifies WebLogic's LoginModule for authentication on the basis of the given username and password: weblogic.security.auth.login.UsernamePasswordLoginModule. When you run the JAAS client, you must specify the location of this configuration file using a system property. Here's how you would run our sample JAAS client:

```
java -Djava.security.auth.login.config=jaas.config \
    com.oreilly.wlguide.security.jaas.SimpleJAASClient system pssst t3://10.0.10.10:
    8001/
```

In this way, we can configure the LoginContext to use WebLogic's LoginModule, which supports authentication using a username-password combination. Later, we'll see how you can use the JAAS configuration file to transparently substitute this with your own LoginModule implementation.

After establishing the login context, we've invoked the loginContext.login( ) method to execute the actual login. Our LoginContext will utilize the configured login module and callback handler objects and attempt to authenticate the client with the server. If this client is authenticated successfully, you can retrieve the authenticated subject from the LoginContext:

```
Subject subject = loginContext.getSubject( );
```

The getPrincipals( ) method on this authenticated Subject retrieves all of the principals associated with the user. For instance, if our JAAS client authenticated using the credentials of the system administrator, the authenticated Subject holds two principals: system, which represents the user, and Administrators, which represents the user's group. Now, we can use this subject to execute one or more "privileged" actions. In other words, these actions are performed within the context of this authenticated subject:

```
weblogic.security.Security.runAs(subject, simpleAction);
```

There is one caveat here—the client must invoke the runAs( ) method on WebLogic's Security class. The runAs( ) method accepts two parameters: the authenticated Subject, and a PrivilegedAction object, which wraps the application-specific interaction with the server. Example 17-3 illustrates the action that our JAAS client wishes to execute.

Example 17-3. A very simple action

```
package com.oreilly.wlguide.security.jaas;

import java.security.PrivilegedAction;
import java.sql.Connection;
import java.util.Hashtable;
import javax.naming.Context;
import javax.naming.InitialContext;
import javax.sql.DataSource;

public class SimpleAction implements PrivilegedAction {
    private static final String JNDI_NAME = "jdbc.xpetstore";
    private String url;

    public SimpleAction(String url) {
        this.url = url;
    }

    public Object run() {
        Object obj = null;
        try {
            Context ctx = null;
            Hashtable ht = new Hashtable();
            ht.put(Context.INITIAL_CONTEXT_FACTORY,
                "weblogic.jndi.WLInitialContextFactory");
            ht.put(Context.PROVIDER_URL, url);
            // Get a context for the JNDI lookup
            ctx = new InitialContext(ht);
            // do any work here
            DataSource ds =(javax.sql.DataSource) ctx.lookup(JNDI_NAME);
            // ...
        } catch (Exception e) {
            e.printStackTrace();
        }
        return obj;
    }
}
```

Here you need to recognize the following significant points:

- The class implements the java.security.PrivilegedAction interface. Any JAAS client can then invoke an instance of this class within the context of the authenticated Subject.

- The run() method encapsulates the client's interaction with the server. Typically, the client will establish a JNDI context, use it to grab resources bound to the JNDI tree, and then invoke/access these resources. In the earlier example, we used the JNDI context to acquire a JDBC data source.

- When we establish the JNDI context within the PrivilegedAction.run() method, we don't provide any user credentials for JNDI authentication. The authenticated Subject supplied by the JAAS client to the runAs() method ensures that the PrivilegedAction object is invoked within the context of this subject. That is, the runAs( ) method is responsible for associating the authenticated Subject with the current thread.

Example 17-4 lists the source code for our CallBackHandler class. In general, the callback handler would interact with the client in some way that prompts the user for the username and password to be used for authentication. In the case of our simple JAAS client, we supply the necessary credentials and URL to the constructor of our callback handler so that the callbacks can easily return this information.

Example 17-4. A simple callback handler

```
package com.oreilly.wlguide.security.jaas;

import javax.security.auth.callback.Callback;
import javax.security.auth.callback.CallbackHandler;
import javax.security.auth.callback.NameCallback;
import javax.security.auth.callback.PasswordCallback;
import javax.security.auth.callback.UnsupportedCallbackException;
import weblogic.security.auth.callback.URLCallback;

public class SimpleCallbackHandler implements CallbackHandler {
    private String username = null;
    private String password = null;
    private String url = null;

    public SimpleCallbackHandler(String pUsername, String pPassword, String pUrl) {
      username = pUsername;  password = pPassword;  url = pUrl;
    }

    public void handle(Callback[] callbacks)
        throws java.io.IOException, UnsupportedCallbackException {
      for (int i = 0; i < callbacks.length; i++) {
        if (callbacks[i] instanceof NameCallback) {
        NameCallback nc = (NameCallback) callbacks[i];
        nc.setName(username);
        } else if (callbacks[i] instanceof URLCallback) {
        URLCallback uc = (URLCallback) callbacks[i];
        uc.setURL(url);
        } else if (callbacks[i] instanceof PasswordCallback) {
        PasswordCallback pc = (PasswordCallback) callbacks[i];
        pc.setPassword(password.toCharArray( ));
        } else {
        throw new UnsupportedCallbackException(
            callbacks[i], "Unrecognized Callback");
        }
      }
    }
  }
}
```

The final piece of the puzzle is the JAAS login module. Earlier, we saw how the JAAS configuration file enabled us to set up our client to use WebLogic's login module for username-password authentication, the UsernamePasswordLoginModule. This Login-Module class expects our callback handler to deal with username and password callbacks, and optionally, the URL callback as well. The login( ) method provides the entry point for the JAAS framework into the LoginModule. It uses the user's credentials to authenticate the client with WebLogic and, if successful, returns an authenticated Subject populated with the appropriate principals.

We could have easily constructed our own login module and modified the configuration file to reference this module. The login( ) method is the most important within the LoginModule implementation class because this method is responsible for performing the actual authentication. Typically, it must use the configured callback handler to retrieve the username, password, and URL. It must then create an Environment object populated with this data, and invoke the authenticate( ) method on WebLogic's Authenticate class to execute the login and generate an authenticated Subject populated with required principals. The following code shows how to accomplish this authentication:

```
weblogic.jndi.Environment env = new weblogic.jndi.Environment( );
env.setProviderUrl(url);
env.setSecurityPrincipal(username);
env.setSecurityCredentials(password);
weblogic.security.auth.Authenticate.authenticate(env, subject);
```

In general, WebLogic's login module should be sufficient for most purposes; it is unlikely that you will need to provide your own LoginModule implementation.

Creating a Custom Authentication Provider

Developing your own security providers is a relatively specialized task—it is necessary only if WebLogic's default providers are insufficient. The majority of custom providers tend to change the default authentication or identity assertion mechanisms. The following sections provide an example of each of these. We recommend that you read WebLogic's well-documented security provider API to understand the life cycle of each provider if you intend to create your own. This information is supplied on the official web site, *http://edocs.bea.com/wls/docs81/dvspisec/index.html*. BEA's dev2dev web site (*http://www.dev2dev.bea.com*) also contains a number of example providers.

MBeans

WebLogic's provider architecture is MBean-based (see Chapter 20)—if you are going to write a new provider, it has to have a corresponding MBean implementation. WebLogic provides tools for creating the necessary MBean deployment files and implementations. At runtime, the MBean representing your provider will be used to create an instance of your provider implementation—the MBean is, in a sense, a factory for the provider implementation that you will have to supply. This, in turn, will use the MBean to read its configuration information. Any provider MBean must extend the appropriate base MBean type, supplied with WebLogic. To facilitate in the creation of these peripheral classes, WebLogic provides a few utilities. They are based around an *MBean Definition File* (MDF), an XML file that describes your MBean implementation. Example 17-5 lists such an XML file.

Example 17-5. A simple MDF (MyAuthentication.xml) for an authentication provider

```
<?xml version="1.0" ?>
<!DOCTYPE MBeanType SYSTEM "commo.dtd">
<MbeanType Name = "MyAuthenticator" DisplayName   = "MyAuthenticator"
 Package       = "com.oreilly.wlguide.security.iap"
 Extends       = "weblogic.management.security.authentication.Authenticator"
 PersistPolicy = "OnUpdate">
<MbeanAttribute Name = "ProviderClassName" Type = "java.lang.String"
  Writeable     = "false"
  Default       =
"&quot;com.oreilly.wlguide.security.iap.MyAuthenticationProviderImpl&quot;"
  />
<MbeanAttribute Name = "Description" Type = "java.lang.String"
  Writeable     = "false"
  Default       = "&quot;O'Reilly Authentication Provider&quot;"
  />
<MBeanAttribute Name = "Version" Type = "java.lang.String"
  Writeable     = "false"    Default = "&quot;1.0&quot;"
  />
</MBeanType>
```

If you are to implement your own authentication provider, copy Example 17-5 verbatim, changing only the lines that have been highlighted (unless you want to add additional attributes). The `ProviderClassName` MBean attribute is the most important. This indicates the class name that represents the custom provider that we will have to implement, in this case, `com.oreilly.wlguide.security.iap.MyAuthentication-ProviderImpl`.

Once you have this file, you can use the `MbeanMaker` utility to take the MDF file and generate the MBean and stubs:

```
java -DcreateStubs="true" weblogic.management.commo.WebLogicMBeanMaker -MDF ..\
MyAuthentication.xml -files outdirectory
```

This generates a number of files, all of which can be ignored unless you implement custom operations and attributes. These are all placed in the *outdirectory*. All you need to do now is supply the actual implementation of the provider, recompile and repackage the whole lot, and deploy it.

Note that to use these utilities, you not only need to execute the *setEnv* script to prepare your environment, but you also have to add an extra JAR file to your classpath. This JAR file is located in *WL_HOME/server/lib/mbeantypes/wlManagement.jar*.

Authentication Provider

Now we turn to the authentication provider implementation itself. Recall that in the MDF, we specified the class name of a class that is to supply the authentication provider (see Example 17-6). This class must implement the `weblogic.security.spi.AuthenticationProvider` interface.

Example 17-6. An authentication provider implementation

```
package com.oreilly.wlguide.security.iap;

import java.util.HashMap;
import javax.security.auth.login.AppConfigurationEntry;
import javax.security.auth.login.AppConfigurationEntry.LoginModuleControlFlag;
import weblogic.management.security.ProviderMBean;
import weblogic.security.provider.PrincipalValidatorImpl;
import weblogic.security.spi.*;

public final class MyAuthenticationProviderImpl implements AuthenticationProvider {
  private String description;
  private LoginModuleControlFlag controlFlag;

  // Our mapping of users to passwords/groups, instead of being in LDAP or in a
  // database, is represented by a HashMap of MyUserDetails objects..
  public class MyUserDetails {
    String pw;
    String group;
    // We use this to represent the user's groups and passwords
    public MyUserDetails(String pw, String group) {
     this.pw=pw; this.group = group;
    }
    public String getPassword() {return pw;}
    public String getGroup() {return group;}
  }

  // This is our database
  private HashMap userGroupMapping = null;

  public void initialize(ProviderMBean mbean, SecurityServices services) {
    MyAuthenticatorMBean myMBean = (MyAuthenticatorMBean)mbean;
    description = myMBean.getDescription() + "\n" + myMBean.getVersion();
    System.err.println("#In realm:" + myMBean.getRealm().wls_getDisplayName());
    // We would typically use the realm name to find the database
    // we want to use for authentication. Here, we just create one.
    userGroupMapping = new HashMap();
    userGroupMapping.put("a", new MyUserDetails("passworda", "g1"));
    userGroupMapping.put("b", new MyUserDetails("passwordb", "g2"));
    userGroupMapping.put("system", new MyUserDetails("12341234",
                                                     "Administrators"));

    String flag = myMBean.getControlFlag();
    if (flag.equalsIgnoreCase("REQUIRED")) {
      controlFlag = LoginModuleControlFlag.REQUIRED;
```

Example 17-6. An authentication provider implementation (continued)

```
    } else if (flag.equalsIgnoreCase("OPTIONAL")) {
      controlFlag = LoginModuleControlFlag.OPTIONAL;
    } else if (flag.equalsIgnoreCase("REQUISITE")) {
      controlFlag = LoginModuleControlFlag.REQUISITE;
    } else if (flag.equalsIgnoreCase("SUFFICIENT")) {
      controlFlag = LoginModuleControlFlag.SUFFICIENT;
    } else {
      throw new IllegalArgumentException("Invalid control flag " + flag);
    }
  }

  public AppConfigurationEntry getLoginModuleConfiguration() {
   HashMap options = new HashMap();
    options.put("usermap", userGroupMapping);
    return new AppConfigurationEntry(
          "com.oreilly.wlguide.security.provider.MyLoginModuleImpl",
          controlFlag, options
    );
  }
  public String getDescription() {
    return description;
  }
  public PrincipalValidator getPrincipalValidator() {
    return new PrincipalValidatorImpl();
  }
  public AppConfigurationEntry getAssertionModuleConfiguration() {
    return null;
  }
  public IdentityAsserter getIdentityAsserter() {
    return null;
  }
  public void shutdown() {}
}
```

The class simply provides a way of getting to the various modules, most of which are optional. For example, we do not provide an identity asserter, so we just return null. Likewise, we simply return WebLogic's default principal validator implementation as the principal validator. All of the action happens in the initialize() and getLoginModuleConfiguration() methods.

Typically, the job of the initialize() method is to set up the resources necessary to perform any authentication. As you can see from the implementation, it has direct access to the MBean—so, if you added extra attributes or operations to the MBean, they can be used here. In our case, we simply set up a local database in the form of a hashmap. It then stores the control flag that is used in the module configuration. This eventually will get passed to the login module.

The getLoginModuleConfiguration() method returns an object that encapsulates the login module—the final piece of functionality that we have to implement. You can think of this method as playing the same role as the JAAS configuration file. It is instructing the provider as to which login module to use, on the server side this time. Note that the login module is wrapped in an object (AppConfigurationEntry) that also captures the control flag and options.

Login Module

We now need to supply a login module, as shown in Example 17-7. This follows the standard JAAS API.

Example 17-7. A login module

```
package com.oreilly.wlguide.security.provider;

import java.io.IOException;
import java.util.*;
import javax.security.auth.Subject;
import javax.security.auth.callback.*;
import javax.security.auth.login.*;
import javax.security.auth.spi.LoginModule;
import weblogic.security.principal.WLSGroupImpl;
import weblogic.security.principal.WLSUserImpl;

/**
 * This login module will be called by our Authentication Provider.
 * It assumes that the option, usermap, will be passed which contains
 * the map of users to passwords and groups.
 */
public class MyLoginModuleImpl implements LoginModule {
    private Subject subject;
    private CallbackHandler callbackHandler;
    private HashMap userMap;

    // Authentication status
    private boolean loginSucceeded;
    private boolean principalsInSubject;
    private Vector principalsBeforeCommit = new Vector();

    public void initialize(Subject subject, CallbackHandler callbackHandler,
                           Map sharedState, Map options) {
        this.subject = subject;
        this.callbackHandler = callbackHandler;
        // Fetch user/password map that should be set by the authenticator
        userMap = (HashMap) options.get("usermap");
    }

    /* Called once after initialize to try and log the person in */
    public boolean login() throws LoginException {
        // First thing we do is create an array of callbacks so that
        // we can get the data from the user
        Callback[] callbacks;
        callbacks = new Callback[2];
        callbacks[0] = new NameCallback("username: ");
```

Example 17-7. A login module (continued)

```
      callbacks[1] = new PasswordCallback("password: ", false);
      try {
        callbackHandler.handle(callbacks);
      } catch (IOException eio) {
        throw new LoginException(eio.toString( ));
      } catch (UnsupportedCallbackException eu) {
        throw new LoginException(eu.toString( ));
      }

      String username = ((NameCallback) callbacks[0]).getName( );
      char [] pw = ((PasswordCallback) callbacks[1]).getPassword( );
      String password = new String(pw);
      if (username.length( ) > 0) {
        if (!userMap.containsKey(username))
          throw new FailedLoginException("Authentication Failed: Could not find user:
" + username);
        String realPassword = ((MyAuthenticationProviderImpl.MyUserDetails) userMap.
get(username)).getPassword( );
        if (realPassword == null || !realPassword.equals(password))
          throw new FailedLoginException("Authentication Failed: Password incorrect
 for user" + username);
      } else {
        // No Username, so anonymous access is being attempted
      }
      loginSucceeded = true;
      // We collect some principals that we would like to add to the user
      // once this is committed.
      // First, we add his username itself
      principalsBeforeCommit.add(new WLSUserImpl(username));
      // Now we add his group
      principalsBeforeCommit.add(new WLSGroupImpl(((MyAuthenticationProviderImpl.
MyUserDetails)userMap.get(username)).getGroup( )));
      return loginSucceeded;
  }

  public boolean commit( ) throws LoginException {
    if (loginSucceeded) {
      subject.getPrincipals( ).removeAll(principalsBeforeCommit);
      principalsInSubject = true;
      return true;
    } else {
      return false;
    }
  }

  public boolean abort( ) throws LoginException {
    if (principalsInSubject) {
      subject.getPrincipals( ).removeAll(principalsBeforeCommit);
      principalsInSubject = false;
    }
    return true;
  }
```

Example 17-7. A login module (continued)

```
  public boolean logout( ) throws LoginException {
    return true;
  }
}
```

Although long, this is pretty straightforward. Let's go through it. The initialize( ) method has direct access to the options that were configured in the provider. As we put our database in the options, this method provides the ideal place to extract the database. The rest of the action occurs in a combination of the login( ), commit( ), and abort( ) methods. If a login succeeds, and the control flags of the login modules are such that the entire login is to commit, the commit( ) method will be called— otherwise, the abort( ) method will be called. These methods simply ensure that the principals that should be associated with the subject are placed into the subject. The login( ) method does all of the work. First, it sets up a number of callbacks—we need the username and password. Note that the actual callback implementation is going to be handled by WebLogic. For example, WebLogic prompts you for the system user credentials when you try and boot a WebLogic server or access the Administration Console. It is the data from these callbacks that eventually will be supplied to the login method. After handling the callbacks, we extract the username and password of the user and locate it in our database. If successful, we make a list of principals that we want to associate with the user, storing these in the variable principalsBeforeCommit. The principals are added to the subject only if WebLogic calls the commit( ) method.

Deploying the Provider

Once you have created the authentication provider and login module, you can package these together with the generated stub and MBI files. To do this, execute the following command:

```
    java weblogic.management.commo.WebLogicMBeanMaker -MJF myAuth.jar -files .
```

You are now ready to deploy your new provider. Copy *myAuth.jar* to the *WL_HOME/ server/lib/mbeantypes* directory, and then reboot the server. Note that all custom providers have to be located in this directory. Start up the Administration Console and navigate to the Security/myrealm/Providers/Authentication node. In the list of available authenticators and identity asserters, you should find an option for "Configure a new My Authenticator." Selecting this option and clicking Create will configure the authenticator. On the following tab, you will notice that you can change the control flag. If you change this to something such as requisite, make sure that your database has a user in the Administrators group. If not, you won't even be able to boot the server! Use the OPTIONAL flag during development to avoid these problems.

Creating an Identity Assertion Provider

Imagine that you have some external system—say, a Java client or perhaps even an external web server—that authenticates a user, and you now want this user to participate in actions involving WebLogic. Furthermore, you don't want WebLogic to reauthenticate the user. Rather, you want to use some token generated by the external system to be used as an automatic WebLogic login. This is fairly typical of many single sign-on scenarios. The key to implementing this is to use an Identity Assertion Provider. Let's look at how you can implement such a scenario.

We are going to take as an example an external Java client that has presumably performed some user authentication, and who now needs to transfer this identity to WebLogic in order to access a protected web application. First of all, let's configure the web application to use identity assertion. Do this by setting the `login-config` to use a `CLIENT-CERT` authorization method. As this is standard J2EE, you will need to create a *web.xml* file with something such as the following in it:

```
<security-constraint>
  <!-- web resource collection omitted -->
  <auth-constraint>
    <description>nyse</description>
    <role-name>mysecrole</role-name>
  </auth-constraint>
</security-constraint>
<login-config>
  <auth-method>CLIENT-CERT</auth-method>
  <realm-name>myrealm</realm-name>
</login-config>
<security-role>
  <role-name>mysecrole</role-name>
</security-role>
```

Now let's imagine we have a client (written in whatever language you wish) that has already performed some user authentication and now needs to access one of the protected web pages—say, *http://10.0.10.10:8001/index.jsp*. The following client is such an example:

```
URL url = new URL("http://10.0.10.10:8001/index.jsp");
URLConnection connection = url.openConnection();
BufferedReader in = new BufferedReader(new InputStreamReader(
                           connection.getInputStream()));
// Read the input stream
in.close();
```

If you simply run this program, you can expect an IOException when you try and access the input stream. This will be the 401 HTTP error code indicating that you are not authorized. We are going to get around this by making the client supply a token, and then configuring an Identity Assertion Provider to accept this token and authorize the user. Identity Assertion Providers can automatically take advantage of request cookies or headers. If WebLogic finds, for example, a header property with the same name as a token (we will see in a moment how to configure the identity provider with token names), it assumes that the content of the header property is the value of the token. The token we will use is a simple string that we are going to send in the HTTP request header when we create the connection to the server. To this end, modify the preceding code to read as follows:

```
URL url = new URL(urlAddr);
URLConnection connection = url.openConnection( );
connection.setRequestProperty("MyToken",encodedToken);
// Everything as before
```

The name of the request property, MyToken in our example, is significant. This is interpreted as the type of the token, which we will see later. A small caveat here is that WebLogic always expects incoming tokens to be Base 64–encoded. You can do this by using the utility class weblogic.utils.encoders.BASE64Encoder. So, to create an encoded token, you can write something such as this:

```
String token = "jon";
BASE64Encoder encoder = new BASE64Encoder( );
String encodedToken = encoder.encodeBuffer(token.getBytes( ));
```

The text that you place in the token can be anything you please, as long as your Identity Assertion Provider can read it. In our example, we will use a simple string, which we take to represent the authenticated user.

 WebLogic 8.1 allows you to configure the Identity Assertion Provider to use tokens that aren't encoded, in which case you won't need to use an encoder.

All that's left now is to create an Identity Assertion Provider. The MBean definition file used in our example is given in Example 17-8 in full.

Example 17-8. MyA.xml, the MDF file for the assertion provider

```
<?xml version="1.0" ?>
<!DOCTYPE MBeanType SYSTEM "commo.dtd">

<MBeanType  Name = "MyA"   DisplayName  = "MyA"
 Package        = "com.oreilly.wlguide.security.iap"
 Extends        = "weblogic.management.security.authentication.IdentityAsserter"
 PersistPolicy = "OnUpdate"
>
<MBeanAttribute Name = "ProviderClassName"  Type = "java.lang.String"
  Writeable     = "false"
  Default       = "&quot;com.oreilly.wlguide.security.iap.MyAProviderImpl&quot;"
/>
<MBeanAttribute Name = "Description" Type = "java.lang.String"
  Writeable = "false" Default = "&quot;My Identity Assertion Provider&quot;"
/>
<MBeanAttribute Name = "Version" Type = "java.lang.String"
  Writeable = "false" Default = "&quot;1.0&quot;"
/>
```

Example 17-8. MyA.xml, the MDF file for the assertion provider (continued)

```
<MBeanAttribute Name = "SupportedTypes" Type = "java.lang.String[]"
  Writeable = "false" Default = "new String[] { &quot;MyToken&quot; }"
/>
<MBeanAttribute Name = "ActiveTypes" Type = "java.lang.String[]"
  Default = "new String[] { &quot;MyToken&quot; }"
/>
</MBeanType>
```

Note the following things:

- Because we are writing an Identity Asserter, it must extend the `weblogic.management.security.authentication.IdentityAsserter` MBean as indicated.

- As always, the `ProviderClassName` attribute must be set to the implementation class.

- The `SupportedTypes` attribute must be set to the token type. In our case, this is `MyToken`.

- The `ActiveTypes` attribute lists the subset of the provider's supported types that you want active. Because we want our only token active, we set it to `MyToken` as well.

You can create the support files as usual. Here we place all the output in the directory *out*:

```
java -DcreateStubs="true" weblogic.management.commo.WebLogicMBeanMaker -MDF MyA.xml
-files out
```

Finally, you need to create the provider class `com.oreilly.wlguide.security.iap.MyAProviderImpl`, which was referred to in the `ProviderClassName` attribute. Example 17-9 lists this class in its entirety.

Example 17-9. The provider implementation

```
package com.oreilly.wlguide.security.iap;

import javax.security.auth.callback.CallbackHandler;
import javax.security.auth.login.AppConfigurationEntry;
import weblogic.management.security.ProviderMBean;
import weblogic.security.spi.*;

public final class MyAProviderImpl
                    implements AuthenticationProvider, IdentityAsserter {
  private String description; // holds our description which we derive from MBean
      attributes

  public void initialize(ProviderMBean mbean, SecurityServices services) {
    MyAMBean myMBean = (MyAMBean)mbean;
    description = myMBean.getDescription() + "\n" + myMBean.getVersion();
  }

  public CallbackHandler assertIdentity(String type, Object token)
                                    throws IdentityAssertionException {
```

Example 17-9. The provider implementation (continued)

```
      if (type.equals("MyToken")) {
       byte[] tokenRaw = (byte[])token;
       String username = new String(tokenRaw);
       return new SimpleSampleCallbackHandlerImpl(username,null,null);
      } else
        throw new IdentityAssertionException("Strange Token!");
    }
    public String getDescription() {
      return description;
    }
    public void shutdown()  {
    }
    public IdentityAsserter getIdentityAsserter() {
      return this;    // this object is the identity asserter
    }
    public AppConfigurationEntry getLoginModuleConfiguration() {
      return null;  // we are not an authenticator
    }
    public AppConfigurationEntry getAssertionModuleConfiguration() {
      return null;  // we are not an authenticator
    }
    public PrincipalValidator getPrincipalValidator() {
       return null;  // we are not an authenticator
    }
}
```

The most important methods are initialize() and assertIdentity(). The initialize() method simply extracts some information from the MBean representing the provider and uses it to create the description. The assertIdentity() method is given two parameters, the type of the token and the token itself. We simply check that the token type is correct and map the token to the username. You could conceivably do a lot more here, such as validate the authenticity of the token for stronger security. The method must return a standard JAAS callback handler, which eventually will be invoked to extract the username (that is, only the NameCallback will be used). We use the callback handler that we defined in Example 17-4. Note that the identity asserter could have been an authenticator too, in which case it could populate the subject with usernames and groups belonging to the user. Because we are doing pure identity assertion, the corresponding methods simply return null.

Place this file and the callback handler in the *out* directory, and then issue the following command to create a packaged provider:

```
    java weblogic.management.commo.WebLogicMBeanMaker -MJF myIAP.jar -files out
```

Copy this to the *WL_HOME/server/lib/mbeantypes* directory, and then reboot the server. Start up the Administration Console and navigate to the Security/myrealm Providers/Authentication node. In the list of available authenticators and identity asserters, you should find an option for "Configure a new MyA...". Selecting this option and clicking Create will configure the identity asserter. On the following tab you will notice that the support token type is set to MyToken and the active token to MyToken too. You will now have to reboot the server for this change to take effect.

If you rerun the client application, you will find that you will no longer get an unauthorized warning (assuming that jon is in the permission group mysecrole, which was granted access to the web resource). To further illustrate the point, you can try accessing a servlet or JSP page in this way, which has a call to request. getUserPrincipal( ). You will find that this call returns jon as you would expect.

So, here is a summary of what happens, as was illustrated in Figure 17-2:

1. The client attempts to access a protected web page. The web container notes that the client does not have any security credentials and that the web application implements identity assertion, so it fires up the Identity Assertion Providers, passing in the appropriate request parameters.

2. The Identity Asserter grabs the username directly from the incoming token and returns it in the form of a callback handler.

3. Any login modules that you have configured for the security realm then fire, using the callback handler to fetch the username. So, for example, the Default Authenticator will fire and log in the user. However, because it knows that the data comes from the Identity Asserter, it will not require a password. As a result, the user is logged in and can now access the web application.

XML

WebLogic provides extensive support for XML and XML-related APIs. Not surprisingly, it comes equipped with modern SAX and DOM parsers based on Apache's Xerces 2.1.0, and an XSLT transformer based on the Xalan 2.2 libraries that is shipped with the JDK 1.4.1 distribution. It also is shipped with a FastParser, which is a high-performance nonvalidating SAX parser. WebLogic's FastParser is optimized for small to medium-size documents, typical of a lot of SOAP and WSDL documents.

WebLogic implements the standard JAXP 1.1 layer, which provides a generic way to access any parser or transformer. Its XML Registry integrates with the JAXP implementation. This allows you to override the built-in parsers and transformers and specify alternative implementations that should be used under different circumstances. For example, you can set up different parsers to be based on the root element or document type information. These XML Registries can be configured on a per-server basis, giving you good control of what XML parsers should be used when. Of course, all these adjustments can be made without changing a single line of Java code.

XML documents often contain references to *external entities*. External entities, such as DTDs, are pieces of text external to the document being parsed. An XML Registry can be used to configure local mappings for these DTDs. If this is done, WebLogic can bypass a potentially time-consuming fetch for the DTD whenever XML data needs to be parsed. The registry also has a configurable cache, which can be used on the results of external entity resolution.

WebLogic's Streaming API offers a parsing paradigm very different from either the DOM or SAX models. Like the SAX model, the program views an XML document as a number of parser events that signify important structural elements within the document. Unlike SAX, the Streaming API supports a *pull model* for parsing XML data, whereby the program must explicitly extract XML events from the stream.

The Streaming API lets you iterate over the stream, pulling off events and processing the XML data depending on the events you encounter. You also can skip ahead over a number of XML events, or just ignore them altogether. You even can apply a filter to the XML stream to ensure that only specific events are allowed through the filter. Finally, you can use the Streaming API to generate XML data and direct this output to various destinations.

WebLogic also provides an XPath API that lets you match XPath queries against a DOM or an XML input stream. WebLogic supports two convenience features as well: a JSP tag library that provides easy access to XSL transformers from within a JSP page, and special-purpose servlet request attributes that automatically can parse the message body of an incoming request.

Finally, WebLogic provides a standalone, Java-based XML editor, which is a simple tool for creating and editing XML documents. It supports both a plain-text view and a tree view of an XML document. The XML Editor also lets you validate a document against a DTD or an XML Schema. WebLogic's JMS implementation includes support for a new type of message that can hold XML data. This is covered in Chapter 8.

BEA has created other XML technologies, not exclusively for use in WebLogic Server, which also deserve a mention. This includes a Streaming API for XML implementation, and XMLBeans, which is an XML Schema to Java Object mapping tool. You can learn more about these from BEA's dev2dev web site.

JAXP

The Java API for XML Processing (JAXP) defines a generic API for processing XML documents and transforming an XML source. The `javax.xml.parsers` package contains classes and interfaces needed to parse XML documents in SAX 2.0 and DOM 2.0 modes, while the `javax.xml.transform` package contains the classes and interfaces needed for transforming XML data (a source) into another format (a result). An XML document can manifest itself in several ways: a stream (`File`, `InputStream`, or `Reader`), SAX events, or a DOM tree representation. The aim of JAXP is to provide applications with a portable way for parsing and transforming XML documents. WebLogic Server is shipped with JAXP 1.1 classes and interfaces—by default, this implementation of JAXP is configured to use WebLogic's built-in parsers and transformers.

The JAXP specification demands that you set the appropriate system properties in order to plug in a custom XML parser (or transformer). However, WebLogic deviates from this model. Instead of using system properties, WebLogic allows you to determine the actual parsers used in two ways:

- You can create an XML Registry that lets you configure server-specific and document-specific parsers and transformers. XML Registries are domain resources configured using the Administration Console.

- You can define application-scoped XML settings in the WebLogic-specific *weblogic-application.xml* deployment descriptor for an EAR. Here you can specify parser and transformer factories that apply to an enterprise application and all its constituent modules.

Both of these mechanisms allow you to configure the parsers and transformers used by your applications at deployment time. This means that you can transparently alter the configuration without changing a single line of code.

In the following sections, we'll show you how to use WebLogic's JAXP to create SAX and DOM parsers, and a transformer based on an XSLT stylesheet. We also will look at WebLogic's support for resolving external entities.

SAX

The Simple API for XML (SAX) is an event-based API for parsing XML documents. The SAX interface defines various events that are triggered while an XML parser is reading an XML document. A custom handler can listen for these events and process the XML document in an easy, event-oriented fashion. A SAX handler implements the relevant callback methods and responds to various events—such as when it encounters start and end tags, character data, or a processing instruction. As the SAX parser reads through an XML document, it invokes the methods on the handler class to mark each particular event. In this regard, the SAX interface is unlike other XML APIs because it relies on a *push model*; the data is pushed to the application as it is encountered.

Example 18-1 shows how to retrieve a SAX parser using the JAXP interface. In order to parse an XML document with SAX, you need to create an instance of a SAX parser. The JAXP interface defines a SAXParserFactory, which manufactures a SAX parser for you. The newInstance( ) method in the SAXParserFactory class creates a new factory object. Call the newSAXParser( ) method on this factory instance to create a new SAX parser.

Example 18-1. Retrieving and using a SAX parser

```
import javax.xml.parsers.SAXParser;
import javax.xml.parsers.SAXParserFactory;
//...
  //Obtain an instance of SAXParserFactory
  SAXParserFactory spf = SAXParserFactory.newInstance( );
  //Obtain a SAX parser from the factory
  SAXParser sp = spf.newSAXParser( );
  //Parse an XML document
  sp.parse(new java.io.StringBufferInputStream("<a><b></b></a>"),
        new org.xml.sax.helpers.DefaultHandler( ) {
          public void startElement (String uri, String localName,
              String qName, Attributes attr)
            { System.err.println(qName); }; }
     );
```

You can now use the SAX parser to parse an XML document. In this example, the SAX handler registered with the parser responds whenever a start tag is encountered. For each start tag, it simply prints out the name of the tag.

By default, WebLogic Server uses its built-in SAX parser factory: `weblogic.apache.xerces.jaxp.SAXParserFactoryImpl`. Later, we'll see how you can override this setting and configure WebLogic to use an alternative SAX parser.

DOM

An XML document is a tree of elements—data elements can be nested within other elements and optionally have attributes attached. The Document Object Model (DOM) defines an object hierarchy that represents the structure of an XML document as a recursive tree of elements. This means that you need to read and parse the entire XML document in order to build this data structure. Because a DOM representation of an XML document needs to be held in memory, many DOM implementations can be memory-intensive.

As its name suggests, DOM parsing uses a hierarchical, object-based model. XML parsing in DOM mode is useful when you need frequent, random access to different parts of the document, or if you want to manipulate its structure in complex ways. However, the DOM API is not suitable for applications that need to parse XML data incrementally; in these cases, you should use SAX.

Example 18-2 shows how you can use the JAXP interface to create a DOM parser. In order to parse an XML document in DOM mode, you need to obtain an instance of `DocumentBuilder`. Once again, the JAXP interface provides a factory, called the `DocumentBuilderFactory`, which manufactures a DOM parser for you. The `newInstance()` method on the `DocumentBuilderFactory` class creates a new DOM parser factory. Call the `newDocumentBuilder()` method on the `Document-BuilderFactory` instance to create a new DOM parser.

Example 18-2. Retrieving and using a DOM parser

```
import javax.xml.parsers.DocumentBuilder;
import javax.xml.parsers.DocumentBuilderFactory;
import org.w3c.dom.Document;
//...
//Obtain an instance of the DocumentBuilderFactory
DocumentBuilderFactory dbf = DocumentBuilderFactory.newInstance();
// Get a DOM parser
DocumentBuilder db = dbf.newDocumentBuilder();
System.err.println(db.getDOMImplementation().getClass().getName());
//Parse the document
Document doc = db.parse(/*..*/);
System.err.println(doc.getDocumentElement().getNodeName());
```

Once you create a `DocumentBuilder` object, you can parse an XML document and build a DOM tree. The `parse()` method returns an `org.w3c.dom.Document` object, which represents the hierarchical view of the XML document. Now that you have built the DOM tree in memory, you can access the elements within the `Document`, or perhaps even modify the structure. In the earlier example, we simply print the name of the root element of the document.

By default, WebLogic uses the built-in DOM parser factory. Later, we will see how you can configure WebLogic to use a third-party DOM parser.

XSL Transformers

XSL Transformations (XSLT) are XML-formatted rules that define how one XML document can be transformed into another. You typically would assemble templates specifying a particular transformation and place these in an XSLT stylesheet. Then, an XSLT processor uses the templates defined in the stylesheet to process matching elements in the input XML source and writes the template conversion into an output tree. The source and sink (or output target) of an XSL Transformation can be a stream, a DOM tree, or SAX events. JAXP provides a standard way for acquiring an XSL transformer. The same XSL transformer can process XML data that originates from a variety of sources and can write the output of the transformation to a variety of sinks. For instance, using the same XSLT stylesheet, you could easily transform a stream of input SAX events to a DOM tree representation of the output XML document.

The JAXP interface enables you to capture XSLT stylesheets in two ways:

- A Transformer object that is created via the newTransformer( ) factory method on an instance of the TransformerFactory.

- A Templates instance that encapsulates runtime-compiled information about the XSLT stylesheet. You can create a Templates object via the newTemplates( ) method on an instance of the TransformerFactory.

A Templates object can be shared across multiple concurrent threads and may be used multiple times during its lifetime. However, an XSL Transformer isn't thread-safe and must not be shared across multiple concurrent threads. Typically, a single Templates object will spawn multiple Transformer instances, one for each thread that needs to use the XSLT stylesheet. Example 18-3 shows how you can create an XSL transformer for a given stylesheet.

Example 18-3. Using JAXP to access a transformer

```
import javax.xml.transform.Transformer;
import javax.xml.transform.TransformerFactory;
import javax.xml.transform.dom.DOMSource;
import javax.xml.transform.stream.StreamSource;
import javax.xml.transform.stream.StreamResult;
import org.w3c.dom.Document;
//...
TransformerFactory tf = TransformerFactory.newInstance( );
Transformer t =
  tf.newTransformer(new StreamSource(new java.io.File("foo.xsl")));

// apply stylesheet to a DOM tree and write the
// output of transformation to System.out
t.transform(new DOMSource(doc), new StreamResult(System.out));
```

Alternatively, you could create a `Templates` object that captures all the transformation instructions specified in the stylesheet. For example, you could create a `Templates` instance in the `init( )` method of a servlet:

```
TransformerFactory tf = TransformerFactory.newInstance( );
Templates tmpl =
    tf.newTemplates(new StreamSource(new java.io.File("foo.xsl")));
```

Then, when you need to apply the XSLT stylesheet to an XML document (for instance, in the `doPost( )` method of a servlet), you need only to create a new `Transformer` instance using the same `Templates` object:

```
// Needs to be applied to an XML document
Transformer t = tmpl.newTransformer( );
t.transform(domSource, streamResult);
```

By default, WebLogic uses its built-in factory for processing XSLT stylesheets: `org.apache.xalan.processor.TransformerFactoryImpl`.

External Entity Resolution

External entities are portions of text external to the XML file being parsed. An external entity resembles a macro replacement facility. The replacement text can either be *parsed*, which means the text is incorporated into the XML document, or *unparsed*, which means the declaration points to external data. A typical external entity declaration uses the `SYSTEM` keyword and the URI of the substitution text:

```
<!ENTITY header SYSTEM "http://www.oreilly.com/templates/header.xml">
```

Alternatively, the declaration also could specify a relative URL:

```
<!ENTITY header SYSTEM "/templates/header.xml">
```

Whenever a parser encounters an entity reference &header;, it replaces the reference with the actual contents of the document located at the specified URI. A DTD reference is another example of an external entity reference. An XML document uses a `DOCTYPE` declaration to reference a DTD:

```
<!DOCTYPE oreilly SYSTEM "http://www.oreilly.com/dtds/wl.dtd">
<oreilly> <!-- --> </oreilly>
```

The preceding declaration indicates that the root element for the document is oreilly, and its DTD is located at *http://www.oreilly.com/dtds/wl.dtd*. In addition, the `DOCTYPE` declaration may use a *public identifier*, which is a publicly declared name that identifies the associated DTD. When a validating XML parser processes an XML document that includes a `DOCTYPE` declaration, the parser needs to fetch the DTD file referenced by the URI.

The SAX interface allows you to associate a custom entity resolver with the parser, which can intercept parser requests for external entities (including an external DTD) and determine how the entity references are resolved. To do this, you need to register an instance of the `org.xml.sax.EntityResolver` interface with the `XMLReader` before you begin to read from an XML source. Whenever the SAX parser encounters an entity reference, it will invoke the resolveEntity( ) method on the registered EntityResolver instance.

 SAX's XMLReader interface is encapsulated by the JAXP SAXParser class.

Typically, an application uses an EntityResolver to substitute a reference to a remote URI with a local copy. The resolveEntity( ) method returns an input source for the XML entity based on either a character or a byte stream. If the method returns null, the parser tries to open a connection to the URI referenced by the system identifier. A custom entity resolver is very useful if your application parses XML documents that need to be retrieved from a database or other nonstandard locations.

WebLogic's XML Registry provides several enhancements that improve the performance of external entity resolution:

- It allows you to map an external entity to a local (or remote) URI that contains a copy of the substitution text for the entity.
- It allows you to retrieve a copy of the remote resource associated with the external entity and cache the text, either in memory or on disk.
- It allows you to specify the duration after which a cached item becomes stale and needs to be refreshed.

Each entry in the XML Registry uses a public or system identifier to identify the external entity. Each entry also may specify various caching options for entity resolution. For instance, you could instruct the server to fetch an external entity the first time it is required, and cache it for 120 seconds. Whenever an XML parser reads a document that uses an entity reference configured in the registry, WebLogic Server fetches a local or a cached copy of the substitution text.

Built-in Processors

The WebLogic distribution comes equipped with a number of standard XML parsers and transformers: the Apache-based Xerces and Xalan libraries, which provide the SAX and DOM parsers as well as the XSLT transformer. You also can use WebLogic's own FastParser, which is a fast, nonvalidating SAX parser.

WebLogic's FastParser

WebLogic's FastParser is a high-performance, nonvalidating SAX parser. It has been designed for processing small to medium-size documents—documents that contain no more than 10,000 elements. This is typical of many web service applications, in which SOAP and WSDL documents tend to be small. The Streaming API, which we'll cover later, is based on WebLogic's FastParser.

Because the FastParser supports the SAX interface, you can use it instead of WebLogic's default SAX parser, Apache Xerces. By configuring an XML Registry to use the FastParser factory, you ensure that your JAXP code automatically uses the FastParser for processing an XML document.

Clearly, you cannot use the nonvalidating FastParser to validate XML documents.

Using JAXP-Compliant Parsers

The default parsers supplied with WebLogic are based on Apache's Xerces 2.1.0 and Xalan 2.2 libraries. They provide full support for SAX and DOM parsing, as well as XSL transformers. However, you are not required to use these parsers. For instance, you could upgrade the Xerces parser to a newer version that supports the current W3C XML Schema recommendation.

All parser implementations work on a factory design pattern, as we saw in the examples earlier in this chapter. The JAXP interface hides the actual parser class being used, but it also can be exposed in certain situations. For instance, the print statement in Example 18-2 yields weblogic.apache.xerces.dom.DOMImplementationImpl as its output. This indicates that we were using WebLogic's default DOM parser, based on Xerces.

When you configure WebLogic to use a particular parser or transformer implementation, it is important to know the fully qualified class names of the factories that manufacture the parsers or transformers. Table 18-1 lists the class names for WebLogic's default DOM, SAX, and transformer factories.

Table 18-1. Default XML factories for WebLogic Server

XML factory	Class name
DOM parser	weblogic.apache.xerces.jaxp.DocumentBuilderFactoryImpl
SAX parser	weblogic.apache.xerces.jaxp.SAXParserFactoryImpl
XSL Transformer	org.apache.xalan.processor.TransformerFactoryImpl
FastParser	weblogic.xml.babel.jaxp.SAXParserFactoryImpl

In some cases, you may want to bypass the JAXP layer and instantiate a parser directly. For instance, you could instantiate WebLogic's DOM parser directly as follows:

```
import weblogic.apache.xerces.parsers.*;
...
DocumentBuilderFactory dbf = DocumentBuilderFactoryImpl.newInstance();
DocumentBuilder db = dbf.newDocumentBuilder();
```

However, it also means that your applications are less portable and you need more code changes when you need to change the DOM parser implementation. The following code snippet shows how you can use the Xerces-derived SAX parser implementation directly:

```
import weblogic.apache.xerces.parsers.*;
...
SAXParserFactory spf = SAXParserFactoryImpl.newInstance();
SAXParser sp =  spf.newSAXParser();
```

Ideally, you should use the generic JAXP interfaces to create an XML parser or an XSL transformer. If you want to use another library, you should configure WebLogic separately with the desired parser factories. In fact, the XML Registry allows you to configure this on a per-server basis.

In some situations, you may need to use more than one parser implementation. For example, you may want to use the FastParser for SOAP documents, and a standard SAX parser for other XML processing within your application. There are two ways in which to achieve this:

- Use the XML Registry to target a parser to a particular document, based on its root element (for instance). This allows you to continue using the standard JAXP interface to retrieve parsers and processors.

- Bypass the JAXP interface altogether and directly use the API provided by the parser implementation. This approach means sacrificing application portability.

The XML Registry

An *XML Registry* provides domain-wide configuration settings for XML parsers and XSL transformers, as well as resolution of different external entities. It is a domain resource that can be administered on a per-server basis using the Administration Console. Once you associate an XML Registry with a server instance, the settings apply to all applications running on that server. A WebLogic domain may define multiple XML Registries, but one XML Registry only may be assigned to a server instance. Of course, the same XML Registry may be shared by multiple servers in the domain. If a server instance doesn't have an XML Registry targeted to it, any server-side application that uses the JAXP interfaces will use the default parsers and XSL transformers shipped with your WebLogic distribution.

An XML Registry allows you to configure alternative parsers and transformers, instead of WebLogic's built-in parsers and transformers.

 The XML parsers and XSL transformers you've defined in the registry are available only to server-side applications that use the standard JAXP interface. The XML Registry doesn't affect applications that directly use the API provided by the actual parser implementation.

As we saw in earlier examples, an application that relies on JAXP does not need to use any code specific to the parser or transformer. The XML Registry lets you plug in different parsers and transformers without changing any code. The parser implementation returned by JAXP depends on the following conditions:

- If you have defined application-scoped parsers or transformer factories for an application EAR, WebLogic will use these configuration settings to determine the parser or transformer.
- If an application EAR doesn't have any such application-scoped XML configuration, WebLogic will look for an XML Registry that may be targeted to the server. If it exists, then the following occurs:
  - If the XML Registry defines a parser specific to the XML document being parsed, WebLogic will use this configured value.
  - Otherwise, WebLogic will choose from the default parsers defined in the registry.
- If there is neither an application-scoped configuration nor any XML Registry targeted to the server, WebLogic will use its built-in parsers.

Thus, an XML Registry is a server-specific, domain-wide resource. It determines the actual parser and transformer implementations used by *all* applications running on a server, provided they use the JAXP interface and don't have an application-scoped configuration! An XML Registry consists of the following:

- A list of default factories that will be used to create a parser or transformer.
- A list of external entity resolvers that map external entities to possible local URIs, with options for caching the entities as well.
- A list of XML factories that will be used for particular XML applications. Each such XML document is identified either by its root element or by its public and system identifiers.

An XML Registry acts as a deploy-time parser configuration for server-side applications running on a particular server instance. Document-specific parsers provide a simple yet powerful way to transparently alter the actual parser, without any change to the code.

Creating an XML Registry

In order to create an XML Registry, open the Administration Console, move to the Services/XML node in the left pane, and then select the "Configure a new XML Registry" option from the right pane. You will need to supply a name for the registry and the fully qualified class names for the SAX and DOM parser factories, as well as an XSL transformer. If any of these fields are left blank, WebLogic's default parsers will be used. As it is, the fields are initialized with the default values for WebLogic's built-in parser and transformer factories. After creating an XML Registry, select the Target and Deploy tab to associate the registry with particular server instances and make it available.

Suppose you've set `weblogic.xml.babel.jaxp.SAXParserFactoryImpl` as the SAX parser factory for an XML Registry, and the registry is targeted to server A. If no other configuration overrides this setting, any server-side application running on server A that uses JAXP will automatically use the FastParser as its SAX parser.

Configuring Document-Specific Parsers

Once you configure the default parsers for an XML Registry, you can further specify document-specific parser factories. You can configure this by setting up a new Parser Select Registry Entry. This option is available from the Parser Select Entries node under the selected XML Registry. Once again, you will need to specify the fully qualified class names of the XML factories (you can ignore the defunct Parser Class Name field). In addition, you need to associate these XML factories with a specific document. You can specify the document type information in two ways:

- You can supply the public or system identifier that corresponds to a DTD. If a server-side application parses a document that includes a DTD reference with the same public or system ID, it will use the associated parser factories.

- You can supply the name of a root element. Because XML is case-sensitive, be sure to use the correct case for the tag name. If the XML document defines a namespace, include the namespace-prefix for the root element.

Remember, the Parser Select Entries associated with an XML Registry apply only to server-side applications that use the JAXP interface to acquire parser factories. When an application is about to parse a document, WebLogic tries to determine the document type by searching through the first 1000 characters of the document. If it does find a public or system identifier, or a root element that matches one of the parser select entries, WebLogic uses the parser specified for that document type.

This document-based selection of a parser is useful when you want to use parsers that are more optimal for specific document types (e.g., the FastParser for SOAP messages). Another benefit of document-specific parsers is that you can override the default XML configuration transparently, without requiring any code changes. However, because WebLogic needs to inspect the document type for any XML document, this feature may carry a small performance penalty.

Configuring External Entity Resolution

An XML Registry also can define a number of entity resolution mappings. Each mapping associates an external entity with either a local file or contents of a remote URL. It also provides additional cache settings that determine when the external entity is fetched, and the length of time it will be cached. Creating an entity resolution mapping requires a little more effort than defining a document-specific parser. Select an

XML Registry entry and then select the Entity Spec Entries option. You can now configure an entity resolution mapping by mapping a public or system identifier to an entity URI.

The URI specifies the location from which the external entity can be fetched. Its value is either the path to a local copy of the external entity, or a URL that refers to a remote copy. If the entity URI refers to a local file, the path is interpreted relative to the directory associated with the XML Registry: *domainRoot/xml/registries/registryName,* where *registryName* is the name of the registry. You have to create this directory manually. It will stock local copies of files that will be used to resolve external entities configured in the XML Registry.

As an example, let's add external entity resolution to our XML Registry, *MyRegistry*. Start by creating a directory in the domain root called *xml/registries/MyRegistry*. Now create a file, called *ext.txt*, which holds the text <side><in/></side>. Next, configure an external entity mapping, with a system identifier of example, and specify a URI of *ext.txt*. We have now effectively mapped an external entity with a system identifier of example to substitution text contained in the *ext.txt* file. We can test this configuration by creating a server-side application (servlet, JSP, etc.) that parses an XML fragment that includes this entity reference:

```
// Grab the SAX parser using JAXP
SAXParserFactory spf = SAXParserFactory.newInstance();
SAXParser sp = spf.newSAXParser();

sp.parse(new java.io.StringBufferInputStream(
    "<!DOCTYPE outside[ <!ENTITY a SYSTEM \"example\"> ]> <outside>&a;</outside>"
    ), new org.xml.sax.helpers.DefaultHandler() {
    public void startElement (String uri, String lName,
            String qName, Attributes attr){
        System.err.println(qName);}; }
        );
```

Here, the SAX handler simply prints the name of each element encountered during the parse. If the external entity is resolved successfully, the resulting XML should be:

```
<outside><side><in/></side></outside>
```

The parse yields the following output, as expected:

```
outside
side
in
```

So, an Entity Spec Entry allows you to map an external entity to a local file that holds the replacement XML. This kind of mapping also is useful for DTD references, which are treated like external entities. For example, you could create another mapping under MyRegistry that associates a document type with system identifier *http://oreilly.com/dtds/foo* to a local entity URI */dtds/foo.dtd*.

```
<!DOCTYPE someroot SYSTEM "http://oreilly.com/dtds/foo">
<!-- rest of XML document -->
```

Then, any XML document that includes a DTD reference with the same system ID will resolve the DTD to the local copy held under the */xml/registries/MyRegistry* folder.

Caching Entities

WebLogic provides a caching facility that improves the performance of external entity resolution. You can configure WebLogic's support for caching by adjusting when the external entity is fetched, and the period after which it is considered stale. The When to Cache field for an Entity Spec Entry determines when an external entity is fetched. If you select an XML Registry from the left pane of the Administration Console and then choose the Configuration tab from the right pane, you can set a value for the When to Cache field. WebLogic permits the following values for this setting:

cache-on-reference
> This setting ensures that WebLogic caches the item after it has been referenced for the first time while parsing a document.

cache-at-initialization
> This setting ensures that WebLogic caches the item when the server starts up.

cache-never
> This setting instructs the server never to cache the item

defer-to-registry-setting
> This setting instructs the cache to use the value set in the XML Registry's main configuration page.

The When to Cache field can take any one of the first three values explained earlier. By default, the XML Registry is configured to cache an external entity when it is first referenced, and if an entity resolution mapping doesn't override the XML Registry setting, it will inherit the value of its cache setting.

Finally, you can adjust the Cache Timeout Interval setting for an entity resolution mapping, which determines the duration (in seconds) after which the cached entity is considered stale. A subsequent request to a cached entity that has become stale causes WebLogic to fetch the resource from the location specified by the URI. Otherwise, the server will continue to use the cached value of the entity resolution. Although you may specify a timeout interval for each entity mapping, you also can specify a value of -1 for the timeout interval. In this case, the actual timeout will be determined by the value of the Cache Timeout Interval setting associated with the server instance that the XML Registry is targeted to. All entity mappings with a timeout value of -1 will inherit the cache timeout setting for the targeted server itself.

The Cache Timeout Interval server setting can be found by clicking on the server in the left pane of the Administration Console and then selecting the Services/XML node. This setting determines the timeout period for all entity mappings whose

Cache Timeout Interval has a value of -1. Three other settings on this screen are of interest:

XML Registry
> This setting determines the name of the XML Registry targeted to the server instance—you can choose from any one of the XML Registries defined in the domain. Of course, you can change this value by selecting an XML Registry and assigning the server from the Targets panel. Make sure that you do not target more than one XML Registry to the same server.

Cache Memory Size
> WebLogic can cache some of the external entities in memory. This setting specifies how much memory (in kilobytes) to set aside for this cache. It defaults to 500 KB.

Cache Disk Size
> When the memory cache has reached its maximum allotted size, WebLogic persists the little-used external entities to disk. This setting determines the maximum size (in megabytes) for the disk cache. It defaults to 5 MB.

Using these settings, you can specify on a per-server basis the size of the cache for external entities, both in memory and on disk, and when to refresh a cached external entity.

The final option on this screen, Monitor XML Entity Cache, allows you to monitor how the cache is being used. Select this option if you need to access usage statistics such as the total number of cached entries, the frequency of timeouts, and the resource usage.

XML Application Scoping

The XML Application Scoping mechanism in WebLogic allows you to configure XML resources such as parsers, transformers, and entity resolvers on a *per-application* basis. This is different from the XML Registry settings that we covered earlier—they apply to a server instance and all applications running on it. An application-scoped XML configuration has two major benefits:

- It allows you to configure different parsers for different applications. You can covertly change the parsers that will be used by the enterprise application simply by editing a deployment descriptor.

- It makes the resultant EAR file less dependent on the server configuration. If you do not specify an application-scoped factory, the application is at the mercy of the target server. You need to ensure that all servers that will host the enterprise application are configured identically. A scoped XML configuration defined for an application EAR removes this dependence.

To use this mechanism, you have to include an XML deployment descriptor, *weblogic-application.xml*, within the *META-INF* directory of the application EAR file, as shown in Example 18-4. You also can use this descriptor file to configure application-specific parameters, JDBC pools, security settings, EJB-wide settings, etc. For now, we focus only on the XML configuration settings.

Example 18-4. A typical weblogic-application.xml configuration

```
<weblogic-application>
   <!-- ... rest of weblogic-application ... -->
   <xml>
      <parser-factory>
         <saxparser-factory>
            weblogic.xml.babel.jaxp.SAXParserFactoryImpl
         </saxparser-factory>
         <document-builder-factory>
            weblogic.apache.xerces.jaxp.DocumentBuilderFactoryImpl
         </document-builder-factory>
         <transformer-factory>
            org.apache.xalan.processor.TransformerFactoryImpl
         </transformer-factory>
      </parser-factory>
      <entity-mapping>
         <entity-mapping-name>My Mapping</entity-mapping-name>
         <public-id>-//OReilly & Associates//DTD WL//EN</public-id>
         <system-id>http://www.oreilly.com/dtds/wl.dtd</system-id>
         <entity-uri>dtds/wl.dtd</entity-uri>
         <when-to-cache>cache-at-initialization</when-to-cache>
         <cache-timeout-interval>300</cache-timeout-interval>
      </entity-mapping>
   </xml>
</weblogic-application>
```

Example 18-4 shows how the *weblogic-application.xml* descriptor file allows you to set up application-scoped XML resources. The configuration is split into two parts— a parser factory configuration that specifies the default parsers and transformers to use, and multiple entity mappings that associate external entities with local or remote URIs. The entity mappings also include cache settings, which are analogous to the external entity resolution mappings that may be specified for an XML Registry. The easiest way to set up this configuration is to use the WebLogic Builder tool.

Configuring Factories

The parser factory configuration is quite straightforward. If the parser-factory element declares any XML or transformer factories, these settings will be used to manufacture a parser (or transformer) whenever the application uses JAXP. If you don't specify a factory in the *weblogic-application.xml* descriptor file, the factory in the XML Registry will be used instead. If there is no application-scoped factory setting, nor any corresponding setting in the XML Registry targeted to the server, WebLogic will then use its built-in XML factory.

To specify an XML factory, you need to provide its fully qualified class name. You can define any of the following three subelements:

saxparser-factory

> This element specifies the factory to use for generating SAX parsers. In Example 18-4, we configured the application to use the WebLogic FastParser.

document-builder-factory

> This element specifies the factory to use for generating DOM parsers. In Example 18-4, we configured the application to use the default built-in DOM parser factory.

transformer-factory

> This element specifies the factory to use for generating XSL transformers. In Example 18-4, we configured the application to use the default built-in XSL transformer factory.

Now any server-side component in the application that uses the JAXP interface will automatically use the factory settings declared in the *weblogic-application.xml* descriptor file:

```
SAXParserFactory spf = SAXParserFactory.newInstance();
//Create a parser using the factory
SAXParser sp = spf.newSAXParser();
```

Given the XML configuration in Example 18-4, the preceding code for retrieving a SAX parser will use WebLogic's FastParser.

Configuring Entity Resolution

As Example 18-4 illustrates, the *weblogic-application.xml* descriptor may also define multiple entity-mapping elements. Each entity-mapping element specifies a name for identification purposes, and includes the following optional subelements:

public-id

> This element specifies the public identifier of the external entity.

system-id

> This element specifies the system identifier of the external entity.

entity-uri

> This element specifies the location of a file that holds the substitution text for the external entity. The file path is relative to the root directory of the EAR. When parsing an XML document, WebLogic uses the entity-uri setting to resolve a reference to an external entity with a matching public or system identifier.

Given the configuration in Example 18-4, any request for an external entity matching the specified system or public ID will resolve to the file *dtds/wl.dtd*, where this path is relative to the root directory of the EAR.

Just like entity resolution mappings in an XML Registry, you can specify the cache settings for an application-scoped entity mapping:

`when-to-cache`
> This element determines when the external entity should be cached. It can accept three valid values:
>
> `cache-on-reference`
>> This setting ensures that WebLogic will cache this entity the first time the entity is referenced. This is the default value for the `when-to-cache` setting.
>
> `cache-at-initialization`
>> This setting ensures that WebLogic will cache this entity during server initialization.
>
> `cache-never`
>> This setting guarantees that WebLogic will never cache this entity.

`cache-timeout-interval`
> If an item is cached, this setting determines the duration (in seconds) after which the cached entity should be considered stale. After a cached entity becomes stale, the next request for the entity causes WebLogic to retrieve it again from its location. The default value for this setting is 120 seconds.

WebLogic's Streaming API

WebLogic's Streaming API offers a simple and intuitive way to parse and generate XML data. Compared to the SAX or DOM parsing models, it presents a fundamentally different viewpoint on an XML document. As the name suggests, parsing with the Streaming API is based around a stream. This stream is, in fact, a stream of XML events generated as the XML document is parsed. These events are similar to the events defined in the SAX API because they represent the same fundamental information about the XML data.

BEA is involved in the standardization of the Streaming API for XML (StAX), which has an API very similar to that described here. As a result, you can consider using BEA's implementation of StAX, available from the dev2dev web site.

When an XML document is parsed in SAX mode, the program registers a handler that can listen for SAX events as they occur. The SAX parser then automatically invokes the different callback methods of the event listener. In contrast, a program using the Streaming API pulls events off a stream, whereby each event represents some fundamental information about the XML being parsed. The Streaming API supports events that mark the occurrence of start and end tags, character data, whitespace characters, processing instructions, and several other document characteristics. These parser events enable you to step through the XML document, filter out certain event types, perhaps skip ahead in the document, and stop processing at any point. Parsing an XML document entails iterating over the stream of events and processing the XML data depending on the type of parse event. Thus, parsing with the Streaming API is demand-driven because you need to explicitly iterate over the stream and extract the events of interest. For this reason, it is often referred to as *pull* parsing.

Assume that `xmlInput` is a string variable holding the XML fragment shown in Example 18-5.

Example 18-5. Sample XML

```
<out>
  Hello <inOne>  <simple/>  </inOne>
  <inTwo>  World  </inTwo>
</out>
```

The following piece of code illustrates how you can parse the XML data using the Streaming API:

```
import weblogic.xml.stream.*;
//
String xmlInput = /* as in Example 18-5 */;
// Create a stream
XMLInputStreamFactory factory = XMLInputStreamFactory.newInstance( );
XMLInputStream stream = factory.newInputStream(new StringReader(xmlInput));
// Iterate over the stream
while (stream.hasNext( ))
    // Ask for the next event off the stream
    XMLEvent e = stream.next( );
    // Do something with the event
    System.out.print(e.getTypeAsString( ));
}
stream.close( ); // Always close your streams
```

Notice how we create the XML input stream, then iterate over the stream of events and process each event that is encountered. Here, the program simply lists the type of XML event generated during the parse. Example 18-6 lists the output generated as a result of running this program. (Note that we have indented the list for readability purposes.)

Example 18-6. Events generated while parsing the sample XML

```
START_DOCUMENT
  START_ELEMENT
  CHARACTER_DATA
    START_ELEMENT SPACE
      START_ELEMENT
      END_ELEMENT
      SPACE
    END_ELEMENT
    SPACE
    START_ELEMENT
```

Example 18-6. Events generated while parsing the sample XML (continued)

```
      CHARACTER_DATA
    END_ELEMENT
  END_ELEMENT
END_DOCUMENT
```

You now can see the similarity between the events generated using the Streaming API and SAX events generated by a SAX parser. The Streaming API generates events that indicate the start and end of the document, the start and end of an XML element, whitespace characters, and character data used in a tag's body. Later, we shall look at all the XML event types that can be generated when parsing with the Streaming API.

The Streaming API provides a number of useful enhancements to iterating over a stream of events:

- Instead of handling all events, you can apply a filter to the stream so that only specific event types permeate through.

- The Streaming API also allows you to skip a number of events, or skip until a particular event occurs.

You also can use the Streaming API to generate XML data. In this case, the entire process is reversed. Instead of requesting events from the stream, you create an XML output stream and then write elements to this stream. The Streaming API provides an ElementFactory class that manufactures the XML elements that you'll need. When writing to the XML output stream, you need to construct the XML document in a serial fashion. For each element, you need to create the start tag, its attributes, the body that may include other elements, and finally the end tag.

These features make the Streaming API a very useful addition to the current arsenal of SAX and DOM parsers. Each model has its own niche—the Streaming API is best suited when you need to process only a subset of the events generated during the parse. Because the Streaming API relies on WebLogic's FastParser, you cannot use it to validate an XML document. Remember, the Streaming API is proprietary and not yet supported by the JAXP interface. This means you cannot use the JAXP interface to create a streaming parser. Therefore, neither the XML Registry nor the application-scoped parser factories can impact how you use the Streaming API.

Creating a Stream

With the Streaming API, the parsing occurs implicitly as you iterate through the stream of events. So, you don't even explicitly create a streaming parser; instead, you create an XMLInputStream instance, which then acts as source of parse events:

```
XMLInputStreamFactory factory = XMLInputStreamFactory.newInstance( );
XMLInputStream stream = factory.newInputStream(someSource);
```

This stream can be created from a number of different sources, including the following:

java.io.File, java.io.InputStream, *or* java.io.Reader
> The source XML data is read from a file, byte stream, or character-based reader (as we saw in the earlier example).

org.w3c.dom.Document *or* org.w3c.dom.Node
> The source XML data is read from a DOM tree, perhaps created previously by a DOM parser.

XMLInputStream
> It may seem odd that the source for a stream may be a stream itself, but as we shall see later in this chapter, the Streaming API allows you to snap off a substream to be used for a different parse. The substream can be created by calling the getSubStream( ) method on an existing stream.

Once you create a stream, you can start parsing the XML data by iterating over the stream. The XMLInputStream provides the familiar iterator pattern for retrieving the next parse event:

```
while(stream.hasNext( )) {
    XMLEvent event = stream.next( );
    // Do something with the event
}
```

Events

As an XML document is parsed, the XMLInputStream object generates a stream of parser events. A typical handler will determine the event's type and then process the event accordingly. As we have already seen, the Streaming API supports a number of different types of events. In fact, the Streaming API provides an interface that corresponds to each event type, and all these interfaces extend the XMLEvent interface (one way or the other). Table 18-2 provides a complete list of XMLEvent subinterfaces provided by the Streaming API.

Table 18-2. XMLEvent subinterfaces

XMLEvent subclass	Description	Constant identifier
StartDocument	Indicates the start of an XML document	START_DOCUMENT
EndDocument	Indicates the end of an XML document	END_DOCUMENT
StartElement	Indicates the start tag for an element has been encountered	START_ELEMENT
EndElement	Indicates the end tag for an element has been encountered	END_ELEMENT
CharacterData	Indicates character data from the body of an element has been encountered	CHARACTER_DATA
Space	Indicates whitespace characters have been encountered	SPACE

Table 18-2. XMLEvent subinterfaces (continued)

XMLEvent subclass	Description	Constant identifier
Comment	Indicates an XML comment has been encountered	COMMENT
ProcessingInstruction	Indicates an XML processing instruction has been encountered	PROCESSING_INSTRUCTION
StartPrefixMapping	Indicates prefix mapping has started its scope (triggered before the StartElement event)	START_PREFIX_MAPPING
EndPrefixMapping	Indicates prefix mapping has ended its scope (triggered after the EndElement event)	END_PREFIX_MAPPING
ChangePrefixMapping	Indicates transition from one prefix mapping to another	CHANGE_PREFIX_MAPPING
EntityReference	Indicates an entity reference has been encountered	ENTITY_REFERENCE

The Constant Identifier column indicates the name of an integer constant in the XMLEvent interface that identifies each event type. The getType( ) method on an XMLEvent object returns a value that matches one of these constants.

The XMLEvent interface also defines an is<XMLEvent>( ) method for each of the XML events, which allows you to identify the actual event subclass. Once you determine its type, you can cast the XMLEvent object to the correct subinterface and process the event accordingly. For example, when a new namespace prefix is introduced, the XML stream returns a StartPrefixMapping event. It provides various methods for accessing the namespace data—e.g., the getNamespaceUri( ) and getPrefix( ) methods. Similarly, a StartElement instance has methods for accessing the attributes of an element:

```
//alternative check:
// if (event.getType( ) == XMLEvent.START_ELEMENT) {
//   ...
// }
if (event.isStartElement( )) {
  StartElement startElement = (StartElement) event;
  AttributeIterator attributes = startElement.getAttributesAndNamespaces( );
  while(attributes.hasNext( )){
    Attribute attribute = attributes.next( );
    System.out.print("Name of attr: " + attribute.getName( ).getQualifiedName( ));
    System.out.print("Value of attr: " + attribute.getValue( ));
  }
}
```

The preceding piece of code illustrates how you can access an element's attributes once you have encountered its start tag.

Filtering a Stream

At this point, we know how to create an XML stream from a document, step over the stream of events, and provide custom handling depending on the event's type. The

Streaming API also enables you to filter an XML stream so that only the events of interest are pulled from the stream. This means that when you do iterate over a filtered stream, you need to deal with only those events that have passed the filter. WebLogic's Streaming API allows you to register your interest in several ways. You can apply a filter based on an event's type, a subset of the elements, or the URI/type of a namespace. You even can apply a custom filter, whereby you decide which XML events will pass through the filter.

Earlier in this section, we saw an example of how you can use the newInputStream( ) methods on an XMLInputStreamFactory instance to create a stream from an XML document. The Streaming API supports an alternative two-argument version of the same methods. In this case, you use the second parameter to supply a filter. It could be a custom filter you have created or one of the default filters provided with WebLogic Server. The default filters are available in the weblogic.xml.stream.util package. Each of the TypeFilter, NameFilter, NameSpaceFilter, and NamespaceTypeFilter classes implement the ElementFilter interface.

The TypeFilter class takes a bit mask of all the event types that you want to let through. For instance, if you need to retrieve only the character and whitespace data in a document, you could apply the type filter as follows:

```
XMLInputStream stream =
    factory.newInputStream(someSource,
            new TypeFilter(XMLEvent.CHARACTER_DATA | XMLEvent.SPACE));
```

Now when you iterate over the XML stream, you'll encounter only events for whitespace and character data:

```
while (stream.hasNext( )) {
    XMLEvent e = stream.next ( );
    switch (e.getType( )) {
        case XMLEvent.SPACE: //Handle whitespace here and break
        case XMLEvent.CHARACTER_DATA: //Handle character data here and break
        default: // You will never reach here
    }
}
```

The NameFilter class filters the stream based on the name of the element. For example, if you need to deal with only inOne elements in the XML data, you would apply a name filter as follows:

```
XMLInputStream stream =
    factory.newInputStream(someSource, new NameFilter("inOne"));
```

The NameSpaceFilter class lets you filter a stream based on the URI of a namespace, while the NamespaceTypeFilter class allows you to filter on both the namespace and type of an element. For example, if you want to retrieve only the XSLT start elements of an XSLT document, you would create a NamespaceTypeFilter as follows:

```
XMLInputStream stream = factory.newInputStream(someSource,
        new NamespaceTypeFilter ("http://www.w3.org/1999/XSL/Transform",
                        XMLEvent.START_ELEMENT));
```

Custom Filters

Custom filters can be applied to an XML stream in the same way as built-in filters. In order to create a custom filter, you need to register an instance of a class that implements the ElementFilter interface with the XML stream:

```
package weblogic.xml.stream;
public interface ElementFilter {
    public boolean accept(XMLElement event);
}
```

A custom filter needs to implement the accept( ) method, which determines whether an incoming XMLEvent can be let through.

Example 18-7 shows how to implement a custom filter that wraps multiple filters. The wrapping filter accepts an element if it is accepted by any one of its component filters.

Example 18-7. A custom filter

```
package com.oreilly.weblogic.xml.filters;

import weblogic.xml.stream.XMLName;
import weblogic.xml.stream.ElementFilter;
import weblogic.xml.stream.events.NullEvent;

public class OrFilter implements ElementFilter {
  protected ElementFilter [] filters;

  public OrFilter(ElementFilter [] filters) {
    this.filters = filters;
  }
  public setFilters(ElementFilter [] filters) {
    this.filters = filters;
  }

  // Only permit elements that pass any of the filters
  public boolean accept(XMLEvent e) {
    for (int i=0; i<filters.length; i++)
      if (filters[i].accept(e))
        return true;
    return false;
  }
}
```

We then can apply an OrFilter to an XML stream so that only elements with the name a or b are let through:

```
ElementFilter myFilter = new OrFilter(
    new ElementFilter[] {new NameFilter("a"), new NameFilter("b")});
XMLInputStream stream = factory.newInputStream(someSource, myFilter);
```

Positioning the Stream

The ability to skip ahead while iterating over a stream of parse events is a powerful feature of the Streaming API. You can skip ahead by *n* events or until a particular element has been encountered. Later in this chapter, we will examine how you can use this feature in conjunction with a buffered XML stream, whereby you can mark a position within the stream and later reset the stream to an earlier mark.

WebLogic provides three mechanisms for skipping within a stream. All of these methods are invoked on an XMLInputStream instance:

skip( ) *and* skip(int)

> These methods allow you to skip ahead by one or a specified number of events. It does not matter what type of events are present in the stream. This method will just skip over as many events as you specify.

skip(XMLName) *and* skip(XMLName, int)

> These methods allow you to skip ahead to an event with the specified name, or an event with the specified name and type. For instance, you could skip to the next end tag for element b as follows:

```
skip(ElementFactory.createXMLName("b"),XMLEvent.END_ELEMENT)
```

skipElement( )

> This method simply skips over the start/end tag pair for the next element, avoiding all its subelements. If the current XML element contains no subelements, the method skips ahead past its end tag. For instance, if you create an XML stream using the following XML fragment "<c> foo </c><a> <b/>bar </a>", you can expect the following behavior:
>
> - If you invoke the skipElement( ) method just after processing the Start-Element event for a, the stream will skip past the space and element b, and the next event will be the CharacterData event marking bar.
>
> - If you invoke the skipElement( ) method just after processing the Start-Element event for c, the stream will skip past the character data, and the next event will be the StartElement event marking the start tag for a.

An XML stream supports an additional peek( ) method, which allows you to look ahead at the next event. Because this method returns the next XMLEvent, you then can make a decision based on the event's type or any information that you can extract from it.

Substreams

At any point while you are stepping over an existing XML stream, you can invoke the getSubStream( ) method on the XMLInputStream instance to return a copy of the next element and all of its subelements. The new XML substream will generate all XML events between (and including) the start/end tag pair for the next element. The parent stream remains unaltered and you can continue to iterate over the existing stream as before. If you want to step over the element that generated the substream, you can invoke the `skipElement( )` method. The `getSubStream( )` method returns a new `XMLInputStream` instance, which now can be used as the basis for parsing the next element and all its subelements. This substream extends over all XML events and stops only after it encounters an `EndElement` event that matches the initial `StartElement` event for the substream.

Buffered Streams

A buffered input stream can be created by wrapping an `XMLInputStream` instance by a `BufferedXMLInputStream` instance. When using a buffered XML stream, you can mark a particular position in the stream and later reset the stream back to the marked spot. Effectively, this feature allows you to reparse the stream—this is very useful in situations in which you need to process the same XML fragment more than once.

The following code sample shows how you can mark a position within a stream, process that stream, and later reset it back to the earlier position:

```
XMLInputStreamFactory factory = XMLInputStreamFactory.newInstance( );
BufferedXMLInputStream bstream =
    factory.newBufferedInputStream(factory.newInputStream(someSource));
skip(4); // go somewhere
// mark the current position
bstream.mark( );
// perform some work on the stream
workOne(bstream);
// go back to our mark
bstream.reset( );
// perform some more work on the stream
workTwo(bstream);
```

Creating Output Streams

WebLogic's Streaming API also enables you to generate XML documents on the fly. Here you need to create an XML output stream and send various XML events to this stream. The Streaming API has an `ElementFactory` class, which provides factory methods for the various elements of an XML document: character data, comments, attributes, start and end tags, etc. Because XML data is structured hierarchically, you will be sending a linear stream of events based on a flattened representation of the XML. This means that for each element you need to construct a start tag, add any attributes, then build its body (which may include other elements) and finally its end tag.

The following code shows how to create an XML output stream, write XML data to the stream, and finally flush the contents of the stream:

```
XMLOutputStreamFactory factory = XMLOutputStreamFactory.newInstance( );
XMLOutputStream output =
    factory.newOutputStream(new PrintWriter(System.out,true));
```

```
// ...
output.add(ElementFactory.createCharacterData("avi"));
// ...
output.flush();
output.close();
```

You can construct an output stream from a number of different sinks:

`java.io.OutputStream` *and* `java.io.Writer`
> The XML data is written to the binary stream or character writer, as you would expect. In the earlier example, the XML output stream wraps the writer System. out, so the XML data is written to the console screen.

`org.xml.sax.ContentHandler`
> The output is written to a SAX content handler, which eventually generates a stream of SAX events.

`org.w3c.dom.Document`
> The XML output is written to a DOM document. The following code snippet shows how to create an XML output stream that wraps a DOM tree:
>
> ```
> XMLOutputStreamFactory factory = XMLOutputStreamFactory.newInstance();
> Document doc =
>   DocumentBuilderFactory.newInstance().newDocumentBuilder().newDocument();
> XMLOutputStream output = factory.newOutputStream(doc);
> ```

Do not forget to use the `flush()` method on the output stream. Only then will the current contents of the XML output stream be written to the actual sink. For instance, if you are writing to a DOM document, you must flush the output stream before you start manipulating the DOM tree. If you don't flush the XML stream, you may have to suffer the consequences of a partially constructed DOM!

Writing to the Stream

The XML output stream provides various `add()` methods that enable you to generate XML data and write various elements to the stream. All elements are created via factory methods provided by the `ElementFactory` class:

```
output.add(ElementFactory.createStartElement("myelement"));
output.add(ElementFactory.createAttribute("a","1"));
output.add(ElementFactory.createCharacterData("Hello World"));
output.add(ElementFactory.createEndElement("myelement"));
```

The preceding code sample generates the following XML data:

```
<myelement a='1'>Hello World</myelement>
```

The output stream is nonvalidating, so you need to guarantee that the XML document is well-formed. For instance, you need to ensure that all elements are properly nested and that each start tag for an element has a matching end tag.

In fact, the `add()` method supports adding four types of objects: plain markup, elements, attributes, and an `XMLInputStream`. You can supply an `XMLInputStream` to the add( ) method—this allows you to easily insert XML data from another source. Recall an XMLInputStream instance can wrap several different sources: a file, character reader, or DOM tree. The next example shows how you can insert XML data that has been parsed from a file:

```
output.add(ElementFactory.createStartElement("example"));
XMLInputStreamFactory factory = XMLInputStreamFactory.newInstance( );
XMLInputStream stream = factory.newInputStream(new FileInputStream(somefile));
output.add(stream);
output.add(ElementFactory.createEndElement("example"));
```

As you can see, writing to the XML output stream is quite straightforward. The ElementFactory class can manufacture all of the obvious elements in an XML document: start and end tags, attributes, character data, processing instructions, etc. It is quite cumbersome having to use the XMLOutputStream to write XML data. You need to generate the hierarchical XML data in a serial fashion, much like how the XML input stream delivers its XML events during a parse. This is quite *unlike* the more natural approach of constructing a DOM tree.

WebLogic's XPath API

WebLogic XPath API lets you match XPath expressions against an XML document, represented either as a DOM tree or an XMLInputStream. The API is contained in the weblogic.xml.xpath.* package. Though the XPath syntax and semantics follow the W3C standard, there is still no standard Java API for manipulating XPath expressions, so this is a welcome API.

Using the API with a DOM

To use the API, construct DOMXPath instances representing your XPath. Here are a few examples:

```
DOMXPath threeDebt = new DOMXPath("sum(//co[@type='3']/debt)");
DOMXPath haveFirst = new DOMXPath("count(//co[@type='1']) > 0");
DOMXPath biggestDebt = new DOMXPath("//co[debt > 1000]/debt");
```

We will use the following XML as test input:

```
<world>
  <co type='1'><debt>100</debt></co>
  <co type='3'><debt>1000</debt></co>
  <co type='3'><debt>2000</debt></co>
</world>
```

You can match the XPath expressions against either a DOM node or the entire document itself. Use a node if you intend to just search a portion of the document. To evaluate the XPath expression, you must invoke one of the following evaluate methods on the DOMXPath instance:

```
public boolean evaluateAsBoolean(Document|Node);
public java.util.Set evaluateAsNodeset(Document|Node);
```

```
public double evaluateAsNumber(Document|Node);
public String evaluateAsString(Document|Node);
```

The actual evaluate method you invoke will depend on the type of the expected result(s) of your XPath expression. For example, we would invoke the earlier XPath expressions as follows:

```
/** evaluate the total third-world debt */
double e_debt = threeDebt.evaluateAsNumber(doc);
/** evaluate if there are any developed countries */
boolean e_haveFirst = haveFirst.evaluateAsBoolean(doc);
/** find the countries with a serious debt problem */
Set biggest = biggestDebt.evaluateAsNodeset(doc);
```

The evaluateAsNodeSet( ) method returns a set of org.w3c.dom.Node objects that match the XPath expression, so, you could iterate over the set of nodes as follows:

```
if (biggest!= null) {
  Iterator i = biggest.iterator();
  while (i.hasNext()) {
     Node n = (Node)i.next();
     // Process the node
  }
}
```

The result of running this little test will indicate that the total third-world debt (e_debt) is 3000, that it is true that there is a first-world country, and that there is one member in the set of countries with a major debt problem.

Using the API with a Stream

Matching XPath expressions against an XML document that is read as an XML stream is just a little more involved. You would expect this because the document that you are matching against is read only incrementally. Thus, instead of waiting for the XPath expression to complete its evaluation, the API lets you register a set of "observers" before the XML stream is processed. These observers then are invoked whenever an XPath match is found as you incrementally parse the XML stream, in the order in which the observers were assigned. Because you're going to match an XPath expression against an XML stream, you need to create a StreamXPath instance (instead of a DOMXPath object) to represent your XPath expression:

```
StreamXPath pops = new StreamXPath ("//co/pop");
```

Now you must create an XPathStreamFactory instance and register one or more observers that are invoked whenever something within the XML stream matches the XPath expression:

```
XPathStreamFactory factory = new XPathStreamFactory();
factory.install(pops,
    new XPathStreamObserver () {
       public void observe(XMLEvent event) {
          System.out.println("Population event matched: "+event);
```

```
        }
        public void observeAttribute(StartElement e, Attribute a) {} //ignore
        public void observeNamespace(StartElement e, Attribute a) {} //ignore
    });
```

In this case, we've registered an observer that responds to any XML events that match the XPath expression. This means that as we pull events of the XML stream, WebLogic automatically calls the appropriate observe( ) methods whenever an XML event matching the XPath expression //co/pop is found. Remember, if you configure a StreamXPath instance with multiple observers, they will be called (during the parse) in the order in which they were installed.

Once you've installed the observers with the XPath expression, you then can initiate the evaluation. To achieve this, you need to simply use the XPathStreamFactory instance to construct an XML stream that can trigger the XPath observers, whenever you pull XML events that may match the XPath expression. In fact, the XPathStreamFactory instance provides the createStream( ) method, which accepts a single parameter: an XMLInputStream or an XMLOutputStream object. This method then returns an XML stream that can match the events in the source stream with the installed XPath observers. The following example shows how to enable XPath matching on an XML stream:

```
//src represents the location of an XML document
XMLInputStream sourceStream =
    XMLInputStreamFactory.newInstance( ).newInputStream(new File(src));
XMLInputStream matchingStream =
    factory.createStream(sourceStream);
```

Now when you iterate over this XML stream, you get the same XML events as if you had iterated over the source stream, but in addition, the events are matched against the configured observers and the appropriate observe( ) methods are invoked. The following example shows how you would evaluate the XPath expression against the source stream:

```
while(matchingStream.hasNext( )) {
    XMLEvent event = matchingStream.next( );
    // Do nothing if you are only interested in the XPath observations
}
```

As you can see, we simply pull XML events from the stream—the configured observers are executed transparently during this iteration. Note that because the Streaming API observes a set of events, a node such as debt will have two events associated with it (i.e., the start and end events). Both of these events will match the XPath expression, and both will trigger the appropriate observe( ) methods.

One of the disadvantages of using the Streaming XPath API is that you cannot use the full XPath expression syntax. For instance, if you attempt to match the following XPath expression against an XML stream, you will surely encounter a weblogic.xml. xpath.XpathUnsupportedException:

```
StreamXPath cost = new StreamXPath ("//co[debt > 1000]/debt");
```

The reason should be obvious. Since the Streaming XPath API iterates over a stream of XML events without any "look ahead" capability, it cannot possibly match against child elements. For this reason, you cannot use the *child* axis in the XPath predicate. The same reasoning can be applied to several other XPath expressions, leading to the following natural limitations:

- You may not use the XPath functions `last()`, `size()`, `id()`, `lang()`, and `count()` when constructing a `StreamXPath` object. In addition, the `string()` function is not fully supported because the string value of a node with offspring depends on its child nodes.

- The Streaming XPath API doesn't support XPath predicates that use the following axes: `self`, `child`, `descendant`, `descendant-or-self`, `following`, `following-sibling`, `attribute`, and `namespace`.

Miscellaneous Extensions

WebLogic provides a number of miscellaneous extensions that ease the processing of XML data. For instance, WebLogic extends the standard SAX input source. Instances of the `weblogic.xml.sax.XMLInputSource` class enable you to retrieve document header information such as the name of the root element or the public and system identifiers:

```
package weblogic.xml.sax;
public class XMLInputSource extends org.xml.sax.InputSource {
  public String getNamespaceURI();
  public String getPublicId();
  public String getRootTag();
  public String getSystemId();
  //...
}
```

This is useful when you need to decide how to process the XML data without having to complete a lengthy parse of a potentially large document. The following code snippet shows how to retrieve the root tag of an incoming XML document:

```
XMLInputSource xis =
  new XMLInputSource(new java.io.StringBufferInputStream("<theroot></theroot>"));
System.err.println(xis.getRootTag());
```

In addition, WebLogic provides a JMS extension whereby XML messages may be filtered on the value of an XPath expression. We covered this in Chapter 8.

Parsing XML in a Servlet

WebLogic provides a proprietary but convenient way for parsing the message body of an HTTP POST request made to a servlet. It allows you to use the `setAttribute` and `getAttribute` methods on the `HttpServletRequest` object to parse XML documents. However, it is not a feature supported by other J2EE-compliant servlet engines. WebLogic provides two special-purpose attributes in the request object. When you retrieve the value of the particular attribute, instead of returning its value, WebLogic parses the message body of the HTTP request.

WebLogic automatically uses the JAXP interface to create the appropriate parser, and lets the parser run through the contents of the body of the HTTP POST. To use the DOM parser, you need to retrieve the value of the org.w3c.dom.Document attribute from the HTTP request object and cast the return value to Document:

```
org.w3c.dom.Document doc =
        (org.w3c.dom.Document) request.getAttribute("org.w3c.dom.Document");
```

To use the SAX parser, you need to assign a SAX handler instance as the value of the org.xml.sax.helpers.DefaultHandler request attribute. WebLogic then will automatically parse the message body of the HTTP POST request using the SAX handler you've supplied:

```
request.setAttribute("org.xml.sax.helpers.DefaultHandler", someHandler);
```

Example 18-8 illustrates how a simple servlet can parse the message body of an incoming POST request. In response, the servlet outputs the names of all the start elements found in the XML document.

Example 18-8. Parsing the body of a POST request

```
import weblogic.servlet.XMLProcessingException;
import org.xml.sax.helpers.DefaultHandler;
// ...
public void doPost(HttpServletRequest request,
                              HttpServletResponse response)
  throws ServletException, IOException  {
  try {
    final PrintWriter out = response.getWriter();
    DefaultHandler printName = new DefaultHandler() {
     public void startElement (String uri, String lName, String qName,
                            Attributes  attr){
         out.println(qName);};
               };
    request.setAttribute("org.xml.sax.helpers.DefaultHandler",
                       printName);

  } catch(XMLProcessingException ex) {
    ex.printStackTrace();
  }
}
```

A Java client may send a POST request to the servlet, using an instance of the java. net.URLConnection class. Example 18-9 shows how a program can send XML data to an HTTP servlet. Once the client has established a connection with the servlet and delivered the XML data, it prints the response data returned from the servlet.

Example 18-9. Sending data to the XML servlet

```
// Connect to our servlet
URL u = new URL("http://10.0.10.10:7061/B");
URLConnection uc = (URLConnection) u.openConnection();
uc.setRequestProperty("Content-Type","text/xml");
uc.setDoOutput(true);
uc.setDoInput(true);
// Send some XML
PrintWriter pw = new PrintWriter(uc.getOutputStream());
pw.print("<fine>I am <dandy/>You are</fine>");
pw.close();
// Read the result
BufferedReader in =
 new BufferedReader(new InputStreamReader(uc.getInputStream()));
String inputLine;
while ((inputLine = in.readLine()) != null) {
    System.out.println(inputLine);
}
in.close();
```

Running this code will yield the following output in the console window:

```
fine
dandy
```

Using the JSP Tag Library for XSL Transformations

WebLogic supplies a JSP tag library to help with XSL Transformations from within a JSP page. You can make the tag library available to a web application by placing the tag library *xmlx-tags.jar* under the *WEB-INF/lib* folder of the web application. Before this, however, you need to extract the tag library JAR from the *WL_HOME\ server\ext\xmlx.zip* file. Finally, you need to specify a taglib element in the standard *web.xml* descriptor file to make the tag library visible to the web application:

```
<taglib>
  <taglib-uri>xmlx.tld</taglib-uri>
  <taglib-location>/WEB-INF/lib/xmlx-tags.jar</taglib-location>
</taglib>
```

Given this declaration, you now can reference the tag library from within a JSP page as follows:

```
<%@ taglib uri="xmlx.tld" prefix="x"%>
```

The tag library defines the main xslt tag, and two tags that can be used within its body: the xml and stylesheet tags. The xslt tag can be used in several different ways:

- The XML data can be supplied within the body of the xml tag.
- You can reference multiple XSLT stylesheets and, at runtime, determine which one is used for the transformation.
- If the JSP uses an empty xslt tag, the XML data is grabbed from the URL used to access the JSP.

In all these cases, the JSP tag automatically uses the JAXP interface to acquire an XSL transformer and then apply the correct stylesheet to the XML data.

Using an interceptor

You can set up a mechanism whereby a request for an XML file automatically triggers an XSLT conversion, and the result of the transformation is then returned back to the client. In this case, the XML file references the XSLT stylesheet that ought to be used for the transformation. The trick is to map a servlet (or JSP) to a URL pattern so that the servlet (or JSP) can intercept the requests for the XML file and run the transformation. In this case, we'll use a JSP to intercept requests for the XML file(s). The JSP page intercepts the HTTP request. A simple JSP tag then automatically passes the requested file through an XSLT processor and sends the output of the transformation back to the client.

The JSP page looks quite simple—it merely includes an empty xslt tag. The following code snippet lists the source for the *interceptor.jsp* file:

```
<%@ taglib uri="xmlx.tld" prefix="x"%>
<x:xslt/>
```

Next, you need to register this JSP as a servlet and map it to a URL pattern—say, */xslt/*. Do this by modifying the standard *web.xml* descriptor for the web application:

```
<!-- web.xml entry -->
<servlet>
   <servlet-name>interceptor</servlet-name>
   <jsp-file>interceptor.jsp</jsp-file>
</servlet>
<servlet-mapping>
   <servlet-name>interceptor</servlet-name>
   <url-pattern>/xslt/*</url-pattern>
</servlet-mapping>
```

This will ensure that all requests that match the URL pattern */xslt/* are now delegated to the interceptor JSP. Because the *interceptor.jsp* contains an xslt tag with an empty body, the tag implementation will fetch the contents of the resource automatically. The location of the resource is determined implicitly by the rest of the URI that follows the servlet path. The JSP tag will read the XML data from the resource and then use the referenced XSLT stylesheet to execute the transformation, before returning the output back to the client. Now, suppose the web application contains an XML file *test.xml*:

```
<?xml version="1.0"?>
<?xml-stylesheet type="text/xsl" href="test.xsl"?>
<a>Hello World!</a>
```

Here, the XML file includes a reference to the XSLT stylesheet *test.xsl*:

```
<?xml version="1.0"?>
<xsl:stylesheet xmlns:xsl="http://www.w3.org/1999/XSL/Transform" version="1.0">
```

```
<xsl:template match="a">
  <html><h1>
    <xsl:value-of select="."/>
  </h1></html>
</xsl:template>
</xsl:stylesheet>
```

If you place both *test.xml* and *test.xsl* under the root of the web application, a request for the URL *http://server:port/webapp/xsl/test.xml* will be redirected to the interceptor JSP automatically. The JSP will invoke the xslt tag, which will fetch the resource using the URI that follows the servlet path (i.e., */test.xml*) and send this file through the configured XSLT processor. The HTML generated as a result of the transformation then will be returned to the client:

```
<html><h1>
  <a>Hello World!</a>
</h1></html>
```

Of course, you can reduce the cost of XSLT processing by relying on WebLogic's support for caching, via either the JSP cache tags or the cache filters.

Using the XSLT tag

The XSLT tag also can be used in a more traditional manner—i.e., in nonintercept mode. The following code sample shows how to execute a transformation when the URIs for the XML document and the XSLT stylesheet are attributes of the xslt tag:

```
<%@ taglib uri="xmlx.tld" prefix="x"%>
<x:xslt xml="test.xml" stylesheet="test.xsl"/>
```

In this case, the result of the XSL transformation also will be the output of the xslt tag. You can specify a number of subelements within the body of the xslt tag:

- You can specify the source XML data within the body of an xml tag. If the xslt tag doesn't define an xml attribute or include an xml tag, the XML data is grabbed from the URI that follows the servlet path, as described earlier.

- You can specify one or more stylesheet elements, whereby each tag declares a media attribute and a uri attribute that references an XSLT stylesheet. You also can define the XSL templates within the body of the stylesheet tags.

If the xslt tag declares a media attribute, its value determines which one of the stylesheets is eventually used. Example 18-10 illustrates how to use the media attribute to select from one of the stylesheets. Here, the JSP decides based on whether the output is meant for an HTML browser or a WAP browser (which supports WML).

Example 18-10. Using the xslt tag

```
<%@ taglib uri="xmlx.tld" prefix="x"%>
<%
  String mediaType = "html"; // Usually dynamically computed
  String content = "<a>Hello World!</a>";
```

Example 18-10. Using the xslt tag (continued)

```
%>

<x:xslt media="<%=mediaType%>">
  <x:xml><%=content%></x:xml>
  <x:stylesheet media="html" uri="test.xsl"/>
  <x:stylesheet media="wml"  uri="wml.xsl"/>
</x:xslt>
```

In this case, the JSP generates the same output as *interceptor.jsp*:

```
<html><h1>
    <a>Hello World!</a>
</h1></html>
```

The media attribute acts as a selector variable for stylesheets listed in the body of the xslt tag. This way, the JSP can decide at runtime which stylesheet should be used for the XSL transformation.

CHAPTER 19

Web Services

Web services can be characterized by three properties. First, web services are accessed over the Web through standard Internet protocols, such as HTTP or HTTPS. Second, web services describe themselves using XML and typically rely on registries to aid the lookup and invocation of the services. Finally, web services talk to their clients (and other web services) using an XML-based protocol—i.e., remote procedure calls to a web service operation are transmitted in the form of XML messages.

The combination of these properties is quite powerful—distributed applications that span heterogeneous hardware and software platforms can now interoperate using a cross-platform language (XML) over standard Internet protocols. Web services provide an environment for building loosely coupled, decentralized applications where the diverse services can collaborate in a platform-independent and language-agnostic way. Application interoperability is the primary motivation for adopting web services. Given an environment in which a number of applications written in different programming languages running on diverse platforms need to communicate with each other, web services can help bridge language barriers and overcome these platform differences. As long as the participating applications adhere to the published standards that determine the formats of the XML messages, processing rules, and more, it is possible to expose the different application services in the form of web services, all of which can be accessed by peer applications using a standard XML-based protocol.

There is a plethora of standards in the world of web services. WebLogic supports the following standards:

SOAP 1.1 with Attachments
  Simple Object Access Protocol (SOAP) is a lightweight, XML-based communications protocol for exchanging messages. WebLogic Server comes equipped with its own implementation of the SOAP 1.1 and "SOAP with Attachments" specifications. In fact, WebLogic web services accept both SOAP 1.1– and SOAP 1.2– compliant message requests, but produce only SOAP 1.1–compliant message responses. In addition, WebLogic supports the various XML Schema datatypes

used to describe the format for data that is being exchanged. WebLogic 8.1 also can be configured to use SOAP 1.2. As this is not a W3C recommendation at the time of writing, this implementation is subject to change.

WSDL 1.1

The Web Services Description Language (WSDL) is the XML application that is used to describe a web service. A WSDL document describes the various operations exposed by a web service, their input and output parameters, and how to access the web service. WebLogic supports WSDL 1.1–compliant descriptions for web services.

JAX-RPC

Sun Microsystems has developed the Java API for XML-based RPC (JAX-RPC) standard, which defines the client API needed for invoking a web service. WebLogic supplies a client JAR that includes an implementation of the JAX-RPC 1.0 specification, thereby allowing Java clients to access both WebLogic and other non-WebLogic web services. The JAX-RPC standard is central to understanding WebLogic's web services framework.

UDDI 2.0

The Universal Description, Discovery and Integration (UDDI) specification defines a standard way to describe a web service, publish web services over a registry, and discover other registered web services. WebLogic supports the UDDI 2.0 standard for publishing web services over a registry and for inquiring about other registered web services.

In this chapter, we focus on how to build and deploy web services to WebLogic, which supports the implementation of a web service using ordinary Java classes and standard J2EE components such as EJBs and JMS. We also examine how to create clients for these web services. These clients can talk to other standards-compliant web services, not just those deployed to WebLogic Server. We also look at how to secure access to your web services and how to invoke web services that use SSL.

Web services are not part of the J2EE 1.3 standard. WebLogic implements many specifications that probably will form the heart of J2EE 1.4 support for web services. You can expect much of the material in this chapter to become standard in future releases. This chapter exposes the core web service material. Much of this is at the developer level. Some application builders and architects may prefer a higher-level approach to building web services, which is supported by WebLogic Workshop.

Using the Web Services Framework

WebLogic provides a rich framework for the development and deployment of web services. Here is a brief outline of the capabilities of WebLogic's web services framework:

- WebLogic automatically provides a web home page for each deployed web service. The home page includes links to the WSDL document for the web service, the client JAR file that you can download to invoke the web service, and a mechanism for testing each operation exposed by the web service. This last feature is useful particularly during development stages because it lets you debug your web service and inspect the incoming SOAP message requests and outgoing SOAP responses.

- WebLogic lets you expose standard J2EE components as web services. This means that you can implement web service operations using different backend components. For instance, a call to a web service operation may translate to a method call on a standard Java object. Alternatively, the web service operation may be implemented via one of the remote methods of a stateless session EJB. Web service operations also can trigger specific JMS actions—for example, send a JMS message to a JMS destination, or receive a message from a JMS queue.

- WebLogic lets you configure a chain of SOAP message handlers for each operation on a web service. These message handlers can intercept incoming message requests or outgoing SOAP responses, and potentially alter the body of the message. Typical applications of SOAP message handlers include encryption and decryption, response caching, content transformation, and more.

- WebLogic provides a number of Ant tasks and command-line utilities that allow you to quickly build and package your web services within an enterprise application. For instance, you can point the servicegen utility to an existing stateless session EJB, and it will automatically generate a web service that exposes each public method of the EJB. It also provides Ant tasks that handle specific jobs during the development of a web service such as automatically generating the Java support classes and XML schema definitions needed for any custom data types, assembling all components of the web service into a deployable EAR, and manufacturing a client JAR that can be used by Java or Java 2 Micro Edition (J2ME) clients to invoke the web service.

- WebLogic includes a UDDI registry over which web services may be published and searched. WebLogic also supplies a UDDI Directory Explorer that lets you hunt for web services on different UDDI registries and publish your own web services over the local UDDI registry. Of course, WebLogic supports the client API that lets you publish and look up web services from UDDI registries.

- You can comfortably integrate web services into your existing security framework. This means you can restrict external client access to the web service (and the WSDL document), secure access to the various backend components that support your web services, and permit only HTTPS connections to the web services.

There are many orthogonal and overlapping aspects to designing and implementing web services. Before we take a closer look at WebLogic's web services framework, we need to understand how your deployed web services operate at runtime.

Web Services Architecture

A web service is composed of one or more operations, whereby each operation may be implemented using different backend components. You even can associate a separate set of message handlers for each operation. For example, a web service operation may be implemented by a single method of a standard Java object, or perhaps by a combination of SOAP message handlers and a remote method of a stateless session EJB. Because web services extend the capabilities of your web applications, WebLogic requires that you define a *web-services.xml* deployment descriptor that captures the vital information describing a web service. This XML-formatted descriptor file is located under the */WEB-INF* folder of a web application and includes the following information on each web service:

- It specifies the backend components used to implement the various operations of the web service.

- It defines any SOAP handler chains that intercept incoming and outgoing SOAP messages.

- It specifies the XML Schema definitions for any custom datatypes that are used as parameters and return values for web service operations. It also provides the XML-to-Java datatype mappings that specify the serialization class and Java classes for the custom datatypes.

- It declares the actual operations supported by the web service and associates each operation with a backend component and/or SOAP handler chain.

The *web-services.xml* descriptor file is crucial to properly configuring your web services. Even though WebLogic provides various Ant tasks for automatically generating the *web-services* deployment descriptor, often you will need to return to the *web-services.xml* descriptor file and manually tweak its configuration settings. During the course of this chapter, we'll cover the different configuration elements of the web services deployment descriptor. WebLogic can use the *web-services.xml* descriptor file to automatically generate the WSDL document for the deployed web service.

As illustrated in Figure 19-1, WebLogic's web services are packaged into standard J2EE enterprise applications (EAR).

The EAR file includes the web application (WAR) that contains the *web-services.xml* descriptor file and any Java classes that implement the web service, the message handlers, and support classes for handling custom datatypes. It also packages any EJB JAR files for any stateless session EJBs or JMS consumers and producers that implement the web service operations. Fortunately, WebLogic provides several Ant tasks for assembling the various components of the web service into an EAR file.

Because WebLogic's web services are packaged within enterprise applications, they can integrate easily with the rest of the J2EE framework. Your web services can automatically benefit from WebLogic's support for various J2EE features: access to JDBC connection pools and JTA transactions, the business objects within the enterprise application, and a simple and unified security model.

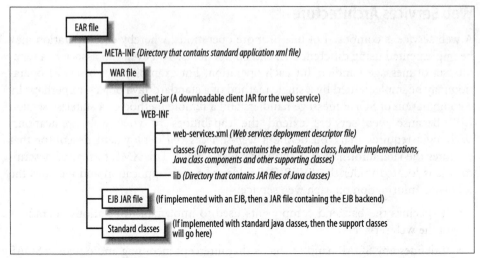

Figure 19-1. Package structure of a typical web service

Typical behavior of a web service

Like EJB interfaces, a web service exposes a set of operations that can be invoked by remote clients. Instead of using RMI-IIOP to invoke the EJB's methods, the operations are accessed through SOAP calls passed over standard HTTP. Instead of the traditional marshalling of Java objects to a bit stream, client-side stubs now serialize the method arguments to an XML stream. On the server side, WebLogic parses the incoming XML stream and deserializes the method arguments. WebLogic uses this information to invoke an operation on a backend component that implements the particular web service. If the operation generates a response for the client, the client-side stubs deserialize it to extract the return values before passing them on to the client.

Along the way, the incoming SOAP request or the outgoing SOAP response may be processed by a number of message handlers that transform the message body. In fact, a web service operation may simply go through a chain of message handlers, without actually invoking a backend component! Figure 19-2 depicts the activity surrounding a client application that invokes an operation on a web service. You can think of this diagram as representing the runtime behavior of a JAX-RPC call.

When a client invokes an operation exposed by a web service, the following actions occur:

1. The client-side libraries translate the JAX-RPC call to a SOAP request, which is then sent to WebLogic.

2. WebLogic inspects the URI of the incoming request to determine which web service ought to be invoked. The web service also needs to parse the SOAP message to determine which operation needs to be invoked.

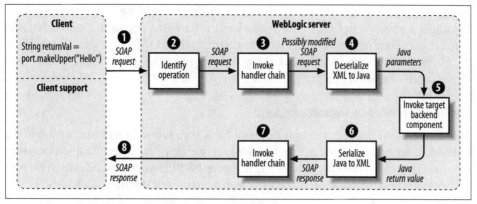

Figure 19-2. Architecture of a typical web service operation

3. If the operation is associated with a chain of message handlers, the SOAP message must go through the sequence of message handlers. Each message handler may potentially alter the SOAP message or even abort the operation.

4. Using the appropriate deserializer classes, WebLogic builds a Java representation of the inbound parameters from their XML representation. This deserialization logic relies both on WebLogic's support for handling built-in datatypes, and on your deserialization classes that handle any custom datatypes you've used.

5. The web service now invokes the backend component associated with the operation, passing it the Java parameters.

6. WebLogic then converts the return values from Java to XML using the appropriate serializer classes and creates a SOAP message response for the client.

7. If the operation is associated with a chain of message handlers, the SOAP response must again pass through a chain of SOAP message handlers, but this time in reverse order. Once again, each message handler may alter the outgoing SOAP response or abort the operation.

8. WebLogic finally sends the resulting SOAP message back to the client. At the client's end, the client-side stubs intercept the returned SOAP message and extract the returned value(s) before passing them on to the client.

How the backend component is invoked depends on the *web-services.xml* descriptor file. You can configure the "invocation style" for individual operations on a web service, and enable clients to invoke an operation without waiting for a SOAP response. Alternatively, you can mark a web service as being "document-centric," in which case each operation accepts a single XML document as an incoming parameter. Later in this chapter, we discuss similar design considerations in more detail once we've looked at how to build a web service.

Figure 19-2 describes the typical behavior of a web service that is implemented by some backend component. However, a SOAP message handler chain need not be associated with the web service at all. In that case, all incoming SOAP requests from the client and any outgoing SOAP responses to the client remain unaltered because no message handlers are configured to intercept the SOAP messages. Thus, if no SOAP interceptors are configured for a web service operation, you can disregard steps 3 and 7 depicted in Figure 19-2.

Web service operations without a backend

Just as the SOAP handler chain is optional for a web service operation, so too is the backend component. This means that a web service may implement an operation simply through a chain of SOAP interceptors. Figure 19-3 illustrates the behavior of a web service operation implemented purely through a chain of SOAP message handlers.

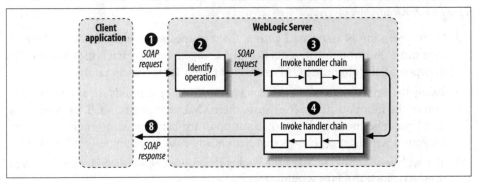

Figure 19-3. Behavior of an operation without a backend component

After the last SOAP interceptor in the chain has processed the incoming SOAP request, the SOAP message then continues directly with the "response chain" of SOAP handlers, but this time in reverse order of the chain. Each SOAP handler in the chain has direct access to the SOAP message and may alter the message before passing it to the next handler in the chain. A common use of SOAP message handlers is to decrypt and encrypt SOAP messages that enter and leave a web service operation.

Building Your First Web Service

Let's now survey the web services framework by constructing a simple web service that wraps a standard Java class. Example 19-1 provides the definition of the Java class that will implement the web service.

Example 19-1. A simple backend Java component for a web service

```
public class Simple {
    public String makeUpper(String arg) {
        return arg.toUpperCase();
    }
}
```

It exposes a single method, makeUpper( ), that simply returns an uppercase equivalent of the input string. Recall that all web services in WebLogic are packaged within an EAR file that includes the web application (WAR), which holds the *web-services. xml* descriptor file, and any Java classes that implement the web service. If your web service is implemented using EJBs, then the EAR file also packages the required EJB JARs. In the case of our example, the EAR file will simply package the web application (*myWar.war*) that hosts the actual web services:

```
META-INF/MANIFEST.MF
META-INF/application.xml
myWar.war
```

Our web application will be a standard J2EE web archive that can hold the static content (HTML, images, text files, JARs, etc.), JSP pages, and compiled Java classes for any servlets, JSP tags, and filters. In addition, the web application will include the following files under the document root:

```
WEB-INF/web-services.xml
WEB-INF/classes/com/oreilly/wlguide/webservices/pojo/Simple.class
WEB-INF/web.xml
```

So, simple Java backends are packaged with the web application. The *web-service. xml* descriptor file is essential because it completely describes all the web services hosted by the web application. Example 19-2 describes the web service that wraps our Java class.

Example 19-2. The web-services.xml descriptor file

```
<web-services>
  <web-service protocol="http" name="Simple" uri="/Simple"
      targetNamespace="http://www.oreilly.com/webservices/Simple" style="rpc">
    <components>
      <java-class name="jcCompo"
                  class-name="com.oreilly.wlguide.webservices.pojo.Simple">
      </java-class>
    </components>
    <operations>
      <operation method="makeUpper(java.lang.String)"
                  component="jcCompo" name="makeUpper">
        <params>
          <param location="body" class-name="java.lang.String" style="in"
              name="arg" xmlns:xsd="http://www.w3.org/2001/XMLSchema" type="xsd:string">
          </param>
          <return-param location="body" class-name="java.lang.String" name="result"
              xmlns:xsd="http://www.w3.org/2001/XMLSchema" type="xsd:string">
          </return-param>
        </params>
      </operation>
    </operations>
  </web-service>
</web-services>
```

Notice how the *web-services.xml* descriptor file defines the operations that are supported by the web service and the components that are used to implement the web service. Our Simple web service exposes a single operation, makeUpper, that is mapped to the makeUpper( ) method on the standard Java class. The operation accepts a single in parameter of type xsd:string and returns a single out parameter, again of type xsd:string. In this way, the deployment descriptor specifies the parameters and return values of each operation and maps it to a particular method on one of the backend components. The *web-services.xml* descriptor file is quite similar to the WSDL document for a web service, though it provides additional deployment information. WebLogic lets you automatically generate the *web-services.xml* deployment descriptor in several ways:

- You can invoke the servicegen task, which automatically generates the *web-services.xml* descriptor file before creating a deployable EAR for the web service.

- You can invoke the source2wsdd task, which simply generates the *web-service.xml* descriptor file after introspecting the backend Java class. This is essentially what happens when you run the servicegen task before it generates the EAR file.

- You can run the wsdl2service task that uses a WSDL document to generate both the *web-services.xml* descriptor file and a template for a Java class that implements the web service.

All of these tools have their limitations, which become even more debilitating when you need to build multiple web services that are supported by different backend components or are associated with a chain of SOAP handlers. For now, we can safely rely on the servicegen Ant task to generate both the deployment descriptor and the actual EAR file that packages our web service. Example 19-3 shows how to invoke the servicegen task from within an Ant build script.

Example 19-3. Ant script for invoking the servicegen task

```
<project name="simple" default="create" basedir=".">
  <property name="namespace" value="http://www.oreilly.com/webservices/Simple" />
  <property name="build" value="/classes" />
  <target name="create">
    <servicegen destEar="myPOJOEar.ear" warName="myWar.war" contextURI="pojoService">
      <service
        javaClassComponents="com.oreilly.wlguide.webservices.pojo.Simple"
        targetNamespace="${namespace}"
        serviceName="Simple"
        serviceURI="/Simple"
        expandMethods="True">
      </service>
      <classpath>
        <pathelement path="${build}"/>
      </classpath>
    </servicegen>
  </target>
</project>
```

In order to invoke the servicegen task, we need to specify the name of the deployable EAR file that is generated and the name of the WAR file that hosts the web service and classes for the backend component. By running the preceding build script, you manufacture a deployable EAR file, *myPOJOEar.ear*, which in turn contains the WAR, *myWar.war*, which contains the web service and the Java implementation class. By deploying the EAR file to WebLogic Server, you also deploy all web services that are packaged within its web applications.

Note that the serviceURI attribute for the web service is set to */Simple*, and the contextURI attribute for the EAR is set to *pojoService*. This means that you can access the web service by pointing a browser to the following address: *http://hostname:port/pojoService/Simple*, where *hostname* and *port* refer to the listen address and port number of a running WebLogic instance to which the web service has been successfully deployed. Here you can view the home page for the web service and also access the automatically generated WSDL by clicking the Service Description link. Example 19-4 lists the WSDL that describes our web service.

Example 19-4. Autogenerated WSDL for our web service

```
<definitions targetNamespace="http://www.oreilly.com/webservices/Simple">
  <message name="makeUpper">
    <part name="string" type="partns:string"/>
  </message>
  <message name="makeUpperResponse">
    <part name="result" type="partns:string"/>
  </message>
  <portType name="SimplePort">
    <operation name="makeUpper">
      <input message="tns:makeUpper"/>
      <output message="tns:makeUpperResponse"/>
    </operation>
  </portType>
  <binding name="SimplePortSoapBinding" type="tns:SimplePort">
   <soap:binding style="rpc" transport="http://schemas.xmlsoap.org/soap/http"/>
    <operation name="makeUpper">
      <soap:operation soapAction="" style="rpc"/>
      <input>
       <soap:body use="encoded" namespace="http://www.oreilly.com/webservices/Simple"
                  encodingStyle="http://schemas.xmlsoap.org/soap/encoding/"/>
      </input>
      <output>
       <soap:body use="encoded" namespace="http://www.oreilly.com/webservices/Simple"
                  encodingStyle="http://schemas.xmlsoap.org/soap/encoding/"/>
      </output>
    </operation>
  </binding>
  <service name="Simple">
    <port name="SimplePort" binding="tns:SimplePortSoapBinding">
      <soap:address location="http://10.0.10.10:8001/pojoService/Simple"/>
    </port>
  </service>
</definitions>
```

The home page also provides a customized environment where you can test the operations of the web service. If you click the *makeUpper* link, you navigate to a screen where you can invoke the makeUpper operation of the web service. Enter some random string value in the Value text box and then hit the Invoke button. The web service will return the uppercase equivalent of the same string. You also can view the SOAP request and response envelopes exchanged during the invocation. Here's a sample request envelope used to invoke the web service operation:

```
<env:Envelope  xmlns:xsd="http://www.w3.org/2001/XMLSchema"
   xmlns:soapenc="http://schemas.xmlsoap.org/soap/encoding/"
   xmlns:env="http://schemas.xmlsoap.org/soap/envelope/"
   xmlns:xsi="http://www.w3.org/2001/XMLSchema-instance">
  <env:Body>
   <m:makeUpper xmlns:m="http://www.oreilly.com/webservices/Simple"
      env:encodingStyle="http://schemas.xmlsoap.org/soap/encoding/">
     <string xsi:type="xsd:string">everything here should be in uppercase really!</
string>
   </m:makeUpper>
   </env:Body>
  </env:Envelope>
```

Finally, the home page provides a link to the client JAR that you can download to build your own static JAX-RPC clients for the web service. In fact, you also could invoke the clientgen Ant task to manufacture a client JAR that can be used by JAX-RPC clients. Example 19-5 shows how to use the clientgen task to generate a client JAR that includes the required JAX-RPC interfaces and client-side stubs for the web service.

Example 19-5. Invoking the clientgen Ant task

```
<!-- build target within an Ant Script -->
<target name="createClient">
   <clientgen
     ear="myPOJOEar.ear"
     warName="myWar.war"
     packageName="com.oreilly.wlguide.webservices.pojo.client"
     clientJar="myClient.jar">
     <classpath>
       <pathelement path="${build}"/>
     </classpath>
   </clientgen>
</target>
```

Using *myClient.jar*, which is generated by invoking the previous Ant target, you then can write a Java client that invokes the web service. Example 19-6 lists the code for a JAX-RPC client that invokes the makeUpper operation exposed by the web service.

Example 19-6. Invoking a web service

```
public class Invoke {
    public static void main(String[] argv) throws Exception {
        // Set up the global JAXM message factory
```

Example 19-6. Invoking a web service (continued)

```
        System.setProperty("javax.xml.soap.MessageFactory",
          "weblogic.webservice.core.soap.MessageFactoryImpl");
        // Set up the global JAX-RPC service factory
        System.setProperty( "javax.xml.rpc.ServiceFactory",
          "weblogic.webservice.core.rpc.ServiceFactoryImpl");

        Simple ws = new Simple_Impl("http://10.0.10.10:8001/pojoService/Simple?WSDL");
        SimplePort port  = ws.getSimplePort( );
        String returnVal = port.makeUpper("Hello There");
        System.out.println("The service returned: " + returnVal);
    }
}
```

As you can see, the web service client needs to do very little to contact the web service. The client JAR packages the interface and implementation for each SOAP port defined in the WSDL. The Simple_Impl stub implements the JAX-RPC Service interface and is created using the URI */pojoService/Simple?WSDL*, which fetches the WSDL for the target web service. The getSimplePort( ) method relies on the Service.getPort( ) method to then return an instance of the SimplePort stub implementation. Once you create the client-side port, you can use the local methods on the SimplePort interface to invoke the operations of the web service. In this case, the makeUpper( ) method is invoked. You can expect the following output:

```
java com.oreilly.wlguide.webservices.pojo.client.Invoke
The service returned: HELLO THERE
```

We've just looked at the important aspects of WebLogic's web services framework. It is essentially a tool-driven environment that enables you to rapidly build deployable web services using different starting points—the backend implementation of the web service or, as we shall see later in this chapter, the WSDL document itself.

Using the Administration Console

The Administration Console lets you view any web services deployed to WebLogic Server. Web services typically are deployed as a part of another application, either a WAR or EAR. To view the web service, expand the Deployments/Applications node and click the name of the container component in the left pane of the Administration Console. For example, if the web service was part of the EAR called demo, clicking demo will expand the EAR to show you the components contained within the EAR. Clicking the web service then will provide you with a number of tabs with which to manage the service. WebLogic 7.0 provides a Deployments/Web Service Components node with similar functionality.

Mapping your web service to an alternative URL

Notice how we used the URL *http://10.0.10.10:8001/pojoService/Simple* in order to access our web service. By default, any web service deployed to WebLogic Server is accessible through the URL *http://server:port/<web-app-context>/<service-URI>*.

However, you may also modify the default endpoint for the web service. Because all requests to a web service deployed to WebLogic Server are handled by an internal servlet, `weblogic.webservice.server.servlet.WebServiceServlet`, this means that you can use the servlet-mapping element in the *web.xml* descriptor file to expose your web services via an alternative URL scheme.

The following portion from the *web.xml* descriptor shows how to map the Web Service servlet to a custom URL pattern:

```
<!-- web.xml entry -->
<servlet>
    <servlet-name>InternalWebServiceServlet</servlet-name>
    <servlet-class>weblogic.webservice.server.servlet.WebServiceServlet</servlet-class>
</servlet>
...
<servlet-mapping>
    <servlet-name>InternalWebServiceServlet</servlet-name>
    <url-pattern>/CustomersComeHither/*</url-pattern>
</servlet-mapping>
```

Any web service packaged within the web application then is accessible through the URL *http://server:port/<web-app-context>/CustomersComeHither/<web-svc-name>*. If you modify the *web.xml* descriptor file for *myWar.war* to include a similar URL mapping, clients need to use *http://10.0.10.10:8001/pojoService/CustomersComeHither/Simple* in order to access the web service.

Using the WSDL to Create a Web Service

Recall how the WSDL document describing your web service is generated automatically from the *web-services.xml* descriptor file and then made available as a download link on the home page for the web service. In the example, the WSDL is accessible through the URL *http://10.0.10.10:8001/pojoService/Simple?WSDL*. You can, however, reverse the roles and generate the web service from an existing WSDL document using the `wsdl2service` task. This generates a *web-services.xml* descriptor file and a template for the backend that implements the operations of the web service. You then can modify the Java source template and include the business logic that supports each web service operation.

The `wsdl2service` Ant task generates the support files for only a single web service described by the WSDL file. By default, the task chooses the first web service it finds in the WSDL document. You can use the `serviceName` attribute to specify a particular web service. The following Ant target shows how to generate a web service from a WSDL file:

```
<target name="gen-websvc-from-wsdl">
    <wsdl2service wsdl="myWSDL.wsdl" serviceName="Simple"
        destDir="myEarWSDL" typeMappingFile="types.xml"
        packageName="com.oreilly.wlguide.webservices" />
</target>
```

The typeMappingFile attribute is needed only if the web service defines operations that use custom types for parameters and return values. If so, you must use the autotype task to generate the type mapping file for all custom types from the WSDL file. On invoking this Ant target, you get a *web-services.xml* descriptor that describes the web service Simple found in the WSDL file *myWSDL.wsdl*. In addition, the task creates a Java class located under the com.oreilly.wlguide.webservices package that implements the web service. This Java class contains skeleton code, with empty methods that correspond to the operations exposed by the web service. You can now build on the *web-services.xml* descriptor and Java class backend as required.

Publishing a static WSDL file

Instead of using the automatically generated WSDL that WebLogic provides for each web service, you could make a static WSDL file available through an alternate URL, perhaps apply different security constraints, bundle it with a J2ME client, or even extend the documentation in the WSDL file. While the automatically generated WSDL for a web service is always in sync with the deployed web service, you need to explicitly ensure that the static WSDL file also is kept up-to-date with changes in the web service. Of course, you could always use the automatically generated WSDL as a starting point for the static WSDL file, modify it as appropriate, and then publish the WSDL document.

To publish the WSDL file, you need to include it in the EAR file that packages the web service and define a suitable MIME type mapping. Thus, the WSDL file (say, *myWSDL.wsdl*) can be placed anywhere under the document root of the web application that hosts the web service. Then you should edit the *web.xml* descriptor file for the web application and map all documents with the suffix *.wsdl* to the text/xml MIME type:

```
<!-- portion from the web.xml descriptor file -->
<mime-mapping>
    <extension>wsdl</extension>
    <mime-type>text/xml</mime-type>
</mime-mapping>
```

The static WSDL file for the web service will now be accessible through the URL *http://host:port/webAppContextRoot/myWSDL.wsdl*.

Using Ant Tasks to Build Web Services

In order to assemble a web service, you need to collect all the different components of the web service: the backend Java classes, any EJB JARs used to implement one or more operations of the web service, possible SOAP message handlers, datatypes and their support classes, and the *web-services.xml* descriptor file that completely describes the web service. Only then can the web service be packaged into a standard

J2EE enterprise application. If you intend to assemble the web service manually, you need to execute the following steps:

1. Compile and package the backend components into their respective modules. For instance, any standard Java classes used to implement the web service typically are deployed under the *WEB-INF/classes* folder, or as a JAR under the *WEB-INF/lib* folder of your web application. Any EJBs used to implement the operations of the web service must be packaged into one or more EJB JARs. Refer to Chapter 12 for more information on packaging J2EE applications for WebLogic.

2. Manually create the *web-services.xml* deployment descriptor for the web service. In particular, you would need to supply information about the backend components that implement the web service, the custom datatypes used as parameters and return values, any SOAP message handlers that are used to intercept incoming or outgoing messages, and the actual operations themselves.

3. If the web service implementation uses one or more custom datatypes, you need to generate the serializer/deserializer classes and any support classes needed to handle the custom datatypes.

4. Package all of these components into a deployable EAR file.

In general, you would not assemble the web service manually because the process can be quite time-consuming and error-prone. Instead, you should rely on the various Ant tasks WebLogic provides to generate all the necessary components of the web service and then assemble them into a deployable EAR file. By automating many of the tasks required to assemble the web service, WebLogic removes some of the tedium and allows you to focus on the task of implementing the web service. In some cases, it can even eliminate the need to look inside the *web-services.xml* descriptor file. Let's now review how the various Ant tasks automate the job of assembling a web service:

servicegen

This Ant task takes an input EJB JAR (or a list of Java classes), generates all the necessary web service components, and packages them into a deployable EAR. servicegen actually subsumes the functionality of several other Ant tasks that focus on smaller aspects of assembling the web service. This Ant task introspects the Java code and looks for public methods that can be converted into web service operations, and for any custom datatypes that are used as parameters and return values. Based on the attributes passed to the Ant task and the information gleaned from the introspected code, it generates the *web-services. xml* descriptor file.

For any custom datatypes, it also generates the support classes for converting the datatypes between their XML and Java representations. Finally, it packages all the generated web services into a web application (WAR), and then packages the WAR and any EJB JARs into a deployable EAR file. Example 19-3 showed how to invoke the servicegen task to build a web service. Later, we'll examine other important attributes of the servicegen Ant task.

source2wsdd

Use the `source2wsdd` task to generate the *web-services.xml* descriptor file for a web service that wraps a standard Java class. The same process also occurs when the servicegen Ant task is invoked. This Ant task provides a quick and easy way to generate the deployment descriptor for a web service whose Java implementation class is prepared already. The following build script shows how to generate the *web-services.xml* descriptor from the Java source file *MyService.java*:

```
<project name="gen-web-svc" default="gen-wsdd">
    <target name="gen-wsdd">
        <source2wsdd
            javaSource="c:\source\MyService.java"
            typesInfo="c:\autotype\types.xml"
            ddFile="c:\ddfiles\web-services.xml"
            serviceURI="/Simple" />
    </target>
</project>
```

Here, *c:\autotype\types.xml* refers to a file that includes the XML Schema definitions for any custom datatypes used as parameters and return values, and maps these types to appropriate serialization classes. You often can generate this file by using the autotype Ant task.

autotype

If your web service defines operations whose parameters and/or return values use custom datatypes, you may use this Ant task to generate the Java representation of the type, the XML Schema and type mappings, and the serialization classes that convert the data between the XML and Java representations. Note that you can also invoke the servicegen Ant task so that the same support for custom datatypes is generated during the assembly of the web service.

The following build script shows one way of using the autotype task to generate the required support for handling custom datatypes:

```
<project name="gen-web-svc" default="gen-type-info">
    <target name="gen-type-info">
        <autotype schemaFile="mytypes.xsd"
            targetNamespace="http://oreilly.com/wlguide/auto"
            packageName="mypackage.name"
            destDir="c:\outtypes"/>
    </target>
</project>
```

Here *mytypes.xsd* holds the XML Schema definitions for any custom datatypes, and the value of the `packageName` attribute allows you to specify the package name for the generated serialization classes. The input for this Ant task can come from either a schema file representing the custom datatypes, a URL to a WSDL file containing a description of the datatypes, a Java class that represents the datatypes, or a Java class file that implements a web service. In the latter case, the Ant task will inspect the Java code for custom datatypes used in parameters or return values.

wsdl2service

Use this Ant task to generate a partial implementation of a web service from an existing WSDL file. This task generates the *web-services.xml* descriptor file and the Java source file for one of the web services it finds in the specified WSDL file. The output Java source provides a template upon which you can build the implementation for the web service. The following example shows how to use the wsdl2service task to generate the Java implementation from the specified WSDL file:

```
<project name="gen-web-svc" default="gen-from-wsdl">
    <target name="gen-from-wsdl">
        <wsdl2service
            wsdl="c:\wsdls\simple.wsdl"
            destDir="c:\simple\impl"
            typeMappingFile="c:\autotype\types.xml"
            packageName="com.oreilly.wlguide.webservices.simple" />
    </target>
</project>
```

Once again, this task does not generate any type information or any serialization classes for any custom datatypes used to implement the web service operations. Instead, you need to use the autotype task first, and use the generated type mappings as input for this task.

wspackage

This is a useful Ant task for packaging the various components of a web service into a deployable EAR. Typically, you will invoke this Ant task if you have chosen to manually assemble all the pieces of the web service. It assumes that you've already generated the *web-services.xml* descriptor, the Java classes and any EJB JARs that implement the web service, a client JAR that users can download, SOAP handler classes, and necessary support for handling custom datatypes.

The following script shows how to package all the components of a web service implemented by a standard Java class:

```
<project name="build-web-svc" default="pkg-web-svc">
    <target name="pkg-web-svc">
        <wspackage
            output="c:\output\myEar.ear"
            contextURI="CustomersComeHither"
            codecDir="c:\autotype"
            webAppClasses="com.oreilly.wlguide.webservices.simple.Simple.class"
            ddFile="c:\dd\web-services.xml" />
    </target>
</project>
```

Here the Ant task creates an EAR called *c:\output\myEar.ear* that packages the web service whose context URI is now *CustomersComeHither*. The webApp-Classes attribute is used to specify the list of Java classes that are placed under the *WEB-INF/classes* folder of the web application. In addition, we've specified the location of the deployment descriptor and the folder that holds all the required serialization classes for handling any custom datatypes. This task can also be used with the `overwrite` attribute set to `false` to add additional components to an existing EAR. This will attempt to merge the contents of the EAR with the *web-services.xml* file.

clientgen

This Ant task generates a client JAR that clients can use to invoke both WebLogic and non-WebLogic web services. The `clientgen` task generates the client JAR either from an EAR file that packages the web service, or from the WSDL document of an existing web service, not necessarily running on WebLogic Server. The client JAR includes the JAX-RPC client API and the necessary stubs needed to statically invoke the web service. It also includes serialization classes for any custom datatypes used by the web service and a client-side copy of the WSDL file.

Example 19-5 showed how to generate the client JAR from an existing EAR file that hosts one or more web services. The following script shows how to generate the client JAR from the WSDL file of an existing web service:

```
<project name="gen-web-svc" default="gen-web-svc-client">
    <target name="gen-web-svc-client">
        <clientgen wsdl="http://foobar.com/myapps/simple.wsdl"
            packageName="com.oreilly.wlguide.webservices.simple.client"
            clientJar="c:/myapps/simple_client.jar" />
    </target>
</project>
```

Here the task generates the client JAR *simple_client.jar* from the WSDL file located at *http://foobar.com/myapps/simple.wsdl*. The packageName attribute specifies the name of the package used for the generated client interface and stub files.

wsdlgen

This Ant task generates a WSDL file from the EAR and WAR files that make up a web service. The following example generates a WSDL file for the web service myWebService, which should be in the referenced WAR:

```
<wsdlgen ear="myEar.ear"
        warName="myWAR.war"
        serviceName="myWebService"
        wsdlFile="output.wsdl"
/>
```

This task is not available in WebLogic 7.0.

Remember, in order to invoke these Ant tasks, you need to first establish the appropriate shell environment by invoking the setEnv command-line script located under the root directory of your domain. You also can run the servicegen and clientgen tasks from the command line:

```
java weblogic.webservice.clientgen
java weblogic.webservice.servicegen
```

The documentation for these tools is available if you simply run these tasks without supplying any additional command-line options.

The Ant tasks supplied by WebLogic will go a long way toward easing the process of building your web services. However, many of these Ant tasks are limited in scope. For instance, the source2wsdd task can generate the *web-services.xml* descriptor file only for a web service that wraps a standard Java class. The wsdl2service task generates the skeleton code for a Java backend that implements only one of the web services described in the WSDL file. Neither of these Ant tasks provides support for web services that can wrap stateless session EJBs or JMS destinations. Moreover, the servicegen task creates a deployable EAR for a web service that simply wraps the supplied backend component. If you need to build rich web services in which individual operations are implemented by separate backend components, then you have no choice but to manually author the *web-services.xml* deployment descriptor and ensure it accurately describes your web services. The same holds true if you need to associate specific operations of the web service with a chain of SOAP message handlers. None of the Ant tasks that we've examined provides any support for SOAP interceptors.

Still, it is important to be aware of the capabilities of these Ant tasks, and to be able to use them as the situation demands. We cover many scenarios in which the Ant tasks prove to be quite effective and circumvent the need to even look at the layout of the *web-services.xml* descriptor file. Depending on your needs, you can rely on Ant tasks such as servicegen and clientgen to generate a deployable EAR and client-side JAR files. Alternatively, you could use some combination of other available Ant tasks: autotype, wspackage, wsdl2service, and source2wsdd. WebLogic also offers a visual approach to building web services in the form of WebLogic Workshop. The Workshop IDE abstracts away many of the underlying details and greatly simplifies web service construction.

We believe that a proper understanding of the innards of the *web-services.xml* descriptor file and a judicious application of these Ant tasks will go a long way toward the development of your web services. In the rest of this chapter, you'll learn more about how to use the *web-services.xml* descriptor file to configure the different aspects of your web services. For instance, we examine how the *web-services.xml* descriptor file lets you configure a particular backend component for a specific operation. This information is intended to further your understanding of the *web-services. xml* descriptor file, which is crucial when you need to configure real-world web services that wrap diverse backend components.

Web Service Design Considerations

You need to consider several architectural design choices when building a web service for WebLogic:

- You need to carefully architect the "signature" for each operation of the web service and decide whether the operation will be invoked in a synchronous request-reply fashion, or in a one-way asynchronous manner.

- You need to decide what type of backend components (if any) will be used to implement the operations of the web service.

- You need to determine whether your web service is designed to be process- or data-oriented. Based on this, you can decide whether the web service implementation is better suited to handling traditional RPC-style invocations or a single XML document that is exchanged between the client and the web service.

- If the SOAP request/response messages need additional processing before/after they are handled, you need to configure the chain of SOAP message handlers that will be associated with the web service operations.

- If the web service is designed to use custom datatypes, you need to determine the structure for these datatypes and how they can be converted between their Java and XML representations.

All these factors influence how you design the operations of a web service and choose a best-fit implementation.

RPC-Oriented Versus Document-Oriented Web Services

When creating a WebLogic web service, you can specify whether its operations are *RPC-oriented* or *document-oriented*. In the case of an RPC-oriented operation, the SOAP message encapsulates the parameters and return values using SOAP encoding. In the case of a document-oriented operation, the SOAP message encapsulates a single XML document using literal encoding. For this reason, methods that support RPC-oriented operations can declare any number of parameters, whereas methods that implement document-oriented operations must declare only *one* parameter (of any supported type, though typically an XML document). In addition, a document-oriented web service cannot declare out or in-out parameters. Thus, the choice between an RPC-oriented web service versus a document-oriented web service not only determines the structure of the SOAP message, but also impacts how its operations are implemented. WebLogic 8.1 introduces a variation of the standard document-oriented operations, namely *document-wrapped* operations. A document-wrapped operation can take any number of parameters. All of the parameters are wrapped into one complex datatype in the SOAP message.

By default, a WebLogic web service is RPC-oriented. In order to change the default behavior so that it's document-oriented, you need to adjust the style attribute of the web-service element in the *web-services.xml* descriptor file. The following example illustrates how you can declare a document-oriented WebLogic web service:

```
<!-- webservices.xml fragment -->
<web-service protocol="http" name="Simple" uri="/Simple"
```

```
        targetNamespace="http://www.oreilly.com/webservices/Simple"
        style="document">
<!-- ... -->
</web-service>
```

Set the style to documentwrapped for document-wrapped operations. You also can use
the servicegen task to generate document-oriented web services by adding a
style="document" attribute. The following example shows how to create a document-
oriented web service that wraps the specified Java class:

```
<servicegen destEar="myEar.ear" warName="myWar.war">
    <service  javaClassComponents="com.oreilly.wlguide.webservices.simple.Simple"
        targetNamespace="${namespace}" serviceName="Simple"
        serviceURI="/Simple" generateTypes="True" expandMethods="True"
        style="document"
    </service>
    <!-- ... -->
</servicegen>
```

Note that WebLogic does not allow you to mix both RPC-oriented and document-
oriented operations in the same web service. You can mark the web service as either
RPC-oriented or document-oriented only, in which case the setting applies to all
operations exposed by the web service. Thus, any method that implements an operation of a document-oriented web service must declare only one parameter of any
supported type. Of course, this restriction is relaxed for any methods that implement the operations of an RPC-oriented web service.

Synchronous Versus Asynchronous Operations

Web service operations can be either synchronous or asynchronous. The "synchronous request-response" behavior, which is the default, means that the client waits for
a SOAP response each time the operation is invoked. Web service operations usually
exhibit synchronous request-response behavior, which is analogous to traditional
RPC-style communication. The client always receives a SOAP response in synchronous communications, even if the method that implements the operation has a void
return type.

If an operation is marked as asynchronous, the client *never* receives a SOAP
response, even if an exception or a SOAP fault is raised. Because no response is sent
back to the client, asynchronous operations must not declare any out or in-out
parameters. They can use only "in" parameters. Besides this, any method that implements an asynchronous operation must explicitly return a void type. For example,
this is a valid implementation for an asynchronous web service operation:

```
public void async(String arg) {
    // no response is returned to the client, so it will not wait for the method to
    complete.
}
```

In order to configure an asynchronous operation, you need to adjust the invocation-style attribute of the operation element in the *web-services.xml* descriptor file. The default value for the invocation-style attribute is "request-response," which means the operation receives a SOAP request and sends back a SOAP response to the client. The following portion of the *web-services.xml* descriptor shows how to mark a web service operation as being asynchronous by setting this attribute to "one-way":

```
<operation invocation-style="one-way" method="async(java.lang.String)"
           component="jcComp0" name="async">
  <params>
    <param location="body" class-name="java.lang.String" style="in" name="string"
           xmlns:xsd="http://www.w3.org/2001/XMLSchema" type="xsd:string">
    </param>
  </params>
</operation>
```

Remember, the method that implements an asynchronous operation must use a void return type and can accept only "in" parameters.

Datatypes

WebLogic supports a rich mixture of built-in and custom datatypes that can be used to define the parameters and return values for web service operations. Built-in datatypes are those that are natively supported by WebLogic's framework, which means all datatypes defined by the JAX-RPC specification. Using built-in datatypes is fairly straightforward because WebLogic is able to automatically convert the data between its Java and XML representations.

WebLogic also supports web services whose operations rely on custom datatypes— any complex datatype that can be represented using an XML Schema.

Stateful Web Services

WebLogic's web services are inherently stateless because the only components that can live behind these web services are stateless. If a web service operation is implemented using a public method of a standard Java class, WebLogic uses a single instance of the class across all client invocations of the web service. Similarly, if the web service is supported by a stateless session EJB or a JMS destination, again no conversational state is maintained across client invocations.

Therefore, if you need to implement stateful web services, you must explicitly engineer the stateful behavior. One way is to require clients to pass a unique ID whenever they invoke a web service operation. The ID will uniquely identify the client that initiated the request. The backend code could then use the client's ID to persist any conversational state and later use the same ID to recover the client-specific state information from the persistent store.

Creating an HttpSession for a web service

WebLogic 8.1 provides a great feature for maintaining server-side session state for a web service, which avoids the need for explicitly passing some token to and fro during web service invocations. Simply use the weblogic.webservice.context. WebServiceSession class to access WebLogic's internal HTTP session infrastructure. Your web service implementation can obtain the session object from a weblogic. webservice.context.WebServiceContext object, and then use the setAttribute( ), getAttribute( ), and invalidate( ) methods as usual. Here is an example of a Java class backend for a web service that maintains session information:

```java
public class Simple {
  public int getSessionValue() {
    WebServiceSession session = null;
    session = WebServiceContext.currentContext().getSession();
    Integer count = (Integer) session.getAttribute("count");
    if (count == null)
      count = new Integer(0);
    session.setAttribute("count", new Integer(count.intValue() + 1));
    return count.intValue();
  }
}
```

Here, an operation backed by the getSessionValue( ) method increments a counter stored in the session each time the operation is invoked. All of the session-handling code is hidden in the web service implementation. The client doesn't need any special code to take advantage of the session state. It can simply invoke the web service operation as usual:

```java
Simple ws = new Simple_Impl(where);
SimplePort port = ws.getSimplePort();
System.out.println(port.getSessionValue());
System.out.println(port.getSessionValue());
System.out.println(port.getSessionValue());
//prints out 0,1,2...
```

Because the WebServiceSession object relies on an HTTP session to maintain the state, any client of the web service also must support HTTP cookies for this to work. You can also use it in a standalone client application, in which case the state is maintained on the client itself.

JMS Transport

The standard approach for invoking an operation on a web service is to use either the HTTP or HTTPS protocol. WebLogic 8.1 lets you use JMS as a transport too. The client need not create an HTTP connection to the server running the web service. Instead it can look up a JMS connection factory, interact with a destination for invoking an operation, and then receive any results through a temporary destination. All of this occurs under the hood though, and your client is mostly unchanged.

The JMS transport can be configured for any web service, regardless of whether it is implemented using a JMS, EJB, or plain Java class backend. It merely alters the transport that is used to invoke the operations on the web service. Because this facility is nonstandard, your clients will be able to use this transport mechanism only for web services running on WebLogic.

To use the JMS transport, you need to first set up a JMS connection factory and JMS destination on the WebLogic instance that hosts the web service. The JMS server hosting the destination also must support temporary destinations—so, you must ensure that you have set up a Temporary Template for the JMS server, as outlined in Chapter 8. Let's assume that a WebLogic instance hosts a connection factory myCF, and a JMS server with a destination called myQ.

Unfortunately, the servicegen Ant task doesn't let you set up a web service to use the JMS transport. You have to manually edit the *web-services.xml* descriptor file, and make the necessary changes. We suggest that you create the web service using supplied tools, and then modify the generated deployment descriptor. The only change needed to support JMS transport is to include the jmsUri attribute in the web-service element:

```
<web-service protocol="http" name="Simple" style="rpc" uri="/Simple"
             targetNamespace="http://www.oreilly.com/webservices/Simple"
             jmsUri="myCF/myQ">
<!-- -->
</web-service>
```

Here, the value of the jmsUri attribute matches the pattern connection-factory-name/ queue-name. You can now go ahead and repackage and deploy the web service to WebLogic. The WSDL of the deployed web service will in fact have *two* ports for the web service—a standard port for HTTP traffic, and an additional port for JMS traffic.

The client application JAR can be created in the usual way—the clientgen task will use the jmsUri attribute to automatically create an additional port. Usually you get the port for a service—say, Simple—by calling the getSimplePort( ) method on a service object. WebLogic will provide an additional method, getSimplePortJMS( ), which lets the client invoke a web service using the JMS transport. Here, the code invokes a web service, first using the standard HTTP transport and then using the JMS transport:

```
Simple ws = new Simple_Impl(where);
SimplePort portHTTP = ws.getSimplePort( );
String reply1 = portHTTP.makeUpper("hello World");
SimplePort portJMS = ws.getSimplePortJMS( );
String reply2 = portJMS.makeUpper("hello World");
```

The client application is now also a JMS client because it looks up a JMS connection factory and interacts with a JMS destination. So, you need to package the client with the appropriate libraries. In WebLogic 8.1, you need to include *wlclient.jar* and *wljmsclient.jar*, and in WebLogic 7.0 you must include the monolithic *weblogic.jar*.

Implementing the Backend Components

WebLogic permits three choices for a backend component: a simple Java class, a stateless session EJB, or a JMS destination. Remember, a web service is composed of a number of operations, and you can implement each operation using any one of these backend component types. Quite often, the operations of a web service are implemented using the remote methods of a stateless session EJB. In a sense, the web service simply wraps the corresponding EJB interface. Stateless session EJBs allow you to encapsulate well-defined business processes, and web services built around a stateless session EJB can provide SOAP clients with an elegant conduit to this business functionality.

Thus, stateless session EJBs are a good choice for implementing the operations of a web service, especially if it is process-oriented and needs to benefit from other J2EE services such as the support for distributed transactions, persistence, security, and concurrency. A Java class is a suitable backend for a process-oriented web service. Creating a Java class requires less effort than building a stateless session EJB. In general, you should consider using standard Java classes for implementing the operations of a web service if you don't need the support for additional EJB features such as persistence, security, transactions, and concurrency. However, Java classes used as backends for web service operations have certain limitations, which we examine in the next section.

Web service operations can also wrap JMS actions. For example, a client can invoke an operation that triggers the delivery of a message to a JMS destination. A JMS consumer—say, an MDB—then can process the message. Alternatively, the client can invoke an operation that pulls messages from a JMS queue. In this case, some JMS producer regularly feeds messages into the JMS queue. The client then can poll the web service for a response that wraps the received message. JMS backends are ideal because they allow you to decouple the web service from its actual implementation. Moreover, if the underlying application is built over the asynchronous messaging paradigm, web services allow you to transparently expose your existing JMS destinations to other SOAP clients. BEA, however, discourages the use of JMS-backed web services.

Java Class Backends

A Java class is quite possibly the simplest backend that you can create for a web service. As we have seen already, WebLogic's servicegen Ant task can easily manufacture a deployable EAR file that packages a web service from any Java class that exposes one or more public methods. In this case, each operation of the web service is bound to a public method of the Java class, so when a client invokes the web service operation, it actually is handled by the associated Java method. However, you do need to obey certain rules when creating a Java class that serves as a backend for a web service operation:

- The Java class must define a default, no-argument constructor. WebLogic uses the default constructor to create an instance of the class.

- WebLogic creates a single instance of the Java class that handles all requests to the web service. This means that whenever a client invokes an operation that is backed by a method of a Java class, WebLogic uses the same instance to service the SOAP request. For this reason, you must write thread-safe Java code.

- Any method that is exposed as a web service operation must be declared `public`.

Most importantly, because the backend Java class runs within WebLogic's J2EE framework, the Java class must never start any threads. Once you create the Java classes, you need to modify the *web-services.xml* descriptor file and list all the Java components:

```
<components>
  <java-class name="compA" class-name="com.oreilly.wlguide.ws.ClassA" />
  <java-class name="compB" class-name="com.oreilly.wlguide.ws.ClassB" />
  <!-- other backend Java classes -->
</components>
```

The names that you specify for these Java components are important. They are used later when you bind an operation to a method in the component. The following portion from the *web-services.xml* descriptor file shows how to associate web service operations with Java methods:

```
<operations>
  <operation method="methodX(java.lang.String)" component="compA" name="opX" />
  <operation method="methodY(java.lang.Integer)" component="compA" name="opY" />
  <!-- More operations -->
  <operation method="methodZ(java.lang.Double)" component="compB" name="opZ" />
</operations>
```

Notice how we've used multiple Java classes to implement the different operations of the same web service. One important use of the operation element is that it lets you describe the parameters and return values of a web service operation. The following fragment from the *web-services.xml* descriptor file describes the signature of a web service operation that is implemented via the method String methodX(java.lang. String):

```
<operation method="methodX(java.lang.String)" component="compA" name="opX">
  <params>
    <param name="string" style="in" type="xsd:string" location="body"
        class-name="java.lang.String" xmlns:xsd="http://www.w3.org/2001/XMLSchema"/>
    <return-param name="result" type="xsd:string" location="Header"/>
  </params>
</operation>
```

Use the params element to explicitly specify the list of parameters and return values for the operation. If you omit the params element, WebLogic introspects the target method to automatically determine how the web service operation ought to be invoked. Each parameter is specified using the param element, while the return value is specified using the return-param element. A single web service operation may declare, at most, one return value. For each parameter (or return value), you can specify the name, the associated datatype, and whether the parameter is located in the "header" or the "body" of the SOAP message. By default, parameters and return values are located in the body of the SOAP message. For each parameter, you can use the style attribute to specify the direction of flow: in, out, or in-out. The following XML fragment shows how to specify an input-output parameter of integer type located in the body of the SOAP message:

```
<param name="myParam" style="in-out" type="xsd:int" location="body" />
```

Later in this chapter, we examine how the operation element lets you associate a chain of SOAP handlers with a web service operation.

Note that you don't need to explicitly declare each operation of the web service. If the web service is implemented by a stateless session EJB or a standard Java class, WebLogic can automatically introspect the backend component and construct a list of operations using all of the public methods in the backend component. The following portion of the *web-services.xml* descriptor file shows how you can expose all the public methods of ClassA as web service operations:

```
<components>
    <java-class name="compA" class-name="com.oreilly.wlguide.ws.ClassA" />
    <java-class name="compB" class-name="com.oreilly.wlguide.ws.ClassB" />
    <!-- other web service backends -->
</components>

<!-- ... -->

<operations>
    <operation component="compA" method="*"/>
    <operation method="methodZ(java.lang.Double)" component="compB" name="opZ" />
    <!-- more operations -->
</operations>
```

Stateless Session EJB Backends

Stateless session EJBs provide another alternative for implementing web services. They allow you to build web services over existing business operations encapsulated within a J2EE application. Furthermore, stateless session EJBs can benefit from all the standard J2EE services such as support for object pooling, persistence, transactions, security, and concurrency. It also is neater from an architectural viewpoint because the web service is designed based on an EJB interface rather than being based on the EJB's implementation class.

Assume that you've generated an EJB JAR that packages one or more stateless session EJBs, and the EJB JAR has been assembled into a J2EE enterprise application. This means that all stateless session EJBs are available to any deployed web applications as well. Once again, you need to first modify the *web-services.xml* descriptor file for a web application and make these stateless session EJBs available to your web services. The following portion from the *web-services.xml* descriptor shows how to use the stateless-ejb element to specify a stateless session EJB that will be used to implement the operations of the web service:

```
<components>
    <stateless-ejb name="FooEJB">
      <ejb-link path="myEJBServices.jar#FooEJB" />
    </stateless-ejb>
    <stateless-ejb name="FooBarEJB">
      <ejb-link path="myEJBServices.jar#FooBarEJB" />
    </stateless-ejb>
    <!-- other web service backend components -->
</components>
```

Here we used the ejb-link element to refer to the stateless session EJBs FooEJB and FooBarEJB, both bundled within the *myEJBServices.jar* EJB JAR file. You also could use the jndi-name element to refer to a particular EJB through its JNDI name:

```
<components>
    <stateless-ejb name="FooEJB">
      <jndi-name path="myEJBs.FooEJB" />
    </stateless-ejb>
    <stateless-ejb name="FooBarEJB">
      <jndi-name path="myEJBs.FooBarEJB"/>
    </stateless-ejb>
    <!-- other web service backend components -->
</components>
```

In this case, the EJB deployment descriptor *weblogic-ejb-jar.xml* in *myEJBServices.jar* must assign the JNDI names for all EJBs packaged within the EJB JAR:

```
<weblogic-ejb-jar>
    <weblogic-enterprise-bean>
      <ejb-name>FooEJB</ejb-name>
      <jndi-name>myEJBs.FooEJB</jndi-name>
    </weblogic-enterprise-bean>
    <weblogic-enterprise-bean>
      <ejb-name>FooBarEJB</ejb-name>
      <jndi-name>myEJBs.FooBarEJB</jndi-name>
    </weblogic-enterprise-bean>
    <!-- ... -->
</weblogic-ejb-jar>
```

Refer to Chapter 10 for more information on how to implement stateless session EJBs. Now that you've declared the stateless session EJBs, you can map the web service operations to the desired EJB methods:

```
<operations>
    <operation name="opX" method="methodX(java.lang.String)" component="FooEJB" />
    <operation name="opY" method="methodY(java.lang.Integer)" component="FooEJB" />
    <!-- More operations -->
    <operation name="opZ" method="methodZ(java.lang.Double)" component="FooBarEJB" />
</operations>
```

Once again, if the web service operation is asynchronous, the corresponding EJB method must be declared to return void. Similarly, if the EJB method uses custom data types for the parameters and return values, you need to generate the serialization classes that convert these datatypes between their XML and Java representations.

You also can use the servicegen Ant task to create a web service that blindly exposes all EJB methods of a stateless session EJB. The following build script shows how to invoke the servicegen task to generate this web service:

```
<project name="build-web-svc" default="gen-web-service" basedir=".">
    <property name="namespace" value="http://www.oreilly.com/webservices/Foo" />
    <property name="build" value="/classes" />
    <target name="gen-web-service">
        <servicegen destEar="myEar.ear" warName="myWar.war">
            <service ejbJar="build_dir/myEJBServices.jar"
                targetNamespace="${namespace}" serviceName="FooService"
                serviceURI="/FooService" generateTypes="True" expandMethods="True" />
        </servicegen>
    </target>
</project>
```

The expandMethods="True" attribute indicates whether servicegen should create a separate operation element for each EJB method in the *web-services.xml* descriptor file, or simply refer to all EJB methods using the generic <operation component="FooEJB" method="*"/>. The attribute generateTypes="True" instructs servicegen to also generate the serialization classes, the schema definitions, and the type mappings for any custom datatypes used as parameters or return values of the EJB's methods.

JMS Backends

Two kinds of JMS actions can be triggered when a client invokes a web service operation: the operation may *send* data to a JMS destination, or it may *receive* data from a JMS queue. If the web service defines an operation that sends data to a JMS destination, you also need some JMS consumer to process any messages delivered to the JMS destination. So, when a web service receives a SOAP request from a client, the parameters encapsulated in the request are sent to the target JMS queue or topic. Any JMS consumers listening on the JMS destination will receive the message, extract the incoming parameters from the message body, and process it accordingly. If the web service defines an operation that receives data from a JMS queue, you also need some JMS producer to feed messages to the queue. A web service client must then poll the web service at regular intervals for a SOAP response in order to receive the messages placed on the queue.

Operations that receive data from a JMS *topic* are a deprecated feature of WebLogic 7.0. We don't recommend that you implement web services that receive data from a JMS topic because this feature has been removed from WebLogic 8.1.

In the case of an operation supported by a JMS backend, the only refinement to the event sequence illustrated in Figure 19-1 is how the operation is handled. When the client invokes a JMS-implemented operation, WebLogic converts the incoming XML data to its Java representation using the appropriate serializer classes. It then wraps the resulting Java object within a `javax.jms.ObjectMessage` instance and places this object on the JMS destination. Thus, any JMS listener bound to the JMS destination needs to process the `ObjectMessage` instances that are delivered to the JMS topic or queue. A similar process occurs in reverse when a client invokes a web service operation that receives data from a JMS queue.

Note that although WebLogic's JMS backends provide an easy way to interface with a JMS queue, the resulting code is proprietary and won't be portable. Writing your own interface to a JMS queue using a stateless session bean or Java class isn't that much more difficult, and the result will be more portable and flexible.

Designing a JMS backend

If the operation sends data to a JMS destination, you need to decide whether you want to use a JMS topic or a queue. A JMS queue provides support for point-to-point messaging, whereby the message is delivered to exactly one JMS consumer. A JMS topic provides support for publish/subscribe messaging, whereby the message is delivered to a number of recipients. Once you've decided on the type of JMS destination, you need to implement the listener that retrieves messages from the JMS destination and processes them. For instance, you could implement an MDB that processes all the messages delivered to the JMS destination. The MDB could even delegate some of the handling to other EJBs. The operation completes its handling once the backend listener processes the message delivered to the JMS destination.

Furthermore, you need to decide whether the operation sends data to a JMS destination or receives data from a JMS queue. The same operation cannot do both simultaneously. If you want the client to be able to both send and receive data, you need to define two web service operations:

- A *send* operation that is associated with a JMS destination to which a JMS listener is attached (say, an MDB). Chapter 8 examines the various ways to implement a listener for a JMS destination.

- A *receive* operation that is associated with a JMS queue. After the JMS listener retrieves and processes the incoming message, it delivers a response message to this JMS queue.

So, for instance, you could implement an MDB that listens to a JMS topic (associated with the *send* operation) for an incoming message, process it, and then place a response on the JMS queue (associated with the *receive* operation). Thus, in order to simulate typical request-response behavior, you need to set up two JMS destinations, one for receiving request messages from the client and another JMS queue for delivering response messages for the client. And, in order to support any web service operation that is implemented by a JMS backend, you need to complete the following tasks:

1. Create the JMS consumers (or producers) that retrieve (or deliver) messages to the JMS destination.

2. Configure the JMS destinations that the web service will use to receive data from a client or send back data to the client.

3. Configure the JMS connection factory that is used by the web service to connect to WebLogic's JMS server.

Chapter 8 provides more information on how to use the Administration Console to set up various JMS resources for WebLogic.

Building a web service over a JMS backend

Once again, the servicegen Ant task lets you automatically create a deployable EAR that packages a web service that interacts with a JMS destination. It also can be used to generate the necessary support for a client JAR that lets you statically invoke the web service. The following portion of a build script shows how to assemble a web service that sends XML data to a JMS queue:

```
<servicegen destEar="myJMS.ear" warName="myJMSService.war" contextURI="WebServices">
    <service
        JMSAction="send"
        JMSDestination="InQueue"
        JMSDestinationType="queue"
        JMSConnectionFactory="oreilly.myConnectionFactory"
        JMSOperationName="makeUpper"
        targetNamespace="${namespace}"
        serviceName="SimpleJMS"
        serviceURI="/SimpleJMS"
        expandMethods="True">
    </service>
    <client
        clientJarName="myJMSClient.jar"
        packageName="com.oreilly.wlguide.webservices.simple.SimpleClient" />
</servicegen>
```

Here, we've instructed the servicegen task to create a web service that exposes a single operation, makeUpper, that sends data to a JMS queue. Because the web service wraps a JMS backend, you need to supply values for the following JMS-specific attributes of the service element:

JMSAction
> This attribute indicates whether the web service sends data to the JMS destination or receives data from the JMS destination.

JMSDestination
> This attribute specifies the JNDI name of the JMS destination that sits behind the web service.

JMSDestinationType

This attribute indicates whether the JMS destination is a queue or a topic.

JMSConnectionFactory

This attribute specifies the JNDI name of the connection factory used to connect to the JMS destination.

JMSOperationName

This attribute specifies the name of the web service operation in the generated WSDL file. If no value is specified, the name of the operation defaults to the value of the JMSAction attribute.

Another attribute that we didn't use in the preceding example is the JMSMessageType attribute, which specifies the fully qualified name of the Java class that defines the type for the single parameter to the send (or receive) operation. By default, the web service sends or receives JMS messages that wrap a java.lang.String parameter. If you have specified a nonbuilt-in data type for the web service, then you also should include the generateTypes="True" attribute when you invoke the servicegen task.

The Ant task must be run from within a staging directory that contains a JAR file that bundles together the compiled Java classes for any JMS producers and consumers. This JAR file should be placed directly under this staging directory, along with other EJB JARs that package any MDBs. The generated EAR file bundles together all of these JAR files, and a WAR file that also includes the appropriate *web-services.xml* descriptor file. Remember, the client subelement is optional and should be used only when you also need to generate the client JAR during the assembly of the web service. Of course, you also can use the clientgen task to generate the client JAR file.

 Any input parameters passed to a web service operation, or any return values generated by the operation implemented through a JMS backend, must implement the java.io.Serializable interface.

The following portion from an Ant script shows how you can generate a web service that receives data from a JMS queue:

```
<servicegen destEar="myJMSRead.ear" warName="myJMSService.war"
                                    contextURI="WebServices">
    <service
        JMSAction="receive"
        JMSDestination="OutQueue"
        JMSDestinationType="queue"
        JMSConnectionFactory="oreilly.myConnectionFactory"
        JMSOperationName="getMakeUpperResult"
        targetNamespace="${namespace}"
        serviceName="SimpleJMSResult"
        serviceURI="/SimpleJMSResult"
        expandMethods="True">
    </service>
</servicegen>
```

Given these two web services, you now can simulate a call to the makeUpper( ) method using the two JMS queues. Example 19-7 lists the code for an MDB that retrieves JMS messages from InQueue, processes the incoming parameter, and then sends back the result in a JMS message to OutQueue.

Example 19-7. Using an MDB to implement the makeUpper() operation

```
// Assume the MDB is listening for messages delivered to the JMS queue "InQueue"
// and uses the JMS connection factory bound to oreilly.myConnectionFactory
public void onMessage(Message message) {
   ObjectMessage o = (ObjectMessage) message;
   if (o != null) {
     String inparam = (String) o.getObject( );
     String result = inparam.toUpperCase( );

     //send message response to the "OutQueue"
     QueueConnectionFactory factory =
        (QueueConnectionFactory) ctx.lookup("oreilly.myConnectionFactory");
     Queue queue = (Queue) ctx.lookup("OutQueue");
     QueueConnection qconn = factory.getQueueConnection( );
     QueueSession qs = wconn.createQueueSession(false, Session.AUTO_ACKNOWLEDGE);
     QueueSender qsender = qs.createSender(queue);
     Message response = qsession.createObjectMessage(new String(result));
     qconn.start( );
     qsender.send(response);
     qsender.close( );
     qs.close( );
     qconn.close( );
   }
}
```

Once you've deployed the web services, you can use the generated client JAR to invoke the web services:

```
import com.oreilly.wlguide.webservices.simple.SimpleClient.SimpleJMS;
import com.oreilly.wlguide.webservices.simple.SimpleClient.SimpleJMSPort;
import com.oreilly.wlguide.webservices.simple.SimpleClient.SimpleJMS_Impl;

//Send JMS message to "InQueue"
SimpleJMS wsj = new SimpleJMS_Impl(args[0]);
SimpleJMSPort p = wsj.getSimpleJMSPort( );
p.makeUpper("Hello World");

SimpleJMSResult wsj2 = new SimpleJMSResult_Impl(args[0]);
SimpleJMSResultPort p2 = wsj2.getSimpleJMSResultPort( );

//Keep polling "OutQueue" for a response
while (!quit) {
   String result = (String) p2.getMakeUpperResult( );
   if (result != null) {
     System.out.println("TextMessage:" + result);
     if (result.equals("")) {
        quit = true;
```

```
            System.out.println("Done!");
        }
        continue;
    }
    try { Thread.sleep(1000); } catch (Exception ignore) {}
}
```

Remember, web services implemented by a JMS backend either accept a single parameter or return a single value. If the web service needs to support a custom datatype, then you should use the `JMSMessageType="com.foo.bar.myType"` attribute of the service element when invoking the servicegen Ant task. In this case, you must ensure that the Java type is available to the classpath before invoking the Ant task.

Configuring the web-services.xml descriptor

Let's examine the changes you need to make to the *web-services.xml* descriptor file in order to describe a web service implemented by a JMS backend. Once again, you need to use the components element to describe the JMS destinations that live behind the web service:

```
<components>
    <jms-send-destination name="JMSSend"
            connection-factory="oreilly.myConnectionFactory">
      <jndi-name path="InQueue"/>
    </jms-send-destination>
    <jms-receive-queue name="JMSReceive"
            connection-factory="oreilly.myConnectionFactory ">
      <jndi-name path="OutQueue" />
    </jms-receive-queue>
    <!-- other web service backends -->
</components>
```

Here, the `jms-send-destination` element defines the JMS destination (InQueue) to which a *send* operation can deliver its messages, whereas the `jms-receive-queue` element defines the JMS queue (OutQueue) from which a *receive* operation can retrieve the response messages. In both cases, you need to specify the fully qualified JNDI names of the JMS destination, and the JMS connection factory used by the web service to connect to the destination. Once you've set up the JMS backends in the *web-services.xml* descriptor file, you can define the web service operations in terms of these backend components:

```
<operations>
    <!-- "send" operation that delivers to InQueue -->
    <operation component="JMSSend" name="makeUpper" invocation-style="one-way">
        <params>
            <param location="body" class-name="java.lang.String" style="in" name="arg"
xmlns:p1="http://www.oreilly.com/webservices/Simple" type="p1:makeUpper" />
        </params>
    </operation>
    <!-- "receive" operation that retrieves from OutQueue -->
```

```
<operation component="JMSReceive" name="getMakeUpperResult"
                invocation-style="request-response">
    <params>
      <return-param location="body" class-name="java.lang.String" name="result"
                                          type="xsd:string" />
    </params>
  </operation>
  <!-- other web service operations -->
</operation>
```

Notice how the *send* operation declares a single inbound parameter, while the *receive* operation defines a single return value. This is an essential requirement of JMS-implemented web service operations—the operation must define either a single inbound parameter or return value. The *send* operation is marked as asynchronous because the client doesn't expect a response when it invokes the *send* operation. On the other hand, the *receive* operation must be invoked in the typical request-response fashion.

Raising a SOAPFaultException

Web services can propagate exceptions back to the client. Any stateless session EJB or Java class used to implement a web service operation should throw a `javax.xml.rpc.soap.SOAPFaultException` exception to indicate an error during processing. WebLogic then serializes the exception to the appropriate XML structure and generates a SOAP response that wraps this SOAP fault before sending the message back to the client. Remember, asynchronous operations cannot propagate SOAP faults back to the client because no response is ever returned to the client. If the backend component throws any other type of Java exception, then WebLogic still tries its best to map the exception to a SOAP fault. However, in order to ensure that the client receives accurate information on any exceptions raised by the web service, the backend should explicitly throw a `SOAPFaultException`.

Datatypes

WebLogic supports a number of different Java types that can be used as parameter and return values for your web service operations. If you rely on these types, WebLogic automatically converts between their XML and Java representations. If a web service relies on complex types—for instance, an operation accepts an input parameter representing an instance of a custom Java class—you need a set of serialization classes that can convert between their XML and Java representations. There are two ways to generate this set of serialization classes:

Auto-generation of serialization classes
    Given a class definition that adheres to certain reasonable constraints, WebLogic's Ant tasks let you automatically generate the required serialization classes and XML Schemas that represent the class.

Manual creation of serialization classes

If the class definition doesn't comply with these constraints, you must manually implement the serialization logic and specify the XML Schemas that represent the datatypes.

In this section, we look at how to work with the built-in types, to automatically create the required serialization classes and XML Schemas for any custom types, and to manually provide this support if needed.

Built-in Types

The built-in datatypes are those supported by the XML Schema specification (see the XML Schema datatype specification at *http://www.w3.org/2001/XMLSchema*). This mandates that all the built-in datatypes have the namespace name *http://www.w3.org/2001/XMLSchema*. The Java SOAP type will have a namespace name of *http://schemas.xmlsoap.org/soap/encoding/*. Figure 19-4 depicts the hierarchy of datatypes supported by the XML Schema standard. Let's look at how these built-in XML Schema datatypes map to the equivalent Java types:

- The primitive Java types boolean, byte, short, int, long, float, and double (and their wrapper Java classes) map to the XML Schema datatypes with the same name.

- anyURI, NOTATION, and all the subtypes of string map to the Java type java.lang.String. All array types NMTOKENS, IDREFS, and ENTITIES map to the Java String[] type. The primitive Java type char (and its wrapper class) maps to the XML datatype string with a facet of length=1.

- All date/time XML Schema types map to java.util.Calendar. In the case of the types gYearMonth, gYear, gMonthDay, gDay, and gMonth, only the relevant portion of java.util.Calendar is used. For example, the gYear type maps to the "year" attribute of the equivalent Calendar object. Conversely, the Java types java.util.Calendar and java.util.Date both map to the XML Schema type datetime.

- hexBinary and base64Binary map to the Java byte[] type.

- The XML Schema types integer and decimal map to the Java types java.map.BigInteger and java.math.BigDecimal, respectively. The integer subtypes also map to java.math.BigInteger.

- The unsigned XML Schema types map to their higher Java equivalents. For instance, unsignedLong maps to java.util.BigInteger, unsignedInt maps to the Java type long, and so on.

- Finally, QName maps to the Java class javax.xml.namespace.QName, and duration maps to weblogic.xml.schema.binding.util.Duration.

Refer to *http://www.w3.org/TR/xmlschema-2/* for more information on XML Schema datatypes.

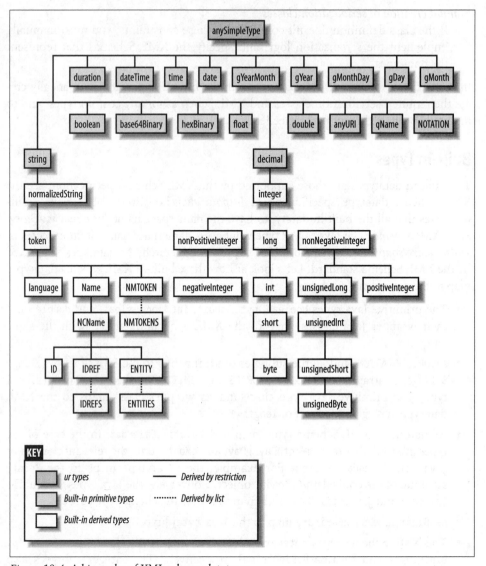

Figure 19-4. A hierarchy of XML schema datatypes

Custom Types

If a web service defines operations that uses custom datatypes or those that are not provided for by the XML Schema specification, you need the following support files for each such datatype:

- A Java class that represents the datatype.
- A serialization class that converts between the Java and XML representation of the data.

- Holder classes, if you intend to use the custom type as an out or in-out parameter.

- An XML Schema representation of the type, which is later included in the *web-services.xml* deployment descriptor.

- A datatype mapping, which maps the XML Schema to the actual serialization class. This mapping must be placed in the *web-services.xml* descriptor file.

You often will begin with a Java class that represents a custom datatype. For instance, you could wrap a web service around an existing backend component whose methods use custom Java classes as their parameters or return values. Conversely, if you need to interact with already published web services, the XML Schema representation of the datatype serves as the starting point for generating the other support files. In either case, WebLogic provides tools that can easily create the necessary files.

Generating Support Files for a Custom Java Class

If a web service operation defines parameters or return values that use custom datatypes, WebLogic can generate the required support files automatically from a given Java class if the following conditions are met:

- Your class must define a default, no-argument constructor.

- Your class must define a get*XXX*( ) method and a set*XXX*( ) method for each member variable that needs to be serialized.

- The type of any member variable that needs to be serialized must be either a built-in datatype, a collection of a supported datatype as described in Table 19-1, or a datatype for which you already have generated the serialization classes and XML Schema definitions.

If a custom type adheres to these requirements, WebLogic's servicegen and autotype Ant tasks let you generate the required support classes and schema. Table 19-1 lists the custom XML Schema types that WebLogic supports by default.

Table 19-1. List of other custom types supported by WebLogic, and their equivalent XML Schema types

Java type	Equivalent XML schema type
An array of any supported datatype	SOAP array
A JavaBean whose properties are declared to be of a supported datatype	<xsd:sequence>
java.util.List	SOAP array
java.util.ArrayList	SOAP array
java.util.LinkedList	SOAP array
java.util.Vector	SOAP array

Table 19-1. List of other custom types supported by WebLogic, and their equivalent XML Schema types (continued)

Java type	Equivalent XML schema type
java.util.Stack	SOAP array
java.util.Collection	SOAP array
java.util.Set	SOAP array
java.util.HashSet	SOAP array
java.util.SortedSet	SOAP array
java.util.TreeSet	SOAP array
java.lang.Object	<xsd:anyType>
JAX-RPC-style enumeration class	<xsd:simpleType> with enumeration facets

Thus, WebLogic supports an array or collection of any supported datatype. It also supports java.lang.Object, so long as the type of the runtime object matches one of the built-in datatypes, or a custom type for which the required support files have been generated. The Java class in Example 19-8 satisfies these constraints:

Example 19-8. A suitable candidate for automatic generation

```
public class MyType implements java.io.Serializable {
  String name;
  ArrayList myPets; // ArrayList of type String
  public void setName(String name) { this.name = name; }
  public String getName() { return name; }
  public void setPets(ArrayList myPets) { this.myPets = myPets; }
  public ArrayList getPets() { return myPets; }
}
```

In order to generate the necessary support files, you should use the autotype Ant task. The following portion from an Ant script shows how to invoke the task:

```
<target name="build-customtype" description="Auto Generate Type">
  <autotype
    javatypes="com.oreilly.wlguide.webservices.simple.MyType"
    targetNamespace="http://oreilly.com/wlguide/auto"
    packageName="package.name"
    destDir="outtype" />
</target>
```

This Ant task requires you to specify the name of the Java class that represents the custom type, the target namespace to be associated with the custom type, the package name to be used by the generated Java classes, and the destination directory in which the output files should be placed. There are other attributes you can specify when invoking the autotype task, which we cover later in this chapter. The example Ant task generates the following files in the output directory:

types.xml

> This file contains the XML Schema definition for the Java class and the type mappings. Other Ant tasks, such as servicegen, can take this file as a parameter and use it to include support for the custom datatypes.

mypackage/name/MyTypeCodec.java

> This file includes the Java source for the serializer/deserializer that can be used to convert between XML and Java representations of the custom type.

com.oreilly.wlguide.webservices.simple.holders.MyTypeHolder.java

> This file includes the Java source for the type holder classes, and is needed if the custom datatype is used to define out and in-out parameters of a web service operation.

In order to use these generated files, you must execute the following tasks:

1. Compile the Java source files and package them along with other compiled classes used by your web services.

2. Splice the generated *types.xml* file into the *web-services.xml* file. This means that the types element in the *web-services.xml* descriptor should be changed to include the XML Schema generated in the *types.xml* file.

3. Modify the type-mapping element in the *web-services.xml* descriptor to include the type mappings generated in the *types.xml* file.

Using the servicegen Ant task

The servicegen task can also perform all of these responsibilities when generating a deployable EAR from a backend component. You can instruct the servicegen task to generate the necessary support files using the generateTypes="True" attribute. Suppose you extend the backend Java class illustrated earlier in Example 19-1 to include a method that accepts a parameter of type MyType. For example, suppose you modify the Simple class to include the following Java method:

```
public String foo(MyType mytype) {
    return mytype.getName( );
}
```

Then you need to change the servicegen task to generate the necessary support files for the custom type. In fact, the servicegen task will perform the same tasks as the autotype task, and also insert the necessary XML to the *web-services.xml* descriptor file and include the generated Java classes in the output EAR file. So, you need to invoke the following Ant target to generate a deployable EAR:

```
<target name="create">
  <servicegen destEar="myEar.ear" warName="myWar.war">
    <service
      javaClassComponents="com.oreilly.wlguide.webservices.simple.Simple"
      targetNamespace="${namespace}" serviceName="Simple" serviceURI="/Simple"
      generateTypes="True" expandMethods="True">
    </service>
```

```
        <classpath>
          <pathelement path="${build}"/>
        </classpath>
      </servicegen>
    </target>
```

The servicegen task used with this attribute automatically detects any nonbuilt-in datatypes that are used as parameters or return values and generates the appropriate XML Schema definitions and Java classes that handle the serialization of these datatypes.

You also can test operations that use custom types from the automatically generated home page. However, for custom-type parameters, WebLogic provides an input area where you can specify your own XML for creating an instance of the data type. In fact, WebLogic provides a sensible template for modeling an instance of the custom type. In the case of the earlier MyType, the template will resemble this XML fragment:

```
<myType  xmlns:xsd="http://www.w3.org/2001/XMLSchema"
  xmlns:ns100="java:com.oreilly.wlguide.webservices.simple"
  xmlns:soapenc="http://schemas.xmlsoap.org/soap/encoding/"
  xmlns:xsi="http://www.w3.org/2001/XMLSchema-instance"
  xsi:type="ns100:MyType">
 <pets soapenc:arrayType="xsd:anyType[0]">
    <!-- define the elements of the "pets" array here -->
 </pets>
 <name xsi:type="xsd:string">sample string</name>
</myType>
```

Autotyping

The autotype task is quite versatile because it can generate the required support classes from three sources:

- It can examine a Java class that represents the custom datatype and generate the required serialization classes, holder classes, XML Schema, and type mappings, provided the class adheres to certain conditions. We already saw an example of this in which the javatypes attribute of the Ant task lets you specify the Java class that represents the custom type.

- It can generate the necessary support classes from an XML Schema that defines the custom type. Use the schemaFile attribute to supply the name of the schema file in this case.

- It also can examine a WSDL file and generate the support classes from the relevant portions of the WSDL. In this case, you must use the wsdl attribute to supply the pathname or the URI of the WSDL file:

```
<!-- portion of Ant build script -->
<target name="build-customtype-s" description="auto build type">
  <autotype wsdl="mywsdl.xml"
            targetNamespace="http://oreilly.com/wlguide/auto"
            packageName="mypackage.name"
```

```
                   destDir="outtypew"/>
        </target>
        <!-- ... -->
```

The preceding Ant target generates the same output: the *types.xml* file, the Java class that represents any custom datatypes, and the serialization classes. Let's now examine how the autotype task can generate the required support classes from an XML Schema.

Using an XML Schema

Consider the XML Schema representation for a custom type, as shown in Example 19-9.

Example 19-9. Schema representation of a datatype

```
<xsd:schema xmlns:xsd="http://www.w3.org/2001/XMLSchema"
            attributeFormDefault="qualified"
            elementFormDefault="qualified"
            targetNamespace="http://oreilly.com/wlguide/auto">
  <xsd:complexType name="SimpleSchemaBean">
    <xsd:sequence>
      <xsd:element name="name"
                   type="xsd:string"
                   nillable="true" minOccurs="1" maxOccurs="1">
      </xsd:element>
      <xsd:element name="age"
                   type="xsd:positiveInteger"
                   nillable="true" minOccurs="1" maxOccurs="1">
      <xsd:simpleType>
        <xsd:restriction xsd:base="xsd:positiveInteger">
          <xsd:maxInclusive value="144"/>
        </xsd:restriction>
      </xsd:simpleType>
      </xsd:element>
    </xsd:sequence>
  </xsd:complexType>
</xsd:schema>
```

The schema defines two properties for a custom type: a string-valued property name, and an age property that accepts any integer value in the range 1-144. Thus, WebLogic can also handle restrictions imposed on property types, as we have done in this example. If the *mytypeschema.xsd* file holds this XML Schema definition, you can use the autotype task to generate the required support classes using this file:

```
    <!-- portion of Ant build script -->
    <target name="buildCustomTypeFromSchema" description="Create custom type">
        <autotype schemaFile="mytypeschema.xsd"
                  keepGenerated="True"
                  targetNamespace="http://oreilly.com/wlguide/auto"
                  packageName="com.oreilly.wlguide.webservices.customtype"
                  destDir="outtypes"/>
    </target>
    <!-- ... -->
```

Here the schemaFile attribute refers to a file that holds a valid schema definition for a custom type. In this case, the Ant task will generate the appropriate serializer and deserializer classes, as well as the JavaBean class that represents this type and the *types.xml* mapping file. The JavaBean class for the XML Schema defined in Example 19-9 will look something like this:

```
public class SimpleSchemaBean implements java.io.Serializable {
  public SimpleSchemaBean( ) {}
  public SimpleSchemaBean(java.lang.String p_name,  java.math.BigInteger p_age) {
     this.name = p_name;
     this.age = p_age;  }
  // ...
}
```

Note how the age property of the JavaBean uses the java.math.BigInteger type. This is in accordance with the mapping rules for XML Schema types described earlier. The generated serializer and deserializer classes will also include checks to ensure that the XML Schema restrictions are adhered to.

This mechanism for generating the required support classes is quite robust. Let's examine the rules that determine the eventual structure of the JavaBean for the XML Schema:

- A JavaBean is created for each <xsd:complexType> element found in the XML Schema. The <xsd:complexType> element may include both simple and complex types, or just simple content. Abstract datatypes are mapped to an abstract Java class.
- Any <xsd:attribute> element within an <xsd:complexType> element is mapped to a property of the JavaBean. Any <xsd:attribute> element that relies on a <xsd:simpleType> that is derived by restriction from an existing simple type is mapped to a property whose type corresponds to the equivalent Java datatype. However, the serialization and deserialization routines are augmented to handle any restrictions placed on the existing simple types.

  If one or more facets are associated with an <xsd:restriction> element, you may use only the following base primitive types: string, decimal, float, and double. However, the pattern facets are not enforced by the associated serializer and deserializer classes.
- A complex type derived from a simple type is mapped to a JavaBean property called simpleContent of type String. A complex type derived from another by extension is mapped through Java inheritance.
- The <xsd:anyType> element is mapped to the java.lang.Object type.

Table 19-2 lists how some of the other XML Schema types are mapped to their equivalent Java types.

Table 19-2. Mapping XML Schema types to their equivalent Java datatypes

XML schema datatype	Equivalent Java datatype
`<xsd:anyType>`	`java.lang.Object`
`<xsd:nil>` or `<xsd:nillable>`	A Java `null` value. If the XML datatype is built-in or maps to a primitive Java type, the XML datatype maps to the equivalent Java object wrapper type (e.g., `java.lang.Integer`).
`<xsd:list>`	An array of the list datatype.
Enumeration	A typesafe enumeration pattern as described by the JAX-RPC standard.
Array derived from `soapenc:Array` by restriction using the `wsdl:arrayType` attribute	An array of the Java equivalent of the `arrayType` attribute.
Array derived from `soapenc:Array` by restriction	An array of the Java equivalent.

Round-tripping

Suppose you use the servicegen task to generate a web service that relies on the Java class *MyType.java* illustrated earlier in Example 19-8. Suppose that later you use the autotype task to manufacture the required support classes from the WSDL file generated for the web service. You'll find that the MyType class generated by the autotype task doesn't exactly match your original definition for the MyType class. The original definition for the custom type included a property myPets of type java.util.ArrayList:

```
ArrayList myPets;
//...
public void setPets(ArrayList myPets) { this.myPets = myPets; }
```

The generated Java class that represents the custom datatype includes a slightly different declaration:

```
private java.lang.Object[] pets ;
//...
public void setPets(java.lang.Object[] v) {this.pets = v; }
```

Even though the custom datatype isn't represented in the same way, both versions of the Java class that represents the custom type are functionally equivalent. Thus, you cannot always round-trip the process of generating the XML Schema from the Java class and then re-create the same Java class from the generated XML Schema. Similarly, if you use the autotype task to generate the Java equivalent of an XML Schema definition, and again use autotype to create an XML Schema from the generated Java class, the original and generated versions of the XML Schema that represents the custom type may not be identical. Thus, even though the autotype task works in both directions, round-tripping doesn't guarantee the same results, only a version that is functionally equivalent to the original.

This side effect of round-tripping has important implications. Suppose that you use the servicegen task to create a deployable EAR for a web service that wraps a standard Java class. The task also creates the serializer classes and the Java/XML representations of any custom datatypes used by the web service. Later, you may use the clientgen task to generate a client JAR for the web service, and the client JAR also includes the serializer class and Java/XML definitions for any custom types. Because the clientgen task (by default) looks at the generated WSDL to create these support files, you are essentially trying to round-trip. Thus, the client-side Java/XML representations may not be compatible with the server-side Java/XML definitions of the custom type, which will create potential problems.

Rather than maintain separate versions of the Java and XML representations of the custom type, it would be desirable if the client JAR could reuse the server-side support classes generated for the custom type. Fortunately, by using the useServerTypes="true" attribute, you can instruct clientgen to rely on the server-side generated serializer class and the Java/XML representations of the custom type included within the EAR file that packages the web service. Of course, you must then ignore the wsdl attribute and simply use the ear attribute to refer to the existing EAR file. Alternatively, you also could use the client subelement of the servicegen task to generate the client JAR during the assembly of the web service. In this case, the client JAR automatically will use any server-side support classes generated for the custom datatypes.

Manually Creating the Support Classes for a Custom Type

Recall that in order for WebLogic to support web services that use custom types, you need to supply the following information:

- An XML Schema that defines the structure of the custom datatype
- A Java class that describes a Java representation of the datatype
- A serialization class that converts between the XML and Java representations of the data
- Mapping information for the custom type in the *web-services.xml* descriptor file

As we've seen already, WebLogic's support for autotyping can generate these items for you by introspecting the backend components for your web service. In fact, the servicegen and autotype Ant tasks can handle many custom types. Still, there may be situations in which the Ant task is unable to correctly support your custom type, or perhaps you need to control how the data is converted between its XML and Java representations. In such instances, you must manually create the support files required for the custom datatype.

Creating the XML Schema and Java class for a datatype

Consider the XML Schema for a nonbuilt-in type, defined earlier in Example 19-9. The XML Schema defines the structure of a custom type, SimpleSchemaBean, in terms of two properties: name, which is a string-valued property, and age, whose value is any positive integer no greater than 144. Thus, the following XML is a valid instance of the custom type defined by the XML Schema:

```
<SimpleSchemaBean>
  <name>Mountjoy</name>
  <age>43</age>
</SimpleSchemaBean>
```

Example 19-10 depicts the source for a JavaBean that can hold the data captured by the XML Schema defined earlier.

Example 19-10. A JavaBean representation of the XML Schema

```
package com.oreilly.wlguide.webservices.fromJavaType;
public class MySimpleSchemaBean implements java.io.Serializable {
  private String surname;
  private int age;
  public MySimpleSchemaBean( ) {};
  public String getSurname( ) { return surname; }
  public void setSurname(String surname) { this. surname = surname; }
  public int getAge( ) { return age; }
  public void setAge(int age) { this.age = age; }
}
```

A quick glance at the source code reveals two points:

- The name of the JavaBean isn't the same as the value of the name attribute of the `<xsd:complexType>` element in our XML Schema.

- The XML Schema defines a complex type, SimpleSchemaBean, which exposes a name property, whereas the corresponding JavaBean exposes a surname property. The two property names are not identical.

These differences are superficial and were included intentionally to illustrate the flexibility you have when designing the Java class and XML Schema for the custom type. The *web-services.xml* descriptor file will map the XML Schema to the corresponding Java class, thus you are free to specify different names for the custom type. Moreover, your custom serialization logic will ensure that the XML Schema property name is mapped to the JavaBean property surname.

Creating the serialization class

Once you've defined the XML Schema and the Java class for the custom type, you must define the serialization class that converts between instances of the XML Schema to instances of the Java class, and vice versa. This conversion relies on WebLogic's XML Streaming API, which provides an event-driven mechanism for handling incoming XML documents and an intuitive way for building new XML documents (the XML Streaming API is covered in more detail in Chapter 18). Typically, the serialization class will extend the weblogic.webservice.encoding.AbstractCodec class, which also implements several interfaces: weblogic.xml.schema.binding. Serializer, javax.xml.rpc.encoding.SerializerFactory, and others.

Our serialization class will effectively build on the following skeleton code:

```
public class MyCodec extends weblogic.webservice.encoding.AbstractCodec {
    public void serialize(Object obj, XMLName name, XMLOutputStream writer,
                          SerializationContext ctx) throws SerializationException {
        // convert the incoming obj to an XML stream
    }
    public Object deserialize(XMLName name, XMLInputStream reader,
                          DeserializationContext ctx) throws DeserializationException {
        // convert the XML stream to a Java object
    }
    public Object deserialize(XMLName name, Attribute att,
                          DeserializationContext ctx) throws DeserializationException {
        // convert the XML attribute to a Java object
    }
}
```

Use the serialize method to convert data from Java to XML. Here, the Object parameter holds an instance of the Java type MySimpleSchemaBean. The XMLOutput-Stream parameter allows you to use the Streaming API to generate a valid instance of the XML Schema for the datatype. The XMLName parameter specifies the name of the resulting element that is generated. Here is a straightforward implementation of the serialize( ) method:

```
public void serialize(Object obj, XMLName name, XMLOutputStream writer,
                      SerializationContext ctx) throws SerializationException {
    MySimpleSchemaBean m = (MySimpleSchemaBean) obj;
    //add start element
    writer.add(ElementFactory.createStartElement(name));
    //add name element
    writer.add(ElementFactory.createStartElement("name"));
    writer.add(ElementFactory.createCharacterData(m.getSurname( )));
    writer.add(ElementFactory.createEndElement("name"));
    //add age element
    writer.add(ElementFactory.createStartElement("age"));
    writer.add(ElementFactory.createCharacterData(Integer.toString(m.getAge( ))));
    writer.add(ElementFactory.createEndElement("age"));
    //add outer start element
    writer.add(ElementFactory.createEndElement(name));
}
```

Use the deserialize( ) method to convert the data from XML to its Java equivalent. Our implementation maps the incoming XML contained in the XMLInputStream parameter to an instance of the Java type MySimpleSchemaBean. Again, the XMLName parameter specifies the expected name of the XML element MySimpleSchemaBean. Here is a simple implementation that skips over XML elements until it finds the name and age elements. It then extracts the character data and uses this to construct an instance of the Java type MySimpleSchemaBean:

```
public Object deserialize(XMLName name, XMLInputStream reader,
                      DeserializationContext ctx) throws DeserializationException {
    MySimpleSchemaBean m = new MySimpleSchemaBean( );
    try {
```

```
    if (reader.skip(ElementFactory.createXMLName("name"))) {
      reader.next( ); // skip over name start element
      CharacterData cdata = (CharacterData) reader.next( );
      m.setSurname(cdata.getContent( ));
    } else {
      throw new DeserializationException("name not found");
    }
    if (reader.skip(ElementFactory.createXMLName("age"))) {
      reader.next( ); // skip over age start element
      CharacterData cdata = (CharacterData) reader.next( );
      m.setAge(Integer.parseInt(cdata.getContent( )));
      if (m.getAge( ) > 144)
        throw new DeserializationException("age value not valid");
    } else {
      throw new DeserializationException("age not found");
    }
    // Always read the entire XML representing your data
    if (reader.skip(name, XMLEvent.END_ELEMENT))
      reader.next( );  // skip over the last element
    else
      throw new DeserializationException("end element not found");
  } catch (XMLStreamException e_xs) {
    throw new DeserializationException("problem deserializing");
  }
  return m;
}
```

The deserialize( ) method also includes extra logic to enforce the restrictions on the age property, defined earlier in the XML Schema for the custom type. Typically, you will use the deserialize( ) method to perform additional checks and ensure that the Java instance is a valid instance of the Java type. The method implementation also reads until the end of the last element in the incoming XML. This is important because otherwise, the deserialization of subsequent XML elements may fail.

The second version of the deserialize( ) method is required only if you need to map an XML attribute to a Java object. In this case, we don't need to implement this method.

Including type information in the web-services.xml descriptor

At this stage, you've created the Java and XML Schema representations for the custom type, and the serialization class that converts between the two forms. Now you need to specify this type information for each custom type used by a web service. As always, this information must be embedded within the *web-services.xml* descriptor file. If you are going to create your web service with the servicegen task, place the type mappings in a separate file (say, *types.xml*) and refer to this file from the task. If you've already created a *web-services.xml* descriptor for the web application, for each nonbuilt-in datatype you need to make the following changes in the *web-services.xml* descriptor:

- Include the XML Schema for the custom type within the types element:

```
<!-- a portion of the web-services.xml descriptor -->
<web-service protocol="http" name="Simple" uri="/Simple"
      targetNamespace="http://www.oreilly.com/webservices/Simple" style="rpc">
   <types>
     <!-- XML schema for the custom type "MySimpleSchemaBean" goes here -->
     <xsd:schema xmlns:xsd="http://www.w3.org/2001/XMLSchema"
           attributeFormDefault="qualified"
           elementFormDefault="qualified"
           targetNamespace="http://oreilly.com/wlguide/auto">
       <xsd:complexType name="MySimpleSchemaBean">
        <xsd:sequence>
          <xsd:element name="name" type="xsd:string" nillable="true"
                     minOccurs="1" maxOccurs="1">
          </xsd:element>
          <xsd:element name="age" type="xsd:positiveInteger" nillable="true"
                     minOccurs="1" maxOccurs="1">
            <xsd:simpleType>
               <xsd:restriction xsd:base="xsd:positiveInteger">
                  <xsd:maxInclusive value="144"/>
               </xsd:restriction>
            </xsd:simpleType>
          </xsd:element>
        </xsd:sequence>
       </xsd:complexType>
     </xsd:schema>
   </types>
   <!-- define the backend components and operations here -->
</web-service>
```

- Use the type-mapping element to map the XML datatypes to the equivalent Java types. Each type-mapping-entry element includes a namespace declaration for the custom type, the fully qualified name of the Java class, the name of the XML Schema type, and the name of the serializer and deserializer classes. For the XML datatype MySimpleSchemaBean, you must specify the following type-mapping information:

```
<types>
   <!-- XML Schemas for any custom types go here -->
</types>
<type-mapping>
    <type-mapping-entry
        xmlns:s2="java:com.oreilly.wlguide.webservices.fromJavaType"
        class-name="com.oreilly.wlguide.webservices.fromJavaType.
MySimpleSchemaBean"
        type="s2:MySimpleSchemaBean"
        serializer="com.oreilly.wlguide.webservices.fromJavaType.MyCodec"
        deserializer="com.oreilly.wlguide.webservices.fromJavaType.MyCodec" />
    <!-- other type mapping entries go here -->
</type-mapping>
```

Once you make these changes to the *web-services.xml* descriptor, you can define web service operations that use these custom types as parameters and/or return values.

Using the servicegen task

WebLogic's servicegen task lets you assemble a web service for which you have manually created the required support files for each nonbuilt-in type. This includes the Java class and XML Schema that describe the structure of the custom type, as well as a file that holds the type-mapping information. In such cases, you need to disable the autotyping feature when invoking the servicegen task. The following portion from an Ant script shows how to use the servicegen task to assemble a web service while relying on the support files that were created manually for any custom types:

```
<target name="create">
  <servicegen destEar="../out/myjavatypeEar" contextURI="javatypeService"
          warName="myWar">
    <service
      javaClassComponents="com.oreilly.wlguide.webservices.fromJavaType.Simple"
      serviceName="Simple"  serviceURI="/Simple" targetNamespace="${namespace}"
      generateTypes="False" typeMappingFile="types.xml"
      protocol="http" expandMethods="True">
    </service>
    <classpath>
      <pathelement path="${build}"/>
    </classpath>
  </servicegen>
</target>
```

Notice how the generateTypes="False" attribute lets you disable the autotyping feature. The typeMappingFile attribute specifies the location of the file that includes the mapping information for all custom types used by the web service. Now imagine that a web service operation is implemented through the following method of the back-end component:

```
public String getName(MySimpleSchemaBean mytype) {
    return mytype.getSurname();
}
```

The getName( ) method accepts an input parameter of type MySimpleSchemaBean. When you invoke the servicegen task to package the web service into a deployable EAR, it uses the supplemented mapping information in the *types.xml* file to generate any references to the support classes. So, if you examine the *web-services.xml* descriptor file generated by the servicegen task, you find the following definition for the web service operation:

```
<operation
  method=
    "getName(com.oreilly.wlguide.webservices.fromJavaType.MySimpleSchemaBean)"
  component="jcComp0" name="getName">
  <params>
```

```
            <param location="body"
                class-name="com.oreilly.wlguide.webservices.fromJavaType.MySimpleSchemaBean"
                style="in" name="mySimpleSchemaBean"
                xmlns:myns="http://www.oreilly.com/webservices/Simple"
                type="myns:SimpleSchemaBean">
            </param>
            <return-param location="body" class-name="java.lang.String" name="result"
                xmlns:xsd="http://www.w3.org/2001/XMLSchema" type="xsd:string">
            </return-param>
        </params>
    </operation>
```

Moreover, you'll notice that the type-mapping element in the *web-services.xml* descriptor file contains the mapping information held in the *types.xml* file. Unfortunately, the generated *web-services.xml* descriptor does not include the XML Schema definitions for any of the custom datatypes. This means that you must manually edit the *web-services.xml* descriptor file and explicitly include the XML Schemas for any custom types. As explained earlier, these XML Schemas must be placed verbatim within the types element, which occurs before the type-mapping element. To accomplish this change, you must unpack the *myEar.ear* file, edit the *web-services.xml* file to include the XML Schemas, and then repackage the EAR file.

Implementing Multiple Return Values

Usually, a web service operation returns a single value, which is the return value of the EJB method or a method on a Java class used to implement the operation. If the operation must return multiple values, you can redesign the backend method so that it returns an instance of a complex type—say, an object with multiple attributes or an array itself. Alternatively, the operation could define one or more parameters to be out or "in-out" parameters. The JAX-RPC standard lets you define web service operations with parameters that are either in, out, or in-out. An in parameter specifies the type of data input into the web service operation. An out parameter specifies the type of data output from the web service operation. Finally, an in-out parameter is used by the client to send data to and receive data from the operation.

It is the out and in-out parameters that let you explicitly define multiple return values from the web service operation. An out parameter has an undefined value when the operation is invoked, but acquires a value before the backend method completes. In contrast, an in-out parameter behaves like an in parameter and an out parameter at the same time. It is assigned a value before the operation is invoked, and a new value before the backend method completes servicing the web service operation. An out parameter can be treated just like a return value. By defining multiple out parameters, a web service operation is able to return multiple values to the client. An in-out parameter allows the web service operation to return a value of the same type as the incoming value.

Suppose we wish to add a holderExample( ) method to Example 19-1, which accepts an in-out parameter and an out parameter of type String. The following fragment from the *web-services.xml* descriptor file depicts the signature for this operation:

```
<!-- portion from the web-services.xml descriptor -->
<operation component="jcComp0" name="holderExample"
method="holderExample(javax.xml.rpc.holders.StringHolder,javax.xml.rpc.holders.
StringHolder)" >
  <params>
    <param style="inout" xmlns:xsd="http://www.w3.org/2001/XMLSchema"
           type="xsd:string" location="body" name="stringHolder"
           class-name="javax.xml.rpc.holders.StringHolder">
    </param>
    <param style="inout" xmlns:xsd="http://www.w3.org/2001/XMLSchema"
            type="xsd:string" location="body" name="stringHolder0"
            class-name="javax.xml.rpc.holders.StringHolder">
    </param>
  </params>
</operation>
```

In such a case, you need to specify the corresponding holder class as the types of the parameters. The use of out or in-out parameters always requires you to change the backend code to use holder classes. The holderExample( ) method must therefore be implemented as follows:

```
public void holderExample(StringHolder inout, StringHolder out) {
    inout.value = inout.value.toUpperCase( );
    out.value = "someOutValue";
}
```

Effectively, the method returns two values, inout and out. It also could have returned a standard value using a return type. All out and in-out parameters must implement the javax.xml.rpc.holders.Holder interface. The backend method can use the Holder. value attribute to obtain the input value passed to the in-out parameter and use it to assign the output value for the out and in-out parameters. The following code fragment shows how a client would invoke the modified holderExample operation:

```
javax.xml.rpc.holders.StringHolder oString =
  new javax.xml.rpc.holders.StringHolder( );
javax.xml.rpc.holders.StringHolder ioString =
  new javax.xml.rpc.holders.StringHolder( );
ioString.value = "Incoming";
Simple ws = new Simple_Impl("http://10.0.10.10:7001/pojoHolderService/Simple?WSDL");
SimplePort port = ws.getSimplePort( );
port.holderExample(ioString, oString);
System.err.println("in/out string is now: " + ioString.value);
System.err.println("out string is now: " + oString.value);
```

Notice how the client uses the Holder.value attribute to obtain the results of the web service operation. The output should look like this:

```
in/out string is now: INCOMING
out string is now: someOutValue
```

WebLogic provides support for in-out parameters if you use the servicegen Ant task. When you use this task to generate a service from a backend that you provide and your backend uses the Holder classes in its implementation, WebLogic will automatically ensure that the *web-services.xml* file describes the relevant parameters as in-out. If you want the parameter to be an out parameter instead, you will have to edit the generated descriptor file manually.

Creating holder classes

The JAX-RPC standard defines a number of holder classes for the built-in types. Table 19-3 lists the holder classes WebLogic provides for the various standard types.

Table 19-3. Built-in holder classes

Java datatype	Built-in holder class
boolean	javax.xml.rpc.holders.BooleanHolder
byte	javax.xml.rpc.holders.ByteHolder
short	javax.xml.rpc.holders.ShortHolder
int	javax.xml.rpc.holders.IntHolder
long	javax.xml.rpc.holders.LongHolder
float	javax.xml.rpc.holders.FloatHolder
double	javax.xml.rpc.holders.DoubleHolder
java.math.BigDecimal	javax.xml.rpc.holders.BigDecimalHolder
java.math.BigInteger	javax.xml.rpc.holders.BigIntegerHolder
byte[]	javax.xml.rpc.holders.ByteArrayHolder
java.util.Calendar	javax.xml.rpc.holders.CalendarHolder
javax.xml.namespace.QName	javax.xml.rpc.holders.QnameHolder
java.lang.String	javax.xml.rpc.holders.StringHolder

In general, the autotype Ant task can generate the holder classes for any custom types that a web service uses as parameter or return values. You may, of course, implement the holder classes for your custom datatypes manually. Example 19-11 illustrates the holder class for the custom Java type SimpleSchemaBean.

Example 19-11. Holder class for the SimpleSchemaBean type

```
package com.oreilly.wlguide.webservices.simple.holders;
import com.oreilly.wlguide.webservices.simple.SimpleSchemaBean;
public final class SimpleSchemaBeanHolder
                    implements weblogic.xml.schema.binding.Holder {
  public SimpleSchemaBean value;
  public SimpleSchemaBeanHolder() {}
  public SimpleSchemaBeanHolder(SimpleSchemaBean value) {
    this.value = value;
  }
}
```

Besides implementing the `javax.xml.rpc.holders.Holder` interface, this class also adheres to the following guidelines:

- The holder class is named *Type*Holder, where *Type* represents the name of the custom Java type.

- The holder class is placed in a "holders" subpackage, just below the package for the custom Java type. For instance, if the custom type Foo is located in the package `a.b.c`, the FooHolder implementation class must be located within the `a.b.c. holders` package.

- The class must declare a public field called "value" that represents an instance of the custom Java type. In addition, the class defines a default constructor that initializes the value of the field to some default, and another constructor that sets the value of the field to the value of the incoming parameter.

SOAP Attachments

Some datatypes are transported as SOAP attachments, with the appropriate MIME type, rather than as elements within the body of the SOAP message. For example, a `java.awt.Image` object is transported as an attachment with MIME type image/gif or image/jpeg. Similarly, a `javax.mail.internet.MimeMultipart` object is transported as a message attachment with MIME type multipart/*, and a `javax.xml.transform.Source` object is transmitted as an attachment with its MIME type set to either text/xml or application/xml. If your code uses any of these datatypes for a parameter or return value, servicegen automatically will ensure that the instance data is transferred as a SOAP attachment. As a result, the location attribute of a param element within the generated *web-services.xml* descriptor file will be set to attachment.

By default, servicegen treats `java.lang.String` as a built-in datatype. Thus, any string parameter or return value will be sent in the SOAP body as an XML Schema string type. Instead, if you wish to send a string value as a SOAP attachment with the text/plain MIME type, you must edit the *web-services.xml* descriptor file manually and then change the location attributes accordingly.

Note that WebLogic's SOAP message encryption cannot be configured to encrypt SOAP attachments. It can encrypt only selected parts of a SOAP message body.

Implementing Clients

Web service clients can be built on any platform in any language, so long as they adhere to the existing standards for invoking web services. In this section, we look at how to use WebLogic's JAX-RPC implementation to build Java clients that can invoke a web service. WebLogic lets you generate a web service–specific client JAR that can be used by clients to statically invoke the operations of the web service. In addition, WebLogic allows you to build standard JAX-RPC clients that can discover and invoke web service operations dynamically. Finally, WebLogic provides client-side libraries that let you invoke web services over SSL and build J2ME clients over the CDC profile.

Because WebLogic's web services implementation conforms to all of the existing standards in the world of web services, clients we construct in this section are capable of interacting with any web service, not only those hosted by WebLogic. The JAX-RPC standard provides several ways to implement a web service client. For instance, the web service client can use a statically generated stub that acts as a proxy for the remote service. Such clients also are called *static* because the client is aware of the operations exposed by the web service. Alternatively, a client can invoke operations through a dynamic proxy generated at runtime using the WSDL for the web service. Such clients are called *dynamic* because the client needs to dynamically discover the operations exposed by the web service and then use this information to construct an "invocation."

Client-Side Libraries

WebLogic comes with several client libraries that package all the classes needed by Java clients to interact with web services:

webserviceclient.jar
> This client-side JAR includes the runtime implementation of the JAX-RPC standard.

webserviceclient+ssl.jar
> This client-side JAR includes all of the classes provided by *webserviceclient.jar*, and additional support for invoking web services protected by SSL.

webserviceclient+ssl_pj.jar
> This client-side JAR includes the runtime implementation of JAX-RPC over SSL for the CDC profile of J2ME.

All of these client libraries can be found in the *WL_HOME\server\lib* directory of your WebLogic installation. If you are building a client application that invokes one or more web services, you can bundle the appropriate JAR along with your client.

If you intend to create dynamic clients, you need to choose only from one of the preceding client JARs. However, if you intend to build static clients, then you must use the clientgen Ant task to generate a client JAR specific to the web service that packages the stubs allowing clients to statically invoke operations exposed by the web service. Dynamic clients don't need this client JAR; they simply can rely on the JAX-RPC API to invoke both WebLogic and non-WebLogic web services. If you want to invoke a web service from within an EJB or a servlet hosted by WebLogic, you do not need to supply the *webserviceclient.jar* or any of its variations. However, if you want to make use of static clients, you need the JAR representing the client side stubs to be placed in the appropriate directory. For example, you could place the JAR in the *WEB-INF/lib* directory for a web application, or reference it from within the manifest file in an EJB.

Building a Client JAR for Static Clients

In order to create static clients, you must use the clientgen Ant task to generate a client JAR that web service clients can use to statically invoke the web service. The clientgen task can be invoked in two ways: either by referring to an existing EAR file that packages a WebLogic web service, or by pointing to the WSDL for an existing web service.

Example 19-5 showed how you can generate the client JAR from an existing EAR file that packages a WAR file representing a web service component:

```
<!-- build target within an Ant Script -->
<target name="createClient">
  <clientgen
    ear="myPOJOEar.ear"
    warName="myWar.war"
    packageName="com.oreilly.wlguide.webservices.pojo.client"
    clientJar="../out/myPOJOClient.jar">
    <classpath>
      <pathelement path="${build}"/>
    </classpath>
  </clientgen>
</target>
```

This clientgen task examines the specified EAR file (and the WAR file it packages) and creates a client JAR called *myPOJOClient.jar*, placing the generated classes into the oreilly.wlguide.webservices.pojo.client package. This deployable EAR file packages a WebLogic web service, possibly generated from a backend component using the servicegen task. The clientgen task also supports other features that we looked at earlier, including autotyping and the use of a type-mapping file.

Instead of pointing to an existing EAR file, you also could invoke the clientgen task by pointing to the WSDL file for an existing web service. The following portion from an Ant script shows how to generate an identical client JAR from an existing WSDL file:

```
<!-- build target within an Ant Script -->
<target name="createClientFromWSDL" >
  <clientgen
    wsdl="http://10.0.10.10:7001/pojoService/Simple?WSDL"
    packageName="com.oreilly.wlguide.webservices.pojo.client"
    clientJar="../out/myPOJOClientFromWSDL.jar">
    <classpath>
      <pathelement path="${build}"/>
    </classpath>
  </clientgen>
</target>
```

In this case, the task creates a client JAR that allows clients to statically invoke operations on the web service described by the WSDL. Once again, the generated classes are placed in the oreilly.wlguide.webservices.pojo.client package. If the WSDL file describes multiple web services, you should use the serviceName attribute to identify the web service for which the client JAR should be generated. The same applies to a deployable EAR that packages multiple WebLogic web services.

You can also use the servicegen Ant task to generate the client JAR. In this case, the client JAR is packaged into the deployable EAR itself, and is made available as a download on the home page for the web service. If you've created the client JAR manually and would like to make it available on the web service home page, you must ensure that it is named correctly. If a web service named Foo is packaged within the EAR file, the corresponding client JAR within the EAR must be named *Foo_client.jar*. The following portion from a build script shows how to use the servicegen Ant task to *also* generate the client JAR:

```
<servicegen destEar="myEar "warName="myWar" contextURI="pojoService">
  <service
    javaClassComponents="com.oreilly.wlguide.webservices.pojo.Simple"
    targetNamespace="${namespace}"
    serviceName="Simple" serviceURI="/Simple">
    <client packageName="com.oreilly.wlguide.webservices.pojo.client" />
  </service>
</servicegen>
```

In this case, the client JAR *Simple_client.jar* will be made available as a download on the home page for the web service. Because it will be packed within the generated WAR, it can be fetched using a URL such as *http://10.0.10.10:7001/pojoService/Simple_client.jar*. Java clients can then use this JAR to statically invoke any operation exposed by the Simple web service.

Static Clients

A client that statically invokes an operation relies on a strongly typed interface to interact with the web service. Once you've generated a client JAR specific to the web service, a static client can use the stubs generated specifically for that web service. These stubs serve as client-side proxies for the web service, exposing methods that let you directly invoke the operations of the web service.

As depicted in Figure 19-5, when a client invokes one of the methods on the stub, the call is forwarded via the JAX-RPC runtime to the server hosting the web service. At the server end, the JAX-RPC runtime decodes the request and invokes the appropriate web service operation. In WebLogic, these stubs are packaged within the client JAR generated specifically for the web service, while the server-side ties are generated automatically when the web service is deployed.

When writing a static client for a web service, you must include the web service–specific client JAR in your classpath. Example 19-6 illustrated how a client can statically invoke a web service operation. Let's take a closer look at the sequence of steps needed to interact with the web service.

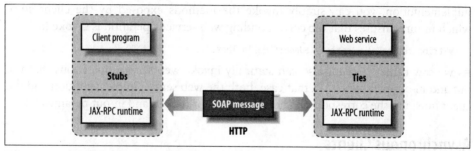

Figure 19-5. Static invocation

First, the client configures WebLogic's implementation of the JAXM message factory and the JAX-RPC service factory:

```
System.setProperty("javax.xml.soap.MessageFactory",
                   "weblogic.webservice.core.soap.MessageFactoryImpl");
System.setProperty("javax.xml.rpc.ServiceFactory",
                   "weblogic.webservice.core.rpc.ServiceFactoryImpl");
```

These factory classes are available in the client JAR generated for the web service. When you use the clientgen task to generate the client JAR for a web service, WebLogic creates a Java interface that represents the web service and its operations. For our example, it is named SimplePort and it looks like this:

```
public interface SimplePort extends java.rmi.Remote {
  public String makeUpper(String arg) throws java.rmi.RemoteException;
}
```

Notice how the SimplePort interface reflects the structure of the web service. In addition, WebLogic creates a Java interface that offers a convenient way of accessing the service port:

```
public interface com.oreilly.wlguide.webservices.pojo.client.Simple
                extends javax.xml.rpc.Service {
  public SimplePort getSimplePort()   throws javax.xml.rpc.ServiceException;
  public SimplePort getSimplePort(String un, String pw)
                                    throws javax.xml.rpc.ServiceException;
}
```

Finally, the client JAR packages the classes that implement both of these interfaces. The Simple_Impl class implements the Simple interface and ensures that when a client invokes the getSimplePort( ) method it actually acquires the stub implementation that also implements the SimplePort interface. Given this background, it is clear the client must use the SimpleImpl object to obtain the SimplePort stub implementation in order to interact with the web service:

```
Simple ws = new Simple_Impl("http://10.0.10.10:8001/pojoService/Simple?wsdl");
SimplePort port = ws.getSimplePort();
```

In this case, we've created the javax.xml.rpc.Service instance from a URI that refers to the WSDL for the web service. Once you've obtained the SimplePort stub implementation, you can simply invoke the methods exposed by the client stub, which in turn ensures that the corresponding web service operation is invoked:

```
String returnVal = port.makeUpper("Hello There");
```

As we saw earlier, a client also can statically invoke web service operations that use out and in-out parameters. In that case, both the web service implementation and the client must use the corresponding holder classes for the out and in-out parameters.

Asynchronous Clients

WebLogic 8.1 lets clients invoke web service operations asynchronously. Instead of waiting for the operation to return a value, the client simply can continue and fetch the result of the operation later. In other words, WebLogic offers a non-blocking way of invoking an operation. This mechanism is ideal for long-running operations, provided you can architect your client application to retrieve the result at a later stage. This form of method invocation works regardless of whether the operation's invocation style is one-way (asynchronous) or request-response (synchronous).

To enable asynchronous invocations of web service operations, you need to generate client stubs that support this form of invocation for the web service. You can do this simply by adding a generateAsyncMethods attribute to the standard clientgen task:

```
<clientgen ear="../out/myPOJOAsyncEar" warName="myWar"
           packageName="com.oreilly.wlguide.webservices.pojoAsync.client"
           clientJar="../out/myPOJOAsyncClient.jar"
           generateAsyncMethods="true">
   <classpath>
     <pathelement path="${build}"/>
   </classpath>
</clientgen>
```

There are, in fact, three ways in which the client can behave after invoking an operation:

- The client can continue execution and call a blocking method later to fetch the result of the web service operation. The next example shows how to use a blocking fetch:

```
FutureResult fr = port.startMakeUpper("hello World", null);
// Do some work here, twiddle your thumbs
String result = port.endMakeUpper(fr);    // blocks
```

The weblogic.webservice.async.FutureResult class, together with the other related classes, acts as a placeholder for the impending result of the operation. Given any web service operation named operation that takes the argument args and returns a result result, WebLogic adds the following two methods to the client-side stubs:

```
FutureResult startOperation (args, AsyncInfo asyncInfo);
result endOperation (FutureResult fr);
```

Use the startOperation( ) method to asynchronously invoke the operation and use the endOperation( ) method to block until the value is returned.

- The client can poll to check whether the result has arrived. So, instead of calling the blocking endOperation( ) method, it can simply check for the result by calling the isCompleted( ) method on the FutureResult object. Here is an example that shows how to poll for the result of the operation:

```
FutureResult fr = port.startMakeUpper("hello World", null);
while (!fr.isCompleted( )) {
  // Twiddle thumbs, update graphics
}
String result = port.endMakeUpper(fr);    // should return immediately
```

The FutureResult class also supports a waitFor(long timeout) method, which blocks for a length of time or until the result becomes available.

- The client can register a listener that gets notified when the result arrives. To do so, the client needs to pass an AsyncInfo object to the startOperation( ) method. The previous two examples simply passed a null value, indicating that the client didn't wish to be notified when the operation returns a result. Here is the example rewritten to make use of the listener:

```
AsyncInfo asyncInfo = new AsyncInfo( );
asyncInfo.setResultListener( new ResultListener( ){
    public void onCompletion( InvokeCompletedEvent event ){
        SimplePort source = (SimplePort)event.getSource( );
        try{
        String result = source.endMakeUpper ( event.getFutureResult( ) );
         System.err.println("Message Received and Understood");
        } catch ( RemoteException e ){
          e.printStackTrace ( System.out );
        }
    }});
// Perform the operation
FutureResult fr = port.startMakeUpper("hello World", asyncInfo);
// Assuming client continues to run, the listener will get notified.
```

This code simply registers a listener, which implements a single callback method, onCompletion( ), that gets invoked when the result arrives.

Dynamic Clients

Dynamic clients simply follow the JAX-RPC specification. Instead of using a statically generated stub to invoke an operation, these clients interact with the web service through a dynamic proxy, generated at runtime by examining the WSDL. The code in Example 19-12 shows how to use this dynamic approach to invoke the makeUpper operation exposed by our web service:

Example 19-12. A dynamic client

```
System.setProperty("javax.xml.soap.MessageFactory",
            "weblogic.webservice.core.soap.MessageFactoryImpl");
System.setProperty("javax.xml.rpc.ServiceFactory",
```

Example 19-12. A dynamic client (continued)

```
            "weblogic.webservice.core.rpc.ServiceFactoryImpl");

// Create the service factory
ServiceFactory factory = ServiceFactory.newInstance();

// Now specify the names for the service, port, and operation
String targetNamespace = "http://www.oreilly.com/webservices/Simple";
QName serviceName = new QName(targetNamespace, "Simple");
QName portName = new QName(targetNamespace, "SimplePort");
QName operationName = new QName("makeUpper");

// Create the service
URL wsdlLocation = new URL("http://10.0.10.10:8001/pojoService/Simple?WSDL");
Service service = factory.createService(wsdlLocation, serviceName);

// Create the call
Call call = service.createCall(portName, operationName);
// Invoke the operation, passing in a parameter
String result = (String) call.invoke(new Object[] {"lowercase string"});
```

This example illustrates the typical sequence of steps needed to invoke any web service. After initializing the JAXM and JAX-RPC factories, you create a `ServiceFactory` instance, which lets you construct a `Service` instance that represents the available web service. The `Service` object allows you to interact with the web service and create a `Call` object for invoking a web service operation. Remember, you do not need to use the clientgen task to generate the web service–specific client JAR because this client JAR is needed only by static clients. All of these standard JAX-RPC classes are located within the `javax.xml.rpc` package and are available within the *webserviceclient.jar* client library that includes WebLogic's JAX-RPC implementation. If your client makes use of custom datatypes, you still need to provide serialization classes to the client, which you can create conveniently using the autotype task.

If a dynamic client doesn't use the WSDL to create a `Service` instance, it must explicitly supply the information that is usually gleaned from the WSDL. This includes the parameters expected by the operation, the return value, the target endpoint address, and so on. The following example again shows how to invoke the `makeUpper` operation, this time without using the WSDL that describes the web service:

```
// Specify the names for the service, port, and operation as above
// Create the service
Service service = factory.createService(serviceName);
// Create the call
Call call = service.createCall(portName, operationName);

// Now we need to specify the parameters and the return type
call.addParameter("string",
        new QName("http://www.w3.org/2001/XMLSchema", "string"), ParameterMode.IN);
call.setReturnType(new QName("http://www.w3.org/2001/XMLSchema", "string"));
```

```
// Specify the endpoint of the web service
call.setTargetEndpointAddress("http://10.0.10.10:8001/Simple");

// Now invoke the operation in the same way
String result = (String) call.invoke(new Object[] { "lowercase string" });
System.out.println("Result of call is:" + result);
```

Clearly, you can write such a client only if you have all the information needed to invoke the web service operation, such as the name and type of the parameters. In this case, we've obtained this information by inspecting the WSDL that describes the web service.

There are certain caveats you should be aware of when building dynamic clients for a web service:

- The dynamic client that doesn't use the WSDL to interact with the web service needs to explicitly supply information about the parameters and the return type for the web service information. In such cases, the client can invoke the following methods on the javax.xml.rpc.Call interface:

  ```
  getParameterTypeByName( )
  getReturnType( )
  ```

  However, if a dynamic client does rely on the WSDL to interface with the web service, the client cannot invoke these methods on the Call object. The Call object is oblivious to the parameters and return type of the operation because that information is already captured by the WSDL.

- Similarly, a client can invoke the getTargetEndpointAddress( ) method only if it has already executed the setTargetEndpointAddress( ) method. This is true even if the target endpoint address is available in the WSDL file.

- A dynamic client that uses the WSDL to interact with a web service can invoke the getPorts( ) method on the javax.xml.rpc.Service object to obtain a list of service ports available for the web service. If the dynamic client ignores the WSDL that describes the web service, the getPorts( ) method always returns null.

Introspecting the WSDL

As Example 19-12 illustrates, when you create a dynamic client, you must manually construct the parameters and return values for the calls, based on the WSDL for the web service that is being invoked.

WebLogic provides a weblogic.webservice.extensions.WLCall interface that can be used to conveniently introspect the WSDL of the web service. It extends the standard javax.xml.rpc.Call interface with three additional methods:

- Use the getParameterNames( ) method to retrieve the names of the parameters for the call.

- Use the getParameterMode( ) method to retrieve the mode of a particular parameter (in, out, or in-out).

- Use the getParameterJavaType( ) method to get the Java type of a particular parameter.

These methods ease the task of creating dynamic clients against an unknown WSDL. To illustrate the interface, we will simply continue with Example 19-12:

```
WLCall wlCall = (WLCall) call;
for (Iterator i = wlCall.getParameterNames( ); i.hasNext( );) {
    String parm = (String) i.next( );
    System.out.println("Parameter name is: " + parm);
    System.out.println("Type is: " + wlCall.getParameterJavaType(parm));
    System.out.println("Mode is: " + wlCall.getParameterMode(parm));
}
```

This yields the following output:

```
Parameter name is: string
Type is: class java.lang.String
Mode is: IN
```

Note that the parameter names enable you to access the type and mode information, and reflect the names used in the *web-services.xml* descriptor (not the parameter names used in the implementation of the web service operation).

Registering datatype mapping information

When clientgen creates a client JAR for a static client, it ensures that any custom and WebLogic datatypes and their serialization classes are registered with the standard type-mapping machinery. Clients then can seamlessly use custom datatypes.

For dynamic web service clients however, the custom datatypes will not be registered automatically. Instead, you must use the JAX-RPC API to register custom datatypes manually. Using this API is cumbersome, as the dynamic client must register a number of datatypes, including some internal WebLogic serialization classes. For example, given a type implemented by a class MyType and its codec MyTypeCodec, a dynamic client must register the type as follows:

```
TypeMappingRegistry registry = service.getTypeMappingRegistry( );
TypeMapping mapping = registry.getTypeMapping(
                        SOAPConstants.URI_NS_SOAP_ENCODING );
mapping.register( SOAPStruct.class,
        new QName( "http://typeurl.org/xsd", "MyType" ),
        new MyTypeCodec( ),
        new MyTypeCodec( ) );
```

A dynamic client can then use the custom type. For example, it can register the custom type as the return type for a web service call:

```
call.setReturnType(new QName( "http://typeurl.org/xsd", "MyType" ) );
```

Recall how the autotype task generates a type-mapping file *types.xml*, together with the serialization and deserialization classes and custom datatype. WebLogic provides a utility class, weblogic.webservice.encoding.DefaultTypeMapping, which can conveniently use this type-mapping file to register all of the listed custom datatypes in one call. Here is an example:

```
TypeMappingRegistry registry = service.getTypeMappingRegistry();
registry.registerDefault(new DefaultTypeMapping("types.xml"));
```

You also can use the GenericTypeMapping class to associate all custom XML datatypes to the generic datatype SOAPElement, though this is usually less useful than the previous approach.

SOAP 1.2

By default, both WebLogic 7.0 and WebLogic 8.1 use SOAP 1.1, although both can accept SOAP 1.1– and SOAP 1.2–compliant message requests from clients. WebLogic 8.1 can be configured to produce SOAP 1.2 compliant messages too. To do this, modify your servicegen task as follows:

```
<servicegen destEar="../out/myPOJOEar" contextURI="pojoService" warName="myWar">
  <service javaClassComponents="com.oreilly.wlguide.webservices.pojo.Simple"
    serviceName="Simple" serviceURI="/Simple"  targetNamespace="${namespace}"
    useSOAP12="true">
  </service>
</servicegen>
```

This task generates a *web-services.xml* that includes an additional useSOAP12 attribute:

```
<web-service protocol="http" useSOAP12="true" name="Simple" style="rpc" uri="/Simple"
        targetNamespace="http://www.oreilly.com/webservices/Simple" >
```

When you create the client JAR using this web definition, WebLogic generates two ports in the Service implementation:

- A get*ServiceName*Port( ) method that still can be used for SOAP 1.1 message exchanges
- An additional get*ServiceName*PortSoap12( ) method that can be used for generating SOAP 1.2 messages

The following code sample shows how a client can interact with the web service using SOAP 1.2 exchanges:

```
Simple ws = new Simple_Impl(where);
SimplePort port = ws.getSimplePortSoap12();
System.out.println("The service returned: " + port.makeUpper("hello there"));
```

J2ME Clients

You also can use the clientgen Ant task to generate a web service–specific client JAR for J2ME clients running on the CDC and Foundation profiles. In order to generate a client JAR for J2ME clients, you simply need to add a j2me="True" attribute to the clientgen Ant task.

```
<clientgen wsdl="http://10.0.10.10/pojoService/Simple?WSDL"
           packageName="com.oreilly.wlguide.webservices.pojo.client"
           clientJar="../out/j2me_client.jar"
           j2me="True" />
```

Unlike the client JAR generated for non-J2ME clients, the web service–specific stub does not implement the java.rmi.Remote interface, and thus its methods do not throw a java.rmi.RemoteException either.

If you intend to build dynamic J2ME clients that don't need to talk over SSL, you simply can use the *webserviceclient.jar* library. However, if the J2ME client needs to interact with a web service that is using SSL, the *webserviceclient+ssl_pj.jar* library must be included in your classpath instead. Moreover, if the client uses the WSDL to invoke a web service, you must package a local copy of the WSDL for the client. A J2ME client cannot access a remote WSDL using a URLConnection object. Besides these issues, writing web service clients for J2ME devices is identical to writing non-J2ME clients.

Client Portability

Suppose you've created a web service client that runs on WebLogic and relies on client JARs—either the standard client libraries provided by WebLogic or the web service–specific client JARs generated by the clientgen Ant task. In such a case, you may observe that the Java classes in the client JAR collide with the JAX-RPC implementation classes in WebLogic itself. This problem becomes even more apparent when the client JAR is deployed to a WebLogic release that is different from the one from which it was generated. In other words, the client JARs used to support the web service client actually conflict with WebLogic's JAX-RPC implementation classes.

To get around this problem you need to run the client through a conversion program that renames any accessed packages to a version-specific package name that doesn't collide with any of the server-side classes. For instance, in a WebLogic 8.1 environment, the tool renames all *weblogic.** packages to *weblogic81.**. You then can include the *wsclient81.jar** library in your classpath instead of the *webserviceclient.jar* library. This client JAR contains the same files as the *webserviceclient.jar* library, but under the modified package name. Both client JARs are located under the *WL_HOME/ server/lib* folder. To execute this change, you must run the *setenv* script to set up the environment and then invoke the conversion tool as follows:

```
java weblogic.webservice.tools.versioning.VersionMaker \
    output_directory yourClient.jar yourSupportingLibs.jar
```

---

* Include the *wsclient70.jar* for the equivalent functionality in WebLogic 7.0.

This will modify the client and any supported library JARs, and place the modified version in the output directory. Remember, this conversion tool merely avoids any potential conflicts for web service clients running on WebLogic itself. For stand-alone web service clients, this change is unnecessary.

Client System Properties

Table 19-4 lists the system properties that Java clients can utilize when interacting with a web service. The weblogic.webservice.verbose property also can be specified on the server side and is particularly useful during debugging. It may cause some performance degradation, so you should enable it only during debugging.

Table 19-4. System properties useful for web service clients of WebLogic 8.1

System property	Description
weblogic.webservice.transport.http.full-url	Set this property to true if you want the full URL of the web service, rather than its relative URL, to be specified in the Request-URI field of the HTTP request.
weblogic.webservice.transport.https.proxy.host and weblogic.webservice.transport.https.proxy.port	If your client makes HTTPS connections that have to go through a proxy, use these properties to specify the hostname and port of the proxy server.
weblogic.webservice.verbose	Set this property to true to cause the SOAP request and response messages to be written to the console.
weblogic.webservice.client.ssl.strictcertchecking	This property, which defaults to false, enables or disables strict certificate validation when using WebLogic's SSL implementation.
weblogic.webservice.client.ssl.trustedcertfile	Set this property to the name of the file that contains the certificates of the CA, which allows you to trust the certificate issued by WebLogic Server. It also can contain certificates that you trust directly.
weblogic.webservice.client.ssl.adapterclass	If the client uses a third-part SSL implementation to interact with an SSL-protected web service, set this property to the fully qualified name of the SSL adapter class.

WebLogic 8.1 runs on the JDK 1.4, which provides a number of additional properties that you may want to use in your clients. For example, you can use http.proxyHost and http.proxyPort to specify the proxy server characteristics, http.keepAlive to determine whether persistent connections may be used, sun.net.client.defaultConnectTimeout to specify the millisecond timeout used to establish a connection, and sun.net.client.defaultReadTimeout to specify the timeout during a read.

Table 19-5 lists the system properties that Java clients can utilize when interacting with a web service. These are in addition to the properties listed in Table 19-4.

Table 19-5. System properties useful for web service clients of WebLogic 7.0

System property	Description
`weblogic.webservice.transport.http.proxy.host` and `weblogic.webservice.transport.http.proxy.port`	If your client makes HTTP connections that have to go through a proxy, use these properties to specify the hostname and port of the proxy server.
`weblogic.http.KeepAliveTimeoutSeconds`	This determines the number of seconds to maintain HTTP keepalive before timing out the request. It defaults to 30 seconds. Set this to 0 to disable HTTP keepalive.

Reliable SOAP Messaging

WebLogic 8.1 supports a reliable SOAP messaging framework that enables an application hosted by one WebLogic instance to reliably invoke a web service hosted by another WebLogic instance. *Reliability* means that the sender will eventually know whether the SOAP message was received by the web service or if it was unable to deliver the message. In other words, WebLogic provides the sender with a transport guarantee *only*, and does not indicate whether the web service operation was invoked successfully. The sender must invoke the web service asynchronously and then either poll or register a listener to know whether the SOAP message was delivered.

WebLogic provides this reliability in the following ways:

- Both WebLogic instances that are involved store the message after it has been sent by the sender application and before it is received by the web service.
- The reliable SOAP messaging information is embedded in the headers of the SOAP message that must be delivered to the web service. For this reason, reliable SOAP messaging is independent of the transport mechanism used to invoke the web service—it can be used alongside either HTTP(S) or JMS transport.
- To ensure that the transport guarantees are enforced correctly at the web service end, WebLogic ensures that all actions at the receiver's end are executed within a transaction context.
- If the receiver's runtime fails to acknowledge the receipt of the SOAP message, the sender's runtime can resend the message transparently.

Reliable SOAP messaging also imposes certain restrictions on its use:

- It operates only between two WebLogic instances—i.e., when an application on one server invokes a web service deployed to another. This means that both WebLogic instances must be configured to support reliable SOAP messaging. Behind the scenes, WebLogic augments both the client and server runtimes to facilitate reliable SOAP messaging. Of course, reliable SOAP messaging is a proprietary mechanism, so you lose interoperability with other web service implementations if you employ this feature.

- The sender application must invoke the web service operation asynchronously. So, even though a sender won't know immediately if the message was delivered, it still can actively poll for a result, or establish a listener that notifies the application if the message was received, or if it could not be delivered.

- The web service operation must return a void type and must be two-way (synchronous). One-way (asynchronous) operations cannot be reliably invoked.

Other than these restrictions, the reliable transport mechanism is transparent to both the application and the web service. WebLogic embeds all the reliable SOAP messaging logic in the runtime systems of the sender application and receiving web service.

Architecture

Reliability stems from the fact that both the sender and the receiver use JMS stores to keep a copy of the SOAP message until it has been delivered successfully. JMS stores can be kept in either the filesystem or the database, and you can read more about their setup in Chapter 8. A transaction context at the receiver's end further ensures that the receiver's runtime can correctly acknowledge the receipt of the SOAP message. In addition, the server's runtime can resend the SOAP message if its receipt hasn't been acknowledged. Let's take a closer look at the sequence of events that occur when a web service operation is reliably invoked:

1. An application asynchronously invokes a reliable operation. Its runtime stores the SOAP message in a JMS store before sending it to the WebLogic instance hosting the web service.

2. The receiver's runtime checks the incoming message against those already saved in its own JMS store. If the message is new (i.e., it is absent from its JMS store), the message ID is recorded in the store, the appropriate web service operation is invoked, and the message is acknowledged. If the message is not new (i.e., it already exists in the JMS store), the web service operation is skipped and the message simply is acknowledged. Note that all of the actions at the receiver's end occur within a transaction context.

3. When the sender's runtime receives an acknowledgment, it removes the message from its JMS store to ensure that it is not delivered again. The sender's runtime also ensures that the application is notified if the SOAP message has been sent or was never delivered successfully, either through polling or via a registered listener.

Note that the receiver does not store the entire message, only its message ID. The sender runtime can be configured to retry a send automatically if the message was not acknowledged. The combination of the sender's retries, stored messages, and receiver's acknowledgment provides for a guaranteed delivery.

For example, even if the WebLogic instance hosting the web service is not available, the outgoing messages will be kept in the sender's JMS store, and the sender's runtime will try periodically to send them to the receiver. The transaction context at the receiver's end plays a key role in coordinating its activities. When the receiver's runtime receives a SOAP message, it performs a number of activities in a transaction context to preserve the integrity of the message IDs in its store. After a message has been received, the following actions occur:

1. A transaction context is started.
2. The receiver's runtime checks the message ID for duplicates in its JMS store. If a duplicate is found, it sends an acknowledgment back to the sender and rolls back the transaction. No further actions occur.
3. If a duplicate isn't found, it saves the message ID in the JMS store.
4. The web service operation is invoked.
5. An acknowledgment is sent back to the sender's runtime.
6. The transaction is committed.

The backend component that implements the web service operation can roll back the receiver's transaction. A rollback forces the sender's runtime to redeliver the SOAP message. It also ensures that the sender application is aware that the operation was not invoked. Note that ordinary application exceptions do not cause a rollback. For example, if a Java backend throws an exception, or if an EJB throws an application exception, the transaction isn't rolled back. Instead, the Java class or EJB must explicitly roll back the existing transaction context. An EJB can also throw a system exception (e.g., RemoteException) to cause a rollback. Finally, the transaction is rolled back if the WebLogic instance hosting the web service crashes.

Implementing Reliable Web Service Backends

If you implement the reliable web service with a Java backend, you must use the standard JTA to roll back the receiver's transaction context, as shown here:

```
try {
  //get the transaction context at the receiver's end
  tx = (UserTransaction)
  ctx.lookup("javax.transaction.UserTransaction");
  //...
}
catch (Exception e) {
  //something went wrong
  tx.rollback();
}
```

If you implement a web service using a stateless session EJB backend, you must remember the following:

- The stateless session EJB must use container-managed transactions and not bean-managed transactions. Moreover, you should set the transaction attribute for the EJB method that implements the web service operation to either Required, Supports, or Mandatory.

- The stateless session EJB can explicitly roll back the transaction either by invoking the `EJBContext.setRollbackOnly( )` method or by throwing a system exception such as `RemoteException`.

The rest of the section looks at how to set up the WebLogic instances to use the reliable transport, configure the JMS stores, and finally write the sender application.

Building the sender and receiver

To enable reliable messaging at the web service's end, use the servicegen Ant task to build the web service, but also include the reliability subelement:

```
<servicegen
    destEar="../out/myReliableEar" contextURI="reliableService"
    warName="myWar">
    <service
      javaClassComponents="com.oreilly.wlguide.webservices.reliable.Simple"
      targetNamespace="${namespace}" serviceName="Simple" serviceURI="/Simple"
      generateTypes="True" protocol="http"expandMethods="True">
      <reliability duplicateElimination="True" persistDuration="120"/>
    </service>
</servicegen>
```

The reliability element has two optional attributes:

duplicateElimination
Use this attribute to determine whether the service should ignore duplicate invocations by keeping track of the message IDs. If you set this attribute to false, the message IDs are not recorded and you run the risk of an operation being invoked more than once.

persistDuration
Use this attribute to set the minimum number of seconds that the receiver should persist the history of a reliable SOAP message. It defaults to 60000.

If you specify the reliability subelement within the servicegen task, each operation that returns void will be configured for reliable invocations. If you want only specific operations to be reliably invoked, you must manually edit the *web-services.xml* descriptor. For example, here is an excerpt that highlights this:

```
<!-- configure a reliable operation -->
<operation name="reliableOperation" method="reliableOperation(java.lang.String)"
           component="jcComp0">
    <params> <!-- As usual --> </params>
    <reliable-delivery persist-duration="120" duplicate-elimination="true"/>
</operation>
```

The sender must invoke the reliable operation asynchronously, so remember to set the generateAsyncMethods attribute to true when employing clientgen to create the client JAR.

Configuring the servers

Both servers participating in reliable SOAP messaging must be configured with a JMS store. In other words, you must configure the web service system on both servers to use a JMS store. You can do this by selecting the server from the Administration Console and then navigating to the Services/Web Services tab. Use the drop-down list in the Store attribute to select the JMS store to be used.

For the sender, you also can set the Retry Count and Retry Interval attributes. The retry count determines the maximum number of times a sender should try to deliver an unacknowledged message, while the retry interval determines the minimum duration (in seconds) to wait between attempting to redeliver. For the receiver, you can set the Default Time To Live attribute, which determines the duration (in seconds) that a receiver should store the history of the message. The Default Time To Live setting determines how long the sender's runtime will attempt to resend a message with the same message ID. If the sender's runtime cannot send a message successfully before the Default Time To Live duration, it reports a delivery failure.

The persist-duration attribute that you specify for the reliable-delivery element when using servicegen can be set on a per-operation basis and corresponds to the time-to-live attribute that you can set for the server. The server setting defines the default value and always should be larger than the duration specified for any operation.

Writing the receiver

An application can invoke an operation in the standard way, without using the reliable delivery mechanism. If you want the benefit of a reliable invocation, however, the sender also must supply an AsyncInfo object to the operation. Here is an example:

```
AsyncInfo asyncInfo = new AsyncInfo( );
asyncInfo.setReliableDelivery(true);
FutureResult fr = port.startReliableOperation("hello World", asyncInfo);
port.endReliableOperation(fr);
```

Except for the call to setReliableDelivery( ), the rest of the code is identical to how you would create asynchronous clients. Because this is an asynchronous client, you could either poll for a return or register a ResultListener object.

SOAP Message Handlers

As depicted earlier in Figure 19-2, you may associate a chain of SOAP message handlers with a web service operation. SOAP message handlers are a part of the JAX-RPC standard. A SOAP message handler can be tied to a web service endpoint either on the client side or on the server side. It is used simply to provide additional logic for handling the SOAP messages. Each SOAP handler in the chain intercepts the request and response SOAP messages, and processes the SOAP message before passing it on to the next member in the chain. Each message handler has access to the

SOAP message and can transform the incoming request or outgoing response before passing it on to the next SOAP handler. For this reason, SOAP handlers are best suited to implement a number of useful add-on features such as logging, encryption and decryption, and caching.

The rest of this section describes how to write and deploy SOAP message handlers, and how to associate a chain of SOAP handlers with operations of WebLogic web services. If you need to create message handlers that process SOAP messages on the client side, you should refer to the JAX-RPC specification for more information.

Life Cycle of a SOAP Handler

Every SOAP handler implements the javax.xml.rpc.handler.Handler interface. Example 19-13 describes the methods exposed by the Handler interface.

Example 19-13. The javax.xml.rpc.handler.Handler interface

```
package javax.xml.rpc.handler;
public interface Handler {
   public boolean handleRequest(MessageContext ctx);
   public boolean handleResponse(MessageContext ctx);
   public boolean handleFault(MessageContext ctx);
   public void init(HandlerInfo hi);
   public void destory();
   public QName [] getHeaders();
}
```

WebLogic invokes the init( ) method to create an instance of the Handler object, and invokes the destroy( ) method when it determines that the SOAP handler is no longer needed. These methods give you the opportunity to acquire and release any resources needed by the Handler object. The init( ) method is passed a HandlerInfo object, which lets you access any information about the SOAP handler—in particular, any initialization parameters configured in the *web-services.xml* descriptor file. In fact, you should invoke the HandlerInfo.getHandlerConfig( ) method to obtain a Map object that holds a list of name-value pairs, one for each of the initialization parameters. These parameters are quite useful for several things—for instance, to enable debugging, or perhaps to specify the name of the web service with which the SOAP handler is going to be associated (there is no other way of accessing this information).

The handleRequest( ) method is invoked to intercept incoming SOAP requests before they are processed by the backend component, and the handleResponse( ) method is invoked to intercept outgoing SOAP responses before they are delivered back to the client. If a single SOAP handler implements both the handleRequest( ) and handleResponse( ) methods, it intercepts both incoming and outgoing SOAP messages. The handleFault( ) method is invoked when WebLogic needs to process any SOAP faults generated by the handleRequest( ) or handleResponse( ) methods, or even by the backend component. These methods also have access to a

MessageContext object that models the message context in which the SOAP handler has been invoked. Typically, you would use the SOAPMessageContext subinterface to access or update the contents of the SOAP message. Remember, a SOAP handler is free to update the contents of the incoming SOAP request or the outgoing SOAP response before it forwards the message to the next SOAP handler in the chain.

Once the handleRequest() method has processed the incoming SOAP request, it can determine how the SOAP message is subsequently handled in the following ways:

- If the method returns true, the next handler in the chain is invoked. If there are no more handlers in the chain, depending on how the web service operation has been designed WebLogic either invokes the backend component, passing it the final SOAP request, or sends the SOAP message through the handlers in the response chain by invoking the handleResponse() method of the last handler in the chain.

- If the method returns false, WebLogic aborts the remaining handlers in the request chain. It also means that any backend component will not be executed for this particular invocation of the web service operation. Instead, the SOAP message is sent through to the handlers in the response chain, by first invoking the handleResponse() method on the current Handler object.

- If the method throws a javax.xml.rpc.soap.SOAPFaultException to indicate a SOAP fault, WebLogic intercepts this exception, blocks the execution of the rest of the handler chain, and instead invokes the handleFault() method.

- If the method throws a javax.xml.rpc.JAXRPCException to indicate runtime errors, WebLogic handles the exception in the same way as a SOAP fault, except that it also logs the exception to the server's log file before invoking the handleFault() method.

In the same way, once the handleResponse() method has processed the outgoing SOAP response, it can determine how the SOAP message is subsequently handled in the following ways:

- If the method returns true, the next Handler object in the chain is invoked. If there are no more handlers in the chain, the final SOAP message response is sent back to the client.

- If the method returns false, the remaining handlers in the response chain are skipped (for this particular invocation of the web service operation), and the current SOAP message is sent back to the client.

- If the method throws a javax.xml.rpc.JAXRPCException, WebLogic intercepts this exception, blocks the execution of the remaining handlers in the chain, and instead invokes the handleFault() method after logging the exception.

Remember, the handleFault() method is used to handle any SOAP faults generated during the processing of the SOAP message request/response. The handleFault() methods can be invoked in a chain: if the handleFault() method on a Handler object returns `true`, the `handleFault()` method of the next handler in the chain is invoked. Otherwise, the rest of the chain is skipped.

WebLogic also provides a convenient abstract base class that lets you easily create your own handlers: `weblogic.webservices.GenericHandler`. Example 19-14 shows how to construct a simple handler in this way.

Example 19-14. Using the GenericHandler interface

```
public class MyHandler extends GenericHandler {
  public boolean handleResponse(MessageContext ctx) {
    SOAPMessageContext sMsgCtx = (SOAPMessageContext) ctx;
    SOAPMessage msg = sMsgCtx.getMessage();
    SOAPPart sp = msg.getSOAPPart();
    try {
      SOAPEnvelope se = sp.getEnvelope();
      SOAPHeader sh = se.getHeader();
      sh.addChildElement("TheStorkBroughtMe");
    } catch (SOAPException e) {
      e.printStackTrace();
    }
    return true;
  }
}
```

Note how the `handleResponse()` method uses the `SOAPMessage` class. This class is part of the SOAP with Attachments API for Java 1.1 (SAAJ) specification, and gives you access to all parts of the SOAP message. In this case, we used it simply to add a child element to the SOAP header of the response.

Configuring a Handler Chain

A *handler chain* represents an ordered group of SOAP message handlers. Any SOAP handler that needs to participate in a web service must be defined in the *web-services. xml* descriptor file. In fact, the descriptor file also lets you configure the sequence in which the SOAP handlers are invoked. The following excerpt from the *web-services. xml* descriptor shows how to declare a chain of SOAP message handlers:

```
<!-- portion from the web-services.xml descriptor -->
<web-services>
  <handler-chains>
    <handler-chain name="myChain">
      <handler class-name="a.b.c.H1">
        <init-params>
          <init-param name="webservicename" value="myWebService"/>
        </init-params>
      </handler>
      <handler class-name="a.b.c.H2"/>
      <handler class-name="a.b.c.H3"/>
    </handler-chain>
  </handler-chains>
  <!-- ... -->
</web-services>
```

Notice how we've defined an initialization parameter for the first handler in the chain. The order in which the handlers are defined is very important because it determines the sequence in which the handlers are invoked; that order is detailed here:

1. The `handleRequest( )` methods of all SOAP handlers in the chain are invoked in the order in which they're defined. In case of the preceding SOAP handler chain, the handlers will be invoked in the following sequence:

   ```
   H1.handleRequest( )
   H2.handleRequest( )
   H3.handleRequest( )
   ```

2. Once the `handleRequest( )` method of the last `Handler` object in the chain has completed, WebLogic then invokes the backend component that implements the web service. This occurs only if a backend component has been configured for the web service operation.

3. When the backend component has finished processing, the `handleResponse( )` method of all SOAP handlers in the chain are invoked, this time in the reverse order in which they're defined. In case of the preceding SOAP handlers, the response chain will be invoked in the following order:

   ```
   H3.handleResponse( )
   H2.handleResponse( )
   H1.handleResponse( )
   ```

4. Once the `handleResponse( )` method of the first `Handler` object in the chain has completed, the final SOAP message then is sent back to the client.

Creating and Registering SOAP Handlers

A SOAP message handler can either directly implement the Handler interface or can extend the abstract class `GenericHandler` provided by WebLogic. This class offers a simple and sensible implementation of the `Handler` interface and maintains a reference to the `HandlerInfo` object passed during the initialization of the `Handler` object. The following example shows how a SOAP message handler can access the SOAP message and its headers:

```
public class MyHandler extends weblogic.webservice.GenericHandler {
    public boolean handleRequest(MessageContext ctx) {
        System.err.println("In MyHandler.handleRequest( )");

        // type cast MessageContext to access the SOAP message
        SOAPMessageContext sMsgCtx = (SOAPMessageContext) ctx;
        SOAPMessage msg = sMsgCtx.getMessage( );
        SOAPPart sp = msg.getSOAPPart( );
        SOAPEnvelope se = sp.getEnvelope( );
        SOAPHeader sh = se.getHeader( );
        // ...
        return true;
    }
    public boolean handleResponse(MessageContext ctx) {
```

```
                System.err.println("In MyHandler.handleResponse( )");
                return true;
        }
    }
```

Once you create the SOAP message handler, you must modify the *web-services.xml* descriptor file in order to register the handler. In WebLogic 8.1, you simply need to modify the servicegen Ant task as follows:

```
<servicegen destEar="../out/myHANDLEREar" contextURI="handlerService"
            warName="myWar">
    <service javaClassComponents="com.oreilly.wlguide.webservices.handler.Simple"
            serviceName="Simple" serviceURI="/Simple" targetNamespace="${namespace}"
            generateTypes="True" protocol="http" expandMethods="True">
        <handlerChain name="myChain"
                handlers="com.oreilly.wlguide.webservices.handler.MyHandler"/>
    </service>
</servicegen>
```

The handlers attribute can take a comma-separated list of fully qualified class names. When you update the servicegen task in this way, every operation will be associated with the handler chain. If you want to be more selective, you have to edit the *web-services.xml* by hand. Likewise, if you are using WebLogic 7.0, you must edit the *web-services.xml* descriptor manually, as WebLogic 7.0's servicegen Ant task doesn't support handler chains. In these cases, you will need to edit the descriptor file to look something like this:

```
<web-services>
    <handler-chains>
        <handler-chain name="myChain">
            <handler class-name =
                "com.oreilly.wlguide.webservices.handler.MyHandler" />
            <!-- define other handlers in the chain -->
        </handler-chain>
        <!-- other handler chains can be defined here -->
    </handler-chains>
</web-services>
```

Only after you've registered the handler chain can you bind it to a web service operation. For this, you need to modify the particular operation element in the *web-services.xml* descriptor file to which the handler chain will be linked. Here you can see how the handler-chain attribute allows you to associate the handler chain myChain with the makeUpper operation defined earlier:

```
<operation  method="makeUpper(java.lang.String)"  component="jcComp0"
        name="makeUpper"  handler-chain="myChain">
    <!-- ... -->
</operation>
```

Once you've deployed the web service with these changes to the descriptor file, any SOAP requests and responses for the makeUpper operation will pass through the configured handler chain (myChain).

Using only SOAP handlers to implement an operation

Typically, a web service operation is implemented by a backend component. However, a web service operation also may be implemented through a handler chain alone, without the aid of any backend component. This means a SOAP message is processed by the handleRequest( ) methods of each handler in the chain, and then by the handleResponse( ) methods of each handler in the chain, but in reverse order. A web service operation implemented solely through a chain of SOAP message handlers can be configured as follows:

```
<operation name="myChainService" handler-chain="myChain">
  <!-- ... -->
</operation>
```

In this case, you can completely ignore the component and method attributes for the web service operation.

Security

There are three aspects to securing WebLogic web services:

Access control security
> You can secure the entire web service by restricting access to the URLs that invoke the web service (or its WSDL). This approach automatically secures any backend components used to implement the web service. Alternatively, you can secure the individual components that make up the web service: the web application that hosts the *web-services.xml* descriptor file, the stateless session EJBs, a subset of the methods of the EJB, and so on. You also can prevent access to the home page and WSDL, which is by default publicly accessible.

Connection level security
> You can modify the *web-services.xml* descriptor file to indicate that clients can invoke the web services only over HTTPS. Moreover, if the client authenticates itself using SSL, you need to configure SSL security for WebLogic as well.

Message security
> WebLogic 8.1 lets you use a mixture of digital signing, data encryption, and security token propagation to provide you with message integrity and confidentiality.

Like other J2EE components, WebLogic allows you to assign a security policy to a web service component. These policies allow WebLogic to enforce authorization checks on clients who invoke the web service. Because a web service relies on multiple backend components for its implementation, you can independently secure the web service backends as well. Configuring SSL security for a web service is equally easy—most of the work lies in building clients that can invoke web services over SSL. WebLogic 8.1 provides SOAP message data encryption and signing, based on OASIS' draft Web Services Security Core Specification. As this is not yet an OASIS standard, WebLogic's implementation is subject to change.

Access Control

WebLogic's web services are packaged into standard J2EE enterprise applications. This means that you can secure a web service with access control settings on the various J2EE components that constitute the web service. WebLogic lets you control access to a web service in the following ways:

- You can assign a security policy to a web service component (i.e., the web application that hosts the web service), which permits access to only the authorized users, groups, or roles.

- You can restrict access to the web service URL by configuring additional security constraints on the URL in the web application's deployment descriptors. You also may set up separate access restrictions on the URL for obtaining the WSDL for the web service.

- You can assign a security policy to the backend components used to implement the web service. Unfortunately, this protection can be enforced only for stateless session EJBs that implement the web service. If a Java class or a JMS destination is used to implement the web service, WebLogic doesn't provide any built-in mechanisms to secure the backend. Your only recourse is to either programmatically secure the backend Java class or JMS listener or persist with securing the web service URL.

- You can prevent the web service home page and WSDL data from being generated.

Let's take a closer look at these various mechanisms for securing access to a web service.

Assigning a security policy to the web service

You can use the Administration Console to assign a security policy to a deployed web service component—i.e., a web application that hosts one or more web services. This policy determines the set of users, groups, and roles that are authorized to access the web service. Of course, this also means that the client needs to authenticate itself when interacting with the web service. Only then can WebLogic enforce these authorization checks on the web service.

In order to view or modify the security policy assigned to a web service, you need to right-click the web service component in the left pane of the Administration Console and select the Define Security Policy option from the pop-up menu. If you select "Define policies and roles for individual services" instead, you will be able to set a role or policy for each individual operation within a selected service. Chapter 17 provides more information on how to apply security policies to WebLogic resources.

Securing the web service URL

Clients need a URL to access the web service. For instance, our Simple web service is available via the URL *http://10.0.10.10:8001/myWar/Simple*. Similarly, the WSDL for the web service is available via *http://10.0.10.10:8001/myWar/Simple?WSDL*. This means that you could secure access to the entire web service and its operations by simply restricting access to the web service URL. To set up this access control, you need to configure a security constraint over the web service URL by modifying the deployment descriptors of the web application that hosts the *web-services.xml* descriptor file.

Chapter 2 provides more details on how to set up security constraints on a web resource collection. Because you need to enforce access control over the web service URL itself, you must restrict all GET and POST requests to URLs that match the */Simple/** pattern:

```
<security-constraint>
  <web-resource-collection>
    <web-resource-name>Simple Web Service</web-resource-name>
    <url-pattern>Simple/*</url-pattern>
    <http-method>POST</http-method>
    <http-method>GET</http-method>
  </web-resource-collection>
  <!-- ... -->
</security-constraint>
```

This ensures that any client that attempts to invoke the protected web service or access the WSDL that describes the web service must authenticate itself. Later in this chapter, we examine how the client can authenticate itself when invoking an operation on a web service protected in this way.

Securing a stateless session EJB and its methods

If a stateless session EJB serves as the backend component for a web service, you can use the EJB's deployment descriptors to restrict access to the EJB methods. Chapter 17 explains how you can use the assembly-descriptor element in the *ejb-jar. xml* descriptor file to associate security roles with individual EJB methods, and the security-role-assignment element in the *weblogic-ejb-jar.xml* descriptor file to list WebLogic users and groups that belong to the role. You can use this to restrict access to individual operations of the web service by applying security constraints on the EJB methods that implement the operations. Other clients can continue to access the web application, the WSDL, and the home page for the web service.

Any unauthorized client that attempts to invoke an operation implemented by a method on a protected stateless session EJB will be denied access:

```
java.rmi.RemoteException: SOAP Fault:javax.xml.rpc.soap.SOAPFaultException:
Security Violation: User: '<anonymous>' has insufficient permission to access EJB:
type=<ejb>, application=_appsdir_myEarEJB_dir, module=webserviceEJB.jar, ejb=Case,
method=makeUpper, methodInterface=Remote, signature={java.lang.String}.;
```

Removing access to the home page and WSDL

You can prevent the home page and WSDL of a web service from being exposed by editing the *web-services.xml* descriptor file. Simply add an exposeWSDL or exposeHomePage attribute, as shown in the following example:

```
<web-service protocol="http" name="SimplePOJO" style="rpc" uri="/SimplePOJO"
             targetNamespace="http://www.oreilly.com/webservices/Simple"
             exposeWSDL="False"
             exposeHomePage="False">
   <!-- -->
</web-service>
```

Authenticating client access to a protected web service

Once you've restricted the access to a web service, the client can no longer anonymously invoke a web service operation over plain HTTP. The client now needs to authenticate itself as well. For instance, if you secure the URL for the Simple web service and then point your browser to the home page for the web service, you will be greeted with an HTTP 401 (Unauthorized) response. Instead, you need to specify a modified web service URL that includes the username and password of an authorized WebLogic user:

```
http://username:password@10.0.10.10:8001/myService/Simple
```

Similarly, if you've configured access restrictions over the URL for obtaining the WSDL for the web service, again you need to specify the login credentials of a WebLogic user authorized to view the WSDL:

```
http://joebloggs:pssst123@10.0.10.10:8001/myService/Simple?WSDL
```

For a static client that needs to authenticate itself when invoking an operation on a secure web service, the only change that's required is how the client creates an instance of the SimplePort stub implementation:

```
Simple ws = new Simple_Impl("http://10.0.10.10:8001/myService/Simple?WSDL");
SimplePort port = ws.getSimplePort(username, password);
String returnVal = port.makeUpper("Hello There");
```

Here, we've supplied the username and password of an authorized WebLogic user to the web service–specific implementation of the getSimplePort( ) method. Remember, if you've restricted access to the web service URL, you must also modify the URL for the WSDL to include the user's login credentials. Once the client has authenticated successfully, WebLogic is able to enforce any authorization checks placed on the web service, the URLs, or even the backend stateless session EJBs.

In fact, the standard JAX-RPC approach for a client that invokes a secure web service and needs to authenticate itself is to specify values for two authentication properties:

- javax.xml.rpc.security.auth.username
- javax.xml.rpc.security.auth.password

The client JAR generated by WebLogic for a particular web service already contains the stub classes that automatically set these login credentials when the Java client invokes the get*Service*Port( ) method. The following example shows how a JAX-RPC client would submit its credentials before invoking a web service:

```
SimpleStub stub = // ... get the stub;
stub._setProperty("javax.xml.rpc.security.auth.username", "juliet");
stub._setProperty("javax.xml.rpc.security.auth.password", "mypassword");
String returnVal = stub.makeUpper("lower case string!");
```

Using SSL

WebLogic lets you configure a web service so that it's accessible only through the HTTPS protocol, in which case plain HTTP clients will not be able to access the service. This connection-level security provides you with point-to-point security, which is securing communication between two endpoints. If your SOAP messages are going to pass through unsecured intermediaries, such as caches, you may want to also use the more advanced end-to-end security measures, such as SOAP message encryption and digital signing.

To force the use of HTTPS, modify the *web-services.xml* descriptor file by specifying a protocol attribute for the web-service element:

```
<web-service protocol="https" name="Simple" uri="/Simple"
             targetNamespace="http://www.oreilly.com/" style="rpc">
   <!-- the rest unchanged -->
</web-service>
```

WebLogic's servicegen task also can let you adjust the protocol constraint for a web service, by simply adding a protocol attribute as follows:

```
<servicegen destEar="myEar.ear" warName="myWar.war">
  <service
      javaClassComponents="com.oreilly.wlguide.webservices.simple.Simple"
      targetNamespace="${namespace}"
      serviceName="Simple"
      protocol="https"
      serviceURI="/Simple"
      expandMethods="True">
  </service>
  <classpath>
    <pathelement path="${build}"/>
  </classpath>
</servicegen>
```

When you configure a web service in this way, clients *must* create HTTPS connections when invoking a web service operation. Without the HTTPS protocol constraint, clients are free to create either HTTP or HTTPS connections when invoking the web service. Of course, HTTPS connections may be used only if you've properly configured SSL at the server's end. For a web service that accepts only HTTPS connections, a client must use SSL to access the web service operations.

Client access using WebLogic's SSL

WebLogic provides a client runtime JAR, *webserviceclient+ssl.jar*, which includes the standard JAX-RPC runtime classes and the SSL implementation classes. Thus, in order to configure a client application to use WebLogic's SSL implementation, you need to make a note of the following issues:

- Ensure that the client library *webserviceclient+ssl.jar* (and not *webserviceclient. jar*) is included in the classpath before running the client application.
- Specify the name of the file that contains the trusted CA certificates by setting the -Dtrustedfile=filename system property from the command line.
- Indicate the home directory of your BEA installation (the directory that holds the license file). The -Dbea.home=c:\bea_home system property allows you to configure the BEA home directory from the command line.
- Configure the client to use WebLogic's SSL implementation by setting the -Djava.protocol.handler.pkgs=com.certicom.net.ssl system property from the command line.
- During development stages, it is sometimes useful to disable strict validation of certificates. You can configure this by setting the -Dweblogic.webservice.client. ssl.strictcertchecking=false system property from the command line.

The following example summarizes these points and shows how you would run a client that needs to interact with HTTPS-protected web services:

```
java
    -classpath %WL_HOME%\server\lib\webserviceclient+ssl.jar;%CLASSPATH% \
    -Dbea.home=c:\bea_home \
    -Djava.protocol.handler.pkgs=com.certicom.net.ssl \
    -Dweblogic.webservice.client.ssl.strictcertchecking=false \
    oreilly.wlguide.webservices.secure.client.MyApp
```

Using a proxy server

If the client sits behind a firewall and must use a proxy server to invoke the web service, it can specify the host and port of the proxy server using the following two system properties:

```
java -Dweblogic.webservice.transport.https.proxy.host=10.0.0.1  \
    -Dweblogic.webservice.transport.https.proxy.port=4567 \
    ...
```

By specifying these two system properties, the client can make HTTPS connections to the web service via the configured proxy server.

Configuring SSL programmatically

While you can configure a client to use WebLogic's SSL implementation through the command-line options, you also can achieve the same results programmatically by using the weblogic.webservice.client.WLSSLAdapter class. The following code sample shows how to modify the client-side code so that it can use WebLogic's SSL implementation when invoking an SSL-protected web service:

```
System.setProperty("java.protocol.handler.pkgs", "com.certicom.net.ssl");
SSLAdapterFactory adapterFactory = SSLAdapterFactory.getDefaultFactory();
WLSSLAdapter adapter = (WLSSLAdapter) adapterFactory.getSSLAdapter();
adapter.setStrictChecking(false);                    //optional
adapter.setTrustedCertificatesFile("trusted-ca.pem");
adapterFactory.setDefaultAdapter(adapter);
adapterFactory.setUseDefaultAdapter(true);
Simple ws = new Simple_Impl(argv[0]);
SimplePort port = ws.getSimplePort("system", "12341234");
String returnVal = port.makeUpper("Hello There");
// ...
```

If the client uses the generic JAX-RPC interfaces, it also can choose WebLogic's SSL adapter for a particular web service invocation:

```
ServiceFactory factory = ServiceFactory.newInstance();
Service service = factory.createService(serviceName);
Call call = service.createCall();
call.setProperty("weblogic.webservice.client.ssladapter", adapter);
String result = (String) call.invoke( new Object[]{ "SOMEPARAM" } );
```

If the client statically invokes a web service using the Stub interface, it also needs to set the following property:

```
((javax.xml.rpc.Stub)stubClass)._setProperty(
                    "weblogic.webservice.client.ssladapter", adapterInstance);
```

Using two-way SSL

If the WebLogic server hosting the web service is configured for two-way SSL, you will need to modify your client to load its identity, much like that described in Chapter 16. In this case, we need to modify our client code like this:

```
SSLAdapterFactory adapterFactory = SSLAdapterFactory.getDefaultFactory();
WLSSLAdapter adapter = (WLSSLAdapter) adapterFactory.getSSLAdapter();
adapter.setStrictChecking(false);
adapter.setTrustedCertificatesFile("x:/server/lib/cacerts");
FileInputStream fs = new FileInputStream(CERT_CERTCHAINFILE);
adapter.loadLocalIdentity(fs, CERT_KEYPASSWORD.toCharArray());
adapterFactory.setDefaultAdapter(adapter);
adapterFactory.setUseDefaultAdapter(true);
```

The loadLocalIdentity() method expects a FileInputStream that references an encoded certificate chain. You can create such a certificate chain by simply appending the *mycertfile.pem* and *mykeyfile.pem* (in that order) generated in Chapter 16.

Rolling your own SSL implementation

In the previous examples, we saw how the client uses an instance of WebLogic's SSLAdapterFactory to manufacture an object that implements the SSLAdapter interface—in this case, a WLSSLAdapter class provided by WebLogic:

```
import weblogic.webservice.client.WLSSLAdapter;
import weblogic.webservice.client.SSLAdapterFactory;
//...
SSLAdapterFactory adapterFactory = SSLAdapterFactory.getDefaultFactory();
WLSSLAdapter adapter = (WLSSLAdapter) adapterFactory.getSSLAdapter();
```

It is this adapter class that enables the client to interact with that SSL-protected web service. Thus, in order to use a custom SSL implementation, you need to first create your own SSL adapter class. Example 19-15 provides a sample adapter class that implements the SSLAdapter interface while relying on the standard JSSE implementation of SSL.

Example 19-15. Custom SSL adapter class

```
import java.net.URL;
import java.net.Socket;
import java.net.URLConnection;
import java.io.IOException;
public class JSSEAdapter implements weblogic.webservice.client.SSLAdapter {
  // Use Java's standard SSL socket factory
  javax.net.SocketFactory factory = javax.net.ssl.SSLSocketFactory.getDefault();

  // Use Java's implementation to return an SSL connection to the
  // server hosting the web service
  public Socket createSocket(String host, int port) throws IOException  {
    return factory.createSocket(host, port);
  }
  // Assumes that you have set the java.protocol.handler.pkgs property
  public URLConnection openConnection(URL url) throws IOException {
    return url.openConnection();
  }
  public void setSocketFactory(javax.net.ssl.SSLSocketFactory factory) {
    this.factory = factory;
  }
  public javax.net.ssl.SSLSocketFactory getSocketFactory() {
    return (javax.net.ssl.SSLSocketFactory) factory;
  }
}
```

A client then can create an instance of this custom SSL adapter in two ways:

- You can use the default SSL adapter factory and simply instruct the client to use the custom adapter class you've created:

  ```
  java  -Dweblogic.webservice.client.ssl.adapterclass=
        oreilly.wlguide.webservice.client.JSSEAdapter
     ...
        oreilly.wlguide.webservices.client.MyApp
  ```

- You can create your own SSL adapter factory that manufactures and configures an instance of the custom SSL adapter class. In order to use a custom SSL adapter factory, you must write a class that extends:

  ```
  weblogic.webservice.client.SSLAdapterFactor
  ```

In particular, you must override the method that creates a new SSL adapter instance:

```
public SSLAdapter createSSLAdapter();
```

The client then needs to create an instance of the custom SSL adapter factory and set it as the default using the following method:

```
SSLAdapterFactory.setDefaultFactory(factory);
```

Subsequently, the client can use this default adapter factory to manufacture an instance of the custom SSL adapter:

```
SSLAdapterFactory myfactory = SSLAdapterFactory.getDefaultFactory();
JSSEAdapter adapter = (JSSEAdapter) myfactory.getSSLAdapter();
```

SOAP Message Security

WebLogic's implementation of SOAP message security is based on the OASIS draft specification WSS: SOAP Message Security, which is based on the WS-Security draft specification. These specifications aim to secure SOAP message exchanges through a flexible set of mechanisms based on security token propagation, message integrity, and message confidentiality.

Architecture

WebLogic augments three aspects of web services in order to implement SOAP message security:

WSDL

WebLogic augments the WSDL of a web service to indicate which operations should be secured and how they should be secured. As usual, you can either use the servicegen Ant task or modify the *web-services.xml* descriptor file to effect these changes. Because there is no standard specification, WebLogic's changes to the WSDL are necessarily proprietary.

Client runtime

The client runtime is augmented with WebLogic's implementation of SOAP message security. It also requires access to a key file and a certificate file, which are used to sign outgoing messages. The runtime performs any encryption and signature tasks just before the SOAP message is sent to the server, after all of the client handlers are executed.

Server runtime

The server runtime also is augmented with WebLogic's implementation of SOAP message security. The runtime performs any encryption and signature tasks just after receiving the SOAP message, before passing it on to the web service. It requires *two* key/certificate pairs—one for encrypting and one for signing.

When a client invokes a web service operation, it reads the WSDL of the service. If the service has added SOAP message security, the WSDL will reflect this. For example, the WSDL will contain the server's public certificate for encrypting any messages that are sent to it! When such an operation is invoked, certificates, signatures, and tokens are sent back and forth many times. Don't be overawed by the following description because most of these actions occur transparently to the client and web service implementation. When a client invokes a web service operation that needs additional message security, the following actions occur before the SOAP message is actually sent:

1. The client generates its SOAP message in the usual fashion, and then adds a Security element to the header (in a different namespace), which holds the information about the security measures applied to the SOAP message.

2. If a user token is supplied, this also is embedded in the Security element.

3. If the SOAP message must be signed, the client runtime generates a signature using its own private key and adds this to the Security element. The client also adds its own public certificate, as the server will use this later to verify the signature.

4. If the SOAP message needs to be encrypted, the client runtime uses the server's public key that was grabbed from the encryption certificate embedded in the WSDL to encrypt the relevant parts of the message. It then records in the Security element the fact that encryption has taken place.

When the server runtime receives a SOAP message and finds that additional security information has been included in the SOAP message, it performs the following actions:

1. If the SOAP message was encrypted, it decrypts the message using its encryption private key.

2. If the SOAP message was signed, it extracts the client's certificate and the signature from the Security element in the header and verifies the signature. At this point, WebLogic also asserts the identity of the client certificate to ensure that it maps to a valid WebLogic user.

3. It extracts the username token from the Security header, if it is present. It also verifies the associated password and ensures that the web service operation is invoked using this username and password.

4. The Security element then is removed from the SOAP message, and the client's certificate is saved in case any responses need to be encrypted. The SOAP message then is passed on to the web service runtime system, and the operation is invoked.

Note that WebLogic asserts the identity of the client certificate so that it doesn't accept invocations from just any client. Only those clients with certificates that can be validated in this way may invoke the operations of the web service. So, for a client to use WebLogic's SOAP message security, it must possess a valid public certificate and WebLogic must have an Identity Assertion Provider installed.

The username and password supplied by the client in the username token help establish the identity of the WebLogic user for executing the web service operation.

When WebLogic sends a SOAP response, the same actions occur, but in reverse order:

1. It encrypts the SOAP message response using the client's certificate.
2. It signs the message using its own signature key and certificate, and it embeds its public certificate in the response.
3. It includes a username token in the SOAP response, if this is specified in the *web-services.xml* descriptor. This step is omitted by default.

When a client runtime receives a message from the web service, the following sequence of actions take place:

1. If the message is encrypted, it decrypts the message using its private key. Recall how WebLogic saves the client's public key that was sent in the original request and uses it to encrypt the response.
2. If the message is signed, it checks the signature of the message using the server's public signature certificate that was embedded in the SOAP message.

The following sections examine how to set up SOAP message security and then put it all into action. For the sake of the discussion, we assume that you have an existing web service—say, the Simple web service described earlier in Example 19-1—that needs to be secured through username tokens, encryption, and signing. Although you also can choose which parts of the SOAP message ought to be encrypted instead of just the entire body, we will not consider this here because it involves lengthy changes to the *web-services.xml* descriptor file.

Configuring SOAP message security

To enable SOAP message security for a web service, you need to first add a security element to the servicegen task used to build the web service, as shown in Example 19-16.

Example 19-16. Using the servicegen task to enforce SOAP message security

```
<servicegen destEar="../out/mySECURESOAPEar" contextURI="secureSOAPService"
        warName="myWar">
  <service targetNamespace="${namespace}"
          javaClassComponents="com.oreilly.wlguide.webservices.secureSOAP.Simple"
          serviceName="Simple" serviceURI="/Simple"
          generateTypes="True" protocol="http" expandMethods="True">
    <security signKeyName="signKeyAlias" signKeyPass="mypassword"
            encryptKeyName="encryptKeyAlias" encryptKeyPass="mypassword"
            enablePasswordAuth="True" />
  </service>
</servicegen>
```

By supplying the `signKeyName` and `signKeyPass` attributes, you enable the signing mechanism on outgoing SOAP messages. Likewise, by supplying the `encryptKeyName` and `encryptKeyPass` attributes, you enable the encryption of the body of the SOAP messages. The values of these attributes determine the aliases and passwords of the key and certificate pairs for signing and encryption. We also have set the `enablePasswordAuth` attribute to `true`, to force any client of the web service to supply a username token.

The security subelement here ensures that SOAP message security is enabled on all operations of the web service. In addition, it secures (encrypts and signs) the entire SOAP message body. If you want to secure only a subset of operations, or only parts of the message body, you must manually edit the *web-services.xml* descriptor file.

Creating the certificates

The server needs two key pairs. One is used for digitally signing a SOAP message, and another for encrypting the message. WebLogic's current SSL implementation for web services requires that the key length of certificates used for encrypting and signing be at least 1024. In this case, we will use the keytool to create the two keys referenced in Example 19-16. Refer to Chapter 16 to see how you can configure WebLogic to use this store as its identity store. We simply will add the two certificates to a keystore called *myIdentityStore.jks* developed in that chapter. The following commands create and store the key pairs:

```
keytool -genkey -keysize 1024 -keyalg RSA -dname "cn=system, ou=OR, o=UH, c=US"
        -alias encryptKeyAlias -keypass mypassword -keystore myidentitystore.jks
        -storepass mykeystorepass
keytool -selfcert -keystore myidentitystore.jks  -alias encryptKeyAlias
        -storepass mykeystorepass -keypass mypassword
keytool -genkey -keysize 1024 -keyalg RSA -dname "cn=system, ou=OR, o=UH, c=US"
        -alias signKeyAlias -keypass mypassword -keystore myidentitystore.jks
        -storepass mykeystorepass
keytool -selfcert -keystore myidentitystore.jks  -alias signKeyAlias
        -storepass mykeystorepass -keypass mypassword
```

Notice how we have set the CN field to system. Later in this chapter, we shall configure the username mapper in the default Identity Assertion Provider to extract the WebLogic username from this field. A production environment would use something more robust.

Any client application that needs to interact with the web service must possess its own key pair too. Simply create a new keystore using similar commands—the client then can extract the key pair from the keystore.

Setting up the Identity Assertion Provider

SOAP messages that are signed by the client will also have the client's public certificate embedded in the message. WebLogic uses the certificate to verify both the signature and the client's identity so as to prevent anonymous clients from invoking the operations of the web service. WebLogic does this by invoking the Identity Assertion Provider configured for the security realm. For our example, we simply will use WebLogic's Default Identity Asserter. (Chapter 18 explains how you configure this provider). The client-supplied token in this case is an X.509 certificate, so you must add this to the list of supported token types for the provider. Select the Default Identity Asserter from the left pane of the Administration Console, and in the Types option, move the X.509 to the Chosen column. This enables WebLogic to consider X.509 certificates as a form of identity assertion.

You also need to set up a username mapper that can extract some data from the certificate and map it to a WebLogic user. You can either write your own, similar to that in Example 18-2, or use WebLogic's default username mapper. For the running example, the latter approach will suffice. Select the Details tab of the Default Identity Asserter, and then the Use Default User Name Mapper option. Because the username can be extracted from the certificate's CN field, you should choose CN as the Default User Name Mapper Attribute Type and then blank out the Default User Name Mapper Attribute Delimiter. Finally, ensure that Base64Decoding Required is not selected.

Writing the client

A client that uses SOAP message security must be modified to support it. First, you need to include BEA's SOAP message security implementation in the client's classpath. In other words, you must add the *WL_HOME/server/lib/wsse.jar* library to the client's classpath. This library doesn't contain the web services JAX-RPC classes, so you still must keep the existing *webserviceclient.jar* in the classpath. Our Java client needs to load its security identity into the context and supply the username and password of a valid WebLogic user because we have forced the client to supply a username token. To do this, you must set the relevant attributes on the WebServiceSession object. Example 19-17 illustrates the code for a Java client that can invoke a web service operation securely.

Example 19-17. Client code to interact with secure SOAP messages

```
package com.oreilly.wlguide.webservices.secureSOAP.client;

import java.io.FileInputStream;
import java.net.URL;
import java.rmi.RemoteException;
import java.security.KeyStore;
import java.security.PrivateKey;
import java.security.cert.X509Certificate;
import javax.xml.namespace.QName;
import javax.xml.rpc.Call;
import javax.xml.rpc.Service;
import javax.xml.rpc.ServiceFactory;
import weblogic.webservice.context.WebServiceContext;
import weblogic.webservice.context.WebServiceSession;
```

Example 19-17. Client code to interact with secure SOAP messages (continued)

```
import weblogic.webservice.core.handler.WSSEClientHandler;
import weblogic.xml.security.UserInfo;
public class Invoke {
  private static final String KEYSTORE = "myIdentityStore.jks";
  private static final String KEYSTORE_PASS = "mystorepass";
  private static final String KEY_ALIAS = "myalias";
  private static final String KEY_PASS = "mypassword";

  static void invoke(String where) throws Exception {
    // First get hold of the keystore that holds our key/cert pair
    KeyStore ks = KeyStore.getInstance("JKS");
    ks.load(new FileInputStream(KEYSTORE), KEYSTORE_PASS.toCharArray());
    // Use the keystore to load the certificate and private key
    X509Certificate myCert = (X509Certificate) ks.getCertificate(KEY_ALIAS);
    PrivateKey myKey = (PrivateKey) ks.getKey(KEY_ALIAS, KEY_PASS.toCharArray());
    // Now retrieve the web service context, and its session, from the service
    Simple ws = new Simple_Impl(where);
    WebServiceContext wsCtx = ws.context();
    WebServiceSession session = wsCtx.getSession();
    // Finally, set the attributes
    session.setAttribute(WSSEClientHandler.CERT_ATTRIBUTE, myCert);
    session.setAttribute(WSSEClientHandler.KEY_ATTRIBUTE, myKey);
    // Since we set enablePasswordAuth, we have to supply token and define user
    UserInfo ui = new UserInfo("someWLUser", "somePassword");
    session.setAttribute(WSSEClientHandler.REQUEST_USERINFO, ui);
    SimplePort port = ws.getSimplePort();
    System.out.println("The service returned: " + port.makeUpper("hello there"));
  }

  public static void main(String[] argv) throws Exception {
    invoke(argv[0]);
  }
}
```

The first part of the code simply retrieves the client's private key and certificate from a keystore. After creating the service object, Simple, the code then retrieves WebLogic's context and session. These objects maintain any server-side state associated with the client. The session then is populated with the digital certificate, private key, and username token into predefined attributes. After this, you should be able to invoke a secured web service operation. Note that the user token information determines which WebLogic user is used to actually invoke the operation.

Running the client

Clients that use SOAP message security can be executed in the same way as ordinary web service clients, except that you should include the *wsse.jar* in the classpath. During development, you may find it useful to enable the debugging flags provided by WebLogic. Use the `weblogic.xml.encryption.verbose` and `weblogic.xml.signature.verbose` system properties to obtain debugging information about the encryption and signing processes. For example, you can use the following mouthful when running the client during development:

```
java -Dweblogic.xml.encryption.verbose=true -Dweblogic.xml.signature.verbose=true
    -Dweblogic.webservice.verbose=true
    -Dweblogic.webservice.client.ssl.strictcertchecking=false
    -cp mysecureSOAPclient.jar;classes;y:\server\lib\wsse.jar;
        y:\server\lib\webserviceclient+ssl.jar
    com.oreilly.wlguide.webservices.secureSOAP.client.Invoke
        http://10.0.10.10:7001/secureSOAPService/Simple?WSDL
```

Encrypting passwords

The security element used to include the server's key, certificate, and password information, creates a number of additional elements in the *web-services.xml* descriptor file. By default, the key passwords are not encrypted in this file. You can encrypt them using the weblogic.webservice.encryptpass utility. This tool encrypts the passwords salted with the domain name. As a result, the EAR or WAR with the encrypted data can be deployed only to the same domain from which you encrypted the passwords in the first place.

The following command encrypts the secureSOAPService in the EAR file:

```
java weblogic.webservice.encryptpass -serviceName secureSOAPService
                    out/secureSOAPService.ear
```

You must either run this command from the root of the domain so that it has access to the *config.xml* file, or specify the –domain argument to point to the root directory.

UDDI

The Universal Description, Discovery and Integration (UDDI) specification defines a way to publish and discover information about web services. UDDI relies on a distributed registry of different businesses and the descriptions of their services implemented using a common XML format. This framework allows you to access public UDDI sites and search for information on the available web services. This information includes the technical programming interfaces (i.e., the WSDL) for interfacing with the business. The details about what kind of information you should store in a UDDI registry and the APIs that can be used to access this registry are documented in the specification, which can be found by visiting *http://www.uddi.org/*.

WebLogic implements the UDDI 2.0 specification. In fact, it comes equipped with three UDDI features:

- A UDDI registry runs on every WebLogic instance, and can be used to store references to any web service.
- A web-based UDDI Directory Explorer is distributed with your WebLogic installation. The UDDI Explorer lets you search and browse any UDDI registry on the Web, including any private UDDI registries running on WebLogic. Authorized users also can publish new services over WebLogic's UDDI registry.

- WebLogic provides a set of client APIs that allow you to programmatically publish and inquire about information stored in a UDDI registry.

The UDDI Registry

WebLogic's UDDI registry is deployed automatically when the server starts. It provides a public interface that lets you query and publish web services. A client can access this private registry through the URL *http://host:port/uddi/uddilistener*, where host and port refer to the listen address and port of a running WebLogic instance. Generally you won't access the UDDI registry directly from a browser. Later, in the section "The Client API," we examine how to use the client API to interact with UDDI registries.

The UDDI Directory Explorer

The UDDI Directory Explorer is a web-based utility that lets you search UDDI registries for published web services and advertise your own web services over the local UDDI registry. In order to invoke the UDDI Explorer, you need to point your browser to the following address: *http://host:port/uddiexplorer*, where host and port refer to the listen address and port of a running WebLogic instance. Here you can use the console to browse and/or manipulate the configured UDDI registries.

Public registries

The UDDI Directory Explorer can be configured with a number of public UDDI directories. Select the Setup UDDI Directory Explorer option from the UDDI Explorer to add a new public registry. In order to configure a new registry, you simply need to specify a name and the URL for the registry. In fact, the UDDI Explorer comes preconfigured with a number of public registries. This configuration page also lets you set up the default address of the private registry for publishing and inquiring about web services. By default, the UDDI Explorer uses the private UDDI registry running on the local server, so its value will be a URL similar to *http://10.0.10.10:8001/uddi/uddilistener*.

Once you have configured the public registries, select the "Search public registries" option from the UDDI Explorer to search an existing public registry. You can search the selected public registry using various search options: the business name, a service key, or the value of a specified registry field such as the business location, t-Model name, business URL, or D-U-N-S number. After executing the search, the UDDI Explorer returns a list of web services that match the query. You then can select any of the search results to further explore the web service and discover more information about the access points and the WSDL.

Private registries

The UDDI Explorer also lets you search private WebLogic registries. If you select the Search Private Registry option, you can locate specific web services that match search criteria. The search query can be built using the name of the service, department, or project. Alternatively, you can simply list all of the web services published over the private registry.

Select the Modify Private Registry Details option to modify or create a registry entry. After the system ensures that you are an authentic WebLogic user equipped with the necessary privileges, you are presented with a list of projects/departments and options to create, remove, or edit a registry entry. You also can click a project to further drill down into its contact and service information, changing or adding to any of the details along the way.

You can use the Publish to Private Registry option to create a new registry entry. In either case, you need to supply a project name, service name, the URL for the WSDL, and a service description. In case you wish to publish the WebLogic web service that we developed earlier, the WSDL URL for the registry entry *http://10.0.10.10:8001/myWar/Simple?wsdl*.

The Client API

WebLogic's UDDI registry also can be accessed programmatically. In fact, WebLogic provides two types of APIs for UDDI clients: a publisher's API for storing and manipulating data in the registry, and an inquiry API for accessing the registry for information about published web services. These API functions actually are exposed as SOAP messages over HTTP. However, all publisher API calls must be made over HTTPS. You should refer to the online JavaDoc for a detailed coverage of the API. WebLogic's API for interfacing with UDDI registries can be found in the set of packages rooted at `weblogic.uddi.client.*`.

Let's now look at how a client can programmatically publish a web service over the private UDDI registry. Here is the main entry point for our client `UDDIPublish`:

```
UDDIPublish x = new UDDIPublish( );
// default to WebLogic's SSL implementation
System.setProperty("java.protocol.handler.pkgs", "weblogic.net");
// authenticate the client
Publish p = new Publish( );
p.setURL(LISTEN_URL);
AuthInfo ai = x.doLogin(p, "system", "pssst123");
// publish the web service over the private registry
x.pub(ai, p, "businessName", "businessDescription", "serviceName",
    "serviceDescription", "http://10.0.10.10:8001/myWar/Simple?wsdl");
// log out after you're done
x.doLogout(p, ai);
```

The doLogin( ) method establishes the client's identity and allows WebLogic to later ensure that it is authorized to create or modify entries in the local UDDI registry. The following excerpt illustrates the implementation for the doLogin( ) method:

```
// Log in
private AuthInfo doLogin(Publish p, String username, String password)
                                                    throws Exception {
    GetAuthToken gat = new GetAuthToken( );
    gat.setUserID(username);
    gat.setCred(password);
    AuthToken at = p.getAuthToken(gat);
    return at.getAuthInfo( );
}
```

When the client is authenticated successfully, it acquires an authentication token that it can subsequently use whenever it needs to interact with the UDDI registry. The doLogout( ) method simply releases the authentication token and is invoked once the client has finished manipulating the UDDI registry. The following code sample shows how to discard the authentication token obtained after login:

```
// Log out
private void doLogout(Publish p, AuthInfo ai) throws Exception {
    DiscardAuthToken dat = new DiscardAuthToken( );
    dat.setAuthInfo(ai);
    p.discardAuthToken(dat);
}
```

Let's now examine the pub( ) method, which performs the bulk of the work. It publishes a new service over the private registry. Its signature accepts parameters that allow the client to configure the new web service—i.e., the name and description of the business, the name and description of the service, and a URL that points to the WSDL for the web service:

```
public void pub (AuthInfo ai, Publish p, String businessName, String
businessDescription, String serviceName, String serviceDesc, String serviceWSDL)
throws Exception {
```

First, you need to create a new business entity and publish it over the private registry:

```
// Publish a new business entity
BusinessEntity be = new BusinessEntity( );
be.setBusinessKey("");
be.setName(businessName);
be.addDescription(businessDescription);
Vector vbe = new Vector( );
vbe.add(be);
SaveBusiness sb = new SaveBusiness( );
sb.setAuthInfo(ai);
sb.setBusinessEntityVector(vbe);
BusinessDetail bdtls = p.saveBusiness(sb);

// Now access the business entity and retrieve its key
be = (BusinessEntity) bdtls.getBusinessEntityVector( ).elementAt(0);
String key = be.getBusinessKey( );
```

Once you create the new business entity, you can attach a new service to the business entity:

```
BusinessService bs = new BusinessService();
bs.setBusinessKey(key);
bs.setServiceKey("");
bs.setName(new Name(serviceName));
bs.addDescription(serviceDesc);

// provide information about the technical entry point
BindingTemplate btemp = new BindingTemplate();
btemp.addDescription("");
btemp.setBindingKey("");
btemp.setAccessPoint(new AccessPoint(serviceWSDL, "http"));
BindingTemplates btemps = new BindingTemplates();
TModelInstanceDetails tmidls = new TModelInstanceDetails();
btemp.setTModelInstanceDetails(tmidls);
btemps.addBindingTemplate(btemp);
bs.setBindingTemplates(btemps);
```

Finally, you are ready to publish the business service over the private registry:

```
Vector bss = new Vector();
bss.add(bs);
SaveService ss = new SaveService();
ss.setAuthInfo(ai);
ss.setBusinessServiceVector(bss);
ServiceDetail sd = p.saveService(ss);
```

Once you publish the web service, a client can inquire about the web service. For example, using the same business key created earlier, we can search for the business service given its name:

```
BusinessKey businessKey = new BusinessKey(key);
// define the search parameters—i.e., name and find qualifiers
Name name = new Name(serviceName);
FindQualifiers fqs = new FindQualifiers();
fqs.addFindQualifier("sortByNameDesc");
fqs.addFindQualifier("caseSensitiveMatch");
// build the search query using the business key, service name, and find qualifiers
FindService fs = new FindService();
fs.setBusinessKey(businessKey.getValue());
fs.setFindQualifiers(fqs);
fs.setName(name);
// execute the query and inspect the list of services that match the query
Inquiry i = new Inquiry();
i.setURL(LISTEN_URL);
ServiceList rServiceList = i.findService(fs);
ServiceInfos rServiceInfos = rServiceList.getServiceInfos();
// iterate through the list of services and process each
Vector rServiceInfoVector = rServiceInfos.getServiceInfoVector();
ServiceInfo rServiceInfo;
for (int x = 0; x < rServiceInfoVector.size(); x++) {
    rServiceInfo = (ServiceInfo) rServiceInfoVector.elementAt(x);
    System.out.println("Found service " + rServiceInfo.getName().getValue());
}
```

These client APIs provide a complete way of interacting with the UDDI registry, allowing you to mimic the capabilities of the UDDI Directory Explorer.

Internationalization and Character Sets

The default character sets installed with WebLogic, and its default handling, are sufficient in most cases. If a client interacts with a web service specifying its preferred character set, WebLogic will respond using that character set requested by the client. This section looks at how you can take more control over which character set should be used for a web service.

Configuring Web Services

You can explicitly configure the character set to be used by a web service. In effect, this determines the value of the HTTP Content-Type header embedded in the responses sent back to clients of the web service. You can specify the character set in two ways:

- Modify the *web-services.xml* descriptor file by adding a charset attribute. Once deployed, the web service will be forced to always use the specified character set:

```
<web-service protocol="http" useSOAP12="false"
             targetNamespace="http://www.oreilly.com/webservices/Simple"
             name="Simple" style="rpc" uri="/Simple"
             charset="Shift_JIS">
<!-- ... -->
</web-service>
```

- Set the -Dweblogic.webservice.i18n.charset system property in WebLogic's startup script. However, this character set then will apply to all web services deployed to the server, and you must set this property on each server that hosts the web service.

The character set used for any web service is determined by the following precedence rules. If the charset attribute is set for a web service, it is used. Otherwise, if the client explicitly requests a character set, it is used instead. If neither of these values is set, the weblogic.webservice.i18n.charset system property is used (if it is set). If none of these conditions holds, WebLogic use the default character set for the JVM. If the JVM property user.language is set to en, the US-ASCII character set it used. If the property is set to anything else, UTF-8 is used instead.

Thus, if the Content-Type HTTP header of the SOAP request has been set, WebLogic will use the specified character set. If the Accept-Charset HTTP header has been set instead, WebLogic will use this preferred character set, provided you've not configured a charset attribute for the web service. SOAP 1.2 requests may have an encoding attribute in their XML declaration, such as <?xml version="1.0" encoding="UTF-8"?>. The character set specified by this attribute is used, provided there is no

Content-Type header in the SOAP request. For SOAP 1.1 requests, the encoding attribute is ignored.

Configuring Client Applications

Clients can use the `weblogic.webservice.binding.BindingInfo` class to set the `Content-Type` or `Accept-Charset` HTTP headers. As we just learned, these headers don't guarantee that the same character set will be used for the response. Here is how to specify the preferred character set:

```
BindingInfo info =
    (BindingInfo)stub._getProperty("weblogic.webservice.bindinginfo" );
info.setCharset("UTF-8" );        // This sets the Content-Type
info.setAcceptCharset("UTF-8");   // This sets the Accept-Charset
port.makeUpper("Lang maande lê die reënboog in 'n miershoopgat gekrul");
```

JMX

The Java Management Extensions (JMX) specification defines the architecture, services, and API for the distributed management of resources using Java. JMX can be used to instrument everything from network hardware to applications, enabling you to build your own applications that manage these instrumented resources. This chapter focuses on how WebLogic Server is itself instrumented, and how this enables you to create applications that monitor and manage various aspects of a WebLogic domain and its deployed applications.

WebLogic's JMX implementation, and the specification itself, comprise three levels: an instrumentation, agent, and distribution level. The *instrumentation level* provides a design for implementing JMX-manageable resources. Within WebLogic, the manageable resources include just about everything, ranging from connection pools and security realms to the domain configuration and the state of a deployed application. The instrumentation of a resource is provided by MBeans, which expose an interface for the management and control of that resource. For instance, the MBeans for a JDBC connection pool expose attributes such as the pool's name and size, as well as operations such as resetting the pool or shutting it down. Runtime statistics are also made available, such as the maximum number of connections to the pool and the connection delay time.

The *agent level* builds upon the instrumentation level to provide a standardized way of managing MBeans. In WebLogic, this is realized by an MBean Server, which hosts the MBeans on an individual WebLogic instance and lets clients access, retrieve, and modify MBeans on the MBean Server. You typically would write management applications that interact with the MBean Server and its hosted MBeans. For example, you can write an application that locates all JDBC connection pool MBeans and ensures that they don't have unacceptable connection time delays. WebLogic supports two ways of interacting with MBeans. You could either adopt the standard approach put forward in the JMX specification or use a WebLogic-specific type-safe interface. The standard approach provides a generic interface for accessing any MBean. For example, in order to invoke an operation on an MBean, you need to pass the operation name and an array of arguments to an invocation method. WebLogic's type-safe implementation exposes an individual interface for each MBean, thereby making manipulating MBeans as easy as using traditional JavaBeans.

As WebLogic domains are distributed, the manageable resources are themselves spread across a number of server instances. WebLogic's JMX architecture provides each WebLogic instance with its own MBean Server. WebLogic's *distribution level* defines precisely how MBeans are made accessible through this distributed management architecture. For example, when a Managed Server instance starts up, it contacts the Administration Server for a set of MBeans that describes its local configuration. The Managed Server then uses these local configuration MBeans to establish the services that have been configured for the server.

The JMX specification provides two powerful additions to this framework that allow you to build effective management applications. The MBean notification model allows MBeans to broadcast management events, called *notifications*. By registering a listener class with an MBean, you can be alerted when a notification has been broadcast and can react to it appropriately. The Monitor MBean architecture provides the second management enhancement. This architecture defines a set of MBeans that monitor other MBeans, observing specific attribute values as they vary over time and automatically firing notifications when these values exceed specified thresholds. For instance, you could configure a monitor MBean to observe the connection count value on a connection pool and alert you when the pool exceeds specified thresholds.

All of these facilities provide you with the means to create applications that enable you to remotely configure, monitor, and manage the different aspects of your WebLogic domain and the applications deployed to it. You can programmatically monitor and manipulate a WebLogic deployment, leading to exciting opportunities. For instance, a management application could constantly monitor the status of JMS servers, and in the case of failure, automatically migrate the service to an alternate WebLogic Server—a service not provided by the standard JMS tooling in WebLogic. The Administration Console is itself an example of a remote management application. In fact, it is nothing more than a web-based tool that allows Administrators and Deployers to remotely manipulate MBeans.

WebLogic has literally hundreds of instrumented services, and it would be senseless to explain each one in detail. In addition, any deployments such as EJBs or servlets become manageable resources as well. Instead of looking at each MBean in detail, something that is covered by the JavaDoc APIs, this chapter will teach you how to effectively use WebLogic's JMX implementation. You will learn about WebLogic's distributed JMX architecture, and how to access and manipulate MBeans to configure, manage, and monitor a wide range of managed services. En route, a number of code examples will demonstrate how to use particular MBeans. You will also see an example of using the WLShell tool, which provides a scripting environment for navigating the MBeans in a running WebLogic instance. You can use this tool to script MBean actions, such as modifying a domain configuration, or simply to view MBean attributes and invoke operations.

The MBean Architecture

Every WebLogic instance owns an MBean Server that hosts a number of MBeans. The MBean Server acts as a registry for the MBeans and provides services for accessing and manipulating MBeans running on the server. Because a WebLogic domain may be distributed across multiple machines with differing deployments and domain resources targeted to different servers, the MBean Server for each WebLogic instance will hold different types of MBeans. For instance, the runtime statistics for a JDBC connection pool on a server can be obtained only from an MBean running on that server. WebLogic makes a distinction between three different sets of MBeans:

Configuration MBeans
  These expose attributes and operations for the configuration of a resource.

Runtime MBeans
  These provide information about the runtime state of a resource.

Security MBeans
  These reflect the SSPIs, providing direct access to the configuration of WebLogic's security framework.

To fully understand the MBean architecture as implemented in WebLogic, you need to understand the different types of MBeans and how WebLogic distributes these MBeans across MBean Servers within a domain.

Configuration MBeans

A Configuration MBean holds the configuration for a managed resource or service within a WebLogic domain. WebLogic captures the configuration settings for all kinds of domain resources and services: web servers, clusters, JDBC connection pools, J2EE components (EJBs, web applications, resource adapters), JMS destinations, XML Registries, web services, and many more. The definitive list of Configuration MBeans can be found within the API documentation under the `weblogic.management.configuration` package. Here are a few examples:

`DomainMBean`
  This MBean represents a WebLogic Domain. You can use it to access various attributes of the domain (e.g., Administration Port), or even explore subcategories of configuration settings such as JTA, Security, Logging, and others. In addition, you can access the configuration settings for the managed servers within the domain.

`ServerMBean`
  This MBean represents a WebLogic Server instance. You can use it to access virtually all the attributes for the server: server name, listen address and port, external DNS name, and many more. You also can use the MBean to acquire configuration settings for the web server, the cluster to which the server belongs, the machine that hosts the server, the XML Registry, and other related resources that have been configured for the server.

JDBCConnectionPoolMBean

This MBean represents a JDBC connection pool configured within a domain. It can be used to access the various configuration settings for a connection pool, such as its capacity, driver name, and database URL.

The configuration of a managed resource is described entirely by the state of the MBean representing that resource. As we learned in Chapter 13, the Administration Server is responsible for managing the configuration of a domain and distributing the relevant portions of the configuration to different Managed Servers. The *config.xml* file that is used by the Administration Console to persist the current state of the domain's configuration is nothing more than a serialization of all the Configuration MBeans on the Administration Server. When the Administration Server starts up, it reads this domain configuration file and reconstructs the set of Configuration MBeans in its local MBean Server. So, the Administration Server is the prime host for all Configuration MBeans, and using the Administration Console is one of the easiest ways of manipulating these MBeans.

When a Managed Server starts up, it asks the Administration Server for its own server configuration. The Administration Server responds by sending back a subset of those MBeans that are relevant to the Managed Server. This includes the MBeans that reflect the configuration of all resources and services deployed to that server. Hence, the Administration Server holds the master copy of all Configuration MBeans for all resources within a domain, while the MBean Server on each Managed Server hosts local replicas for all resources that are targeted to the Managed Server.

This replication of Configuration MBeans hosted on the Administration Server occurs for performance reasons as well. Local clients of the Managed Server can simply use the local replicas of the Configuration MBeans, without having to contact the MBean Server running on the Administration Server. Figure 20-1 illustrates this process.

The Configuration MBeans hosted by the Administration Server are called *Administration MBeans*, while the replicas hosted on the Managed Servers are called *Local Configuration MBeans*. Any permanent changes to the configuration of a domain must be made through the Administration MBeans. These changes then will propagate through to the Local Configuration MBeans on all running Managed Servers.

The Administration Server periodically serializes the state of its Administration MBeans to the domain's *config.xml* configuration file, making them permanent. This serialization also occurs when the Administration Server detects that one or more configuration settings have been changed. Sometimes, a domain resource instantly is updated to reflect any changes made to its configuration settings. In other cases, the resource may define configuration settings whose value changes come into effect only after you restart the server that hosts the resource. In this case, the changes to the configuration won't dynamically alter the behavior of a resource. The Administration Console gives you an indication of which configuration settings require a

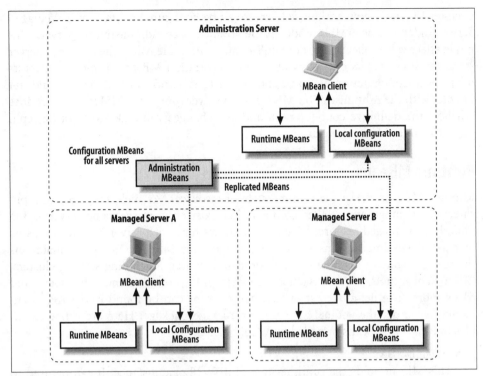

Figure 20-1. *Distribution of Runtime and Configuration MBeans in a domain*

server restart by placing a caution icon (a yellow triangular icon) next to the attribute name. Although the changes to these attributes are persisted instantly, the actual change to the resource occurs only after you restart the server to which the resource or service has been targeted. The JavaDoc documentation also indicates explicitly which attributes of the MBean are dynamically configurable.

Though Administration MBeans have a persisted state, the Local Configuration MBeans are transient. If the server instance hosting the Local MBeans is shut down, then their in-memory state is lost. This is not a problem because the Local MBeans are reinitialized the next time the server boots and makes contact with the Administration Server. You can, however, make temporary changes to particular server instances. For example, you could use the command-line option -Dweblogic. ListenPort=7501 during server startup to change the listen port of a Managed Server. This option temporarily updates the listen port information in the local ServerMBean running on that Managed Server only, and the change lasts as long as the server is alive. Moreover, this setting has no effect on the master copy of the ServerMBean on the Administration Server.

The same distinction between Local and Administration MBeans is maintained even if you deploy applications to the Administration Server. In this case, the Administration Server hosts both Administration and Local Configuration MBeans.

Chapter 13 shows how a Managed Server can be configured to start up in Managed Service Independence (MSI) mode, in the absence of an Administration Server. This mode effectively replicates the domain's configuration file; when the Managed Server starts up, it creates its own copy of the Administration MBeans. It then extracts its own Local Configuration MBeans, allowing it to start up as usual. You should not interact with the Administration MBeans on a server running in MSI mode, as it does not host the definitive configuration, and any changes you make will not be replicated to the rest of the domain.

Runtime MBeans

Runtime MBeans reflect the runtime state of resources. As such, they are not replicated like Configuration MBeans, but rather exist only on the same server as the underlying managed resource. Figure 20-1 shows how each server instance holds its own set of Runtime MBeans and Local Configuration MBeans. WebLogic maintains the runtime state of a whole range of domain resources, including servers, clusters, EJB instance pools, JTA transactions, servlets, JMS producers and subscribers, and many more. The definitive list of Runtime MBeans can be found in the API documentation under the `weblogic.management.runtime` package. Here are a few examples of Runtime MBeans provided by WebLogic:

ServerRuntimeMBean
> This MBean holds the runtime state of a WebLogic instance. It can be used to find the state of the server instance and the number of open sockets.

EJBPoolRuntimeMBean
> This MBean can be used to access the runtime state of an EJB pool, providing access to an array of runtime statistics, including the total number of bean instances in use and the number of threads waiting for a bean instance to be made available.

JDBCConnectionPoolRuntimeMBean
> This MBean can be used to access the runtime information of a JDBC connection pool, providing access to the total number of current connections.

A Runtime MBean provides runtime information on a resource, as well as operations that can modify its runtime state. For instance, the ServerRuntimeMBean allows you to restart a suspended server. Runtime MBeans are transient, so when the hosting server instance is shut down, all of the MBean's associated state is lost.

Security MBeans

The third category of MBeans reflects the SSPIs provided by WebLogic's security framework, which we covered earlier in Chapter 17. These MBeans can be found in the `weblogic.management.security` package hierarchies. The security framework uses the MBeans to access and configure the security within a domain, so any implementation of the SSPIs must be accompanied by an implementation of the MBeans as well. Naturally, the default security implementation that ships with your WebLogic distribution does just this.

The Security MBeans comprise sets of required and optional MBeans. The required MBeans provide access to the main interfaces. For instance, the `AuthenticatorMBean` is used by the authentication services. The base MBean implementation merely lets you retrieve and set the control flag setting. Custom implementations of the Authenticator SSPI also are required to provide an MBean with which to manage the implementation. This custom Security MBean must extend the `AuthenticatorMBean`, and may even provide additional management attributes and operations. Security SSPI implementations may implement additional MBean interfaces, such as the `UserAddEditorMBean` and `UserRemoverMBean` that can be used to create, edit, and remove users from the security realm.

Accessing MBean Servers

Now that you know how WebLogic organizes MBeans across MBean Servers, we can turn to accessing MBean Servers. The first point of entry is to find a home interface for the MBean Server. The home interface provides access to the underlying MBean server and enables you to reach the MBeans hosted on the server.

Local and Administration Home Interfaces

The MBean Server running on a WebLogic Server instance can be reached through the `weblogic.management.MBeanHome` interface. Two implementations of this home interface can be obtained:

Local Home interface
> This interface provides access to the local MBeans hosted on the MBean Server itself. This means that you can use the Local Home interface to access the Local Configuration and Runtime MBeans on that server instance, but not interact with any of the Administration MBeans.

Administration Home interface
> This interface, exposed only by the Administration Server, provides access to the Administration MBeans and all other MBeans on all other server instances within the domain.

Figure 20-2 illustrates this architecture.

As indicated in Figure 20-2, you also can reach the Runtime MBeans on any Managed Server through the Administration Home interface itself, instead of using the Local Home interface of the Managed Server directly. Clearly, it is slower to access the local MBeans through the Administration interface rather than to access them directly through the Local interface. You incur an additional performance penalty due to the overhead imposed by the RMI communication with the local server

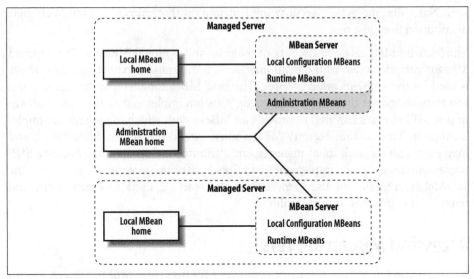

Figure 20-2. Home interfaces and their hosted MBeans

MBeans. If you need to manipulate the local MBeans of a particular Managed Server, you should contact that server directly through its Local Home interface.

Retrieving the Home Interface

The home interfaces can be retrieved either by looking up the server's JNDI tree or by using a WebLogic-specific helper class. In both cases, you need to supply the authentication details of a user who is authorized to access the domain resource and the URL of the server that you wish to contact. If you intend to access a local home, you also need the name of the server that you would like to contact.

Use the getMBeanHome( ) method on the weblogic.management.Helper class to access the Local MBean home, and use the getAdminMBeanHome( ) method on the Helper class to access the Administration MBean home. The following code sample shows how to use these helper methods to retrieve the Local and Administration home interfaces:

```
public MBeanHome findLocalHomeHelper(String url, String serverName) {
    weblogic.management.MBeanHome localHome = null;
    localHome =
        (MBeanHome) Helper.getMBeanHome(USERNAME, PASSWORD, url, serverName);
    return localHome;
}

public MBeanHome findAdminHomeHelper(String adminURL) {
    weblogic.management.MBeanHome adminHome = null;
    adminHome =
        (MBeanHome) Helper.getAdminMBeanHome(USERNAME, PASSWORD, adminURL);
    return adminHome;
}
```

Now, if you need to access the Local home of ServerB, you need to simply issue the following call:

```
MBeanHome localHomeB = findLocalHomeHelper("t3://10.0.10.14:7001", "ServerB");
```

Using the JNDI to obtain a home is just as easy. The locations of the Local and Administration homes are stored in the constants MBeanHome.LOCAL_JNDI_NAME and MBeanHome.ADMIN_JNDI_NAME, respectively. Once you establish an initial context with a server, you simply look up the home interface using these names:

```
InitialContext ctx = new InitialContext();
MBeanHome localHomeB = (MBeanHome) ctx.lookup(MBeanHome.LOCAL_JNDI_NAME);
```

An initial JNDI context obtained from the Administration Server also allows you to access the Local home from any of the Managed Servers. In this case, the JNDI name used to look up the Local home matches the following string:

```
"weblogic.management.home" + "." + ServerName
```

This prefix weblogic.management.home is conveniently bound to the constant MBean-Home.JNDI_NAME. The following code sample shows how to locate the Local Home interface of ServerB via the initial JNDI context obtained from the Administration Server:

```
//create an initial JNDI context using the URL of the Admin Server
Hashtable env = new Hashtable();
env.put(Context.INITIAL_CONTEXT_FACTORY,
        "weblogic.jndi.WLInitialContextFactory");
env.put(Context.PROVIDER_URL, "t3://adminserver:8001");
//set other environment properties for the initial JNDI Context
InitialContext ctx = new InitialContext(env);
//now look up Local home by prefixing MBeanHome.JNDI_NAME to "ServerB"
MBeanHome localHomeB = (MBeanHome) ctx.lookup(MBeanHome.JNDI_NAME + "." + "ServerB");
```

Accessing MBeans

Once you obtain a home interface, there are several ways to access the underlying MBean Server. The first approach is to use the MBeanHome interface to retrieve an instance of javax.management.MBeanServer, the standard JMX interface for interacting with an MBean Server. It provides a generic way for accessing the attributes and invoking the operations exposed by an MBean. The onus is on you to supply the correct number of parameters, of the correct type, when you use an MBeanServer instance to issue method calls to an MBean.

The second approach is to use a proprietary type-safe interface, which is implemented as a wrapper around the MBeanServer interface. At the cost of portability, you gain very simplified and compact access to MBeans and their attributes and operations. WebLogic's Administration Tool provides another nonprogrammatic approach to accessing MBeans. In addition, the new WLShell tool provides a shell environment for accessing and manipulating MBeans on a particular WebLogic instance.

Naming of MBeans

Before you can use the `MBeanServer` interface to locate MBeans, you need to understand how WebLogic names its MBeans. Each MBean hosted by an MBean Server is uniquely named, and every MBean name is constructed using an instance of the JMX `ObjectName` class. WebLogic uses instances of the `WebLogicObjectName` class, which extends `ObjectName` to carry additional information. When printed, the name of an MBean follows this format:

```
domain:Name=name,Type=type[,Location=servername][,attr=value]* ...
```

So, a name contains a domain name, followed by an unordered list of property/value pairs, explained here:

- A domain name identifies the domain to which the MBean belongs. For most MBeans, this is just the name of the WebLogic administration domain. For Security MBeans, the name of the domain must be Security.

- A `Name` property identifies the name of the resource associated with the MBean. For instance, if you've created a JMS server with the name My JMS server, the name used to locate the associated MBean may use the `Name=My JMS Server` property. Note that this property does not represent the JNDI name to which the resource is bound.

- A `Type` property points to the interface implemented by the MBean's class. It also indicates whether the MBean is an Administration, Local Configuration, or Runtime MBean.

- A `Location` property identifies the name of the server instance on which the MBean is running. You don't need to specify this property when locating Administration MBeans.

- MBeans that are in a parent-child relationship with other MBeans use an additional `TypeOfParentMBean=NameOfParentMBean` property/value pair to express this relationship.

For example, if you defined a data source in the `myClusterDomain` domain, the name of the associated Administration MBean is:

```
myClusterDomain:Name=My Data Source,Type=JDBCDataSource
```

To construct a name object representing such an MBean, use the three-argument `WebLogicObjectName` constructor, which takes the name, the type, and the domain of the object:

```
WebLogicObjectName oname = new WebLogicObjectName("My Data Source",
                           "JDBCDataSource", "myClusterDomain");
```

Determining MBean type

Every MBean within WebLogic is an instance of a class that implements one of the `weblogic.management.configuration` or `weblogic.management.runtime` interfaces.

When constructing the MBean's name, the value for the Type property that you need to supply is determined by a mangling of the name of the interface implementing either of the aforementioned interfaces.

For WebLogic's Runtime MBeans, the value for the Type property corresponds to the name of the MBean interface, but without the MBean suffix. So, for the ServletRuntimeMBean, the MBean's name must include the name/value pair Type=ServletRuntime. Similarly, for the JDBCDataSourceMBean, you must specify Type=JDBCDataSource.

For WebLogic's Configuration MBeans, the value for the Type property that you supply indicates whether the name refers to an Administration or a Local Configuration MBean. For an Administration MBean, the type corresponds to the name of the MBean's interface but, as before, without the MBean suffix. For a Local Configuration MBean, its type is obtained by appending Config to the type of its Administration MBean counterpart. For example, the MBean name for a ServerMBean on the Administration Server must use the name/value pair Type=Server. If you need to refer to a Local Configuration MBean, you must specify Type=ServerConfig.

Let's assume that our myClusterDomain domain has an Administration Server and two Managed Servers, ServerA and ServerB. If a data source is targeted to both Managed Servers, the names of the Local Configuration MBeans associated with the data source will be:

```
myClusterDomain:Location=ServerA,Name=My Data Source,Type=JDBCDataSourceConfig
myClusterDomain:Location=ServerB,Name=My Data Source,Type=JDBCDataSourceConfig
```

To construct a name object representing such an MBean, which has a location, use the four-argument WebLogicObjectName constructor, which takes the object's name, type, domain, and location:

```
WebLogicObjectName oname = new WebLogicObjectName("My Data Source",
        "JDBCDataSourceConfig", "myClusterDomain", "ServerA");
```

Determining parent-child relationships

Except for the DomainMBean, all MBeans inherit either directly or indirectly from the DomainMBean. Sometimes you need to explicitly state this inheritance when constructing the MBean's name in order to uniquely identify it. For instance, consider the LogMBean, which represents the configuration of a log file. Log configuration can occur at several levels. At the domain level, you could set up the domain log configuration. At a server instance level, you could adjust the server log's configuration. Different instances of the LogMBean represent the configuration at different levels. You can differentiate between these configuration MBeans by indicating the fact that the server log Configuration MBean is a child of the server Configuration MBean running within the domain. The domain log Configuration MBean is an implicit child of DomainMBean and *not* a child of the server Configuration MBean.

To emphasize this point, let's take a look at an excerpt from the domain's *config.xml* configuration file:

```
<Domain ConfigurationVersion="8.1.0.0" Name="myDomain">
  <!-- etc. etc. etc. -->
  <Log FileName=".\wl-domain.log" Name="myDomain"/>
  <Server Name="Admin" ListenAddress="10.0.10.10" ListenPort="8001">
    <!-- etc. etc. etc. -->
    <Log FileName="Admin\Admin.log" Name="Admin"/>
  </Server>
  <Server Name="ServerA" Cluster="MyCluster" InterfaceAddress="10.0.10.10"
        ListenAddress="10.0.10.10" ListenPort="7001">
    <!-- etc. etc. etc. -->
    <Log Name="ServerA"/>
  </Server>
  <Server Name="ServerB" Cluster="MyCluster" InterfaceAddress="10.0.10.14"
        ListenAddress="10.0.10.14" ListenPort="7001">
    <!-- etc. etc. etc. -->
    <Log Name="ServerB"/>
  </Server>
</Domain>
```

Here we can clearly see the log configuration for the domain and the two Managed Servers within the domain. The domain LogMBean does not need to express a relationship with the domain. It is unambiguous. The server's LogMBean instance does have to express a parent-child relationship. In this case, the parent is the ServerMBean instance associated with its Managed Server. The relationship between the Log MBeans for the domain and for the Administration Server is expressed in Figure 20-3.

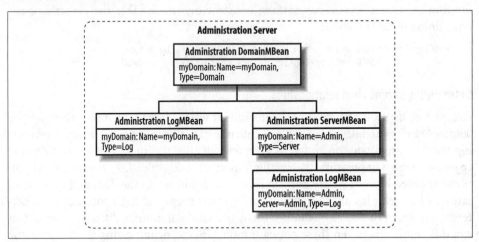

Figure 20-3. Relationships in the MBean hierarchy

There are a two additional points to note from this figure.

- The child MBeans use the same name as the parent MBean, unless there are multiple children of the same type. Thus, the name of the domain's LogMBean is myDomain because the name of the parent MBean also is myDomain.

- The server's LogMBean is in a parent-child relationship, so its name also must include a *TypeOfParentMBean=NameOfParentMBean* property/value. In this case, we have an additional Server=Admin part to the LogMBean's name so that we can identify the parent MBean.

To construct a name object representing such an MBean, first create one for the parent and then another for the child. As shown in Figure 20-3, the parent MBean is of type ServerMBean. Constructing the name object for the parent uses the constructor that we have seen before:

```
WebLogicObjectName parent =
        new WebLogicObjectName("Admin", "Server", "myDomain");
```

Now, to construct the name of the child, we use the constructor that additionally takes the name of a parent. This time, of course, the type of the MBean is Log:

```
WebLogicObjectName childlog =
        new WebLogicObjectName("Admin", "Log", "myDomain", parent);
```

Though the MBean naming schema may seem tedious, it often makes it a lot easier to find the MBean you want either programmatically or by using the Administration Tool.

Using the Administration Tool

The weblogic.Admin tool can be used to view and manipulate JMX data. You can use this tool for quick, nonprogrammatic access to the MBeans. WebLogic's Administration Tool supports three options pertinent to manipulating MBeans: the GET, SET, and INVOKE options. The GET option can be used to retrieve attribute values of an MBean, the SET to modify attribute values, and the INVOKE to invoke any operation on the MBean. Each command provides two ways in which you can identify the MBean on which to operate. The -mbean argument requires you to specify the name of the MBean, and the -type option requires you to specify the MBean's type.

The following example shows how to use the GET option to retrieve the attribute values of a named DataSource MBean:

```
java weblogic.Admin -url http://10.0.10.10:7001 -username system -password pssst
  GET -pretty -mbean
  "myClusterDomain:Location=ServerA,Name=My DataSource,
Type=JDBCDataSourceConfig"
```

This outputs the full list of attributes and values:

```
MBeanName: "myClusterDomain:Location=ServerA,Name=My Data Source,
  Type=JDBCDataSourceConfig"
        CachingDisabled: true
        ConnectionWaitPeriod: 1
```

```
DeploymentOrder: 1000
JNDIName: DS
Name: MyJDBC Data Source
Notes:
ObjectName: MyJDBC Data Source
PoolName: MyJDBCTool
Registered: false
RowPrefetchEnabled: false
RowPrefetchSize: 48
StreamChunkSize: 256
Targets: ServerB,MyCluster
Type: JDBCDataSourceConfig
WaitForConnectionEnabled: false
```

The tool can also help you determine the name of an MBean if you know its type only. The following example prints out the configuration settings encapsulated by the Log MBeans, which we explored in the previous section:

```
java weblogic.Admin -url http://10.0.10.10:7001 -username system -password pssst
   GET -pretty -type Log
```

In our example domain, which consists of an Administration Server and two Managed Servers, this command outputs the settings for four Configuration Log MBeans, one for the domain Log MBean and one for each Log MBean associated with the servers.

Using WLShell

BEA's dev2dev web site contains several tools for manipulating and viewing MBean data. The most flexible is *WLShell*, a powerful shell environment that lets you script actions to create, view, monitor, or modify MBeans. You will need to download and install the tool before you can use it. The latest version, together with many useful scripts, can be obtained from *http://www.wlshell.com/*.

After starting the tool, you will be presented with a command prompt that allows you to enter commands using the shell's scripting language. *WLShell*'s scripting language uses a filesystem analogy, whereby directories correspond to MBeans. In this analogy, creating a new directory is akin to creating a new MBean. It also provides the familiar get, set, and invoke commands on MBeans, as well as flow control and various other features. The following script illustrates these concepts. It creates a new connection pool, configures the relevant attributes of the pool, and assigns it to a server:

```
connect 10.0.10.10:7001 system password

targetServer = /Server/MyServer

mkdir /JDBCConnectionPool/MyJDBCTool
cd /JDBCConnectionPool/MyJDBCTool
set DriverName "com.microsoft.jdbcx.sqlserver.SQLServerDataSource"
set InitialCapacity 5
```

```
set MaxCapacity 10
set PreparedStatementCacheSize 15
set Properties (Properties) "user=sa;url=jdbc:microsoft:sqlserver://
;password=pw;PortNumber=143;SelectMethod=cur
sor;ServerName=10.0.10.10;dataSourceName=lsiPool;DatabaseName=Galactica"
set SupportsLocalTransaction true
set TestConnectionsOnRelease false
set URL "jdbc:microsoft:sqlserver://"
invoke addTarget $targetServer
cd /
```

The following script retrieves a few MBean attribute values and then invokes the stop operation on the Server MBean:

```
get -r ServerRuntime/myserver/State
get JTARuntime/JTARuntime/TransactionCommittedTotalCount
invoke Server/myserver/stop
```

The tool can also be used with a graphical MBean explorer. To invoke the Explorer, use the explore command in the shell. Figure 20-4 illustrates the Explorer window, showing the MBean structure together with the attributes and values for a selected JMS server.

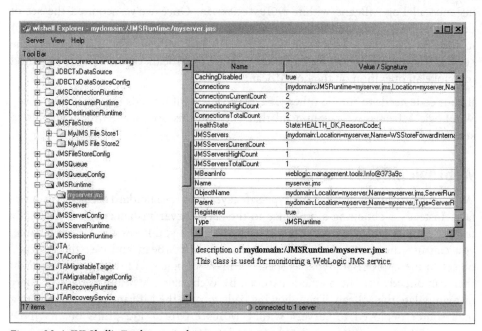

Figure 20-4. WLShell's Explorer window

A great feature of the tool is its ability to reverse-engineer a domain's *config.xml* file. This creates a script file that reconstructs the domain's configuration. For any JMX-related work in WebLogic, we recommend that you use this tool because it is far more convenient than the weblogic.Admin tool, and its scripting language lets you create complex scripts for monitoring and configuring WebLogic resources.

Standard MBean Access

A typical JMX client will use the generic methods to interact with an MBean Server and the MBeans it hosts. As we mentioned earlier, an MBeanServer instance is the primary point of contact with an MBean Server. Once you've obtained an Administration or Local home, you can invoke the getMBeanServer( ) method on the MBean home object to retrieve the MBeanServer. Subsequent interaction with the MBeanServer follows the JMX specification.

The following example locates all Log MBean instances and prints out the log filenames:

```
MBeanServer mbs = adminHome.getMBeanServer();
Set s = mbs.queryMBeans(new ObjectName("myClusterDomain:*,Type=Log"), null);
for (Iterator i=s.iterator();i.hasNext();) {
    Object o = i.next();
    ObjectInstance m = (ObjectInstance) o;
    System.err.println(mbs.getAttribute(m.getObjectName(),"FileName"));
}
```

Here, we've used the queryMBeans( ) method to find all MBeans of interest, in this instance all Log MBeans within myClusterDomain. Once we've acquired the set of desired MBeans, we can iterate over the collection and use the getAttribute( ) method to read the FileName property of each Log MBean. You also can use the setAttribute( ) method to set attributes on the Log MBean, or the invoke( ) method to invoke an operation on the Log MBean.

If your code needs to run on other J2EE platforms, or if it needs to interact with non-WebLogic MBeans, we recommend that you use this approach, which adheres to standard JMX conventions.

WebLogic MBean Access

WebLogic provides a proprietary, type-safe layer over the standard MBeanServer interface. Instead of obtaining a reference to the MBeanServer instance, you can directly use the MBean home to find or retrieve an MBean. If you know the MBean's name, you can use the getMBean( ) method to retrieve the MBean and cast the returned object to the appropriate type, as specified in WebLogic's API documentation. You then can directly use the methods exposed by WebLogic's MBean interface to query or manipulate the MBean. The following code locates the MBean corresponding to a data source deployed to ServerA within myClusterDomain and prints out its JNDI name and the name of its associated connection pool:

```
WebLogicObjectName name = new WebLogicObjectName(
        "MyJDBC Data Source","JDBCDataSourceConfig",
        "myClusterDomain", "ServerA");
JDBCDataSourceMBean pf = (JDBCDataSourceMBean) localHomeA.getMBean(name);
System.err.println(pf.getJNDIName());
System.err.println(pf.getPoolName());
```

Notice how the MBean's name is specified using a `WebLogicObjectName` instance. The `JDBCDataSourceMBean` interface (and any WebLogic-specific Configuration or Runtime MBeans) explicitly exposes all the necessary attributes and allowed operations. In general, the MBean's interface will expose get*XXX*( ) and set*XXX*( ) methods to read and write each MBean attribute and sensible names for each allowed operation on the target resource or service. Thus, WebLogic-specific MBeans give you a straightforward, type-safe way of exploring MBeans.

If you don't know the MBean's name, you still can query the MBean home for all MBeans using the `getAllMBeans( )` method and then operate on the one(s) you want. The following code prints out the JNDI name for all data sources, though it's rather inefficient:

```
Set s = adminHome.getAllMBeans( );
for (Iterator i=s.iterator( );i.hasNext( );) {
    WebLogicMBean o = (WebLogicMBean) i.next( );
    if (o instanceof JDBCDataSourceMBean) {
        JDBCDataSourceMBean p = (JDBCDataSourceMBean)o;
        System.err.println(p.getJNDIName( ));
    }
}
```

Alternatively, you can query the home interface for all MBeans of a particular type directly using the `getMBeansByType( )` method and instantly filter out unwanted MBeans. The following code sample shows how to query the MBean home for all data source Configuration MBeans and iterate over the result:

```
Set s = adminHome.getMBeansByType("JDBCDataSourceConfig");
for (Iterator i=s.iterator( );i.hasNext( );) {
    JDBCDataSourceMBean p = (JDBCDataSourceMBean)i.next( );
    System.err.println(p.getJNDIName( ));
}
```

If your JMX client needs to run on other J2EE platforms or access non-WebLogic MBeans that you have developed and incorporated into WebLogic, you should use the standard MBean access methods and not this WebLogic-specific type-safe approach.

Examples

WebLogic contains hundreds of MBeans. The following sections cover examples of some of the Runtime, Configuration, and Security MBeans and examines common ways of manipulating these MBeans. Other MBeans provided by WebLogic may be manipulated similarly.

Runtime MBeans

A prime example of a Runtime MBean is the `ServerRuntimeMBean`, which provides information on the operational status of a server and other details such as its listen

address and port. The following code uses WebLogic's type-safe approach to connect to a Managed Server, print out its listen address and port, and then shut it
down:

```
serverRuntime = (ServerRuntimeMBean)
    localHomeB.getRuntimeMBean("ServerB", "ServerRuntime");
System.out.println("Listens on " +
    serverRuntime.getListenAddress( )+":"+serverRuntime.getListenPort( ));
serverRuntime.shutdown( );
```

You can do the same thing using the weblogic.Admin tool:

```
java weblogic.Admin -url http://serverb.x:7001 -username system -password pssst
    INVOKE -mbean "myClusterDomain:Location=ServerB,Name=ServerB,Type=ServerRuntime"
    -method shutdown
```

The ServerRuntimeMBean will exist on the Local Home of each server instance. To
find all of the server runtimes, we will have to contact the Administration Server:

```
Set mbeanSet = adminHome.getMBeansByType("ServerRuntime");
Iterator mbeanIterator = mbeanSet.iterator( );
while (mbeanIterator.hasNext( )) {
    ServerRuntimeMBean serverRuntime = (ServerRuntimeMBean)mbeanIterator.next( );
    System.err.println("Found server: " + serverRuntime.getName( ));
}
```

Runtime MBeans often hold a lot of useful information when it comes to monitoring
a resource and its usage. Here, for example, we list the maximum capacity and current connection count for a JDBC pool targeted to a Managed Server, using the standard JMX interface to the JDBCConnectionPoolRuntimeMBean:

```
MBeanServer mbs = localHomeB.getMBeanServer( );
WebLogicObjectName parent = new WebLogicObjectName("ServerB", "ServerRuntime",
                                                    "myClusterDomain");
WebLogicObjectName oname = new WebLogicObjectName("NoTxPool",
    "JDBCConnectionPoolRuntime", "myClusterDomain", "ServerB", parent);
Set s = mbs.queryMBeans(oname,null);
for (Iterator i = s.iterator( ); i.hasNext( );) {
    Object o = i.next( );
    ObjectInstance m = (ObjectInstance) o;
    System.err.println(mbs.getAttribute(m.getObjectName( ), "MaxCapacity"));
    System.err.println(mbs.getAttribute(m.getObjectName( ),
                "ActiveConnectionsCurrentCount"));
}
```

In this case, we found the name of the desired MBean by issuing the following
command:

```
java weblogic.Admin -url http://10.0.10.10:8001 -username system -password pssst
    GET -pretty -type JDBCConnectionPoolRuntime
```

Similar statistics are available for all kinds of managed resources, including EJBs,
JMS servers, web applications, and more.

Administration MBeans

The Administration MBeans hosted by the Administration Server completely define the configuration of the domain. You can manipulate the Administration MBeans to alter the configuration of the domain. The following example locates a JDBC connection pool and changes its maximum capacity:

```
WebLogicObjectName n = new WebLogicObjectName("MyJDBC Connection Pool",
                                 "JDBCConnectionPool", "myClusterDomain");
JDBCConnectionPoolMBean cp = (JDBCConnectionPoolMBean) adminHome.getMBean(n);
cp.setMaxCapacity(20);
```

If you take a closer look at the JavaDoc documentation, you will find that the setMaxCapacity( ) method on the JDBCConnectionPoolMBean is dynamic. This means that the effect of changing the maximum capacity will be immediate, something you can verify for yourself using the Administration Console. In addition, the change is persisted so that the next time the server is started, the new configuration will be in place.

You also can create new Administration MBeans dynamically by using the home methods createAdminMBean( ) or findOrCreateAdminMBean( ). The latter variant returns an existing MBean if it finds one. There are two main variations of this method call:

findOrCreateAdminMBean(String name, String type, String domain)
> This creates an Administration MBean in the given domain with the appropriate name and type.

findOrCreateAdminMBean(String name, String type, String domain,
                       ConfigurationMBean parent)
> This also creates an Administration MBean with the given name and type, but in addition it makes the newly created MBean a child of the parent.

In the following code sample, we use both variants to create a JMS Connection Factory, Server, and Queue:

```
String domain="myClusterDomain";
JMSConnectionFactoryMBean cf = (JMSConnectionFactoryMBean)
                    ahome.findOrCreateAdminMBean("oreillyConnectionFactory",
                                         "JMSConnectionFactory", domain);
cf.setJNDIName("oreilly.CF");
JMSServerMBean server = (JMSServerMBean)
                          ahome.findOrCreateAdminMBean("oreillyJMSServer",
                                              "JMSServer", domain);
JMSDestinationMBean queue = (JMSDestinationMBean)
            home.findOrCreateAdminMBean("oreillyQ", "JMSQueue", domain, server);
queue.setJNDIName("oreilly.Q");
```

In this case, both the JMSConnectionFactory and the JMSServer MBeans are implicit children of the DomainMBean, while the JMSDestination MBean associated with the JMS queue is a child of the JMSServer MBean.

Security MBeans

In order to manipulate the Security MBeans, you need to be familiar with WebLogic's SSPI architecture as outlined in Chapter 17. For instance, suppose you need to provide a facility to programmatically add a new WebLogic user to the default security realm. Then, you need to know how to find an Authentication Provider that also implements the optional UserEditorMBean interface. Using WebLogic's type-safe interface, the following method shows how to programmatically add new users to WebLogic's default security realm:

```
public void createUsers(MBeanHome ahome, String un, String pw) {
  // First we locate the default security realm for the domain
  RealmMBean securityRealm = ahome.getActiveDomain()
                                   .getSecurityConfiguration()
                       .findDefaultRealm();
  // We then find all the authentication providers
  AuthenticationProviderMBean[] providers =
                              securityRealm.getAuthenticationProviders();
  for (int i = 0; i < providers.length; i++) {
    // We look for a provider that implements UserEditorMBean
    if (providers[i] instanceof UserEditorMBean) {
      UserEditorMBean editor = (UserEditorMBean) providers[i];
      try {
        editor.createUser(un, pw, pw);
        System.out.println("Created User " + un);
      } catch (Exception e) {
        System.err.println("Exception " + e.toString());
      }
    }
  }
}
```

It is important to remember that the Security MBeans live in their own Object Name domain called Security. For instance, the name of the default Authenticator MBean is Security:Name=myrealmDefaultAuthenticator. Using this information, we can quite easily use the Administration Tool to create a new WebLogic user from the command line:

```
java weblogic.Admin -username system -password pssst -url http://10.0.10.10:7001
   INVOKE -mbean "Security:Name=myrealmDefaultAuthenticator"
          -method createUser username password password
```

MBean Notifications

The Administration, Local Configuration, Security, and Runtime MBeans allow us to view and modify the configuration and runtime statistics of resources being managed by the MBean Server. Notifications and Monitoring go one step further—they allow you to react to changes in the runtime state of the underlying managed resources. This is critical if you want to build a management application that is able to react and respond to runtime state changes of WebLogic resources and services.

The JMX specification defines a model that allows MBeans to broadcast management events called notifications. You then can create applications that listen for JMX notifications. Your applications may also filter out unwanted notifications. Each WebLogic MBean directly or indirectly extends the javax.management.NotificationBroadcaster interface, thereby allowing you to add or remove notification listeners.

Creating a Notification Listener

A *notification listener* is a handler that is triggered when the MBean it is registered with sends one or more JMX notifications. A notification listener is an instance of a class that implements the javax.management.NotificationListener interface. For remote applications, the listener object should instead implement the weblogic.management.RemoteNotificationListener interface, which merely extends the previous interface and java.rmi.Remote as well, making the JMX notifications available to external clients via RMI.

The listener interface is simple—it exposes a single method, handleNotification( ), that gets called when a notification is received. Here is an example of a remote notification listener:

```
public class SimpleListener implements RemoteNotificationListener {
    public void handleNotification(Notification notification, Object hb) {
        System.err.println("Received Notification");
        System.err.println("Source=" + notification.getSource( ));
        System.err.println("Message=" + notification.getMessage( ));
        System.err.println("Type=" + notification.getType( ));
    }
}
```

Registering a Listener

In order to receive notifications from an MBean, you need to register a listener object with the MBean. If you already hold a reference to the MBean, you simply can invoke the addNotificationListener( ) method to register the listener object. An alternative is to use the addNotificationListener( ) method on the MBeanServer, which takes the name of the MBean and the listener object and registers the listener for you. The following code registers a listener with the JDBCConnectionPoolMBean called My Connection Pool:

```
SimpleListener sl = new SimpleListener( );
WebLogicObjectName oname = new WebLogicObjectName("My Connection Pool",
"JDBCConnectionPool", "myClusterDomain");
mb.getMBeanServer( ).addNotificationListener(oname, sl, null, null);
```

If we then change the runtime state of the JDBC connection pool (e.g., modify the initial capacity of the pool), and if the program that registered the listener object is still running, the listener will receive a notification of the change. Here is the output that is generated when the initial capacity was raised from 2 to 3 using the Administration Console:

```
Received Notification
Source=myClusterDomain:Name=My Connection Pool,Type=JDBCConnectionPool
Message=WebLogic MBean Attribute change for InitialCapacity from 2 to 3
Type=jmx.attribute.change
```

The MBean fires notifications whenever attributes are modified, or whenever new attributes are added or existing ones are removed from an MBean. WebLogic provides two subclasses of the standard Notification class that represent notification events that are fired when attributes are added or removed from an MBean:

weblogic.management.AttributeAddNotification

> An instance of this class is fired whenever an addXXX( ) method is called on an MBean.

weblogic.management.AttributeRemoveNotification

> An instance of this class is fired whenever a removeXXX( ) method is called on an MBean.

Notifications also are used by the Monitor MBeans that we explore in the next section, and by the distributed logging framework covered in Chapter 21.

Monitor MBeans

To further enhance your control over the management of an application, JMX provides Monitor MBeans that allow you to observe attribute values as they vary over time and to fire notifications when these values exceed specific thresholds.

Monitor MBeans monitor attributes in other MBeans at specified intervals and derive a value from this observation called the *derived gauge*. The derived gauge is either the exact value of the attribute, or optionally the difference between two consecutive observed values of a numeric attribute. Depending on the Monitor MBean and its setup, it then can emit an MBean Notification. Monitors can also send notifications when error cases are encountered during monitoring.

Monitors are MBeans as well, and so can be created or destroyed dynamically. Typically, Monitor MBeans are used in combination with the statistics captured by the Runtime MBeans. For example, you could write an MBean to monitor the connection delay time of connections in a JDBC connection pool, or the number of messages dropped in a JMS destination. The Monitor MBean could then send a notification when certain thresholds are crossed. This gives you the opportunity to listen for those notifications and take some appropriate action.

Types of Monitors

There are three types of Monitor MBeans, each explained in depth in the JMX specification:

`CounterMonitor`

This can observe Integer attributes that behave like a counter. That is, the attribute value is always greater than or equal to zero, they can only be incremented, and they may roll over. This monitor sends a notification when the derived gauge exceeds a threshold, after which you can have the monitor automatically increase the threshold by some offset.

`GaugeMonitor`

This can observe Integer, Float, or Double attributes that behave like gauges, arbitrarily increasing or decreasing. Notifications are sent when values exceed a high or low threshold. A hysteresis mechanism ensures that repeated triggering of notifications doesn't occur.

`StringMonitor`

This can observe String attributes. The derived gauge is always the value of the attribute, and the monitor fires events when the observed attribute differs from some initialized String value.

Notifications sent by these monitors are all instances of the `MonitorNotification` class. This subclass of the usual `Notification` event class includes information such as the observed MBean's object name, attribute name, derived gauge, and threshold value or string that triggered the notification. Note that the type property of the `Notification` class is a string that represents the type of monitor notification. This notification type is a string of the form `jmx.monitor.*`. For example, the Gauge monitor will send notifications of two possible types: `jmx.monitor.gauge.low` or `jmx.monitor.gauge.high`.

An Example Monitor

As mentioned earlier, the JMX specification provides an in-depth description of these standard JMX monitors. Here, we'll look at how to create a Monitor MBean for WebLogic. This example creates a Counter Monitor MBean that observes the invocation count on the `FileServlet`, which is responsible for serving requests for static files within a particular web application.

The first thing we want to do is create a new `NotificationListener` specialized to handle Monitor notifications so that we can access the additional information available:

```
public class MyMonitorListener implements RemoteNotificationListener {
  public void handleNotification(Notification notification, Object obj) {
    System.err.println("Received Notification");
    System.err.println("Message: " + notification.getMessage());
    System.err.println("Type: " + notification.getType());
    if (notification instanceof MonitorNotification) {
        MonitorNotification monitorNotification =
            (MonitorNotification) notification;
        System.out.println("This is a MonitorNotification");
```

```
        System.out.println("Observed Attribute: "
                    + monitorNotification.getObservedAttribute());
        System.out.println("Observed Object: "
                    + monitorNotification.getObservedObject());
        System.out.println("Trigger value: " + monitorNotification.getTrigger());
        }
    }
}
```

When you monitor something, you need to construct ObjectNames for both the Monitor MBean and the target MBean that needs to be monitored. Here, we've created names for both the Counter Monitor MBean and FileServlet MBean:

```
WebLogicObjectName monitorObjectName = new
    WebLogicObjectName("myClusterDomain:Type=CounterMonitor,Name=OurCounter");

WebLogicObjectName myServlet = new
    WebLogicObjectName("myClusterDomain:Location=ServerB,Name=ServerB_ServerB_" +
                    "DefaultWebApp_weblogic.servlet.FileServlet_94," +
                    "ServerRuntime=ServerB,Type=ServletRuntime");
```

In this case, the FileServlet MBean is deployed under the DefaultWebApp on ServerB. Its exact name may differ depending on your deployment.

Our Counter Monitor needs to observe the InvocationTotalCount property, whose value gets incremented every time the DefaultWebApp serves up a static file. We now can create a CounterMonitor and configure it to send a notification only if more than 15 requests have been made, and subsequently with an offset value of 10:

```
CounterMonitor monitor = new CounterMonitor();
monitor.setObservedAttribute("InvocationTotalCount");
monitor.setThreshold(new Integer(15));
monitor.setOffset(new Integer(10));
monitor.setNotify(true);
monitor.setObservedObject(myServlet);
```

Finally, we need to instantiate our listener object, bind it to the monitor, register our monitor with the register, and start the monitor:

```
MyMonitorListener listener = new MyMonitorListener();
monitor.addNotificationListener(listener, null, null);
monitor.preRegister(mb.getMBeanServer(), monitorObjectName);
monitor.start();
```

After requesting a static file (say, *index.html* within the web application) a number of times, the code produces the following output:

```
Received Notification
Message:
Type: jmx.monitor.counter.threshold
This is a MonitorNotification
Observed Attribute: InvocationTotalCount
Observed Object: myClusterDomain:Location=ServerB,Name=ServerB_ServerB_DefaultWebApp_
weblogic.
    servlet.FileServlet_94,ServerRuntime=ServerB,Type=ServletRuntime
Trigger value: 15
```

In fact, we observe that further notifications are fired when the same static file receives 25 hits, again when it receives 35 hits, and so on.

Timer MBeans

JMX provides a standard timer service API, which can be used to generate notifications at set times or intervals. WebLogic 8.1 implements this service by extending the standard JMX timer service, enabling it to run with WebLogic execute threads and any associated security context.

To use this service, you must use an instance of the `weblogic.management.timer.Timer` class. The following example illustrates how to create an instance, register a listener, register a notification for when an event should be emitted, and start the timer:

```
Timer timer= new Timer( );
// Register a standard notification listener
timer.addNotificationListener(someListener,
                              null, "handback object");
// Start in one second
Date start =
   new Date((new Date( )).getTime( ) + 1000L);
// Repeat every minute, please
notificationId = timer.addNotification("eggTimer",
            "someString", this, start, 3*Timer.ONE_MINUTE
);
// Start the timer
timer.start( );
```

Note that you may register any standard notification listener that we have already encountered. The type of the notification is `TimerNotification`. The only tricky bit is the call to the `addNotification( )` method, which lets you set up the timer schedule. You can invoke this method as many times as you like to add multiple schedules to the timer. One of the method signatures looks like this:

```
Integer addNotification (java.lang.String type, java.lang.String message,
            java.lang.Object userData,java.util.Date startTime,
            long period, long numOccurences)
```

Other versions of the same method let you omit the period and/or the number of occurrences. Let's take a closer look at the arguments of this method:

- Use the type argument to identify the type of notification.
- Use the message argument to set the string that should appear in the message attribute of the TimerNotification.
- Use the userData argument to pass an object to the listeners. This can be anything that a listener needs to be able to access. In our example, we simply used this.
- Use the startTime argument to set the time and date after which notifications should start being sent.

- If you specify a period (.), this argument determines the number of milliseconds between notifications. Repeat notifications are disabled if you set this argument to 0.

- Use the `numOccurrences` argument to set the total number of times that the notification is fired. The MBean keeps track of the number of notifications that are yet to be fired, and you can invoke the `Timer.getNbOccurrences()` method to retrieve this information. If this value is set to 0 and you have specified a period, the notification will repeat indefinitely.

The `Timer` class also defines constants that make it easier for you to specify the time period: `ONE_SECOND`, `ONE_MINUTE`, `ONE_HOUR`, `ONE_DAY`, `ONE_WEEK`. For example, `ONE_WEEK` resolves to the number of milliseconds in a week.

hod, which simply removes all notifications assigned to a timer.

 Timers are not persistent. If you reboot your server, all timers will be lost and you will have to reinitiate them.

The `addNotification()` method returns an `Integer` identifier that can be used later to remove the notification from the timer. For example, you could write the following:

```
// Later
timer.stop();
timer.removeNotification(notificationId);
//alternatively
timer.removeNotification("eggTimer");
```

Alternatively, you may use the `removeNotification(type)` method to remove all notifications of the given type, or else you can use the `removeAllNotifications()` method, which simply removes all notifications assigned to a timer.

Logging and Internationalization

WebLogic's logging infrastructure plays an important role in the administration and management of a domain. Every important subsystem within WebLogic supports the logging framework, sending informational, warning, and error notifications. These notifications can help you understand the state of a server instance and its subsystems, and are critical when handling any errors and failures. These notifications are made easier because of the distributed nature of WebLogic's logging architecture, which allows it to be managed centrally. This chapter begins by looking at how the logging architecture is distributed throughout a WebLogic domain and at how the separate server logs eventually combine into a domain log on the Administration Server. We'll also look at how to access the various log files and interpret them so that you can detect errors and the source of these errors.

The logging architecture in WebLogic 8.1 is implemented using a combination of WebLogic's JMX services and the JDK 1.4 logging API, making it a perfect partner to the management and control facilities provided by the JMX framework. Indeed, we describe how to use the JMX services to write your own applications that listen for log events, allowing you to create powerful management applications that can react to critical notifications. We also show you how to manipulate logging by writing standard log handlers and filters.

Two important features of the logging architecture are its extensibility and support for internationalization. We show you how to create your own catalog of log messages, and how to use WebLogic-supplied tools to automatically generate Java classes that can be used within your own code. This makes it very easy to instrument your own applications. The log messages generated from your applications fit in seamlessly with the internally generated log messages, thereby ensuring that your code can take full advantage of the distributed logging architecture. The log message catalogs that you create can be written in any language and can be accompanied by translations for different locales. The built-in support for internationalization ensures that the log messages are presented in the appropriate language for the current locale under which WebLogic is running.

The Logging Architecture

WebLogic provides various facilities to create, view, and listen for log messages. Its internal subsystems, such as its web and EJB containers, constantly generate a number of informational, error, and warning log events while a server is running. These log events are visible on the console window for the server, and also may be found in the appropriate log files.

WebLogic manages a distributed log infrastructure. A typical domain is composed of an Administration Server and one or more Managed Servers. The logging infrastructure supports a Logger on each server, which collects the log events generated by your own applications and WebLogic's internal subsystems. These messages then are written to a log file and console that is local to each server instance. In addition, the Logger forwards all but the debug-level messages to a Log Broadcaster. The Log Broadcaster then sends these messages through an optional filter to the Domain Logger on the Administration Server. The Domain Logger gathers all of the messages received from the different servers in the domain and writes these messages to a unified log called the domain log file. This distributed logging infrastructure is depicted in Figure 21-1.

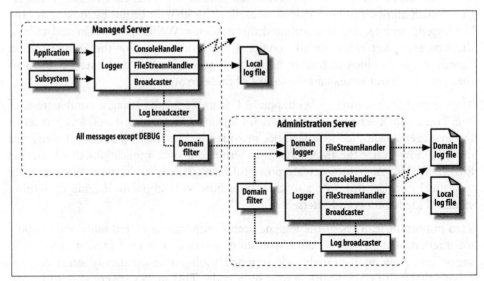

Figure 21-1. The distributed logging architecture

The logging architecture is extensible, letting you create your own set of log messages. You then can instrument your code with the necessary log messages as you see fit. A major advantage of integrating your application logging with WebLogic's logging framework is ease of management. If an application sends log events in this way, its notifications will be treated in the same way as WebLogic's notifications are. This unified handling of your application's log messages will make it easier to manage your application and the WebLogic platform on which it runs. As you shall see later in this chapter, you can write applications that listen for particular log events. The same application can quite easily listen to events generated by WebLogic's internal subsystems or by your own applications.

Under the Hood

Let's examine how WebLogic 8.1 implements its logging infrastructure. The logging in WebLogic 7.0 is similar in structure, though it doesn't rely on the JDK 1.4 API. As a result, it doesn't have the extensible handler system. The logger, sitting on each WebLogic instance, is in fact implemented by a java.util.logging.Logger instance. Each logger instance is equipped with a number of handlers; it is these handlers that provide the ability to stream the messages to a combination of local log files, the console, and the domain log file. The Administration Server has an additional logger that is responsible for the domain log.

WebLogic's ConsoleHandler is responsible for writing the messages to the console, and the FileStreamHandler is responsible for writing the messages to the log files. The JMX MBean LogBroadcasterRuntimeMBean handles message distribution from the Logger in each Managed Server to the Administration Server.

WebLogic provides direct access to the logger on each server. Because these loggers are a part of the JDK 1.4 Logging API, you can easily benefit from other features of the API, such as log filters. In particular, note that loggers and handlers can be assigned a logging level. For a logger, this log level determines the lowest-level message that the logger will publish. For a handler, this log level determines the lowest-level message that the handler will process. Likewise, loggers and handlers can be assigned filters, which determine the subset of messages that will be published by the logger or accepted by the handler.

As the placement of the domain filter in Figure 21-1 suggests, only those log messages that pass through the log level or filter assigned to the logger on the Managed Server will reach the domain filter. So, the logger filter and level settings supersede any domain filter.

Viewing Log Files

You can view all the log files from the Administration Console. Right-click any server name in the left frame and choose View Server Log to view the local log for that server. Right-click the domain name and choose View Domain Log to view the central log for the domain. If you choose the "Customize this View" option, you can determine which subset of messages you wish to see. For instance, you can restrict the view to only those error-level messages that occurred in the past 60 minutes.

The local log files are stored on each server instance in a subdirectory under the domain's root directory named after the server. For instance, the server logs for a Managed Server ServerA, which belongs to the WebLogic domain myclusterdomain, can be found in the *myclusterdomain/ServerA/ServerA.log* file. This naming scheme avoids any potential conflicts if you have several WebLogic instances that use a shared directory. The domain log file can be found under the domain's root directory in a file called *wl-domain.log*. This domain log file lives on the machine that hosts the Administration Server.

Anatomy of a Log Message

Each log message emitted by WebLogic adheres to the following pattern:

```
####<Timestamp> <Severity> <Subsystem> <Machine Name> <Server Name> <Thread ID>
    <User ID> <Transaction ID> <Message ID> <Message Text>
```

Table 21-1 lists each of these attributes and their meanings.

Table 21-1. Log message attributes and their meanings

Attribute	Meaning
Timestamp	This attribute registers the time and date when the log message was sent.
Severity	This attribute indicates the degree of seriousness of the event.
Subsystem	This attribute indicates which subsystem generated the event. For example, its value could be EJB, JMS, Clustering, or any custom subsystem name that you've chosen for your own events.
Machine Name	This attribute indicates the machine on which the message was generated.
Server Name	This attribute indicates which server instance generated the message.
Thread ID	This attribute determines the ID of the thread that ran the code that generated the message.
User ID	If the log message was generated by a thread with an active security context, this attribute indicates the ID of the user used to create the security context.
Transaction ID	If the message was generated from within a transaction, this attribute represents the transaction ID.
Message ID	This attribute is a unique six-digit message identifier identifying the message template. Messages generated by WebLogic's internal subsystems begin with the string BEA-. Messages generated by noncatalog loggers always have a Message ID of 000000.
Message Text	This attribute generally provides a description of the event.

Each message has a severity level, indicating the degree of seriousness of the message. Table 21-2 provides a list of the different severity levels supported by WebLogic.

Table 21-2. Severity levels and their meanings

Severity	Integer value	Meaning
INFO	64	This indicates that the message represents a general information notification.
WARNING	32	This indicates that something suspicious may have happened, though it will probably not affect normal operation.
ERROR	16	This indicates that an error has occurred, and that the system has handled the error with little interruption of service.

Table 21-2. Severity levels and their meanings (continued)

Severity	Integer value	Meaning
NOTICE	8	This is an INFO or WARNING level message that is useful for monitoring the server.
CRITICAL	4	This indicates that a system or service level error has occurred. The system should be able to recover, but there may be a loss or degradation of service.
ALERT	2	This indicates that a service is in an unusable state and that automatic recovery is not possible.
EMERGENCY	1	This indicates that the server is in an unusable state.

As you'll see later in this chapter, the integer representation for the severity level of log messages is quite useful when you build your own applications that listen for log messages.

Managing the Domain Log

The Administration Console lets you manage all of the log files and related options. To configure logging for the domain, select the domain name from the left frame of the Administration Console and then select the Configuration/Logging tab. Table 21-3 lists the various configuration options available for domain-level logging.

Table 21-3. Configuration options for the domain log file

Attribute	Description	Default
File Name	This specifies the name of the file to which the central domain log entries will be written.	*domainName.log*
Rotation Type	This can be set to either None, By Size, or By Time. If set to None, the single domain file continues to grow until you delete it. If set to By Time, a new log file is created according to the value of File Time Span. If set to By Size, a new file is created when the log file reaches a specified size.	By Size
Minimum File Size	If the rotation type is set to By Size, the log file is rotated when it reaches this size.	500 kb
Rotation Time and File Time Span	If the rotation type is set to By Time, the log files are rotated at an hourly interval determined by the File Time Span attribute. Such a rotation will begin at the time specified by the Rotation Time attribute.	00:00 and 24 hours
Limit Number of Retained Logs and Log Files to Retain[a]	If you have file rotation configured, choosing to limit the number of files will ensure that no more than the specified number of files is retained.	No limit

[a] In WebLogic 7.0, these options are labeled Limit Number of Files and File Count respectively.

It is important to properly configure your log file rotation so that your files do not consume unnecessary space.

Managing the Local Log

You can find the logging options for a server by selecting the desired server from the left pane of the Administration Console and then navigating to the Logging tab. Table 21-4 describes the various settings that can be configured from the Logging/Server tab.

Table 21-4. General logging options for a server

Attribute	Description	Default
File Name	This specifies the file to which the local log entries will be written.	*ServerName/ServerName.log*
Log to Stdout	This writes log output to the standard output. It allows you to enable or disable the console handler on the logger.	Selected
Debug to Stdout	This writes messages with DEBUG severity to the standard output.	Selected
Stdout Severity Threshold	This determines the minimum severity of a message that the server sends to standard output.	WARNING[a]
Minimum File Size	If the rotation type is set to Size, the log file is rotated when it reaches this size.	500 kb

[a] The default value in WebLogic 7.0 is ERROR.

The remaining options on this tab configure the log file rotation policy and were explained earlier in Table 21-3. The Stdout Severity Threshold sets up a log filter for the messages that are sent to the standard output stream (by the FileStreamHandler) and does not affect which messages are sent to the domain log.

Creating a Domain Log Filter

As depicted in Figure 21-1, each server can filter the events that are sent to the Domain Logger on the Administration Server. The Logging/Domain tab for a server instance has a Log to Domain Log File option that determines whether log messages generated by a server instance should be forwarded. In addition, you can create and target a Domain Filter to server instances to determine the exact subset of log messages that should be delivered to the domain log.

To create a Domain Filter, click the Domain Log Filters in the left frame of the Administration Console and select the "Configure a new Domain Log Filter" link. The severity level that you set here determines the minimum severity level for messages that will be forwarded to the central log. You also can select which subsystems and user identifiers ought to be filtered. For instance, by choosing the EJB subsystem, only log messages generated in the EJB subsystem will be forwarded to the domain-wide log.

The Targets tab lets you target the domain filter to various server instances. Log messages generated by the loggers on these servers must then pass through this configured domain filter before they can reach the Domain Logger.

WebLogic Message Catalogs

The list of message catalogs that describe all of the messages that can be emitted by the various WebLogic subsystems is available on the Web at the following address: *http://edocs.bea.com/wls/docs81/messages/index.html*. Use these pages to look up any errors generated by WebLogic. Each entry includes a detailed description of the error, a possible cause, and a recommended action to avoid or fix the error.

Listening for Log Messages

There are two ways to listen for log messages. You can either take advantage of the JMX infrastructure and register a notification listener with the LogBroadcaster-Runtime MBean, or you can attach a custom log handler (using the JDK 1.4 Logging API) to the server's Logger directly using a startup class. Using the Logging API is simpler and lets you benefit from other features of the API, such as filtering and message formatting.

JMX Listeners

WebLogic distributes log messages as JMX notifications. Thus, writing an application that listens and responds to log events is no different from writing any other notification listener, which we covered in Chapter 20. As Figure 21-1 illustrates, each server hosts a log broadcaster. This is implemented by the LogBroadcasterRuntime MBean. The following command retrieves the name of the LogBroadcasterRuntime MBean on a Managed Server:

```
java weblogic.Admin -url t3://servera.x:7001/ -username system -password pssst
    GET -pretty -type LogBroadcasterRuntime
```

In this case, the name of the MBean on ServerA is:

```
myClusterDomain:Location=ServerA,Name=TheLogBroadcaster,Type=LogBroadcasterRuntime
```

You can use the MBean's name to register a NotificationListener with the Log-BroadcasterRuntime MBean:

```
WebLogicObjectName name = new WebLogicObjectName("TheLogBroadcaster",
                    "LogBroadcasterRuntime", "myClusterDomain", "ServerA");
MyLogListener mll = new MyLogListener();
ah.getMBeanServer().addNotificationListener(name, mll, null /*no filter*/, null);
```

Here we used the MBeanServer interface to register the log listener with the desired Log Broadcaster MBean. All notifications that are generated by the log system are of type weblogic.management.logging.WebLogicLogNotification. This interface lets you access crucial attributes about the nature of the log event. Example 21-1 shows how the log listener can extract the attributes of the generated log notification.

Example 21-1. Listening for log notifications

```
public class MyLogListener implements RemoteNotificationListener {
 public void handleNotification(Notification notification, Object hb) {
    WebLogicLogNotification wln = (WebLogicLogNotification) notification;
    System.out.println("Message ID = " + wln.getMessageId( ));
    System.out.println("Server name = " + wln.getServername( ));
    System.out.println("Machine name = " + wln.getMachineName( ));
    System.out.println("Severity = " + wln.getSeverity( ));
    System.out.println("Type = " + wln.getType( ));
    System.out.println("Timestamp = " + wln.getTimeStamp( ));
    System.out.println("Message = " + wln.getMessage( ));
    System.out.println("Thread ID = " + wln.getThreadId( ));
    System.out.println("User ID = " + wln.getUserId( ));
    System.out.println("Transaction ID = " + wln.getTransactionId( ));
  }
}
```

If the client that registers the listener object is still running, and we fire a log message, the listener generates the following output to the console window:

```
Message ID = 500000
Server name = ServerA
Machine name = xena
Severity = 16
Type = weblogic.log.OREILLY.500000
Timestamp = 1044201543290
Message = I am hungry: 123
Thread ID = ExecuteThread: '8' for queue: 'default'
User ID = kernel identity
Transaction ID =
```

Here, the value for the Type field will be of the format weblogic.logMessage. *subSystem.messageID*, where subsystem refers to the subsystem that generated the log notification. This data is useful particularly if you intend to use a filter in combination with your log event listener.

JDK Logging

In WebLogic 8.1, a java.util.logging.Logger object is responsible for publishing the log messages generated by each server. Each logger can have a number of handlers registered with it. For example, the ConsoleHandler is used to print log messages to the console. If you want to implement a custom listener, you simply can create your own log handler and register it with the server's logger, using the standard JDK Logging API. This approach bypasses JMX altogether. There are three WebLogic classes that you should be aware of:

- Use WebLogic's subclass of `LogRecord`, `WLLogRecord`, to access information on any incoming log messages.
- Use the `weblogic.logging.WLLevel` class to access the logging levels that can be specified for a logger or handler.
- Use the helper class, `weblogic.logging.LoggingHelper`, to access the appropriate logger instances. An external client should rely on the `getClientLogger()` method. A client that runs within a Managed Server should invoke the `getServerLogger()` method to reference the server's Logger, whereas a client on the Administration Server should use the `getDomainLogger()` method to access the Domain Logger.

The following example, which can be executed on a server, shows how easy it is to access the logger and manipulate one of its handlers. It finds the console handler and sets its logging level and filter:

```
Logger serverlogger = LoggingHelper.getServerLogger();
Handler[] handlerArray = serverlogger.getHandlers();
for (int i=0; i < handlerArray.length; i++) {
    Handler h = handlerArray[i];
    if(h.getClass().getName().equals("weblogic.logging.ConsoleHandler")){
        h.setLevel(weblogic.logging.WLLevel.INFO);
        h.setFilter(new InfoFilter());
    }
}
```

Filters are very straightforward. Example 21-2 lists the source for a log filter that permits only log messages with severity level of INFO.

Example 21-2. A simple log filter

```
package com.oreilly.wlguide.logging;

import java.util.logging.Filter;
import java.util.logging.LogRecord;
import weblogic.logging.WLLevel;
import weblogic.logging.WLLogRecord;

public class InfoFilter implements Filter {
    public boolean isLoggable(LogRecord record) {
      return ((WLLogRecord)record).getLevel().equals(WLLevel.INFO);
    }
}
```

Remember, filters and log levels can be assigned to both the loggers and the handlers. If they're assigned to loggers, they determine the set of messages that the logger will publish. If they're assigned to handlers, they determine the set of messages that the handler will accept.

Writing a handler is easy, and Example 21-3 provides a simple implementation.

Example 21-3. A simple handler using the standard JDK 1.4 Logging API

```
package com.oreilly.wlguide.logging;

import java.util.logging.*;
import weblogic.logging.WLLogRecord;

public class WLLogHandler extends Handler {
    public void publish(LogRecord record) {
      WLLogRecord wr = (WLLogRecord) record;
      System.err.println(wr.getServerName()+":" + wr.getLevel()+
                          ":" + wr.getMessage());
    }
  // flush should flush buffered output
    public void flush() {
    }
  // close should close resources.  Will be called at shutdown.
    public void close() throws SecurityException {
    }
}
```

Now you can simply access the logger and register your log handler:

```
Logger l = LoggingHelper.getDomainLogger();
l.addHandler(new MyHandler());
```

Often, a WebLogic startup class provides a convenient point for registering the handler with the loggers. Example 21-4 lists the source code for a startup class that registers a custom handler with the server's Logger.

Example 21-4. A startup class registering a handler

```
package com.oreilly.wlguide.logging;

import java.util.Hashtable;
import javax.naming.*;
import weblogic.common.T3ServicesDef;
import weblogic.common.T3StartupDef;
import java.util.logging.*;
import weblogic.logging.*;

public class InstallLogHandler implements T3StartupDef {
    private T3ServicesDef services;
    public void setServices(T3ServicesDef services) {
        this.services = services;
    }
    public String startup(String name, Hashtable args) throws Exception {
      try {
        Handler h = new WLLogHandler();
        h.setLevel(WLLevel.INFO);  // level that handler accepts
        Logger l = LoggingHelper.getServerLogger();
        l.setLevel(WLLevel.INFO);  // level that logger publishes
        l.addHandler(h);
          // let's rummage around for the console logger
        Handler[] handlerArray = l.getHandlers();
```

Example 21-4. A startup class registering a handler (continued)

```
        for (int i=0; i < handlerArray.length; i++) {
            Handler hh= handlerArray[i];
            if (hh instanceof ConsoleHandler)
                ((ConsoleHandler)hh).setLevel(WLLevel.ERROR);
        }
    } catch (Exception e) {
        e.printStackTrace( );
    }
    return "";
    }
}
```

Notice how the startup class also modifies the severity level of the `ConsoleHandler` attached to the server Logger.

Generating Log Messages

Clearly, it becomes easier to manage your application setup if its log messages can be found in the same places as the log messages generated by WebLogic's subsystems. This is especially true when your applications operate within a distributed environment. There are several ways to generate log messages and integrate them automatically with WebLogic's logging architecture:

- Use WebLogic's tools to build custom log message catalogs and their associated Java APIs. Clients can conveniently invoke these various log methods exposed by these interfaces to generate log messages. These message catalogs can easily be internationalized.

- Use WebLogic's noncatalog logger to generate log messages. This logger doesn't rely on a message catalog, and hence cannot be internationalized. However, it does allow you to publish log messages in a straightforward fashion. When localized log messages aren't a requirement for your applications, the noncatalog logger makes it quick and easy to use WebLogic's logging framework.

- Use one of the `log( )` methods available to an HTTP servlet.

We will also see how you can use WebLogic's catalog and noncatalog logging from a remote Java client. In this case, the log messages are not transmitted to the server's end but are simply logged to a local file and/or the console window.

Log Message Catalogs

WebLogic supports two types of message catalogs: simple text and log message catalogs. Simple text catalogs are collections of internationalized text messages, and their use in WebLogic's environment is not very different from the use of standard Java for outputting internationalized text. For this reason, we will not consider them any further.

Log message catalogs are collections of log messages, instances of which will be recorded in the log files. Each of these catalog types supports locale-specific text versions, thus allowing your messages to be presented in different languages when WebLogic is run under different locales. WebLogic also provides tools that support automatic generation of Java classes and methods that represent the log messages. By invoking these Java classes, you automatically generate the appropriate log messages while utilizing the underlying logging framework.

Creating log message catalogs

Message catalogs are written using two types of XML documents. The top-level, default catalog that describes the various log messages and method names must conform to the *msgcat.dtd* DTD. If you are going to supply localized variants, these must conform to the *l10n_msgcat.dtd* DTD. These DTDs can be found in the *samples* directory in your WebLogic installation, *WL_HOME\samples\server\examples\src\ examples\i18n\msgcat*.

The top-level catalog should contain the definitions of all the log messages that you would like to make available. Each message has a unique ID, a message body containing the text that should be generated, a subsystem name, a severity level (debug, info, warning, or error), and a method name. WebLogic's logging tools use the method names to generate Java methods that you then can use to send instances of the message to the log. These methods can take arguments, allowing you to insert dynamic text into the log message. Messages also can contain other text that will be output when the message is logged. The subsystem name is just a convenient way of grouping related messages together, making it easier for the reader to determine who/what generated the log message—for instance, the default log messages sent to the console window of a WebLogic instance include <HTTP>, <JMS>, <Cluster>, etc. before the actual message.

The easiest way to create a message catalog is to use WebLogic's Message Editor. This GUI-based tool lets you create a top-level catalog, and then it automatically generates the XML representation for you. You can launch the Message Editor by running the following command:

```
java weblogic.MsgEditor
```

Before creating a message catalog, the directory in which you want to store the catalog must hold the DTD files that the Message Editor uses. These can be copied from the *samples* directory referenced earlier.

Let's now look at an example that illustrates all the tooling and formats used. Here, we'll create a new log message catalog file called *ocat.xml*. When creating a new catalog file, you have to supply package names for the code that will be generated from the catalog files. We've chosen the com.oreilly.wlguide.i18n package to provide all the internationalization support, and the com.oreilly.wlguide.i10n package to provide the localization support. You also must choose a subsystem name. We've chosen OREILLY. Using the tool, you now can create a number of messages. As an example, we created a message with a method name of testing(String msg) and message body of I am hungry: {0}. The tool then will generate an XML representation of the log message similar to this:

```
<logmessage messageid="500000" datelastchanged="1044113111822" stacktrace="true"
    datehash="-1538707175" severity="error"  method="testing(String msg)">
  <messagebody>
    I am hungry: {0}
  </messagebody>
  <messagedetail>
  </messagedetail>
  <cause>
  </cause>
  <action>
  </action>
</logmessage>
```

As illustrated in the preceding excerpt, the method can take a number of arguments, thereby allowing you to embed text into the log message dynamically. You may specify up to 10 arguments, and these can be referenced within the message body using {0} {1} ... {9}. Besides string-valued parameters, WebLogic also supports numeric parameters using the {n,number} syntax and dates using the {n,date} syntax.

The master catalog of log messages can be created using any language of your choice. Once you've created the master catalog, you can create other locale-specific translations of these messages. Each translation should be placed in an identically named file within a subdirectory labeled by the two-letter language code. So, for instance, if we were to create a Dutch translation of the earlier message, it has to be placed under the *nl* subdirectory. If you need to support multiple variants for a locale—for instance, the U.S. English variant—you should place the variant under the language directory. Thus, an American English translation for the same message catalog would be placed under the *en/US* subdirectory. The XML representation for the localized translations must include an entry for each message, along with its translation. Here are the contents of the *nl/ocat.xml* catalog file, which specifies the Dutch translation for the original messages:

```
<?xml version="1.0" encoding="UTF-8"?>
<!DOCTYPE locale_message_catalog PUBLIC "weblogic-locale-message-catalog-dtd" "http:/
/www.bea.com/servers/wls600/l10n_msgcat.dtd">
<locale_message_catalog version="1.0">
  <logmessage messageid="500000" datelastchanged="1044113111822">
    <messagebody>
    Ik heb honger: {0}
    </messagebody>
    <messagedetail></messagedetail>
    <cause></cause>
    <action></action>
  </logmessage>
</locale_message_catalog>
```

WebLogic provides two utilities that create Java support for the messages. The `weblogic.i18ngen` utility should be used to generate the Java classes that provide internationalization support, while the `weblogic.l10ngen` utility should be used to generate Java classes that offer localization support. Both utilities accept two command-line arguments: the name of the root catalog file and the location of the directory into which the output classes should be placed. Note that the localization tool automatically scours subdirectories. We used the following commands to generate the Java classes that provide necessary support for i18n and l10n:

```
java weblogic.i18ngen -compile -i18n -l10n -keepgenerated -d x:\out ocat.xml
java weblogic.l10ngen -d x:\out -verbose .\ocat.xml
cd x:\out
jar cvf x:\externalJARs\mylogging.jar .
```

To make the files available to WebLogic, you need to include the support classes within WebLogic's `CLASSPATH`. In the example, we created a JAR that packages all the output Java classes and added the JAR's location to WebLogic's `CLASSPATH` used during startup.

Among other files, WebLogic generates resource bundles representing the localizations, and a class that contains static methods for each of the messages that you defined. The name of the generated Logger class is given by the name of the message catalog with a `Logger` suffix—in our case, `com.oreilly.wlguide.i18n.ocatLogger`.

Generating log messages

Now that WebLogic is aware of the generated support files for generating your own log messages, you can instrument your applications to send these messages. This can be accomplished by invoking the appropriate methods defined for the log messages. For instance, in order to trigger our example log message, you must invoke the following static method:

```
com.oreilly.wlguide.i18n.ocatLogger.testing("123");
```

This will generate a log message on the local server. This simple message call actually invokes the underlying distributed logging facilities, so depending on your log filter settings the message also may be forwarded to the domain-wide log. In our example, the following log message is fired:

```
<01-Feb-03 17:19:49 GMT> <Error> <OREILLY> <500000> <I am hungry: 123>
```

If you run WebLogic under the Dutch locale, the following locale-specific log message is emitted instead:

```
<01-Feb-03 17:24:19 GMT> <Error> <OREILLY> <500000> <Ik heb honger: 123>
```

Noncatalog Logging

Noncatalog logging is, as its name implies, logging without a catalog. Because you don't use a log message catalog, you lose all internationalization support. In addition, your code must explicitly supply the text that needs to be logged. On the other hand, a `NonCatalogLogger` object provides an easy interface for using WebLogic's underlying logging framework. The following example shows how a client (perhaps running within WebLogic) can log messages without the aid of a message catalog:

```
weblogic.logging.NonCatalogLogger wnc =
        new weblogic.logging.NonCatalogLogger("News");
wnc.info("News just in");
wnc.warning("Alien's have landed");
wnc.alert("I'm here, come quickly");
wnc.emergency("Help, I'm trapped")
wnc.critical("Save yourselves!");
wnc.debug("De-bug me man, don't just stand there");
```

The `NonCatalogLogger` constructor takes a string argument that indicates the name of the subsystem that will be used to identify subsequent log messages it generates. The preceding code will result in the following output in your log file, assuming you've not configured any log level or handlers for the server's Logger:

```
<11-Apr-2003 17:17:07 o'clock BST> <Info> <News> <000000> <News just in>
<11-Apr-2003 17:17:07 o'clock BST> <Warning> <News> <000000> <Aliens have landed>
<11-Apr-2003 17:17:07 o'clock BST> <Alert> <News> <000000> <I'm here, come quickly>
<11-Apr-2003 17:17:07 o'clock BST> <Emergency> <News> <000000> <Help, I'm trapped>
<11-Apr-2003 17:17:07 o'clock BST> <Critical> <News> <000000> <Save yourselves!>
<11-Apr-2003 17:17:07 o'clock BST> <Debug> <News> <000000> <Debug me man, don't just
stand there>
```

The various log methods also can take an optional `Throwable` argument, thereby allowing you to include additional information about the error.

Servlet Logging

Because all HTTP servlets indirectly extend the `javax.servlet.GenericServlet` class, a servlet can avail of the following log methods:

```
/** Generate a log message within WebLogic's logs */
log(String message);
/** Use the Throwable object to obtain additional
    information on the exception that generated the log message */
log(String message, Throwable t);
```

A servlet may use either of these methods to output log messages to WebLogic's server logs.

Even though your code is guaranteed to remain portable, these methods are not particularly flexible. For example, you cannot assign a severity level for the log message, or even override the subsystem that generated the log message. In addition, JSPs are unable to use these methods because their implementation class doesn't extend the `GenericServlet` class. For this reason, we recommend that you create your own catalog logger or use WebLogic's noncatalog logger in order to benefit from WebLogic's logging capabilities.

Client Application Logging

Client applications can also use the noncatalog and catalog logging features of WebLogic. The following startup arguments control the behavior of the logging:

weblogic.log.FileName

> Use this argument to specify a filename to which the log messages should be written.

weblogic.StdoutEnabled

> Set this argument to true if you want a subset of the log messages to be written to stdout as well as the log file.

weblogic.StdoutDebugEnabled

> Set this argument to true if you want debug messages written to stdout.

weblogic.StdoutSeverityLevel

> Set this argument to the desired severity level. This can be set to either 64 for info, 32 for warning, 16 for error, 8 for notice, 4 for critical, 2 for alert, or 1 for emergency.

Here is an example:

```
java -Dweblogic.log.FileName=out.log -Dweblogic.StdoutEnabled=true
    -Dweblogic.StdoutSeverityLevel=16 alienClient
```

SNMP

The Simple Network Management Protocol (SNMP) is used to monitor many different types of managed resources, from hardware routers to software products. Network management systems such as monitoring tools use SNMP to gather information from various managed resources and then present this information to the user. These tools usually incorporate alert services that flag anomalies in the runtime state of the system. Any resource that needs to participate in this SNMP framework needs to implement an *SNMP agent*, which serves as the communication endpoint for the management system. Management systems use SNMP to interact with any agents available on the network, polling the agents for required information about their operational state. SNMP also supports trap notifications, event-like data items that SNMP agents automatically broadcast to any listening management systems. WebLogic's SNMP agent supports the SNMPv1 and SNMPv2 protocols.

In this chapter, you will learn how a WebLogic domain can be treated like any other managed resource on the network, thereby allowing you to integrate it with any standard SNMP tools that you may use. For example, you may already have an SNMP framework in place that monitors your network resources. Using WebLogic's SNMP agent, an entire WebLogic domain can be seamlessly integrated with your existing infrastructure, allowing you to treat WebLogic and all its deployments like any other SNMP resource.

WebLogic's SNMP Infrastructure

A WebLogic domain can be configured to support SNMP by enabling the SNMP agent, which runs on the Administration Server. This SNMP agent can be configured to respond to requests about managed resources and deployments within the WebLogic domain. It also can be configured to fire events called *trap notifications* when certain attributes on resources exceed specified threshold values. Much of this sounds very similar to the JMX infrastructure described in Chapter 20, and indeed you will find that the resources that can be managed through the SNMP agent mirror the JMX managed resources. WebLogic's SNMP trap notification mechanism is built around the standard JMX monitoring and notification system. This allows you to configure the SNMP agent to send trap notifications on changes in attribute values, on configured monitor policies, and on log messages. Traps also can be sent when the Administration Server boots, or when any Managed Server comes up or goes down.

In general, a system administrator would configure WebLogic's SNMP agent to monitor information of interest, and then employ some external management system to pull information from WebLogic's SNMP agent and react to the trap notifications sent to it. WebLogic's SNMP agent would typically be part of larger network management framework that is being monitored alongside other distributed SNMP agents. WebLogic's SNMP agent also can serve as a proxy, routing requests for certain resources through to some other SNMP agent. This entire infrastructure is depicted in Figure 22-1.

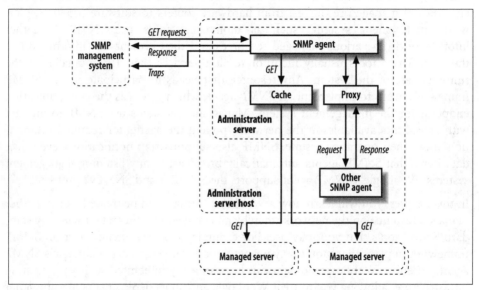

Figure 22-1. WebLogic's SNMP infrastructure

Note that you can configure only a single SNMP agent for a WebLogic domain, and it must run on the Administration Server. When the SNMP agent receives a request for any information on one of its Managed Servers, the agent on the Administration Server fetches the information from the Managed Server. WebLogic's SNMP agent also contains a configurable cache, which it uses to cache the information obtained from Managed Servers in response to queries.

Using the SNMP Agent

In order to use WebLogic's SNMP agent, it needs to be enabled and configured using the Administration Console. To do this, select the Services/SNMP node from the left pane of the Administration Console and then select the SNMP tab. Check the Enabled option and set the SNMP Port on which the SNMP agent will be available. Ensure that the port number for the SNMP agent is available. It may happen that the default value for the port, 161, is already used by the operating system on which you have deployed WebLogic. Table 22-1 lists the other configuration settings that are available for the SNMP agent.

Table 22-1. Configuration options for WebLogic's SNMP agent

Option	Description
Management Information Base (MIB) Data Refresh Interval	The MIB agent caches requested MIB values. This option defines the minimum number of seconds that the values will be cached before the agent attempts to refresh them.
Community Prefix	This option defines the community prefix that is used to form the community name. It defaults to public.
Debug Level	This can configure the agent to output debug information. A value of 0 means that no debug information will be sent, 1 indicates that fatal information will be sent, 2 indicates critical information, and 3 indicates noncritical information.
Trap Version	This option specifies whether the traps that are generated conform to the SNMPv1 or SNMPv2 protocol. It defaults to SNMPv1.
Send Automatic Traps Enabled	This option, which defaults to true, determines whether the automatically generated traps (server start and stop, etc.) are sent to SNMP managers.

Once the agent has been configured and the server restarted, you can start interacting with it using a network management tool. WebLogic comes with a simple utility, snmpgetnext, which can be used to interrogate the SNMP agent. In order to run this utility, you need to supply the community name to use, the port number and host address, and finally the SNMP query itself. Here is an example that shows how to query the domain's SNMP agent for the address of the Administration Server:

```
java snmpgetnext -c public -p 1611 10.0.10.10 .1.3.6.1.4.1.140.625.360.1.30
```

Don't be confused by the string of numbers at the end of the query—it represents an object name that uniquely identifies an MBean attribute for the server. The rest of this section is concerned with naming. In particular, we look at how to construct object names that can be used to identify attributes of managed resources within the domain. We also examine how a community name can be used to identify a particular Managed Server.

The Management Information Base

A Management Information Base (MIB), a standard text file that contains the definitions and properties of all managed resources and services supported by the agent, accompanies WebLogic's SNMP agent. The MIB defines a hierarchy of *objects*, which represent manageable attributes that may be queried using the SNMP interfaces. Each such manageable attribute has a unique identifier, called an *object identifier* (OID), which also is recorded in the MIB. OIDs identify resources of interest and are used when interacting with SNMP agents. All OIDs in SNMP are specified as a sequence of numbers or mnemonic keywords defining a unique path through a global namespace. For example, WebLogic Server is only one of many thousands of devices that are SNMP-enabled. All of these devices can be managed, in principal, by a single agent, so they need to be uniquely named. For this reason, there is an OID for WebLogic Server itself: .1.3.6.1.4.140.625. All OIDs specified in the MIB are relative to this root OID.

You can find the file documenting the MIB in *WL_HOME\server\lib\BEA-WEBLOGIC-MIB.asn1*. It conforms to the standard Abstract Syntax Notation.1 (ASN.1) format. An important aspect of the objects available to WebLogic's SNMP agent is that they all correspond to MBean attributes. Hence, the OIDs listed in the MIB enable you to uniquely identify a particular MBean attribute from the hierarchy of MBeans that are made available for management. You also can find a nicely formatted, searchable, cross-referenced version on the Web at *http://edocs.bea.com/wls/docs81/snmp/index.html*.

Many management tools allow you to search through the information in the MIB to find the resource of interest. You can also construct one by referencing the MIB. In the earlier example, we used an OID for the serverRuntimeListenAddress attribute. Here is how we constructed the OID for this resource:

- The OID for WebLogic Server is .1.3.6.1.4.140.625.
- The ServerRuntimeMBeans are represented in the serverRuntimeTable within the MIB, which has an OID of 360.
- A ServerRuntimeEntry that holds the attributes has an OID of 1, and the serverRuntimeListenAddress is an entry with an OID of 30.

So, the complete OID that identifies the server's listen address is .1.3.6.1.4.140.625.360.1.30, which is what we used in our example when querying the SNMP agent.

Community Names

A *community name* is simply a textual password that can be assigned to an SNMP agent when it is configured. The agent verifies the community name against that supplied by a requesting management agent to ensure that the agent has permission to request data. It also is used when sending trap notifications. If WebLogic's agent receives an incorrect community name, it generates an authenticationFailure trap that is sent to the source of the request.

The community name in WebLogic serves a dual purpose. Because the SNMP agent on the Administration Server serves as the agent for the entire domain, a querying agent needs to be able to identify a Managed Server if it wants information from a particular Managed Server. This can be accomplished by using the following format for the community name when querying the SNMP agent:

```
community_name@server_name
```

Here, `community_name` represents the community name that was assigned to the agent, and `server_name` is the name of the Managed Server within the domain. Thus, if we need to query for the listen address for a Managed Server ServerA within the domain, we could issue the following SNMP query:

```
java snmpgetnext -c public@ServerA -p 1611 10.0.10.10 .1.3.6.1.4.1.140.625.360.1.30
```

To identify manageable attributes on the Administration Server itself, simply use the community name:

```
community_name
```

Finally, if you want to retrieve the values of a manageable attribute for every server within the domain, you can use the following format:

```
community_name@domain_name
```

Here, `domain_name` represents the name of the WebLogic domain. The following example shows how to request the addresses of all the servers in `mydomain`:

```
java snmpwalk -c public@mydomain -p 1611 10.0.10.10 .1.3.6.1.4.1.140.625.360.1.30
```

Traps

WebLogic's SNMP agent can be configured to send a number of notification traps—for instance, when a log message is logged, when an attribute value has changed, or when configured thresholds for a monitor are exceeded.

Each trap notification is sent as a trap protocol data unit (PDU), which includes the following standard information:

Enterprise OID
> The enterprise OID field in all trap notifications sent by WebLogic is set to WebLogic's OID, .1.3.6.1.4.140.625.

Agent address
> The agent address of the PDU is set to the IP address of the WebLogic server on which the trap was generated.

Generic trap type
> The generic trap type of the PDU indicates the generic type of the trap. A value of 0 is used when the trap represents the start of the Administration Server. A value of 4 indicates an authentication failure and is generated when an incorrect community string is sent to WebLogic. Finally, a value of 6 is set for all other traps. Note that the Administration Server coldstart trap (0) and the authentication failure trap (4) are sent automatically in any configured SNMP agent.

Specific trap types
> Different SNMP agents are permitted to further qualify the enterprise trap types by indicating an *enterprise-specific trap type*. Table 22-2 lists the specific trap types used in WebLogic.

Table 22-2. WebLogic-specific trap type values and their descriptions

Value	Description
65	This trap type is sent when a Managed Server that was previously down is started.
70	This trap type is sent when a Managed Server is shut down.
80	This trap type is generated when an observed attribute's value changes.
60	This trap type is generated when a matching log message has been sent.
75	This trap type is generated when a JMX monitor fires.

The trap types for the server starting up and shutting down are set automatically in the event of these servers cycling.

Timestamp

A PDU also can include a timestamp, indicating the length of time between the last reinitialization of WebLogic's SNMP agent and the time at which the trap was issued.

One or more variable bindings

Finally, a PDU may include a number of name/value pairs that convey further information about the trap notification. For instance, the server startup and shutdown traps, type 65 and 70 in Table 22-2, have two name/value pairs that are passed with the trap PDU. The first, trapTime, indicates the time that the event occurred. The second, trapServerName, indicates the name of the server that generated the trap.

Trap Destinations

In order for external management agents to use WebLogic's SNMP, you have to register the management agents with WebLogic as trap destinations. Only then can WebLogic send all notification traps that occur to the registered trap destinations.

To create a trap destination, select the SNMP/Trap Destinations node in the left pane of the Administration Console and choose the "Configure a new SNMP Trap Destination" option. Then you need to enter the address and port of the management agent to which the traps should be sent, as well as the community name that should be used when sending the traps. In this case, the community name is simply the configured password that should be used for the management agent you are using.

In this way, you can create a number of trap destinations that are interested in WebLogic's SNMP notifications. Once you set up a number of trap destinations, select the SNMP node and, using the Targeted Trap Destinations option, select the trap destinations to which the trap notifications ought to be sent.

Attribute Change Traps

Attribute change traps behave like JMX attribute notifications. They are sent when an attribute is added, removed, or updated. For example, you can configure the

SNMP agent to send a trap when the attribute indicating the capacity of a JDBC connection pool changes. The trap types can be sent only for configuration MBeans and cannot be used for runtime attributes. The MIB indicates which attributes belong to the configuration MBeans. Table 22-3 indicates the name/value pairs that are associated with this trap notification.

Table 22-3. Variable name/value pairs for attribute trap notifications

Name	Value
trapTime	This value indicates the time at which the trap was generated.
trapServerName	This value indicates the name of the server that generated the trap, which in general will be the name of the Administration Server.
trapMBeanName	This value indicates the name of the MBean that contains the attribute.
trapMBeanType	This value indicates the type of the MBean.
trapAttributeName	This value indicates the name of the configuration attribute that has changed.
trapAttributeType	This value indicates the type of the attribute.
trapAttributeChangeType	This value indicates the type of change. It will be set to either ADD, REMOVE, or UPDATE.
trapAttributeOldVal	This value indicates the value of the attribute before the change.
trapAttributeNewVal	This value indicates the value of the attribute after the change.

You can create an attribute change trap by using the Administration Console and navigating to the SNMP/Traps/Attribute Changes node from the left pane. Here, you have to fill in either the MBean's type or name and the name of the attribute that you want to monitor. Finally, make sure that you target the servers on which you want the attribute watched. WebLogic displays all of the available MBean types in a drop-down box.

As an example, you can set up the agent to send a trap when the initial capacity of a JDBC connection pool is changed. In order to do this, simply specify the MBean type as JDBCConnectionPoolMBean and the attribute name as InitialCapacity. WebLogic's SNMP agent then will fire a trap notification whenever anybody changes the initial capacity for the connection pool.

Log Message Traps

In Chapter 21, we looked at WebLogic's logging architecture and how the Administration Server collects log messages from all the Managed Servers in the domain and writes them to a domain log. In this context, you can also set up the Administration Server to send SNMP log notification traps. To do this, select the SNMP/Traps/Log Filters node from the left pane of the Administration Console. Here you can configure a log filter by specifying values for the minimum severity level, subsystem names, user IDs, message IDs, and a message substring. For example, if you need to set up a trap so that a trap notification is fired when a Warning log message is sent, then you simply create a new log filter whose Severity Level option is set to Warning. Table 22-4 indicates the name/value pairs that are associated with this trap notification.

Table 22-4. Variable name/value pairs for log trap notifications

Name	Value
trapTime	This indicates the time at which the trap was generated.
trapServerName	This will be set to the name of the server instance that generated the trap.
trapMachineName	This will be set to the name of the machine hosting the server instance.
trapLogThreadId	This indicates the ID of the thread that generated the log message.
trapLogTransactionId	If the log message was generated while in a transaction, this indicates the transaction ID.
trapLogUserId	If the log message was generated while in a security context, this indicates the user ID associated with the security context.
trapLogSubsystem	This indicates the subsystem that generated the log message.
trapLogMsgId	This indicates the ID of the log message.
trapLogSeverity	This indicates the severity level of the message.
trapLogMessage	This contains the text of the log message.

Monitor Traps

WebLogic's SNMP agent can take advantage of the JMX monitors described earlier in Chapter 20. Special JMX monitors can be established that poll MBeans and send notifications when specified conditions occur. These JMX monitor notifications then can be routed automatically to the SNMP agent, which in turn generates a trap notification. WebLogic's SNMP supports all three JMX monitor types:

- String monitors can monitor attributes and generate a notification when the value of an attribute differs from some predefined string.

- Counter monitors can monitor incrementing attribute values and generate a notification when a certain threshold value is reached. In addition, they can optionally add an offset or subtract a modulus to establish a new threshold value.

- Gauge monitors can generate notifications when either the high or low threshold values are exceeded.

In all cases, you need to follow the same procedure to create a monitor trap. Using the Administration Console, choose the SNMP/Traps/Monitors node from the left pane and then select the type of monitor that should generate these traps. You also need to supply the name of the attribute that is to be monitored, the polling interval at which to check if the conditions of the monitor apply, and the MBean type or name. In addition, you have to supply the information necessary for each monitor type. For string monitors, this means the string to compare against, for counter monitors, this means the threshold, offset and, modulus values, and for gauge monitors, this means the high and low threshold values.

In Chapter 20, we looked at how to create a Counter Monitor MBean that monitored the number of times the FileServlet was invoked. To achieve the same behavior using WebLogic's SNMP agent, create a new counter monitor so that the MBean type is set to ServletRuntime, the MBean attribute is set to InvocationTotalCount, and the MBean name is set to ServerB_ServerB_DefaultWebApp_weblogic.servlet.File-Servlet_94. As explained, these values can be obtained easily using the weblogic. Admin tool, and will depend on your particular deployment. Finally, you need to target the monitor to the appropriate server—in our case, ServerB.

Table 22-5 indicates the name/value pairs that are associated with this trap notification.

Table 22-5. Variable name/value pairs for monitor trap notifications

Name	Value
trapTime	This indicates the time at which the trap was generated.
trapServerName	This indicates the name of the server whose attribute value is being monitored.
trapMBeanName	This is the name of the MBean that contains the attribute being monitored.
trapAttributeName	This is the name of the attribute whose value is being monitored.
trapMonitorType	This will be set to either CounterMonitor, StringMonitor, or GaugeMonitor.
trapMonitorThreshold	This is an ASCII representation of the threshold that triggered the trap.
trapMonitorValue	This is an ASCII representation of the values that triggered the trap.

SNMP Proxies

As illustrated in Figure 22-1, WebLogic's SNMP agent also can act as a proxy for other SNMP agents, allowing you to gate traffic from multiple SNMP agents through a single master WebLogic SNMP agent. Each SNMP proxy is configured with a particular branch OID tree. When an incoming request to WebLogic's SNMP agent matches the OID in one of the configured proxies, the request then is forwarded to that agent. To use this proxy functionality, you have to create one or more SNMP proxies from the SNMP/Proxies node in the left pane of the Administration Console. Table 22-6 describes the configuration options available for an SNMP proxy.

Table 22-6. Configuration settings for an SNMP proxy

Option	Description
Port	This is the port number of the other SNMP agent to which WebLogic should proxy.
OID Root	This is the absolute OID for the proxy, indicating the root of the part of the OID tree that will be proxied.
Community	This is the community name that has been configured for the agent to which WebLogic is proxying.
Timeout	This is the length of time that WebLogic will wait for a response to requests proxied to the other agent. If no response is sent in this period, an error is sent to the requesting management system.

WebLogic's SNMP agent cannot be configured as a proxy for Microsoft Windows' SNMP agent. Nor can the SNMP agent in Microsoft Windows 2000 be configured as a proxy for WebLogic.

Of course, in order to use the proxy, you must ensure the agent is listening on a port number that is different from the listen port configured for WebLogic's SNMP agent.

Index

We'd like to hear your suggestions for improving our indexes. Send email to *index@oreilly.com*.

JSTL (Java Standard Template Library), 37
JTA (Java Transaction API), 6, 155
    transactions (see JTA transactions)
    WebLogic extensions to, 167
JTA transactions, 163–165
    data integrity problems with 2PC
        emulation, 166
    XA versus non-XA drivers, 165
JTS driver, 116, 118
    support for distributed transactions, 118
JVM (Java Virtual Machine)
    choosing, 514
    monitoring, 518
    performance tuning, 513–518
        green versus native threads, 518
        heap size/garbage collection, 514–517

K

keep-alive connections, 78
Kerbv5 authentication, 184

L

last-in, first-out (LIFO), 203
LDAP (Lightweight Directory Access
        Protocol)
    authentication and, 10
    authenticators, 586–588
    repository, domain backups, 416
    servers, WebLogic applications and, 15
        (see also embedded LDAP server)
least-recently used (LRU) cache, 136
libraries, client-side, for web services, 704
LIFO (last-in, first-out), 203
Lightweight Directory Access Protocol (see
        LDAP)
load balancing
    affinity-based algorithms, 256
    Application Server, 454
    clustered EJBs, 324
    clustering and, 11, 450
    configuring load balancers, 462
    EJBs, 472
    firewalls and, 482
    via hardware, 57
    heuristics, 263
    JDBC connections and clustering, 153
    JMS clients as consumers/producers, 261
    JMS connections/connection
        factories, 253
    schemes, 465–470
        for avoiding load balancing, 469
        client-server routing, 467

for distributed destinations, 262
    server-to-server routing, 465–467
loadLocalIdentity(SSLContext), 549
loadXML(RowSet), 151
loadXMLSchema(WLRowSetMetaData), 151
local transactions, 129
LocalTransaction level
    resource adapters, 184
    XML deployment descriptors, 181
log files, viewing, 775
log message catalogs, 783–786
    creating, 784
    WebLogic message catalog, 779
log messages
    components of, 776
    generating, 783–788
        client application logging, 788
        log message catalogs, 783–786
        noncatalog logging, 786
        servlet logging, 787
    listening for, 779–783
        JDK Logging API, 780–783
        JMX listeners, 779
logField(CustomELFLogger), 74
log-filename element (weblogic-ra.xml), 190
Logger interface, 780–783
logging
    expired messages, 220
    Node Manager, 441
        client logs, 441
    (see also HTTP access logs; log messages)
logging-enabled element
        (weblogic-ra.xml), 190
LoggingHelper class, 781
LoginContext interface, 597
LoginModule interface, 597
logout(HttpServletRequest), 48
LRU (least-recently used) cache, 136

M

machines, 408
    with multiple CPUs, tuning, 513
Managed Servers, 405, 440
    clustered, using Configuration Wizard to
        create domains with, 412
    health monitoring, 440
    restarting, 418
        Managed Server Independence
            mode, 419
    using Configuration Wizard to create
        domains with, 412

About the Author

Jon Mountjoy has worked with J2EE technologies since their inception and has worked with WebLogic in particular for a number of years. He is employed as a product development manager at a firm specializing in risk management, and also holds posts training and consulting in J2EE and WebLogic technologies. His interests lie in applying enterprise Java technologies, semantics, and the behavior of languages and virtual machines.

Avinash Chugh is presently working as technical lead for a California-based start-up building working-capital management software for leading component, contract, systems manufacturing, and distribution companies. He has over three years experience with J2EE technologies, primarily on WebLogic Server. Avinash holds a post-graduate degree in computer applications from Delhi University.

Colophon

Our look is the result of reader comments, our own experimentation, and feedback from distribution channels. Distinctive covers complement our distinctive approach to technical topics, breathing personality and life into potentially dry subjects.

The images on the cover of *WebLogic: The Definitive Guide* are sand stars. The sand star is a starfish whose main defining feature is the spines that cover the sides of its legs, which differ from the suction cups that most starfish have. The sand star uses these spines to travel. It is chiefly nocturnal and tends to bury itself in sand in daylight hours. Its spines are helpful for allowing it to burrow into and move quickly throughout this sandy environment. The sand star swallows its food whole. Its diet consists of snails, sea urchins, seaweed, other starfish and sand stars, and any dead fish it can find. It often feeds off other creatures it finds buried in the sand alongside it.

Mary Brady was the production editor, and Audrey Doyle was the copyeditor for *WebLogic: The Definitive Guide*. Mary Brady was the proofreader. Reg Aubry and Claire Cloutier provided quality control. Mary Agner provided production support. Nancy Crumpton wrote the index.

Emma Colby designed the cover of this book, based on a series design by Edie Freedman. The cover image is a 19th-century engraving from the Dover Pictorial Archive. Emma Colby produced the cover layout with QuarkXPress 4.1 using Adobe's ITC Garamond font.

David Futato designed the interior layout. This book was converted by Julie Hawks to FrameMaker 5.5.6 with a format conversion tool created by Erik Ray, Jason McIntosh, Neil Walls, and Mike Sierra that uses Perl and XML technologies. The text font is Linotype Birka; the heading font is Adobe Myriad Condensed; and the code font is LucasFont's TheSans Mono Condensed. The illustrations that appear in the book were produced by Robert Romano and Jessamyn Read using Macromedia FreeHand 9 and Adobe Photoshop 6. The tip and warning icons were drawn by Christopher Bing. This colophon was written by Mary Brady.